EUmies Awards

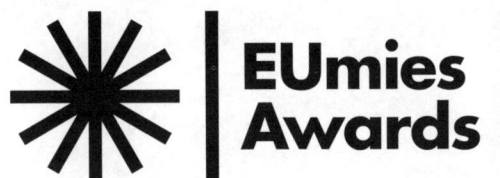

European Union
Prize for Contemporary
Architecture/
Mies van der Rohe Awards

Creative Europe

fundació
mies van der rohe
barcelona

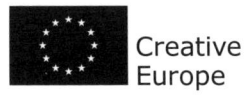

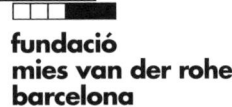

FOREWORD

Architecture is vital for our European culture, sustainable development and overall well-being. The works of the winners of the 2024 European Architecture Prize embody the principles of the New European Bauhaus, integrating the green transition into people's everyday lives and living spaces. I extend my heartfelt congratulations to the architects and clients behind these remarkable achievements at the time of profound change for the European architecture sector.

The EUmies Awards serve as an excellent platform for leading figures in European architecture and the public to engage, share ideas and address common challenges.

They also offer an opportunity to reflect on what unites us in a diverse European community. Culture, arts, heritage and architecture are integral components of the European identity, bringing us together and enriching our shared experience.

Architecture reminds us of what mattered to those that came before us but also reflects current concerns that shape our European identity. For these reasons, it is our duty to ensure that everyone in our community, including the young people and marginalised groups, can enjoy high-quality architecture and living spaces, fostering social cohesion.

Let us continue promoting European values through architecture and supporting our creators through initiatives such as the Creative Europe programme, which celebrates its 10th anniversary this year.

Thank you for your commitment!

Iliana Ivanova

European Commissioner
for Innovation, Research,
Culture, Education and
Youth

FOREWORD

Ever since they were first launched in 1988, the EUmies Awards have challenged us to question what kind of architecture we need and want. Our duty is to continue searching for new solutions to these questions, just as Ludwig Mies van der Rohe did himself, when he designed the marvellous Barcelona Pavilion. While architecture must respond to the immense and inescapable global challenges of our time – social inequality, sustainability and peaceful coexistence – at present we also need architecture that is singular to Europe; that represents the social and urban model, progress, and human and citizen relations that we as Europeans share. All this is symbolised by the Pavilion: a "German Pavilion" in a Mediterranean city, lying at the foot of Montjuïc mountain. A pavilion designed for the 1929 World's Fair in Barcelona, that recalls one of the most dazzling eras of our history. A pavilion that, in response to public demand, Barcelona City Council reconstructed in 1986 with the architect Oriol Bohigas at the helm. Cities are our memory and legacy, and we have to preserve the buildings that, over time, imbue our history with values, meaning and aspiration.

Just as Mies van der Rohe said, "architecture represents the will of an epoch translated into space", and the EUmies Awards – the most prestigious of their kind in Europe – translate the will of our own times, and that of the Europe we are now even more determined to build: a Europe of cities. Although each generation must bring their own vision, there are values and traditions we will continue to maintain as part of European culture: beauty, public service, sustainability and social justice.

We must never forget that, just as Barcelona has done since the reinstatement of democracy, architecture and urban planning must be treated as public policies of the first order. Testament to this are this year's prizewinners – two community projects, and two buildings run by public institutions: Gustav Düsing and Max Hacke's study pavilion at TU Braunschweig, and SUMA Arquitectura's Gabriel García Márquez Library.

The old Europe of cathedrals is also today a Europe of libraries, because what could be more transformative than building a public library in each and every neighbourhood? What could be more revolutionary than access to culture for everyone – regardless of their social and economic class, or origin? What better way to build and create a city, than also doing it while striving for architectural transcendence, through beautiful buildings, that also speak of their time? Through committing to a city model that seeks to bring the best architecture to all neighbourhoods as a driver of regeneration, cohesion and opportunities.

In 2026 we'll have the great opportunity to showcase all these aspirations as the World Capital of Architecture – a designation granted by UNESCO and the International Union of Architects to a city and its architects. This will be an opportunity to show the whole world what we're capable of, and most of all, what we aspire to in the future.

I would like to thank the Fundació Mies van der Rohe for its dedication to the study and promotion of European architecture, and all those participating in this effort to preserve the essential memory and legacy that is to inspire future generations. Mies van der Rohe said that the "new times are a given, they are here whether we like it or not, the only decisive thing is how we assert ourselves towards these givens". We therefore have a duty to assert ourselves fully towards everything we build today.

Jaume Collboni
Mayor of Barcelona

FOREWORD

We are pleased to present you this catalogue for the 2024 European Union Prize for Contemporary Architecture / Mies van der Rohe Awards.

It has been both a pleasure and a privilege to work with so many people and institutions to once again bring this award to light: fifteen architecture museums across Europe, almost a hundred independent experts, the professional institutes of architects from each participating country, the seven members of the jury, architects of over forty nationalities, and all those with an aspiration for architecture to transform and improve their own lives or those of others.

Since it was first launched in 1988 and now in its eighteenth biennial, this award has come of age firmly established as the most significant architecture prize in Europe.

On behalf of us all at Fundació Mies van der Rohe, we'd like to extend special thanks to Barcelona City Council and the European Commission, for jointly entrusting us with this ambitious undertaking of constructing and developing Europe through its architecture: and not an architecture of the historical or monumental kind, vital though this is in establishing our roots and offering a nod to our past, but contemporary architecture, essential because it's what we're producing today as a society, and what defines how we want to live from now on.

The Fundació Mies van der Rohe is the Barcelona City Council entity responsible for driving the discussion, diffusion and awareness of issues related to contemporary architecture and urban development. As well as being charged with conserving and promoting the Mies van der Rohe Pavilion and advocating the study of the work of its creators – Ludwig Mies van der Rohe and Lilly Reich – along with other Modernist architecture that emerged in the early 20th century, the Fundació also heads a range of initiatives such as awards, conventions, conferences, exhibitions, workshops and artistic and cultural events both at the Barcelona Pavilion and throughout the continent, with our sights also now set on the rest of the world.

The merging, superimposing and synthesis of past, present and future that the Mies van der Rohe Pavilion represents, is also a common denominator of the architecture, cities and populated spaces throughout Europe. However, the richness and complexity of European architecture also goes much deeper than this, and the European Union Prize for Contemporary Architecture / Mies van der Rohe Awards, organised in conjunction with the European Commission's Creative Europe programme, provides the very best opportunity for showcasing the architectural solutions proposed in the face of contemporary challenges hailing from all over the continent.

The EUmies Awards help us to understand the climatic and geographical diversity that both enriches and enhances Europe, and to appreciate the different legislative and socio-economic landscapes that inspire us and encourage us to progress, both as a discipline and a society.

This catalogue is a record of, testament to and showcase for the architectural landscape of contemporary Europe, just as it stands today. The catalogue is also further complemented by an open-access online archive (available at eumiesawards.com) – which details each of the 362 works nominated for this year's EUmies Awards along with the 4,512 nominations over its history – as well as the travelling exhibition inaugurated in Barcelona to coincide with the awards ceremony and the city's Setmanes d'Arquitectura ("Architecture Weeks"), and a series of conferences, roundtables and guided tours of the spaces that provide first-hand insights into and foster informed debate on the ways in which architecture can help build a better world.

Anna Ramos
Director
Fundació Mies van der Rohe

Foreword

5   **Iliana Ivanova**
EUROPEAN COMMISSIONER FOR INNOVATION, RESEARCH, CULTURE, EDUCATION AND YOUTH

7   **Jaume Collboni**
MAYOR OF BARCELONA

9   **Anna Ramos**
DIRECTOR FUNDACIÓ MIES VAN DER ROHE

Insights

13   *The Weather Will Be Fine Tomorrow*
Frédéric Druot
JURY PRESIDENT

16   *Three Small Points*
Pippo Ciorra
JURY MEMBER

18   *Posthuman Landscapes*
Martin Braathen
JURY MEMBER

20   *Every Building Has a Story… and a Soul*
Adriana Krnáčová
JURY MEMBER

23   *Temporary Structures rather than Permanent Works*
Tinatin Gurgenidze
JURY MEMBER

25   *An Encouraging Trip through European Architecture*
Sala Makumbundu
JURY MEMBER

27   *A Comprehensive Jury Process and Distinguished Result*
Hrvoje Njiric
JURY MEMBER

362 Works

29   *A Cartography for the EUmies Awards 2024*
Anna Sala
EDITOR

30   Map of Works

49   **Munch Museum**
estudioHerreros

54   **Liljevalchs+**
Wingårdh Arkitektkontor

74   **Son of a Shingle Vaksali Pedestrian Bridge and Underpasses**
PART architects

FINALIST

86   **Hage**
Brendeland & Kristoffersen, Price & Myers

99   *Placing a City*
James Payne

115   **Annesley Gardens**
Metropolitan Workshop

127   **Art Pavilion M.**
Studio Ossidiana

WINNER

132   **Study Pavilion on the Campus of the TU Braunschweig**
Gustav Düsing, Büro Hacke

147   *The TU Braunschweig Study Pavilion*
Peter Cachola Schmal

150   **Building Community Kurfürstenstrasse**
June14 Meyer-Grohbrügge & Chermayeff

156   **Floating University Berlin**
Floating e.V. Association

162   **Targ Blonie / Food Market**
Pracownia Architektoniczna Aleksandra Wasilkowska

176   **Fire Station, Multi-Purpose Space, and Emergency Housing**
Studio SNCDA + Bureau Bouwtechniek

TABLE OF CONTENTS

181	Open Air Swimming Pool Flow POOL IS COOL, Decoratelier Jozef Wouters	316	Black Slavonian Eco Pig Farm SKROZ		FINALIST
186	Amal Amjahid – Community Facility Along the Canal &bogdan	321	Nursery. 1306 Plants for Timișoara MAIO, Studio Nomadic, Studio Peisaj	451	Rebirth of the Convent Saint-François Amelia Tavella Architectes
190	Het Steen noAarchitecten	346	Day Centre for Young People with Autism Spectrum Disorder AV62 Arquitectos	463	*Vortex* Nina Bouraoui
218	Light Rail Tunnel allmannwappner			470	Tbilisi Urban Forest (Narikala Ridge Forest) Ruderal
	FINALIST	353	Média Library Charles Nègre Beaudouin Architectes, Ivry Serres Architecture	483	Living in Lime 42 Social Housing peris+toral arquitectes
226	PLATO Contemporary Art Gallery KWK Promes	374	Escadinhas Footpaths Paulo Moreira Architectures, Verkron	494	Liknon K-Studio
240	*Plato in Ostrava is an art gallery on the crossroads of past and future* Bartosz Haduch, Michał Haduch	378	General Silveira Building ATA Atelier, ENTRETEMPOS		EPILOGUE
			EMERGING FINALIST	504	*Bringing the Conversations Around* Ivan Blasi DIRECTOR EUMIES AWARDS
251	Refurbishment and Extension of a Community Swimming Pool RAUM	386	Piódão Square and Tourist Office Branco del Rio		
		399	*A Difficult Equation for Piódão Square and Tourist Office* Pedro Baía		# Colophon
262	IKEA Vienna Western Station IKEA – the Good Neighbour in the City querkraft architekten	402	Municipal Pools Óscar Miguel Ares. Contextos de arquitectura y urbanismo		INDEXS
				511	Works per Countries
266	Townhouse Neubaugasse PSLA Architekten		FINALIST	521	Works for Studios
273	Reconstruction and Extension of the Slovak National Gallery Architekti B.K.P.Š.	408	Reggio School Andrés Jaque - Office for Political Innovation		EUMIES AWARDS
		423	*Rainforest? Turn left after the drawbridge! Inside Madrid's eye-popping living school* Oliver Wainwright	534	Architecture Winners 1988-2022 Emerging Winners 2001-2022 Young Talent Winners 2016-2023
290	Bivouac Fanton DEMOGO			538	Jury, Advisory Committee, Independent Experts, National Associations, 2024
294	Bohinj Kindergarten KAL A, ARREA architecture	427	Social Housing 1737 HARQUITECTES	540	Credits
300	Covering the Remains of the Church of St. John the Baptist in the Žiče Charterhouse MEDPROSTOR, arhitekturni atelje		EMERGING WINNER	542	Imprint
		434	Gabriel García Márquez Library SUMA Arquitectura	544	Acknowledgements
305	Riding Hall. Land Registry Department of the Municipal Civil Court MORE arhitekture	447	*Shadows and Reflections from the Gabriel García Márquez Library in Sant Martí de Provençals* Josep Lluís Blàzquez		
311	Lonja Wetlands Wildlife Observatories and Visitor Centre roth&čerina				

12

INSIGHTS

The Weather Will Be Fine Tomorrow

362 then 40, then 5+2, and finally 1&1

From the vertigo of the list of 362 works presented to the selection of the lucky ones, everything in the world of nominated architecture reveals something to someone…and it is therefore through a grateful and supportive tribute that I would like, in the name of the jury, to salute all the teams of actors of the winning and non-winning projects of the EUmies Awards 2024. For the most inconsolable among them I would advise to read the last sentences of the myth of Sisyphus by Albert Camus: "The struggle towards the summits is enough to fill a man's heart with pleasure. You have to imagine Sisyphus happy".

Selecting is difficult. A little humbleness and a lot of conviction…

362

To select is to delve into the heterogeneous material of a vast territory to try to extract the most representative characters and features of the present moment in the history of European architecture.

November 2023

Before our eyes, the geography is broad and attractive, European, made of plains, mountains, glaciers, valleys, towns, villages, forests, agricultural landscapes and seasides. The variations of themes and disciplines of architecture are diverse and almost infinite: religions, cultures, leisure, businesses, education, landscape, workplaces, black pig breeding farms, and yes… the contexts and scales are numerous, the economies demonstrative or restrained, the production involves either new creations or the transformation of existing ones. This explicit catalogue demonstrates the formidable place of architecture in world affairs. Like philosophy, it has the power to interest and talk about everything.

Having 362 projects before your eyes is an awareness of an almost unreal amount of work, self-sacrifice, convictions, commitments, time spent focused on subjects with variable and relative implications. The architect is a social animal, his profession often a punishment, his production always a happy contribution to the habitability of the world.

40 then 5+2

To select is also to eliminate and therefore risk leaving behind us the unspeakable truth of a secret and delicate project. But that's how life goes.

To select is to react to words, to intentions, to representations, to drawings, to ideas and contexts. It is to attempt to undermine the power of images, it is to search in all the available material for a grouping of strong lines which will seem to be the most in line with the diversity of the present time.

To select is to verify intuitions and, through the trip that we made with the jury, the meticulous visit to the places, the direct exchanges with the actors, the observation of the contexts and the constructions, to readjust our points of view by accepting to be astonished. 5 intense and deliciously organised days, 5 days with my friends and jury members, Martin, Sala, Pippo, Tinatin, Hrvoje and Adriana at the end of which, in a final debate animated by the pleasure of our disagreements and contradictions, the learning of our differences, our mutual attention and the strength of conviction of each, we were able to put down our suitcases of architects and decide.

And so at the end of the trip and the debates, propose winners.

Frédéric Druot
President of the Jury. Architect, researcher and artist. Founder of Frédéric Druot Architecture (FDA) in Paris.

1&1

The **Study Pavilion on the campus of the Technical University of Braunschweig** by Gustav Düsing and Max Hacke, is rewarded for its ability to challenge the constraints and imagery of sustainability, creating a welcoming and playful environment for study, collaboration and community gathering through an uncompromising and carefully detailed structure. It has taken a clear architectural idea, scrutinized it and pushed it to the limit; more than being a building, it could be understood as a versatile system, merging technological inventions with a flexible and reusable principle.

A project process shaped like a final point at the end of a straight line. Clarity and efficiency.

The **Gabriel García Márquez Library** in Barcelona by Elena Orte and Guillermo Sevillano acts at the scale of the city, contributing to the transformation of the neighbourhood by opening up as a new exterior and interior public space. This wooden structure unfolds as a rich sequence of monumental and domestic spaces that welcome neighbours and citizens, providing them with comfortable atmospheres for learning, teamwork, and community engagement. With meticulous attention to detail, the authors have thoroughly examined and pushed the library programme to its fullest potential.

These two works are relevant and representative artifacts of European architecture today.

However, they need to be associated and combined with the five other shortlisted projects so that the dimension of diversity of European architecture can be truly represented and disseminated.

Diversity of Points of view and attitudes, Diversity of writing, Diversity of expression and context.

+5

The Hage by Brendeland & Kristoffersen is a fantastic mystical public garden on the outskirts of Lund that strives to preserve a small natural area, currently agricultural, around which a residential neighbourhood will rise very soon. Three brick walls and a roof all built using traditional methods create a place for reflection on architecture's relationship with time, urban development principles, and the design of community gathering spaces.

A project process shaped like an interrogation mark. An open work. A mental construction done step by step, with restraint and humility, and a constant concern, to do or not to do.

The Reggio School by Andrés Jaque is a vertical school on the outskirts of Madrid which seeks its place in the face of the privatisation of education and questions architecture, pedagogy, and education. The school is the result of an idiosyncratic imagery, spatial richness, and a reparative ecological aim, all built around a very special pedagogical system.

A project process shaped like an exclamation mark. A generous and truculent attitude clamoring to the world: "Of course it is possible to do like this".

The works of Plato in Ostrava of the team KWK Promes, the Convent of Saint François in Santa Lucia di Tallano of Amelia Tavella, as well as the Square and Tourist Office in Piódão by Branco del Rio preserve with delicate attention an indispensable European cultural heritage – industrial, landscape and urban – granting it a new life that attracts local communities as well as those from neighbouring territories.

In the very existence of the EUmies Awards and its inventory and selection process, we find the things we hope for in a happy vision of Europe. Jean Monnet, one of the founding fathers of the European Union was quoted as saying: "If I had to do it all over again, I would begin with culture." Why not do it today, since the experience we have with the jury of this 2024 prize is a delightful example of it?

The weather will be fine tomorrow.

Long live Europe.

....
FRÉDÉRIC DRUOT

Three Small Points

Apart from the privilege of working together with an uncommonly high-quality institution and group of people, participating in the jury of the European Union Prize for Contemporary Architecture / Mies van der Rohe Awards has been an extraordinary opportunity to reflect on certain questions that surround and remain within the complicated world of contemporary architecture.

The first and most immediate question regards architectural awards and their relevance in our current context, in which it is increasingly more difficult to define shared criteria for quality and excellence. The golden age of architectural awards began in the 1980s, at the start of contemporary architecture's rise to global fame, and it continued into the first years of this century without any major reconsiderations. The Pritzker Architecture Prize was founded in 1979, and it is awarded to an internationally renowned architect every year. Since 1985, to mark the second international architectural exhibition curated by Aldo Rossi, the Biennale di Architettura has followed the line of the Venetian awards system, which had survived with a certain amount of difficulty and interruptions since 1968, and awarded one or more winners with a Stone Lion, a slight understatement compared to the more prestigious Golden Lions of the other disciplines in the Biennale. The choice of stone, halfway between modesty and a love for tectonics, was short lived, however. Since 1996, starting with the *Sensors of the Future* by Hans Hollein, not coincidentally the first with a more artistic structure, the lions awarded for architecture have come in gold. Before the Pritzker Prize, there was the local version of the RIBA Awards, but this is an award given to architects by architects. Later came the Mies van der Rohe Award for European Architecture, recently rechristened the EUmies Awards, starting in 1988. It seems obvious to me that the oldest awards are showing signs of crisis. The initial aim of the Pritzker Prize was to crown young and old masters alike, which is a very rare commodity nowadays. The old master was slowly phased out by that glamorous wave of fame, replaced by the *archistar*, or star architect, who still holds sway in the marketplace, but is no longer seen as a progressive phenomenon. Today the strategy of the Pritzker Prize is to operate in a more situational fashion, creating a list of laureates year by year in which it is no longer easy, and may even be impossible, to draw a sense of coherence. As for the Biennale, rather than an awards crisis, as in reality the awards on the Venetian scene have always had a highly relative impact, the issue is more a structural crisis. The resonance basically lasts over the opening weekend and then gently fades into the background, except for the repercussions at home for the national pavilion awards. Considering that the landscape of national pavilions remains frozen in time together with a geopolitical idea established in the mid-twentieth century and given that there is always a demiurge curator who must choose to distribute their own personal team of architects across 14,000 square metres, the awards problem seems to be the least of their worries. Perhaps, the issue should be about questioning the format of the exhibition, the uniqueness of the curator as well as many other aspects.

The Mies Awards is fortunate to have been founded later, to have certainly recognised in the first part of its existence the charisma of certain individuals of great stature, but also to have the willingness to listen to the latest phenomena in contemporary professional landscape

Pippo Ciorra
Member of the Jury
Architect and curator

architecture. First, the presence of emerging talents and subsequently the partnership with Creative Europe have meant that the search for intriguing projects has increasingly expanded in the direction of greater inclusivity, attention to the environmental and anthropological issues of our time, and an interest in the new forms of agency by young architects and recent laureates. Although the old forms of leadership in architecture are definitely in crisis, the sphere for action of the Mies Awards is certainly a fertile ground to seek out and nurture other forms.

Another interesting character that has come from this selection by Mies, and from having helped to create it, is the emergence of an exciting new generation, capable of bridging the distance between those who remain passionate about the artistic and disciplinary quality of architecture and those who instead understand projects as an ideal opportunity to question the very status of the profession itself. A large part of the shortlisted architects and the finalists were very young designers. By age, a good number of the finalists would have been eligible for both the main award as well as for the emerging category. Many of them have already been operating for some time in a field of action ranging freely between buildings, installations, temporary constructions and performances, thus crafting a space for essential dialogue between the various competing attitudes around architecture today, judging both the intrinsic quality of the projects as well as their ability to contribute to a more comprehensive reconsideration of the contemporary space, whether human or post-human. The Study Pavilion by Düsing and Hacke is a cross between a building and temporary pavilion, the school by Andrés Jaque aims to assemble and reassemble, according to its paradigms, the very process of mediation between architecture and nature, the Plato Gallery in Ostrava straddles the line between building and kinetic installation, while the Hage by Brendendelan & Kristoffersen is a landscape installation.

Going back to the beginning and introducing some form of conclusion, if emphasising these awards also means seeking out a new reference figure and new forms of leadership on a stage in which younger generations view the idea of leadership itself with hostility and a sense of danger, then the team here at the EUmies Awardsis likely following the right tactics. The team does not seek out a resounding ideological statement but rather strives for the ability to discreetly follow what is happening, to map new signs and strategies, and to recognise new forms of talent while never forgetting the legacy upon which the institution itself was founded. Because after all, and perhaps this would be another issue to speculate on, what the Mies van der Rohe Foundation might want to suggest to us with its approach to the prize represents a diverse way of discussing modernity, assessing its fate, and better preserving its legacy.

PIPPO CIORRA

Posthuman Landscapes

To study and discuss the nominations for the 2024 EUmies Awards is also an act of studying today's Europe, and how its cultural production responds to its urgent needs. For this text, I was asked to focus on the projects outside the urban peripheries, but paradoxically, this experience has exemplified how making distinctions between peripheries and centers is unproductive. Instead, this year's works appear to show that crucial issues for the future of Europe are to be found outside of the larger city centers. The integration of architecture in both untouched and cultural landscapes is a recurring theme among this year's shortlisted projects.

This trend reflects posthumanist issues: architecture should be integrated as part of the ecosystems of the already existing landscapes –whether urban, cultural, or natural –and strive to preserve or even rejuvenate those landscapes with all its life forms, from microbes and insects to livestock and human habitats. Behind this notion looms a growing acknowledgment of the vulnerability of landscapes – through climate change and other man-made threats such as the war in Ukraine – which also highlights the issue of sustaining local food production.

Several of this year's shortlisted projects directly address food systems – production, distribution, preservation, and intangible cultural heritage. One example is the Eco Pig Farm designed by SKROZ in Croatia, which addresses the close relationship between production and conservation. With its focus on animal welfare and a more functional planning of spaces, the project offers a solution for the future of livestock farming, contributes to the preservation of the Slovenian black pig breed (which was threatened with extinction a few decades ago), and also preserves the cultural traditions of farming this breed.

Three food markets were also nominated for the awards, among them the Targ Błonie/ Food Market (by Pracownia Architektoniczna / Aleksandra Wasilkowska) in Blonie – a small town amid the vast farmlands surrounding Warsaw – which reinvents the traditional farmer's market with a playful recreational design, new hygiene standards and a direct connection to the landscape. Other agricultural projects include warehouses, the transformation of historical rural farm buildings, and the organic wine museum of Liknon (K-Studio), which is perfectly integrated within the terraced vineyard landscapes of Samos, Greece.

Another common thread can be seen with projects that work towards the preservation of nature through experiencing and interacting with it. There are several large-scale ecopark and wetland projects, among them the Lonja Wetlands Wildlife Observatories and Visitor Centre in Croatia (roth&čerina), which provides facilities for observing and experiencing the effects of seasonal changes. The Floating University of Berlin by the Floating e.V. Association is a symbiotic project integrated into the wetlands of the city's former Tempelhof airport. It provides a platform for learning with nature whilst also filtering the rainwater. Likewise, the large-scale, interventionist replanting of the Tbilisi Urban Forest by Ruderal has managed to regenerate the biodiversity and wildlife of a dilapidated park area, giving new life to the flora and fauna as well as its recreational facilities.

Nature overtaking older buildings (or more specifically, how to deal with landscape ruins) is also a recurring theme. An original solution is the cover for the Church of St. John the Baptist at the Žiče Charterhouse

Martin Braathen
Member of the Jury
Architect and Senior Curator of Architecture at the National Museum, Oslo.

monastery in Stare Slemene, Slovenia, in which a movable roof structure protects the building while still allowing it to be exposed to the natural elements, as it did as a ruin. For the Rebirth of the Convent Saint-François project in Corsica, transformed by Amelia Tavella Architectes, the remnants of the 1480 building are covered with a copper grid, emulating a sort of "ghost from the past".

Among the finalists there are two remarkably strong candidates that touch on the posthumanist issue – one deeply melancholic and one playful and optimistic. The Reggio School by Andrés Jaque, on the outskirts of Madrid, creates a vast microcosmos of nature, air, plants, insects, and birds for the students. Built upon the pedagogical principles developed in Reggio Emilia, Italy, it responds to the pedagogical notion of the school environment as being "the third teacher". The project entails vivid imagery and an architectural grammar comprising different materials and spatial elements, lively sections with varied spaces, and an ever-presence of nature. There are open spaces with airflows, lush indoor vegetation, and gardens for insects and birds. This school provides the perfect medium for learning lessons about our interactions with nature.

A far more melancholic lesson is presented by the Hage project in Lund, Sweden, designed by architects Brendeland & Kristoffersen, in conjunction with Price and Myers. Hage appears as a timeless, simple piece of architecture: three walls with a covered opening standing alone in a field. But the context behind the project is somber and its function will evolve over time: built on church-owned land in the middle of what will soon be a large-scale housing development, this project is protecting some of the last remnants of Sweden's richest soil. The walls are made of repurposed bricks that resemble the local garden walls of Lund, and the roof, finely crafted and engineered with great effort, is constructed using traditional welding techniques. This simplicity imbues the project with earthly materiality and elevated spirituality alike. As the new development rises around it, Hage will become a homage to irreplaceable assets, lost by notions of eternal development and economic growth. But, as an undefined space which can be shaped and utilized by its future residents, it also represents a cautious optimism, and as a principle for urban development it is the subject of a radical proposal: namely, to leave the first part of the development as a void.

MARTIN BRAATHEN

Every Building has a Story... and a Soul

And not just buildings. Human activity, no matter what, must have a story if it wants to communicate something. An authentic and powerful story. If it doesn't, the activity is demeaned; it becomes mediocre and eventually falls into oblivion. This is especially true for buildings that haphazardly try to determine the common space in which we live, work and rest. We can't ignore them, even if we wanted to, because we subconsciously know they're there anyway: they live with us, next to us, and we in turn live within them, each and every day.

Sunday, 8 a.m.: We board the train to Ostrava. I say that "architecture is the mother of all art", and my colleagues stare at me in amazement. They don't understand what I mean.

I reply: "That's what we were taught, long ago in our very first semester when we discussed "ancient art"... somewhere back in the dark days of normalisation, when the faculty was both a refuge and a curse. It gave us young students a glimpse into worlds long forgotten, and worlds that were beyond our reach at the time. It gave us the faint hope that one day we would visit those places; it fostered our imagination. Back then, when everything was different, we escaped into other worlds, only to come to back reality when we left school at the end of the day. Yes, architecture is the mother of all art".

I always remembered this phrase, and later kept coming back to it, seeing it proved to be true.

After three hours, when we got off the train in Ostrava, we headed to the exhibition space called PLATO. Thanks to the city, this former slaughterhouse has been renovated to "process" and showcase contemporary art instead of meat. It's a beautiful sunny day, and the director gives us a warm welcome and shows us around the space. "This building has a strong history and we're trying to build on it", says the director, Marek. There are large spaces shaded by monochrome windows, and a massive revolving entrance. I imagine what it used to be like here, back when animals came in to be turned into food, and compare it to how it is now, serving something completely different - still food, but of another kind: one that cultivates discussion, bridges differences, and fosters mutual understanding.

The bus to Vienna is quiet; everyone is doing something – reading, listening, sleeping... I'm finishing up my proofreading and wondering what the "special something" is that caused these architectural achievements to be finalist. We have discussed this several times – talked about their pros and cons, both individually and in groups. But what is the underlying essence, the underlying common determinator? We pass Brno and more than once Pippo loudly asks how far we are from Villa Tugendhat. His indignation that we passed by the iconic masterpiece by Ludwig Mies van der Rohe - the architect after whom the EUmies Awards is named – without stopping, is great indeed. "Is there no way we can see it?", he tries again. No way, our schedule is tight.

"What's interesting about Braunschweig?", I ask Max, one of the young architects who designed the pavilion for the city's Technical University campus. Apart from the proximity to Wolfsburg and Volkswagen, probably not much – as people are leaving. "We also have a studio in Berlin", adds Max. That's why we created the Pavilion, which is open to everyone – not just university students, but anyone who wants to come here to do their homework, read, study, draw or talk. The light, almost transparent

Adriana Krnáčová
Member of the Jury.
Writer and politician.
In 2014–2018 she served as Mayor of Prague.

structure conceals an ingenious solution to the demanding environmental conditions imposed on new buildings. I ask a student sitting in one of the building's "nests" how he feels here, and whether they disturb each other in this huge open space… "Not at all", he says. In the distance I see a group arguing over something lying in front of them – it looks like a half-finished robot. It's crowded and not at the same time, and sounds like a buzzing hive: white noise, where it's quiet to work and you're in the middle of the action, but respectful.

The drop in temperature is immediately noticeable when we arrive at Copenhagen airport. Inevitably, as we're now much further north. My daughter lives in Copenhagen, so this is not my first time here. On the contrary, I somehow feel at home. The road over the "bron" – the bridge made famous by the crime series of the same name – connects Copenhagen and Malmö: two cities in two countries that couldn't be more different. In the morning, which is sunny but cold, we head to Lund. We're in a land of sparing gestures and muted shows of emotion – yet there's a sparkling warmth, which of course, isn't immediately apparent. Even the meaning of "Hage" isn't obvious at first, though the name intrigued the jury enough to nominate it as a finalist.

A cold wind blows, but the sun attempts to take the edge off the cold, just like Hage, which stands here alone as the first stage of the urban planning project implemented by the city and local church. With its austere structure and highly precise execution through the use of bricks and ironwork, it reflects the character of the local inhabitants, who waste nothing – neither words, nor gestures. Yet the project, which consists of a 40 × 40 m courtyard with a garden in the middle where (chosen by the people) "there will always be something different growing" – as Olaf, one of the project's architects puts it – is filled with future life. Just imagine. "And that long wooden table…that's where everyone gets together for picnics etc.", adds Tim. I wonder what will be there in a few years' time, when the surrounding space is taken up with other projects – mainly housing… Or could this first excavation of the land be the factor that will ultimately determine future development? Maybe. "We have time", says the dean of Lund cathedral, who is both the sponsor and driving force behind the project. "Our cathedral was built in 1123 and celebrated its 900th anniversary last year…we have time, we're in no rush, we're looking after our people and everything around us", she added. How this elderly, frail, reserved, fair-haired lady ended up accepting a goodbye kiss from our charming jury president, Frederic, we'll never know. It was…unexpected.

Before we know it and with an all-female crew we're now flying to Paris. I feel great.

The pace at which we're moving from place to place is beginning to take its toll: always in a hurry, constantly discussing and reassessing what we've seen, talking about talking about the way of the world: about how difficult it is sometimes to all agree in today's Europe; about how we are gradually drifting apart rather than coming together and listening to each other more. At least the jury – even though everyone comes from different places – is able to do that.

Our small plane lands in Adjaccio, Corsica. We have a two-hour inland bus ride to Sainte-Lucie-de-Tallano. Here, the former Franciscan monastery had almost collapsed, and nobody really knew what to do with it. Eventually, the council decided to turn it into a community centre. We are greeted by a ready-laid table on a raised platform between the buildings, and local singers performing Corsican ballads. The bride and the groom were yet to arrive. "As I'm from here, I wanted to come back and give something of myself", says Amelia, the architect behind the renovation. Copper surfaces and light make up the essential components of the project's new visual impression. Inside, there's a library and spaces for social events. It's a start.

Now a stopover in Marseille and a short break with a morning walk to the harbour. "This was also a shortlisted a few years ago", Anna points to the pergola in the middle of the square. "Norman Foster, I think, but it didn't win", she adds.

The last stop in Madrid. Just outside the centre is an elementary school that at first glance conforms to the aesthetic rules of "beauty". "It's so oddly strange as to be intriguing", I thought when I first saw the building in a photo. One student described the school as "a robot made of butter". We meet the "heart and soul" of the building – the school principal, Eva – who instigated the project and drafted in the star architect Andrés Jaque. Parents and children were also invited to put their ideas into action. The school boasts a verdant atrium, recycled materials, open spaces, and a "playground" feel at each level. I wish I was a child again. We walk up one floor and suddenly I hear drumming. In the music room one of the parents is rehearsing something for the school band. "We used prefabs that you can find in the store, and just adapted them...oh, and the yellow cladding on the façade, that's painted cork", says Andrés. "And the bugs, the bugs are important"... he points to one of the overlooks where different plants are growing. Okay...Eva leads us to the ground floor, where there's a preschool for children from the age of two...good concept.

"It's not a competition", Anna points out. Perhaps, but it is *in* a competition...

In a hotel conference room in Madrid, the jury has now met for the last time to decide on the winner. Everyone has, or *had*, a favourite, and everything is different when you see the space in situ: you can sense whether it has a soul, a captivating story to draw you in... and if it can stand up. When you're there, everything changes, and the most valuable part of the process is discussing and listening to each other's arguments.

And so we return to the question of what the common denominator of all the finalist projects is. Professor Mark Hyman, a physician and longevity expert defines living in a community as one of the essential conditions of quality of life and longevity. Whether it's a community centre in Corsica, an art gallery in Ostrava, a community space in Lund, an open study pavilion in Braunschweig or a school on the outskirts of Madrid, all the projects have a strong narrative that is underscored by a fundamental insight – we create spaces for people to feel comfortable in, to realize their dreams and support each other. This is the essence of this European prize – at least this year. And in addition to evaluating architectural qualities, the EUmies Awards also promotes the understanding of architecture as a universal language that tolerates and understands differences, promotes creativity, and opens up spaces for discussing the meaning of mankind's activities in a constantly changing, demanding and polarized world.

ADRIANA KRNÁCOVÁ

INSIGHTS

Temporary Structures rather than Permanent Works

A discussion of architecture through the lens of Actor-Network Theory reveals that social situations are composed of constantly shifting networks, where all factors, whether human or non-human, are equally significant in shaping the outcome. In the context of rapidly evolving urban landscapes, the role of architecture extends beyond mere functionality to actively shape and influence social dynamics. The social aspects of buildings are of significant interest because of their potential for fostering social change and activating their surrounding environments. When might a building be deemed to have been successfully implemented? The influence of the built environment on humans and the potential for people to influence the buildings themselves are key considerations.

The shortlisted projects for this year's EUmies Awards demonstrate a clear focus on revolutionary ideas for changing social environments. Some of the projects are compelling examples of how architecture can act as a catalyst for social change and reshape urban environments, with users playing a crucial role in its success. In some instances, structures are designed to allow users to take centre-stage, thereby emphasizing the active role of individuals in these architectural projects. To gain a deeper understanding of the underlying concepts behind the selected works, I spoke to five individuals involved in the shortlisted projects.

One of the projects shortlisted is a hidden space with utopian-shaped structures that brings together different community practices and creates a public learning laboratory in the heart of the city. Since its inception during the inaugural phase of the Floating University in Berlin and the inaugural ClimateCare Festival in 2019, the Floating University has emerged as a transformative force, challenging traditional educational paradigms, and redefining our relationship with urban landscapes.

"The space looks like the guts of the city", says Rosario Talevi, one of the founders and active members of the Floating e.V.Association. The Floating University is located at a rainwater harvesting basin at the former Tempelhof Airport. This basin serves as both a functional component of the city's water system and a habitat for wetland plants, birds, frogs, bats, and foxes. The architectural design of the space is in a constant state of evolution, in employing a practice of shared construction that takes place annually in a horizontal and collaborative manner.

The other project, the Study Pavilion on the campus of TU Braunschweig, challenges hierarchical structures within educational spaces, and provides a dynamic environment for interdisciplinary collaboration. The design of the structure is intended to facilitate social exchange and interdisciplinary collaboration, creating an environment conducive to knowledge generation among the students and faculty. This self-organized study pavilion for knowledge sharing and the creation of common space, represents a progressive typology of education buildings. At first glance, the structure appears static and solid, but upon closer examination, it becomes evident that it is a living example of dynamic processes of adaptation that occur according to the different situations and needs of its users. The Study Pavilion on the TU Braunschweig campus represents a paradigm shift in educational spaces, by breaking away from traditional hierarchies.

Another example of a shared space is the Escadinhas Footpaths project in Matosinhos. This project is an example of the transformative

Tinatin Gurgenidze

Member of the Jury Architect, urban researcher, curator, and author. Co-founder and one of the artistic directors of the Tbilisi Architecture Biennial.

potential of pedestrian infrastructures to integrate architecture, art, and nature – by revitalizing neglected urban spaces and promoting community engagement. In a similar way to the other projects discussed, the Escadinhas Footpaths project is also a process: a never-ending project that evolves and lives through its users.

As regards the open-air swimming pool, FLOW, Jozef Wouters, one of its creators, describes it as "like a theatre-play that repeats every 45 minutes." The temporary outdoor pool – a 1:1 scale model – is a veritable symbolic space and tool for activism where collective swimming takes place. Serving both as an example and a provocation, the pool highlights Brussels' lack of built open-air swimming spots. The pool, therefore, aims to convince authorities to invest in permanent projects while meanwhile offering a real – albeit small – safe, and inclusive place to cool down in the summer.

The tree-nursery project in Timișoara serves as an illustrative example of the transient nature of social change. It involves the construction of a temporary structure to serve as a nursery for trees and facilitate public discussions. The trees were meticulously cared for in an outdoor temporary installation, with measures taken to protect them from harsh weather conditions. When the installation was dismantled, the trees were all ready to be planted around the city of Timișoara. Throughout the project, community engagement played a vital role. Through citizen engagement and participatory design, this initiative aimed to empower communities to shape their urban environment and cultivate a sense of ownership of shared spaces.

Although the buildings discussed here are all very different, they all have one thing in common: they are, or have the appearance of being, temporary structures rather than permanent works. The temporary nature of the projects is the most significant social aspect of all: in a time of multiple crises, it is a challenging task to think in a permanent and durable manner. Rather than providing the solutions for a sustainable future, the temporality of the structures demonstrates the ability to think critically and discuss architecture. The progressive thinking behind these structures can be seen in their ability to represent a continuous process of testing, playing, caring, learning, unlearning, and experimenting. The buildings are presented as an evolving discussion process, that illustrate new, progressive and open architectural typologies and ideas.

In conclusion, the buildings highlighted in this text offer a glimmer of hope that change is on the horizon. They suggest that we may be entering a new age of architecture, prompting us to reconsider the necessity of our current building practices.

I would like to thank Max Hacke, Gustav Düsing, Rosario Talevi, Alexandra Trofin, Josef Wouters, Paul Steinbrück and Paulo Moreira for taking the time to talk with me about their projects.

An Encouraging Trip through European Architecture

The first visualisation of the 362 projects presented was fascinating. What a kaleidoscope of architecture from different countries and from such varied urban, social and economic contexts!

Despite the differences and diversity of the projects, we clearly feel a common cultural base. Architects offer this range under the influence of the local culture and context. It is reassuring to see this architecture produced by firms of all sizes, some well-known, but the vast majority of them are still under the radar of the European architectural press. What a discovery!

In addition to the particular context of each country, the projects submitted also reflect national economic situations in the construction sector and raise questions about the future of the profession of architecture in certain countries. However, despite contexts that are not always easy, it is encouraging to see how creativity, innovation and the search for proper architectural responses to our societies' needs finds a varied and qualitative expression. The projects express the search for excellence and for new ideas in terms of types, aesthetics and construction methods.

Indeed, architecture can still be innovative! It innovates in terms of space, type, construction, working methods and more. This includes a revival of craftmanship and know-how in some new projects (and not only in those linked to the architectural heritage of the past). In an increasingly complex world, current architecture retains the capacity to move forward to contribute to the broadest possible architectural culture.

While some may lament it, I think it is commendable that most of the projects submitted are not of the 'Bilbao effect' type, but ones that reflect essential architectural production at all scales, often in the context of small and medium-sized towns. The vast majority of architects have understood that it is not the grand architectural gesture that generally matters, but a careful and sensitive architectural approach that will contribute to the quality and consistency of urban and rural areas, as well as to community and social life.

This also translates into great sensitivity towards the existing architectural heritage. A remarkable proportion of the projects submitted for this 2024 edition of the EUmies Awards involves reconversion, transformation and extension. There are different reasons for this: awareness of the richness of heritage and its potential to revive, the search for identity and consciousness of the environmental impact.

Whatever the reason, it is encouraging to see the sensitivity, creativity and courage with which architects approach transformation projects and succeed in continuing to bring to life or revive architectural heritage, often by creating added value for the surrounding neighbourhoods. And it is not only a question of classified built heritage, but also of 'normal' architectural heritage. Fortunately, we can also see that architecture is taking over projects too often left in the hands of 'builders' who often do not focus on creation and architectural quality, as we can observe for many projects in artisanal and industrial areas and the agricultural sector.

The architect's commitment at all levels, his or her exchange with the project owner, the exchange with users, the search for details, new materials or new processes, collaboration with experts and intense inter-

Sala Makumbundu
Member of the Jury.
Architect. Managing partner at Christian Bauer & Associés Architectes in Luxembourg.

disciplinary work results in high-quality architectural projects. The works demonstrate the designers' courage and perseverance to push the idea to the end.

Every architect knows this and the meeting of the stakeholders of the five finalist projects impressively re-confirms it: the role of the project owner is crucial. The project owner's vision for developing a project and their philosophy, trust in designers, open-mindedness, receptive attention paid to the concepts and ideas proposed and involvement in the design process are important for the success of the project, even if too often underestimated.

As an architect and member of the Jury, this intense confrontation with current European architectural production provided enormous inspiration and encouragement to continue the search for architectural excellence, despite a significant increase in the complexity of the profession and all the difficulties that can arise in an architectural project until it is completed. I hope that visiting the exhibition and, even better, the projects, as well as the exchanges and discussions about them and their different approaches, will arouse the same enthusiasm among visitors. Hopefully, this will enable us to have deep exchanges and debates about architecture and convey the profession's passion, desire and commitment to create a quality living environment for all!

SALA MAKUMBUNDU

Mies van der Rohe Award 2024: A Comprehensive Jury Process and Distinguished Results

The Mies van der Rohe Award, formally known as the European Union Prize for Contemporary Architecture - Mies van der Rohe Awards (EUmies Awards), is as a beacon of excellence in architectural innovation and design. The 2024 edition of the award involved a meticulous and multi-faceted jury process that ultimately celebrated some of the most transformative projects in Europe.

The 2024 jury was composed of a diverse group of professionals, each bringing unique expertise and perspectives to the table. Our different backgrounds and shared commitment to sustainability and innovation undoubtedly influenced the selection process in a particular way. I was mostly impressed by the engagement of each and every jury member throughout the whole process.

Our sessions were marked by long and rigorous deliberations. Over several occassions, we engaged in deep discussions, meticulously reviewing each submission to ensure that the projects met the high standards of innovation, sustainability, and social relevance expected of the Mies van der Rohe Award. We reviewed a diverse range of projects, considering factors such as design quality, functionality, environmental impact, and cultural significance. It was very inspiring and stimulating to experience the multifaceted expertise of other jury members which led to enriching debates and discussions, allowing us to carry out a thorough examination of each project's merits and challenges. In particular, we should mention the role of our president Frédéric Druot.

One of the highlights of the jury process was our trip to visit the finalists' projects. This on-site evaluation allowed us to experience the architecture in its true context, providing invaluable insights that are not always evident from drawings and photographs. Visiting the sites made it possible for the jury to appreciate how each project interacted with its environment and community. We met with architects, clients, and users, gaining a deeper understanding of the design intent, execution, and impact of the projects.

The culmination of our extensive work was the selection of the winners, projects that exemplified the pinnacle of contemporary European architecture. Although the jury did not come to a unanimous decision, we awarded the Prize to the German architects Gustav Düsing and Max Hacke for the Study Pavilion TU Braunschweig project that seamlessly integrated innovative design, sustainability, and social impact, setting a new benchmark for architectural excellence. The prize for the best work of emerging architects awarded to the Spanish firm SUMA Arquitectura for the Gabriel García Márquez Library has also brought fresh perspectives and groundbreaking ideas to the field. Finally, as a Croatian, I am particularly proud that this edition ended up with three recognitions for Croatia among the 40 shortlisted projects.

Hrvoje Njiric

Member of the Jury
Architect, professor and lecturer. Founder of njiric+ arhitekti in Zagreb.

28

362
WORKS

From
ILULISSAT
Denmark (Greenland)
69°14'00"N - 51°05'37"W

to
SANTA CRUZ
DE TENERIFE
Spain
28°27'27"N - 16°15'20"W

EDITORIAL

A Cartography for the EUmies Awards 2024

The EUmies Awards 2024 began its 18th cycle in May 2023, with a network of expert nominators and the architecture associations from throughout Europe who submitted 362 projects for the jury's consideration. These 362 works are placed in 38 European countries, corresponding to 125 regions and 240 places. Specific local contexts that share similar climatic conditions or differ in a contrasting manner.

Each of these works can be geolocated through specific coordinates that place them at unique points in the Northern Hemisphere of our planet. The cluster of these projects creates an abstract map of Europe: the map of the EUmies Awards 2024. Following the traces of the meridians, this cartography unfolds into fifteen horizontal bands, stretching from North to South and West to East, offering multiple relational interpretations of the 362 nominated works. Identified by fifteen different colours, from blue to red, including greens, yellows, and oranges, each project is positioned within these bands, from the icy landscape of Greenland (1) to a subtropical banana grove in the Canary Islands (362).

This cartography serves as a navigation chart for this book, in which the 362 nominated works are arranged according to their coordinates within these coloured climatic bands. Thus, each chapter unfolds as a sequence of pages filled with photographs, plans, and texts that, like a collage, illustrate each of the projects. Embedded within this order, the selected, finalist, and winning works are highlighted, taking up more space to be explained in greater depth and detail.

A series of seven unpublished texts accompany the finalist and winning projects: James Payne reflects on Hage "Placing a City"; architects Bartosz Haduch and Michał Haduch discuss the Plato Contemporary Art Gallery; critic Oliver Wainwright delves into the Reggio School; and writer Nina Bouraoui writes about the Rebirth of the Convent Saint-François in her text "Vortex." Pedro Baía reflects on the delicate and invisible intervention of the emerging finalist project, Piódão Square and Tourist Office. Regarding the two winning works, DAM director Peter Cachola Schmal explains the origin of the Study Pavilion TU Braunschweig, while art historian and broadcaster Josep Lluís Blàzquez brings us closer to the local context of the Gabriel García Márquez Library as the emerging winning work.

As an introduction, a series of reflections made by each of the jury members is presented: Frédéric Druot, Martin Braathen, Pippo Ciorra, Tinatin Gurgenidze, Adriana Krnáčová, Sala Makumbundu, and Hrvoje Njiric, a diverse and choral human group, who have been tasked with establishing a framework for reflection on the state of contemporary European architecture based on the 362 works that make up the planetary cartography of the EUmies Awards 2024.

Anna Sala Giralt
Editor, Fundació
Mies van der Rohe

Map of works

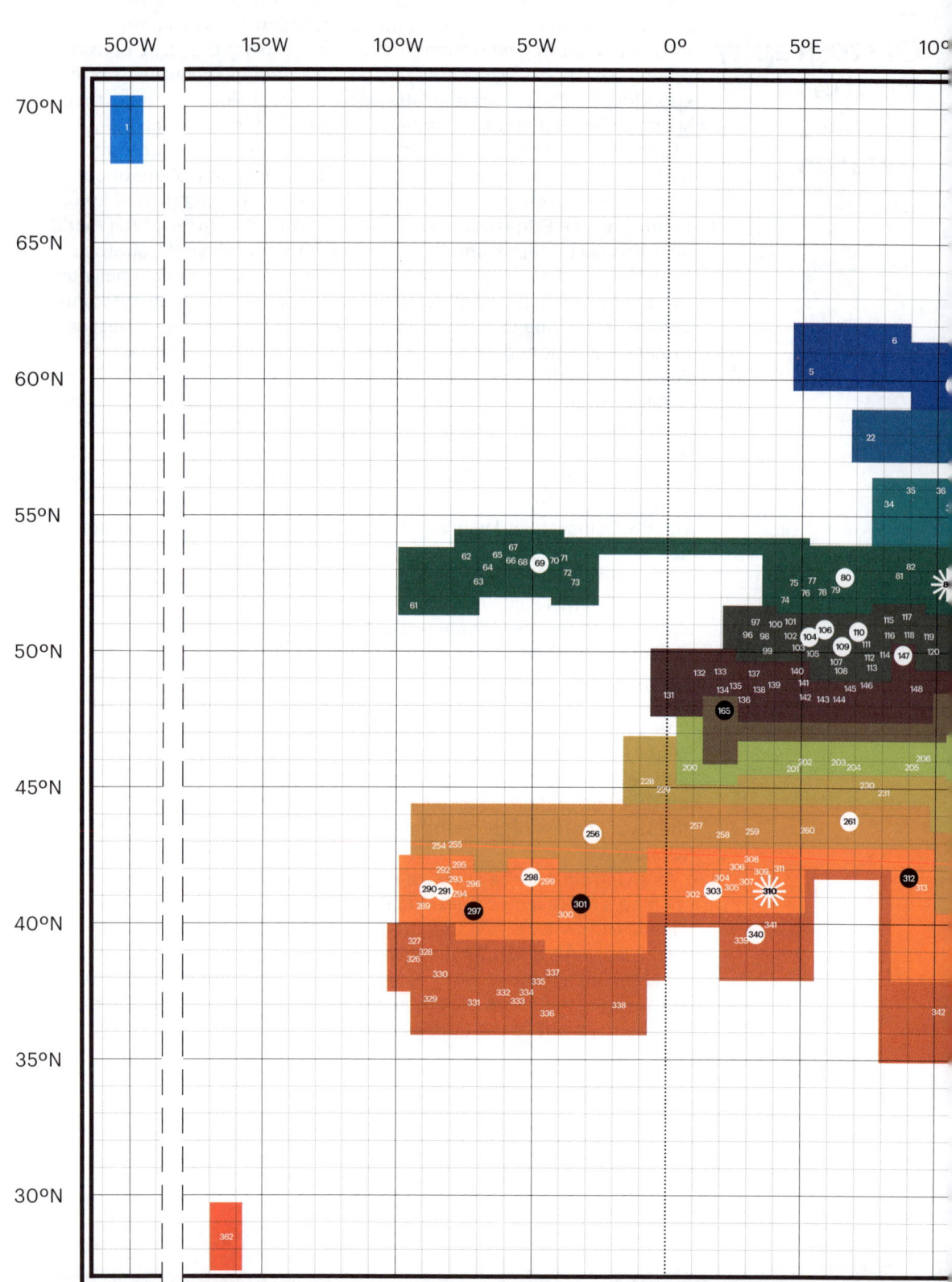

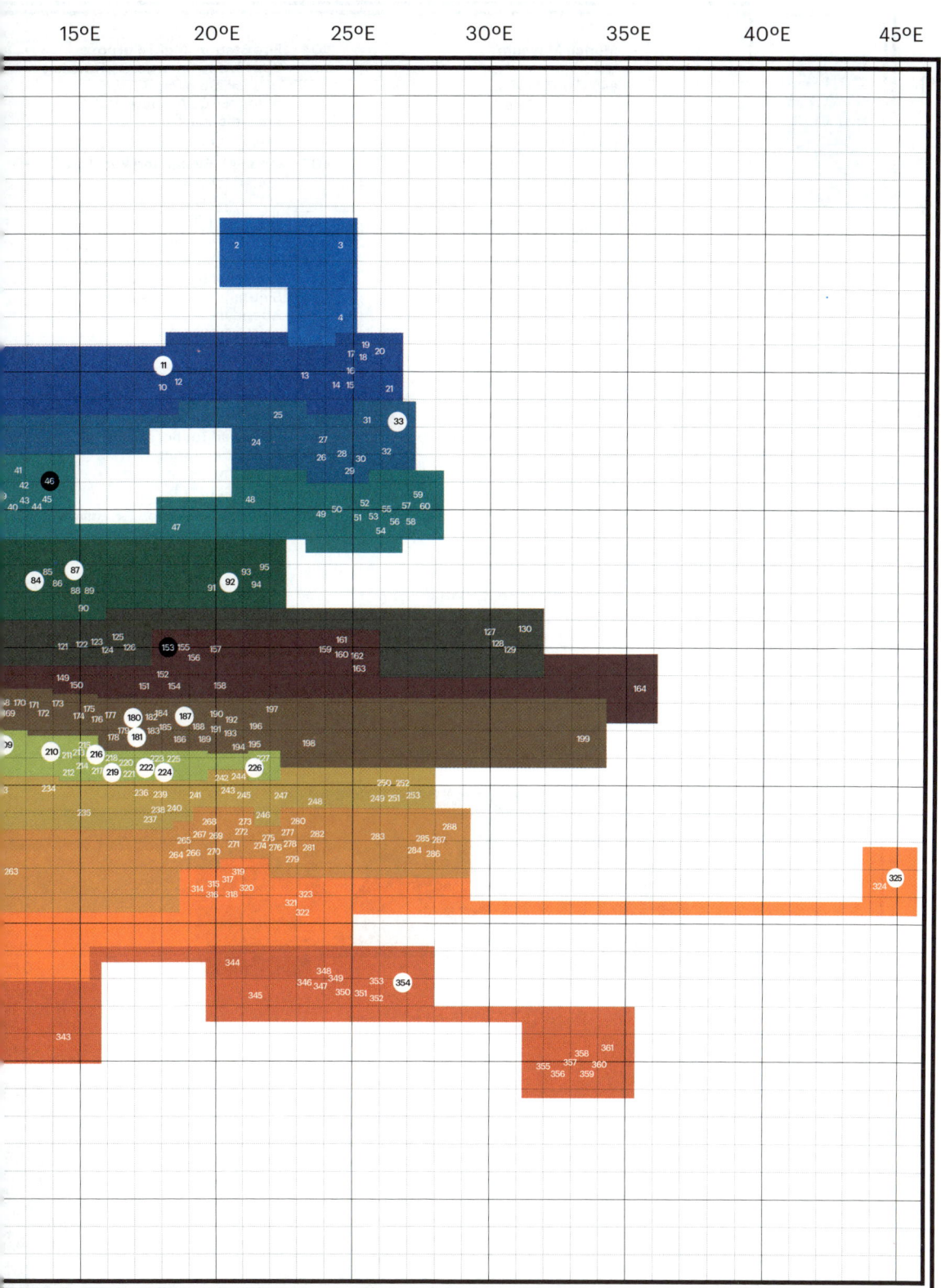

MAP OF WORKS 1/4

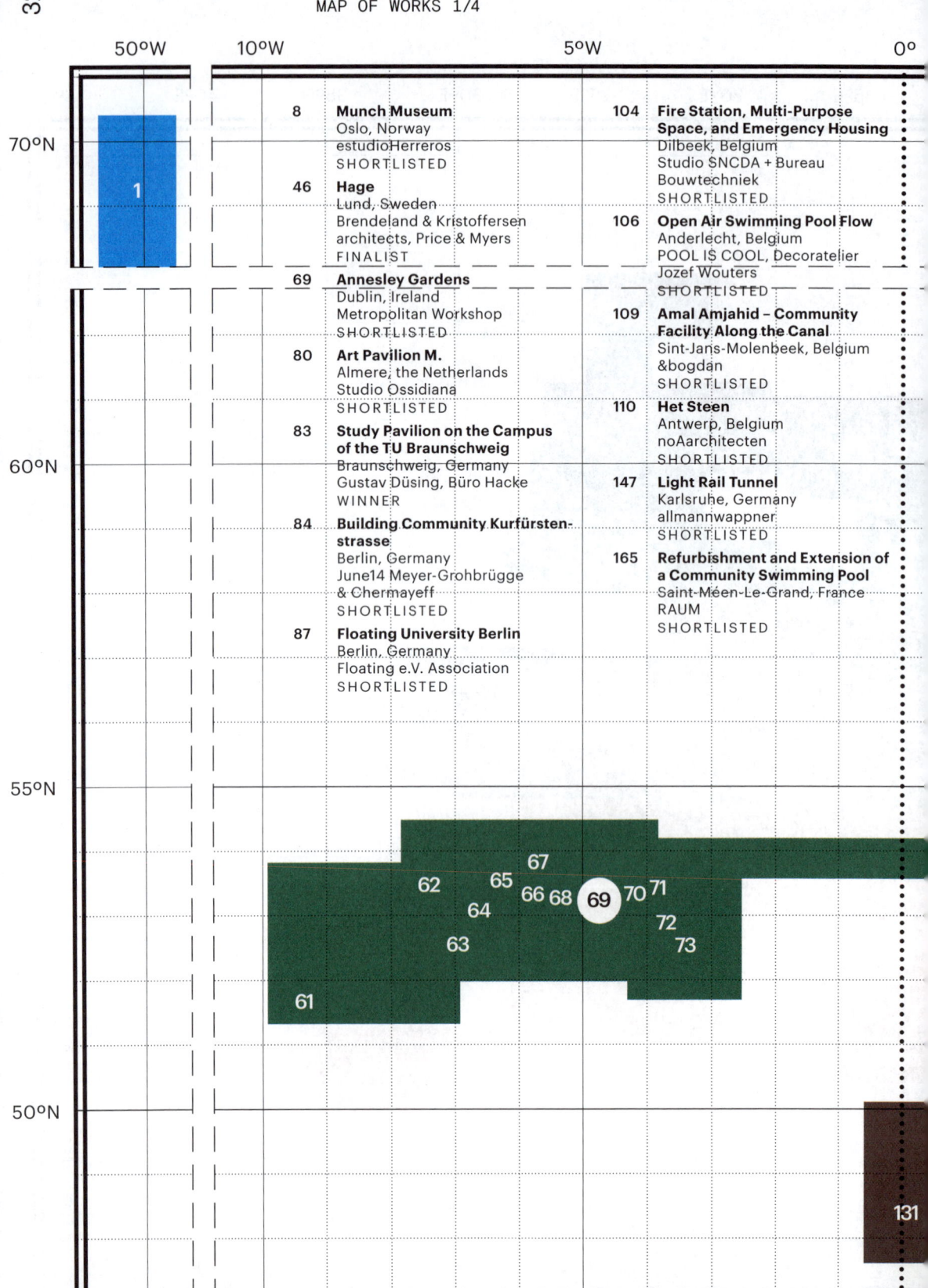

8	**Munch Museum** Oslo, Norway estudioHerreros SHORTLISTED	
46	**Hage** Lund, Sweden Brendeland & Kristoffersen architects, Price & Myers FINALIST	
69	**Annesley Gardens** Dublin, Ireland Metropolitan Workshop SHORTLISTED	
80	**Art Pavilion M.** Almere, the Netherlands Studio Ossidiana SHORTLISTED	
83	**Study Pavilion on the Campus of the TU Braunschweig** Braunschweig, Germany Gustav Düsing, Büro Hacke WINNER	
84	**Building Community Kurfürsten-strasse** Berlin, Germany June14 Meyer-Grohbrügge & Chermayeff SHORTLISTED	
87	**Floating University Berlin** Berlin, Germany Floating e.V. Association SHORTLISTED	
104	**Fire Station, Multi-Purpose Space, and Emergency Housing** Dilbeek, Belgium Studio SNCDA + Bureau Bouwtechniek SHORTLISTED	
106	**Open Air Swimming Pool Flow** Anderlecht, Belgium POOL IS COOL, Decoratelier Jozef Wouters SHORTLISTED	
109	**Amal Amjahid – Community Facility Along the Canal** Sint-Jans-Molenbeek, Belgium &bogdan SHORTLISTED	
110	**Het Steen** Antwerp, Belgium noAarchitecten SHORTLISTED	
147	**Light Rail Tunnel** Karlsruhe, Germany allmannwappner SHORTLISTED	
165	**Refurbishment and Extension of a Community Swimming Pool** Saint-Méen-Le-Grand, France RAUM SHORTLISTED	

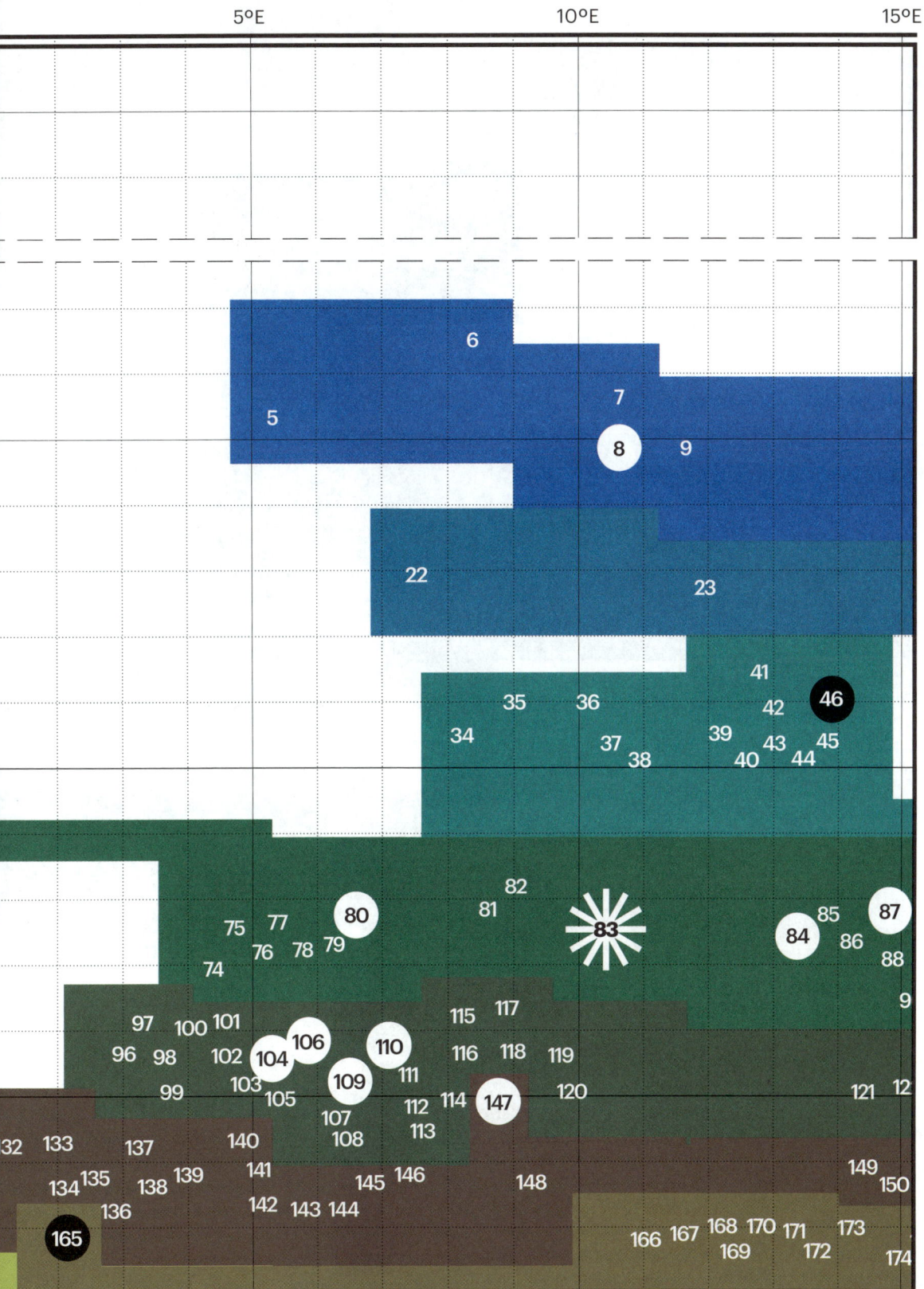

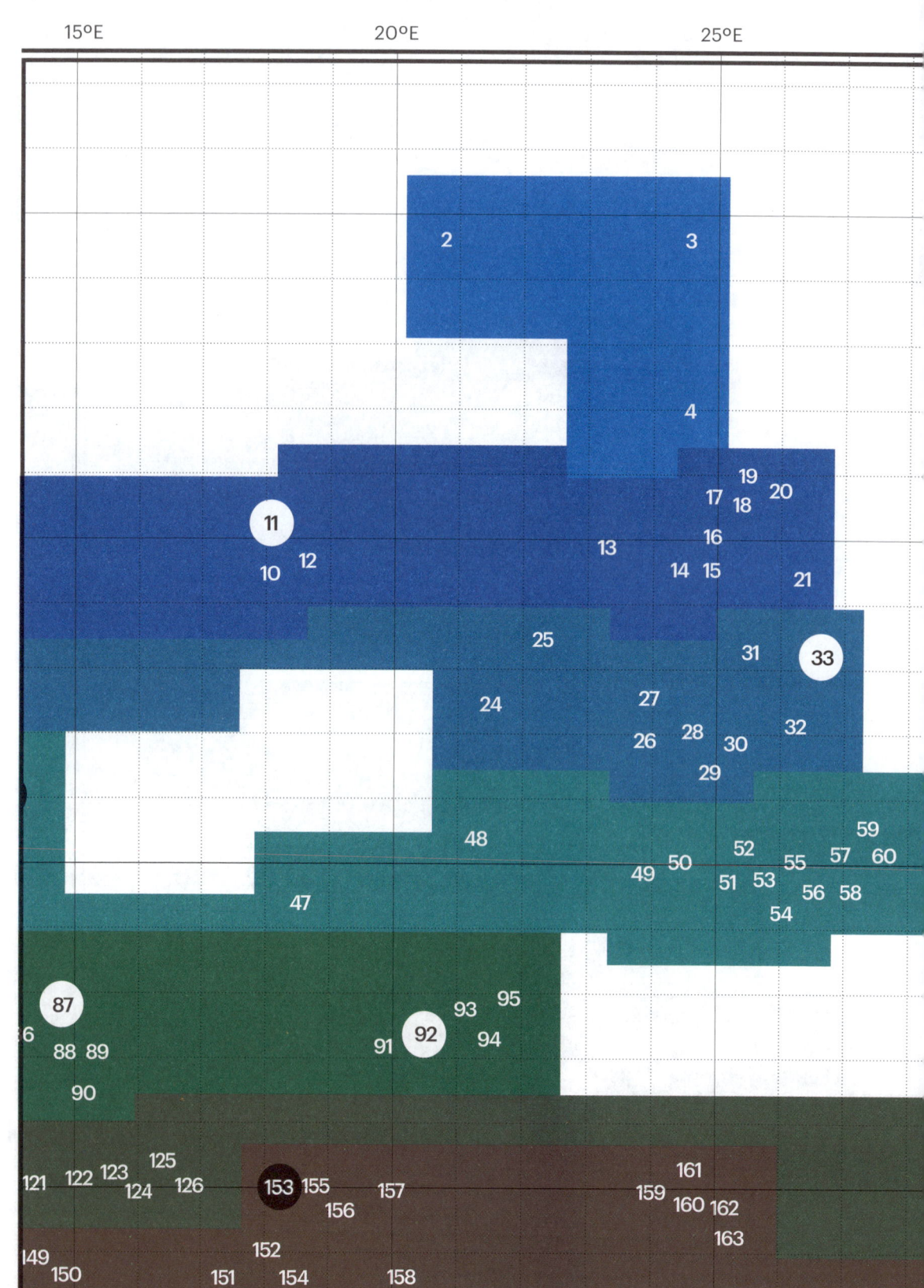

11	**Liljevalchs+** Stockholm, Sweden Wingårdh Arkitektkontor SHORTLISTED
33	**Son of a Shingle – Vaksali Pedestrian Bridge and Underpasses** Tartu, Estonia PART architects SHORTLISTED
87	**Floating University Berlin** Berlin, Germany Floating e.V. Association SHORTLISTED
92	**Targ Błonie / Food Market** Błonie, Poland Pracownia Architektoniczna Aleksandra Wasilkowska SHORTLISTED
153	**PLATO Contemporary Art Gallery** Ostrava, Czech Republic KWK Promes FINALIST

127 130
128 129
164

MAP OF WORKS 3/4

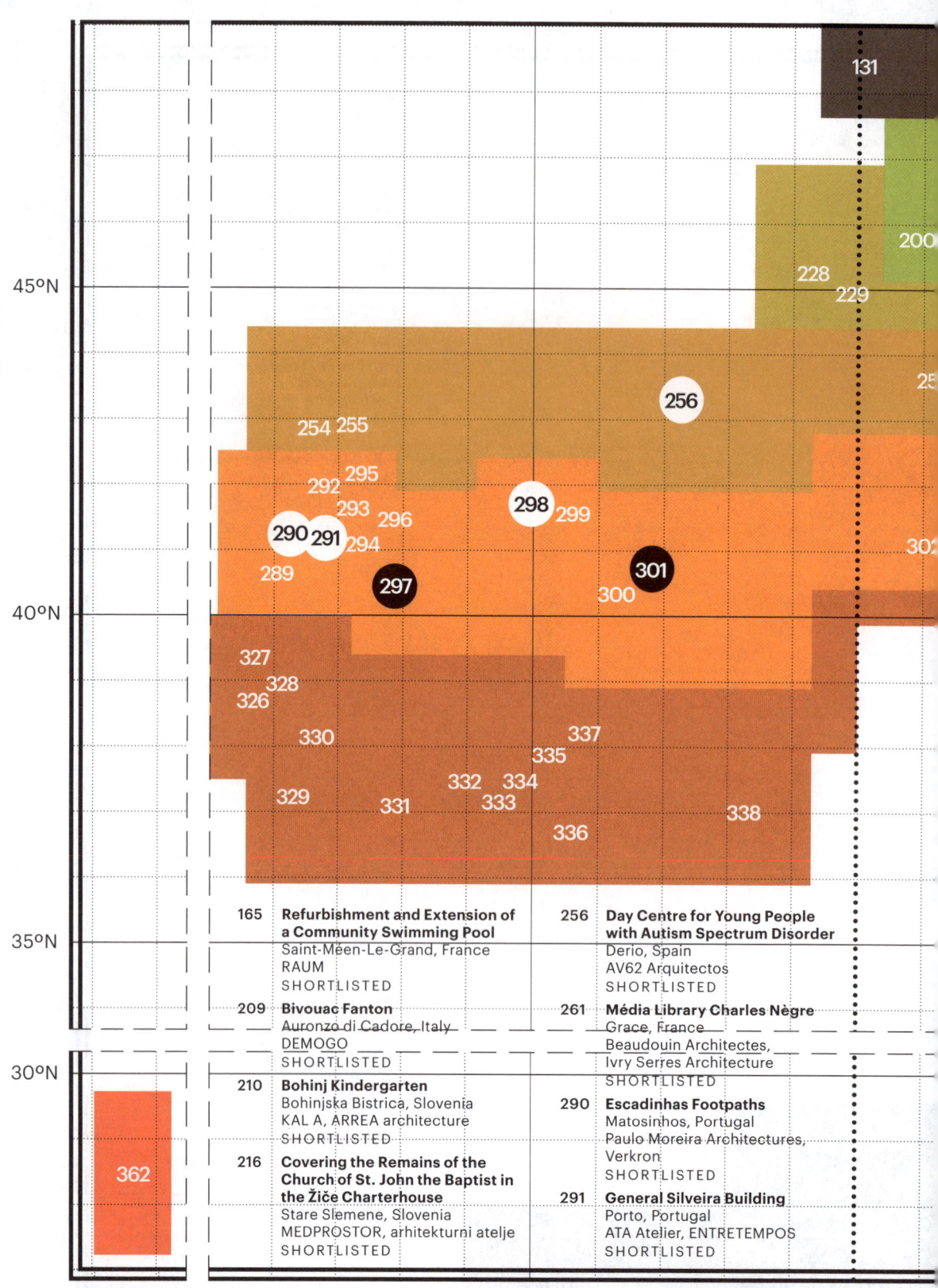

165	**Refurbishment and Extension of a Community Swimming Pool** Saint-Méen-Le-Grand, France RAUM SHORTLISTED	256	**Day Centre for Young People with Autism Spectrum Disorder** Derio, Spain AV62 Arquitectos SHORTLISTED
209	**Bivouac Fanton** Auronzo di Cadore, Italy DEMOGO SHORTLISTED	261	**Média Library Charles Nègre** Grace, France Beaudouin Architectes, Ivry Serres Architecture SHORTLISTED
210	**Bohinj Kindergarten** Bohinjska Bistrica, Slovenia KAL A, ARREA architecture SHORTLISTED	290	**Escadinhas Footpaths** Matosinhos, Portugal Paulo Moreira Architectures, Verkron SHORTLISTED
216	**Covering the Remains of the Church of St. John the Baptist in the Žiče Charterhouse** Stare Slemene, Slovenia MEDPROSTOR, arhitekturni atelje SHORTLISTED	291	**General Silveira Building** Porto, Portugal ATA Atelier, ENTRETEMPOS SHORTLISTED

297 **Piódão Square and Tourist Office**
Piódão, Portugal
Branco del Rio
EMERGING FINALIST

298 **Municipal Pools**
Castromonte, Spain
Óscar Miguel Ares. Contextos de arquitectura y urbanismo
SHORTLISTED

301 **Reggio School**
Madrid, Spain
Andrés Jaque - Office for Political Innovation
FINALIST

303 **Social Housing 1737**
Gavà, Spain
HARQUITECTES
SHORTLISTED

310 **Gabriel García Márquez Library**
Barcelona, Spain
SUMA Arquitectura
EMERGING WINNER

312 **Rebirth of the Convent Saint-François**
Sainte-Lucie-de-Tallano, France
Amelia Tavella Architectes
FINALIST

340 **Living in Lime. 42 Social Housing**
Son Servera, Spain
peris+toral arquitectes
SHORTLISTED

MAP OF WORKS 4/4

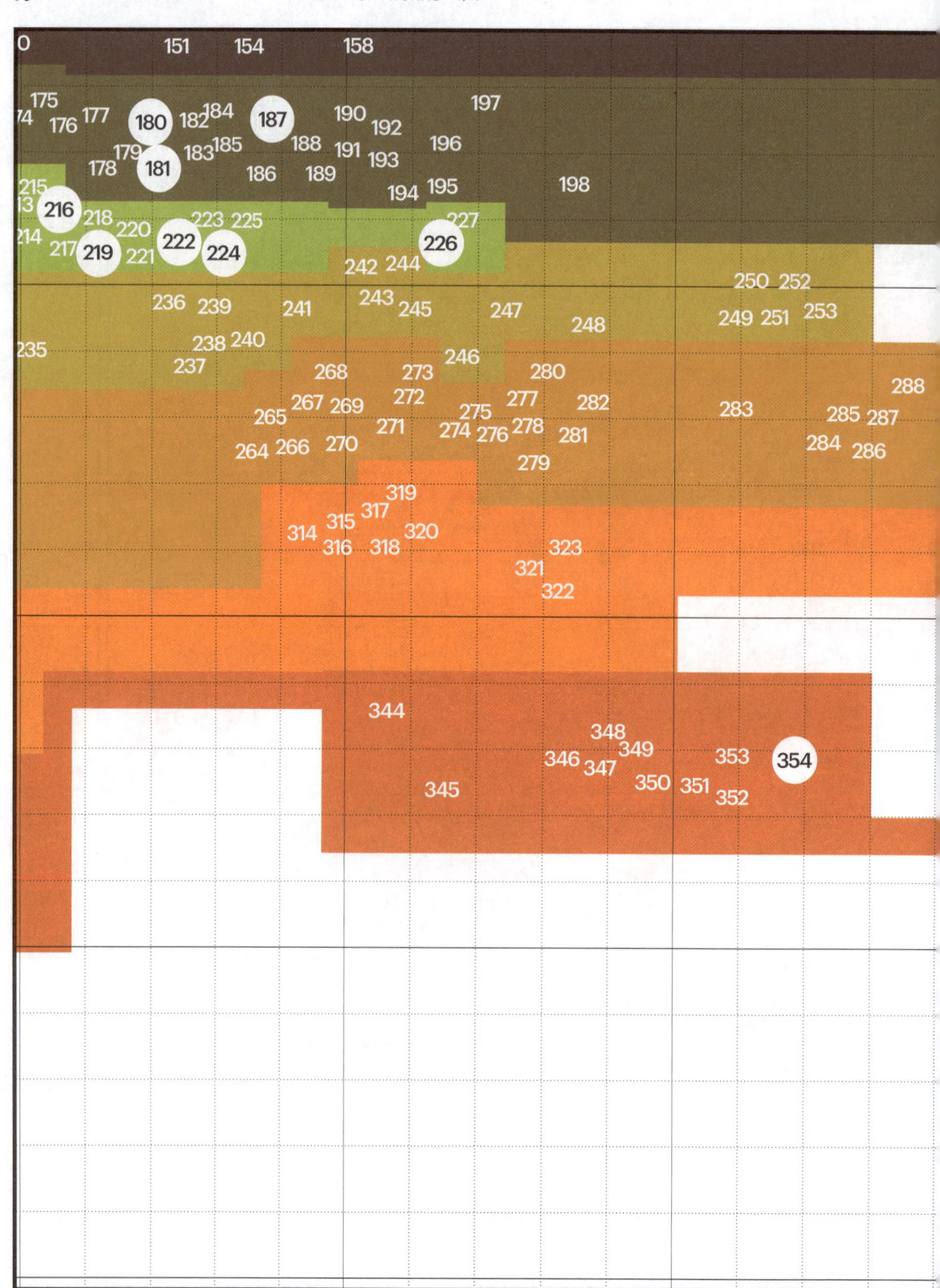

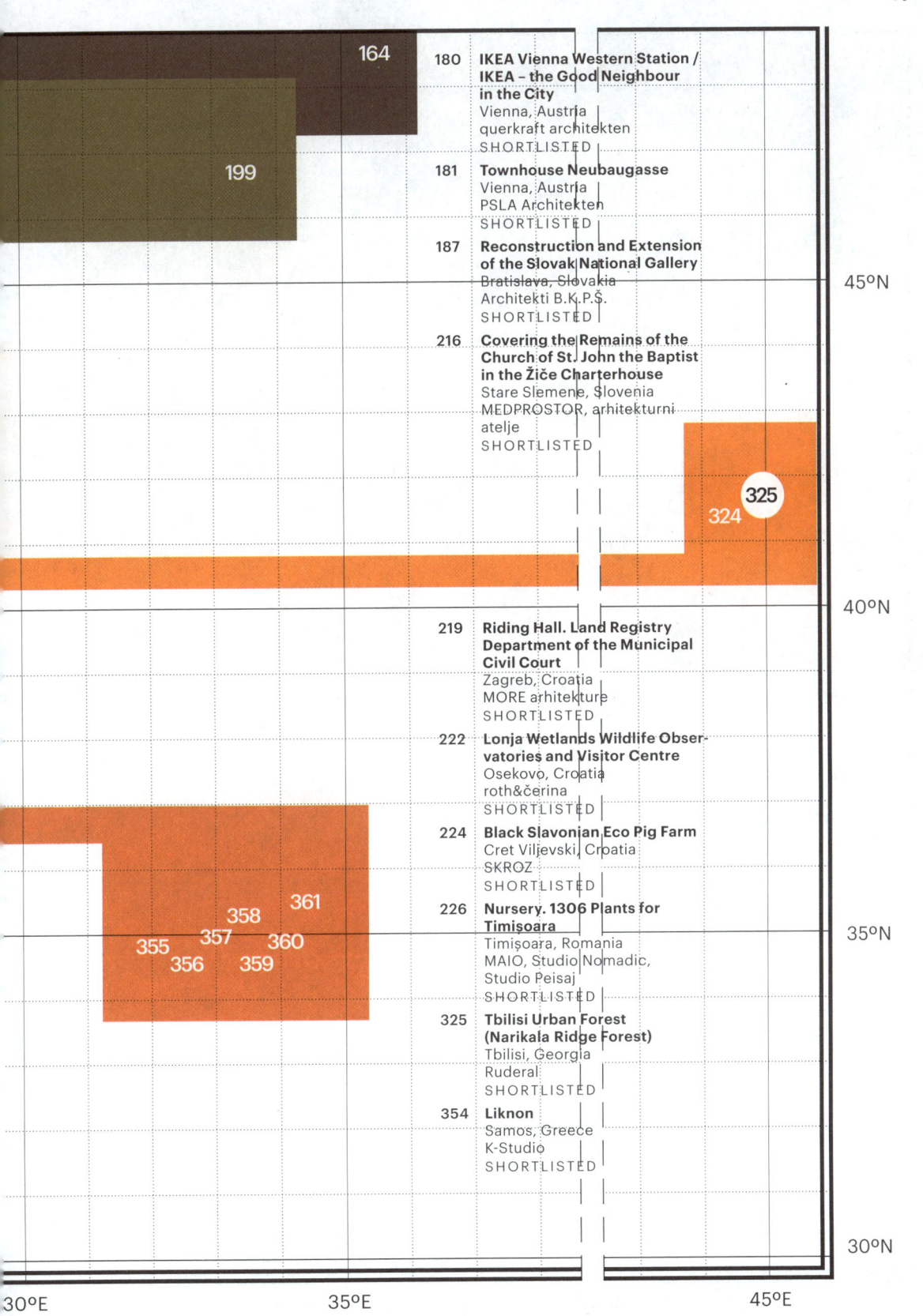

180 **IKEA Vienna Western Station / IKEA – the Good Neighbour in the City**
Vienna, Austria
querkraft architekten
SHORTLISTED

181 **Townhouse Neubaugasse**
Vienna, Austria
PSLA Architekten
SHORTLISTED

187 **Reconstruction and Extension of the Slovak National Gallery**
Bratislava, Slovakia
Architekti B.K.P.Š.
SHORTLISTED

216 **Covering the Remains of the Church of St. John the Baptist in the Žiče Charterhouse**
Stare Slemene, Slovenia
MEDPROSTOR, arhitekturni atelje
SHORTLISTED

219 **Riding Hall. Land Registry Department of the Municipal Civil Court**
Zagreb, Croatia
MORE arhitekture
SHORTLISTED

222 **Lonja Wetlands Wildlife Observatories and Visitor Centre**
Osekovo, Croatia
roth&čerina
SHORTLISTED

224 **Black Slavonian Eco Pig Farm**
Cret Viljevski, Croatia
SKROZ
SHORTLISTED

226 **Nursery. 1306 Plants for Timișoara**
Timișoara, Romania
MAIO, Studio Nomadic, Studio Peisaj
SHORTLISTED

325 **Tbilisi Urban Forest (Narikala Ridge Forest)**
Tbilisi, Georgia
Ruderal
SHORTLISTED

354 **Liknon**
Samos, Greece
K-Studio
SHORTLISTED

40

From
ILULISSAT
Denmark (Greenland)
69°14'00"N - 51°05'37"W

Kangiata Illorsua creates a shelter, a gathering place and a vantage point in the Arctic landscape between the UNESCO-protected Icefjord and small town of Ilulissat. Kangiata Illorsua is located near the Kangia Icefjord, where 35 cubic kilometers of ice per year calves from the icecap at the rapidly retracting Sermeq Kujalleq glacier and floats towards Disco Bay, making it one of the world's most important places for monitoring climate change. The center aims to expand our knowledge of climate change, the influence of the retracting icecap and the unique natural and cultural history of Ilulissat, while contributing to positive societal development and growing Inuit identity. The building sits lightly on the terrain. The roof provides a natural extension to the existing hiking routes and creates an accessible gathering place, a collective shelter and a viewpoint. Inside, visitors can reflect on the story of ice and the Inuit culture while experiencing the vastness of the surrounding landscape.

Ilulissat Icefjord Centre
› **ILULLISAT, DENMARK (GREENLAND)**
 2016/2019-2021
 Food & Accommodation · 1,500m² ·
 7,600€/m²
› **Dorte Mandrup**
 Dorte Mandrup-Poulsen
 Realdania, Avannaata Kommunia and the government of Greeland (Naalakkersuisut) (Mixed)
 © Adam Mørk

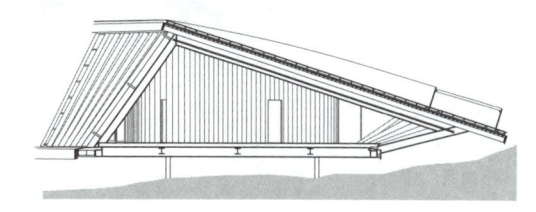

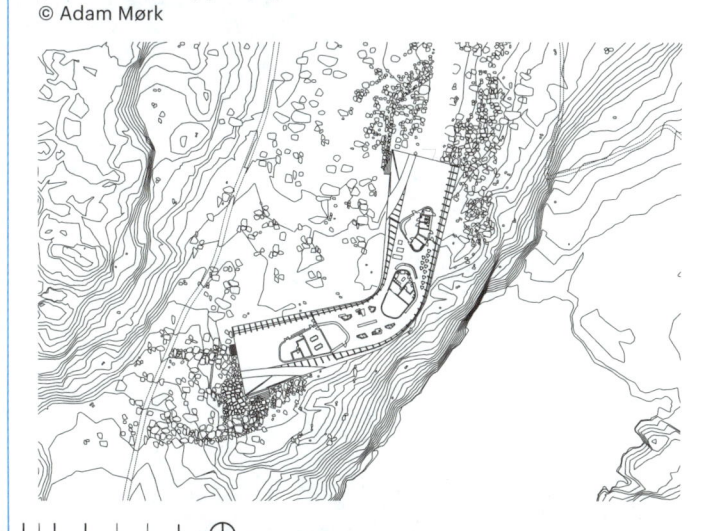

42

From
SKELLEFTEÅ
Sweden
64°45'07"N – 20°57'14"E

to
MÄNTTÄ-VILPPULA
Finland
62°01'37"N, 24°34'23"E

Standing 75-meters tall, this carbon-negative cultural center is one of the world's tallest timber buildings. Located in Skellefteå, which had a rich tradition of timber architecture before the city center was modernized, Sara Cultural Center marks the revival of the city's heritage. Combining traditional materials with modern technology, Sara Cultural Center paves the way for sustainable design and the region's green industry transition with over 3,000 new jobs. Sara Cultural Center is home to the Skellefteå Art Gallery, the Museum Anna Nordlander, the Västerbotten Regional Theater, the new city library and The Wood Hotel with a restaurant, spa and conference center. The cultural center is intended to be a building for collaboration and conversation, so it was important to gather the cultural activities in the same place.

Sara Cultural Centre

› **SKELLEFTEÅ, SWEDEN**
  2016/2018-2021
  Mixed use - Cultural & Social · 30,000m^2
› **White arkitekter**
  Robert Schmitz, Oskar Norelius,
  Maria Orvesten, Patrik Buchinger
  Skellefteå Kommun (Public)
  © Visita Skellefteå

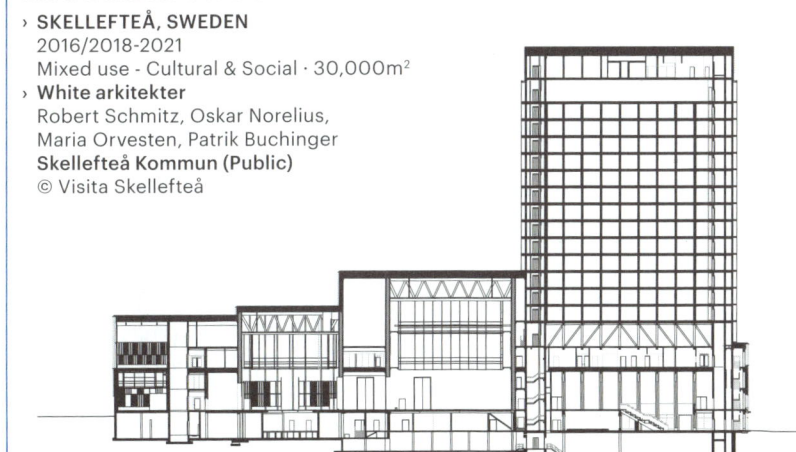

The old church of Ylivieska tragically burned down in 2016. The form of the new church is a continuum of the Finnish church-building tradition, taking the past into future. The new church of Ylivieska forms a landmark and is divided into three parts: the church hall, the vestry and the lobby. The entrance is beveled diagonally, forming an entry plaza together with the war graves and the ruins of the old church.

Ylivieska Church

› **YLIVIESKA, FINLAND**
 2017/2019-2021
 Religion · 1,530m^2
› **K2S Architects**
 Niko Sirola, Mikko Summanen, Kimmo Lintula
 The Parish of Ylivieska (Public)
 © Tuomas Uusheimo

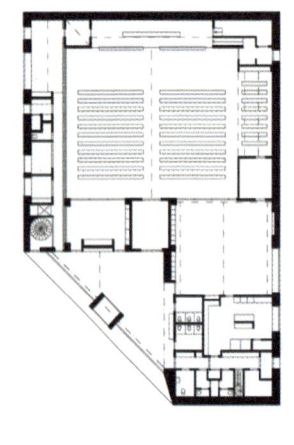

The new art-sauna space is understood as a continuation of the emotional journey of the whole Gösta Serlachius Museum. The museum visitors' experience is more than the act of observing art inside an ad-hoc space. Instead, they are embraced by a chain of moments in which landscape, art and architecture merge. One of the main strategies is to relate the new art-sauna space to the topography and landscape.

Serlachius Art Sauna

› **MÄNTTÄ-VILPPULA, FINLAND**
 2018/2020-2022
 Food & Accommodation · 450m^2
› **Mendoza Partida, BAX studio, Planetary Architecture**
 Héctor Mendoza, Mara Partida, Boris Bežan, Pekka Pakkanen, Anna Kontuniemi
 Serlachius Art Foundation (Private)
 © Marc Goodwin

46

From
BERGEN
Norway
60°22'35"N – 5°21'37"E

to
RAKVERE
Estonia
59°20'37"N – 26°21'54"E

The goal for the Haukeland Station project has been to reconcile high urban ambitions with complex underground technical solutions, with a particular focus on passenger safety and perceived security. The station connects the city's largest workplace, Haukeland University Hospital, and the health clusters in the area with the light rail network in the city. Our design concept for the facility has been to guide passengers through different spatial experiences, characterized by a clear yet varied design, emphasized by changing material choices for each volume.

Haukeland Bybanen (Light-rail Train) Station
› BERGEN, NORWAY
2018/2020-2022
Infrastructure · 8,250m²
› 3RW Arkitekter
Sixten Rahlff, Espen Rahlff, Jerome Picard, Catarina De Almeida Brito, Reka Bankuti-Toht, Lars Cohen, Elida Mosquera
Bybanen Utbygging / Vestland Fylkeskommune (Public)
↑ © Alex Coppo
↓ © Hugo Lutcherath

The number of visitors to the hotel has been growing, making it necessary to expand the restaurant. Near the hotel there is an old pine forest, with many trees around 250 to 300 years old. Due to the quality of the soil, a large proportion of the trees have spreading branches, making them less usable for traditional construction purposes. After evaluating some alternatives, it became clear that using local wood would have many positive effects. Quite quickly, a hypothesis emerged that, due to the proximity of the construction site, within one kilometer, the trees could be transported without removing the branches. To make this process as efficient as possible, all seven trees were accurately scanned by a drone. This was done from chaos to a modular outer layer, so all the cut branches are connected in a rigid cage with a precise shape. This cage forms the support for the glass roof and walls. On the site, the contractor used the model as the primary instruction instead of conventional drawings.

Extension to Raubergstølen Mountain Lodge
› LOM, NORWAY
2020/2021-2022
Food & Accommodation · 140m²
› Jensen & Skodvin Architects
Jan Olav Jensen, Øystein Skorstad, Knut Borgen, Halvard Amble
Amund Mundhjell (Private)
© Jan Olav Jensen

The museum rests on two levels into relation with the existing structure of the city. Together with the two pre-existing buildings, it creates a *piazzetta*: a new entrance forum that introduces the visitor to the museum with objects of art and a space for the café. The building here has a similar eaves size than the pre-existing ones. The idea of pieces of architecture looking at each other and getting into relation with one another is a constant in architectural history. Plato defined beauty in terms of relations. According to him, an object is beautiful if it can relate to us and the world.

The New National Museum in Oslo
› **OSLO, NORWAY**
2010/2014-2022
Culture · 54,600m²
› **Klaus Schuwerk Architect**
Klaus Schuwerk
Ministery of Culture Norway - Staatsbygg (Public)
© Leonardo Finotti

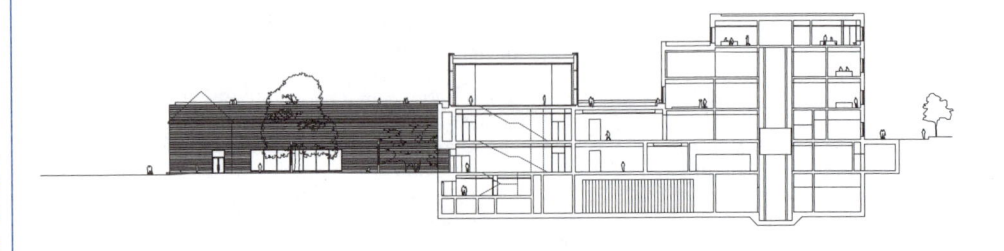

Munch Museum
Oslo, Norway
2009/2013-2021
estudioHerreros
Juan Herreros, Jens Richter
Oslo Kommune, Kultur og idrettsbygg
(Public)
Culture · 26,300m² · 8,717.25€/m²

Located on Oslo's waterfront, MUNCH is the new home to the world's largest collection of works by Norwegian artist Edvard Munch. The new MUNCH is not only a facility to safeguard and exhibit a fundamental part of Norwegian cultural heritage, but also an urban enclave that has helped to transform Oslo into a European metropolis.

Its ascending itinerary connects the public foyer which houses cultural, education, research, and recreational uses with the rooftop terraces, observatory, and club. In parallel to discovering Edvard Munch's work, the museum offers views onto the different historical strata of the city of Oslo. This gesture of conceiving the vertical communications system as a public space and an ascending vantage point is the essence of the heterodox character generated by developing a museum vertically. The museum offers more: as they stroll through the museum visitors get to learn about other programmes such as restauration workshops, the drawings archive, the photography department, administrative offices, and the research library, which denote a programmatic complexity that extends beyond the conventional idea of the museum as a set of exhibition spaces to be visited and a series of invisible facilities from which the institution is managed.

In the 1980s, the port of Oslo, which historically had blocked the city's contact with the fjord, started to be dismantled. The ambitious project involved major infrastructure and construction work to remove any barrier and to recover the desired reconnection of the two environments. The name 'Fjord City' was coined to describe the city that would emerge from the transformation of the former 'Port City'.

In this context, estudioHerreros has created a typological heterodoxy of the museum as a tower with 13 floors of exhibition spaces and vertical circulation routes which connect the lobby, conceived as a grand covered plaza, with a top-floor public space that is open to everyone, offering views over the city. Its clean silhouette remains reverential to the city and aims to express the collective dream of creating a new urban model with the added value of freeing up the ground for pedestrians.

We can boldly claim that this Museum of the future will dedicate merely 40% of the space to exhibition rooms with the rest intended for social contents and new artistic formats. This is the way to transform the Museum into an everyday facility for citizens in contrast with one-time visits by global visitors.

The building is constructed on water. The port-landfill on which it was to be based turned out to have poor loadbearing capacity forcing the soil to be removed and the building to be anchored to the bottom of the fjord using 40-metre-deep piles.

The conception of the framework that splits podium and tower and divides the tower into circulation routes (a dynamic museum) and exhibition rooms and workshops (a static museum) resulted in the coexistence of two structures: one built using recycled steel, and the other built using low CO_2 emissions concrete. A sliding piece of formwork raised the 66 × 18 × 45 m concrete volume in 5 weeks using Norwegian technology originally associated with the construction of offshore oil rigs as a possible way to recycle technologies that will hopefully become obsolete soon.

The construction of the Munch Museum became a research laboratory in sustainability and recycled materials. Some items of this programme include the wooden floors, avant-garde glazing panels, and the undulated perforated recycled aluminium façade that plays an important role in offering protection from sunlight and reducing thermal gains while giving visitors an exciting experience to discover a new pixelized Oslo.

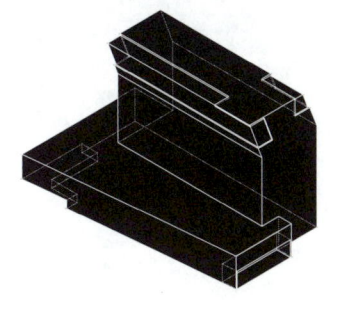

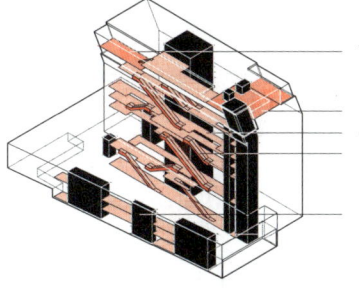

Circulation and
Recreation Zones

Terraces

Restaurant
Circulation Areas
Escalators

Podium Circulations

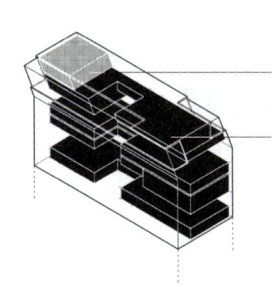

TOWER
Public Zones

Meeting Rooms

Exhibition Rooms

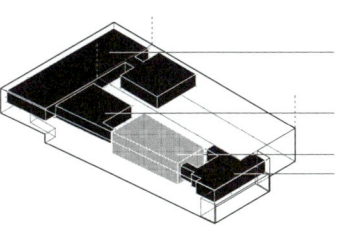

PODIUM
Public Zones

Exhibition Rooms

Library

Auditorium
Classrooms

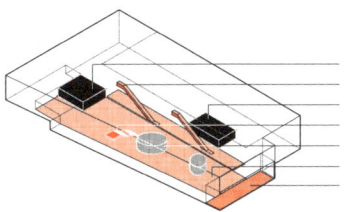

LOBBY
Shop
Museum Access
Toilets
Access to the Auditorium
Cinema
Bar
Terrace

Program diagram

ESTUDIOHERREROS

52

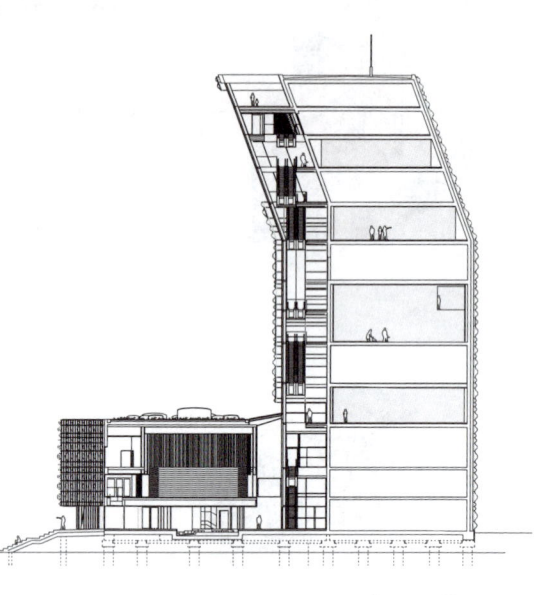

Cross section

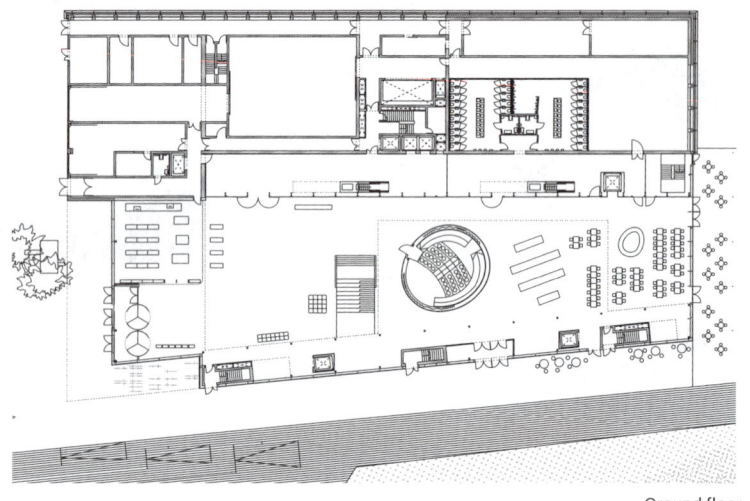

Ground floor

MUNCH MUSEUM 0 5 10 20

We were asked to design a restaurant pavilion at the neighboring excavated site. The brutal excavation soon caught our eye. We proposed a narrow building with the rock wall as part of the large restaurant room, a flat roof with a pool on top and a wall with sliding doors facing the harbor area. The main geometric challenge is how to let a well-behaved modular building structure meet a chaotic rock wall that does not follow any straight lines.

Edholmen Marina and Restaurant
› **FREDRIKSTAD, NORWAY**
2020/2021-2022
Food & Accommodation · 600m²
› **Jensen & Skodvin Architects**
Torunn Golberg, Jan Olav Jensen, Øystein Skorstad, Sigrid Moldestad, Knut Borgen, Thomas Knigge
Jon Brevik (Private)
© Torunn Golberg

The alteration project of St. Paul's Church (1876) aimed to create two new open and flexible squares: an exterior square serving as a meeting place between the city and the church's activities, and an interior square where the church hall becomes a central hub around which new rooms, dining areas and workspaces are arranged. The redesign utilized the spaciousness and spiritual qualities of the church hall to transform the church space from an isolated room into a central hub within the building.

Meeting Place Mariatorget - St. Paul's Church
› **STOCKHOLM, SWEDEN**
2017/2020-2022
Social welfare · 870m² · 9,000€/m²
› **Spridd**
Klas Ruin, Jakob Wiklander, Ola Broms Wessel, Winnie Westerlund
Stockholms Stadsmission (Public)
© Johan Dehlin

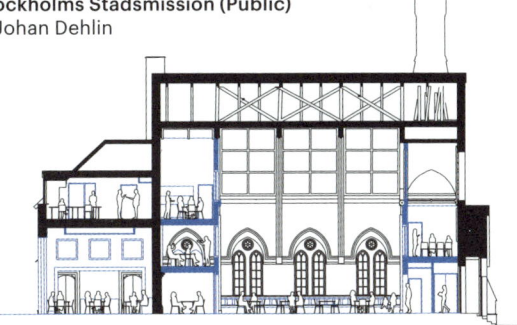

Liljevalchs+
Stockholm, Sweden
2014/2017-2021
Wingårdh Arkitektkontor
Gert Wingårdh
Fastighetskontoret, Stockholms stad
(Public)
Culture · 2,600m² · 16,000€/m²

Liljevalchs+ serves as a complement to an art gallery that dates back to 1916 which continues to welcome visitors through its main entrance. The extension faces another direction. Our addition provides more space for exhibitions, a secondary entrance, a museum shop, and a development for the café.

The Liljevalchs art gallery is located on an island close to the city centre in Stockholm. It is the former Royal hunting grounds, and the area consists of museums and amusement rides. But the context for this building is more urban than archaic. The addition adapts to the roofline of the old building, yet the interior reveals a complex section. The rectangular block contains a split-level plan with floors at six different elevations throughout the building. The volume of the structure is cast like a great concrete block. The glass artist Ingegerd Råman, who has been working with us on the project, has decorated the façades with crystal clear bottle bottoms, creating a glass grid.

The new wing stays one step back in discrete support of the reserved and dignified gallery. It remains in the background, though it does not cower in submission. Like the main building, it has integrity. Toward the main road, Djurgårdsvägen, the old gallery remains in control over the situation, while the new wing faces the smaller Falkenbergsgatan street. The division of roles is more than just visual. The original entrance, an established emblem for Liljevalchs and a fundamental part of the architectural experience, maintains its status. The new addition announces itself primarily as an exhibition building in its own right. One hundred sixty lanterns on the roof provide daylight, structure, and rhythm to the galleries below, creating a two by two metre grid that makes a wide variety of flexible spatial divisions possible. A great deal of effort has been made to keep the exhibition spaces free of openings or other elements that would disturb the exhibitions.

The building is made in concrete cast in situ. The standard concrete is visible in walls, stairs and in the lanterns that constitute the ceiling. The ceilings on the lower floors are made of a steel mesh or, as in the café, of textiles that contrast with the otherwise sturdy materials. A relief of 6860 bottle-ends gives the façades a textile effect with ties to the original building's graceful architecture of slender columns and inset panels. The array of glass studs serves as a modern version of the diamond rustication popular during the Renaissance, like rivets reinforcing a treasure chest.

WINGÅRDH ARKITEKTKONTOR AB

56

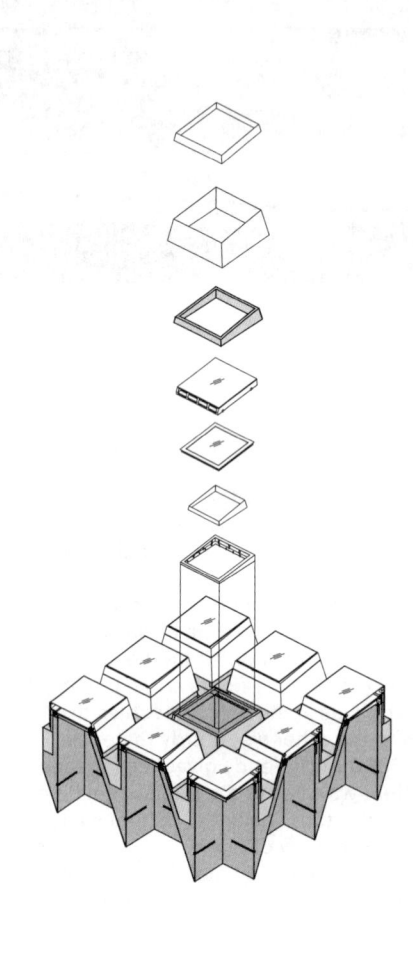

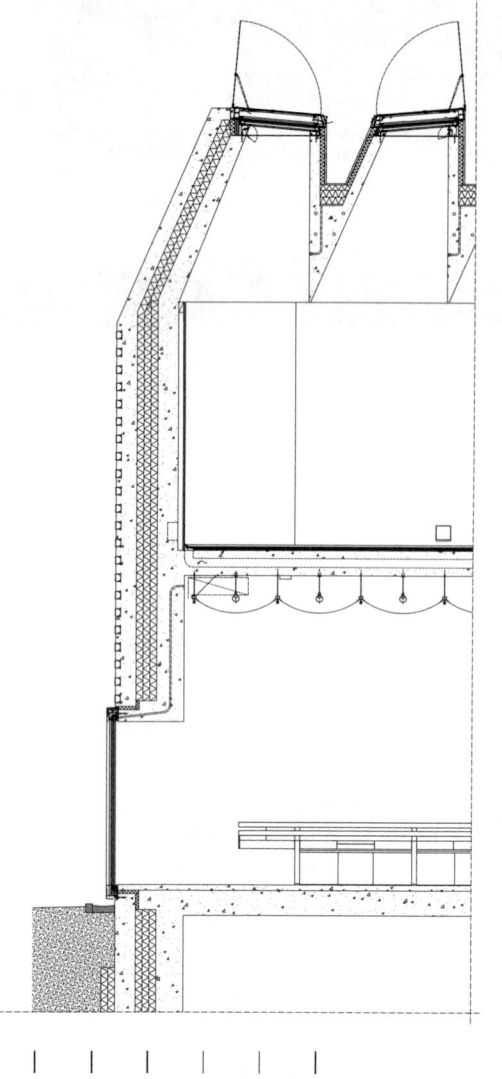

SHORTLISTED

LILJEVALCHS+ 0 1 2   5

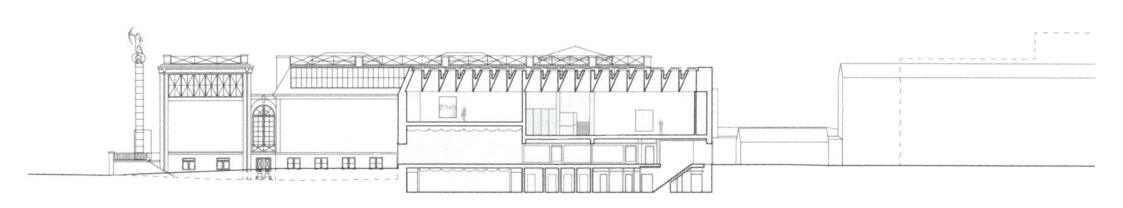

Longitudinal section

WINGÅRDH ARKITEKTKONTOR AB

0 5 10   20

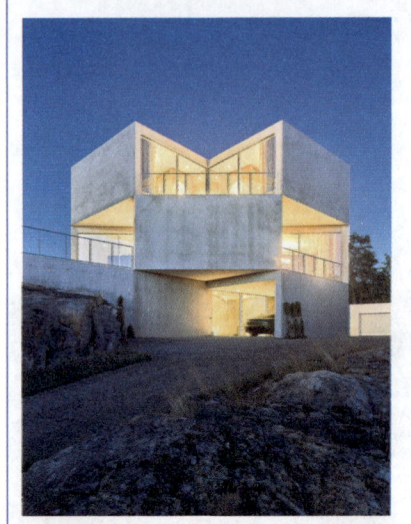

We envisioned the house as reduced to pure structure, where indoor and outdoor spaces mix, and let the emphasis remain on the scenery outside. A vertical figure, freestanding like a lighthouse or a large-scale sundial, and entirely cast in concrete, is firmly anchored on the exposed bedrock.

House on a Hill
› **VÄRMDÖ, SWEDEN**
2023/2017-2022
Single house · 537m²
› **Tham & Videgård**
Bolle Tham, Martin Videgård
Undisclosed (Private)
© Åke Eson Lindman

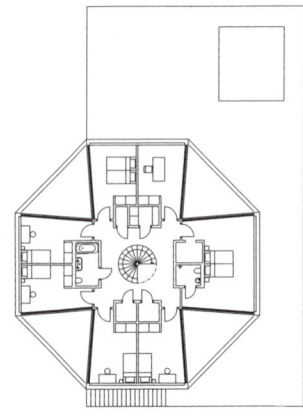

Chappe is a new three-story contemporary art museum located on the southern coast of Finland in the historical town of Tammisaari, known for its timber architecture dating back to the 18th century. Located in the museum quarter in the heart of Tammisaari's old town, Chappe is a 1,210 square meter addition to this mix of cultural attractions. Inspired by the historical surroundings, the black spruce clad elevations of the new art house play on traditional Finnish architecture.

Chappe Art House
› **RASEBORG, FINLAND**
2018/2021-2023
Culture · 1,210m²
› **JKMM Architects**
Asmo Jaaksi, Juha Mäki-Jyllilä, Samuli Miettinen, Teemu Toivio, Teemu Kurkela, Gerrie Bekhuis
Albert de la Chapelle Foundation (Private)
© Tuomas Uusheimo

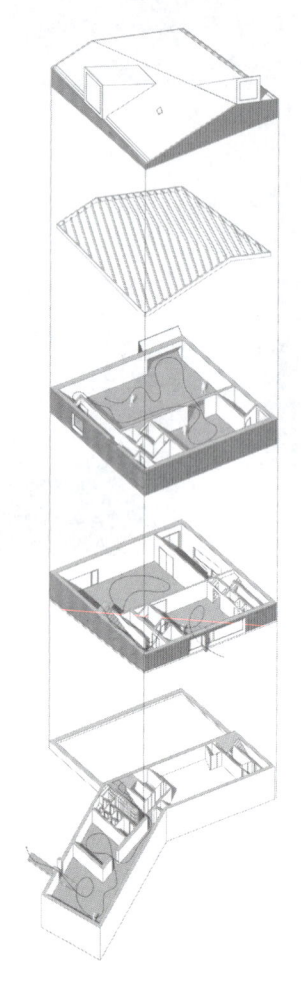

The architecture of Viimsi Artium creates a strong connection with the unique location and the landscape. The Artium building is quite literally a bridge from the suburban stripe into the primeval forest, but it also indirectly bridges wild landscape with contemporary culture and with the experience of them both. The concept is based on creating a connection with the landscape and the cliff creates synergy and cross-use between different functions and activities.

Viimsi Artium
› **VIIMSI, ESTONIA**
  2018/2021-2022
  Culture · 7,000m² · 2,400€/m²
› **KAVAKAVA**
  Indrek Peil, Siiri Vallner
  Viimsi Municipality Government (Public)
  © Tõnu Tunnel

Expanding over 287 hectares, the semi-natural park forms an important link in the backbone of the biggest district in Tallinn, Lasnamäe. The main idea of the landscape architecture was to keep the unique wasteland-like nature somewhat wild and weary, but in a spontaneous and obstinate environment highly characteristic of Lasnamäe, connecting nature with its urban fabric and residents. Providing people with outdoor activities, it increases social sustainability, but also creates free-play space where children can engage with the environment creatively.

Tondiraba Park
› **TALLINN, ESTONIA**
  2020/2021
  Landscape
› **AB Artes Terrae**
  Merle Karro-Kalberg, Heiki Kalberg, Tanel Breede
  Tallinna Keskkonna- ja Kommunaalamet (City goverment of Tallinn) (Public)
  © Kaupo Kalda

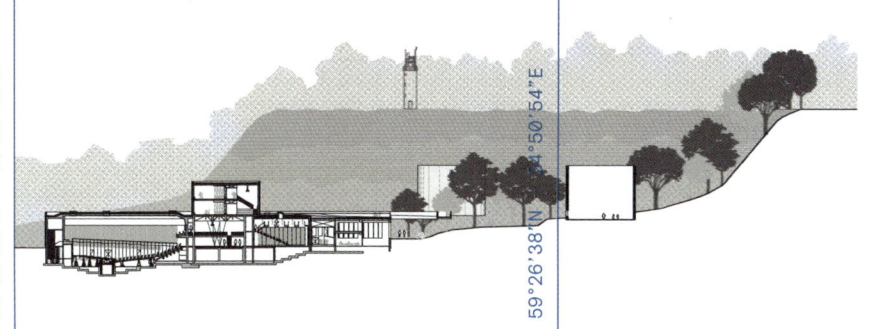

Dance House Helsinki is Finland's first and northern Europe's largest venue exclusively designed for dancing. The impressive new building and renovated premises comprises over 7,000 square meters, offering a world-class setting for performing and experiencing dance, circus and culture. The building is like a huge modern "dance machine" designed to connect to an old factory. The spaces are industrial in scale and the details can be identified as parts of a machine. The main façades consist of two gigantic steel walls lifted from the ground and hovering in the air. One wall is made of rough rusted steel and another of shiny stainless steel.

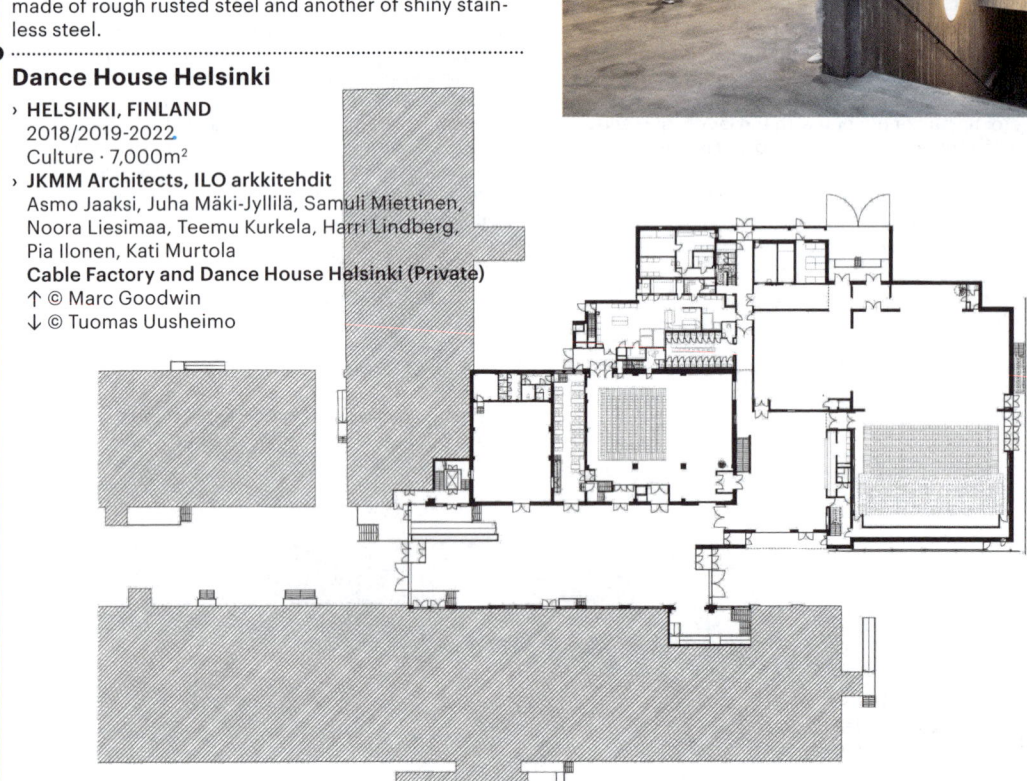

Dance House Helsinki
› HELSINKI, FINLAND
2018/2019-2022
Culture · 7,000m²
› **JKMM Architects, ILO arkkitehdit**
Asmo Jaaksi, Juha Mäki-Jyllilä, Samuli Miettinen, Noora Liesimaa, Teemu Kurkela, Harri Lindberg, Pia Ilonen, Kati Murtola
Cable Factory and Dance House Helsinki (Private)
↑ © Marc Goodwin
↓ © Tuomas Uusheimo

The metabolism of cities and the renovation of cultural heritage call for adaptable architecture. Little Finlandia is a wooden, modular temporary event facility located in central Helsinki's Töölönlahti area, recomposing a public living room in the heart of the city. The critical architectural element of the project is its 95 load-bearing Scots pine columns. On the park side, a colonnade formed by the trunks establishes the public nature of the building and acts as an allegory for a forest margin.

Little Finlandia
› **HELSINKI, FINLAND**
2020/2021-2022
Culture · 2,720m² · 3,640€/m²
› **Pikku-Finlandia Studio, Aalto University**
Jaakko Torvinen, Havu Järvelä,
Elli Wendelin, Pekka Heikkinen
City of Helsinki (Public)
© Mikael Linden

The architecture of the new building of the University of the Arts Helsinki, the Academy of Fine Arts celebrates the imaginative integration of existing structures and pays homage to the history of Sörnäinen, a post-industrial district buzzing with young urban life today. The new campus building has been designed as a direct response to the needs of future visionaries. The ingenuity of the architecture lies in offering students of fine arts, lighting and sound design and design for the performing arts generous, robust, well-lit and clearly defined spaces.

Academy of Fine Arts, Mylly
› **HELSINKI, FINLAND**
2017/2018-2021
Education · 13,000m²
› **JKMM Architects**
Asmo Jaaksi, Juha Mäki-Jyllilä, Samuli Miettinen, Teemu Toivio, Katja Savolainen, Noora Liesimaa, Päivi Meuronen, Teemu Kurkela, Jussi Vepsäläinen
Veritas Pension Insurance (Mixed)
© Tuomas Uusheimo

The main driver for the new departures and arrivals building was the need to improve the passenger experience and functionality at Helsinki Airport, built in multiple phases over the years, and to prepare the airport for future growth. The airport today has all its functions under "one roof", in one combined terminal, instead of the previous division between terminals 1 and 2. The construction of the new building has allowed the departures hall in the former terminal 2 to be transformed into gate areas. This solution provides both passengers and services with plenty of additional space, while also simplifying the airport structure.

Helsinki Airport Departures and Arrivals Building

› **VANTAA, FINLAND**
2017/2019-2021
Infrastructure · 43,600m²
› **ALA Architects**
Samuli Woolston, Antti Nousjoki, Juho Grönholm
Finavia (Public)
© Tuomas Uusheimo

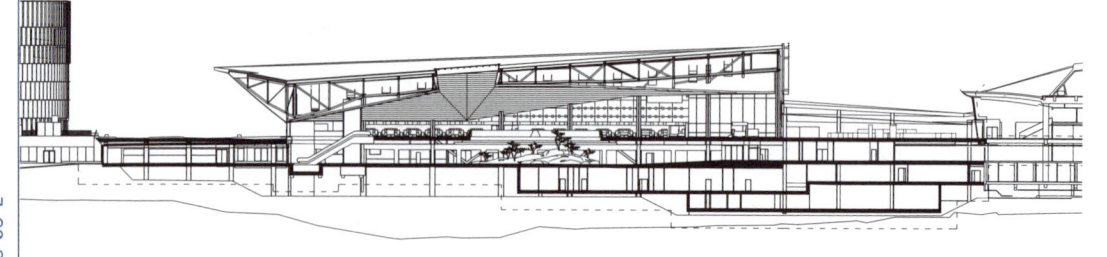

This wooden Daycare Center is the first public building in a new residential area and is a humble monument to everyday life. The architecture explores the possibilities of a massive wooden structure as a frame for early childhood growth and creates a sustainable, healthy and inspiring environment with flexible spaces for varying purposes in the future. The two-story building accommodates 210 children and the residents of the area can use the common areas of the building outside daycare hours.

Hopealaakso Daycare Centre
› **HELSINKI, FINLAND**
2020/2020-2021
Education · 2,400m²
› **AFKS Architects**
Jari Frondelius, Jaakko Keppo, Juha Salmenperä, Mikko Liski, Erika Siikaoja, Soile Heikkinen
City of Helsinki (Public)
© Hannu Rytky

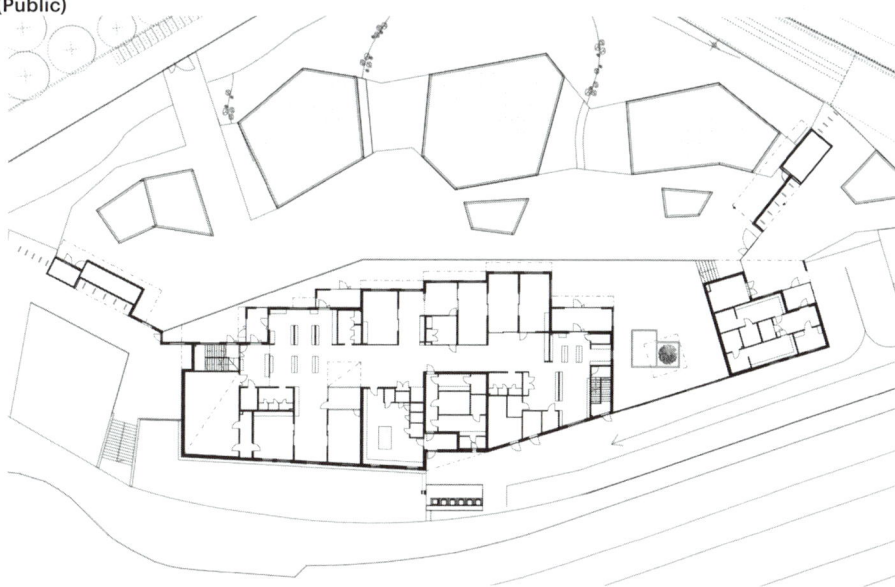

The Rakvere Center for Work and Technology, also known as the joint study building of the middle schools in Rakvere, is designed to accommodate wood and metal workshops. The new workshop building is situated as close to the back of the plot as possible. This creates "air" in the courtyard and the sunlit entrance side. The particular shape of the roofscape of the building takes after the northwest-oriented rooftop windows, which ensure that a necessary amount of daylight reaches the classrooms.

Woodwork and Technology Centre in Rakvere

› **RAKVERE, ESTONIA**
2020/2021-2022
Education · 696m²
› **KUU architects**
Joel Kopli
Rakvere Town Government (Public)
© Tõnu Tunnel

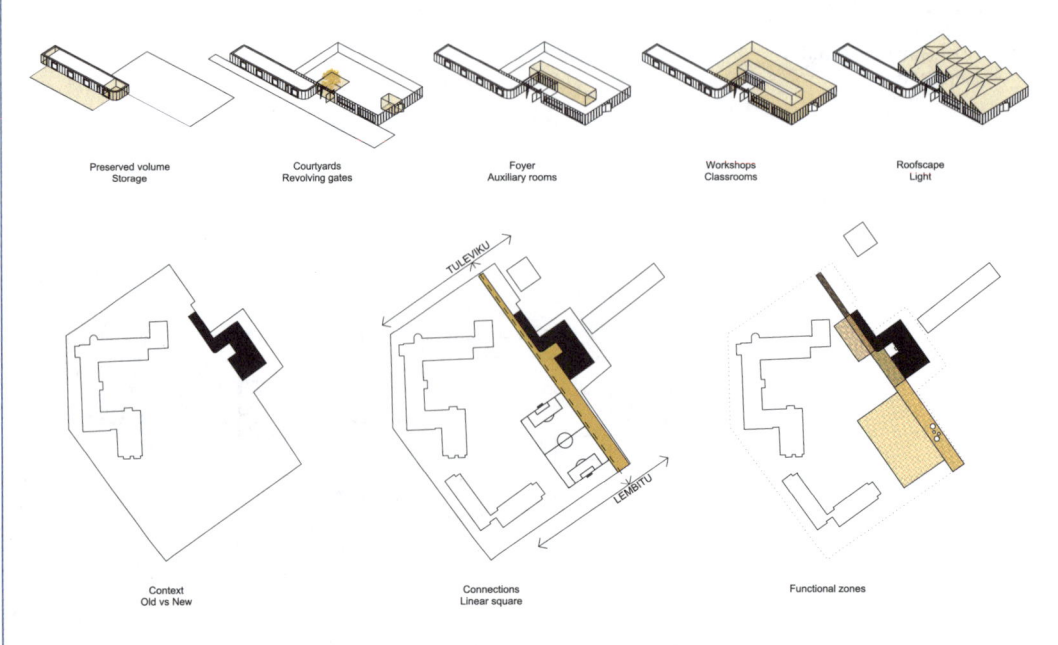

| Preserved volume | Courtyards | Foyer | Workshops | Roofscape |
| Storage | Revolving gates | Auxiliary rooms | Classrooms | Light |

Context
Old vs New

Connections
Linear square

Functional zones

66

From
LINDESNES
Norway
57°59'46"N — 7°33'46"E

to
TARTU
Estonia
58°22'12"N — 26°42'45"E

The plot is located at the center of the small island, at the edge of a little forest. The sea is just barely glimpsed from the site. The program is divided in three separate buildings, a main cabin, an annex and a shed. All three buildings share the same general concept but nuances occur according to their different uses. The three separate buildings establish a series of different outdoor spaces. The sun and wind decide which outdoor space to utilize.

Weekend House Hjeltnes

› **LINDESNES, NORWAY**
 2019/2020-2021
 Single house · 62m²
› **Knut Hjeltnes Sivilarkitekter**
 Knut Hjeltnes
 Knut Hjeltnes (Private)
 © Knut Hjeltnes

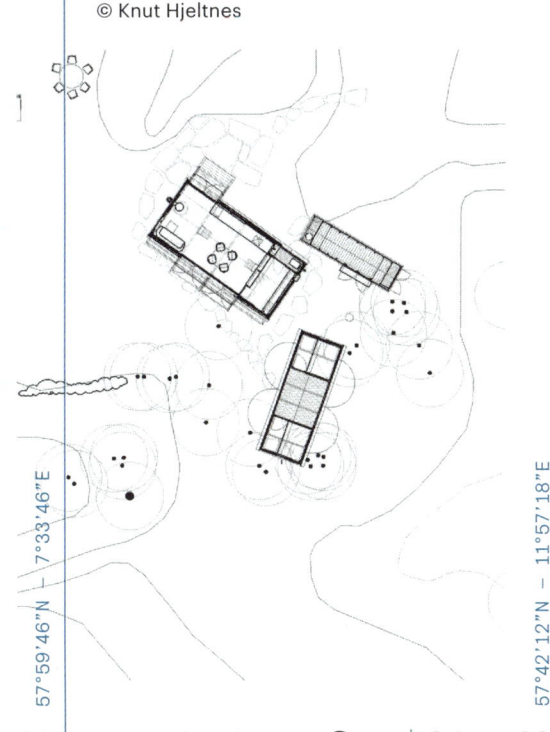

Merkurhuset, located in central Gothenburg, is the final piece of a 19th-century waterfront block. In a compact site, Merkurhuset seamlessly integrates while asserting its presence in harmony with the environment. A simple plan and section concept generates spatial diversity and vitality, imbuing the exterior with dynamism and character. This forms a unique typology that departs from conventional norms, embodying contextual architecture. The interior of the building acts as a representation of the city, with streets and squares.

Merkurhuset

› **GOTHENBURG, SWEDEN**
 2019/2020-2022
 Office · 6,300m² · 2,850€/m²
› **Olsson Lyckefors Arkitektur**
 Andreas Lyckefors, Johan Olsson, Per Bornstein, Fabian Sahlqvist, Viktor Stansvik, Johanna Engloo, Johan Häggqvist, Ergin Can, Rebecca Wallin, Viktor Fagrell, Ainhoa Etxeberria, Karin Pallarp, Marina Pettersson, Joel Gödecke, Edvard Nyman, David Svahn, Ola Sjöberg
 Platzer Fastigheter + Bygg Göta + Forsman & Bodenfors (Public)
 © Mikael Olsson

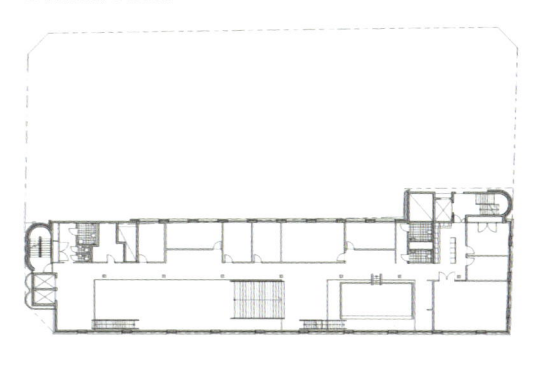

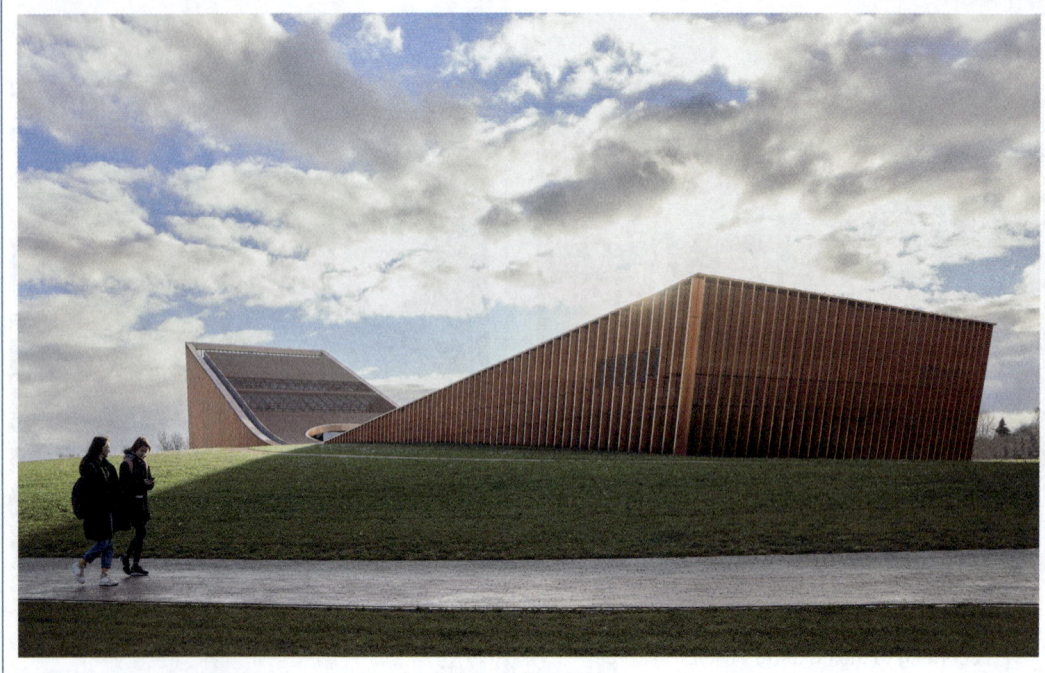

The hill leads to the roof terrace with access to the public facilities on the first floor. Further development of the building continues along the roof slope towards the observation deck, which offers impressive panoramic views. The building itself is also divided into two parts for functional reasons: the science center forms the lower part of the volume, while the innovation center occupies the six floors of the upper part. Instead of proposing a landmark on the bridge axis, we leave it open and inviting. The silhouettes of the building and the hill osculate here. The façade of the building is made of glass with copper finishing sheets.

Science Centre Vizium
› **VENTSPILS, LATVIA**
2018/2019-2022
Culture · 6,653m² · 1,731€/m²
› **Arhitekta J. Pogas birojs, Audrius Ambrasas Architects**
Audrius Ambrasas, Vilma Adomonytė, Justas Jankauskas, Juris Poga, Astra Poga, Jonas Motiejūnas, Viktorija Rimkutė
Municipal Authority of Ventspils City (Public)
© Norbert Tukaj

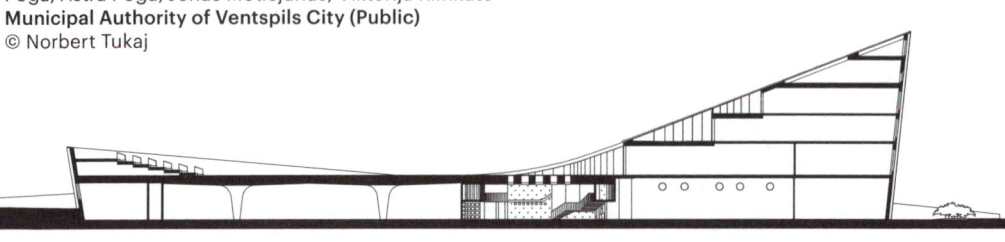

Located in the tiny village of Mustjala, the building references the local architectural culture. The cone-shaped volumes rising from the roof are reminiscent of a traditional farm complex, where multiple buildings with different functions are gathered around a courtyard, marked by the sloping roofs extending from the cubic volume of the buildings. The point of departure for the square shaped building was to create a sense of home, offering an environment where both the indoor and outdoor spaces attract and complement each other.

Mustjala Retirement Home and Daycare Centre
› **MUSTJALA, ESTONIA**
2020/2021-2022
Social welfare · 563m^2 · 2,664€/m^2
› **molumba**
Johan Tali, Karli Luik, Priit Rannik, Annika Lill
Saaremaa Municipality (Public)
© Johan Tali

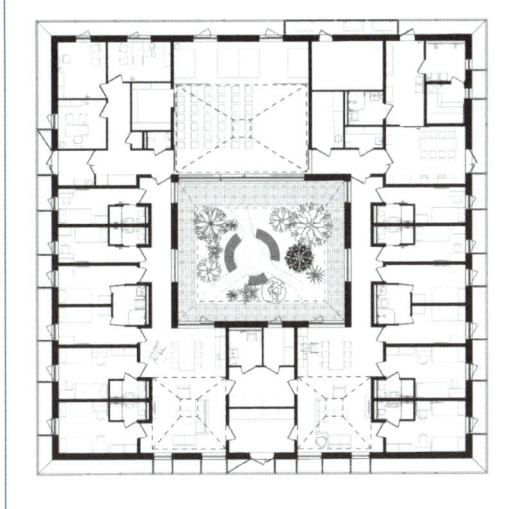

The client of the training center is a local company that has created a place for growth, technology acquisition and training for existing and new employees. In the center of the building is a green courtyard, around which all four functional blocks of the building are located, creating a pure cross shape on the plan. All technical rooms, vent chambers and emergency stairways are brought out of this shape. In the outdoor space, all four front yards are located in the corners of the building. The shape of the building is designed in an industrial style using appropriate design elements: concrete core, metal scaffolding, metal shipping containers and wire mesh for vertical plantings. The building was designed with maximum economy in mind.

Learning Centre in Mārupe
› **MARUPE, LATVIA**
2021/2022-2023
Office · 1,200m^2 · 1,700€/m^2
› **Good Pattern**
Guntis Zingis, Kristina Reinberga
Hagberg (Private)
↑ © Guntis Zingis
↓ © Madara Kuplā

The Ola Foundation is a private foundation whose mission is to promote contemporary culture, architecture, art, music, and education. The central part of the building is made of concrete, while the exterior is of glass. This gives the building a meditative character from the inside, focusing on self-exploration, while its transparent exterior emphasizes its perception in a broader context, breaking down material boundaries and seamlessly merging with nature.

The building spans across three floors, one of which is below ground. The basement houses an exhibition hall, the first floor consists of a complex of conference rooms and the second floor features a music lounge with a vestibule and a unique, electromechanically retractable roof eight meters in diameter.

Ola Foundation
› **RIGA, LATVIA**
2020/2020-2022
Culture · 822.60m²
› **UPB**
Uldis Pīlēns
Ola Foundation (Private)
© Reinis Hofmanis

Manufaktūra adapts an industrial building to the needs of a brewery. Conceptually, the project aims to emphasize the building's long life and transformations, still evident in diverse historical construction techniques and approaches, and to complement this collage with yet another contemporary layer. The leitmotif of this project, with various manifestations, is reuse and adaptation, to establish a positive relationship with the site's past and to reinforce its identity.

Brewery 'Manufaktūra'
› **RIGA, LATVIA**
2019/2020-2022
Food & Accommodation · 694m² · 482€/m²
› **SAMPLING**
Manten Devriendt, Liene Jākobsone
SIA Realto Manufaktūra (Private)
© Madara Kuplā

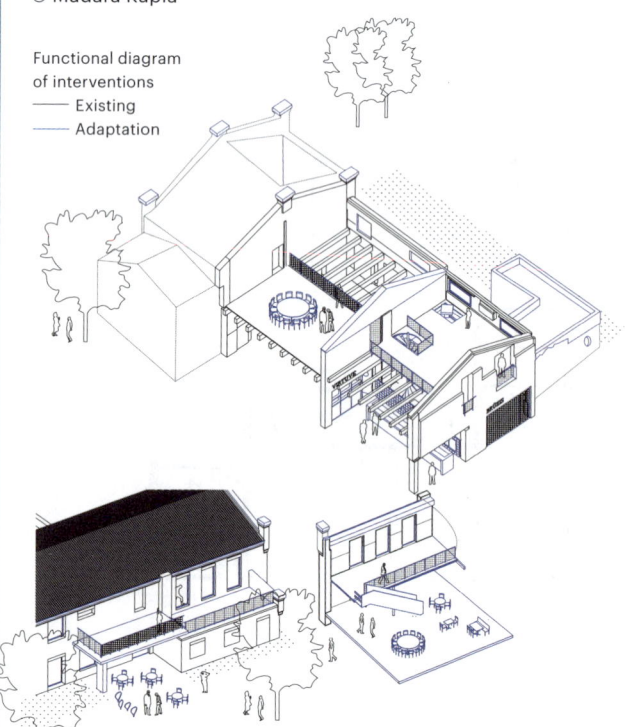

Functional diagram of interventions
— Existing
— Adaptation

The Ogre resort town, which is a home to a lot of wooden summer houses with pitched roofs, nestled amidst the pristine forest and river, served as the muse for the community library. Carefully situated on the hilly terrain, the building harmoniously coexists with the natural forest, reflecting the reserved nature of Latvians. Designed to be more than just an institution, it embodies an open public space for community interaction, learning and relaxation. Its form is inspired by 20th-century resort town summer houses with wooden façades and large sloped metal roofs.

Ogre Central Library and Marriage Registry

› **RIGA, LATVIA**
2019/2020-2021
Mixed use - Cultural & Social ·
2,199m²
› **Office PBR**
Rūdis Rubenis, Valdis Onkelis
Ogre municipality (Public)
© Madara Kuplā

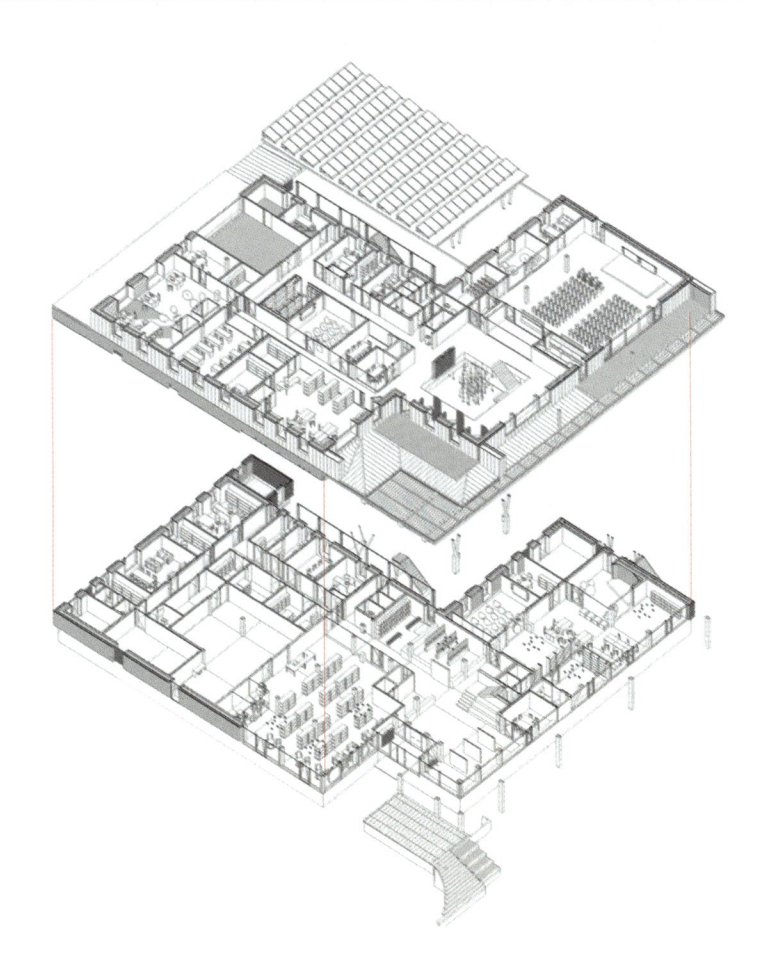

The social services center Perle is located in the municipality of Cēsis right on the city border, between urban environment and nature. The aim was to create a place open to the society and the city but serving as a safe space for users at the same time. The maximum use of daylight, natural materials and constructive clarity where timber structure is space and space is structure, all make the building feel generous. This is a generous bright space with a close connection to nature, a livable terrace with pergola that filters light.

Social Services Centre Perle
› CĒSIS, LATVIA
2019/2020-2021
Social welfare · 720m² · 1,650€/m²
› ĒTER
Dagnija Smilga, Karlis Berzins, Niklavs Paegle
Cēsis Municipality (Public)
© Peteris Viksna

The primary challenge faced by the kuidas. works project was the creation of a restaurant with zero budget, finished in a mere seven days, for the TV series "Restaurant 0". The location was an old sausage shop in Viljandi's historical district. The design showcases a 15-ton table using a rammed earth technique with local clay, complemented by sand-leveled floors and lime-painted walls. The restaurant's primary material was locally sourced clay used to craft the standout 15-ton rammed earth table. This traditional technique, requiring only hand tools, emphasizes sustainability and cost-effectiveness.

Restaurant 0
› VILJANDI, ESTONIA
2021/2021
Food & Accommodation · 100m²
› kuidas.works
Hannes Praks, Henri Papson, Andrea Tamm, Maria Helena Luiga
Estonian Television (Public)
© Tõnu Tunnel

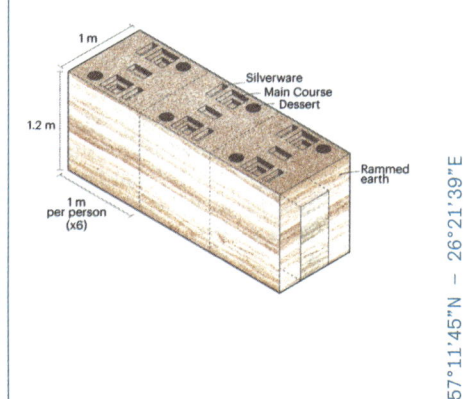

The location of the building was chosen to create good visibility and access from the entrance road and the factory. The laconic and linear construction volume is the result of a simple, rational timber-based construction system. The office building combines various functions (catering, administrative and representative). Its design is inspired by the philosophy of the AVOTI furniture factory, which supplies IKEA. Simple yet sophisticated, it provides excellent indoor comfort with climate-responsive geometry, a structure-integrated HVAC system, renewable materials, zero VOCs and a low CO_2 footprint. Its blend of abstract simplicity and clever details sets an example for the construction industry.

AVOTI Office Building
› LIZUMS, LATVIA
2020/2022-2023
Office · 1,086m² · 1,600€/m²
› MADE ARHITEKTI
Mikelis Putrams, Linda Krumina
AVOTI (Private)
© Ansis Starks

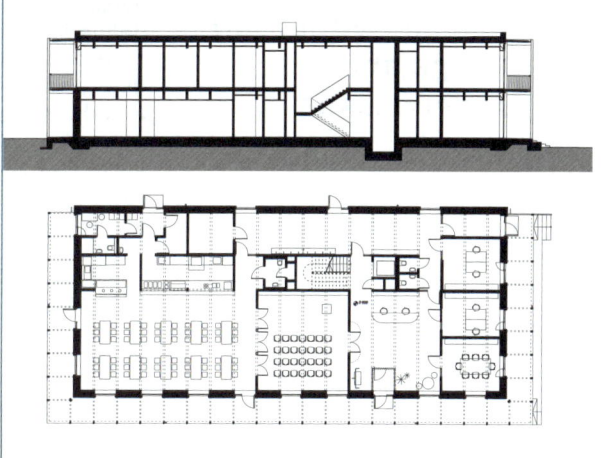

Son of a Shingle Vaksali Pedestrian Bridge and Underpasses

Tartu, Estonia
2017/2020-2021

PART architects
Sille Pihlak, Siim Tuksam

Tartu City
(Public)
Infrastructure · 500m²

This pedestrian junction is a multilevel urban connector, consisting of a bridge and two tunnels. The project is defined by a soft, undulating skin, which pursues the continuity of movement and is covered by 100,000 ceramic shingles. It aims to be a landscape landmark to motivate people to walk and cycle by creating an attractive waypoint.

Over the last few years, this pedestrian junction has proven to strengthen the connections between two neighbourhoods, with more bicyclists and walkers in the region than ever, changing the area's traditional car centred traffic. Above all, this infrastructure project is a landmark for adapting to climate changes and global security issues. Due to climate change, the lower part of the bridge has been flooded for nearly a few months every year making it seem like a monsoon, which made the area impassable for most people. With new two tunnels and a bridge, we were also able to secure faster movement in case of emergencies and better connect Tartu's bicycle network.

Moving in urban space should be smooth and easy, but ideally the environment should also offer diverse experiences. This reduces cognitive distances and perhaps, as a result, more people will go about on foot. Thus, we decided to mould the bridge and tunnel into a single landscaped ensemble, which does not dominate the surroundings, though it still stands out. The structure encourages you to directly experience it, not admire it from a distance.

To achieve the desired result, we have provided an unexpected material for the tunnel and for the guardrail of the bridge: ceramic shingles. In addition to creating form, we wanted to emphasise human scale elements in urban infrastructure. The 100,000 shingles vary between four shades, from silver to honey, depending on the amount of UV radiation that falls on them. As a result, the grey bricks blend in with the outdoor concrete elements, while inside the tunnel there is a warm atmosphere, supported by the curved form of the shingles and the lighting solution.

PART ARCHITECTS

SHORTLISTED

SON OF A SHINGLE - VAKSALI PEDESTRIAN BRIDGE AND UNDERPASSES

77

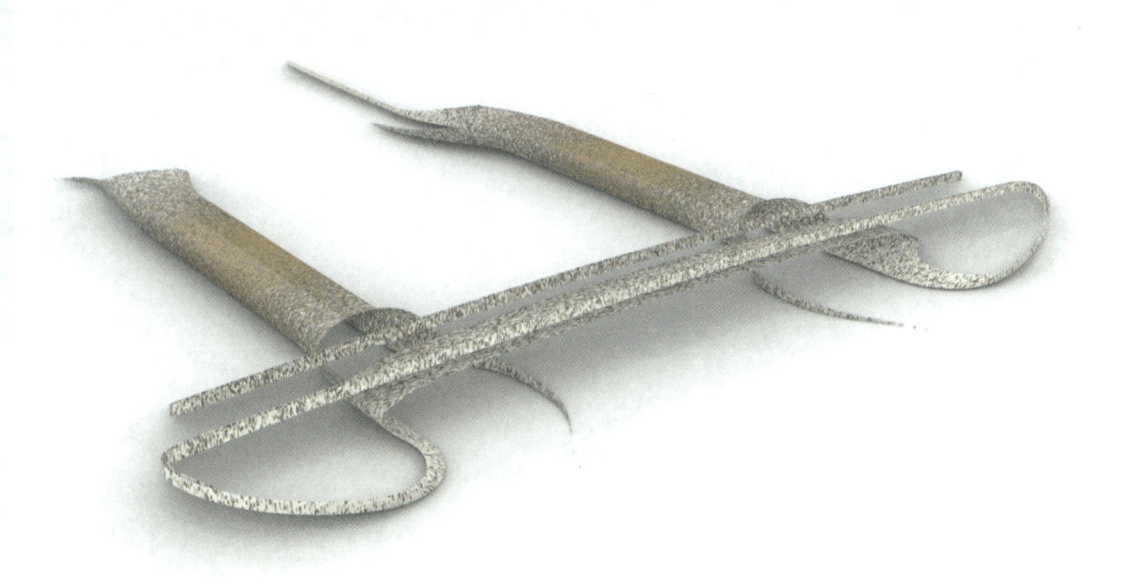

PART ARCHITECTS

78

From
OKSBØL
Denmark
55°38'07"N — 8°16'14"E

to
ZARASAI
Lithuania
55°43'55"N — 26°13'50"E

At the site of Denmark's largest World War II refugee camp, BIG has preserved and extended one of the camp's few remaining structures, a former hospital comprised of two buildings, into FLUGT – Refugee Museum of Denmark. The museum gives a voice and a face to refugees worldwide.
The museum building connects the former hospital buildings architecturally and historically through the addition of a curve-shaped volume. The volume creates a welcoming structure and embraces a courtyard, offering a contemplative space for arrival and breaks for visitors.

Flugt – Refugee Museum of Denmark

› **OKSBØL, DENMARK**
 2015/2020-2022
 Culture · 1,600m²
› **BIG - Bjarke Ingels Group**
 Finn Nørkjær, Ole Elkjær-Larsen, Frederik Lyng, Bjarke Ingels, Frederik Skou Jensen
 Vardemuseerne (Private)
 © Rasmus Hjortshøj

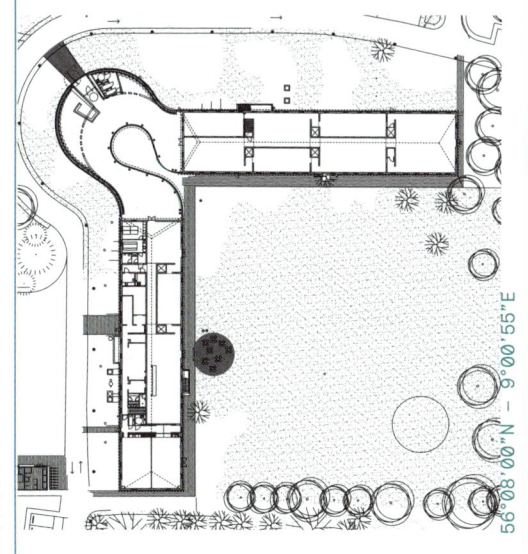

Herning Folk High School was created by visionary industrialists for textile workers to provide a general education in avantgarde art surroundings. Its main contemporary achievement is to successfully revitalize local, living traditions, a community spirit and the modernist architectural heritage in an area of Denmark with few listed buildings. The approach is to use what is already given (materials and values) under the labels of "restoration", "reconstruction" and "renewal".

Herning Folk High School

› **HERNING, DENMARK**
 2020/2021-2022
 Culture · 6,500m²
› **SLETH, HH Herning**
 Søren Leth, Rasmus Therkildsen, Hans Bruun Olesen, Niels Eli Kjær Thomsen, Bente Ulrikke Weinreich, Nanna Østergaard Christensen, Troels Voer Hørup, Anne Marie Mau, Jens Thomas Arnfred
 HH Herning (Private)
 © Laura Stamer

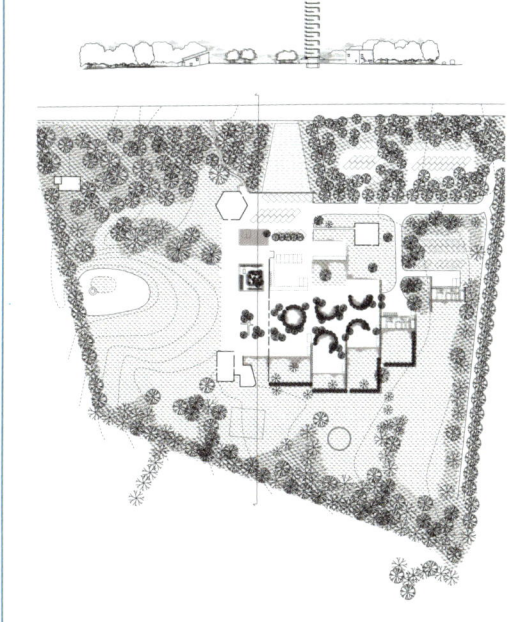

New Aarch brings together 10 former locations into one building. The vision was of a living laboratory, a factory for architecture. This has inspired the workshop-like design that presents itself like an anti-icon: an empty canvas made for ideas, creativity and learning.

The work is located at a former railyard with traces of industrial history forming an unpolished identity. Characterized by its exposed industrial details and MEPs, the building design adapts to this raw environment: the intentional simplicity of the design is a detailed response to the school's need for robust spaces.

New Aarch

› AARHUS, DENMARK
2017/2019-2021
Education · 12,500m^2
› **ADEPT, Danish Building and Property Agency, Aarhus School of Architecture, Rolvung og Brønsted Arkitekter, Vargo Nielsen Palle, A. Enggaard, TriConsult**
Martin Krogh, Martin Laursen, Anders Lonka, Simon Poulsen, Lisa Sørensen, Kristine Leth, Torben Nielsen, Jakob Bronsted, Jonas Snedevind Nielsen, Mathias Palle, Brian Vargo, Gert Hedegaard, Søren Ibsen
Danish Building and Property Agency (Public)
© Rasmus Hjortshøj

To respond to the city's vision to re-connect the old and new part of the city, the purpose of our design was to extend the garden to the full extent of the boulevard and over the light railway to invite and promote quality urban interaction. The journey of the museum would be the narrative, the elements of Anderson's work. The duality of the opposite, dissolving the boundary, will be read through spatial composition. In the sequence of intertwined spaces, visitors will find themselves in between the outside and inside.

H.C. Andersen's House
› **ODENSE, DENMARK**
2016/2019-2022
Culture · 5,000m²
› **Kuma & Associates Europe**
Yuki Ikeguchi, Kengo Kuma
Odense Kommune / Odense Bys Museer (Mixed)
© Rasmus Hjortshøj

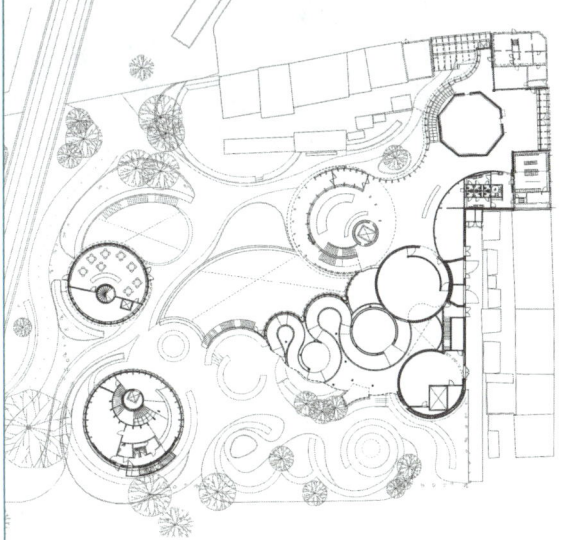

Faber is a privately developed endeavor designed to inspire social and cultural wellbeing: one that connects local, regional and international stakeholders and actions. Our approach to the building and context had two main objectives: the first was to open the building towards the street and the big courtyard of the former industrial compound; and the second was to intervene with simple materials and uniform textures.

Faber's Factories
› **RYSLINGE, DENMARK**
2018/2019-2021
Collective housing · 460m² · 1,341€/m²
› **Arcgency**
Mads Møller, Camilla Lemb Nielsen, David Kofod
Faaborg-Midtfyn Municipality (Public)
© Rasmus Hjortshøj

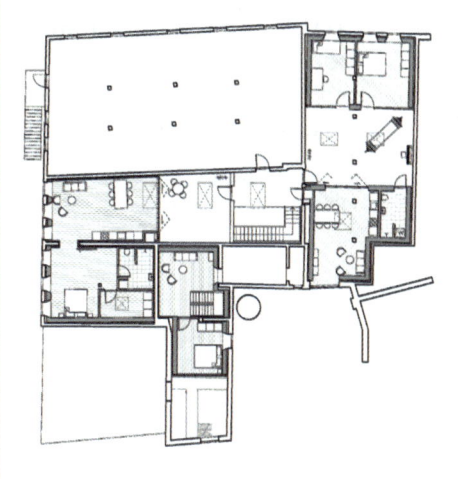

Widely different branches of the pharmaceutical company CODAN are brought together, creating an egalitarian and socially rich community through a maze-like spatial composition. The building is structured as a series of office wings that articulate the internal structure of the company. They envelop the tall warehouse building and nestle into the terrain with slight shifts in level that follow the curvature of the landscape. Through the use of materials, colors and detailing, exterior and interior spaces are intertwined and the connection between built space and landscape is strengthened.

CODAN – Office and Warehouse

› **KØGE, DENMARK**
  2018/2020-2023
  Office · 2,963m^2
› **Johansen Skovsted Arkitekter**
  Sebastian Skovsted, Søren Johansen
  CODAN Companies (Private)
  © Rasmus Norlander

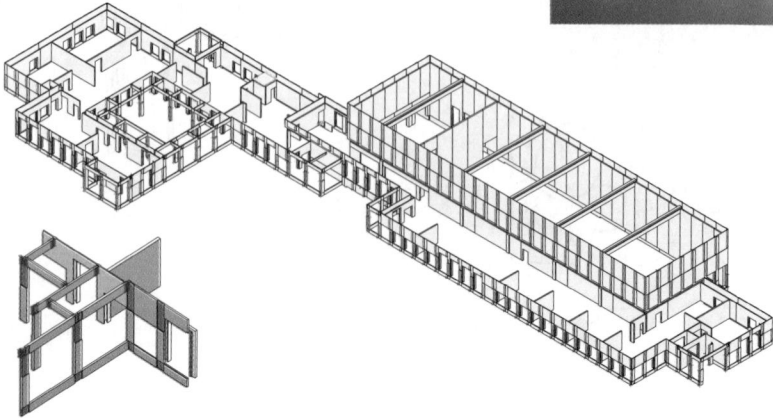

The landscape, the sea and the horizon are and will always be the most commanding aspects of this site. Today the visitors center is situated on an excavated shelf in the slope, below ground, and configured as a hall of columns or portico that frames the view like a large loggia. Here there is a fluid transition between in and out where one can linger on the edge of the landscape. One can step out and look directly down the chalk drop, which has otherwise long been somewhat obscured within the overall site. This somewhat humble approach carries over into the materials and the atmosphere that we have sought to create in this space.

Stevns Klint Experience
› **RØDVIG, DENMARK**
2019/2020-2022
Education · 1,400m²
› **Kristine Jensens Landscape, Praksis**
Mads Bjørn Hansen, Kristine Jensen
Fonden Stevns Klint Besøgscenter (Public)
© Jens Lindhe

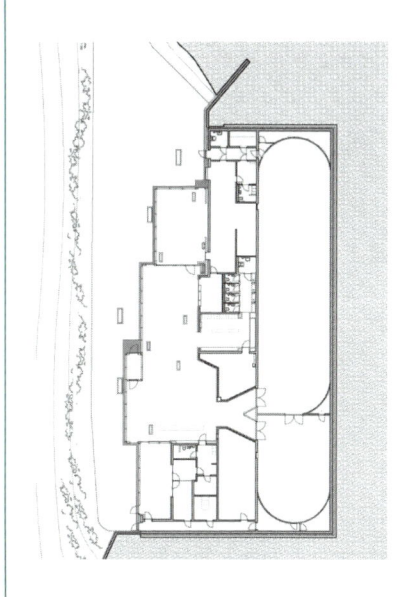

Egedammen is a municipal kindergarten for 144 children. It is a building to be experienced as a series of very different spaces that hopefully give children a better understanding of scale, light, sound and materials. It is a building that looks like a brick house from the outside, but is made of wood on the inside. That's because it is a structure that takes care of both the local building heritage and the planet's climate.

Egedammen Kindergarten
› **GLADSAXE, DENMARK**
2021/2021-2022
Education · 1,200m² · 4,600€/m²
› **BBP Arkitekter**
Ebbe Wæhrens
Gladsaxe Kommune (Public)
© Jens Lindhe

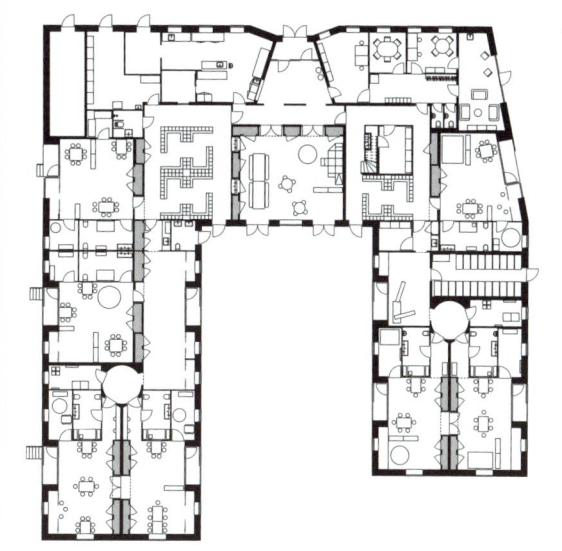

The architectural intent is to create a heavy yet elegant, stable yet dynamic house, where the construction of in situ cast concrete clearly defines the relationship between culture and the individual. The project is about something that is bigger than oneself. Our aim is to create a balance between great heaviness and tactile softness as a picture of a culture meeting a person. The project contributes to the dynamic context by creating urban order outwards along the street.

House of Martial Arts
› COPENHAGEN, DENMARK
2018/2020-2022
Sport & Leisure · 3,007m²
› entasis
Christian Cold, Signe Cold
København Kommune, Kultur og Fritidsforvaltningen (Public)
© Jens Markus Lindhe

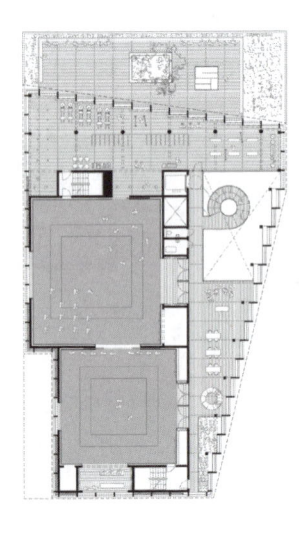

The transformation turns a listed slaughterhouse from 1932 into a food production facility 2.0. Located within the city center, ÅBEN Brewery restores the industrial legacy of the building and turns it inside out by inviting guests into the brewing processes, consequently blurring the contemporary distinction between public and production.

ÅBEN Brewery
› COPENHAGEN, DENMARK
2020/2021-2022
Mixed use - Commercial & Offices · 950m²
› pihlmann architects
Søren Pihlmann, Anna Wisborg
ÅBEN (Private)
© Hampus Berndtson

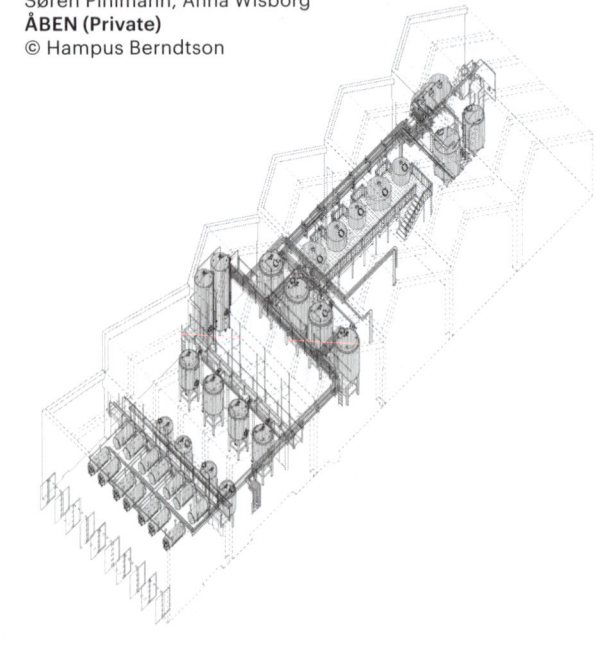

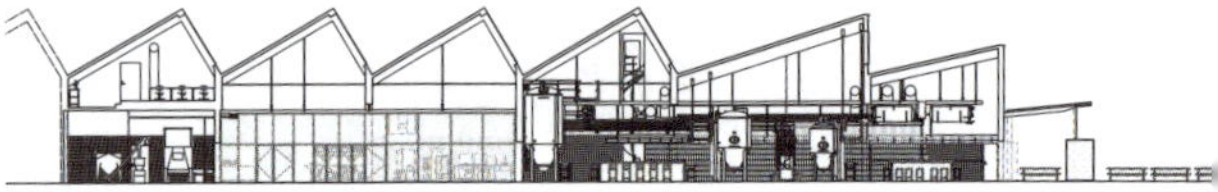

Gjuteriet involves the transformation of industrial heritage into a new creative workplace in Malmö built around social meeting and communal spaces. It is focused on the intensive reuse of repurposed materials, demonstrating how existing buildings can be reimagined based on circular principles. The project is both about the reinvention of the building itself and the wider positive change it brings to the emerging mixed-use sustainable neighborhood.

Gjuteriet

› **MALMÖ, SWEDEN**
2019/2020-2023
Mixed use - Commercial & Offices · 6,030m² · 2,750€/m²
› **Kjellander Sjöberg**
Ola Kjellander, Stefan Sjöberg, Sylvia Neiglick, Johan Pitura, Hannes Haak, Simon Estié, Pär Hädefält, Sebastian Mardi
Varvsstaden (Private)
© Rasmus Hjortshøj

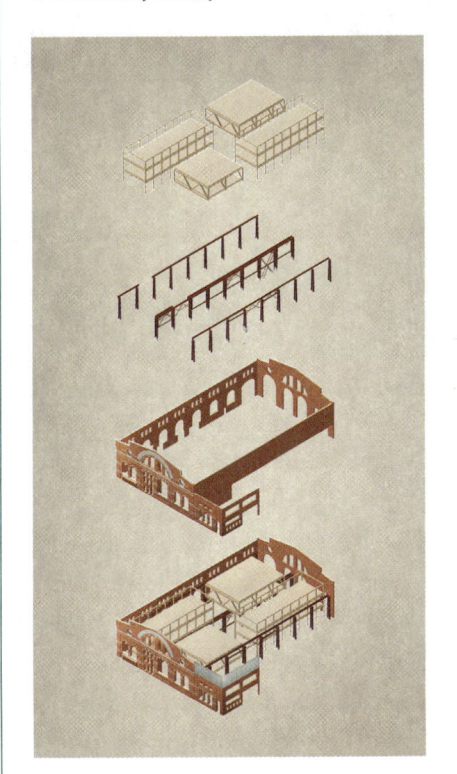

The twelve houses project is a block of town houses comprising three building volumes clad in red brick. Each individual house spans three floors with an exposed cross laminated timber structure on the inside. With six similar openings for each house, the repetitive façades create a framework for the residents to fill with everyday life. The generous width of the individual houses allows for a sequence of spaces around a central bathroom made from larger clay blocks. The main living areas, partially with a double floor height, open toward a garden. The second floor room has an opening towards the double height living space on the ground floor.

Twelve Houses

› **MALMÖ, SWEDEN**
2020/2021-2022
Collective housing · 2,180m²
› **Förstberg Ling**
Mikael Ling, Björn Förstberg
Förstberg Ling, developer-architect (Private)
© Markus Linderoth

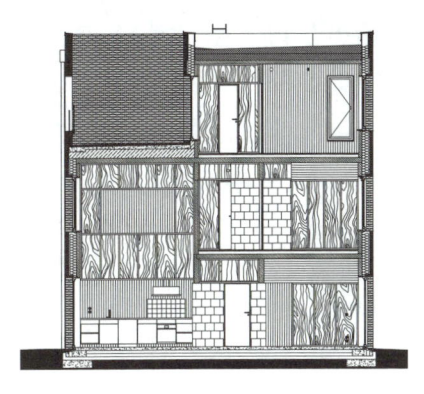

Hage
Lund, Sweden
2018/2019-2021
Brendeland & Kristoffersen architects, Price & Myers
Geir Brendeland, Olav Kristoffersen, Thomas Skinnemoen, Tim Lucas, Ian Shepherd
Lund Cathedral
(Public)
Urban planning · 1,600m² · 700€/m²

FINALIST

Hage is a high-quality public space that should work both as a short-term space for public discussion, events and workshops, while also offer a meditative, beautiful urban space and garden at the heart of a new neighbourhood in the long term. Open to everyone, this project is a response to the question of how to build a new community: start with social space.

The mediaeval city of Lund, located in the south of Sweden, is surrounded by some of the country's most fertile farmland. Following the establishment of a new science park, a large urban development is now taking place on the outskirts of the city. The Lund Cathedral is a large landowner within the new urban development.

The Lund Cathedral has decided to retain a critical distance from this new, large development and to develop their land themselves guided by value-based long-term thinking – rather than handing over the property to a real estate developer.

They have established an alternative long-term planning framework by carefully curating both the art and architecture, and by embracing an open, organic approach to the masterplan involving both the city and its inhabitants in this process.

Hage is the first commission built as part of this plan.

A strong 40 by 40 metre enclosure made of reused bricks in the peri-urban landscape will now transform the fallow fields into a new urban setting. Local residents and groups are invited to inhabit the space and to gradually develop and realise ideas for its future character and use.

Currently, 'Hage' appears as an object in the landscape. Its scale corresponds to the typical farmsteads in the area. In an open windswept landscape, Hage creates a calm environment and protection. A pause.

In time, when a new neighbourhood is gradually established around this public space, it will become a void in the city fabric. The first homes to be built next to Hage – designed by Catalan architects Flores & Prats – will form a direct conversation with 'Hage'. Public spaces in the two buildings, including a communal kitchen, will look out onto 'Hage', creating a generous group of community spaces for all residents and visitors to enjoy.

We hope that the garden will grow along with the children who inhabit the new neighbourhood. We want them to hold birthday parties each year in Hage and create a memory bank of family rituals framed by the garden.

BRENDELAND & KRISTOFFERSEN ARCHITECTS, PRICE & MYERS

Designed as a walled garden for people to meet, talk, play, and exchange ideas, it is enclosed on three sides with a simple, 2.2-metre-high brick wall. The fourth side of the enclosure is open and protected by a 43.2 × 7.2 metre corten steel canopy, beneath which sits a long wooden table, accompanied by two generous benches. The two stones supporting these benches have been sourced from a nearby quarry, while the 48,000 reclaimed bricks came from the recently demolished Björnekulla jam factory.

Working with local fabricators Proswede, the London-based structural engineers Price & Myers devised a beguilingly simple construction system for the canopy using 20,000 rivets. Rather than using a standard welding process, the team elected to take a more hand-crafted approach which reflected the design aesthetic developed through a collaboration between the architects and engineers: simplicity, honesty, and integrity of materials. The design of the canopy is also intended to echo the riveted iron roof structure of Lund Cathedral, creating a conceptual and physical thread between the two structures which sit 5 km apart.

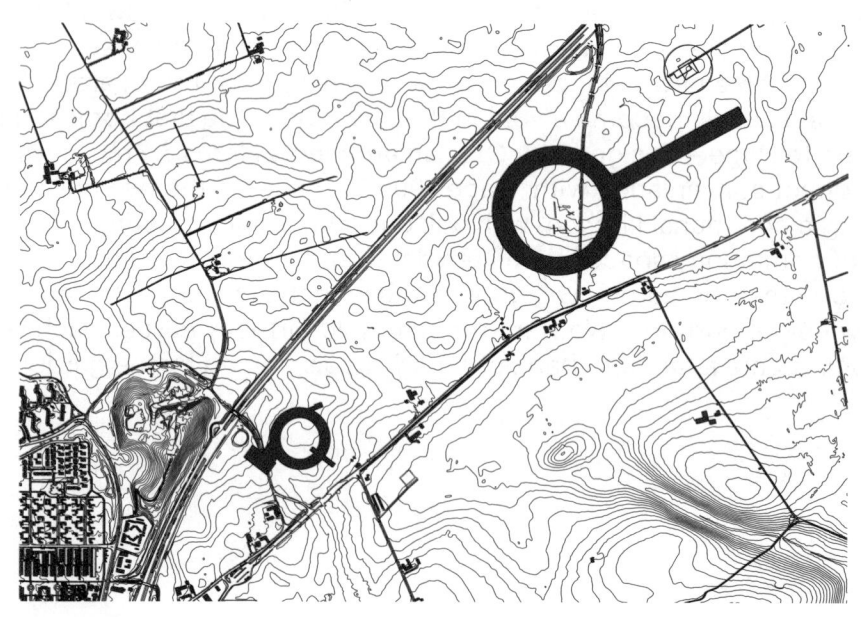

General plan

Sections

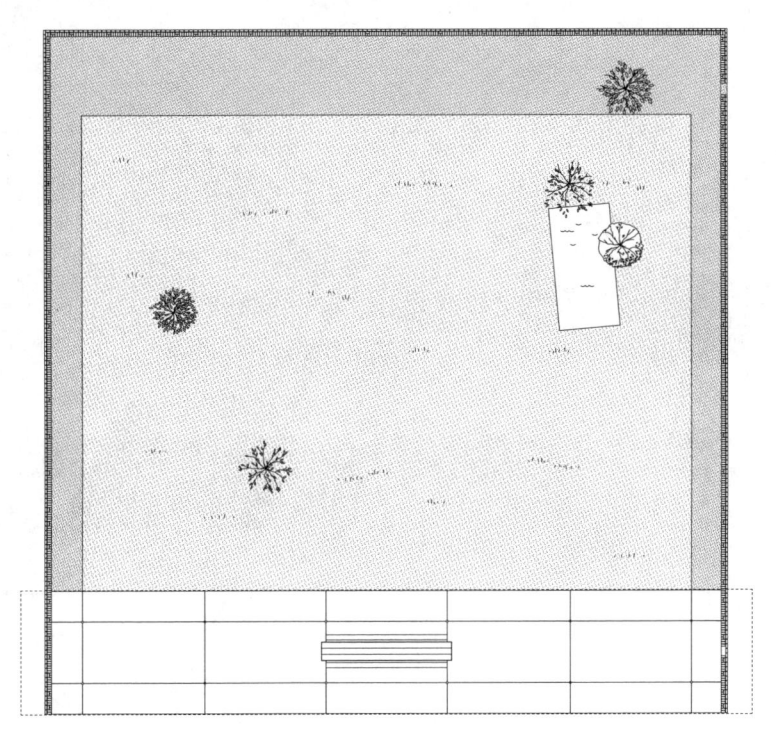

Plan

BRENDELAND & KRISTOFFERSEN ARCHITECTS, PRICE & MYERS

FINALIST

HAGE

BRENDELAND & KRISTOFFERSEN ARCHITECTS, PRICE & MYERS

Drawings by Geir Brendeland

HAGE

BRENDELAND & KRISTOFFERSEN ARCHITECTS, PRICE & MYERS

FINALIST

HAGE

BRENDELAND & KRISTOFFERSEN ARCHITECTS, PRICE & MYERS

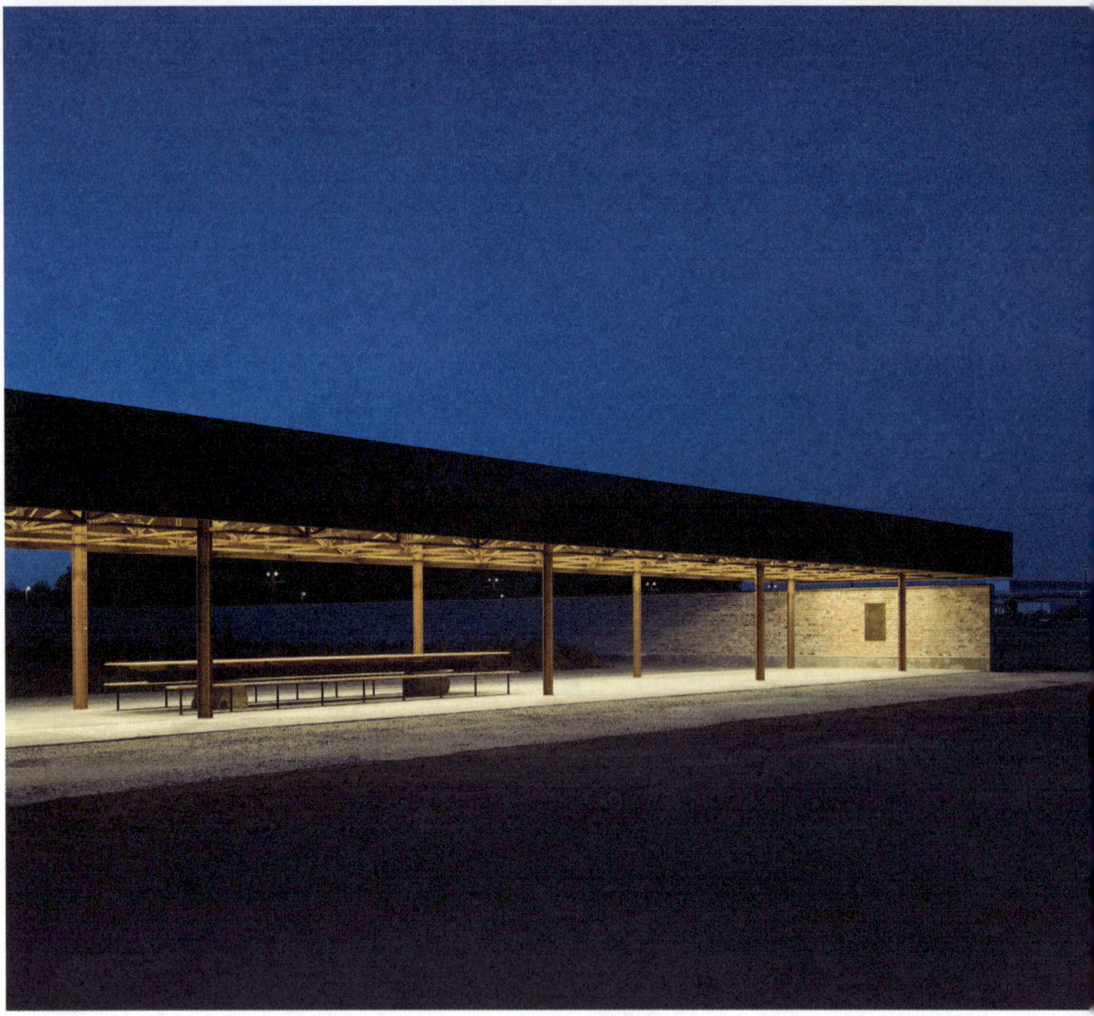

BRENDELAND & KRISTOFFERSEN ARCHITECTS, PRICE & MYERS

FINALIST

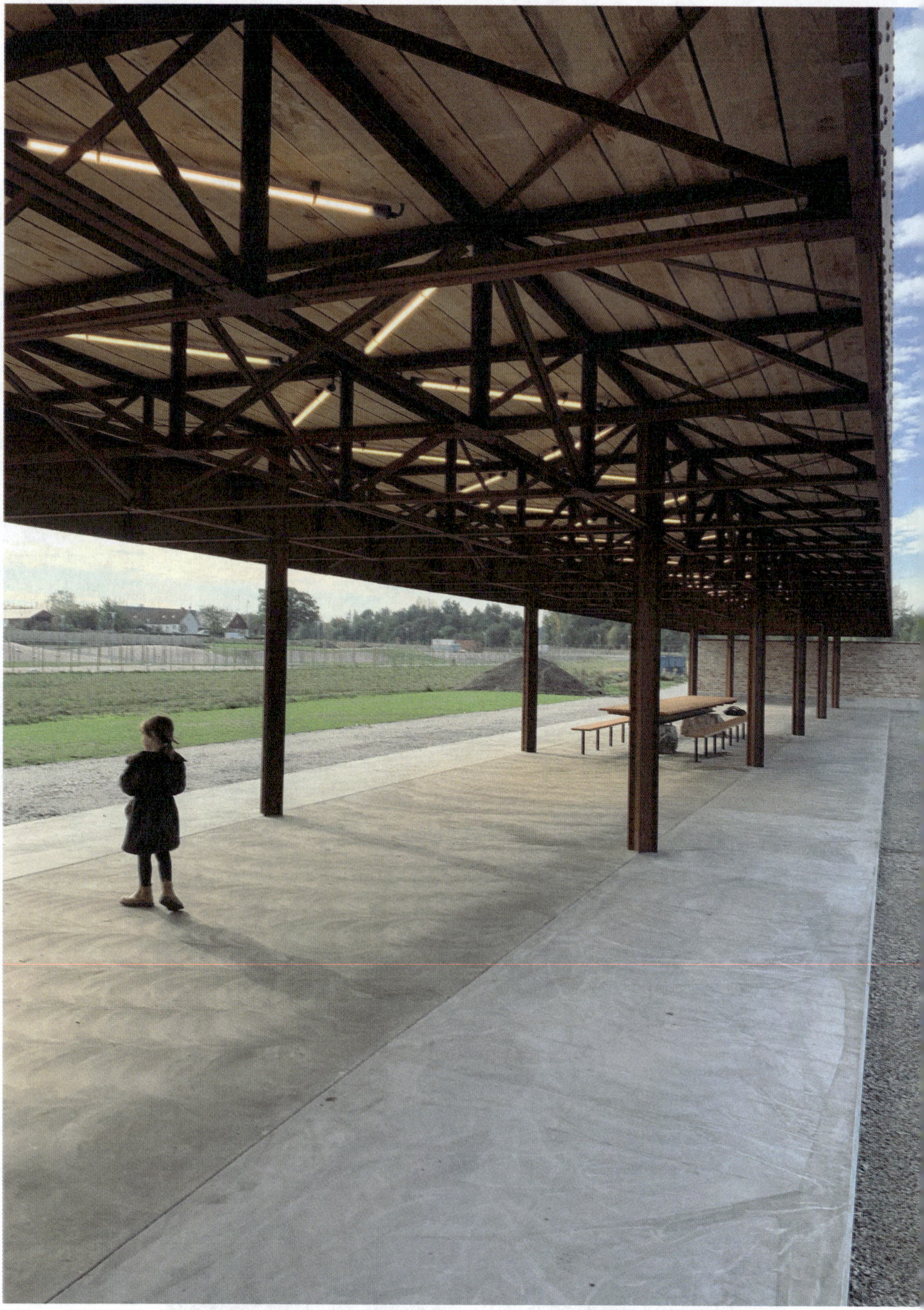

Placing a City

"The construction of Hage thus not only involved gathering materials from the area in the form of bricks, but also the use of local skills and craftsmanship, in the fabrication of the steel roof and through a process that revived the near-extinct technique of riveting."

James Payne

Director of Architects Lundvall Payne, involved in phase 1 of The Råången project.

Gathering around a long table under a broad canopy, a group of people shelter from the rain. Some are local, some have travelled far – here to the middle of a field on the outskirts of Lund in the south of Sweden. They have come to visit "Hage" (Swedish for "clearing") and to hear representatives from Lund Cathedral talk about this first permanent built project – a new public walled garden – on the new Råången development area to be built on fallow farming land owned by the diocese.

Built in 1123, Lund Cathedral lies in the centre of the city 5 km southwest of the site, and celebrated its 900th anniversary in 2023. Constructed in the round-arched Romanesque style, the cathedral originally had a flat ceiling made of wooden planks with tension rods spanning between the thick sandstone walls. Over the centuries a number of structural changes took place, with stone cross vaults added, supported by gothic buttresses. In the late 1800s, Helgo Zettervall restored the cathedral back to the Romanesque style with the help of modern, industrial engineering. Part of this work involved constructing a riveted steel roof structure over the vaults, that would eliminate the need for external buttresses.

An ambitious programme for this new neighbourhood on the northeastern periphery of Lund was established by Lund Cathedral in 2017 together with the art curator Jes Fernie, followed in 2020 with the implementation of a development and commissioning framework alongside Jake Ford and Åsa Bjerndell from White Arkitektur. A gradual process of reflective and discursive intervention from artists, writers, architects, and the community in dialogue with the Cathedral team, has, and will, inform the long-term growth of this place where city meets country. This new area of Råången (Swedish for "wild meadow"), is a 12-acre site earmarked for residential development in various stages within a much larger new neighbourhood called Brunnshög. By 2050, this neighbourhood will host some 6,000 homes, new workspaces and parkland for the city and is connected to the centre by a new tramline. New roads and infrastructures are planned here, to run between a science park in the north and a landscaped park in the south. Beyond the neighbourhood to the east lies flat, fertile farmland and scattered farmsteads typical of this southern Swedish county of Skåne.

In 2021, Hage – the new public space and walled garden – was inaugurated, designed by Norwegian architects Brendeland and Kristoffersen. The

Trondheim-based firm has amassed a portfolio of Norwegian work of great precision, material economy and soul, that deals directly with community concerns. The 40- x 40-metre walled space in the landscape is constructed from 48,000 bricks recuperated from a demolished jam factory. The courtyard is open on the south side, where it is delineated and sheltered by a 44- x 8-metre corten steel roof canopy, that overhangs the flanking walls. The finely tuned engineering on the roof canopy was carried out by structural engineers Price and Myers. 20,000 rivets hold the truss structure together, which is fabricated from 4mm corten steel plate, some of it with customized folded edges. The roof structure is elegantly poised upon 12 slender cruciform columns, overlaid with timber boards to form the ceiling. As well as using similar construction techniques to Zettervall's innovative cathedral roof, the work is also built to last. The construction of Hage thus not only involved gathering materials from the area in the form of bricks, but also the use of local skills and craftsmanship, in the fabrication of the steel roof and through a process that revived the near-extinct technique of riveting.

Lund's roots stem from the church and it boasts one of the oldest universities in northern Europe. During the 20th century, its growth around the medieval town centre saw the population double to around 90,000 inhabitants today. The farming land around Lund has formed a protective barrier to its development, but is now increasingly under pressure to expand.

The apartment buildings that have already been constructed in nearby Brunnshög follow a conventional model of real-estate-market-led urban development. But in Råången, by deciding to develop the land itself, the Cathedral aims to both integrate the new community more deeply and vitally within its surrounding context, and into a thousand-year historical timeframe that stretches far into both the past and future. This kind of stewardship of the land to manage the transition from agricultural to residential aims to foster three long-term values: *landskap* (landscape), *grannskap* (neighbourhood) and *värdskap* (hospitality).

This theme of hospitality was most provocatively explored by Nathan Coley's 2018 installation "And We are Everywhere" – a makeshift church evoking a temporary refugee shelter. Following recent waves of refugees coming into Sweden, this raised difficult questions regarding the displacement of people, not just due to war but also due to the increasing effects of climate change. A process that is clearly a more substantive than the usual artistic window-dressing of pre-approved property deals.

Themes of public gathering, sanctuary and generosity lie at the heart of the Church's ethos, and is reflected in its pragmatic and pastoral role within communities. This ethos can be traced to the history of long-term planning in Sweden in the mid-20th century, a period of democratic social rule that produced the "folkhemmet" ("people's home") concept, which harnessed modern architecture to build this new society. The role of the Lutheran church in Sweden in providing spiritual and community buildings has brought along with it some of the finest architecture of the 20th century, in particular the work of Swedish master Sigurd Lewerentz – which includes his mysterious, archaic-brick Sankt Petri church in nearby Klippan. The Lund school of brick Brutalism also encompasses the work of architects such as Klas Anselm, Bengt Edman and Bernt Nyberg, and this late modernist architecture was at the forefront of much of Lund's postwar expansion.

At Hage, two rugged stone boulders emerge from the smooth concrete ground under the canopy to support a steel beam under the timber tabletop. These natural-looking objects recall the large conch shell baptismal font in

Lewerentz's Klippan church, that is cradled within a steel framework that seems to emerge from the ground. The walled garden may touch upon some obvious biblical themes – such as the Garden of Eden or, indeed, the long table of the last supper – but it also has a more diffuse sense of spirituality, one that is perhaps more earthbound. The garden was originally planned to feature a reflection pool – recalling that of Mies van der Rohe's Barcelona Pavilion – and a formal garden. Eventually, following discussions with the client team, it was decided to leave the ground fallow, and free for future community pioneers to tend the garden or grow fruit and vegetables.

Here there is a powerful sense of the past, present and future: a panoramic portal that frames the landscape to the south and will eventually frame the future buildings that will emerge above the parapet of the wall. When the diagonally arranged strip lights of the canopy illuminate the space at dusk, in bad weather or in darkness, the "charged void" that the project represents as a mark of settlement is particularly present.

The Norwegian architectural theorist Christian Norberg-Schulz wrote in his book *Nightlands* of the particular experiential quality of Nordic space, whose construction is based around the primordial principle of a clearing within a thicket, or a "web" of landscapes at the mercy of the seasons and darkness – as opposed to the figural qualities of brightly lit forms in the Mediterranean South.

"In the North, then, space is not continuous and comprehensive but is an aperture that humans have created in the unsurveyable. As such, this space becomes a home, in that home is precisely a known place of dwelling in an unknown world."

The building accommodates the studios of fashion designers working for the several brands owned by LPP S.A. It is the first stage of development of the campus called LPP Fashion Lab. These workshops are tailored for young creative teams, emphasizing collaboration and the sharing of ideas. The centrally located courtyard serves as the vibrant heart of the envisioned complex, offering a space for relaxation and gatherings. The heavy and Brutalist concrete form of the building is inspired by industrial tradition of the city's shipyard.

LPP Fashion Lab - Fashion Laboratories Building

› **GDANSK, POLAND**
2016/2020-2021
Office · 8,500m²
› **JEMS Architekci**
Maciej Miłobędzki, Jerzy Szczepanik-Dzikowski, Marcin Sadowski, Zygmunt Borawski, Łukasz Kuciński, Katarzyna Kuźmińska, Maria Mermer, Grzegorz Moskała, Anna Świderska, Nina Wójcicka
LPP S.A. (Private)
© Juliusz Sokołowski

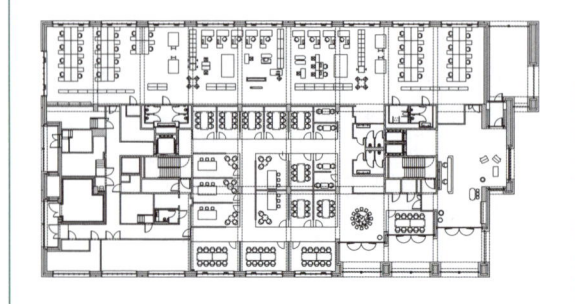

Surrounded by nature reserves, the sensitive landscape of Svencelė is one of the few remaining places where the development of new recreational areas is possible in the Klaipėda region, Lithuania's only access to the Baltic Sea. The abandoned Soviet duck farms and territory are regenerated creating a delicate urban fabric where water and wind are key elements. The area has been transformed into a new center for living and leisure.

Aqua Urban Fabric Salos-1 in Svencele

› **SVENCELE, LITHUANIA**
2020/2020-2022
Mixed use - Infrastructure & Urban · 9,554m²
› **DO ARCHITECTS**
Andre Baldisiute, Sabina Grincevičiūtė, Algimantas Neniškis, Kasparas Žiliukas, Gilma Teodora Gylytė, Ignas Uogintas, Gediminas Aismontas, Milda Gustainė, Justas Paicius, Emilija Deksnytė, Marija Steponavičiūtė, Grasilda Mintaučkytė, Laura Gaudutytė, Edvinas Skiestenis, Emilija Martinkevič
„**Svencelės Salos**" (Private)
©Solds

The Nemunas Island Bridge-Plaza is a hybrid structure that functions as both a bridge connecting areas divided by a river and a public space where people can engage with the city and its natural surroundings. A bridge for pedestrians and cyclists seemingly integrates with the historical city and landscape, enhancing the connectivity and creating an alluring urban space with its elegant curved arches. The project sits over the Nemuno Canal and its two landing points are the essential principles of the design.

Nemunas Island Bridge-Plaza
› **KAUNAS, LITHUANIA**
2018/2020-2022
Infrastructure · 1,100m²
› **Isora x Lozuraityte Studio, Dominykas Daunys, About Architecture**
Petras Išora – Lozuraitis, Dominykas Daunys, Vano Ksnelashvili
Kaunas City Municipality (Public)
© Lukas Mykolaitis

The multifunctional water sports center is a project to expand the existing Žalgiris arena, an entertainment and sports center in Kaunas. The new building is attached to the arena on its western side and a connection is planned between them. The concept of the building and its architectural expression were dictated by the urban context of the island, which contains significant greenery and where an existing park is being further developed. The aim is to preserve the landscape and character of the area. It is a park structure that does not repeat the shapes of the neighboring buildings. By using the terrain, its roof becomes a fifth façade: a green roof.

Žalgiris Arena Multifunctional Water Sports Centre

› **KAUNAS, LITHUANIA**
  2019/2020-2022
  Sport & Leisure · 18,400m² · 1,402€/m²
› **E. Miliūno studija**
  Aurimas Ramanauskas, Vytautas Miliūnas, Vaidas Zabulionis
  Kaunas city municipality (Public)
  ↑ © Gintaras Česonis
  ↗ © Leonas Garbačauskas

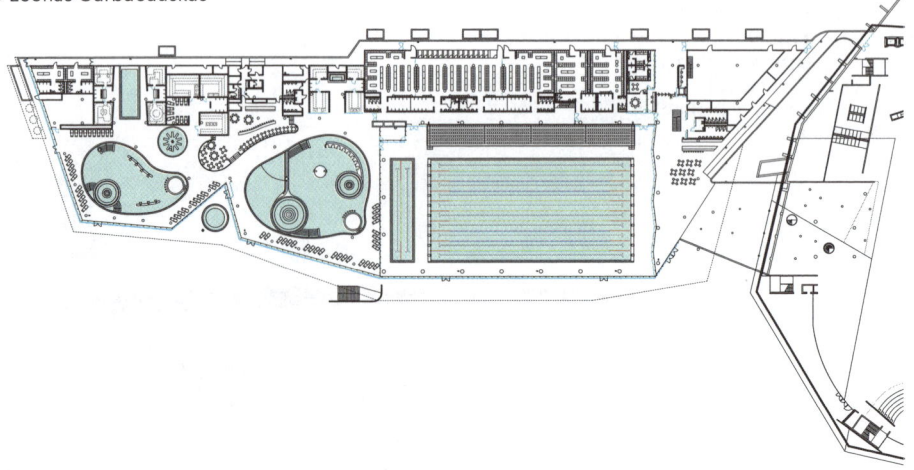

Pilaite Gymnasium is a contemporary high school designed to cater to modern educational needs, turning a school into a community center and developing public spaces. The main goal of the project was to create a school not only as an institution, but also as a community for children. The space that best represents this idea is the monumental amphitheater staircase.

Pilaite High-School (Gymnasium)
› **VILNIUS, LITHUANIA**
2020/2020-2022
Education · 11,782m² · 1,440€/m²
› **DO ARCHITECTS**
Andre Baldisiute, Sabina Grincevičiūtė, Algimantas Neniškis, Kasparas Žiliukas, Gilma Teodora Gylytė, Justas Paicius, Aurimas Lenktys, Solveiga Buozelyte, Karolis Grigaitis, Mikas Kauzonas, Gerda Nevulyte, Roberta Zvirblyte, Vytenis Stasiunas
Vilnius City Municipality (Public)
© Norbert Tukaj

↑ 30

The kindergarten Pelėdžiukas is the first Soviet-built transformation over the past three decades since Lithuania's independence that focused on spatial values rather than energy efficiency without questioning the spatial influence on children, teachers and parents' lives. The kindergarten underwent a remarkable transformation from a closed and divided piece of Soviet spatial propaganda into something communal, unifying, neighborly, human and warm. The main spatial change is the courtyard. Children come out here independently where they engage in games and events. It is where parents, children, teachers and the community gather.

Transformation of Soviet Kindergarten "Peledziukas"
› **VILNIUS, LITHUANIA**
2017/2019-2021
Education · 2,732m²
› **DO ARCHITECTS**
Andre Baldisiute, Sabina Grincevičiūtė, Algimantas Neniškis, Julija Čiapaitė-Jurevičienė, Ignas Uogintas, Justina Jauniškytė, Domantas Baltrūnas, Karolina Čiplytė, Vadim Babij, Gilma Teodora Gylyte, Justas Paicius
Vilnius District Municipality (Public)
© Aistė Rakauskaitė

The main idea of this project is to create a spatial-visual narrative in the central street of Vilnius that connects the historical stages of the area, emphasizing its urban significance and cultural memory. The pavilion building, designed for optical purposes, aims to preserve the layers of the past while providing a modern, multi-layered urban symbol for the avenue and the park in front of it. The semisynthetic landscape penetrates the interior and centers on a yellow stalactite/stalagmite structure that integrates the idea of a landscape with 1990s reconstructions, using a "signal yellow" color to visually reclaim the site's iconic episodes and postmodern manifestations.

FF2 Optics House
› **VILNIUS, LITHUANIA**
 2021/2021-2023
 Commerce · 226m^2
› **Isora × Lozuraityte Studio**
 Petras Išora – Lozuraitis, Ona Lozuraitytė – Išorė
 Friends and Frames (Private)
 © Darius Petrulaitis

The former central post office building is an extraordinary example of Lithuanian modernist architecture from the 1970s, a unique creation of the architects Algimantas and Vytautas Nasvytis. The building is one of the first public architectural objects in Lithuania where the principles of functionalism are combined with historical architecture.

Reconstruction of Vilnius Central Post Office into ISM University
› **VILNIUS, LITHUANIA**
 2021/2022-2023
 Education · 5,758m^2
› **A2SM, Senojo miesto architektai**
 Aurimas Sasnauskas, Sla Malenko, Joris Sykovas, Radvile Samackaite, Diana Sabaliauskiene, Sara Lucinskiene
 Terseta UAB (Private)
 © Norbert Tukaj

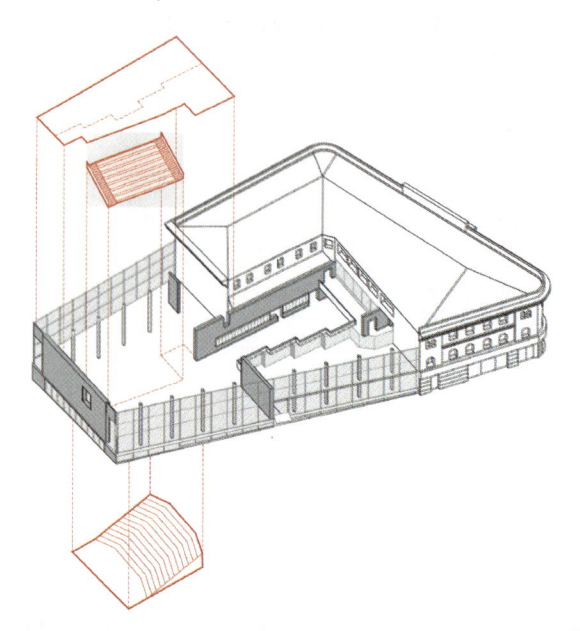

Lojoteka expands the boundaries of a typical school library, being a modern cognitive and educational space that promotes creativity. It is an open space easily adjusted for individual or group learning process, educational experiments and social gatherings. The concept for the reconstruction of the building is based on the image of the carriage house that historically existed on the site, incorporating the existing brick fence into the building and emphasizing open metal structures in the interior. The definition of the building's functions resulted from creative workshops with the school community.

Lojoteka Educational Media Centre

› **Vilnius, Lithuania**
2015/2017-2021
Education · 943m²
› **INBLUM architects, Senamiesčio projektai**
Dmitrij Kudin, Laura Malcaitė, Marija Stonytė-Izdelė, Ramūnas Buitkus, Indrė Šukytė
Vilniaus Jėzuitų gimnazija VŠĮ (Public)
© Norbert Tukaj

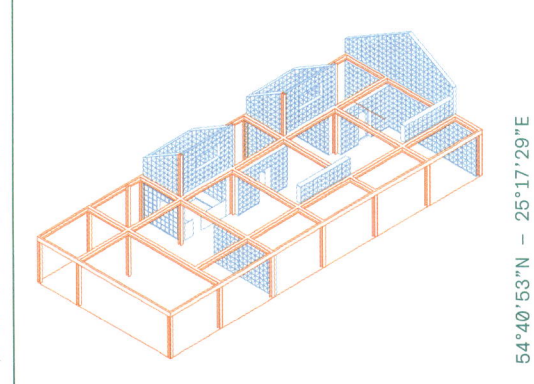

A new high school in the former confectionary factory is an excellent example of adaptive reuse and sustainable design in the historical old town of Vilnius. The reconstruction project re-energized a long neglected building while providing a unique learning environment for the students of Vilnius International School.
The aim was to create a shared space similar to a tech company incubator where students and faculty would be able to freely interact with each other. It was decided to make the former courtyard into an atrium with a glass roof to serve as a multi-functional gathering area.
The result is a light, airy space that belies the prominent views of the building from the street and fits comfortably in the historical quarter.

School Reconstruction Project

› **Vilnius, Lithuania**
2018/2019-2021
Education · 2,171m²
› **Senojo miesto architektai, Senojo miesto architektai**
Daina Ferguson, James Ferguson
Vilnius International School (Private)
© Gedmantas Kropis

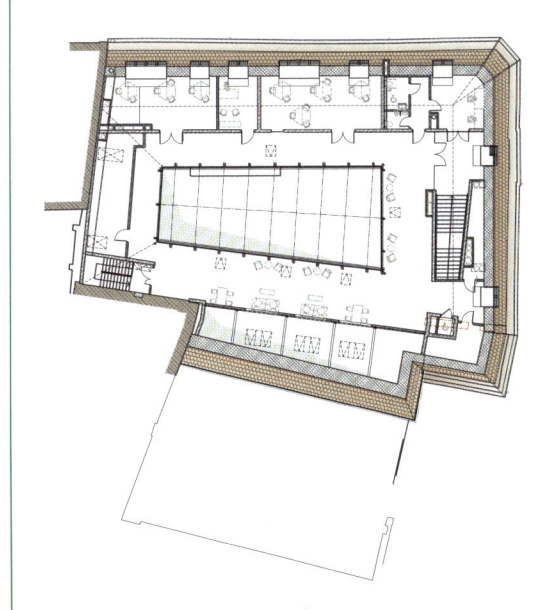

Užupis, located in the old town area of Lithuania's capital city, is characterized by a diverse and mixed architectural expression. While Užupis evolves and modernizes in tandem with Vilnius, it remains dedicated to safeguarding its unique character and individuality. This dual nature of the location served as inspiration for the building's design, which mirrors an embedded splinter or branch, uniting the raw essence of Užupis. The building commences in the depth of the plot, extending the silhouette of a traditional house, branching out into two parts and gracefully hovering above the incline of Krivių Street, creating a presence along the street façade elevation.

House Krivis with Gallery
› **VILNIUS, LITHUANIA**
  2018/2019-2021
  Single house · 167m²
› **Studija Lape**
  Tomas Lape, Edvinas Kaltanas,
  Emilija Liudvinavičiūtė, Ieva Viliūtė
  Tadas Gutauskas (Private)
  © Leonas Garbaciauskas

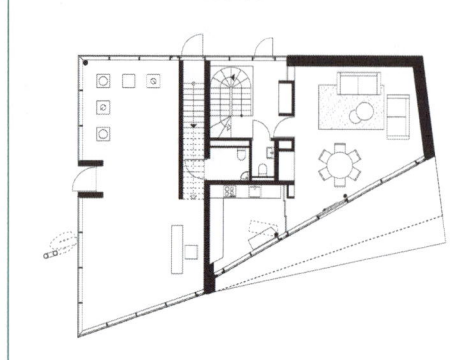

While establishing the museum, it was decided that the most important and valuable exhibit is the building itself. Therefore, the restoration aims to preserve the authenticity of the object as much as possible. The goal of the project was to create a piece of cultural infrastructure in Vilnius that meets the needs of contemporary society by establishing a new Museum of Urban Wooden Architecture that will present creative exhibitions to stimulate interest in and love for wooden urban architecture. MUWA connects the past, present and future of urban wooden architecture and reveals wooden architecture as an integral part of the sustainable and environmentally friendly city. During the restoration works, 80% of the building's exterior decoration elements and 70% of the building's authentic walls and structures were preserved.

Museum of Urban Wooden Architecture
› **VILNIUS, LITHUANIA**
  2018/2019-2022
  Culture · 242m² · 4,888€/m²
› **JSC Vilniaus Planas**
  Vincas Brezgys, Rūta Astasevičiūtė
  Vilnius city municipality (Public)
  © Saulius Žiūra

This building is a pool house in a larger single-family countryside house complex. The idea was to create a space for a family to gather. The movement inside happens around three elements: the fireplace, the kitchen island and the central volume of the utility space, leaving the perimeter of the building completely free. The central focal point of this residence is its distinctive roof, characterized by its robust and timeless design, which stands in sharp contrast to the elegant frameless, rounded corner windows. The design emphasizes a harmonious relationship between the building and its natural surroundings, ensuring a serene atmosphere that can be enjoyed all year round.

Family Retreat House Vasara
› **ZARASAI, LITHUANIA**
2021/2021-2022
Single house · 135m²
› **HEIMA architects**
Povilas Žakauskas, Povilas Daugis, Elena Gaidelytė, Rūta Kazenaitė
Private (Private)
© Norbert Tukaj

The aim of the design was to create a unique space in a unique context with the priority of preserving the natural environment. Designed as a cave for various events and concerts, the multifunctional space was integrated into the terrain of the island. The exterior of the structure joins the unique natural landscape and the interior opens to the lake bay. The building was integrated into the hill preserving the existing terrain. The shape was poured into the landscape so the close connection to the nature is felt from inside, where two glass planes like eyes gaze at the lake and the sky. Countless cultural interdisciplinary events began to take place there.

Multifunctional Hall on Lake Zarasas Island
› **ZARASAI, LITHUANIA**
2016/2017-2021
Culture · 216m²
› **Šarūno Kiaunės projektavimo studija**
Šarūnas Kiaunė, Asta Kiaunienė, Vytis Obolevičius, Ugnė Valatkevičiūtė
Zarasai district municipality (Public)
© Gintarė Marozaitė

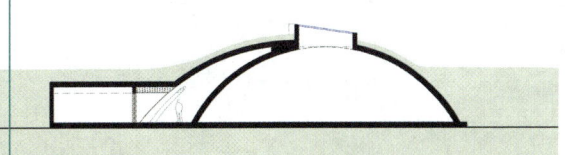

110

From
CORK
Ireland
51°45'50"N – 8°27'06"W

to
WARSAW
Poland
52°12'50"N, 21°20'35"E

This open air pavilion is the first in a planned series of rambling houses. This project aimed to use a built experiment to investigate how contemporary design and traditional materials could be combined to make something meaningful and innovative; explore how non-skilled and highly skilled craftspeople could collaborate together in a working experiment in the crossover between craft and design, all of us learning by doing; and demonstrate how something new and engaging could be made from natural materials and traditional technologies in an outdoor pavilion in a rural Cork setting.

Passage House
› **CORK, IRELAND**
2022/2022
Landscape · 4,100m²
› **O'Donnell + Tuomey**
Sheila O'Donnell, John Tuomey
Joseph Walsh Studio and O'Donnell + Tuomey (Private)
© Stephen Tierney

The challenge of the project was to add a layer of generous living space to the lodge and kennels, while avoiding overwhelming the two diminutive protected (listed) structures. Our approach was to turn the limitation on the scale of any additions to the advantage of making a connection between the new living spaces and the landscape. The new additions were partially sunken into the land so that their overall bulk was diminished. The project has allowed the family to remain on this site and enjoy the landscape more directly, while ensuring the continuity of the historic structures into the future.

Middleton Park Gate Lodge
› **CASTLETOWN GEOGHEGAN, IRELAND**
2017/2020-2021
Single house · 235m²
› **TAKA**
Alice Casey, Cian Deegan
Catriona Hatton & Robbie Nixon (Private)
© Alice Clancy

A new timber frame extension, which evolves a language from the character of local farm buildings, is placed behind the existing house to minimize spatial impact and to open new views to the wider landscape.

Ballyblake House
› BALLYBLAKE, CO.
Carlow, Ireland. 2017/2020-2021
Single house · 260m²
› **Steve Larkin Architects**
Steve Larkin
Dave Murtagh & Thelma Cantlon (Private)
© Shantanu Starick

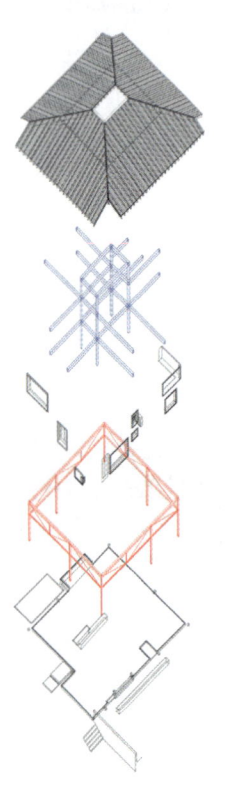

The project involved the restoration and extension of a vernacular thatched cottage built around 1840 for a family of four. The house is situated in a beautiful rural location on a sunny, windy, rolling site. The core concept was to take one on a sensory journey through old to new and to celebrate the character and contrasts of both, completing the journey with a release into the landscape. The cottage is rooted and protective and the extension is open and moving.

The Thatch
› KILDARE, IRELAND
2019/2021-2022
Single house · 260m² · 1,846.15€/m²
› **Karen Brownlee Architects**
Karen Brownlee
Karen Brownlee and Daniel Readman (Private)
© Aisling McCoy

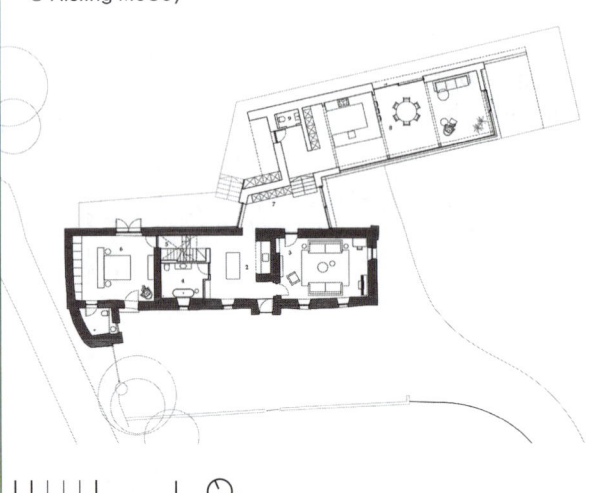

This project looks to find an alternative to the amorphous housing organized around an un-programmed green space that typically makes up suburban development. Referencing 19th-century residential areas in Dublin, we looked to maximize density while maintaining a majority of own-door access typical of Dublin by reducing back-to-back distances between units. The project is organized around a grid that establishes standard party-wall distances, while providing flexibility to accommodate a mix of 2-4 bedroom homes that in turn provided efficiencies in construction.

Ladyswell Square
› DUBLIN, IRELAND
2018/2019-2022
Collective housing · 5,750m^2 · 2,174€/m^2
› **ABK Architects**
John Parker, Criona Nangle
Cluid Housing Association (Mixed)
© Fionn McCann

Devaney Gardens Regeneration Phase is a low-rise medium density housing model. The scheme comprises 56 dwellings in a mix of houses, apartments and duplexes.
The key components of the solution implemented included the enhancement of site connectivity with surrounding neighborhoods, facilities and public transport hubs, the creation of a varied streetscape with a rich mix of types of dwellings providing high quality accommodation and the creation of a high-quality and accessible public realm and a facility-rich walkable neighborhood.

O'Devaney Gardens Regeneration Phase 1
› DUBLIN, IRELAND
2010/2018-2022
Collective housing · 5,176m^2
› **Dublin City Council - City Architects Department**
Ali Grehan, Matt Shelton, Madeline Hallinan
Dublin City Council (Public)
© Donal Murphy

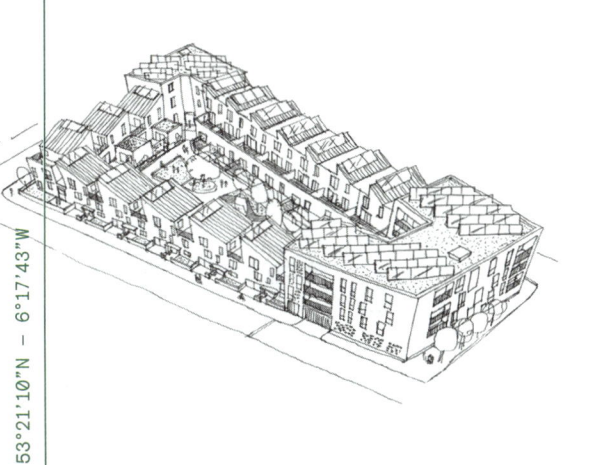

The purpose of the project was initially to find a temporary home for printmaking in TU Dublin using portable modular cabins. However, during the early stages of the design, our team demonstrated better value for both our client and users with a purpose-built, flexible solution offering a multitude of future uses beyond that of a studio. The workshop was not intended as a representation or pastiche of an industrial space. Instead, we were searching for a place with a specific character, a place for production and a place to be robustly engaged with and altered.

Printmaking Studio, Grangegorman
› **DUBLIN, IRELAND**
2019/2020-2021
Education · 320m²
› **Scullion Architects, Plus Architecture**
Gavin Wheatley, Declan Scullion
Grangegorman Development Agency (Public)
© Aisling McCoy

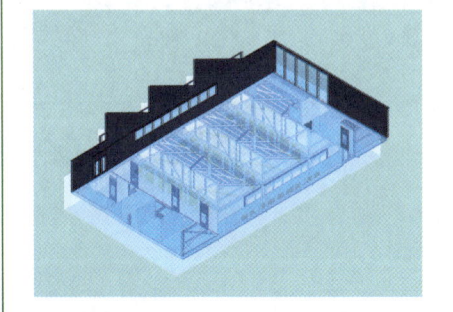

Dominick Hall is the first step in delivering on a long-term ambition for the social, economic and environmental regeneration of this inner-city neighborhood. The mixed-use development delivers energy-efficient and accessible homes, as well as commercial and community spaces to promote a balanced and inclusive community and a sustainable neighborhood. The corner block on Parnell Street has quite a complex urban task, which justifies a more sculptural form. It must negotiate the different scales of Parnell Street and Dominick Street by reading clearly as a separate building with a different language and aesthetics.

Dominick Hall
› **DUBLIN, IRELAND**
2015/2019-2022
Collective housing · 15,810m²
› **Denis Byrne Architects, Cotter & Naessens Architects**
Denis Byrne, Louise Cotter, David Naessens
Dublin City Council (Public)
© Paul Tierney

Annesley Gardens
Dublin, Ireland
2018/2020-2022
Metropolitan Workshop
Neil Deely, Jonny McKenna, Denise Murray, Sharon Chatterton, Ozan Balcik
Seabren Development
(Private)
Collective housing · 3,048m² · 2,559€/m²

Annesley Gardens transformed a backland site into a residential street of 20 homes. Located in an architectural conservation area, the contemporary architecture successfully integrates into the sensitive context not only in terms of its scale but also in its expression and brickwork detailing influenced by the surrounding Victorian architecture.

Annesley Gardens is situated on a backland site overlooked on all sides by Victorian Houses. The site is very well served with a tram stop, shops, and cafes all located nearby. Vehicular access to the site is via an existing laneway and each house has rear pedestrian access via a laneway along the perimeter.

While a number of different approaches were explored to designing homes on the site, the proposed street of terraced houses was deemed to be the most appropriate strategy given the sensitive nature of the surrounding context.

The design of the new terraced street accommodates two key types of houses, each responsive to the peculiarities of the site with individual variances. The architectural expression takes its cue from the surrounding terraces. Panels of patterned brick including stack bonded soldier courses and fluted elements reflect existing decorative brick patterns.

The rich architectural context had a very strong influence on every aspect of the design from the site strategy, to the individual homes, to the architectural detailing. The proposal to create a new street of 2-3 storey homes emerged as the preferred approach as it provided the best opportunity to respond to the challenges of the overlooking and privacy issues posed by the surrounding existing neighbours.

The design of the houses emerged from a deep reading of the context and as a response to the unique peculiarities of the site. This resulted in two types of houses, one with a projecting bay window and the other with a cantilevered first floor over a deeply recessed entrance, the result is a regular rhythm of solid and void along the street. The individual home within the terrace is further articulated through the use of recessed entrance thresholds, dormer roof windows, and individual 'light chimneys' which bring light deep into the heart of the plan. The rear sides of the houses have been sculpted in response to the relationship to their opposing neighbour, ensuring privacy for existing and new residents. The result is a variety of set-backs and brick screened first floor roof terraces.

The external expression emerged from studying the surrounding Victorian architecture and translating this into a contemporary architectural language. The primary material used was brick with two colours selected to reflect the brickwork of the front and rear of the surrounding houses. The traditional detailing was reinterpreted resulting in large areas of sawtooth brickwork, a range of brick bonds and perforated brickwork screens creating a variety of textures and adding depth and interest to the façades. The finishes of the windows and roofs were selected to complement each brick colour.

The project was constructed by a local construction company using conventional construction methods. The structure consists of solid masonry cavity walls, timber posi-joists for the floor structure with some steel required to support cantilevers, and corner windows. The pitched roofs with dormer windows were constructed in solid timber and finished with ventilated standing seam zinc. The homes comply with Irish sustainability regulations, achieving an A2 Building Energy Rating, by having a highly insulated external fabric along with a highly efficient heat pump.

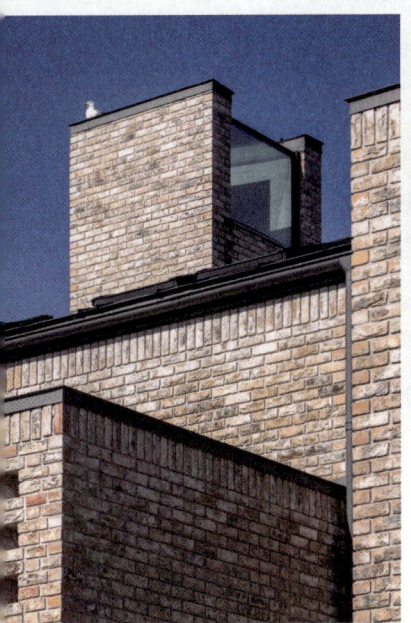

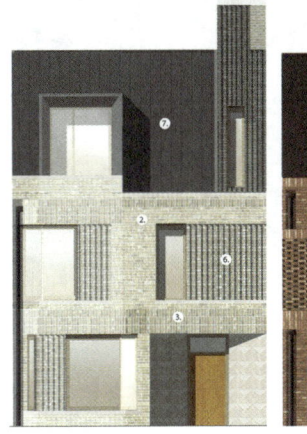

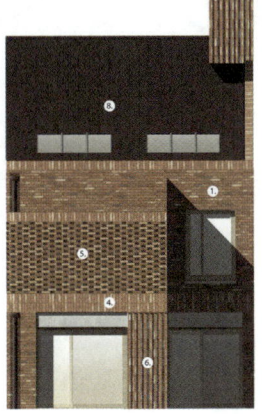

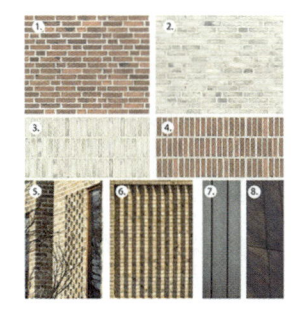

Front and rear elevations. Types of bricks

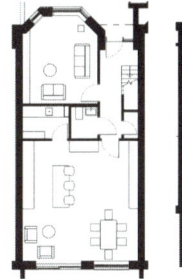

Type A unit. Floor plans

Type B unit. Floor plans

METROPOLITAN WORKSHOP LLP

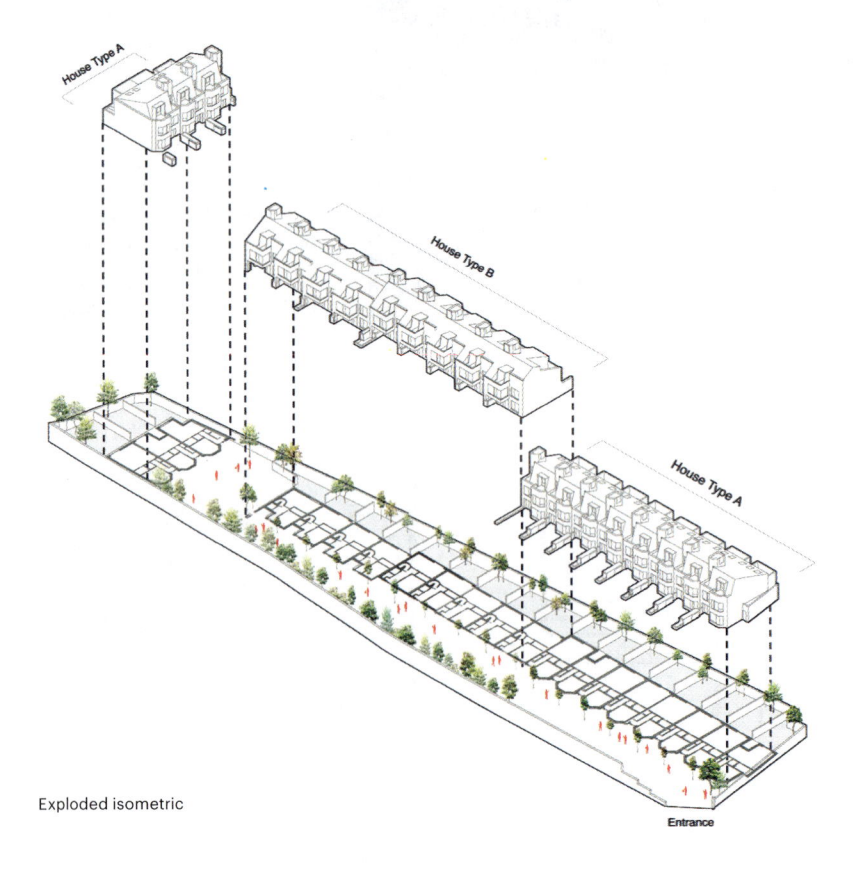

118

SHORTLISTED

Exploded isometric

ANNESLEY GARDENS

Housing for students has reached a crisis point and the university needed a solution. The 18th-century printing house required a sympathetic context. The challenge was to create a building that did not dominate its historic neighbor. The project takes the form of a courtyard and new gateway to Pearse St. The precious city center site was intensively used to provide student accommodation by manipulating levels carefully, providing deep basements for indoor sports, cutting away structure to bring light deep into the Health Centre and Disability Services and making the building section like an iceberg. All levels are accessible via gentle slopes, ramps and external elevators. Optimum conditions are made for students and staff to live, work and learn. The courtyard's shape creates a safe space for everyone. A variety of environments create appropriate settings for people of all abilities: lower convivial households where younger students meet, live and play together and a more monastic top floor that folds calm volumetric rooms into roof spaces like Paris garrets with views through tiny granite courtyards.

Printing House Square
› **DUBLIN, IRELAND**
2015/2017-2022
Education · 12,110m^2 · 3,385€/m^2
› **McCullough Mulvin Architects, O'Mahony Pike Architects**
Valerie Mulvin
Trinity College Dublin (Public)
© Ros Kavanagh

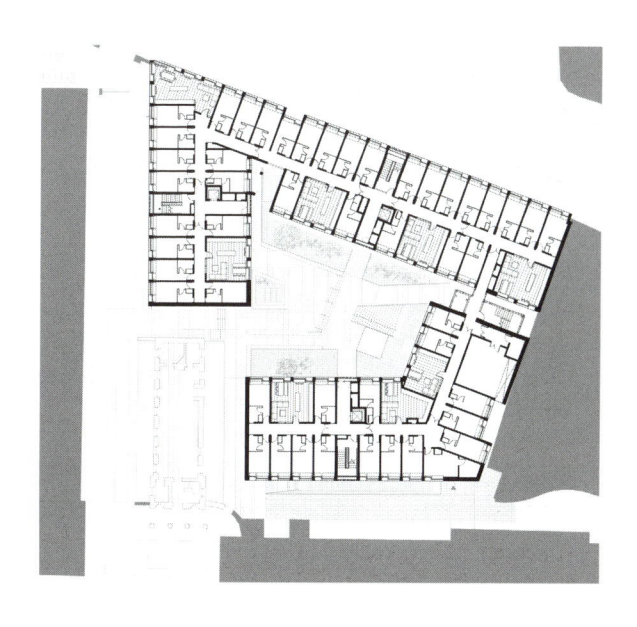

This is a new headquarters for the ESB, which believed in continuing its important presence on its original site. When we make "Dublin" walls, we think of rhythm, surface, light and threshold spaces. The rhythm needs to be in step with the tight grain and rhythm of the city. It is a city of houses, of the same type, though with numerous variations. Our public spaces are made primarily with houses. Six courtyards are diagonally placed to create a sense of spatial rotation, to maximize the distribution of natural light and to create a sense of porosity. A colonnade four meters deep holds the edges of the courtyards. As with the 18th-century city, landscape is embedded into the block. Large-scale sunken gardens bring light to basement levels and make space for large trees to grow.

Electricity Supply Board Headquarters

› **DUBLIN, IRELAND**
2011/2017-2022
Office · 45,000m²

› **Grafton Architects, O'Mahony Pike Architects**
Philippe O'Sullivan, Michael Hussey, Ger Carty, Yvonne Farrell, Shelley McNamara, Matt McCullagh, Donal O'Herlihy, Ivan O'Connell, Shane Twohig, Leah Hogan, Briain Moriarty, Eibhlín Ní Chathasaigh, James Rossa O'Hare, Kieran O'Brien, Simona Castelli, David Healy, Petrina Tierney, Alanah Doyle, Anne Henry, Aonghus Mc Donnell, Fiona Hughes, James Pike, Steven Connolly, Derbhile McDonagh, Eoin Synnot, Dean Wallace, Karen King, Brenda Leonard, Conor McHugh, Terry Murphy, Andrea Doyle, Alex Doran

Electricity Supply Board (Mixed)
↑ © Ros Kavanagh
↗ © Alice Clancy

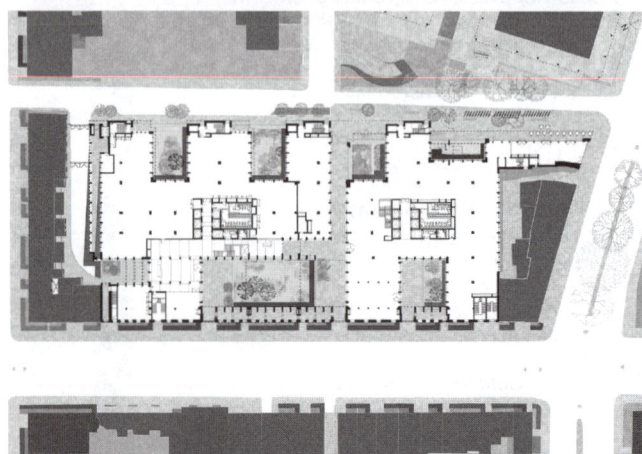

Bottleworks is sensitively shaped by its context and boundaries. Replacing a derelict factory with 3,500m² of light-filled workspace, the design navigates the confined urban site to maximize daylight while minimizing overlooking and overshadowing. The architectural strategy was to replace the factory with a concrete frame of the same footprint that is punctuated by five courtyards. The heavily landscaped voids penetrate the spaces below ground to draw light deep into the heart of the building.

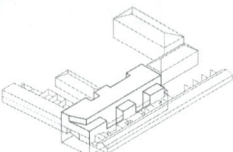

△Axonometric.
Carving Massing

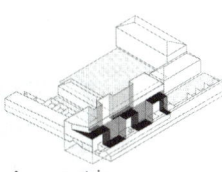

△Axonometric.
Landscaping spaces

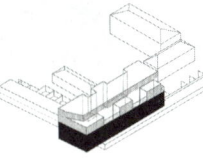

△Axonometric.
Layers transparency

Bottleworks
› DUBLIN, IRELAND
2017/2019-2021
Office · 3,500m²
› Henry J Lyons
Richard Doorly, Miriam Corcoran, Marc Golden
Barrow Street Management Ltd. (Private)
© Aisling McCoy

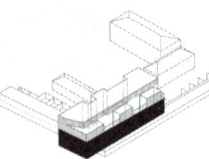

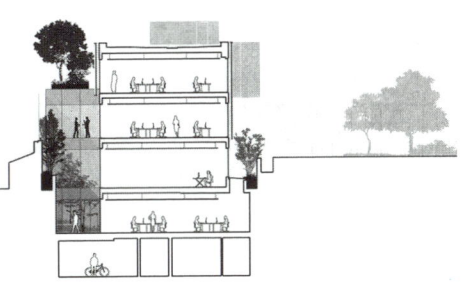

Arising from the COVID lockdowns, this project creates a room for a writer. The site was landlocked and he asked that whatever was built could be taken with him in years to come, so we made it nomadic. The project was dreamed up by thinking of limits, such as the size of the crane that could reach the site, the weight it could bear and the needs of its inhabitant.

Writer's Room
› DUBLIN, IRELAND
2021/2021-2022
Office · 9m² · 4,500€/m²
› Clancy Moore
Andrew Clancy, Colm Moore
Eoin Colfer (Private)
© Fionn McCann

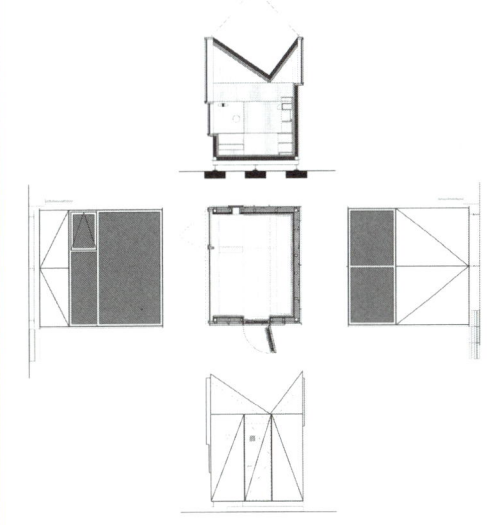

The spatial concept of Little C is a refined high-density and small-grain urban environment made up of 15 compact building volumes. It forms a nice contrast with a generous green park that is being constructed on the water side. With publicly accessible squares and streets, a connecting park and a pedestrian bridge, which provides a direct link with the Erasmus MC, the new district brings cohesion and continuity to the city.

From the different (plinth) programs to the variation in house sizes, from narrow streets to unique types of lofts, from the reuse of materials in public space up to and including the lettering, everything is connected in Little C. The result is a residential area in which urban development, architecture and outdoor space reinforce each other in one story.

Little C
› **ROTTERDAM, THE NETHERLANDS**
2013/2018-2021
Mixed use - Commercial & Offices · 55,000m² · 1,818€/m²
› **INBO, CULD (JVST + Juurlink & Geluk)**
Cor Geluk, Jaakko van 't Spijker, Bert van Breugel
ERA Contour & J.P. van Eesteren / TBI (Private)
© Riccardo De Vecchi

Seven buildings blocks were completely renovated, consisting of 94 renovated residences. They were provided with a new foundation, prepared for district heating and given a floor plan that matches current housing requirements, fulfilling the municipality's wish to restore the 100 year-old houses to their former glory. A cluster of 30 units was dedicated to social housing and forms a housing cooperative.

The houses have been renovated to a high standard, are energy-efficient (A label) and are technically prepared for the district heating system. The historical appearance of the houses has been restored. The residential blocks house a wide variety of homes. The outside of the houses has been restored to their former glory and modernized on the inside. The layouts are completely new. Only load-bearing building walls and stairs have been retained as much as possible. The houses have been made future-proof with modern layouts, including a more spacious bathroom and a good kitchen.

Renovation 94 Houses Van der Pekbuurt Amsterdam
› **AMSTERDAM, THE NETHERLANDS**
2019/2021-2022
Collective housing · 5,005m² · 1,150€/m²
› **Ibelings van Tilburg Architecten**
Marc Ibelings, Tim Schuijt
Dura Vermeer Bouw Midden West BV and Woningcorporatie Ymere (Mixed)
© Petra Appelhof

HAUT is a prototype for building innovative and environmentally friendly high-rise timber structures. Team V designed an ambitious sustainable timber skyscraper, one of the tallest timber towers in the world. This innovative project has helped put timber back on the world map as a structural building material.

"The first reason to use timber, of course, is to build more sustainably, but the second is the architecture. You can really show the timber, especially indoors. You experience the wood as a warm material in your home."

As there are no standard building regulations for high-rise timber construction, the design team has invested time and energy in technical innovation and safety. Floors and walls are constructed in timber, but a structure made completely of timber in wet and windy Amsterdam would be impossible. In combination with HAUT's asymmetrical floor plan, this led to major challenges in the field of torsion. Consequently, the foundations, basement and core are constructed in concrete.

HAUT Amsterdam
› **AMSTERDAM, THE NETHERLANDS**
2016/2019-2022
Collective housing · 14,500m²
› **Team V Architectuur**
Jeroen van Schooten, Do Janne Vermeulen, Thomas Harms, Bart-Jan Hopman, Job Stuijt, Onno van Ark, Coen Ooijevaar
Lingotto (Private)
© Jannes Linders

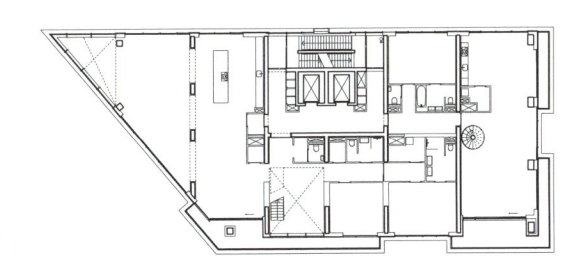

Jonas is a case study for sustainable and collective living in an area of high urban density. It is a building with an innovative housing concept, a spectacular spatial interior and BREEAM Outstanding certification. Jonas aims to create an inviting heart for a new and still developing neighborhood on the outskirts of Amsterdam. Together with its surroundings, the building forms a "living landscape". Yet Jonas' real surprise awaits inside. It expresses a modern and sustainable community life. A communal route, shaped like a canyon, extends through the building, linking together the public and collective program.

Jonas

› **AMSTERDAM, THE NETHERLANDS**
  2017/2019-2022
  Collective housing · 29,500m²
› **Orange Architects**
  Jeroen Schipper, Patrick Meijers, Paul Kierkels, Elena Staskute
  Amvest (Private)
  © Sebastian van Damme

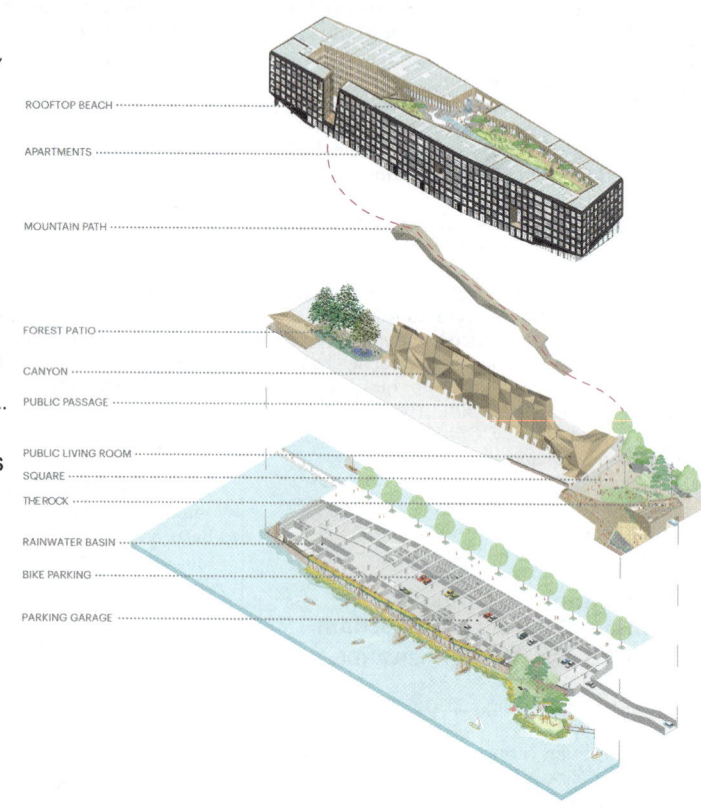

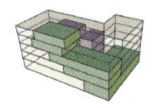

1. collective space woven through
2. origins of the 'Machu Picchu'
3. connecting living kitchens to
4. adding nature-inclusive
5. creating a roofscape with tiny houses

The core idea of De Warren is collective living. With the help of a series of workshops with the future residents, it has been decided that 30% of the building should consist of collective spaces. By placing the collective spaces centrally, they become part of everyone's daily route and contact between residents is maximized.
The facade cladding is made of recycled retaining walls that are untreated. The "Mikado" front façade for balconies and a nature-inclusive approach, with planters that use rainwater from the polder roof, is made of recycled bollards.

De Warren Cooperative Housing
› **AMSTERDAM, THE NETHERLANDS**
 2019/2021-2022
 Collective housing · 3,070m²
› **Natrufied architecture**
 Boris Zeisser, Anja Verdonk
 wooncoöperatie de Warren (Private)
 © Jeroen Musch

The concept rests upon a seamless continuity between spaces and the museum garden. The extension forms the southern border of the museum garden. The two new skylit exhibition spaces are classic in form, matching the existing exhibition spaces. The new wing brings consistency to this collage of elements through its roof, whose pitch, gutter and ridge heights and red slate roofing are similar to that of Hamdorff's museum. In this project, the old and new now tell one story together. By respecting the existing building structure and using it as a blueprint for the renovation, demolition and reconstruction costs were minimized, the use of new materials was limited and the building was embedded in its history and context.

Museum Singer Laren

› LAREN, THE NETHERLANDS
2018/2021-2022
Culture · 2,525m² · 1,875€/m²
› **Bedaux de Brouwer Architecten**
Pieter Bedaux, Joyce Verstijnen, Dennis Schuurkes, Thomas Bedaux, Thom Hoevenaar, Cees de Rooij, Nick van Esch, Luuk Laurijsen, Martijn Rasenberg
Singer Laren (Private)
© Karin Borghouts

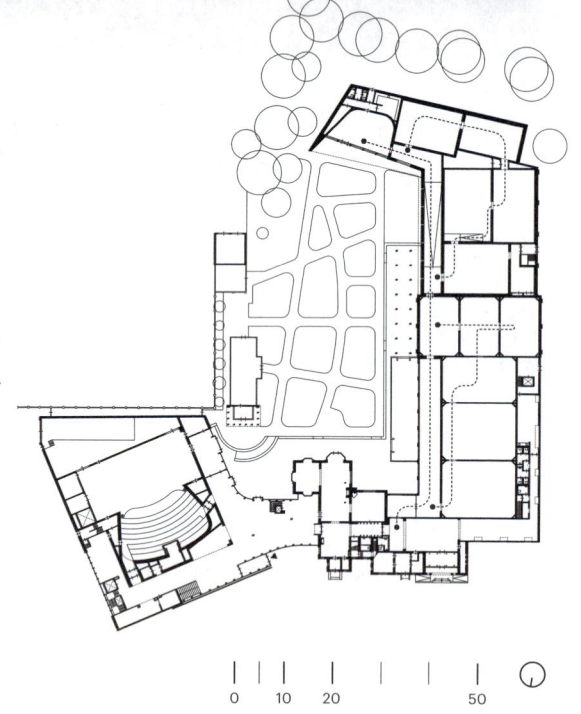

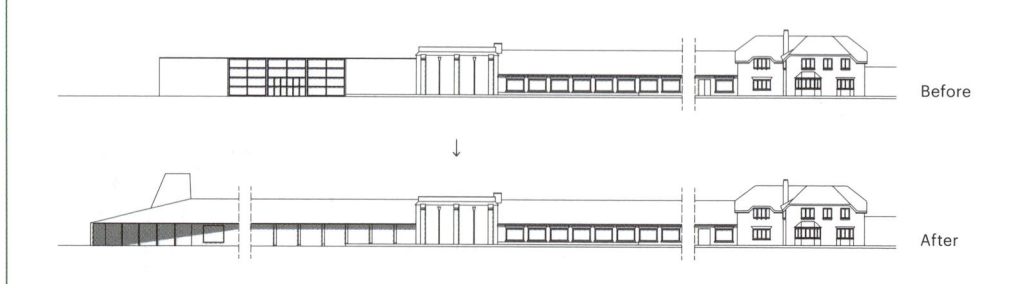

Before

After

Art Pavilion M.
Almere,
 The Netherlands
2020/2021-2022
Studio Ossidiana
Giovanni Bellotti, Alessandra Covini
Almere Municipality and Flevoland Province
(Public)
Culture · 445m² · 2,000€/m²

Art Pavilion M. is a multimedia art museum in Almere. The structure is made up of three circular elements – a pier, a terrace, and a pavilion – opening the institution to performances and installations on water, towards a water plaza framed by the ring.

Art Pavilion M. is a Land Art and Multimedia Museum designed for the waters of Weerwater in Almere. The museum is a sequence of frames: a ring encircles a water plaza, which is to be curated and cultivated, for barges to dock in its outer perimeter, and visitors to arrive by boat. This becomes a public space on water when the museum is closed, where one can swim or fish, and a promenade to the museum during opening hours. The terrace of the museum, within the ring, is the day-to-day museum's terrace, and can become a stage for performances, concerts, and outdoor exhibitions. The pavilion, a lightweight timber and polycarbonate structure enclosing the exhibition rooms, filters the shades of water and surrounds the vegetation like a greenhouse. It is enveloped by a curtain where cut-out shapes create a façade made by the light, with its openings aligned with the dawn and dusk of the summer and winter solstices.

M. began as a competition for a Land Art and Multimedia Museum in Almere, a city in the Netherlands built in the 1980s in Flevoland. The province of Flevoland is the result of the largest 'reclamation' project in the world, an area that was once the Zuider Sea and was transformed into agricultural land in the 1920s. As the sea became land, creating and altering ecosystems, islands became the mainland and sailors became factory workers, while marine ecologies turned into agricultural land. Over time, land art projects were commissioned, shores were redesigned, new lakes were created, such as the one where we worked on M. We proposed an urban project, one that could be read as a water plaza, one that looks outwards, where the pavilion would be an observatory open to other scales, and the path towards it would define a new space for the museum and the city. It was built during COVID, with a spike in construction prices, and an urgency to complete the work before the opening of Floriade. The project turned into a central question about what is necessary: the four openings, the highest number allowed by the budget, look out at planetary alignments, the floor insertions bring back the shells of the marine past, the façade is a game of light, drawn by transparencies in the textile.

M. is conceived as a mineral plinth on water, upon which the pavilion and the artworks rest. The three circles are precast terrazzo and concrete elements, while the pavilion is a timber and polycarbonate structure, circled from within by a two-layered curtain, defining alternating façades during day and night. A functional block, which features bathrooms, an office, and a kitchen, enables free circulation along the perimeter, and the experience of the subtly changing light hue. The roof is covered in loose shells, filtering rainwater.

We carried out research on materials for M., resulting in the 'Surf and Turf' terrazzo, a composite of local shells and horticultural supplies, embodying narratives of the site in its materiality. It has been used as insertions in the flooring of the pavilion, the walkway, the counter, and furniture elements. The Ring is divided into 12 precast segments representing months, a marine calendar of the 'harvest' of shells through terrace inserts with mussels, snails, clams, and oysters.

We do not know if M. will remain in its place form more than 10 years: it has been built so that the pavilion may be disassembled, leaving behind the ring as a water plaza that is open to the city.

ART PAVILION M.

129

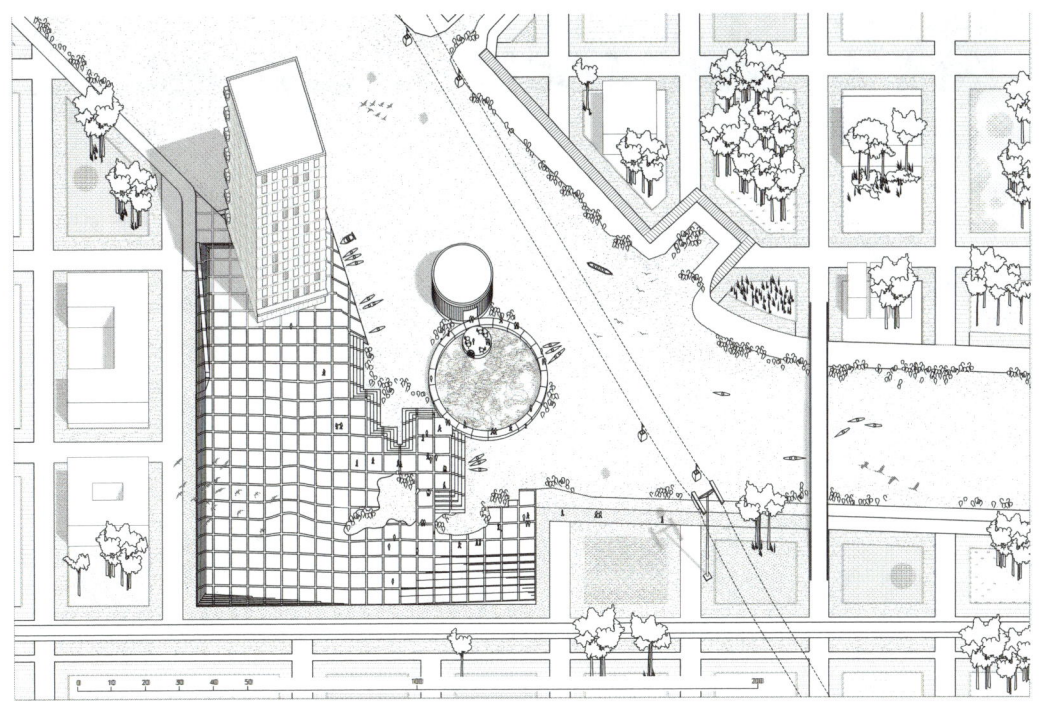

General plan

STUDIO OSSIDIANA

130

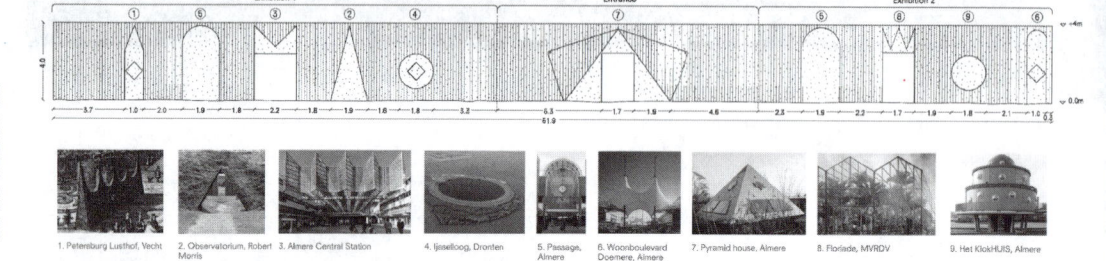

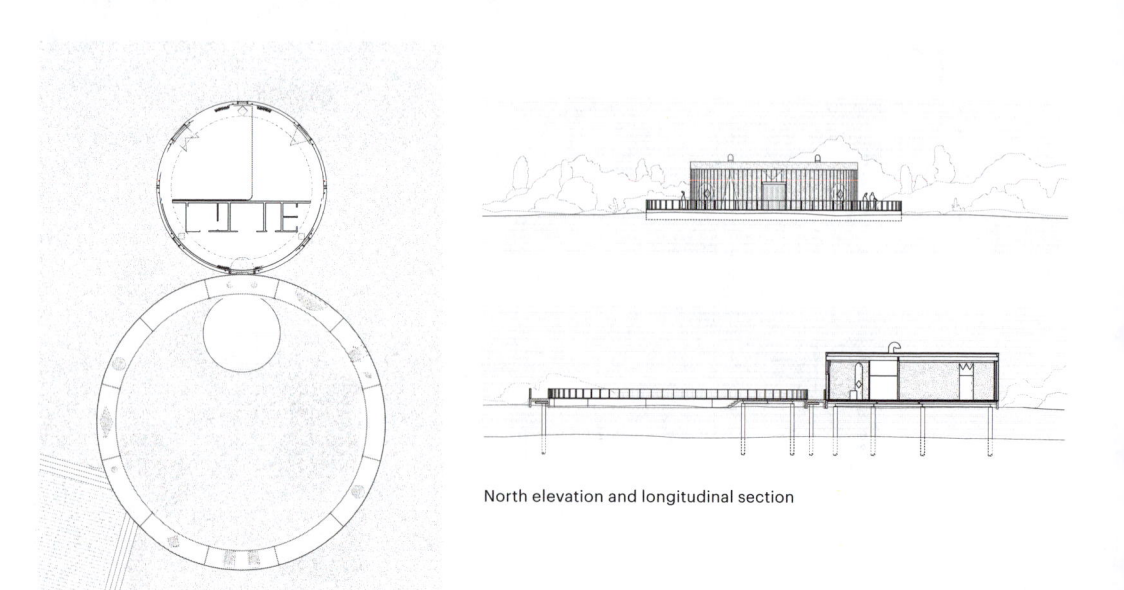

SHORTLISTED

1. Petersburg Lusthof, Vecht
2. Observatorium, Robert Morris
3. Almere Central Station
4. Ijsseloog, Dronten
5. Passage, Almere
6. Woonboulevard Doemere, Almere
7. Pyramid house, Almere
8. Floriade, MVRDV
9. Het KlokHUIS, Almere

Ground floor plan

North elevation and longitudinal section

ART PAVILION M.

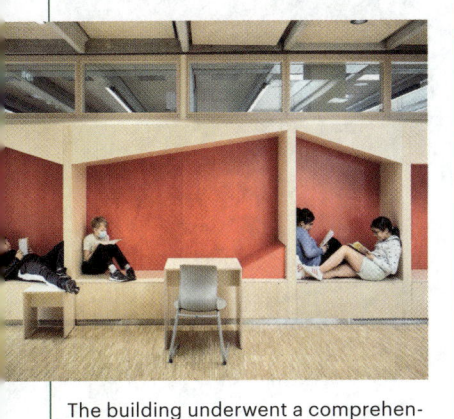

The building underwent a comprehensive core renovation in seven phases while remaining operational, adapting to modern school requirements.
The school is a showcase project for renovation. The generously sized but poorly utilized spatial structure from the 1970s was reinterpreted to make its potential spaciousness both accessible and usable. The renovation took place within a participatory design process.
With the aim of maximizing the preservation of the existing structure while simultaneously enhancing energy efficiency, the "cluster school" utilization concept was implemented in compliance with fire safety regulations within the building's footprint. The core of the design focuses on activating previously unused hallway spaces for educational purposes. Specially designed wood-glass partitions, created and certified specifically for the project, connect these multifunctional areas to the classrooms, forming self-contained learning units characterized by sightlines and natural lighting.

Reorganization and Refurbishment of Leeste Cooperative Comprehensive School

› WEYHE, GERMANY
2017/2018-2022
Education · 14,000m^2 · 1,430€/m^2
› REMKE PARTNER INNENARCHITEKTEN mbB
Dipl.-Ing. Sascha Remke,
Prof. Dr. Tanja Remke
**Gemeinde Weyhe,
Der Bürgermeister (Public)**
© Frank Schinski

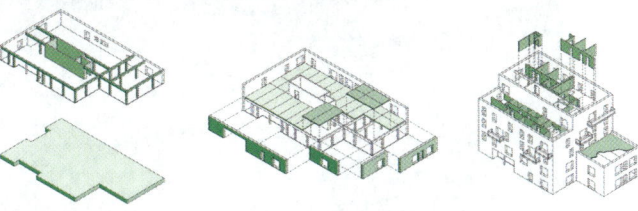

This building ensemble with nine flats and a kindergarten is divided into two buildings to strengthen interaction with the urban space: Woof and Skelle. Skelle is a residential building with five floors, two of which are reserved for a kindergarten. Woof, the smaller building, has two floors and contains additional kindergarten rooms.
Both buildings are characterized by the consistent use of renewable building materials and a high proportion of timber construction. The skeletal structure allows for flexibility for future conversions.

Woof & Skelle: Building Ensemble for Social Housing and Kindergarten | Ellener Hof

› BREMEN, GERMANY
2020/2020-2022
Mixed use - Cultural & Social · 2,400m^2
› ZRS Architekten Ingenieure
Monique Bührdel, Carolin Senftleben, Marine Miroux, Samuel Reichl, Lisa-Marie Kolbinger, Tobias Bieger, Riccardo Fanton
Bremer Heimstiftung (Private)
© Caspar Sessler

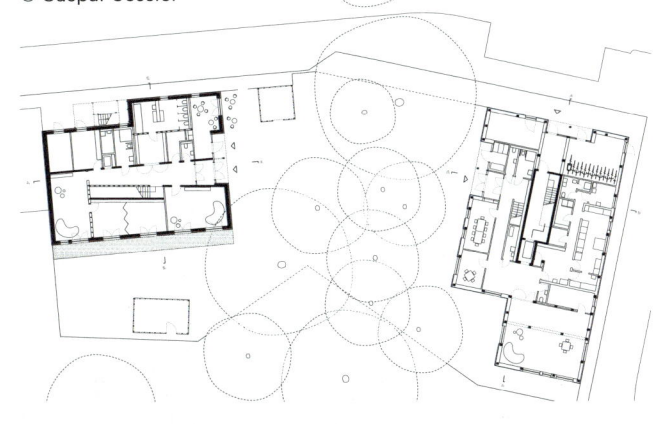

WINNER

Study Pavilion on the Campus of the Technical University of Braunschweig

Braunschweig, Germany

2015/2020-2023

**Gustav Düsing
 Büro Max Hacke**

Gustav Düsing, Max Hacke

TU Braunschweig

(Public)
Education · 1,000m² · 5,200,000€

52°16'20"N – 10°31'44"E

↓119

133

The Study Pavilion on the campus of the Technical University of Braunschweig is a highly flexible, innovative learning environment that promotes social exchange and the generation of interdisciplinary knowledge between students and teachers alike, while also representing an alternative model to spaces of hierarchical knowledge transfer.

The two-story building provides student workspaces for all faculties. With the central campus situated directly next to a river, the pavilion forms a new landmark on the main axis along the Audimax, the historic main building and the Forum Square, thus integrating into the existing pathway of the campus. The compact volume with a square plan is an open space concept with an indeterminate ground floor while the first floor consists of a series of platforms and bridges that extend outside. Decentralized access via 9 doors and 9 stair zones delimit the space, seamlessly blending circulation zones and usable spaces. The building is wrapped in a shaded floor-to-ceiling glass façade that provides views of the natural landscape and campus square.

The post-pandemic academic world is subject to constant change, and the study pavilion as a social space offers answers to the question of what role university campuses can play in the future, when lectures and presentations take place in digital space and AI challenges classical learning models. The building's organizing principle follows the idea of a superstructure that allows for the floor plan to be constantly reconfigured. This flexibility in the floor plan makes the building ephemeral and responsive, ensuring its relevance for a long time. To create a sense of community that transcends individual subjects, a space of equal value was created throughout, with no spatial separation between floors and with equal access to daylight. Instead of fixed walls, zones were developed that are accessed by their own stairs and entrances, creating distinct areas that invite a variety of activities. The structure fosters everything from double-height clearings to intimate retreats and presentation spaces.

The slender steel-wood hybrid structure can be fully dismounted and follows the principle of "design for disassembly". The primary support structure, consisting of beams and columns, is modular and built on a square 3 × 3 m grid, made up of the same hollow 10 × 10 cm square section. The wooden ribbed decks inserted in the beam frames are not mechanically connected, and the façade is not glued, so it can be dismantled. In addition to the possibility to make the structure denser by means of further platforms, the building could also be rebuilt in a different form or at a different location. The building is also in line with the principle of the "future material depot", in which not only can the building materials be reused, but entire architectural elements such as façade panels, stairs and platforms can find a new use following the concept of "circular construction".

135

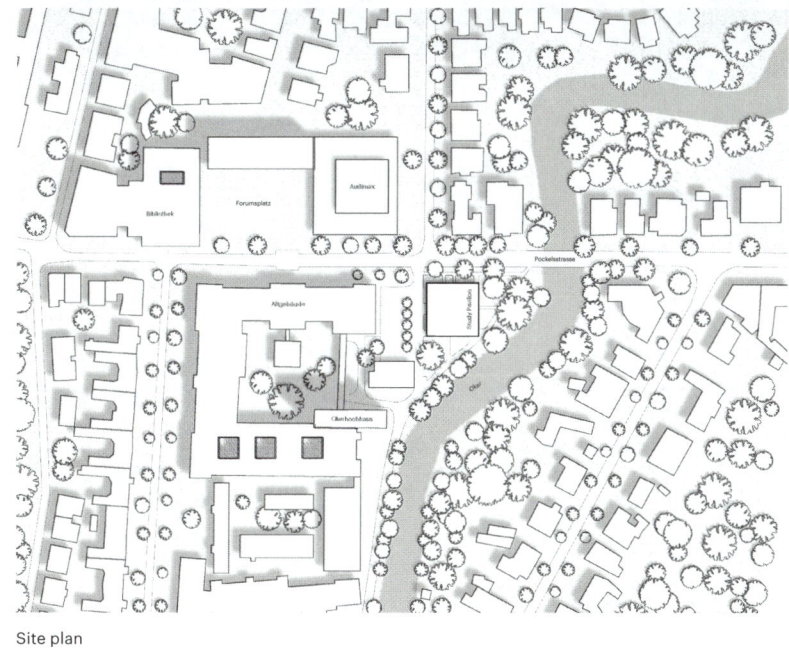

Site plan

GUSTAV DÜSING BÜRO MAX HACKE

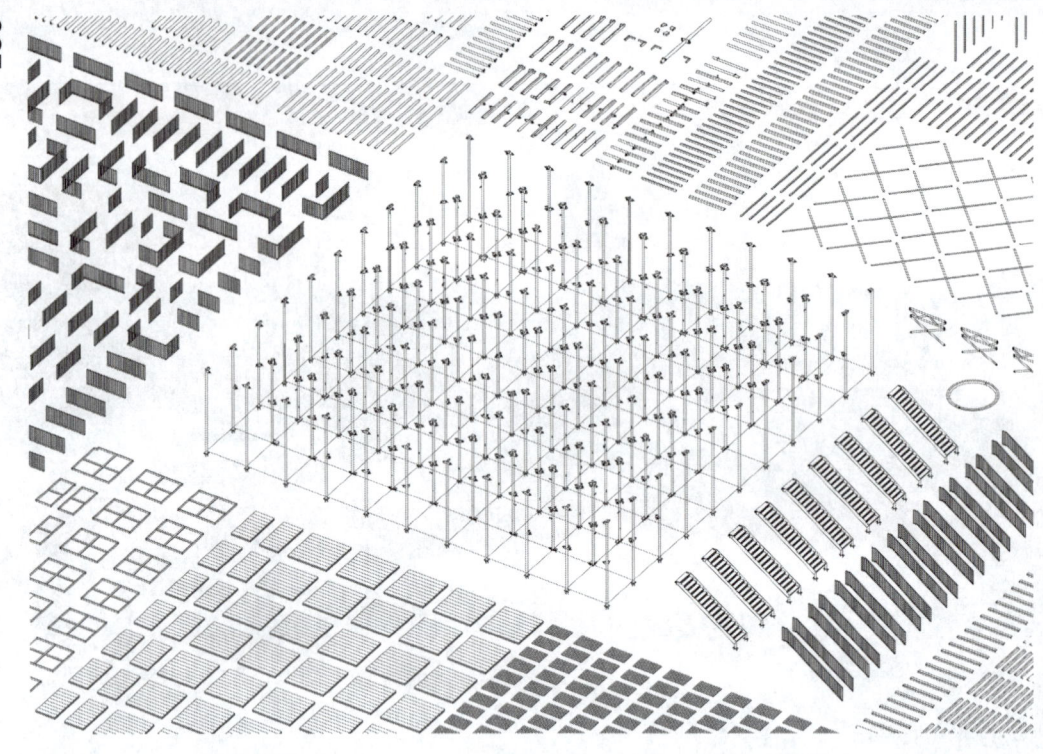

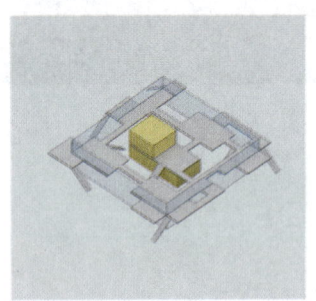

136

FINALIST

Internal logic

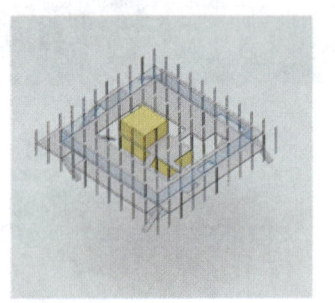

Scalability and flexibility

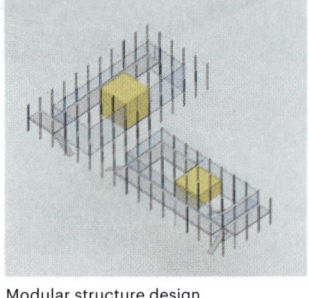

Modular structure design for disassembly

Steel - wood hybrid

Structural bay

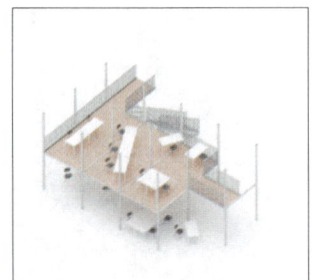

Island principal

Diagrams

STUDY PAVILION ON THE CAMPUS OF THE TECHNICAL UNIVERSITY OF BRAUNSCHWEIG

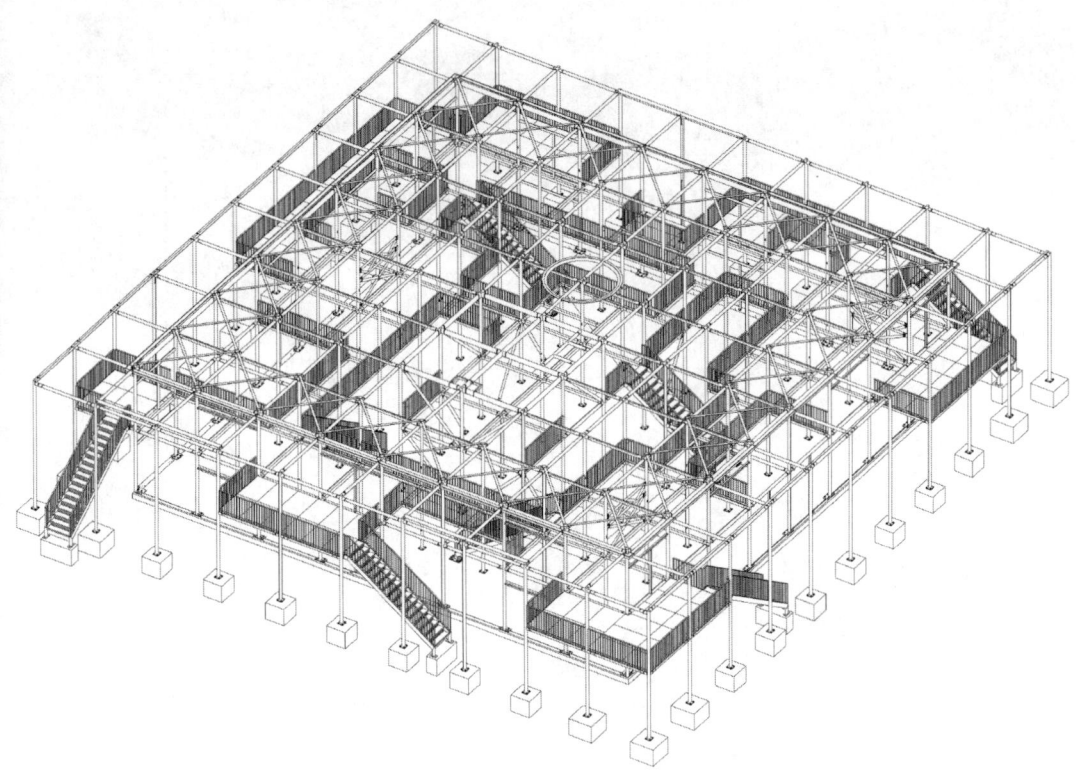

Axonometry

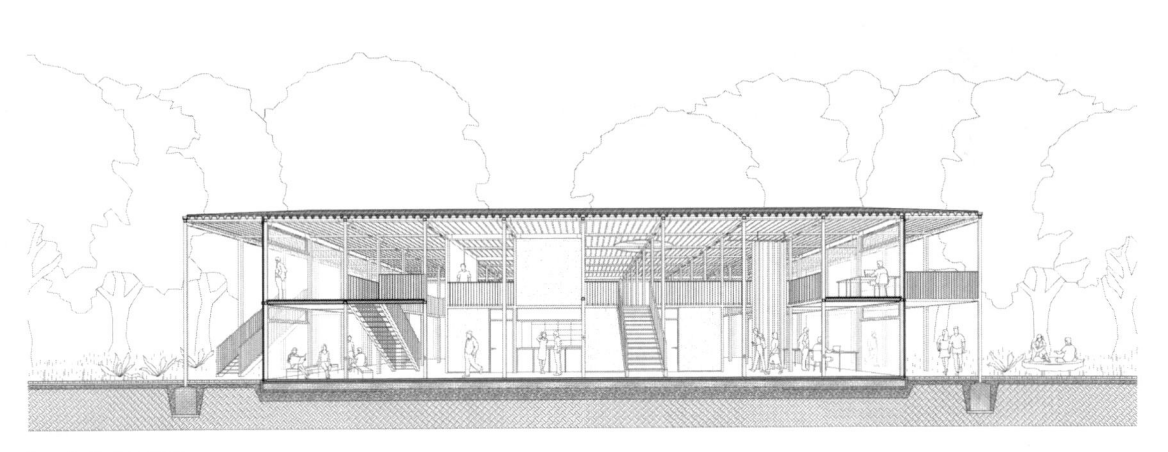

Longitudinal section

GUSTAV DÜSING BÜRO MAX HACKE

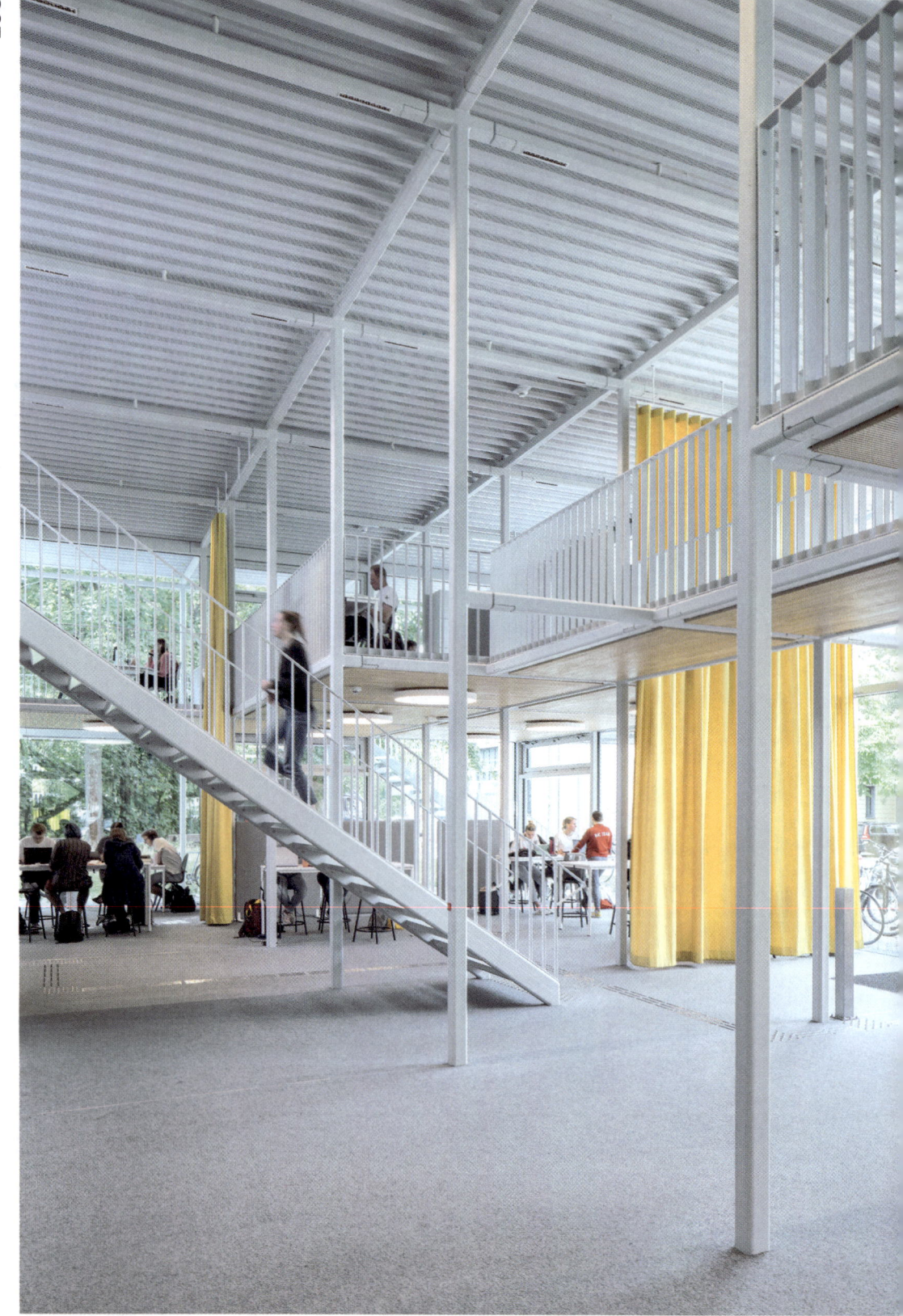

STUDY PAVILION ON THE CAMPUS OF THE TECHNICAL UNIVERSITY OF BRAUNSCHWEIG

GUSTAV DÜSING BÜRO MAX HACKE

140

FINALIST

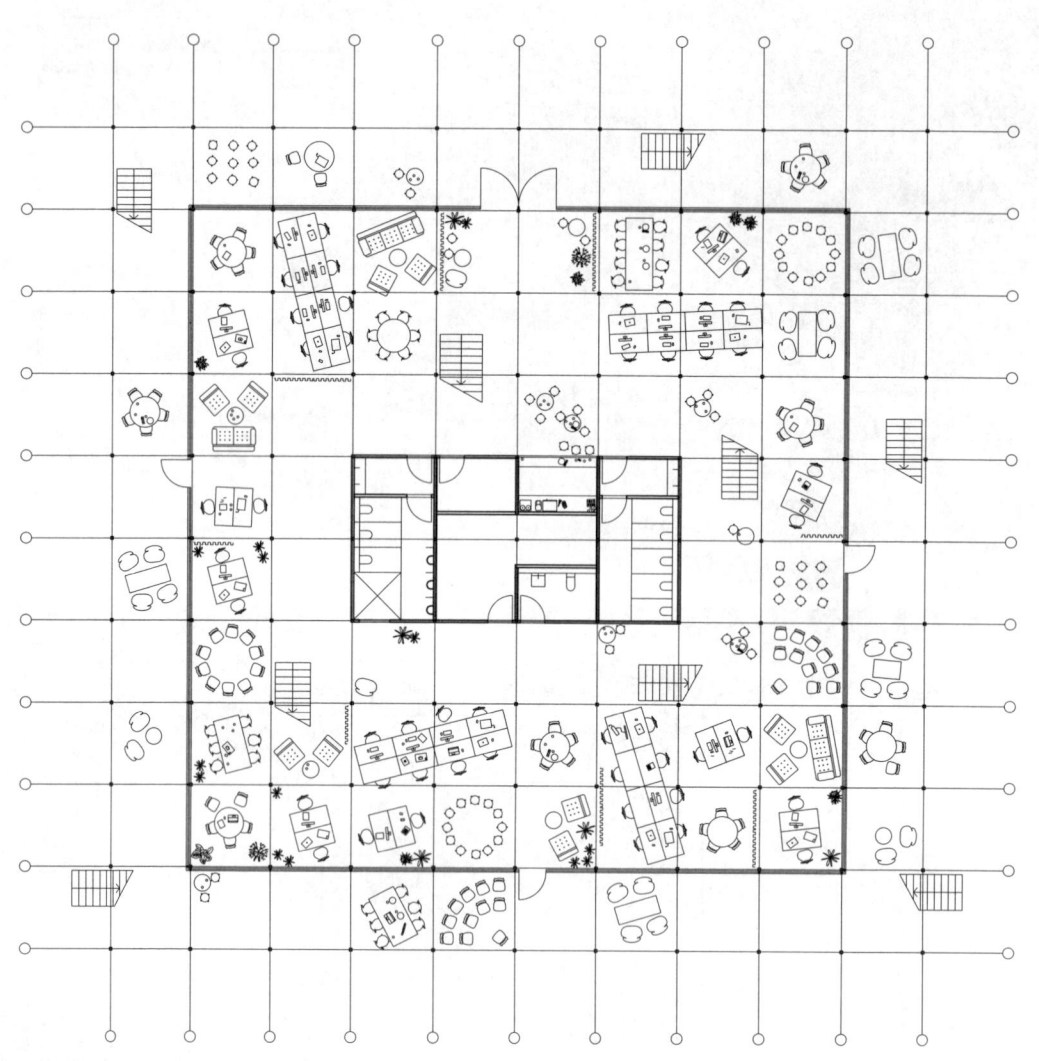

Ground floor plan

STUDY PAVILION ON THE CAMPUS OF THE TECHNICAL UNIVERSITY OF BRAUNSCHWEIG

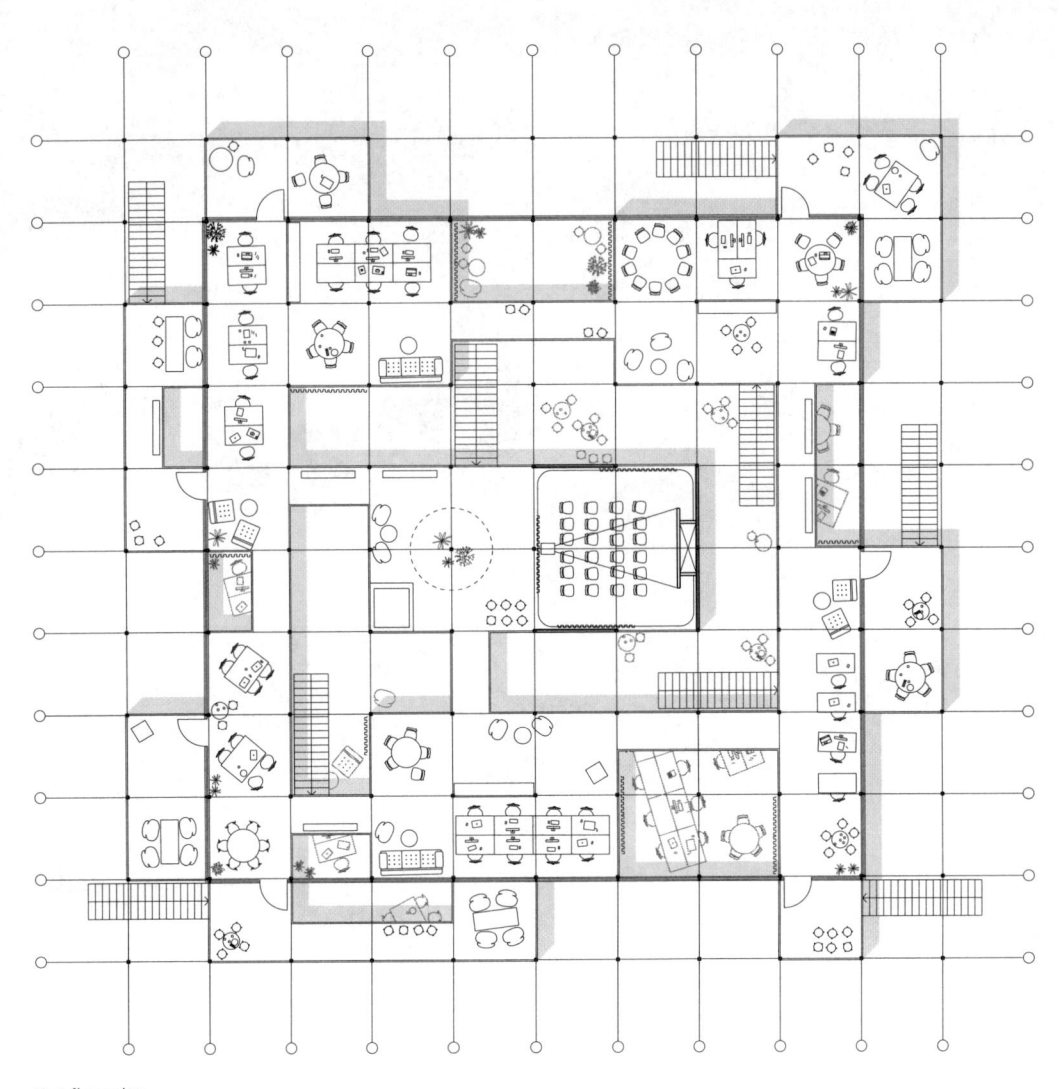

First floor plan

GUSTAV DÜSING BÜRO MAX HACKE

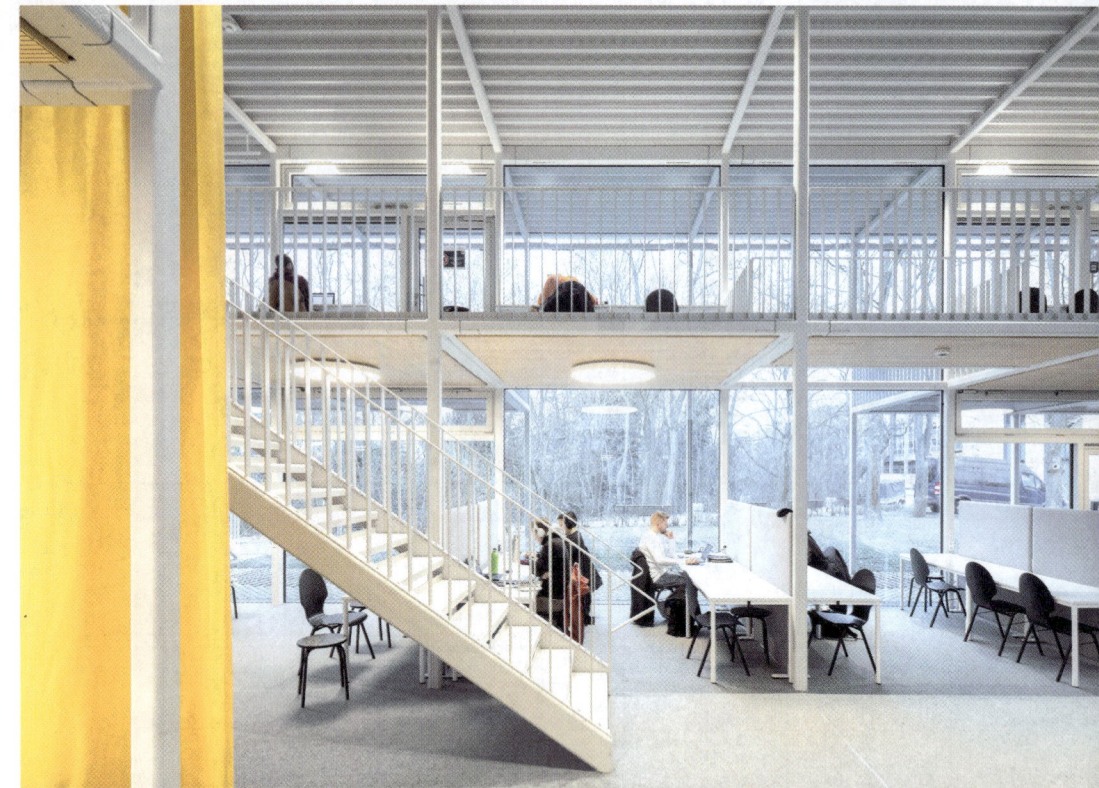

STUDY PAVILION ON THE CAMPUS OF THE TECHNICAL UNIVERSITY OF BRAUNSCHWEIG

Detail

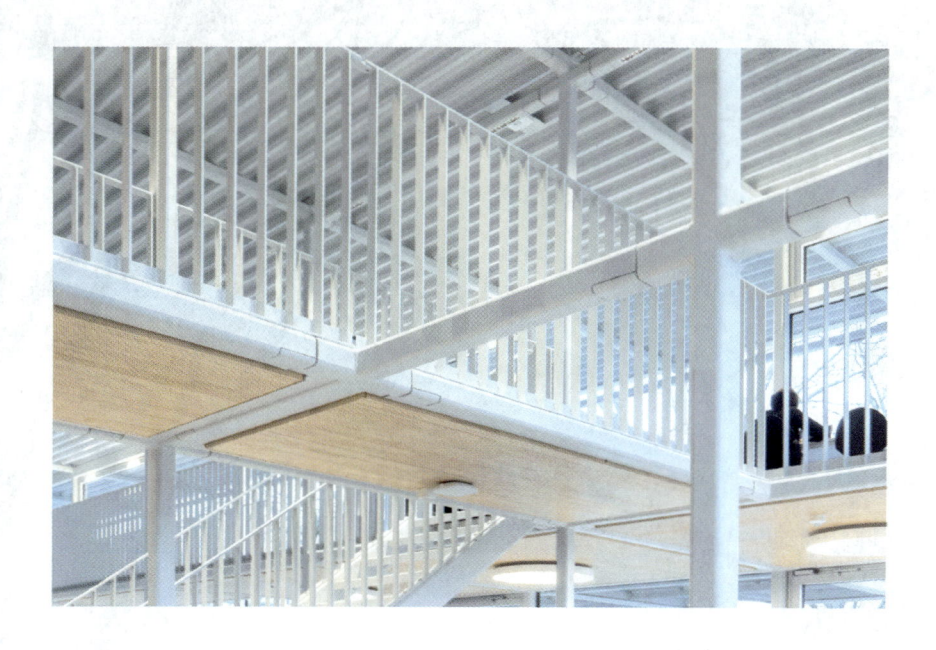

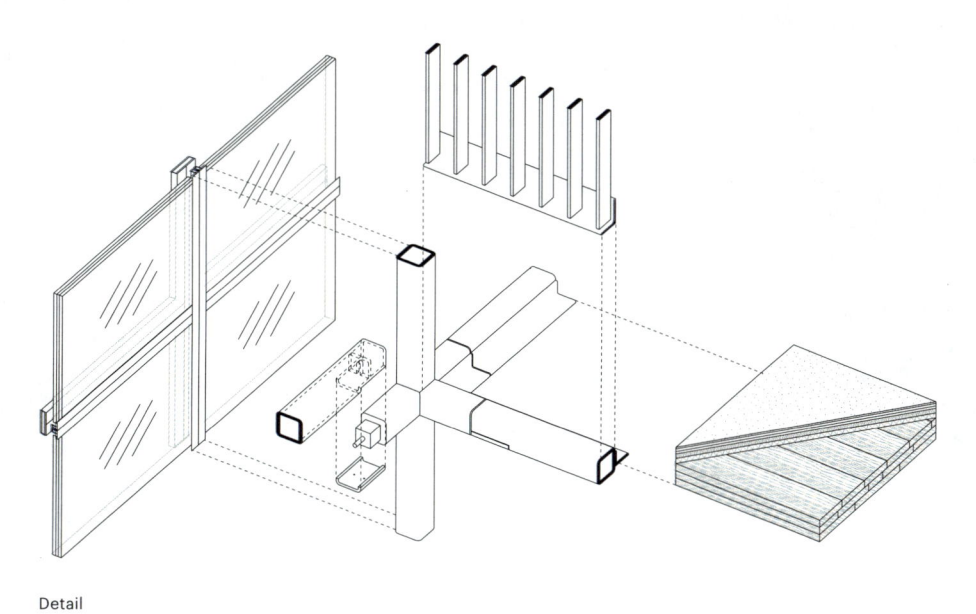

GUSTAV DÜSING BÜRO MAX HACKE

STUDY PAVILION ON THE CAMPUS OF THE TECHNICAL UNIVERSITY OF BRAUNSCHWEIG

GUSTAV DÜSING BÜRO MAX HACKE

FINALIST

STUDY PAVILION ON THE CAMPUS OF THE TECHNICAL UNIVERSITY OF BRAUNSCHWEIG

The TU Braunschweig Study Pavilion

"The objective [of the competition] was to provide up-and-coming architects with an opportunity to demonstrate their abilities within the protective framework of the faculty – given that there are few open architecture competitions, and young architects have limited avenues for proving themselves."

Peter Cachola Schmal

Architect and architecture critic. Director of the German Architecture Museum (DAM). Member of the EUmies Awards Advisory Committee.

Just like the EUmies Awards jury, the jury for the annual DAM Prize once again traveled throughout Germany to visit the sites of its five finalists. The selected projects vary considerably in terms of their building assignments, unique aspirations and message.

One project (also a EUmies Awards 2024 Nominee) is a mass-produced wooden modular apartment block raised on a parking lot in Munich, created by EUmies Awards' "Emerging Architect" of 2001, Florian Nagler. Another contender is a group project for a Brutalist building in an awkward location in Berlin by June14 Meyer-Grohbrügge & Chermayeff, who were also shortlisted for the EUmies Awards 2024. A third – also in Berlin – is a Modernist building by Nalbach + Nalbach, which was threatened with demolition but has been successfully renovated for retail use. A fourth is a transparent student pavilion at Braunschweig Technical University (TU), which is also the first work by its architects Gustav Düsing and Max Hacke. And finally, there is the elegant addition to a Brutalist-style art academy in Kassel, through the construction of a multifunctional exhibition space by Austrian architects Innauer Matt – another EUmies Awards 2024 Nominee.

In what was a novelty for the awards, this year's DAM Prize was awarded for the first time to a first-ever work, as a testament to its remarkable impact. As proudly announced by London's AA School of Architecture, the architects Gustav Düsing and Max Hacke – both previous alumni[1] – were also the youngest ever to receive the EUmies Awards.

This building on the TU Braunschweig campus owes its existence to the TU's former professor, Volker Staab (a ten-times EUmies Awards Nominee), who in 2015 set up a competition together with his Faculty of Architecture teaching staff, to create urgently needed workspaces for architecture students. The objective was to provide up-and-coming architects with an opportunity to demonstrate their abilities within the protective framework of the faculty – given that there are few open architecture competitions, and young architects have limited avenues for proving themselves. Staab determined that the study pavilion project was too small for established firms, too complicated for students, and too expensive to organize as an open competition. Consequently, his department assumed responsibility for its organization. His plan proved to be highly effective. A total of 20 candidates took part in the competition, with the work of Gustav Düsing and Max Hacke

[1] https://www.aaschool.ac.uk/news/aa-alumni-gustav-dusing-and-max-hacke-win-the-2024-mies-van-der-rohe-award

selected as winners by the staff jury and executed with the support of a local engineering firm. Several logistical challenges had to be addressed before construction could commence in 2020.

In the interim, the university decided that the Pavilion should be accessible to all students. The selected site was located opposite the main lecture hall, in a meadow next to the Oker River. The two-story building, constructed with a white steel frame and glass, is a light, airy, and delicate structure. The upper-level features wooden floors, while the shaded facades are covered with wafer-thin panes of glass. This design allows the building to look transparent and translucent not only in the evening and at night, but also during the day. Due to the shading, there is no need for external sun protection. Additionally, diagonal bracing is not required, as the solid core and multiple single-flight steel staircases provide sufficient support. These components do not simply lean into each other, but are connected in a force-fit manner, ensuring stability and durability. The building, of approximately 1,000 square meters with capacity for up to 200 students, is notable for its combination of technical sophistication, and high degree of abstraction and visual reduction. It has received numerous architectural awards, which culminated in the EUmies Awards. And rightly so!

Many architecture critics have noted the impressive construction of the building, which features 10 cm-thick steel tubes with a specially developed joining point, a screwed-on façade with no additional construction, and integrated cabling. Furthermore, the building represents a rare example of circular construction, as it is not glued, but rather screwed in a demountable manner. It can be expanded, modified, and relocated, although it is unlikely that this will ever occur, as all past buildings with reversible designs have stayed where they are, with the first example of this being Ludwig Mies van der Rohe's renowned Lake Shore Drive Apartments in Chicago. Another noteworthy architectural role model for this project could also be Junya Ishigami, with his white, ephemeral glass houses (Kanagawa Institute of Technology, 2008). His structures continue the minimalist tradition of his predecessors, Kazuyo Sejima and Toyo Ito.

Glass houses also address several crucial issues related to contemporary construction. How do we want to live, how do we want to work? What are the characteristics of the so-called "third spaces" – that are neither work nor living spaces, but rather places for meeting and interacting? Who is responsible for organizing such coming togethers, and what types of groups emerge naturally? All of this can be observed in the TU Study Pavilion, which is much loved by its users. However, the inevitable noise-fearing local residents do present a challenge – otherwise the place could be used 24/7. This is an excellent concept that should be emulated by other German universities. We are hopeful that future competitions of this innovative nature will be held, and that our prize – and your prize – along with all the other awards, will garner the significant attention deserving of this building, its unique history, and its message.

As a final note, the Braunschweig Pavilion is also really just lovely, with a modern, functionalist beauty that is also characteristic of the carefully constructed buildings from the early high-tech period of Richard Rogers (House for the Parents, Wimbledon, 1968) and Michael Hopkins (two-story Hopkins House, London, 1975). The design is characterized by a simplicity of form and reduced use of materials. For example, intuitive low-tech building technology is employed, in the automatic ventilation via the central skylight and hinged windows on the ground floor. The design is an elegant solution to contemporary problems, which incorporates energy saving, solar radiation, reversibility and reusability.

I extend my congratulations to the Technical University of Braunschweig – a client that demonstrated remarkable courage – and to Gustav Düsing and Max Hacke, two young architects who have both founded their own architecture firms in Berlin (gustav-duesing.com and burohacke.com). Düsing recently won two competitions – for the campus building at the University of Siegen and the German ambassador's residence in Tel Aviv – while Hacke has just finished an exciting rooftop project in Berlin. We can therefore look forward to hearing much more from them both in the future, which is an encouraging sign for the future of architecture in Germany as a whole.

Building Community Kurfürstenstrasse
Berlin, Germany
2014/2017-2022

June14 Meyer-Grohbrügge & Chermayeff

Johanna Meyer-Grohbrügge, Sam Chermayeff

Kurfürstenstrasse 142 GbR
(Private)
Collective housing · 3,689m²

The building community on Kurfürstenstrasse, located in Berlin Schöneberg, consists of 6 towers that overlap vertically and horizontally. This building was conceived and developed together by the people living and working there. The result is 25 interconnected units that each have a high space and several lower spaces.

The six towers that form the structure on a corner in Berlin are an offset of the given two streets at a 104-degree angle and interlock with the urban space through projections and recesses. The house aims to offer new alternatives for cohabitation and to respond flexibly to individual needs and arrangements. The architecture does not prescribe sharing, but rather enables it both internally and on an urban scale. While they vary in square metres, each unit consists of one double-high space passing through the building with windows facing both the public street and the private courtyard. Except for the bathrooms, there are no interior walls. Privacy and connection thus results from the placement of corners, levels, and sightlines.

In our era of digital atomization, the notion of the commune feels both anachronistic and, perhaps, nostalgically out of reach. Meanwhile, in the real world, we continue to exist amongst other people – side by side on the train, in various cubicles of approximately equal size, or standing in line for any number of reasons. So, we have to ask: How can we live together differently? To invite new possibilities, we've created a house that not only remains open – both to the world and its residents – but by the nature of its design it also has the potential to start a new dialogue with the habits of its residents.

The building is not walled off to its surroundings. Directly in front, on Kurfürstenstrasse, is one of the oldest prostitution strips of Berlin. This northern exposure is loud and provides street life to the building, while also contrasting sharply with the staid, quiet, and sometimes green garden to the south. The architecture responds to these two drastically different aspects of life and is not intended as a moral comment or irony. It simply connects both the urban landscape and nature because both are beautiful and life affirming.

The house is built from a few robust elements with attention paid to an economical and simple use of materials. The project includes a green roof, cross ventilation in every space and careful use of energy but the building is fundamentally a project made by people. The inhabitants, who followed the project from its inception, brought their strengths and weaknesses to the project. The architecture and the community itself reflect the challenges of people working and living together. The structure's flexibility allows residents to create their private and shared spaces according to their own needs. Inhabitants are invited to renegotiate the traditional boundaries between themselves and their neighbours. The building seeks new forms of merging and meeting, challenging the community to use the space in new and different ways.

Steel columns support the concrete floor slabs. The standard bolted aluminium and glass façade is supplemented by opaque sliding aluminium panels for sound insulation, economy, and weight. The polished screed floor and lightweight walls are the only finishes complementing the shell; the interior concrete cores and railings are galvanized steel.

152

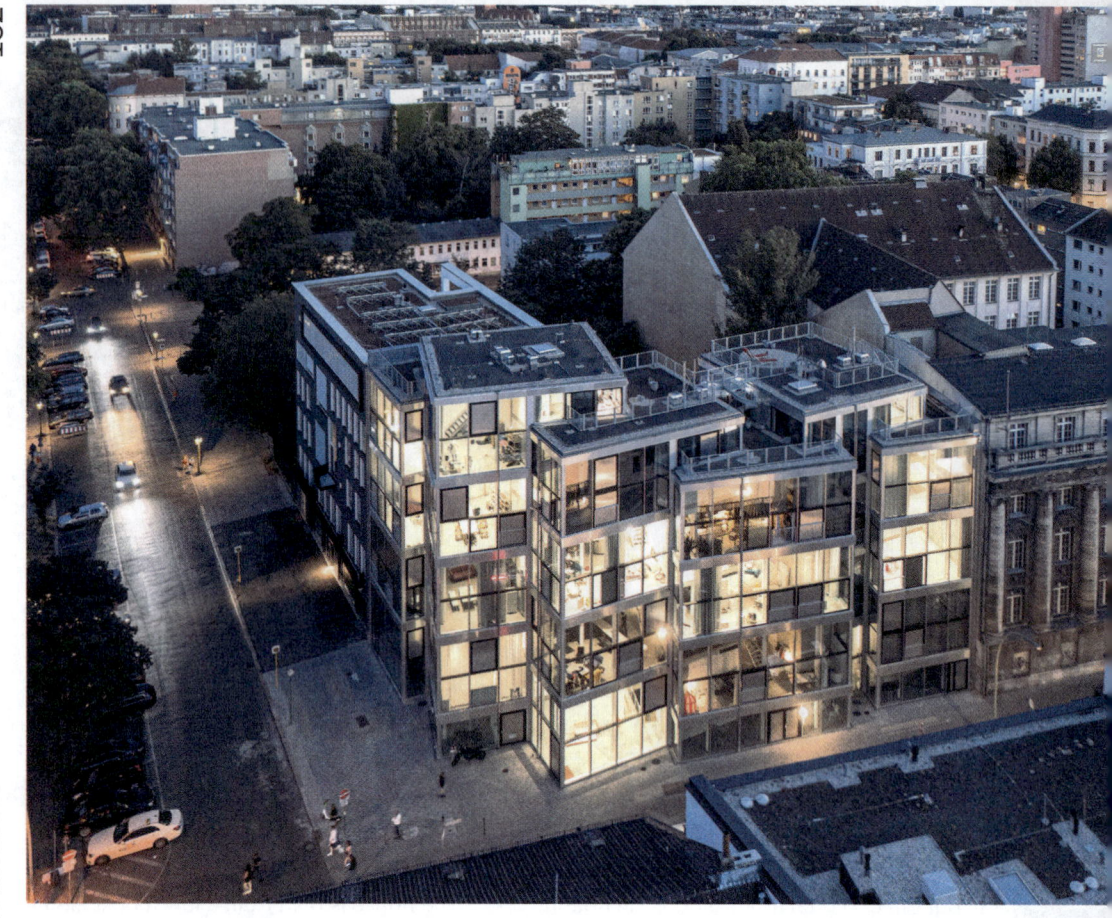

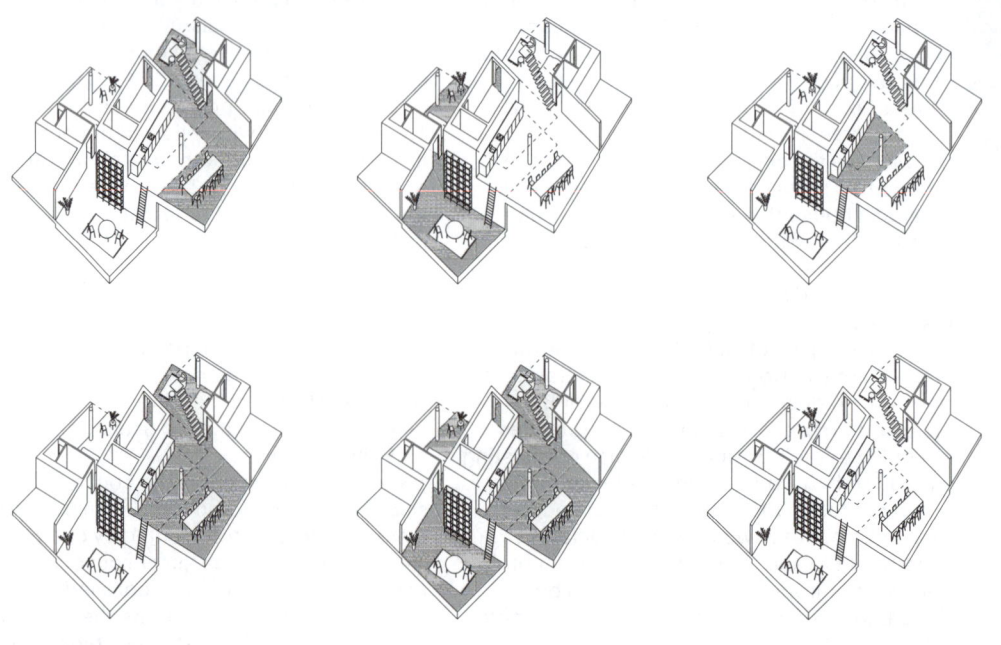

SHORTLISTED

Type units axonometry

BUILDING COMMUNITY KURFÜRSTENSTRASSE

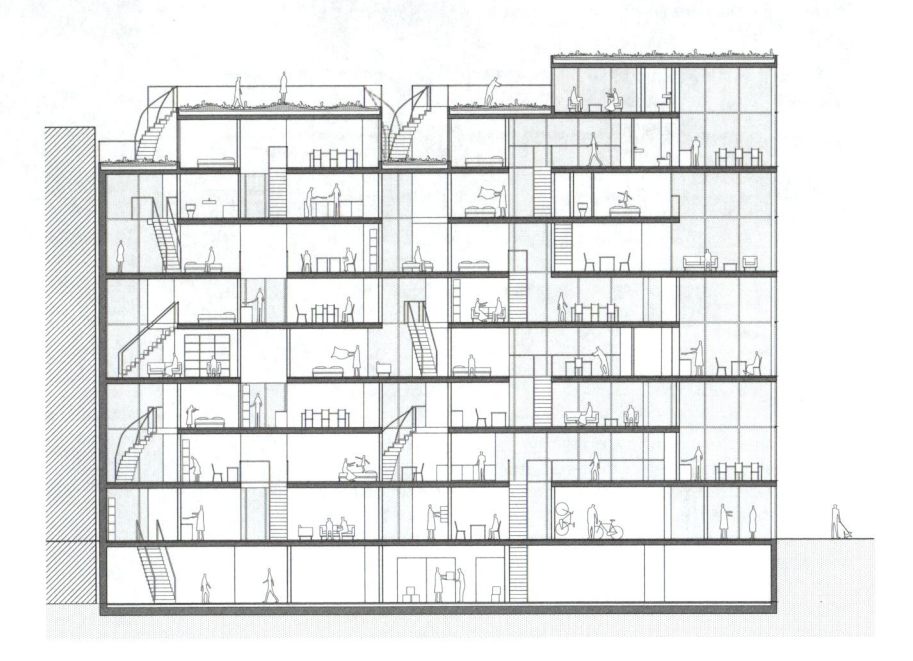

Section

Ground floor plan

JUNE14 MEYER-GROHBRÜGGE & CHERMAYEFF

Ausbauhaus Südkreuz is a collective housing project that consists of owner-occupied flats, social housing units and district-related uses. The facade, built in dry and composite-free construction, and the interior fit-out, made of renewable resources, ensure future reparability and waste-free deconstruction of the materials. The French balconies stretching across the entire facades and the wooden French windows create a generous connection to the outside. This project considers the need for future change and adaptability. The permanent support structure, constructed with concrete, allows for long-term flexibility within the dense urban context. In contrast, the façade has been ingeniously designed as a deconstructible wooden structure. This intentional choice ensures that future remodeling can be carried out in a material-conscious manner.

Ausbauhaus Südkreuz ("House to Be Extended")

› **BERLIN, GERMANY**
 2019/2020-2022
 Collective housing · 2,200m² · 2,600€/m²
› **Praeger Richter Architekten**
 Jana Richter, Henri Praeger
 Baugruppe Ausbauhaus Südkreuz GbR (Private)
 © Lindsay Webb

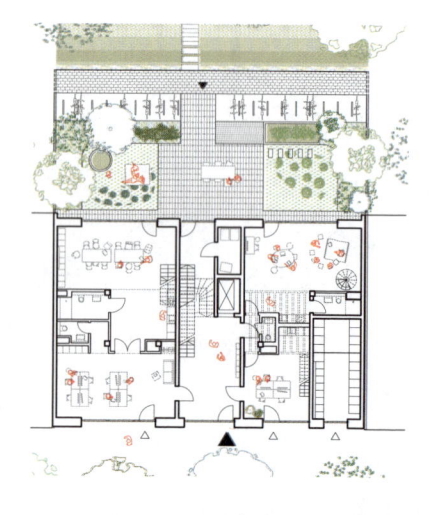

A hybrid prefab concrete and timber building for an efficient and low-impact building process was designed for disassembly according to cradle-to-cradle principles, together with a high-tech ETFE canopy that filters sunlight and makes the building breathe. The central courtyard has the scale of a transit hall, but dialed down to the scale of a lively common space by the intersected vertical circulations with open common spaces. The fluid circulation ends on the rooftop terrace, where the shared rooftop bears witness to the beauty of the technical simplicity of the canopy.

Edge Suedkreuz Berlin
› BERLIN, GERMANY
2016/2019-2022
Office · 32,000m²
› TCHOBAN VOSS Architekten
Sergei Tchoban, Stephan Lohre
SXB S.à r.l. / EDGE (Private)
© HG Esch

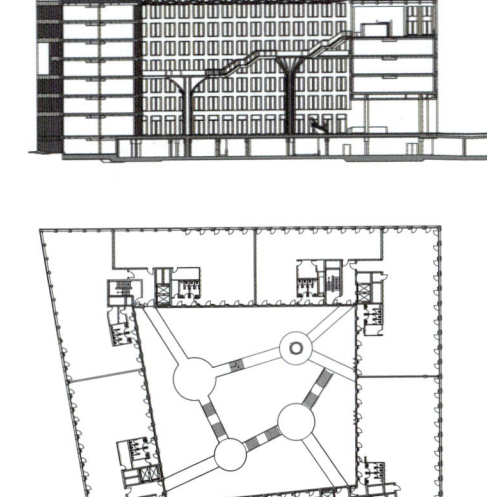

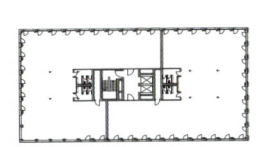

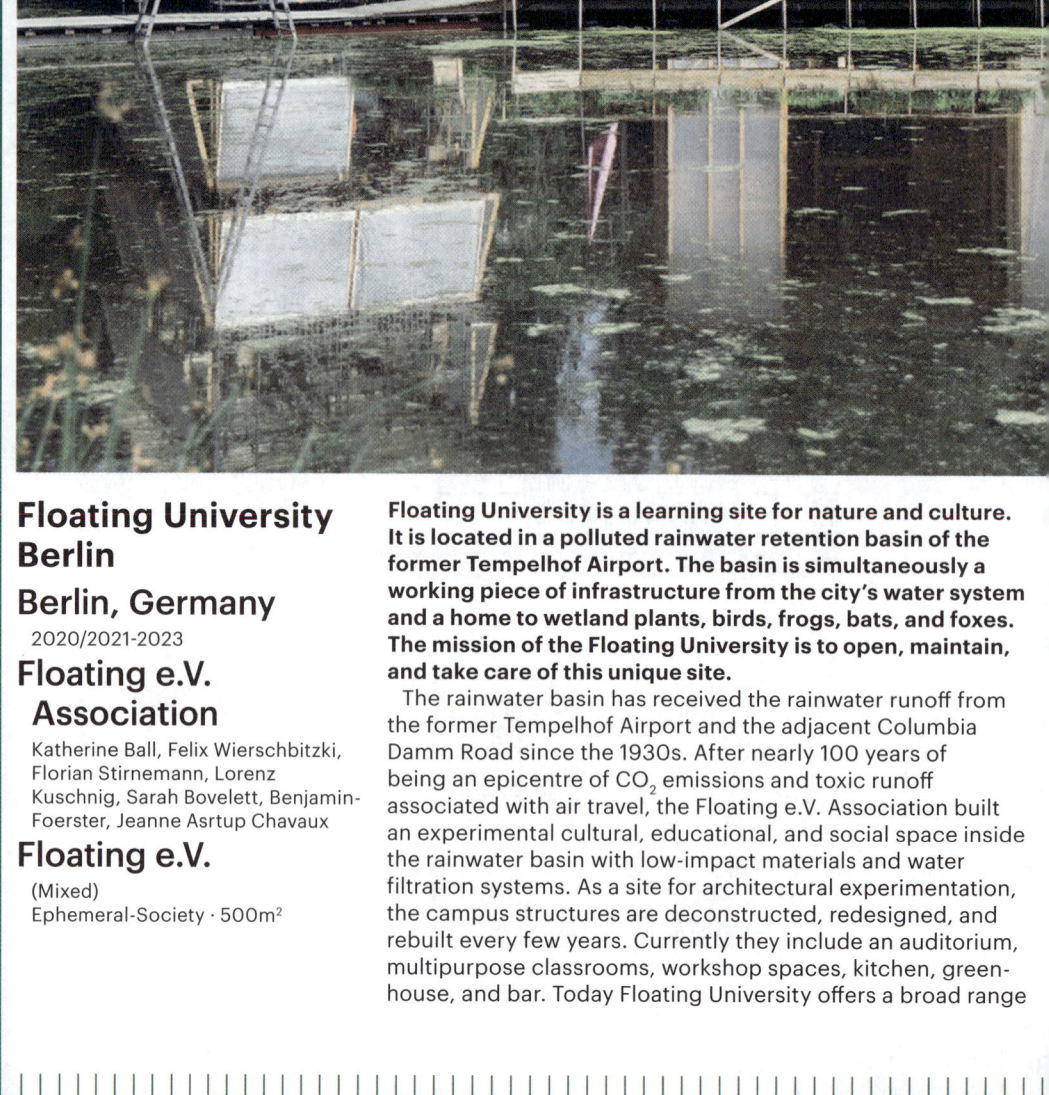

Floating University Berlin

Berlin, Germany

2020/2021-2023

Floating e.V. Association

Katherine Ball, Felix Wierschbitzki, Florian Stirnemann, Lorenz Kuschnig, Sarah Bovelett, Benjamin-Foerster, Jeanne Asrtup Chavaux

Floating e.V.

(Mixed)
Ephemeral-Society · 500m²

Floating University is a learning site for nature and culture. It is located in a polluted rainwater retention basin of the former Tempelhof Airport. The basin is simultaneously a working piece of infrastructure from the city's water system and a home to wetland plants, birds, frogs, bats, and foxes. The mission of the Floating University is to open, maintain, and take care of this unique site.

The rainwater basin has received the rainwater runoff from the former Tempelhof Airport and the adjacent Columbia Damm Road since the 1930s. After nearly 100 years of being an epicentre of CO_2 emissions and toxic runoff associated with air travel, the Floating e.V. Association built an experimental cultural, educational, and social space inside the rainwater basin with low-impact materials and water filtration systems. As a site for architectural experimentation, the campus structures are deconstructed, redesigned, and rebuilt every few years. Currently they include an auditorium, multipurpose classrooms, workshop spaces, kitchen, greenhouse, and bar. Today Floating University offers a broad range of cultural, educational, and discursive programmes for all ages about peoples' relationships with the city and the more-than-human world.

Floating University Berlin re-envisions an urban water infrastructure that welcomes public participation. The architecture on site is constantly evolving, being built, deconstructed, and rebuilt. In the summer of 2020, after a series of workshops that collected spatial desires from association members, a 'space task force' worked towards translating these wishes into reality, as well as maintaining the existing infrastructure of the basin. In its design, the space group tried to take all relationships within the basin into account – talking with association members, observing trees and polluted water levels, discussing with political actors as well as neighbours, children, adults, and nesting birds. The building process is collaborative.

Floating e.V's vision to transform the Tempelhof rainwater basin into an infiltration basin is a design for how to use nature-based solutions to filter the rainwater in the basin and make it possible to reuse it to water local parks and graveyards affected by the drought and to seep into the ground, rather than going unfiltered to pollute the Spree River like it has for the last 100 years.

The built structures at Floating University include mostly reused materials and low-processed, biodegradable materials with small CO_2 footprints, and a self-built water filtration system. The main structures are constructed with scaffolding, metal poles, and beams. Wood is used to envelope the structures as well as for the various walking platforms. Inflatable roofs (some of which are also sliding roofs) are made from fabric and have a ventilation and lighting system incorporated. Some walls are made with straw while the façade of the Rain Palace is made from reeds from the basin and from regional farmers; we plan to compost them and grow mushrooms on it. A milpa garden provides the weight to prevent the kitchen from floating. We use soil as weight and we plant vegetables in it so there is a reciprocal relationship between live matter and architecture.

Since the Floating University is a seasonal space, every winter the soft architectural structures need to be dismantled and stored to be reused/reinflated the next year. Each spring the space group and a group of volunteers run the 'Build+Care+Repair' programme where the structures are repaired, mended, and re-installed.

FLOATING E.V. ASSOCIATION

158

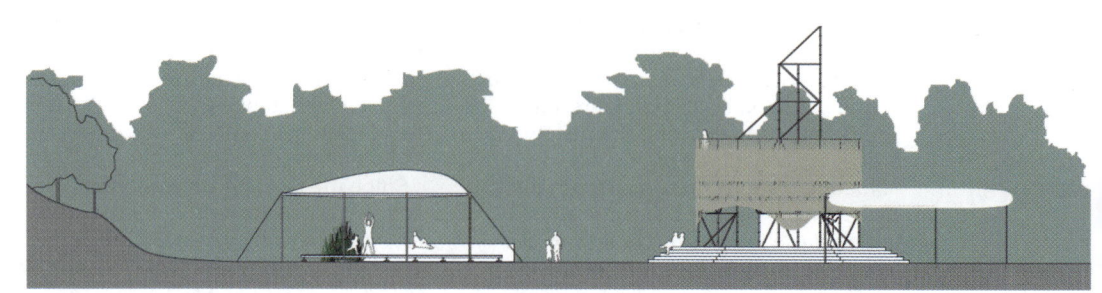

SHORTLISTED

Elevations

FLOATING UNIVERSITY BERLIN

0 1 2   5   10   20

159

General urbanization

FLOATING E.V. ASSOCIATION

Spore House is a culture center that was built for a non-profit foundation. The initiative focuses on communities in nature-based lifestyles and the idea of developing tools via collaboration and local partnerships to record, collect and share knowledge. For all these different stakeholders, the building offers an open, welcoming ground floor, a tranquil community garden, a roof terrace accessible to the public and temporary exhibition spaces. The aim was to create architecturally exciting spaces for appropriation, while at the same time providing access that is as low-threshold as possible. In summary, the result is a house with a concept of use as a robust, urban building block promoting social and cultural dialogue.

Spore Initiative
› BERLIN, GERMANY
2018/2019-2023
Mixed use - Cultural & Social · 4,116m²
› AFF Architekten
Sven Froehlich, Martin Froehlich, Ulrike Dix, Monic Frahn
Schöpflin Stiftung (Private)
© Tjark Spille

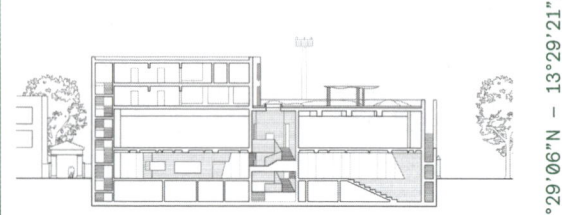

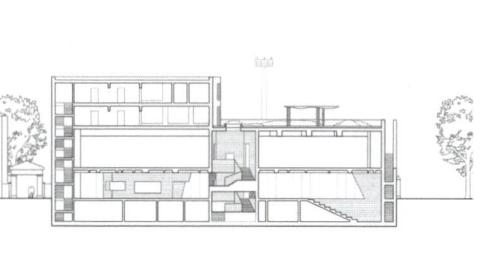

The project transforms the Mero Hall at Spreepark Berlin. Blue Hour is a new hybrid potential space that acts as a host and enables new formats of meeting. The initially temporary installation will now become a permanent part of the new Spreepark after a successful test run. There is no center, so you can sit on the bench and feel comfortable, but it can also become quite dense.

Blue Hour at Spreepark
› BERLIN, GERMANY
2021/2022
Culture · 1,750m²
› modulorbeat
Marc Günnewig, Jan Kampshoff
Spreepark Art Space / Grün Berlin GmbH (Public)
© Jan Kampshoff / modulorbeat

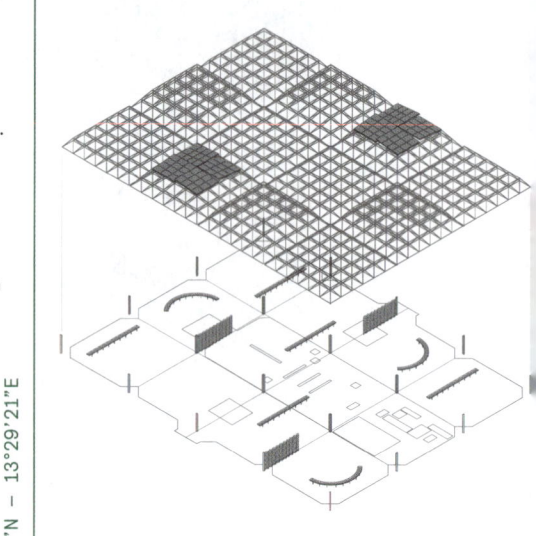

In the transformation from a stable into a photo studio as a temporary workspace, the room initially closes itself off from the outside. It is entirely focused on the production of the images against the abstract setting of a background sweep. The interventions add complexity to the building and retain and celebrate the layers of the past.

Rieckshof Photo Studio
› UCKERMARK, GERMANY
2019/2019-2021
Mixed use - Cultural & Social · 194m² · 150,000€
› HELGA BLOCKSDORF / ARCHITEKTUR
Blocksdorf Helga
Jane Garber, Karel Kuehne (Private)
© Ruben Beilby

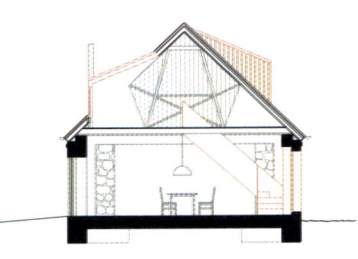

The development consists of three buildings forming a frontage to the street with two together forming a central courtyard and a car-free communal area for the use all residents. It proves that it is still possible to construct low-cost residential buildings while ensuring that aspects often neglected by the commercial market, such as well-proportioned rooms, good natural light and the possibility of cross ventilation, were achieved even in small flats 40 square meters in size.

Public Multi-Family Housing Assembly
› ŁOWICZ, POLAND
2019/2020-2022
Collective housing · 7,228m² · 919€/m²
› PA+U Rafał Mazur, GDA ŁUKASZ GAJ
Rafał Mazur, Łukasz Gaj
PFR Nieruchomości S.A. (Public)
© Maja Wirkus

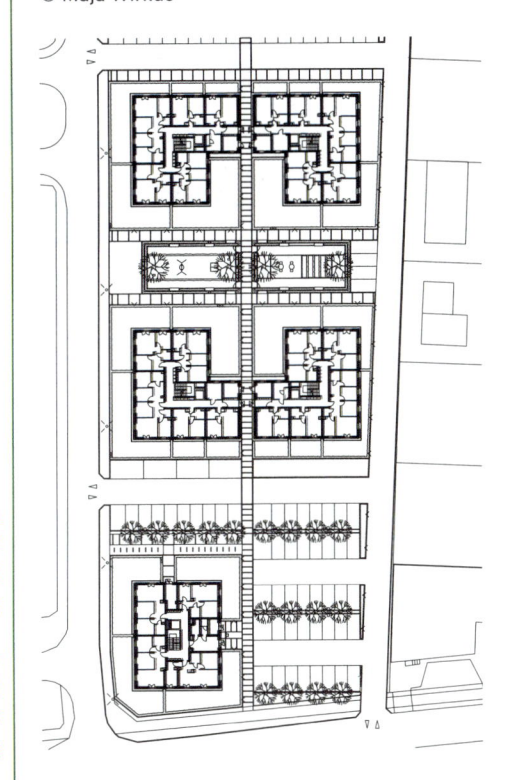

Targ Blonie / Food Market
Błonie, Poland
2021/2022-2022

Pracownia Architektoniczna Aleksandra Wasilkowska
Aleksandra Wasilkowska

Blonie Commune
(Public)
Commerce · 1,453m² · 2,000,000€

Bazaars offering local agricultural products strengthen the city's resilience and encourage equal opportunities for healthy and low-cost food for all social groups, thereby strengthening micro-entrepreneurship and neighbourly bonds.

The renovated open market is located in the commune of Blonie, a small town near Warsaw. The local community boasts a centuries-long tradition of fairs, and the market has been very popular providing access to cheap, good quality food sold directly by producers and farmers for years. The commune of Blonie decided to revamp the market to address poor sanitary standards and the lack of basic market infrastructure.

This hybrid public space combines two social functions: a park and a bazaar. White roofs reflect the sun's rays and provide shelter from the rain. The raised merchant stalls can be used as seats and as a space for spontaneous meetings. A bar can be found in the heart of the market connected with a playground for children and a community table. Naturalistic green islands were designed around the roofing and pavilions. Trees and shrubs that provide food and shelter to birds and insects will offer extra shade for open-air trading posts once they reach a certain height. Rainwater from the roof is retained in rain bowls, and the excess water nourishes the plants and seeps into the soil. Completing the whole design are a variety of street furniture fixtures, such as bicycle racks, boulders, bird and insect houses, and a community table, while a play garden with wood-carved animal-shaped rockers has also been designed. A hybrid park-bazaar structure, Targ Blonie improves the microclimate, strengthens micro-entrepreneurship, and provides residents access to locally produced food in the open air, strengthening the city's resilience in times of food and climate crises.

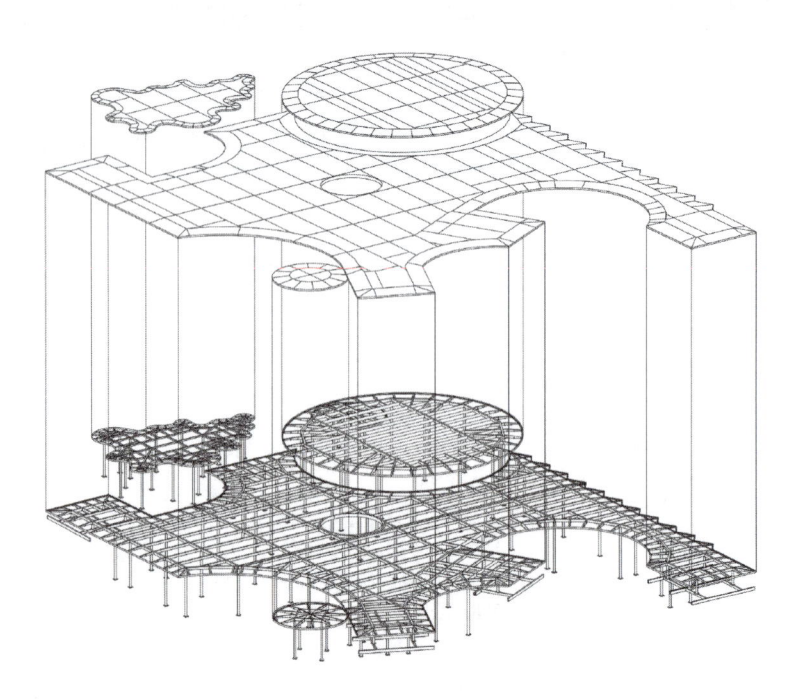

Construction of the roof

TARG BŁONIE / FOOD MARKET

165

General urbanization

PRACOWNIA ARCHITEKTONICZNA ALEKSANDRA WASILKOWSKA

The main idea behind the Warsaw Brewery project was to restore life on the site of the former Haberbusch_Schiele brewing plant. Though forming only a small part of the development, the few historic buildings, or their remains, have become the most prominent features in the new tissue of streets and squares.
A properly functioning city should represent a mix of functions where the boundaries between them are blurred. The breweries are strongly and clearly linked to neighboring parts of the city. The consequences of the basic design assumptions have been translated into major functional and urban planning decisions. As a result, axes, openings, dominants, new streets and squares were shaped. Subsequently, solutions for urban interiors, façade tectonics, greenery management, the shaping of the interiors of the buildings, the choice of materials, textures, colors, small architecture, etc., were detailed. However, none of these components constituted an objective or were self-contained, but interdependent with the others. An important part of the project was the search for proportions and combining them with the newly designed buildings by finding characteristic motifs.

Rebuilding Hope: Turning Empty Offices into a School for Ukrainian War Refugee Children. This school for children from Ukraine in Warsaw is a manifesto and laboratory of circularity in the architecture. The empty office floor has been transformed into the school with the use of the furniture and equipment from the reuse. This school shows that circularity can go in line with a high spatial and formal quality. The project has been created on-site voluntarily by the architects, NGO leaders and many volunteers.

Warsaw Breweries
› **WARSAW, POLAND**
2015/2017-2021
Mixed use - Commercial & Offices · 120,000m²
› **JEMS Architekci**
Paweł Majkusiak, Olgierd Jagiełło, Marek Moskal, Marcin Sadowski, Maciej Rydz, Grzegorz Artymiński, Izabela Bednarska, Zygmunt Borawski, Tytus Brzozowski, Mieszko Burmas, Małgorzata Charazińska, Łukasz Chaberka, Anna Dubois, Aleksandra Dutkowska, Marcin Giemza, Wojciech Gruszczyński, Michał Iwaniuk, Szamil Jachimczyk, Katarzyna Janczura, Rafał Jóźwiak, Radosław Kacprzak, Urszula Kos, Łukasz Krzesiak, Katarzyna Kuźmińska, Magdalena Litaszewska, Beata Momot, Grzegorz Moskała, Marta Najder, Bartłomiej Najman, Maciej Olczak, Mariusz Olszewski, Katarzyna Piotrowska, Maks Potapow, Agnieszka Rokicka, Aleksandra Rusin, Łukasz Stępnik, Bartosz Śniadowski, Marta Świątek-Piziorska, Anna Świderska, Mateusz Świętorzecki, Piotr Waleszkiewicz, Izabela Wencel, Marcin Zaremba, Agata Żak
Echo Investment (Private)
© Juliusz Sokołowski

School for Children from Ukraine - Adaptation of the Floor in the Office Building
› **WARSAW, POLAND**
2022/2022
Social Welfare · 1,240m²
› **xystudio**
Marta Nowosielska, Dorota Sibińska, Filip Domaszczyński
Refugees from Ukraine (Mixed)
© Mikołaj Kwieciński

The main idea of the project was the assumption that the National Library building should become more intuitive, ergonomic and ecological while retaining all its previous advantages and modernist character. We decided to give the interiors of the reading room a new, proper hierarchy through natural materials to emphasize their rank. The most important place of the new library is the central space located at the intersection of the main entrance and the axis of the reading rooms with three key elements: the main brass counter, the skylight and the spiral staircase. The most characteristic element of the reconstruction is the skylight-covered lower reading room.

Redevelopment and Modernization of the National Library of Poland

› **WARSAW, POLAND**
 2015/2018-2022
 Education · 9,484m²
› **KONIOR STUDIO, SOKKA**
 Tomasz Konior, Dominik Koroś, Katarzyna Sokołowska
 Biblioteka Narodowa (Public)
 © Jakub Certowicz

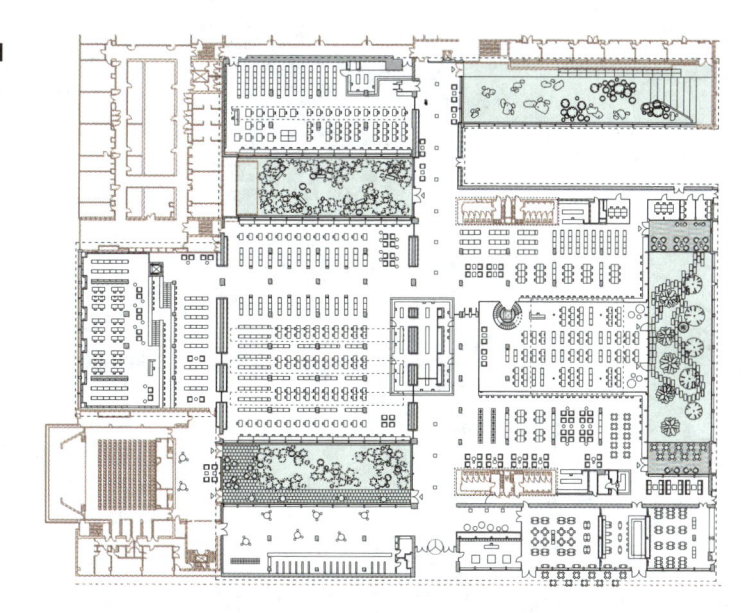

168

From
MARCQ-EN-BAROEUL
France
50°39'59"N – 3°04'32"E

to
STARYI BYKIV
Ukraine
50°35'00"N – 31°38'38"E

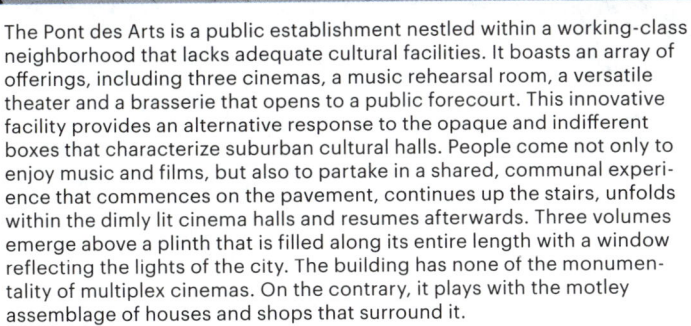

The Pont des Arts is a public establishment nestled within a working-class neighborhood that lacks adequate cultural facilities. It boasts an array of offerings, including three cinemas, a music rehearsal room, a versatile theater and a brasserie that opens to a public forecourt. This innovative facility provides an alternative response to the opaque and indifferent boxes that characterize suburban cultural halls. People come not only to enjoy music and films, but also to partake in a shared, communal experience that commences on the pavement, continues up the stairs, unfolds within the dimly lit cinema halls and resumes afterwards. Three volumes emerge above a plinth that is filled along its entire length with a window reflecting the lights of the city. The building has none of the monumentality of multiplex cinemas. On the contrary, it plays with the motley assemblage of houses and shops that surround it.

Le Pont des Arts – Cultural Pole

› **MARCQ-EN-BAROEUL, FRANCE**
2017/2019-2021
Culture · 3,000m² · 2,600€/m²
› **V+ (Bureau Vers plus de bien-être), Atelier HART BERTELOOT ARCHITECTURE TERRITOIRE (HBAAT)**
Thierry Decuypere, Jörn Aram Bihain, Mathieu Berteloot, Heleen Hart
Ville de Marcq-en-Baroeul (Public)
© Cyrille Weiner

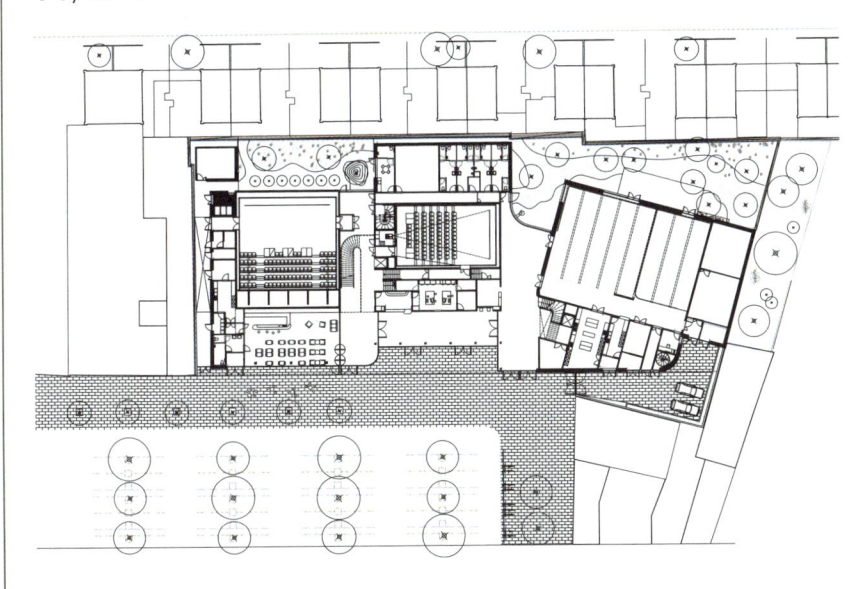

Two functions meet in a common entrance hall preceded by Beursplein square, with a covered outdoor intermediate space between square and building under an imposing cantilever.
The building fits seamlessly in the perimeter of the 50-year-old beech trees. It took great precaution and care to keep the old trees alive during the construction of this new building. The materialization consists of glass to create openness and transparency and red-brown brick to create a robust building that fits in with the environment.
Moreover, it seeks added value by organizing new kinds of events by combining the exhibition hall with a congress facility. The congress part consists of three functions: auditorium, meeting rooms and a catering area.

Bruges Meeting & Convention Centre
› BRUGES, BELGIUM
  2016/2019-2021
  Culture · 21,035m^2 · 1443.44€/m^2
› **Souto Moura - Arquitectos, SA, META architectuurbureau**
  Eduardo Souto de Moura, Deboutte Niklaas, Soors Eric
  Stad Brugge (Public)
  © Filip Dujardin

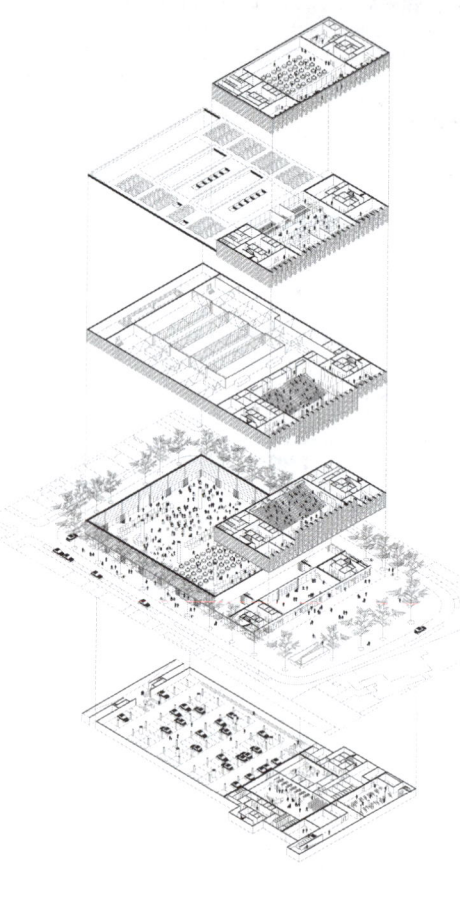

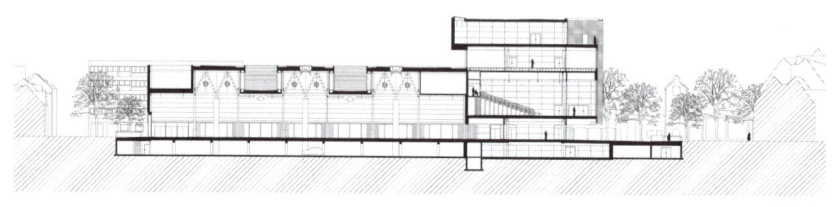

This project is about sharing architecture. In other words, how can new interventions incorporate the existing context and borrow elements from it, but also give something back?
Transforming an introverted site into a publicly accessible ensemble is the essence of the design and is supported by architectural elements.
The hefty concrete columns that appear in the existing façade are interpreted and "reshaped" in the new courtyard façade, aiming to support the public character of this place. The "racing-green" of the existing joinery is reflected in the new buildings. Instead of perpetuating the heritage in pure form, it is observed from a different perspective and updated. In various door openings and along the eaves, the mirrored finish reflects what previously existed in ever-changing and surprising compositions.

Share and Reuse Factory
› **KORTRIJK, BELGIUM**
2020/2021-2023
Mixed use - Cultural & Social · 3,210m² · 1,056€/m²
› **ATAMA**
Carolien Pasmans, Bram Aerts
City of Kortrijk (Public)
© Stijn Bollaert

The original brief for the village of Vendegies-sur-Ecaillon was to move the nursery school to the other side of the main road so the children would no longer have to cross it to get to the canteen. The objective emerged from these characteristics: to clarify the urban structure by developing interactions between programs. The school is crossed via the gallery: a new structure long enough to add quality to the new public space.

The Vendegies-sur-Écaillon Nursery School

› VENDEGIES-SUR-ÉCAILLON, FRANCE
2020/2021-2022
Education · 400 m² · 2,600€/m²
› **Studio RIJSEL**
Edouard Cailliau, Thomas Lecourt
Ville de Vendegies-sur-Écaillon (Public)
© Séverin Malaud

The project is to be viewed as an act of preservation. The factors of time and decay are part of a romantic interpretation of a fantastic building that arose through a complicated historical process. the Winter Circus with its impressive dimensions is a multi-layered architectural gem that on the outside is intended to reflect the constructivist logic of the inside. The ingenious new internal circulation ensures a flow that makes it lively and vivid again. Public programming of the arena and the music venue underneath make the Winter Circus a vibrant hotspot in Ghent.

Repurposing Winter Circus Mahy
› GHENT, BELGIUM
2012/2017-2022
Mixed use - Cultural & Social · 14,297m² · 1,468€/m²
› SumProject, Atelier Kempe Thill, architects and planners, Baro Architectuur, aNNo architecten
Oliver Thill, André Kempe, Paul Lievevrouw, Stijn Cools, Geert Willemyns
sogent (Mixed)
© Ulrich Schwarz

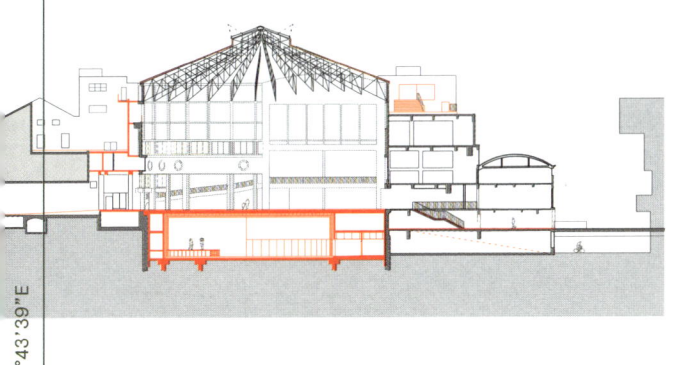

Timelab is conceived as a place where new systems of local production and consumption can be tested and implemented. The design of the project was aimed at reactivating a deserted industrial site as a productive space.

Arthouse Timelab
› Ghent, Belgium
2019/2020-2021
Culture · 1,692m² · 503€/m²
› a2o
Luc Vanmuysen, Jo Berben, Ingrid Mees, Bart Hoylaerts, Stefaan Evers, Wout Sorgeloos, Killian Nekeman, Jonas Knapen, Fréderique Hermans
Timelab (Mixed)
© Stijn Bollaert

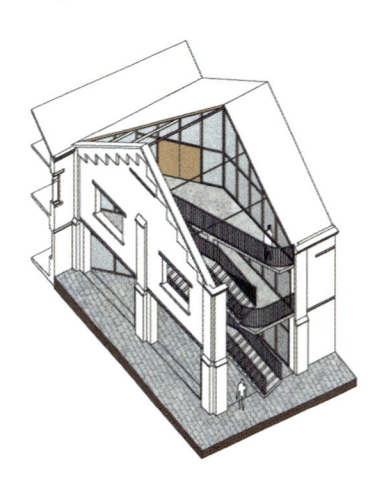

Within a dense building block, the project redevelops a dilapidated mushroom farm into a co-housing project consisting of 10 units supplemented with a variety of shared spaces and a large communal garden. The houses are shallow and wide, so there is enough light and a spacious garden extends in front of the windows. In the wider part, the building forms a hook that closes off the garden. Added to this are the shared spaces, which are tucked under the high parts and as thoughtfully diversified as the living spaces in the houses themselves. The result is a spacious, comfortable living environment. The relations between the private units and the outdoor areas are diverse yet equivalent.

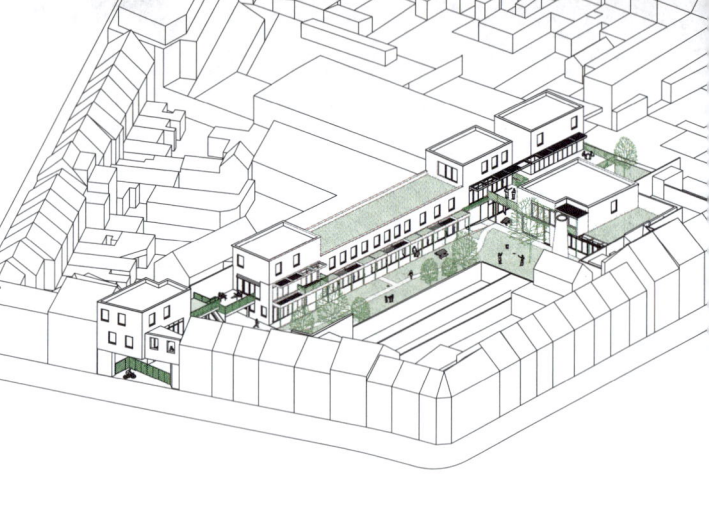

Cohousing Jean
› **GHENT, BELGIUM**
2015/2020-2022
Collective housing · 1,774m² · 1,933€/m²
› **ectv architecten**
Els Claessens, Tania Vandenbussche
Cohousing Jean (Private)
© Filip Dujardin

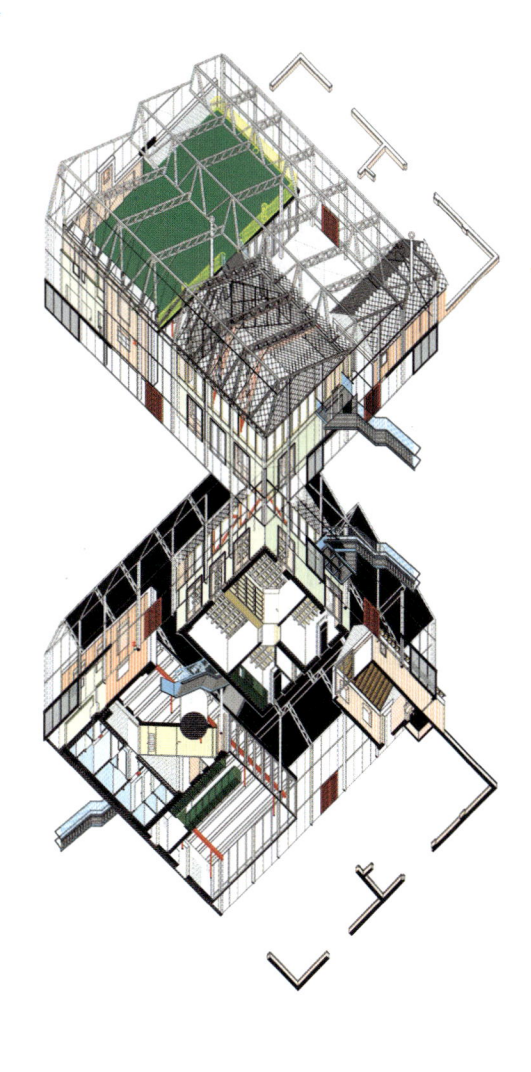

Padenbroek is a reconversion of an old fruit farm into a nature education center in Gooik. It is a powerful building that gives new meaning to the concept of sustainable architecture. The project has a remarkable greenhouse structure that was pushed over the existing buildings. Carefully drawn and custom-made, the three-part stepped white steel roof structure gives the program spaciousness and recognizability, while also meeting important climate requirements.
The ingenuity of this project lies in the surprising way it handles the existing fragments. These were restored, stripped down, cleaned, disconnected and made independent. Sometimes a fireplace was split in two, then a window was bricked up or a sill was kept.

Paddenbroek Educational Rural Centre
› **GOOIK, BELGIUM**
2016/2018-2021
Education · 870m^2
› **jo taillieu architecten**
Jo Taillieu
Gemeente Gooik (Public)
© Filip Dujardin

Fire Station, Multi-Purpose Space, and Emergency Housing

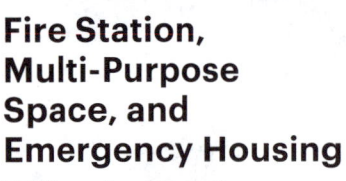

Dilbeek, Belgium
2013/2020-2022

Studio SNCDA + Bureau Bouwtechniek
Sara Noel Costa De Araujo

Gemeente Dilbeek
(Public)
Government & Civic · 5,677m² · 1,500€/m²

Built on the site of the former town hall, this building features 3 distinct programmes: a fire station, a multi-purpose hall, and emergency housing. As part of the master plan for the core of peri-urban Dilbeek, these 3 urban functions constitute an important link in interweaving residential, civic, commercial, hospitality, and employment uses.

The project is located in the outskirts of Brussels in peri-urban Flanders. The site functions as a strategic link between a traffic-intense intercommunal road and the residential heart of the municipality. The plot is divided into public and private sections where 3 distinct urban programmes develop over the depth of the site, each one oriented around its outdoor space. The building has no backside, rather it boasts 2 main façades. The fire station faces traffic, whereas the multi-purpose hall orients its forecourt towards the residential part of the town. The emergency housing is developed around a communal garden, integrated into the existing building fabric of both streets. Seeking to reuse the bricks in the future, the materials were chosen to create a robust building, easy to maintain made fully private for the firemen through a side door that easily connects the two programmes. On the opposite end, meeting rooms can be rendered into public spaces for citizens' activities. The building's intention is to serve as an open flexible sustainable collective infrastructure: a play area that accommodates different uses on a relatively small plot by spatially rethinking the integration of the 3 distinct functions and their public/private characteristics.

The first structure takes the form of a concrete table. It allows for large spans in the truck garage, thereby minimizing the space associated with the columns. The multi-purpose hall is a complementary structure and functions as a large red beam holding the table, i.e. the ceiling slab of the garage. In addition to this structural role, the concrete of the hall allows for acoustic insulation. The structure is a surface for visual experimentation/conversation between SNCDA and KM. The drawing, applied to concrete bricks and formwork concrete, results in a fine work of joints and a perfect grid that allows the same original line of the project to be read both inside and outside. The structure becomes the ornamentation of a robust building that is easy to maintain. The design of the oversized windows with their rounded corner are also extensions of the drawings. Adaptive technologies create environments that meet the users' individual needs. A rainwater recovery system supplies water to the toilets, as well as provides the firemen with water for their exercises. Photovoltaic panels provide electricity, while thermal panels produce hot water. The building is passively cooled using geothermal energy.

while keeping finishings simple. Uncoated, the building shows its structure. Furthermore, we chose not to use any coating, as they are fragile and make the bricks difficult to recycle.

The project ensures specific visibility to each programme in the building and organizes the fire station as a well-oiled machine. Distances are short and spaces are intended to be interconnected like parts of a whole. The large garage, at the centre of the plot, is the heart of the machine. It opens onto the training ground for the fire brigade through large doors. The ground floor needs to accommodate the fire trucks' turning circles. The fire station opens onto two pedestrian passageways from the residential backstreet, through which firefighters can quickly access the town. The multifunctional hall is flexible enough for Dilbeek's citizens to use it for both their private and public events. The multifunctional hall can be

STUDIO SNCDA + BUREAU BOUWTECHNIEK

SHORTLISTED

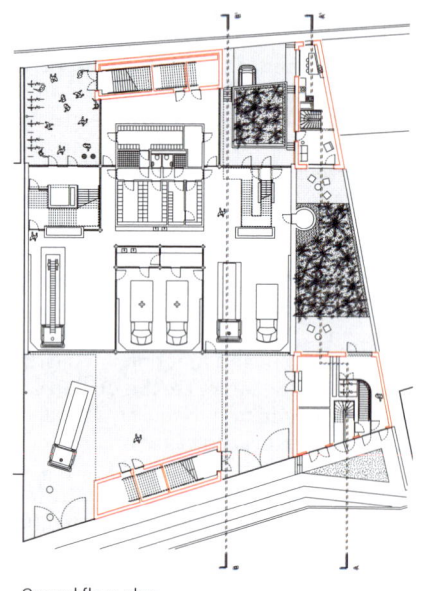

Ground floor plan

Second floor plan

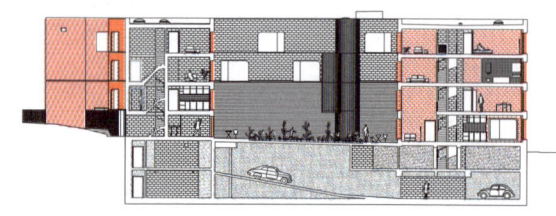

Section AA'

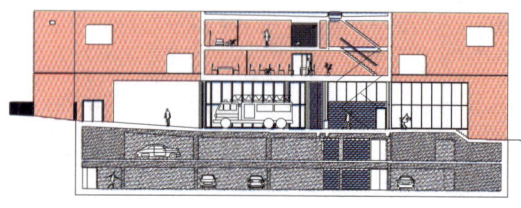

Section BB'

FIRE STATION, MULTI-PURPOSE SPACE, AND EMERGENCY HOUSING

STUDIO SNCDA + BUREAU BOUWTECHNIEK

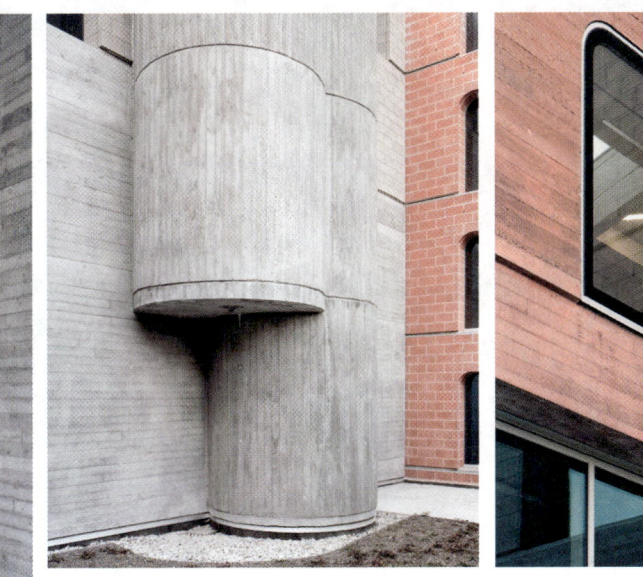

A former office building in a dense, heterogeneous neighborhood was acquired by two neighboring municipalities to remedy the dire lack of space in secondary schools in Brussels. The first phase consisted of setting up a series of classrooms in one of the existing wings, to swiftly welcome the school on site. A new sports hall was placed in a way that allows it to be opened separately outside of school hours, anchoring the project in the social fabric of the neighborhood. Karreveld is a project produced from its constraints. Structural interventions were limited to the barest necessities and material choices were influenced by their quickness of assembly on site.

Karreveld

› **SINT-JANS-MOLENBEEK, BELGIUM**
2018/2020-2022
Education · 7,588m² · 818€/m²
› **AgwA**
Harold Fallon, Benoît Vandenbulcke, Benoît Burquel, Hélène Joos, Nicky Vancaudenberg, Julien Delmotte, Thomas Montulet, Sofie Devriendt, Ali Ismail, Juliette Lucarain, Dorothée Fontignie, Hannelore Thomas, Marie Pirard
Pouvoir Organisateur Pluriel asbl (Public)
© Séverin Malaud

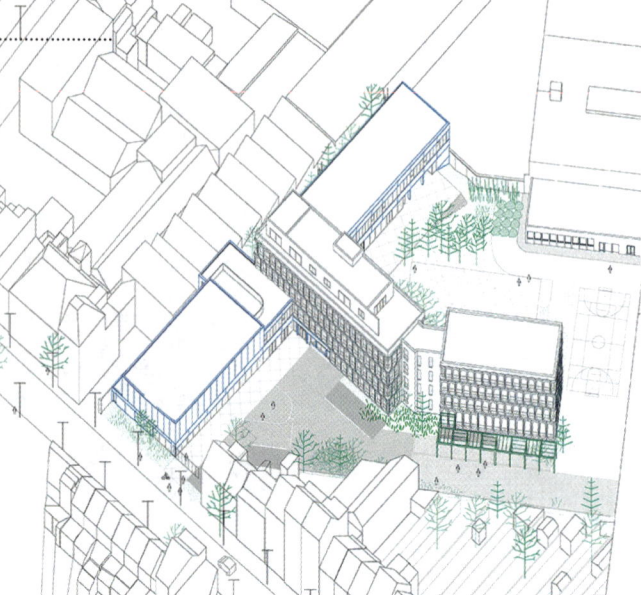

SHORTLISTED

Open Air Swimming Pool Flow
Anderlecht, Belgium
2020/2021

Decoratelier Jozef Wouters, POOL IS COOL

Jozef Wouters, Paul Steinbrück

POOL IS COOL
(Public)
Ephemeral-Society · 540m² · 210€/m²

50°49'55"N – 4°18'56"E

The temporary outdoor swimming pool FLOW is a 1:1 scale model. Serving both as an example and a provocation, the project highlights Brussels' lack of structural open-air swimming spots. Thus, the pool aims to convince authorities to invest in permanent projects while already offering a real, albeit small, safe, and inclusive place to cool down in the summer.

POOL IS COOL is a bottom-up organisation that has been advocating for the reintroduction of outdoor swimming in Brussels since 2015. In 2021, with the support of local organizations and authorities, they created the first public outdoor swimming pool in Brussels in more than 40 years. FLOW was designed and built by Decoratelier Jozef Wouters on a derelict site next to the Brussels canal, with the adjoining traffic-free bridge serving as an access point. It is located in a neighbourhood which is transforming from a former industrial zone to a mixed residential and commercial zone characterized by great diversity. Informed by Jozef Wouters' practice as a set designer, FLOW uses set design as a tool and a language to start a concrete conversation between different stakeholders – beginning with local communities – about the various desires and needs at play in public infrastructure.

FLOW is a process; the building is the result. The pool is an attraction for the whole Brussels region, yet a key objective was to anchor it in the fragile social context of Anderlecht. Decoratelier, located close to the pool, approached the construction as a participatory project, providing education and temporary work to over 50 short-schooled local youth in a neighbourhood where unemployment is a major issue. While building the parts, the participants contributed not only their hands, but also their voices during discussions and panels about privatisation and access to public space. Afterwards, the continued employment of local youth in the pool's daily management has helped to create a sense of shared ownership, as have accessible programmes by local cultural organisations and family-oriented activities such as swimming classes. The building materials were consciously chosen to allow for adaptations and transformation over the years. This includes the addition of new elements such as a staff kitchen and a kiosk. In this sense, the pool is like a blueprint that keeps on changing through a process of continuous research and feedback.

The pool's compact shape, wrapped around a 17 × 7 m basin, incorporates basic facilities such as changing rooms and showers. Characteristic for the design are the multi-tiered sun decks that surround the pool, where visitors can relax without disturbing the swimmers' privacy. Decorative elements by local artists enhance the feeling of the space as a temporary phantasm, a dream made of water. While biological water treatment was initially not possible due to legislative reasons, POOL IS COOL achieved this goal in 2023 through the implementation of an ecological water purification system with plant filters.

Decoratelier developed a design that consists of repeated patterns of identical wooden pieces, made from reclaimed, sustainable wood, that are tailor-made to fit re-used metal racks. This choice was not driven by aesthetic motives, but rather by a desire to build together. The parts are assembled with techniques that can be easily passed on among inexperienced builders in a horizontal learning experience. This way of building also enables future adjustments, disassembly, and reuse, supporting a sustainable vision.

Situation

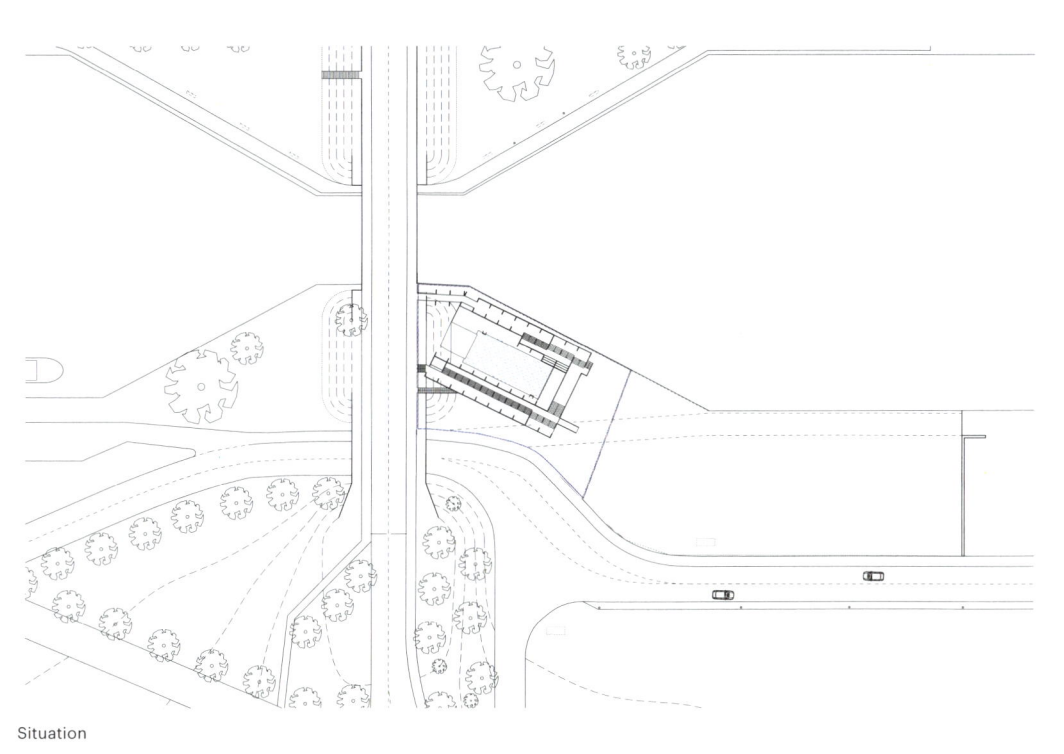

DECORATELIER JOZEF WOUTERS, POOL IS COOL

184

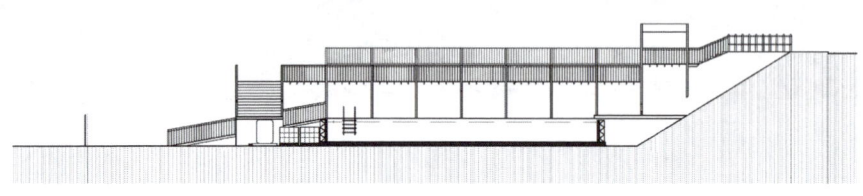

SHORTLISTED

Longitudinal section

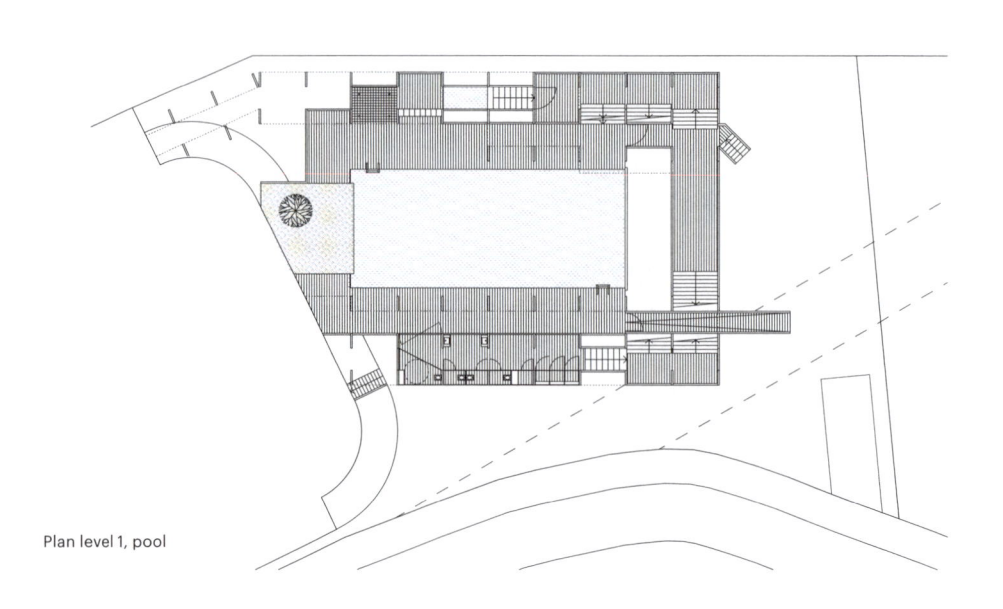

Plan level 1, pool

OPEN AIR SWIMMING POOL FLOW

The building houses the complete beer production process, but is also open to the public. It is conceived as a compact and efficient industrial container, a rectangular box with an inclined roof that reveals its content and expresses the company's graphic identity in the form of stripes in the characteristic colors of BBP beer labels.

Brussels Beer Project
› ANDERLECHT, BELGIUM
2018/2020-2022
Industrial · 1,600m²
› OFFICE Kersten Geers David Van Severen
David Van Severen, Kersten Geers
Brussels Beer Project (Private)
© Bas Princen

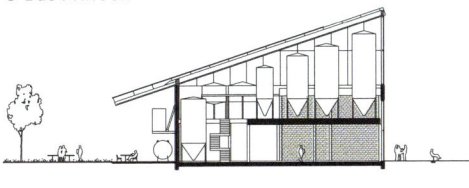

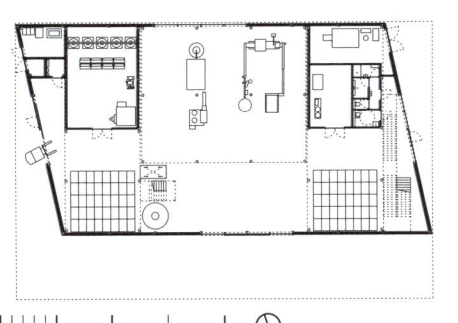

Duchesse is a transformative project turning an industrial site into a dynamic housing complex. Key achievements include meticulous heritage preservation, fostering a strong sense of community, embracing sustainable design principles and exemplifying a harmonious blend of the past and future. The communal garden serves as the heart of the project, hosting essential communal functions while providing a private oasis for residents. In essence, Duchesse strikes a remarkable balance between preserving industrial heritage and creating contemporary living spaces within a dynamic urban context.

Duchesse. Reconversion of Industrial Buildings in Residential Units
› SINT-JANS-MOLENBEEK, BELGIUM
2017/2020-2022
Collective housing · 1,080m² · 1,500,000€
› NOTAN OFFICE
Karam Frédéric
COFIPRIM (Private)
© Stijn Bollaert

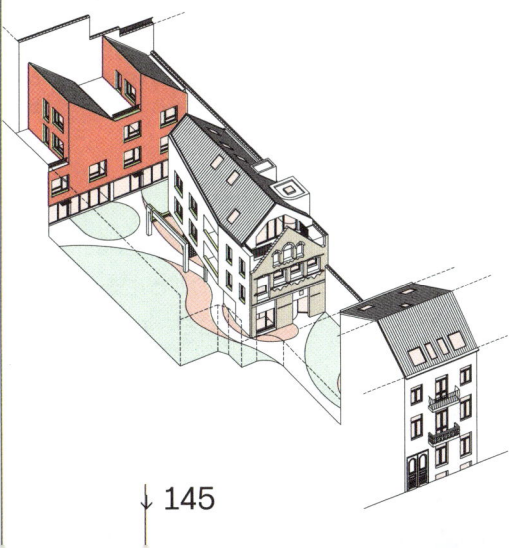

Amal Amjahid Community Facility Along the Canal

Sint-Jans-Molenbeek, Belgium

2016/2017-2021

&bogdan

Oana Bogdan, Leo Van Broeck, Emilie Bechet, Thomas Willemse

Municipality of Sint-Jans-Molenbeek

(Public)
Mixed use - Cultural & Social · 4,086m² · 6,990,393€

Designed for the community as a public passage connecting Molenbeek and the canal, Amal Amjahid optimises land use through the spectacular stacking of 6 functions, voids, and platforms on a small footprint. The structure allows for maximum flexibility over the 5 levels: 2 concrete walls support 4 dismantlable trusses, which were transported by water.

Named by the locals after the martial arts champion Amal Amjahid, this multipurpose public building along the canal in Molenbeek features a café, a sport shall, a boxing club, a martial arts centre, and a daycare centre for 84 children, all connected by shared outdoor spaces.

On the ground floor, a gallery with spacious arcades – the *Galerie des Géants* – continues the urban fabric and accommodates the horizontal and vertical circulation. Its exposed concrete is a sustainable choice for an urban place with heavy foot traffic.

Organised over 3 storeys, the *Patio des Costauds* draws natural light into the heart of the project, makes it possible to expand the activities, and encourages social interaction among users. Thanks to its hanging terraces – the Jardins des Juniors – the daycare centre benefits from outdoor spaces.

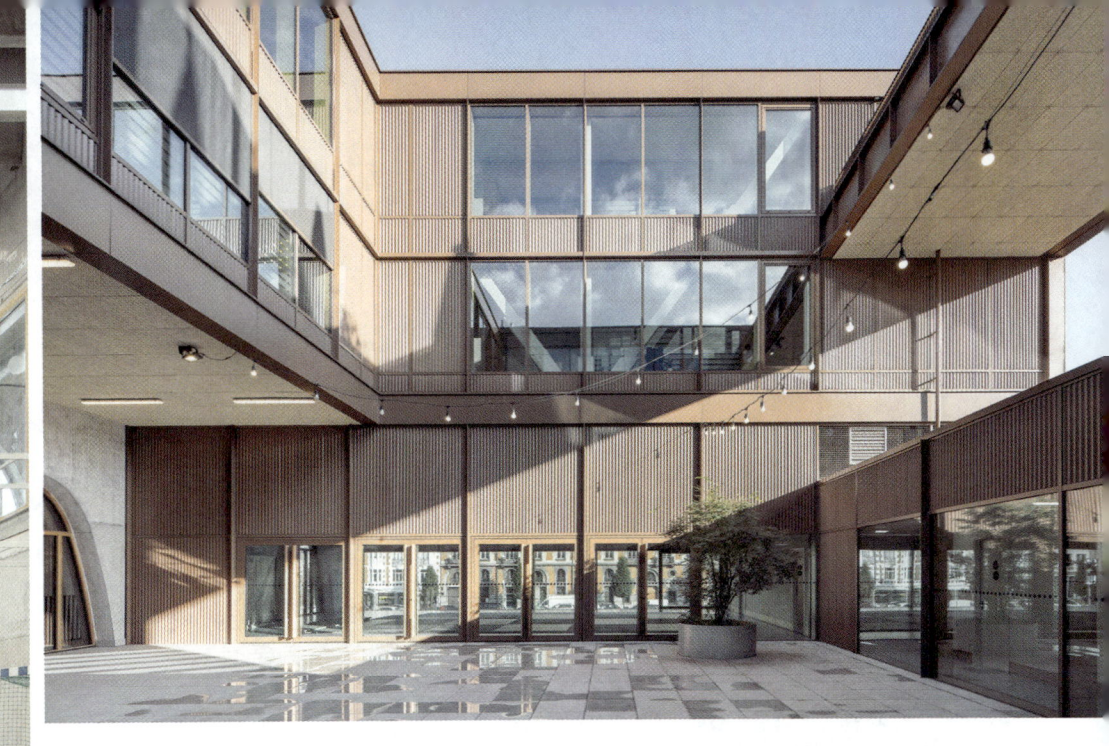

An ingenious visible structure supports this group of functions.

The flagship project of the Sustainable Neighbourhood Contract 'Around Leopold II' and part of the development plan for the canal landscape, Amal Amjahid connects the canal and Molenbeek through public space, sports - including boxing as an antidote against the radicalization of youth - and childcare. Its design and name are the result of a participatory process.

Designing the conditions for collective life is related to the non-quantifiable aspects of architecture. Places that invite people to meet, to interact with their surroundings, which are not found in clients' surface area table. Yet without these places, the other square metres have no value. Here, these places are found in the building's large voids, such as the *Galerie des Géants*, a monumental public passageway on a human scale and a meeting point for locals which overflows into a publicly accessible grandstand from which anyone can watch the sports games. The horizontal and vertical circulation accommodated here brings the public space up into the building. Designed from the users' perspective, this public space nurtures the intangible aspects of collective life, the small encounters that make everyday life so much richer.

To ensure its visibility from the street and facilitate access to it, the sports hall was placed on the building's lower storeys. The 3 storeys reserved for boxing, martial arts and childcare are stacked on top of it. Although more constraining for the structure – since the load distribution would logically have dictated placing this large column-free volume on the upper storeys – this choice ensures that all functions benefit from natural light. The three-storey high concrete wall is punctuated by arcades and a parallel wall support 4 two-storey metal trusses that house the daycare and the concierge's flat. In order to transport the trusses to the construction site, the canal was used as a waterway.

Following the 'smart shell, low tech' concept, the building is energy-efficient but is not reliant on complex technology: a highly insulating prefabricated wooden façade clad in aluminium sheet metal with copper hues envelops the project's volumes; night cooling stacks make it possible to ventilate the halls naturally in summer and to exploit the thermal mass of the concrete structure.

We provided a maintenance manual for end users and the owner when handing over the building.

188

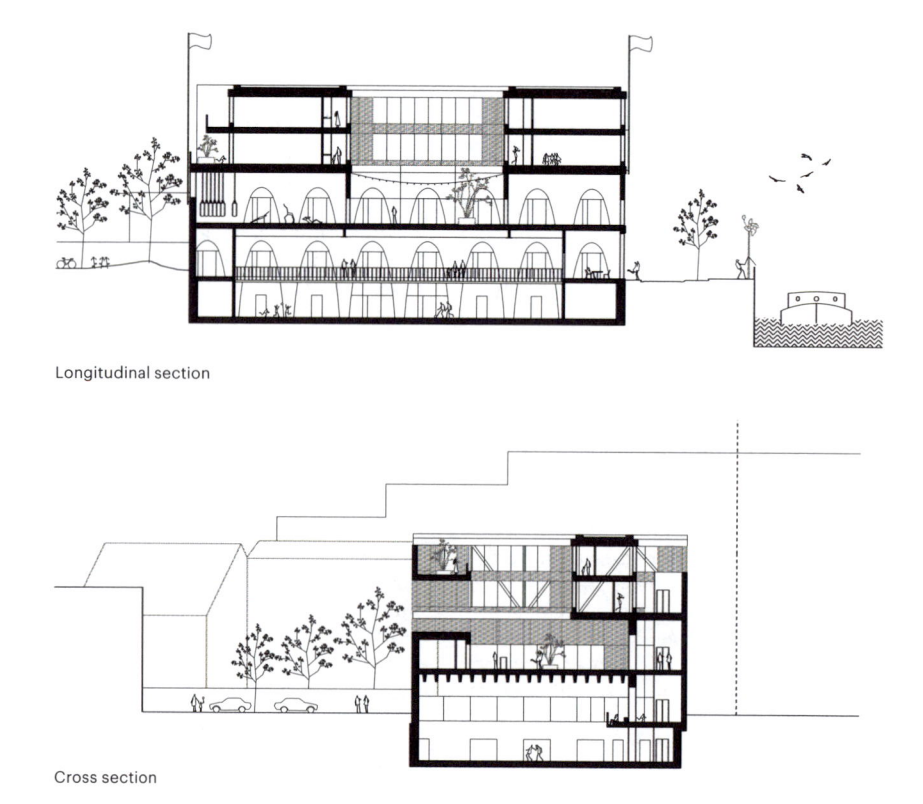

SHORTLISTED

Longitudinal section

Cross section

AMAL AMJAHID COMMUNITY FACILITY ALONG THE CANAL

0 5 10 20

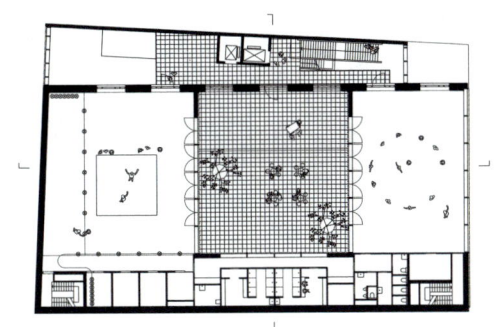

First floor plan

Third floor plan

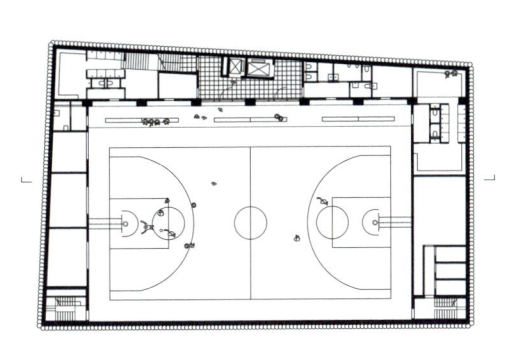

Basement floor plan

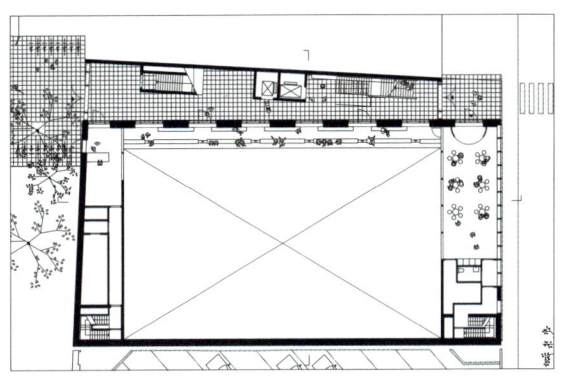

Ground floor plan

Het Steen
Antwerp, Belgium
2016/2019-2021

noAarchitecten
Jitse van den Berg, Philippe Viérin, An Fonteyne

City of Antwerp
(Public)
Culture · 3,700m²

For the last 1000 years, the Steen (listed in 1936) has formed an essential cornerstone and symbol of the city of Antwerp. The building has continuously evolved, adopting new forms, uses, and narratives. The most recent phase contributes strongly to the building's public character and its location along the river, inviting everyone in, tourists and citizens alike.

Prominent on the waterfront, the iconic Steen is the main remnant of historic Antwerp after the course of the river Scheldt was straightened in 1890. After that, the building, which used to be part of a complex city fabric with streets and squares, gained its distinct character as a freestanding castle. The less valuable 1950s annex has been replaced by a new extension, emphasising its role in the public promenade along the river. The new brickwork reflects the colour scheme of the historical stone walls. Closed and robust on the quay level, it forms part of the city's protection against rising water levels.

The Steen now houses the city's main tourist services while remaining equally inviting to its own citizens. The new public tower offers a view over the river and the city. Conscious incisions define the scale and form of the different building parts and offer unexpected spaces and views within its public interior.

Monuments form primal structures in the city; they define its collective memory. Making changes to monuments requires sensitivity as people feel emotionally affected to them. The Steen we see today is the result of centuries of building and rebuilding. The different building periods cannot be sharply distinguished. This ambivalence has fuelled the design strategy, preferring to work with continuity over contrast. The new extension has strengthened the old monument. Together, they have become one building, reconciling different layers of time.

The client, the city of Antwerp, set out to use the building as a central tourist infrastructure, combining a tourist office, a visitor centre about Antwerp's history and future, and a cruise terminal. The design accommodates these wishes, but it simultaneously acknowledges their inevitable temporary character. The design strategy anticipates future change and prepares the Steen for future adaptive re-use. The restoration, renovation, extension and transformation are part of a much longer process. The design is not an end point, but the next addition to the building, a new phase of construction that will also feature a sequel.

The project has combined the goal of preserving the landmark's cultural, historic, and architectural value with defining different comfort zones to reduce energy consumption. The design combines long-term conservation and maintenance with possible future change. This requires an intelligent organisation of the circulation system, a clever integration of technology, and the use of durable materials that age well. The new façades are made of brickwork in colours that follow the palette of the old natural stone walls. Together with artist Pieter Vermeersch, the final colour gradient was determined through a careful selection of bricks and extensive full-scale testing. The interiors unfold as a sequence of elegant halls, where traditional elements such as fireplaces (used for mechanical ventilation), mullions, and bay windows create an intimate yet grand ambiance. The interior materials are modest and long-lasting, featuring brickwork, natural stone, and wooden floors. Multiple staircases and elevators connect the floors throughout the old and new structure, enhancing the sense of continuity, while allowing for plural usage, discoveries, and the ability to lose oneself.

© FelixArchief

192

SHORTLISTED

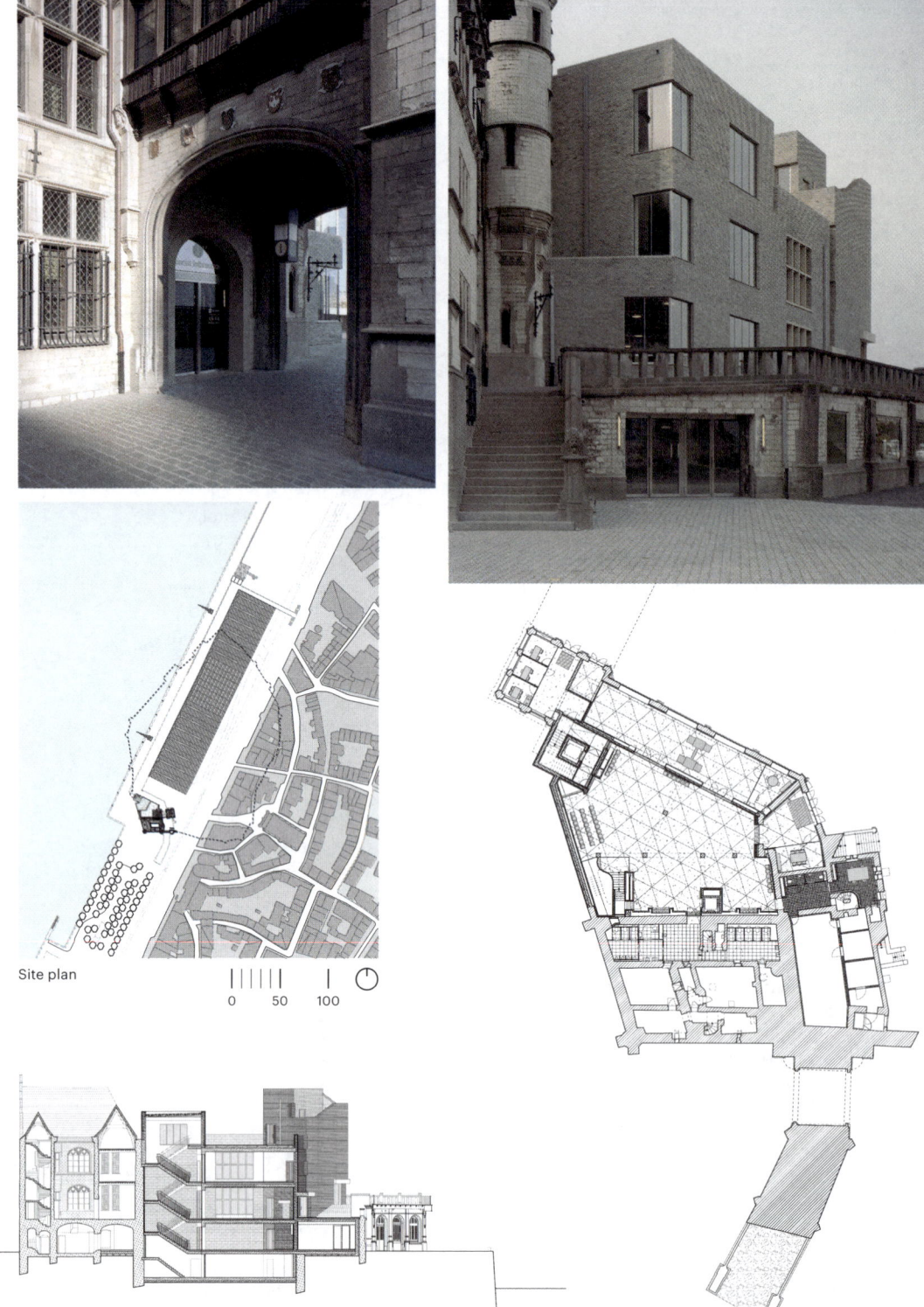

Site plan

0 50 100

Quays plan

HET STEEN

0 1 2   5   10

Photogrammetry

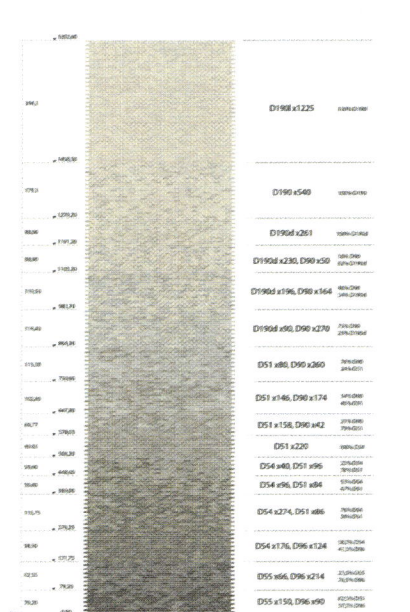

Brick gradient system

NOAARCHITECTEN

The new hospital in Antwerp is a hinge between docks, park and city. The limited area requires the hospital to be organized vertically. It has a layered structure that is bisected horizontally by interweaving the building with its surroundings. The building brings care visibly into the city and repositions itself as a key building that makes the city. It is striking how the hospital, in its vertical form comprising 19 floors, is repeatedly intersected horizontally by a healthcare-related commercial layer at ground level, a panorama floor on the third level and a large number of patios and terraces (despite its dense location). This allows the environment to effectively permeate every level of the hospital.

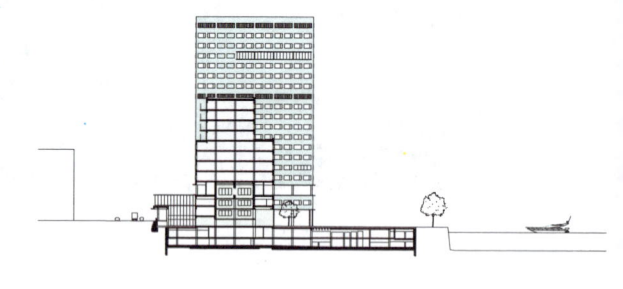

Hospital ZNA Cadix
› **ANTWERP, BELGIUM**
2012/2016-2022
Health · 65,000m²
› **Robbrecht en Daem architecten, VK architects+engineers**
Paul Robbrecht, Hilde Daem, Johannes Robbrecht, Steven Wallays, Tom Debacker, Kim Debeyser
Ziekenhuisnetwerk Antwerpen (Hospital Network Antwerp) - Kairos, Euro Immo Star (Private)
© Filip Dujardin

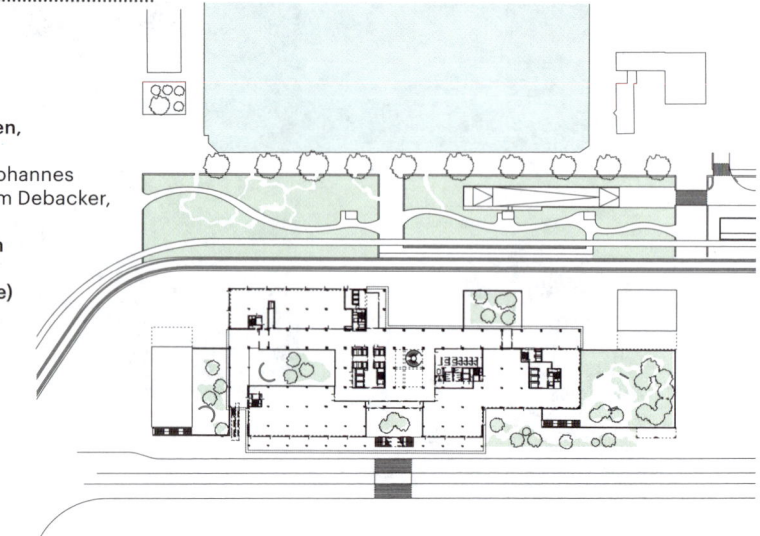

HonkHuis is a small scale collective dwelling for assisted living. It is a house for 13 residents with mental disabilities. It is designed as a contemporary corner town house, marking the entrance to a newly developed neighborhood and public park. The program is small-scale and tailored. Each resident gets their own studio. Cooking and eating are done communally. A shared seating area, garden, multi-purpose therapy room and office/conversation room completes the collective program. We developed a simple section, locating collective living rooms on the ground floor and the personal studios on the upper stories. The top floor houses the multi-use spaces.

Honkhuis - Small-Scale Assisted Living
› LEUVEN, BELGIUM
2019/2021-2023
Collective housing · 1,100m2
› **360 architecten**
Jan Mannaerts, Kris Buyse, Greet Houben, Katrijn De Jonghe
HONK vzw (user) / Resiterra (client) (Private)
© Katrijn De Jonghe

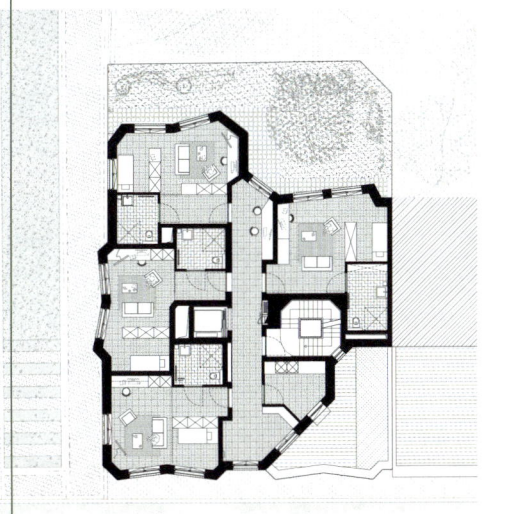

Thanks to its compact hexagonal and equilateral footprint, the volume stands alone in the landscape. Meanwhile, the undeveloped land where its placed remains as open as possible and retains its slightly sloping relief. The hexagonal footprint maintains visual connections from the public domain to the landscape beyond. The project features a wall structure comprising of self-supporting facing brick on the outside and a light timber frame on the inside, eliminating the need for insulation and offering an alternative to petroleum-based wall insulation systems.

Jtb House
› LEUVEN, BELGIUM
2019/2020-2022
Single house · 330m^2
› **BLAF architecten**
Lieven Nijs, Bart Vanden Driessche
Tine Carmeliet & Jasper Vanpaemel (Private)
© Stijn Bollaert

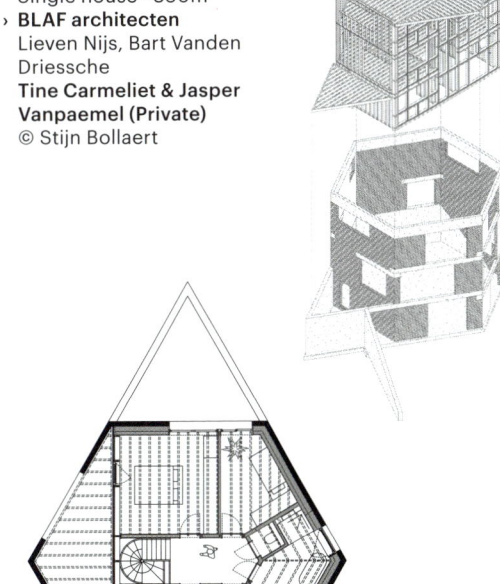

The landscape project must address several challenges: the environment, mobility, functionality and identity. The priority is ecological and hydrological. The project must ensure a strong renaturation of the site. The river sections will be retraced through the center of wet meadows, with meanders and marshes. These areas encourage biodiversity and the water cycle and regulate flow variations. The project must incorporate the crossing of a main road serving all the areas of the domain. Rather than building a bridge, the design allowed the level to be lowered as close to the water as possible, like a ford, thanks to the installation of a hydraulic structure. One and a half kilometers of footpaths have been created to explore, link and extend the site from one end to the other and beyond. Picnic tables and a play area enliven the site for the many walkers. The project creates an open field landscape, putting the infrastructure in the background and offering a kind of immersion in nature.

Before

After

Wetlands - Chevetogne

› CHEVETOGNE, BELGIUM
2017/2020-2022
Landscape · 40,000m² · 37.5€/m²
› **Atelier Paysage**
Etienne Cellier
The Province of Namur (Public)
© Maxime Vermeulen

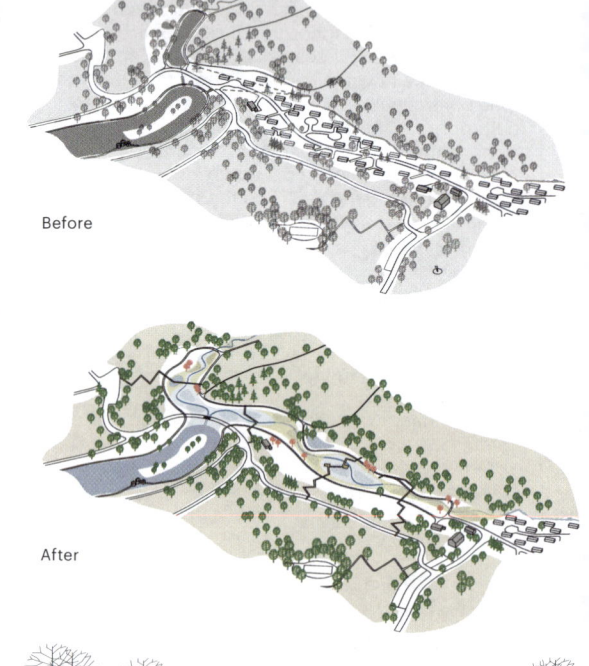

The building has a simple, rational design consisting of two rectangular volumes with a public, landscaped passageway between them with bridges and galleries giving access to the apartments. The passage connects to paths in the park and its design with plants and water elements makes it a continuation of the park. It is the central entrance and meeting place in the building. The apartments face this passage as well as the surrounding park. Most of the apartments have corner windows with expansive views of the park. The balconies are continuous and supported by a colonnade of real tree trunks. The whole forms a kind of collar that provides a comfortable distance between resident and park visitor.

Forest Bath Housing
› **EINDHOVEN, THE NETHERLANDS**
2019/2021-2022
Collective housing · 2,800m²
› **Gaaga**
Stevelink Esther, Arie Bergsma
Kikx Development (Private)
© Melchior Overdevest

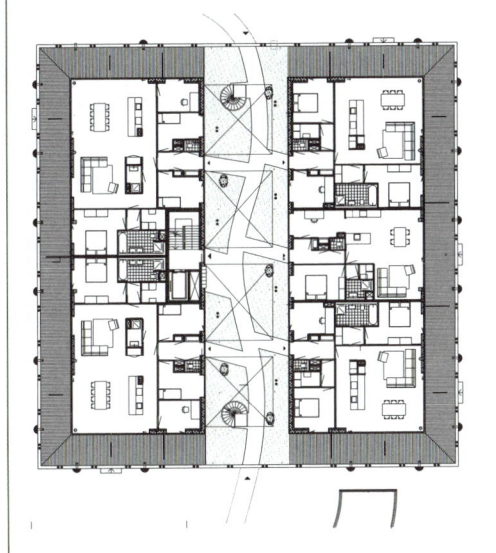

The aim of the project is to maintain a pleasant living experience by enhancing the existing architecture. The concept is a residential project based on the principles of co-living for young people whose lifestyles no longer correspond to traditional rental arrangements. Private cells are complemented by communal spaces to enhance the living environment of the residents. The strategy to achieve this was to transform the site without making external changes to the shell and without affecting the context.

Residence ARC
› **LIÈGE, BELGIUM**
2017/2019-2021
Collective housing · 5,280m²
› **Artau architectures**
Vincent Thiry, Virginie Vinamont, Roland Coulon, Jocelyne Jacobs, Morgan Delvaux, Christophe Klubert
Life (Private)
© Caroline Dethier

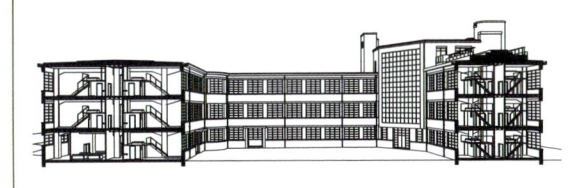

The Kreisarchiv in Viersen, Germany is a sustainable and innovative project. It is prominently located, serving as a welcoming entry point to Duelken. The building is designed to house public areas and a repository for archival materials. It was divided into separate structures for public spaces and the repository, allowing distinct designs for each function while co-existing in the same building.

New Construction of Kreisarchiv Viersen

› **VIERSEN, GERMANY**
2017/2019-2022
Education · 4,410m² · 2,494€/m²
› **DGM Architekten**
Bernd Volkenannt
Kreis Viersen (Public)
© Constantin Meyer

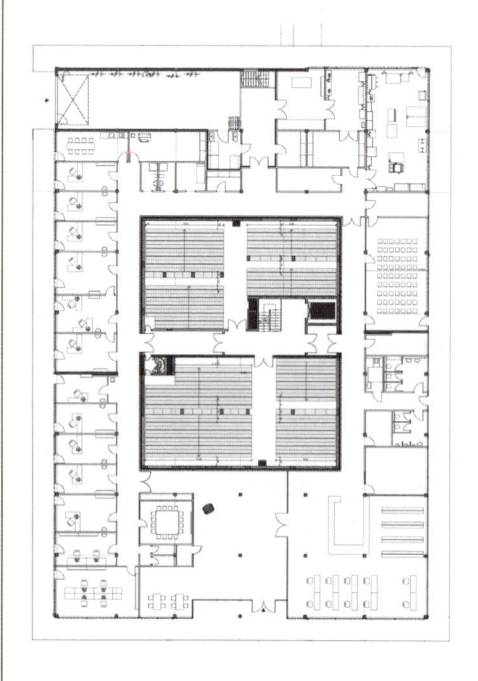

This project transformed a former textile factory site into a vibrant mix-use campus with a public park. As a result of the participatory design process, the project now successfully acts as an urban and social catalyst in a rather disadvantaged Wuppertal neighborhood. The diverse building structures need differentiated responses to requirements for energy refurbishment. In the case of the factory building, this is its new polycarbonate façade. In contrast, the industrial appearance of the older factory hall with its brick facades and the distinctive sawtooth roof was preserved. Newly added elements are always clearly distinguishable from the existing ones.

Bob Campus

› **WUPPERTAL, GERMANY**
2019/2020-2022
Mixed use - Cultural & Social · 8,100m²
› **raumwerk.architekten**
Ragnhild Klußmann, Marc Hübert
Urbane Nachbarschaft BOB gGmbH / a project of Montag Stiftung Urbane Räume gAG (Private)
© Jens Willebrandt

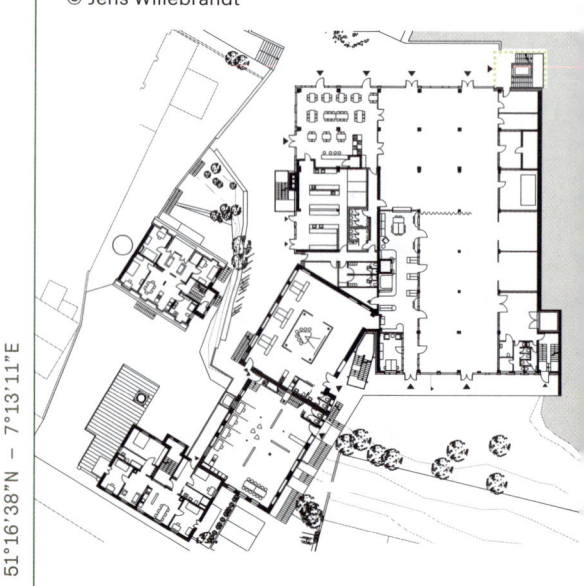

The newly added building is a creative space for students, serving as an "exhibition lab" or place to produce large-scale artworks. Positioned concentrically in the Art Academy's courtyard, Kunstraum Kassel creates various types of quality outdoor spaces. The exhibition hall can be opened to all sides, incorporating the interstices into the exhibition area. With no back side, it equally communicates to all sides and thus fully respects the original architecture. A clear inner structure facilitates the variety of uses, from a full unpartitioned hall to multiple individual spaces for work or exhibition purposes. The edifice appears as a wooden pavilion with a delicate architectural language. Its dark façade design clearly sets it apart from Posenenskes building in terms of material and color, yet it borrows its hue from the original's most striking component: the outer steel structure. The hall's visible wooden framework structure is a clear reference to the historically listed building.

Kunstraum Kassel
› KASSEL, GERMANY
2017/2020-2022
Culture · 470m²
› **Innauer Matt Architekten**
Sven Matt, Markus Innauer
University of Kassel, Department V (Public)
© Nicolas Wefers

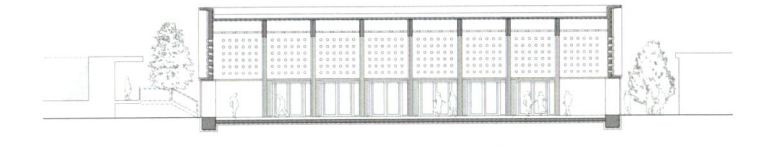

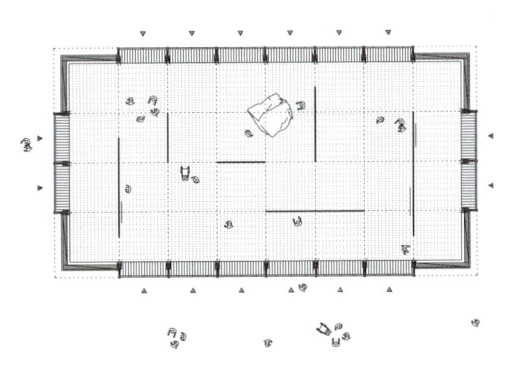

Karlsauge is a place of contemplation, communication and action where people can meet and exchange ideas about climate positive forestry. Young people from the region have come together to plant biodiverse trees in former monoculture woodlands that died due to a bark beetle plague caused by climate change. Four steles located in the center of an elliptical clearing in the forest of the park resemble a huge eye. The blocks are leftover pieces of railway sleepers usually used for heating. Instead of burning this wood and producing emissions, we decided to create an installation for the community where the CO_2 is stored for a long time. Here people can sit face to face and discuss the enormous potential of healthy woodlands to confront the effects of climate change.

Karl's Eye Pavilion
› KASSEL, GERMANY
2022/2022
Ephemeral-Society · 25m² · 100€/m²
› **Christoph Hesse Architects**
Christoph Hesse, Michela Quadrelli
documenta fifteen (Public)
© Laurian Ghinitoiu

Built in neo-Classical style during the 1930s and initially built as a technical facility, the converter station has been transformed into an art gallery with additional amenities. Our objective was to strike a balance between preserving as much of the original building as possible and bringing new life in its core. The outer structure was carefully designed to harmonize with the historical context of its location, while the internal structure represented a modern, function-driven form made of concrete. This contrast became the defining architectural feature of Kunsthalle.

Kunsthalle
› PRAGUE, CZECH REPUBLIC
2014/2018-2022
Culture · 7,605m²
› **Schindler Seko architekti**
Jan Schindler, Ludvík Seko, Zuzana Drahotová
The Pudil Family Foundtaion (Private)
© Filip Šlapal

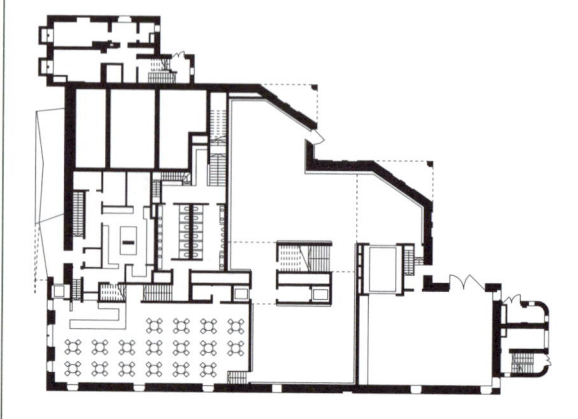

↑ 89

↑ 90

The former rectory could not accommodate all the functions, so it was decided to extend the building with an extension. The rectory is complemented by the contemporary-styled library structure. Both buildings are connected in the basement and by a bridge on the first floor. Its size, shape and location are based on the context of the château garden and the rectory. The result is a building with a narrow, compact three-story upper part and a two-story basement.

IGI Vratislavice - Library and Community Centre
› LIBEREC, CZECH REPUBLIC
2018/2020-2021
Mixed use - Cultural & Social · 1,247m²
› atakarchitekti
Jiří Janďourek, Ondřej Novák
Municipal district Liberec - Vratislavice nad Nisou (Public)
© Tomáš Souček

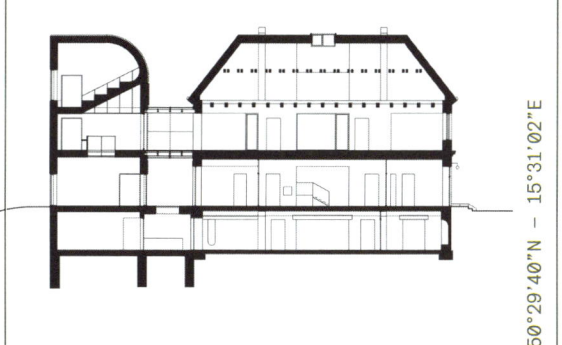

The house will undergo gradual reconstruction, at the end of which it will become a multifunctional center for institutions such as a primary art school, a children's and youth house and, last but not least, a low-threshold club for children and youth at risk of social exclusion. The softness of the project is already evident in the design of the entrance and the wide sandstone staircase between the church and the former school.

Low-Threshold Club
› NOVÁ PAKA, CZECH REPUBLIC
2016/2021-2022
Education · 305m²
› atakarchitekti
Jana Janďourková Medlíková, Jiří Janďourek
City of Nová Paka (Public)
© Upreal Vision

The chosen layout scheme is clear, does not separate the individual workplaces from each other and promotes a feeling of team work. At the same time, it provides adequate space for people waiting and preparing for meetings in the atrium area. The ground-floor spaces can be variably connected according to the needs of different events.

Lázně Bělohrad Town Hall
› **LÁZNĚ BĚLOHRAD, CZECH REPUBLIC**
2018/2021-2022
Government & Civic · 1,200m² · 2,100€/m²
› **re:architekti**
Michal Kuzemenský, David Pavlišta, Ondřej Synek, Jan Vlach, Jiří Žid, Vojtěch Ružbatský
Město Lázně Bělohrad (Public)
© Ondřej Bouška

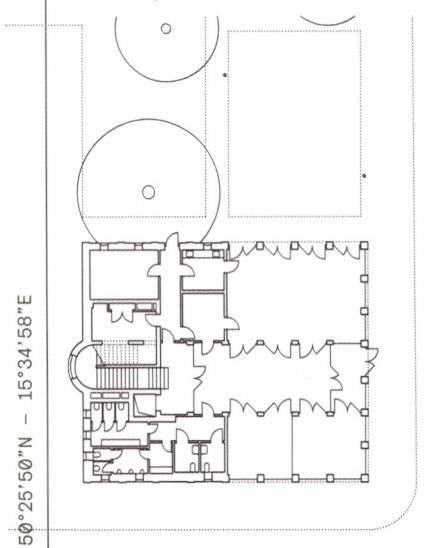

The arrangement of the adjacent external spaces of the embankment, the courtyard and the new square is important for the life of the regional art gallery. To turn the former courtyard into an urban public space, it is newly connected to the embankment by two passages on the ground floor of the gallery. The entrance hall of the gallery is located between the passages in the former mill room. The original building material was consistently preserved during construction.

Gočár's Gallery in Pardubice
› **PARDUBICE, CZECH REPUBLIC**
2017/2020-2022
Culture · 3,808m² · 4,200€/m²
› **TRANSAT architekti**
Petr Všetečka, Robert Václavík, Karel Menšík, Tereza Novotná
Pardubice Region (Public)
© Tomáš Kubelka

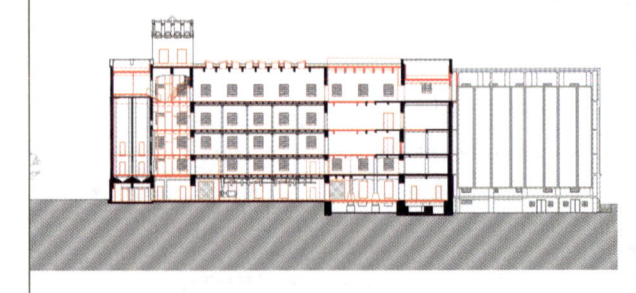

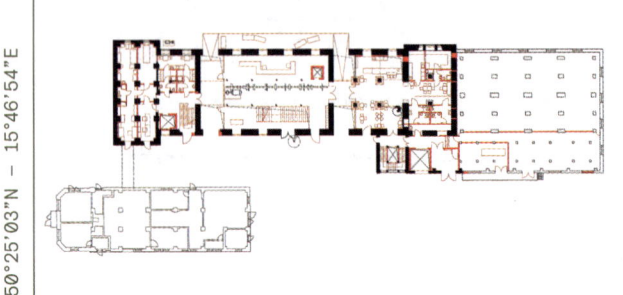

new building in the part of the plot
not at risk of sinkholes

old foundations for an
unbuilt shaft discovered
on the plot

underground tunnels
of the former mine

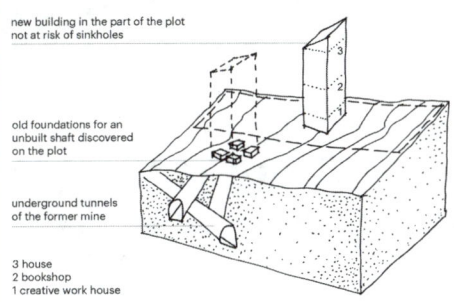

3 house
2 bookshop
1 creative work house

The project was originated in Miedzianka, a town that had sunk underground. A chaotic network of tunnels was created beneath it. Mining shafts sprouted up in between residential buildings. Therefore, all the functions of the project should be piled up in a single vertical structure referring to the form of the shafts. The project draws on this history, brings the community together and offers artistic activities.

Miedzianka Shaft

› MIEDZIANKA, POLAND
2018/2019-2022
Culture · 165m² · 790€/m²
› KWK Promes
Robert Konieczny, Michał Lisiński, Dorota Skóra, Krzysztof Kobiela, Magdalena Orzeł-Rurańska, Klaudia Księżarczyk, Magda Bykowska
Patrycja Rowicka – Masiewicz, Krzysztof Masiewicz (Private)
© Juliusz Sokołowski

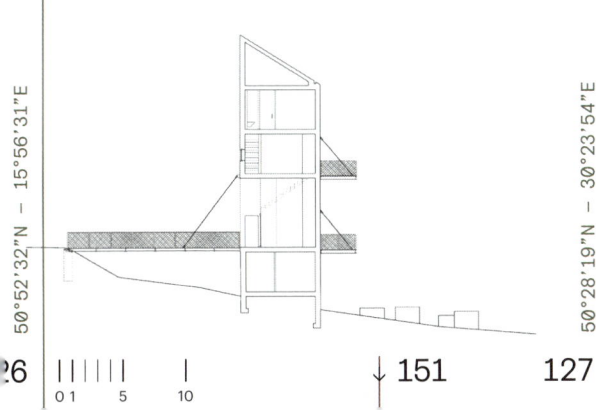

This project moves away from the usual physical layout of the blocks, streets and spaces themselves and plans the metaphysics of emotional relationships. It is important for us to build a cohesive community and create new values. Recently we were invited by the complex dwellers to participate in their charity fair as honorable members, a great honor for architects. The complex became the first to change the residence paradigm in Ukraine and changed the Ukrainian market standards a lot. We paid special attention to the rain garden. Its main practical function is to collect excess rainwater. It will reduce the load on the main sewage system while creating an attractive landscape.

Fayna Town (Stage 5)

› KYIV, UKRAINE
2020/2021-2023
Collective housing · 46,000m²
› Archimatika
Aleksandr Popov, Dmytro Vasiljev, Mykola Morozov, Samir Khuder, Varvara Bebeshko, Anna Kornilova
KAN Development (Private)
© Andrii Avdieienko

Reitarska Circle is a reconstruction of the round point of the modernist complex built in 1986, which had the primary function of a polyclinic for the Union of Writers and was located on Reitarska Street. The main strategy was to bring back the authentic exterior of the building while transforming the entire functionality and interior layout into a modern complex with several restaurants inside and a rooftop terrace arrangement.

Reitarska Circle
› **KYIV, UKRAINE**
2019/2020-2021
Food & Accommodation · 550m²
› **Emil Dervish**
Emil Dervish
Marc Raymond Wilkins, Ihor Farberov, Evgen Lavrenuk, Oleksandr Chernyavskiy, Anton Ruban (Private)
© Evgen Karev

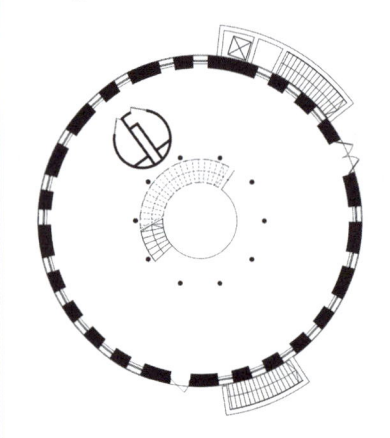

MOT (Module of Temporality) is a temporary cultural space built from 27 shipping containers that can be disassembled, transported and reassembled in less than 10 days. It houses a multimedia exhibition featuring works by 28 artists from 10 countries. MOT is an attempt to capture the fluidity of life and time in art. The goal of the project is to demonstrate that even during times of war, significant cultural projects are possible in Ukraine. With the use of container modules, symbolizing constant movement, we conveyed the idea of temporariness.

MOT (Module of Temporality)
› **KYIV, UKRAINE**
2023/2023
Ephemeral-Society · 417m²
› **balbek bureau**
Slava Balbek, Alla Vitas-Zahargevska, Anastasiia Partyka, Nata Kurylenko
don't Take Fake (Private)
© Andriy Bezuglov

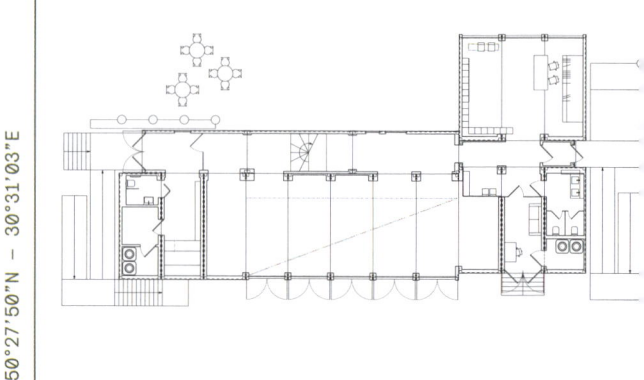

Thirteen private houses for War-Affected Ukrainian IDP Families in De-occupied Village: Fostering Integration and Self-Sufficiency. Within a mere three months, we have achieved something extraordinary: we built 13 private houses in the de-occupied village of Stary Bykiv. This construction was more than just bricks and mortar. It was also about breathing life into the village in post-war devastation, achieving this on a shoestring budget, within traditional temporary plastic module house costs, and infusing the village with fresh energy and skills.

13 Detached Family Houses for IDP

› **STARYI BYKIV, UKRAINE**
2022/2022-2023
Social Welfare · 45.6m²
› **District #1, Individual Intrepreneur Oleksandr I. Petrenko**
Andrii Kopylenko, Oleksandr Petrenko, Andrii Titarenko
Ukrainian IDPs and Nova Basan municipality (Mixed)
© Petro Malai

206

From
SAINT LANGIS-LÈS-MORTAGNE
France
48°29'53"N – 0°32'28"E

to
DNIPRO
Ukraine
48°27'36"N – 35°29'57"E

This studio building was conceived as an architectural tool for the French conceptual artist Jean-Luc Moulène. Located in the countryside, the building is composed of a series of identical volumes distributed in constant offset. Each volume has a north-facing translucent sloping façade; a north-south roof slope terminating in an opaque wall in continuity with the roof. A precise and minimal language was developed around gesture, work and creation.

The Good, the Bad and the Ugly - Artist's Studio

› **SAINT LANGIS-LÈS-MORTAGNE, FRANCE**
2019/2020-2022
Office · 363m^2 · 2,267€/m^2
› **Didier Fiuza Faustino // Mésarchitecture**
Didier Fiuza Faustino, Mazoyer Pascal, Fabre Marie-Hélène
Jean-Luc Moulène (Private)
© David Boureau

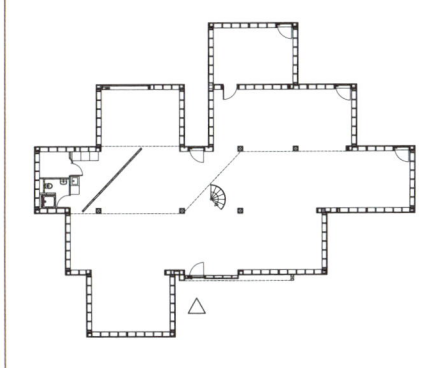

This is a global project in the center of Heudebouville that combines the creation of an expandable positive energy school (Bepos with cep<0), public facilities and the land-scaping of the town center and of the surrounding landscape. The morphology of the houses and farm buildings on the site is reinterpreted, giving rise to large contemporary *longères*. The geography of the site orders the implementation of the work, the houses inserted according to the contours of the land and respect for the natural soil.

School in Heudebouville - Normandy

› **HEUDEBOUVILLE, FRANCE**
2019/2020-2022
Education · 1,500m^2
› **HEMAA ARCHITECTES**
Pierre Martin-Saint-Etienne, Charles Hesters
City of Heudebouville (Public)
© Sergio Grazia

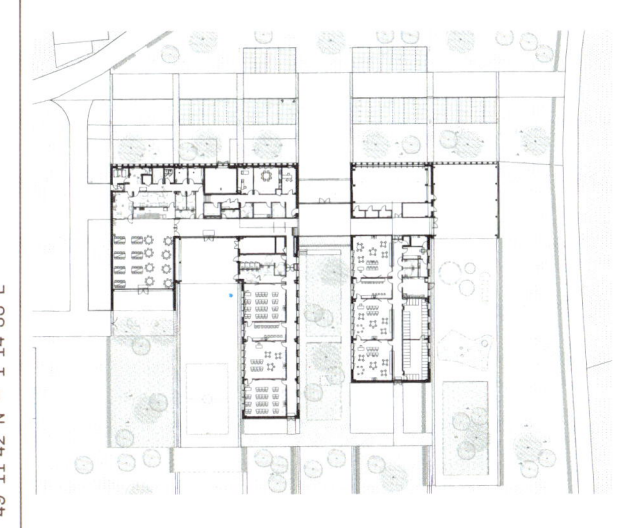

This structure is dedicated to the cultural and artistic awakening of young children. A continuous wall integrated into the natural topography of the site defines the project's perimeter. This domain is shared between a garden and a building. A gently sloping ramp leads through the garden to the building, making it accessible. The building consists of big contiguous rooms, supplemented by small ancillary rooms concealed underground from external view. The plan is divided into four equally sized partitions, each defined by the presence of significant wooden furniture that imparts a specific use-value.

Early Childhood Facilities and a Garden
› MENUCOURT, FRANCE
2018/2020-2021
Education · 451m² · 2,040€/m²
› Nicolas Simon Architectes
Nicolas Simon
Commune de Menucourt (Public)
© Arthur Crestani

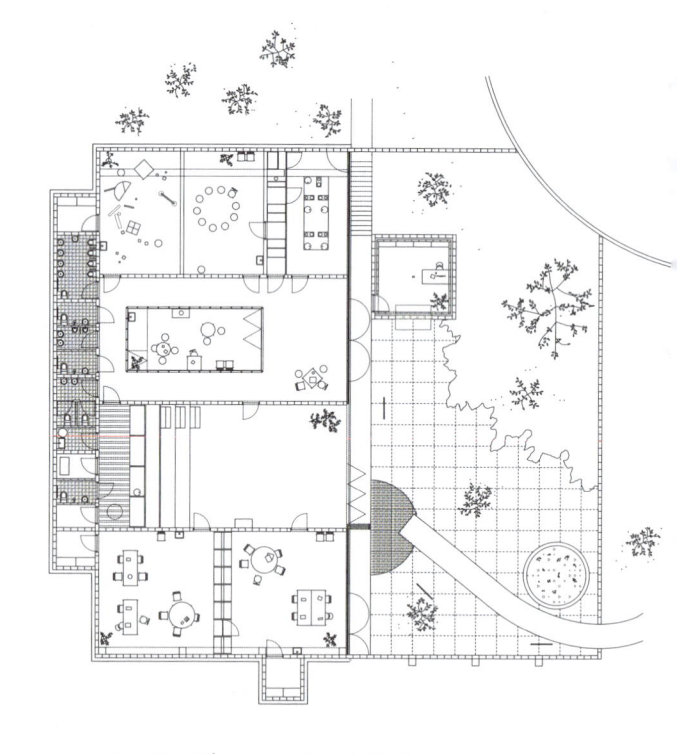

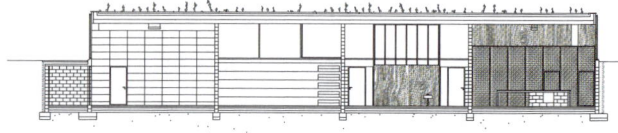

The architectural concept is one of flexibility, sharing and openness. Since this is a shared university building, the architecture is developed to encourage interactions and discussion. The Learning Center's main transparent façade, covered by an origami, breaks the limit between outside and inside to open a vast lobby as public space, invaded by nature and light. Inside, this wide atrium is inhabited by vegetation and a series of walkways and staircases creating many informal spaces for teachers, students and visitors, giving them new places to meet.

Learning Centre for Polytechnic University
› **PALAISEAU, FRANCE**
2015/2019-2023
Education · 9,142m² · 23,566,591€
› **Nicolas Laisné Architectes, DREAM, Sou Fujimoto Architects, OXO architectes**
Nicolas Laisné, Dimitri Roussel, Sou Fujimoto, Manal Rachdi
EPAURIF (Public)
© Sergio Grazia

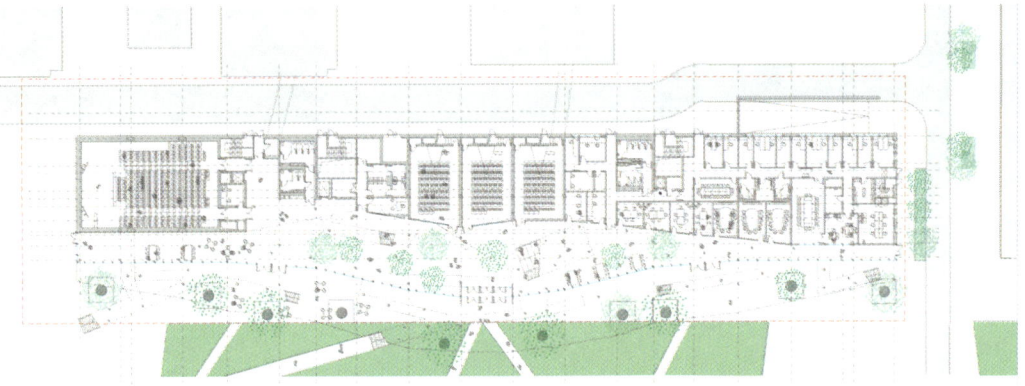

Through heavy restructuration and extension, the project results in a mixed-use building that features a commercial space on the ground floor, office spaces, social and private housing units. While considering the surrounding built environment, the project also improves the building insertion in its urban context. Part of the building also allows for program reversibility, from office space to housing and vice versa, so the spaces can comply with the different needs of each buyer.

From Offices to Housing: 112 Paris Street

› **BOULOGNE-BILLANCOURT, FRANCE**
2018/2021-2022
Mixed use - Commercial & Offices · 1,400m² · 1,860€/m²
› **La Soda**
Bernard Valentin, Latour Helene
Immocades (Private)
© Maxime Verret

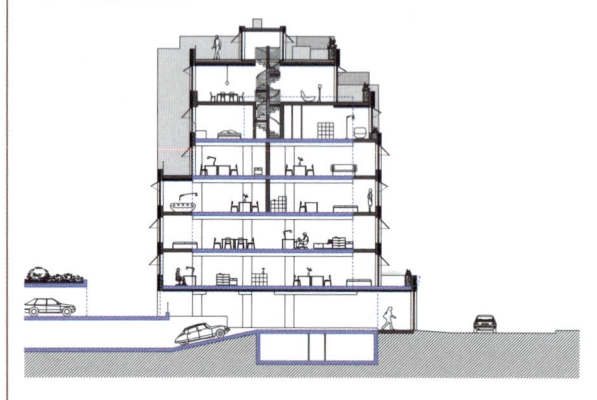

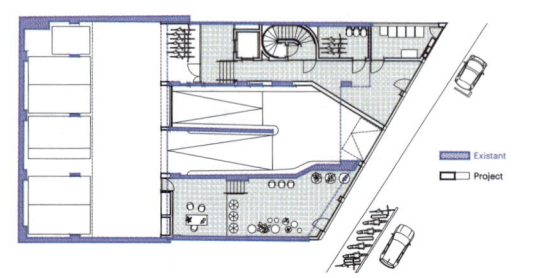

The project aimed to create an inspiring and stimulating kindergarten space to foster kids' growth and development. The building acts as a vessel for young human beings. The building acts as a vessel for young human beings. The additional structure on top of the existing house creates new living spaces and a true extension of the outdoor areas with a terrace offering 360° views.

Roof Extension for a Single-Family House

› **MALAKOFF, FRANCE**
2021/2022-2022
Single house · 215m² · 2,100€/m²
› **Forme**
Clément Maitre, Robinson Neuville
Henri Veillon (Private)
© Giaime Meloni

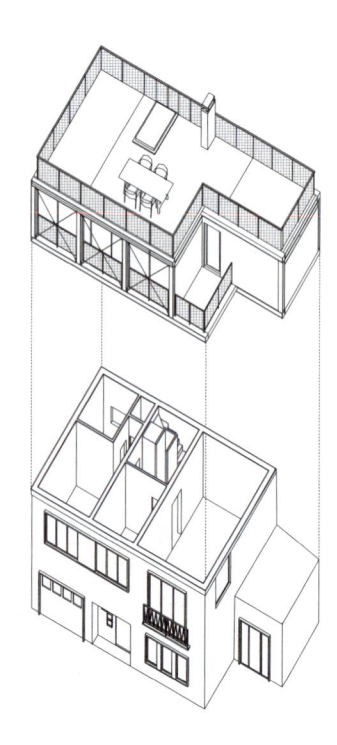

This project was carried out in the center of Alma Palace in a single longitudinal volume. This volume is stretched along the wall surrounding the garden. This inhabited thick wall became the support for the project and was open toward the garden. The site is sensitive due to its purpose and function, as a kindergarten, and provides no direct view from the public space. The notion of courtyard and introverted space is invoked.

Nursery 24-bed
› PARIS, FRANCE
2020/2021-2022
Education · 308m²
› **Atelier Régis Roudil Architectes**
Régis Roudil
Présidence de la République (Public)
© 11h45 - Florent Michel

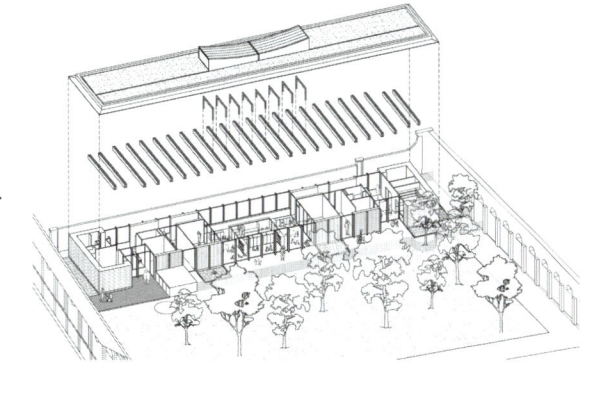

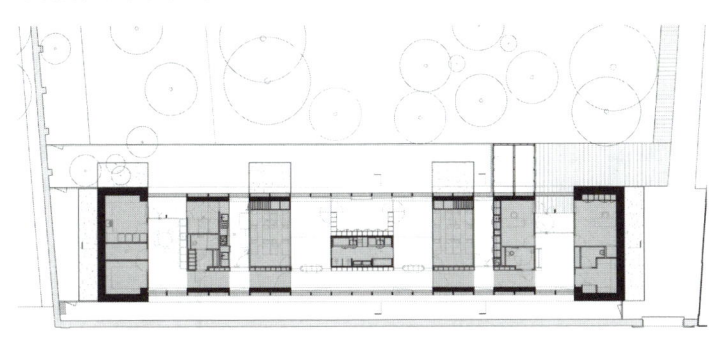

Morland Mixité Capitale is the result of a refurbishment, remodeling and extension of a former administrative building, the Préfecture de Paris. With its mixed-use program, the previously introverted complex was made accessible to the public, transforming it into a lively and open place emanating positive effects for the overall neighborhood. The approach for this project was therefore to transform the overall complex into something new by means of conversion and extension in combination with convincing architectural, programmatic and organizational ideas.

Morland Mixité Capitale
› **PARIS, FRANCE**
2015/2018-2022
Mixed use - Commercial & Offices · 63,500m²
› **David Chipperfield Architects Gesellschaft von Architekten mbH**
David Chipperfield, Felger Christoph
Société Parisienne du Nouvel Arsenal (Private)
© Simon Menges

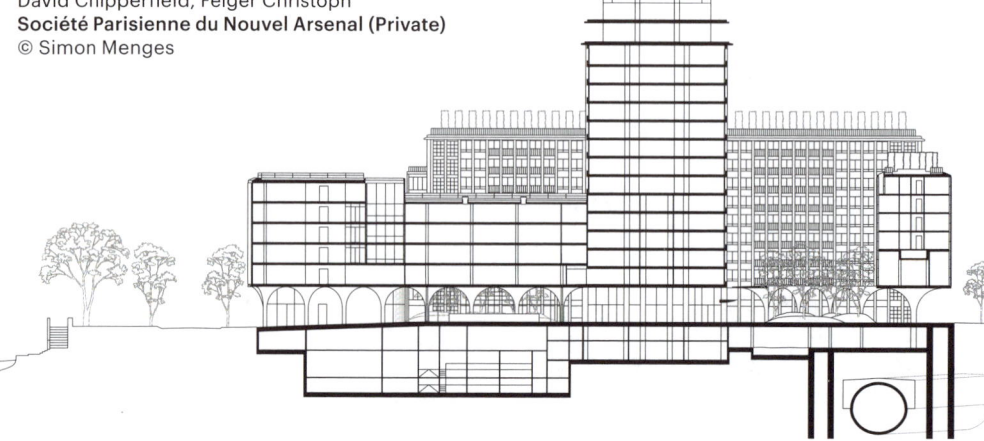

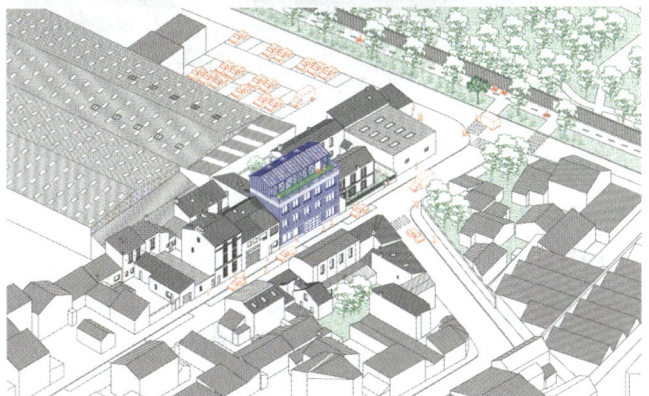

This project involves the construction of a five-unit apartment building, a shared greenhouse and the renovation of a house. Maison Commune is a built manifesto and an open process with its inhabitants. It is a small housing project that defines and highlights a sequence of shared spaces and the joy of everyday life. It provides concrete evidence and a learning tool on how we want to live together. The ratio between domestic spaces (336.7m²) and collective spaces (230.2m²) is exemplary. A sequence of shared and non-heated spaces integrates accesses on all levels.

A Common House
› **PANTIN, FRANCE**
2021/2022-2023
Collective housing · 433m² · 1,800€/m²
› **Plan Común**
Felipe De Ferrari, Nissim Haguenauer, Kim Courrèges, Sacha Discors
SCI Jack Co. (Private)
© Javier Agustín Rojas

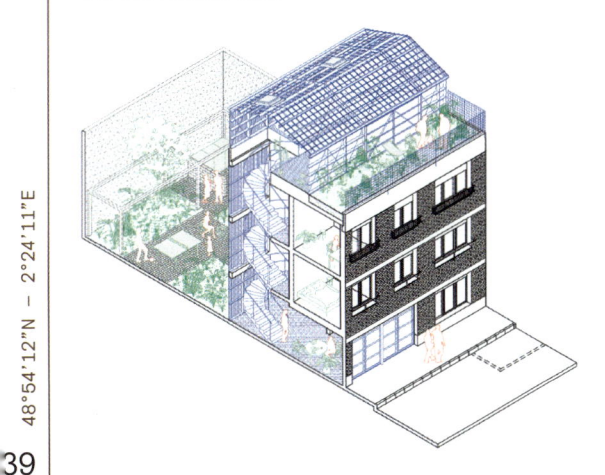

The conversion of part of a former horse stable has created a hostel for walkers and visitors to the Minett region in southern Luxembourg: a *gîte* in the village of Lasauvage. Full of character, the building exceptionally combines architecture and art, nature and community, history and the future. The *gîte* also offers a spacious common room and space for seven beds distributed in three bedrooms of different sizes. One of the main points of focus for the design was the flexible use of the building.

Lodging in Lasauvage
› **LASAUVAGE, LUXEMBOURG**
2020/2021-2022
Food & Accommodation · 170m² · 3,935€/m²
› **Anouck Pesch Architecte**
Anouck PESCH
Ville de Differdange (Public)
© Steve Troes

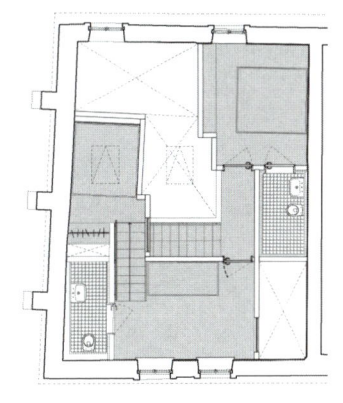

The Esch 22 Space Station is a mobile sleeping hut accommodating six people. It was designed for experiencing the various post-industrial contexts and environments of the city of Esch when it was the European Capital of Culture in 2022. In a mobile setting, the space station is reduced to a stainless steel trailer containing a bath, kitchen and dining space. Once you arrive at a destination, two wings unfold to form a ø9 meter circular platform with a cork cover on top of the trailer. On this platform, a double-shell pneumatic dome is inflated to form a generous sleeping habitat.

E22sspiu!

› **ESCH-SUR-ALZETTE, LUXEMBOURG**
  2020/2021-2023
  Food & Accommodation · 92m² · 8,150€/m²
› **2001**
  Philippe Nathan, Sergio Carvalho, Julie Lorang
  City of Esch-Alzette (Public)
  © Ludmilla Cerveny

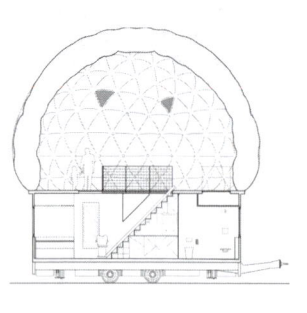

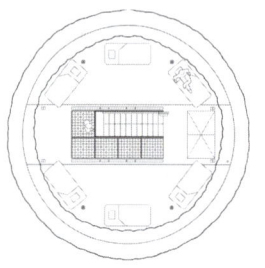

"House Gonner's transformation: Where heritage meets sustainability and artistry". The House Gonner project successfully transformed a historical building into a welcoming hub for hikers along the Minett trail by preserving its historical identity, integrating sustainable materials and creating a harmonious blend of old and new elements. The challenges of a tight deadline, complex health and economic contexts and heritage preservation were met with a strategic approach. The removal of the existing roof and partition wall allowed for the restoration of the building's remnants, preserving its historical authenticity.

Conversion of the Gonner House into a Shelter

› **RUMELANGE, LUXEMBOURG**
  2019/2021-2022
  Food & Accommodation · 74m² · 727,025.13€
› **hsa - heisbourg strotz architectes**
  Michel Heisbourg, Bob Strotz
  town of rumelange (Public)
  © Linda Blatzek

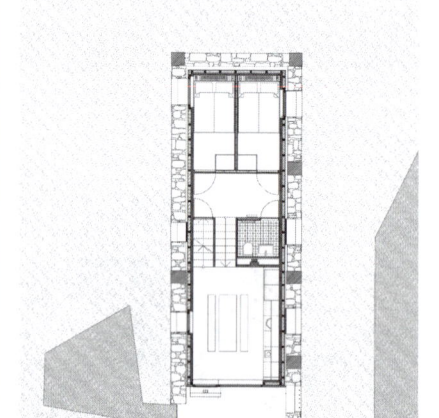

The house was built in 1929 and caused a scandal both for its architectural composition and the color of its façade. Tasked with restoring the house in autumn 2019, we embarked on an intensive search for archived documents and were able to draw up a non-exhaustive list of the architects, ideas and intentions for the transformations that the house underwent between 1937 and 1981. This enabled us to create a restoration project that incorporates contemporary needs and features. The new owners requested a single-family home that could accommodate their children and grandchildren, as well as studios for their artistic work.

"Repairing" Villa Kutter
› LUXEMBOURG, LUXEMBOURG
2020/2021-2023
Single house · 497m² · 3,300€/m²
› **DIANE HEIREND ARCHITECTES**
Diane Heirend
Dominique Cerf & Dominique Dureau
(Private)
© Eric Chenal

Jean Lamour Gymnasium is a large wooden prism lying on a concrete bed. Its wooden framework inspired by agricultural vernacular structures cross long distances, creating vast interior volumes. The building brings acoustic, thermal and visual comfort, unlike other sports facilities, and uses local material and a qualified workforce. Some criteria had to be considered during construction so the building could be more efficient: the surface of the adjacent plot, vehicle access, student access to the building and the importance of green spaces.

Jean Lamour Gymnasium
› NANCY, FRANCE
2019/2020-2023
Sport & Leisure · 1,341m²
› **Studiolada Architects**
Christophe Aubertin, Xavier Géant
Métropole du Grand Nancy
(Public)
© Olivier Mathiotte

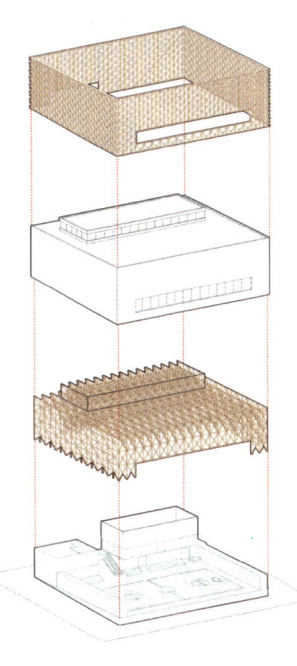

The project is a two-story high, 71-meter-long building made of wood and concrete. It was made to fit a longitudinal and inclined plot of land located between the higher street and the lower standing main building of the winery. It combines commercial and administrative spaces for the winery together with an architecture office and a private apartment. The architecture sought to coherently and elegantly combine the functions and their circulation but also to attract visitors by its own means regardless of the content. This has been achieved through the building's shape and materiality: a metal crown that covers a wooden structure and rests on a concrete table.

Domaine Claude Bentz

› **REMICH, LUXEMBOURG**
2019/2020-2022
Mixed use - Commercial & Offices · 1,500m²
› **Studio Jil Bentz**
Jil BENTZ
Claude Bentz (Private)
© Studio Jil Bentz

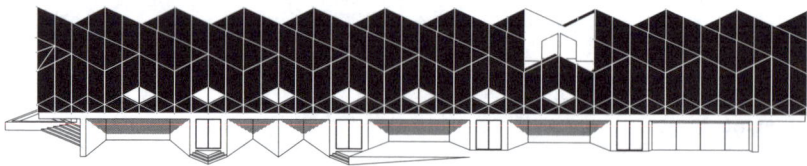

Axonometric projection

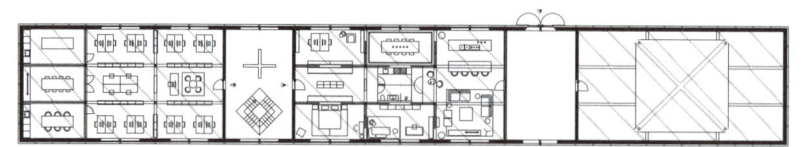

First floor

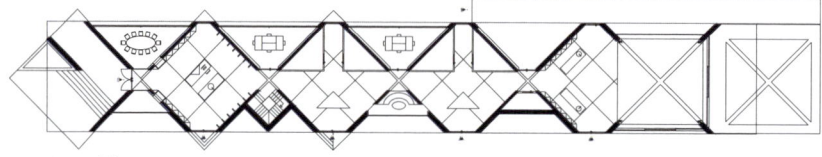

Ground floor

Three independent yet interrelated institutions: the glass museum (Musée du Verre et du cristal), the CIAV and the Cadhame (Halle verrière) are sited at varying floor levels. Our intervention unifies them to define a contemporary institutional identity in dialogue with an industrial heritage. An undulating poured-in-place concrete surface alludes to glass production as it unites the buildings. The surface functions as a roof, ceiling, and wall, connecting the buildings' ground floors to frame a public plaza. The minimal and discreet architectural input is aimed at simplifying and unifying the different programs and avoid any aesthetic conflict with the pre-existing context.

Glass Blowing and Cultural Centre of Meisenthal

› **MEISENTHAL, FRANCE**
2015/2018-2021
Culture · 7,034m²
› **FREAKS, SO-IL**
Yves Pasquet, Cyril Gauthier, Guillaume Aubry, Jing Liu, Florian Idenburg, Ilias Papageorgiou
Communauté de communes du Pays de Bitche (Public)
© Iwan Baan

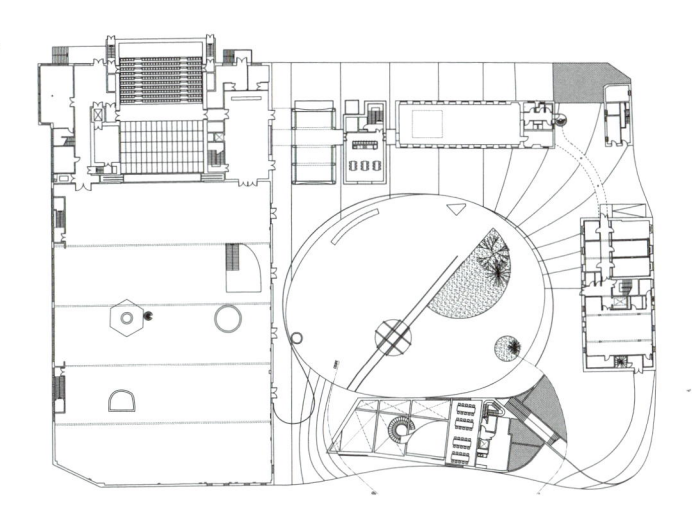

Light Rail Tunnel
Karlsruhe, Germany
2004/2010-2021

allmannwappner

Manfred Sauer (TL), Vasko Petkov (PL), Christian von Arenstorff (PL), Julia Behm (PL), Katrin Bell (PL), Christian Boland (PL), Frank Karlheim (PL), Marion Arnemann, Helge Birke, Tobias Bösl, Ivonne Eitel, Dimitra Giannikopoulou, Nicole Hansmeier, Eva Hartl, Xaver Heltai, Leila Hussein, Henrike Jahns, Eisuke Kawai, Sebastian Kordowich, Kerstin Liese-Schaich, Maria Mesa Izquierde, Marc Ottinger, Mirko Petzold, Bernine Pryor, Muslima Rafikova, Adrian Stadler, Olga Fraile Vasallo, Jakob Wolfrum, Rouven Würfel, Bertram Landwerlin

KASIG mbH

(Public)
Infrastructure

Like a common thread winding its way below ground, our new uniform design ties together the seven light rail stations in downtown Karlsruhe that have been relocated underground. The design is understated, giving a certain potency and poetry to the spaces and providing a contrast to the visual and auditory overload of the busy pedestrian area overhead.

The curvature of the station's interior is largely determined by the form of the respective civil engineering structures and the specific urban location. This gives each station a distinct character and makes them highly recognizable, in allusion to the exterior location. By practicing restraint in the formal design of the spaces, the design underscores the symbolic character of each station's structure. The concept defines two categories of space, each governed by its own design principles. In the transfer area with stairways and mezzanine floors, the design leaves the underlying structure exposed and without cladding. The waiting area at the platform level exudes a calming, almost meditative character with its uniform colour scheme and bright surfaces. The use of the same material on the ceilings, walls, and floors reduces visual noise and places the focus on the essential elements: trains, signs, and symbols. The lighting design for the new light rail tunnel was developed in collaboration with designer Ingo Maurer.

A key design element is the lighting concept designed by Ingo Maurer. As the overhead electrical lines needed to be suspended, a steel cable construction runs freely through the room. In an arrangement of three ropes next to each other and two on top of each other, the light construction - depending on the passengers' line of sight - looks like delicately arranged notes from a symphony. Integrated into it are LED lights that enliven the bus stop area through their shape and distribution and make electricity noticeable. Individual lights create coloured shadows as effect lighting. Passengers and trams are exposed as actors on the light background and atmospherically staged using the light.

The defining material on the platform level is the white cast stone installed as a panel material. This material is laid on the floor and also attached to the reinforced concrete walls via the cove. It forms the lower part of the white space shell.

The joint pattern of the cast stone elements is formed continuously from the floor covering slabs via a groove into the wall cladding. The joints in the wall cladding are not grouted but remain open for structural reasons.

The cast stone facing shell ends below the light web and the contact wire. The transition between the cast stone cladding in the lower wall area and the upper drywall cladding is formed by a shadow gap.

The elements on the walls, such as benches, display cases, line signs, and more, are positioned in relation to the panel format and their clear positioning supports the quiet, tidy character of the station The concrete stone slabs and all other surfaces in the public area have been given anti-graffiti protection.

ALLMANNWAPPNER

220

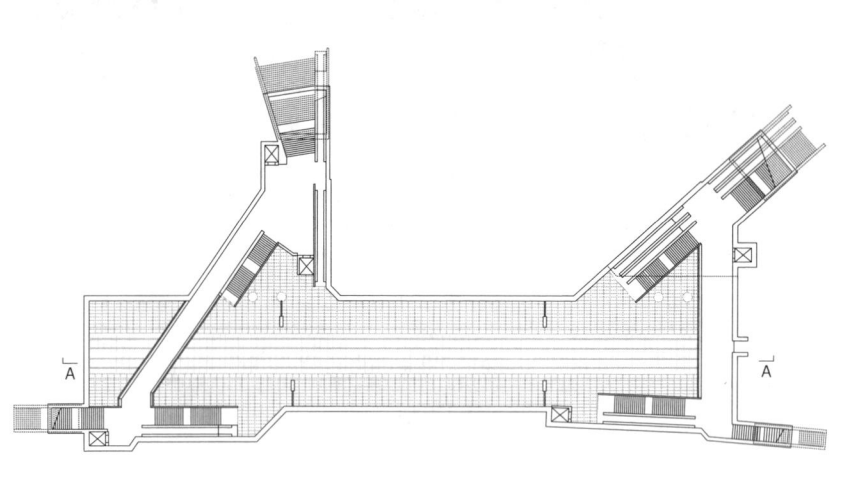

SHORTLISTED

Transfer level floor

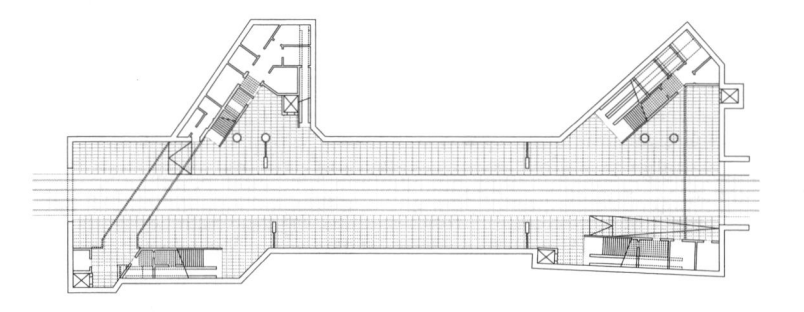

Platform level floor

LIGHT RAIL TUNNEL

0 5 10   20

Cross section

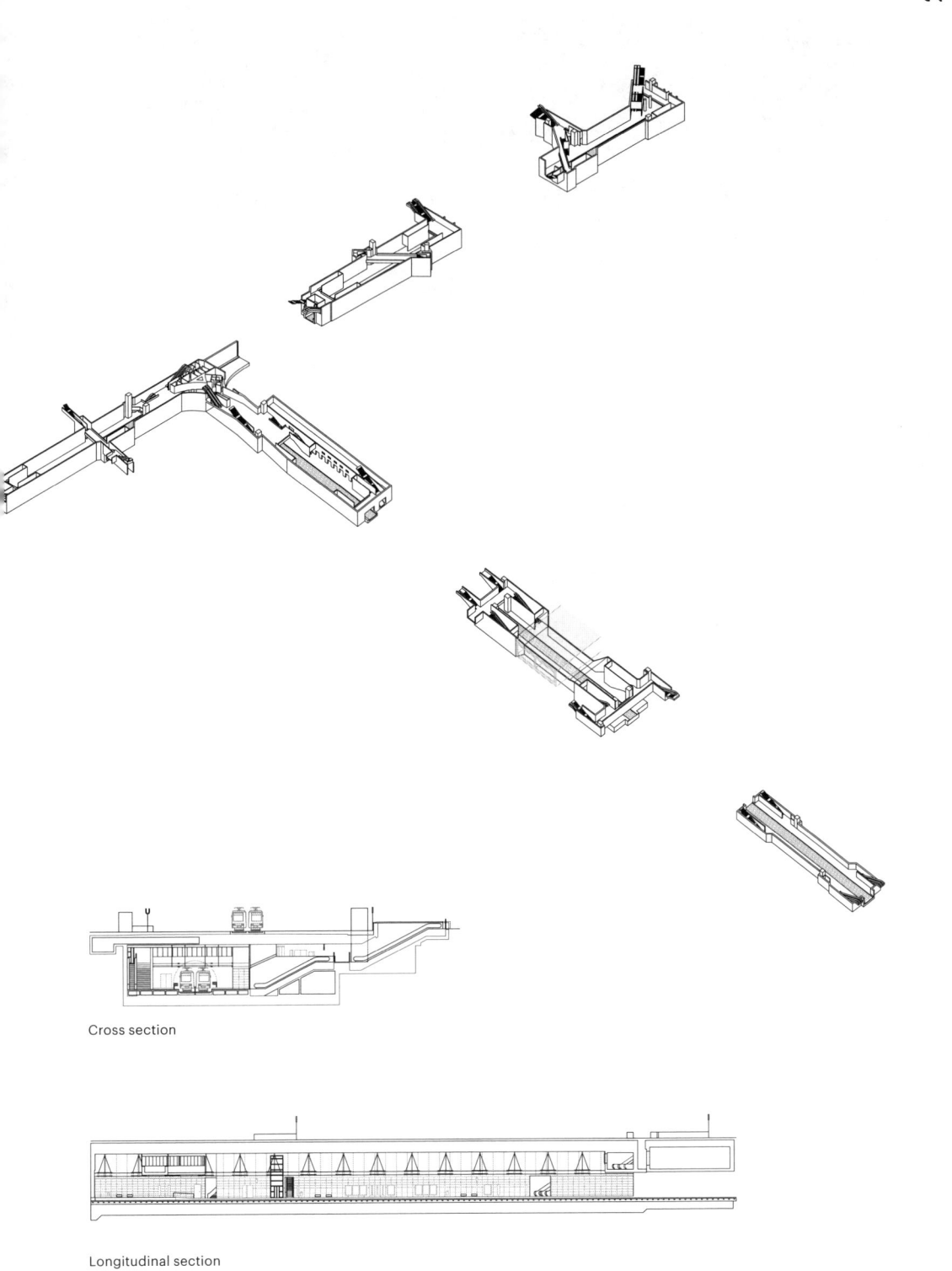

Longitudinal section

ALLMANNWAPPNER

0 5 10   20

Calwer Passage, a listed shopping arcade from 1978 and the adjacent new mixed-use building have undergone a remarkable green transformation. This has significantly improved the microclimate both inside and around the structure. Throughout the year, the lush vegetation changes with the seasons, reflecting this natural rhythm on the building's exterior. In its entirety, this green not only bestows aesthetic beauty, but also champions environmental resilience and well-being.

Calwer Passage
› STUTTGART, GERMANY
2017/2018-2022
Mixed use - Commercial & Offices · 17,500m²
› ingenhoven associates
Christoph Ingenhoven
Ferdinand Piëch Holding GmbH (Private)
© Hans Georg Esch

The studio's philosophy is to bring buildings back to life from a design point of view, but also from a functional point of view, because one cannot function without the other. Therefore, it was essential for the architects to design a multifunctional space that will be able to serve all kinds of events year-round that would enliven the building and enable its operation at the same time. The design of the new pavilion goes hand in hand with functionality, using transparent materials that invite bystanders to visit the space. It is based on the original shape of the building which consisted of three enlarging blocks.

Reconstruction of Pavilion Z
› ČESKÉ BUDĚJOVICE, CZECH REPUBLIC
2019/2019-2021
Culture · 28,500m²
› A8000
Martin Krupauer, Daniel Jeništa, Pavel Kvintus, Petr Hornát
Výstaviště České Budějovice a.s. (Public)
© Ondrej Bouska

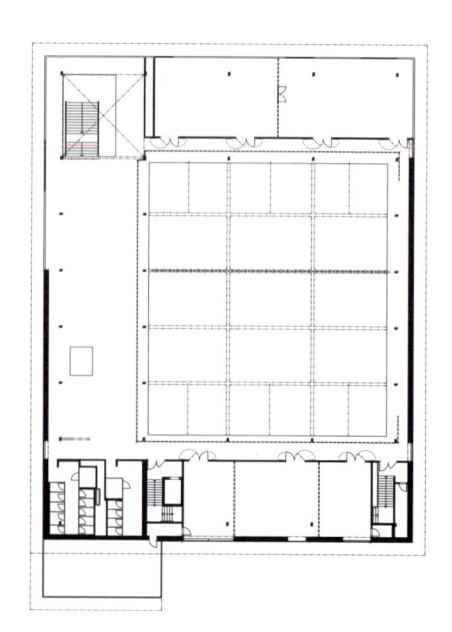

This elementary volume extending the Research Library of South Bohemia responds to the sculptural vertically structured form of the existing building, built in 1970s. The library extension is designed as a single-level pavilion floating above the ground with a fully glazed façade allowing views of the surrounding landscape. The outer skin is created by vertical revolving slats that work as a shading element while separate events take place inside and outside the building at the same time. The inner space of the deep layout of the building is lit by square roof lights located above the study spaces. The connection between both buildings is provided by a ramp of glazed tube. The passage through the park towards the Malše River opens on the side of the building.

Research Library of South Bohemia Extension

› ČESKÉ BUDĚJOVICE, CZECH REPUBLIC
2017/2019-2021
Education · 2,399m^2
› **Kuba & Pilař architekti**
Ladislav Kuba, Tomáš Pilař, Kateřina Jechová, Patrik Obr
Jihočeská vědecká knihovna v Českých Budějovicích (Public)
© BoysPlayNice

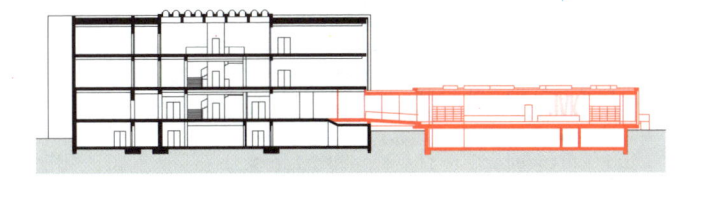

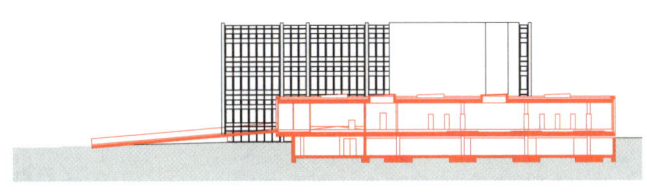

Sections

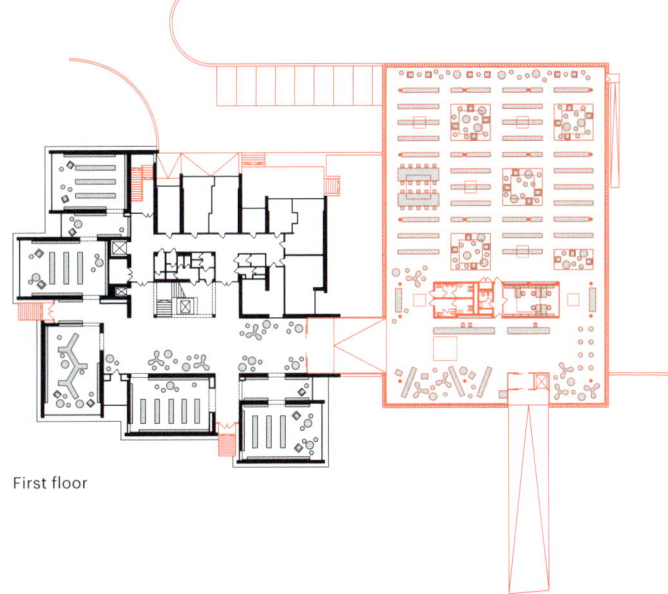

First floor

Leopoldov City Hall is a complex consisting of the original building converted into a municipal library and the new building, integrating all the required functions and the public space in between and around the two buildings. This space is also a stage where old and new stand face to face. One of the initial assumptions of the architectural concept is therefore the dialogue between the original and the new architecture. It is a public administration building that we think should be presented in a pure architectural form, thereby bringing dignity and a civilized presence. The composition is based on an elementary box shape with a simple and easily navigable internal setup, which is exposed externally through a system of regular perforations. In the internal layout, three core functions will be articulated.

City Hall Leopoldov

› **LEOPOLDOV, SLOVAKIA**
2018/2022-2022
Government & Civic · 750m²

› **zerozero**
Irakli Eristavi, Pavol Silla, Juraj Cerveny
Municipality of Leopoldov (Public)
© Matej Hakár

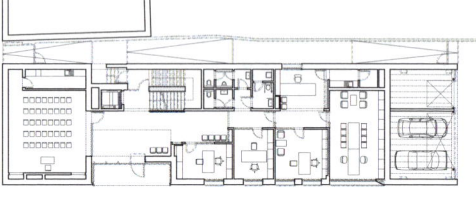

Ground floor

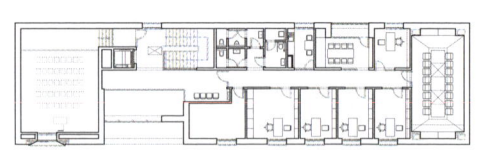

First floor

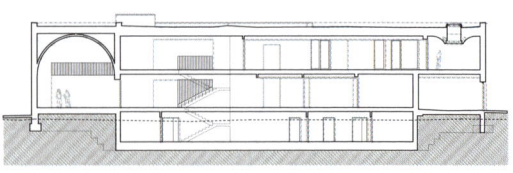

Longitudinal section

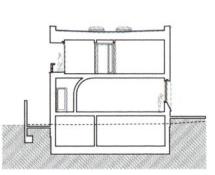

Cross section

The building is shaped like a traditional barn with a gable roof. However, a modern building is hidden in its bowels, serving the needs of a company that takes care of the forest. Imagine a world where the building materials for your house do not travel halfway across the globe and where you know the forest and the timber from which your house came. The new Klboucká lesní headquarters is a laboratory. It studies faster ways of constructing buildings and better ways of working with energy and materials to minimize their environmental impact during their manufacturing, use and disposal at the end of their life cycle.

Klboucká Lesní Company Headquarters
› BRUMOV-BYLNICE, CZECH REPUBLIC
2019/2020-2022
Office · 1,100m² · 3,650€/m²
› **Mjölk architekti**
Jan Mach, Jan Vondrák, Filip Cerha
Klboucká lesní a.s. (Private)
© BoysPlayNice

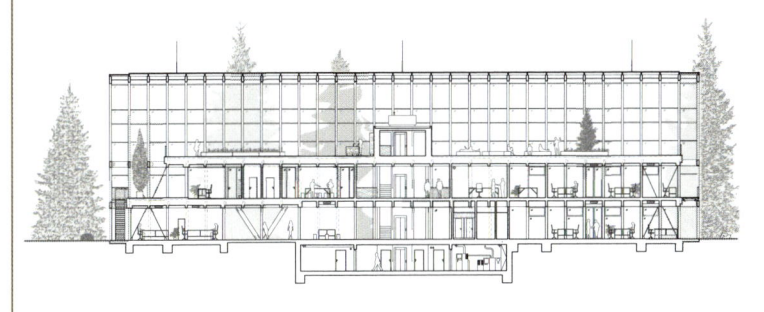

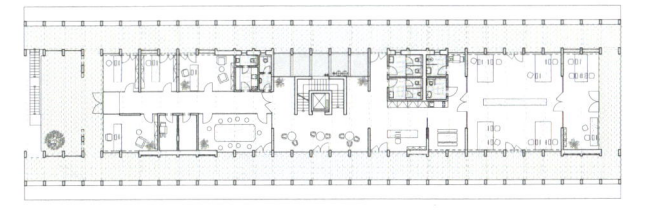

PLATO Contemporary Art Gallery
Ostrava, Czech Republic
2017/2020-2022
KWK Promes
Robert Konieczny, Michał Lisiński, Dorota Skóra, Tadeáš Goryczka, Marek Golab-Sieling, Agnieszka Wolny-Grabowska, Krzysztof Kobiela, Adrianna Wycisło, Mateusz Białek, Jakub Bilan, Wojciech Fudala, Katarzyna Kuzior, Damian Kuna, Jakub Pielecha, Magdalena Orzeł-Rurańska, Elżbieta Siwiec, Anna Szewczyk, Kinga Wojtanowska, Karol Knap

City of Ostrava
(Public)
Culture · 3,601m² · 2,610€/m²

By saving a historic building and turning it into an art gallery, we have introduced a solution that makes art more democratic. By rotating the walls in an unusual way, art extends beyond the building. We transformed the previously polluted space around the gallery into a biodiverse art park for the benefit of local residents.

The realisation is the result of an international competition to transform a dilapidated old slaughterhouse in the Czech city of Ostrava into the PLATO Gallery of Contemporary Art. The walls of the slaughterhouse were run down and battered in many places by huge holes. The soot-reddened brickwork bore witness to the city's industrial history. We took these deficiencies at face value and added another layer to the history of the building, which is under conservation protection. We were allowed to preserve the character of the soiled brick and the windows, and to fill in the openings in the walls with contemporary material while retaining the old ornamentation of the brick walls. We also used the adopted principle of recreating all non-existent elements of the building from micro-concrete to rebuild the collapsed section of the slaughterhouse.

The main idea of the project is based on maintaining the functionality of the openings as shortcuts connecting the building to the city. Hence the idea that their new infills could rotate and open the exhibition rooms directly to the outside. This has provided artists and curators with entirely new exhibition possibilities and allows art to literally 'go out' into the space around the building.

Mobility has meant that culture, in the broadest sense, has the potential to become more democratic, as well as accessible to new audiences.

We were involved not only in saving the former slaughterhouse building, but also in the design of the outdoor areas even though this was not our task. We convinced the authorities to abandon the concrete paving. The contaminated soil there was rehabilitated and replaced by a biodiverse park with water-permeable floors, flower meadows, and retention basins. The layout of the greenery refers to the location of the buildings that once supported the slaughterhouse, and edible crops, also inside the gallery, complete the transformation of the site. The result is an inclusive space that sensitises not only to art but also to environmental issues.

The building's original dominant material is brick. The destroyed bricks have been mostly replenished with those salvaged from a collapsed section of the building. The new glazing has a ceramic screen print, making it appear dark and dull, attenuating the light in the galleries. The interiors were whitewashed for hygienic purposes, so the exhibition rooms are finished with white lime plaster laid over mineral board insulation. The building's soiled brickwork appears in the former atrium, now covered. The partially collapsed wooden roofs covered with dark felt have been replaced with steel structures and covered with a light-coloured membrane. This allows the roofs to heat

KWK PROMES

up less, without creating a heat island effect around them. The colour refers to the micro-concrete from which all the new and reconstructed elements are made. The most important of these are the six revolving walls. Two are the entrances to the building, while the others connect the galleries to the outside. Despite their considerable size, they give a complete seal when closed, and the maintenance of the mechanisms hidden under the floor is simple and required only once a year.

KWK PROMES

230

FINALIST

PLATO CONTEMPORARY ART GALLERY

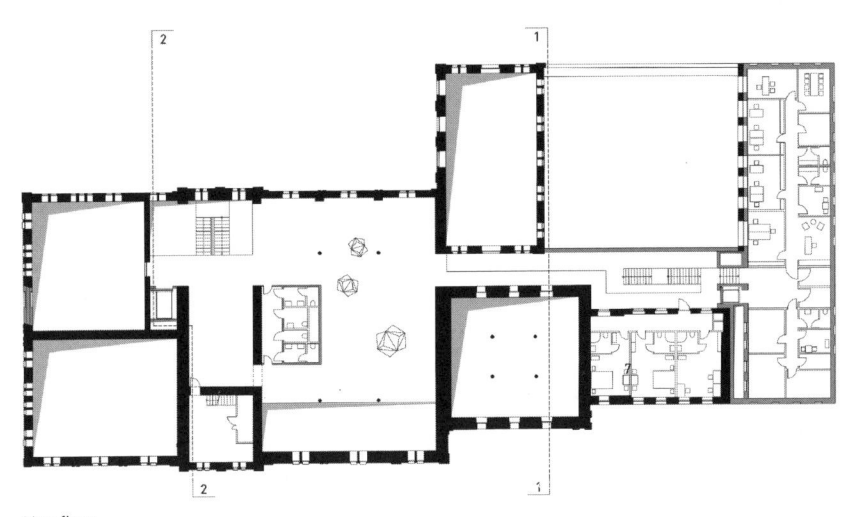

First floor

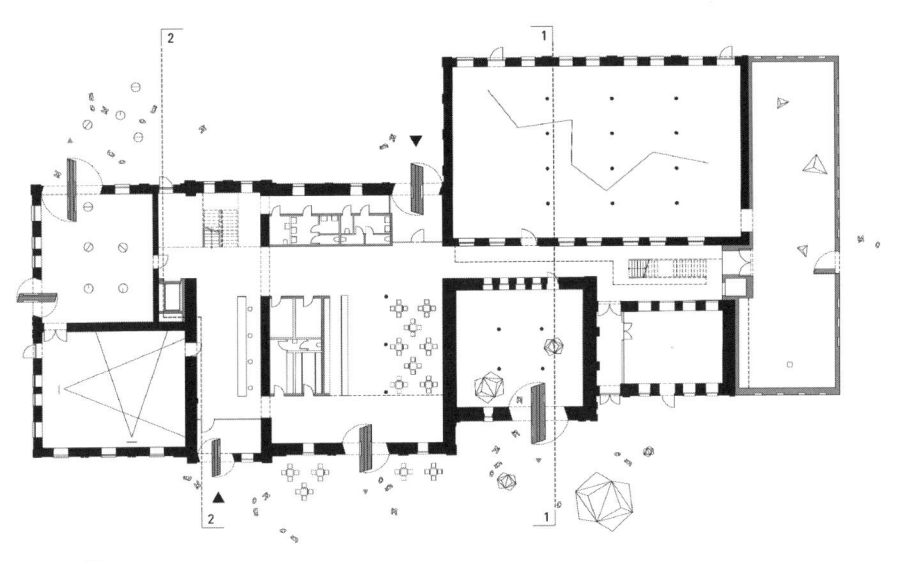

Ground floor

KWK PROMES

0   5   10   20

232

FINALIST

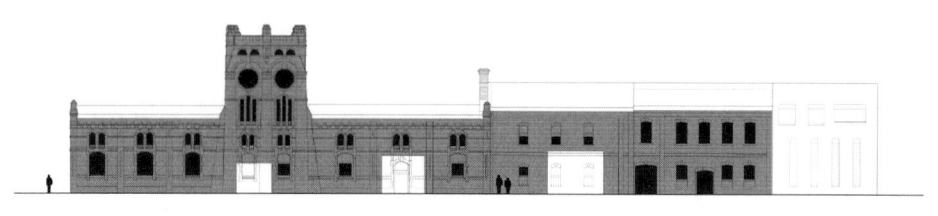

West elevation

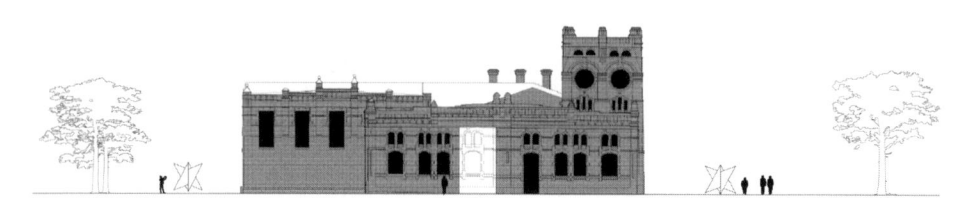

North elevation

PLATO CONTEMPORARY ART GALLERY

0 5 10   20

Section 1-1

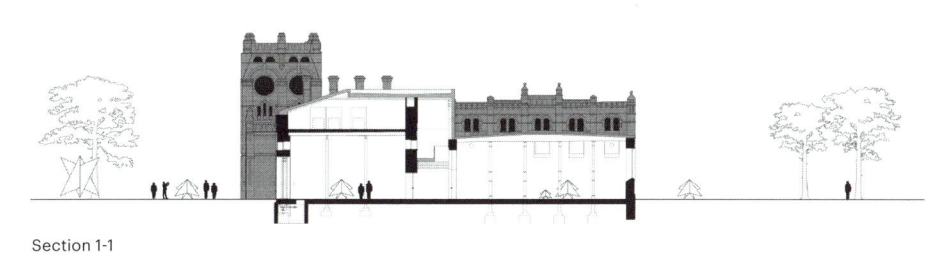

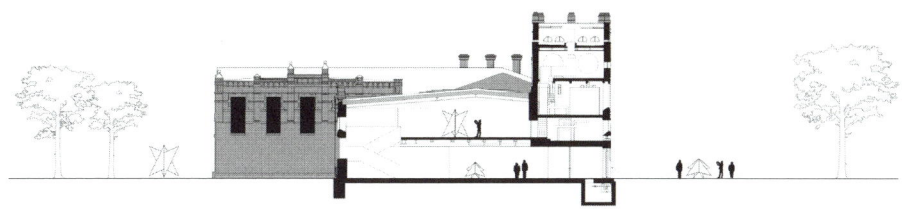

Section 2-2

KWK PROMES

PLATO CONTEMPORARY ART GALLERY

KWK PROMES

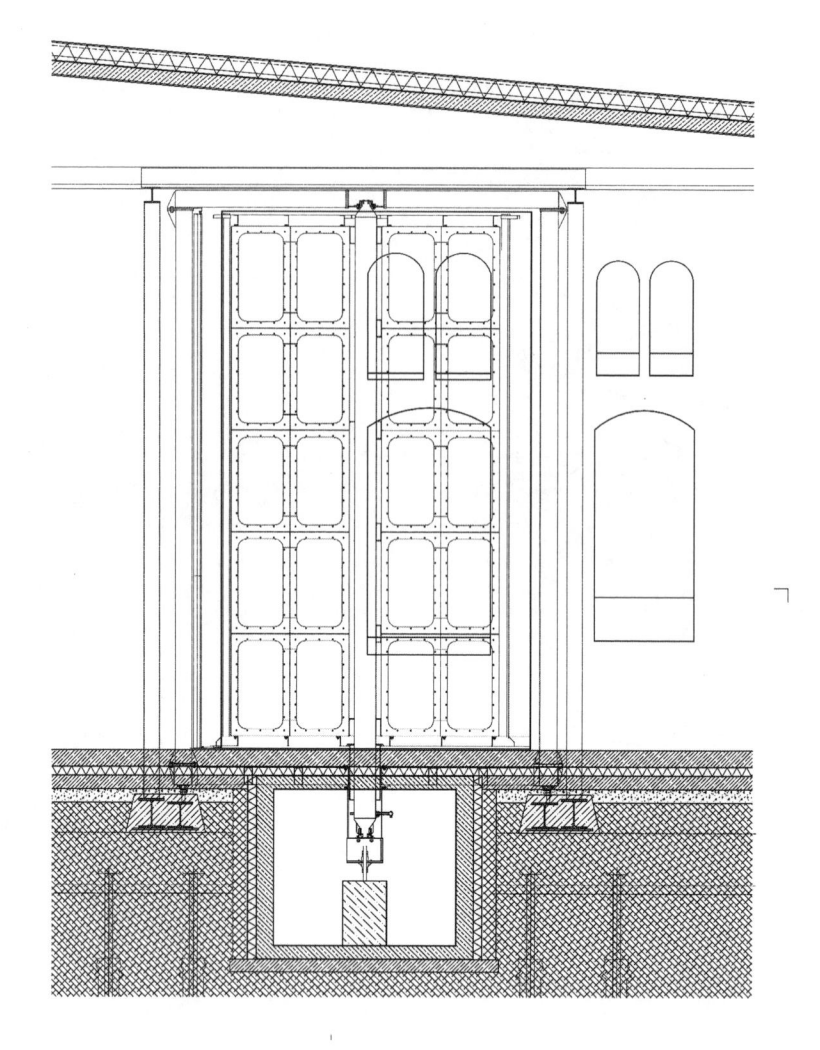

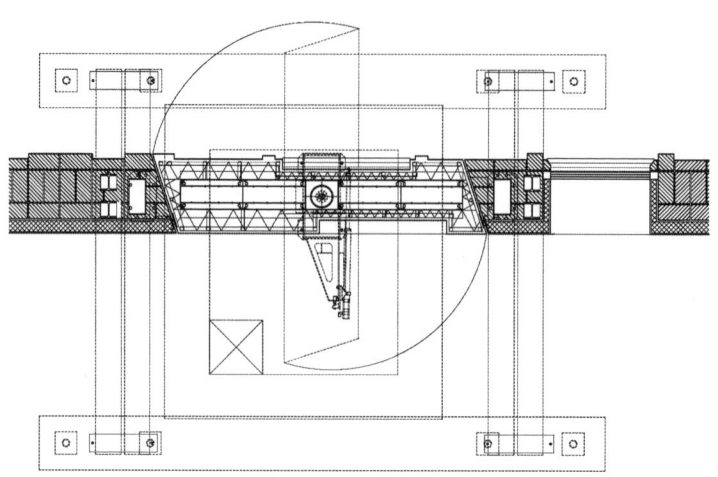

236

FINALIST

PLATO CONTEMPORARY ART GALLERY

0 0.5 1   2

KWK PROMES

FINALIST

PLATO CONTEMPORARY ART GALLERY

KWK PROMES

Plato in Ostrava is an art gallery on the crossroads of past and future
Plato Contemporary Art Gallery in Ostrava by KWK Promes is a modern rebirth celebrating a Czech building's heritage

Bartosz Haduch, Michał Haduch

NArchitekTURA

Article previously published in *Wallpaper** 3rd May 2023
https://www.wallpaper.com/architecture/plato-ostrava-kwk-promes-czech-republic

Plato Contemporary Art Gallery is the newest chapter in the redevelopment story of Ostrava, which is slowly being transformed into an extensive cultural hub. Situated in the north-eastern part of the Czech Republic, Ostrava is the country's third largest metropolis, founded in the Middle Ages, but only flourished in the 19th century thanks to its then-booming coal-mining and metallurgy sectors. Nowadays, the city has embraced an era of post-industrial transformation, launching an extensive cultural programme. This includes museum complex on its Dolní Vítkovice old industrial grounds, and a concert hall by Steven Holl Architects, currently being built, while Plato is the latest addition to be completed.

Plato Contemporary Art Gallery: a history

The new exhibition venue is located in a 19th-century former slaughterhouse. The building served its original function until the 1960s and was subsequently used as a warehouse and garage. Over the decades, the historical complex has undergone substantial architectural changes (for example, with large openings being carved out in its outer walls) and has even partially collapsed. In the 1990s, the industrial ruin was finally added to the country's protected monuments list. In 2017, the local authorities launched an international design competition for the modernisation of the complex, and Polish office KWK Promes was entrusted with the task.

Designing an icon reborn

KWK Promes founder Robert Konieczny and his team decided to expose rather than hide traces of the complex's turbulent past. The architects preserved and stabilised the remaining soot-darkened brick walls and complemented the collapsed southern wing with a new concrete volume. Consistently, six large openings in the old structure were filled in with light-grey cement panels. These are adorned with an abstract interpretation of

> "The complex successfully reconciles past and present, inside and outside, art and architecture. The reclaimed building has the potential to become a new landmark for Ostrava, catering to locals and tourists alike."

historical detailing and can be used as rotating gates. Two of them serve as entrances to the building's lobby, one as a shortcut to its café, and three as possible extension portals of the exhibition area.

The interior design follows a restrained palette in both colour (mainly shades of white and grey) and materials (comprised almost exclusively of cement, concrete and brick). Nothing feels superfluous in the space and nothing serves as an ornament. Apart from the exhibition halls, the former slaughterhouse also hosts educational spaces, guest rooms, administration offices, as well as a small hydroponic farm. Ongoing plans in the area mean the complex will soon be complemented by a small, green, sustainable park that will replace an existing large, open plaza on site.

A new landmark for Ostrava
The Plato gallery by KWK Promes constitutes a bold statement about the conservation and adaptation of industrial heritage. The complex successfully reconciles past and present, inside and outside, art and architecture. The reclaimed building has the potential to become a new landmark for Ostrava, catering to locals and tourists alike. Most importantly, though, with its partially movable walls, it will offer a flexible, playful space of unprecedented creative opportunities for artists and curators, enabling unusual interactions with the public and symbolically underlining the message that culture should be open and accessible to all.

The renovation of the late Renaissance operational building in the lower courtyard of the castle is a milestone in its further renovation. At the same time, it sets new criteria for monumental restoration in our region. The three-story building with a mixed function serves as an exhibition space with a common room and accommodation facilities for visitors, as well as people involved in further systematic renovation. Traditional building materials, classic craftsmanship and many details that seemed to be lost have brought life back to the abandoned complex.

Uhrovec Castle – Operation Building
› **UHROVSKÉ PODHRADIE, SLOVAKIA**
 2016/2018-2021
 Food & Accommodation · 165m² · 1,962€/m²
› **ō, Slovak Technical University – Faculty of Architecture and Design - Institute of History and Theory of Architecture and Restoration of Monuments**
 Martin Varga, Martin Kvitkovsky, Pavol Paulíny
 Občianske združenie Hrad Uhrovec (Public)
 © Peter Čintalan

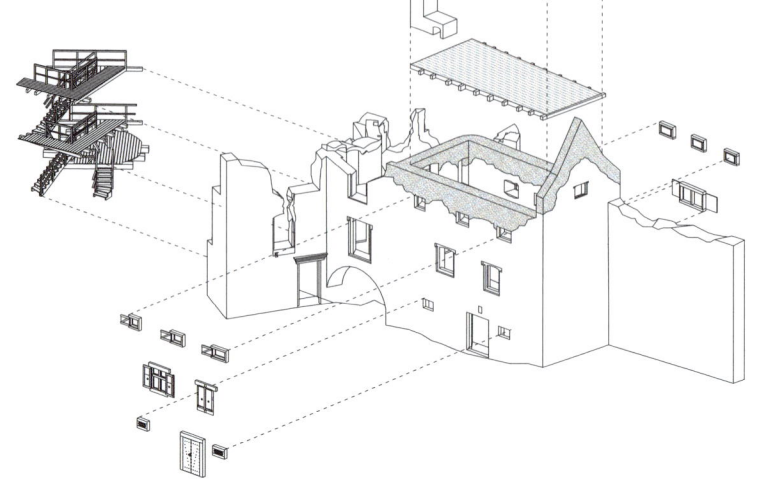

The new building is an extension of the existing music school with a concert hall. The urban design assumption of the project was to determine mutual relations and appropriate proportions between the main elements of the given building program: the concert hall, foyer and school and the created public space. A small square in front of the building is also a public space used by local residents every day. The new concert hall building reorganizes and tidies up the existing space, giving it a multi-threaded, public character. Reduction has become the main tool or even a method of design work in which financial constraints encourage thoughtful spending of public funds, redirecting them to the most important elements of the building.

Extension of the Building of the State Music School in Jastrzębie-Zdrój with a Concert Hall

› **JASTRZĘBIE ZDRÓJ, POLAND**
 2016/2018-2021
 Education · 1,695m² · 2,530€/m²
› **SLAS architekci**
 Aleksander Bednarski, Mariusz Komraus
 Państwowa Szkoła Muzyczna I i II stopnia im. prof. J. Świdra w Jastrzębiu-Zdroju (Public)
 © Jakub Certowicz

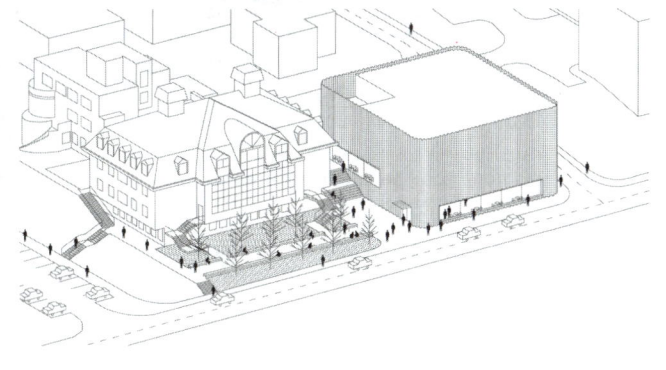

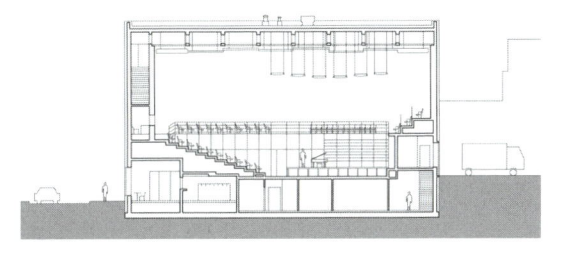

Cross section

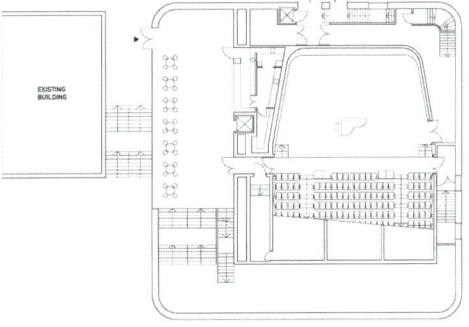

Level +1 floor

The house is three stories high, consisting of two above-ground and one underground floor, with each floor representing a formally different spatial organization. The characteristic spiral staircase connecting all three floors of the house is located outside the square floor plan of the central part of the house. Other specific elements of the villa are the western "utility" façade, forming a filter between the street and the interior, and the triangular roof marking the entrance to the house on its northern side.

Villa Bôrik
› ŽILINA, SLOVAKIA
2018/2019-2021
Single house · 315m²
› PLURAL, LABAK
Martin Jančok, Michal Janák, Zuzana Kovaľová, Ruslan Dimov, Michal Marcinov
Private
© Maxime Delvaux

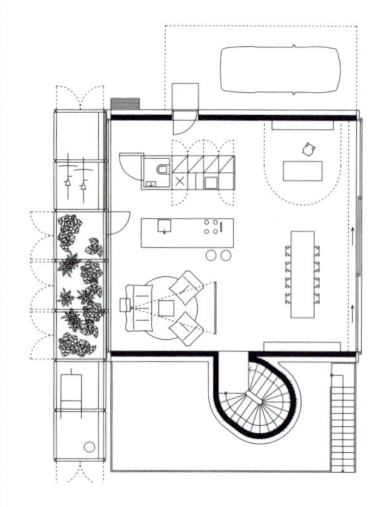

The purpose of the design was to create the shortest possible connection of the dam on the Raba River reservoir with Castle Hill while respecting the value of the location. These two aims (the first, typical for bridges, of connecting point A with point B, and the second, integrating it into a multi-element composition) reinforced each other throughout the design. As a result, a pedestrian and bicycle bridge was created, forming part of a local bike trail supplemented by pedestrian traffic and integrated into the network of existing paths.

Footbridge for Bikes and Pedestrians
› DOBCZYCE, POLAND
2014/2019-2021
Infrastructure · 180m²
› Biuro Projektów Lewicki Łatak
Kazimierz Łatak, Piotr Lewicki
Gmina Dobczyce (Public)
© Juliusz Sokołowski

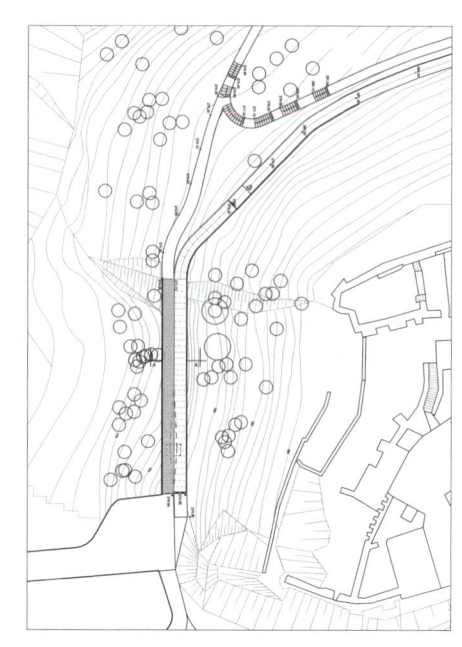

Visitors can now book overnight stays in the building and experience all its authentic features. Architects installed glass cabins and metal gangplanks for the public. The cabins are positioned so as not to impede construction work at the same time as facilitating restoration of this part of the building. The cabins provide the basic comforts of tourist accommodation together with hot showers and a kitchenette. Inside there is space for up to six people. The cabins and gangways can be removed with no damage to the building and are arranged so that the original construction and gradual repair work are fully visible and create a separate level with its own design principles.

Jelšava Cabins
› JELŠAVA, SLOVAKIA
  2019/2020-2022
  Food & Accommodation · 40m²
› **2021 Architects**
  Peter Lényi, Ondrej Marko, Marián Lucky, Lenka Borecká
  Čierne diery (Private)
  © Matej Hakár

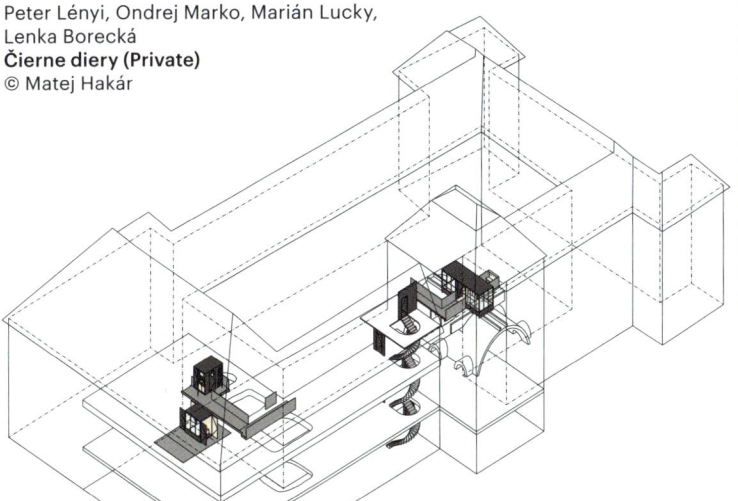

The designed house is located in a quiet area of beautiful Lviv in a block of low-rise buildings and villas and occupies a favorable place in the infrastructure system of the block. The project combines two styles that continue to shape modern world architecture. The constant combination of blank walls and glass with more traditional materials such as wood and stone is dictated by the style of Organic Architecture. The distinctive feature of the house is its openness and simplicity of forms: this is minimalism.

Dwelling House "Baltiyska Hall"
› LVIV, UKRAINE
2018/2018-2023
Collective housing · 570m² · 1,200-2,500€/m²
› SHEREMETA ARCHITECT GROUP
Mykola Sheremeta, Oles Kuzo, Ostap Halko
Volodymyr Yanchynskyy (Quantum) (Private)
© Mykola Korsun

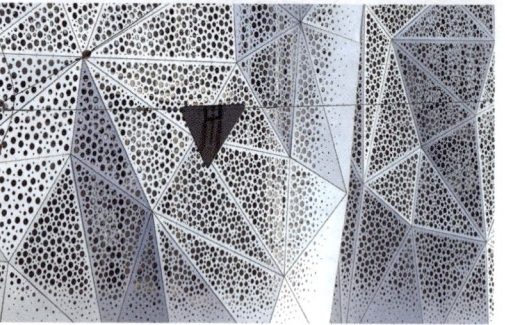

Creating a multifunctional environment is the development strategy that is recognized as successful according to the "soft city" concept. We followed the same vector when designing the object, which itself is different in filling. Although our object is also actively different from the surrounding buildings, we took care of proportionality with the surroundings so that the new volume complements the formed architectural area. When forming an architectural image, we set ourselves the goal of saving energy. Therefore, a perforated façade was used to prevent overheating, given the southern orientation.

Office Centre On 5 sq. Petrushevych
› LVIV, UKRAINE
2017/2014-2021
Office · 1,101m²
› **Andriy Asanov architecture&design studio**
Andriy Asanov, Yuriy Nazaruk, Taras Salo, Vitalii Nesterenko, Taras Andrushko, Oleksandr Davydyuk
Товариство з обмеженою відповідальністю «КОМПАНІЯ РІЕЛ-ЕСТЕЙТ ГРУП» (Private)
© Oleh Babenchuk

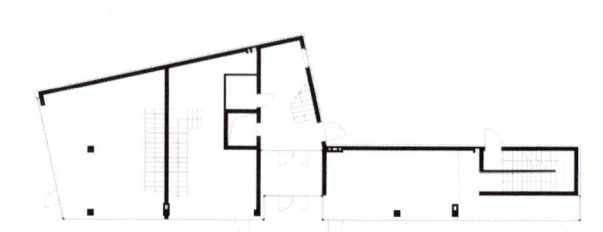

This temporary housing project for internally displaced persons aims to humanize housing for refugees. This social project rethinks the appearance of a typical temporary dwelling. Moving away from common container solutions, it shows how temporary housing can become a part of a city's urban fabric and provide a sense of home and security. Two houses, mirroring each other, are united by the common space of the courtyard. The silhouette of the building in the form of a traditional hut is subconsciously perceived as a basic image of home, especially for the children who live here.

Temporary housing for refugees "Unbroken Mothers"
› LVIV, UKRAINE
2022/2022
Social welfare · 1,300m^2
› **Sulyk Architects**
Taras Sulyk
Lviv City Council (Public)
© Galyna Kuchmanych

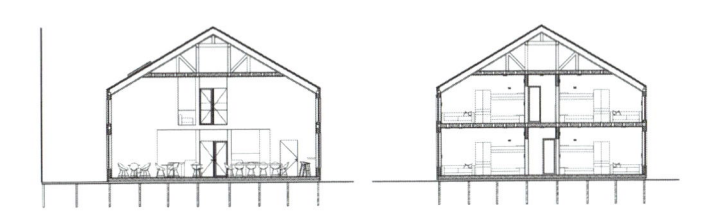

CO-HATY, an adaptation of a vacant dormitory for IDP housing, converts vacant spaces into emergency temporary accommodation for internally displaced people in western Ukraine. CO-HATY is a co-housing project for people who lost their homes due to war.

Co-haty – Pilot Project of Adaptation of a Vacant Dormitory for IDP Housing

› IVANO-FRANKIVSK, UKRAINE
2022/2022
Social Welfare · 575m² · 60€/m²
› **Urban Curators, METALAB**
Anastasiya Ponomaryova, Varvara Yagnysheva, Anna Pashynska, Tetyana Pashynska, Nasar Dnes, Maryana Baran, Bohdan Volynskyi
Ivano-Frankivsk National Technical University of Oil and Gas (Public)
↑ © Anastasiya Kubert
↗ © Anastasiya Ponomaryova

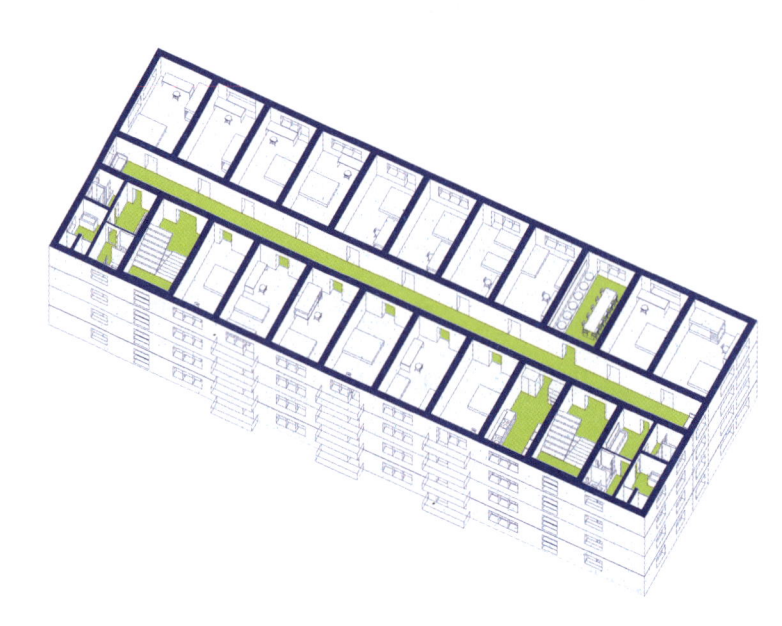

Club Town 12 is a unique residential complex that includes twelve sections of low-rise buildings within walking distance to the river. Most residential apartment buildings have four floors. Individual green recreation areas are provided for residents of apartments on the first floors and roof terraces are arranged for apartments on the upper floors.

Club Town 12

› IVANO-FRANKIVSK, UKRAINE
2018/2019-2023
Collective housing · 22,297m²
› **GaidART, Atelier Architecture+**
Volodymyr Gaidar, Yaroslav Doroshenko
VAMBUD (Private)
© Gaidar Volodymyr

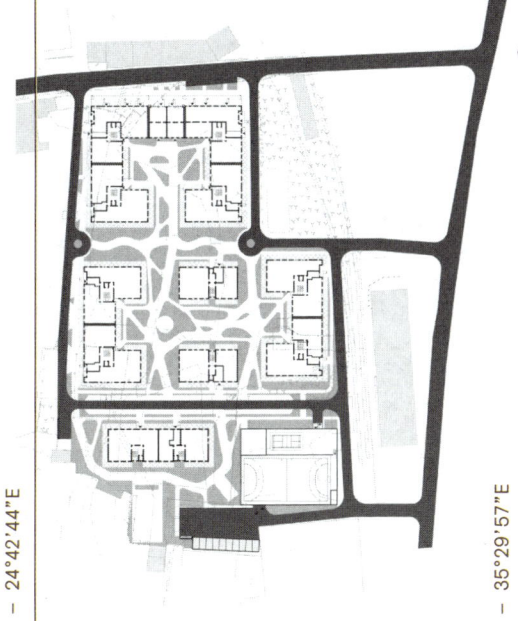

The object is unique for the city because it organizes a high-quality environment. The height of the building emphasizes the intersection of streets and its form connects the building with the surroundings. Its landscaping has an artificial stream, symbolizing the underground river. There is a sculpture of Atlas at the crossroads, taking his first step to freedom.

Katerynoslavski Residential Complex

› DNIPRO, UKRAINE
2016/2017-2021
Collective housing · 11,500m² · 750€/m²
› **Filimonov&Kashirina Architects**
Sergij Filimonov, Natalia Kashirina
Alef Estate (Private)
© Andrey Avdeenko

250

From
SAINT-MÉEN-LE-GRAND
France
48°11'19"N − 2°11'41"W

to
NOVA KAKHOVKA
Ukraine
46°45'20"N − 33°22'05"E

Refurbishment and Extension of a Community Swimming Pool

Saint-Méen-Le-Grand, France

2019/2021-2022

RAUM

Julien Perraud, Benjamin Boré, Thomas Durand

Local Community of Saint Méen Montauban

(Public)
Sport & Leisure · 3,650m²

The town's existing public swimming pool could no longer accommodate the inhabitants or meet the requirements needed by the youngest learners. The resulting project addresses both issues of restoration (a contemporary issue necessary in order to save resources) and extension in the immediate proximity of a listed cultural heritage site.

The project directly addresses the existing structure, composed of a cluster of compact wood and slate buildings. A black wooden skin offers thermal insulation for the entire project while also providing architectural continuity and legibility to this otherwise heterogenous site.

Respectful toward the existing structures while offering a certain degree of abstraction, the new indoor pool remains mostly open toward the surrounding landscape with a large solid volume floating on top.

As a gesture of goodwill toward the community, the architectural project questions how to address heritage sites by combining contemporaneity and environmental qualities and by reusing as many of the various constructions built over the years as possible.

The status of the existing buildings and the necessity to economize on resources present in contemporary architecture have imposed a position that preserves the superstructure to the greatest extent possible.

This line of thinking about construction has allowed for 3 main founding principles to emerge:
- A contemporary architecture that responds to and integrates the volumetric diversities of the existing building,
- The implementation of the structure and the insulation act to restore coherence in the public building while facilitating control over the performance of the new envelope,
- The enhancement in light of the site's topography, connecting the interior spaces to the vast landscape and its horizon.

The full renovation and extension of the public swimming pool demanded the implementation of an architecture that proliferates. Complementary elements, coherent with the heterogeneity on site, are placed in association with the existing structures. The buildings as found are looked not objectively finding the embedded volumetric qualities while seeking a transformation able to affirm, though its coherence and a certain abstraction, the distinct status of new public facility, sized to the needs of the local community.

The existing pool hall is made with concrete load-bearing walls and a traditional wooden frame.

The small extensions (administration area, paddling pool, and collective showers) are made with concrete walls and traditional wooden frames.

The extension of the sports pool hall consists of a large-span glued laminated timber frame made up of double lattice beam trusses. The bracing is provided by a series of horizontal and diagonal beams and in the plane of the trusses.

For the cladding of the façades, exterior thermal insulation is added under wooden cladding with a black saturator made for Douglas fir battens, originating in France (Breton wood).

The existing natural slate roofs are completely overhauled and cleaned. In line with the project's uniform logic, the new roofs are also covered using natural slate with a black stainless steel hook installation.

The renovated interior spaces are unified by 12.5 × 12.5 cm tiles.

The acoustic correction is treated with wood fibre panels (locker rooms, administration area, leisure pool hall, and paddling pool). The ceiling of the sports pool hall is covered with openwork wood battens and rigid rock wool slabs.

REFURBISHMENT AND EXTENSION OF A COMMUNITY SWIMMING POOL

Cross section

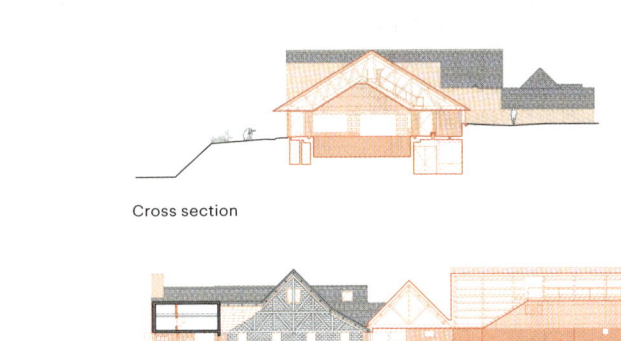

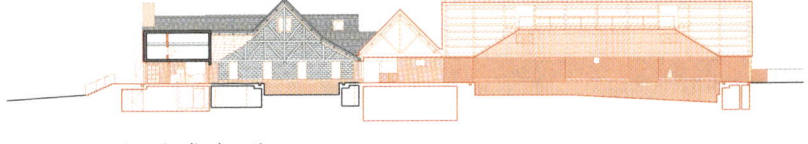

Longitudinal section

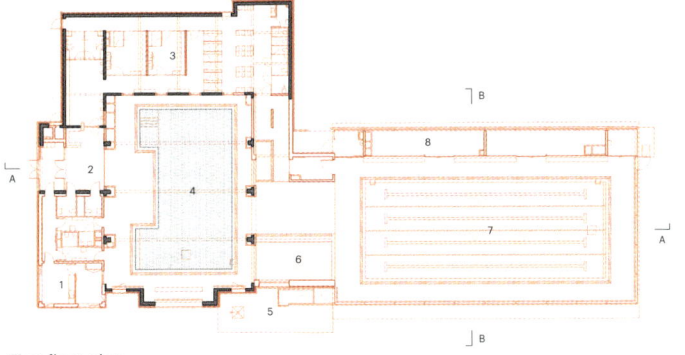

First floor plan

1 - Offices
2 - Entrance
3 - Lockers
4 - Recreation pool
5 - Solarium
6 - Children pool
7 - Sport pool
8 - Storage

254

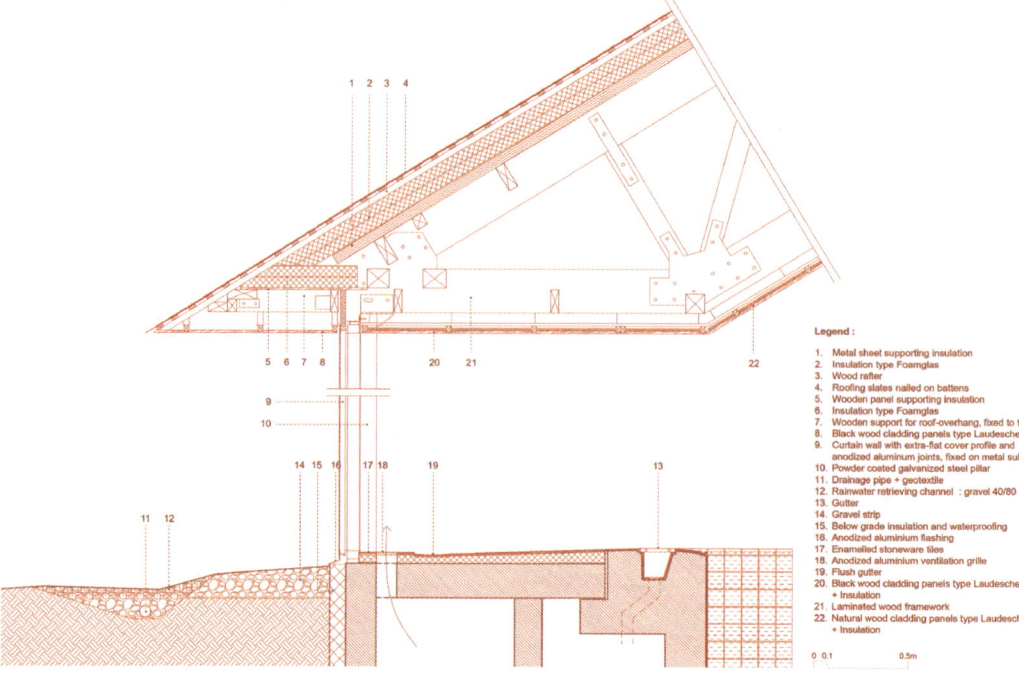

SHORTLISTED

Roof section detail

Legend:
1. Metal sheet supporting insulation
2. Insulation type Foamglas
3. Wood rafter
4. Roofing slates nailed on battens
5. Wooden panel supporting insulation
6. Insulation type Foamglas
7. Wooden support for roof-overhang, fixed to the framework
8. Black wood cladding panels type Laudescher linea P 4.2.1
9. Curtain wall with extra-flat cover profile and anodized aluminum joints, fixed on metal sub-frame
10. Powder coated galvanized steel pillar
11. Drainage pipe + geotextile
12. Rainwater retrieving channel : gravel 40/80 + grass
13. Gutter
14. Gravel strip
15. Below grade insulation and waterproofing
16. Anodized aluminium flashing
17. Enamelled stoneware tiles
18. Anodized aluminium ventilation grille
19. Flush gutter
20. Black wood cladding panels type Laudescher linea P 4.2.1 + Insulation
21. Laminated wood framework
22. Natural wood cladding panels type Laudescher linea P 4.2 + Insulation

REFURBISHMENT AND EXTENSION OF A COMMUNITY SWIMMING POOL

The southwestern area of the site was chosen as the location for the extension to preserve the existing permeability for the public. The two-story ridge structure with its generous green spaces was adopted, adapted and adjusted to current requirements. Thus, among other things, the subtle differences between the existing building and the extension become visible and perceptible in the corridor walls, the glass railings and the façade.

Extension Starnberg District Office
› STARNBERG, GERMANY
2019/2019-2021
Government & Civic · 4,530m^2
› Auer Weber Assoziierte
Landkreis Starnberg (Public)
© Aldo Amoretti

The machine hall on a scenic agricultural plot of land was to be suitable as a parking garage for agricultural equipment and as a storage facility for wood chips. The roof surfaces were covered with PV elements and the construction and façade of the building with the owner's own wood. The hall forms a simple ensemble with the existing barn, which fits into the topography and opens up to the landscape.

Machine Hall
› IRSCHENHAUSEN, GERMANY
2021/2021-2021
Industrial · 815m^2
› Florian Nagler Architekten
Florian Nagler
Andreas Wach (Private)
© Pk Odessa

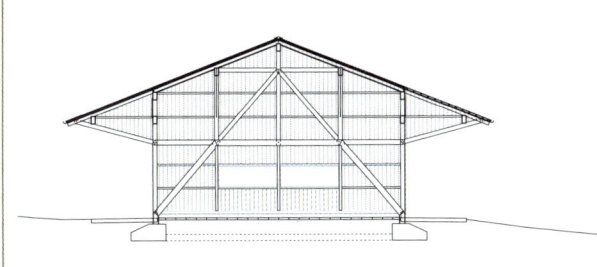

The project was intended to quickly provide further living space. It was an attempt to show that you do not have to reinvent everything in every building project and that it is possible to transfer proven principles from one project to another. In this case, we wanted to apply the "construction kit" of Dante I to Dante II as well.

The aim was to preserve as many of the existing parking spaces as possible, on which the actual residential building rests as a wooden structure. The building only touches the ground with four staircases and the attached technical and storage rooms. There is also a spacious roof terrace with play areas and sunbathing decks.

Dantebad II - Housing

› **MUNICH, GERMANY**
2020/2020-2021
Collective housing · 12,871m²
› **Florian Nagler Architekten**
Florian Nagler
GEWOFAG Holding GmbH (Public)
© Stefan Müller-Naumann

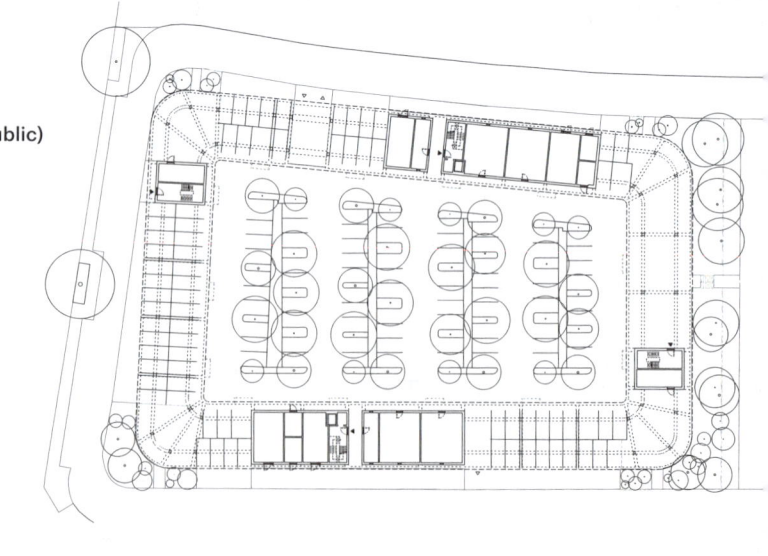

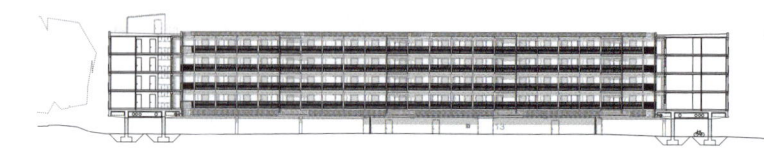

The Volkstheater forms a focal point in a new urban quarter that is being created on Munich's former slaughterhouse site and cattle yard. With its striking architecture, the new building with all its stages, foyers, workshops and restaurant lives up to the demand for representation and identification.

Munich Volkstheater
› **MUNICH, GERMANY**
2016/2018-2021
Culture · 30,134m² · 4,300€/m²
› **LRO Lederer Ragnarsdóttir Oei**
Arno Lederer, Jórunn Ragnarsdóttir, Marc Oei, Katja Pütter
Landeshauptstadt München (Public)
© Roland Halbe, Stuttgart

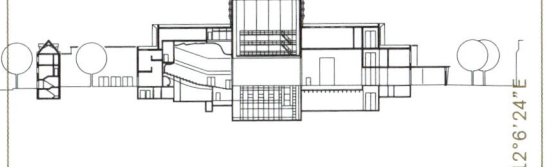

This project is aimed at creating urgently needed student housing in the immediate vicinity of the university and a mixed residential area for a wide variety of social groups that strengthens social integration. The vertical and horizontal development structure is defined by an external pathway that links the communal, greened meeting places. A new type of green and stacked village was created. The individual apartments offer differentiated private and semi-public space zones despite a minimized footprint.

Campusro
› **ROSENHEIM, GERMANY**
2019/2020-2022
Collective housing · 9,580m²
› **ACMS Architekten**
Christian Schlüter-Vorwerg, Laura Heidelauf, Jonathan Vogt
CampusRO Projektentwicklungs GmbH & Co. KG (Private)
© Sigurd Steinprinz

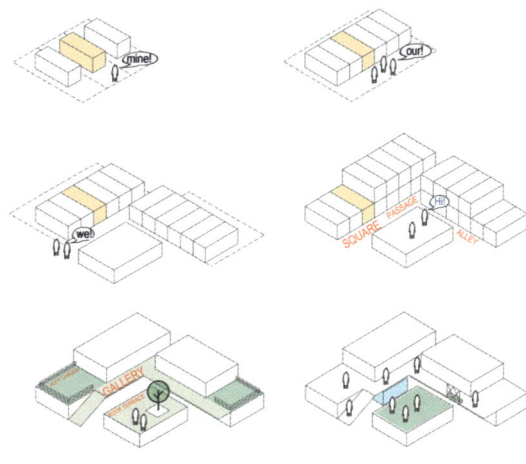

Starting with vacant warehouses, the team developed the Handelszentrum 16, a multifunctional center for commerce, production, research and culture. Contrary to common practice, the new use was not determined in advance and for all time, but developed during the process and is still flexible. For the area to come alive, the right selection and combination of tenants was essential. This diversity is key and critical to building a thriving community of people in a formerly misanthropic environment.

Possibility Space instead of Building Waste

› BERGHEIM, AUSTRIA
2017/2019-2021
Mixed use - Commercial & Offices · 61,600m²
› **smartvoll Architekten**
Christian Kircher, Philipp Buxbaum, Dimitar Gamizov, Olha Sendetska, Viola Habicher
Handelszentrum 16 Projekt GmbH (Private)
© Dimitar Gamizov/smartvoll

The essence of the new object that occupies the gap between the two existing buildings can be described as a paradox. It is a building that does not see itself as such, but as a walkable structure whose transparency forms a bridge between the massive structures it connects. From a functional point of view, there are two foyers: a city foyer on the ground floor and a second foyer on the first floor, which is assigned to the Great Hall of the concert hall and can be opened generously to both sides of the city.
Two aspects are decisive for the generosity of these two new foyers. Firstly, all service rooms could be accommodated either in newly created basement rooms or in the existing buildings, so that no facilities interfere with the spaciousness of the halls. Secondly, all technical facilities must be integrated.

New Mozarteum Foyers

› SALZBURG, AUSTRIA
2018/2020-2022
Culture · 650m²
› **maria flöckner und hermann schnöll**
Maria Flöckner, Hermann Schnöll
Internationale Stiftung Mozarteum (Private)
© Andrew Phelps

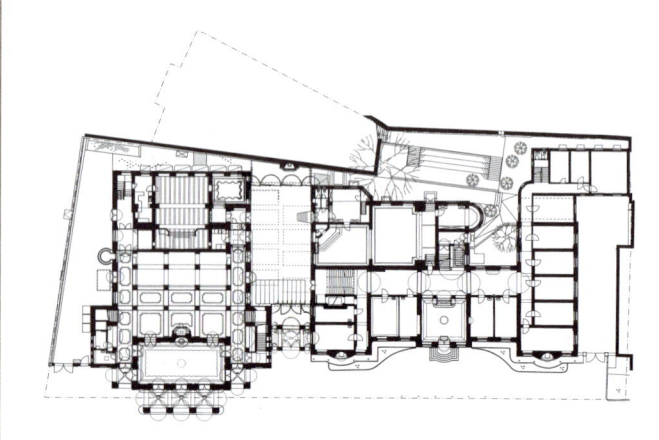

↑ 149

The mortuary is located at the threshold between the streets of the village and the humble silence of the cemetery. The space enables a dignified ambience for memorial services, using pure materials and simple, yet ingenious shapes. An intriguing roof floats over the construction and stretches over a forecourt. The wooden wall panels can be rotated on asymmetrically positioned axes to create two large openings shielded by the wooden panels.

Mortuary
› **KEMATEN AN DER KREMS, AUSTRIA**
2018/2020-2021
Funerary · 195m² · 2,500€/m²
› **Moser und Hager Architekten**
Michael Hager, Anna Moser
Gemeinde Kematen an der Krems, Verein "Aufbahungshalle Neu", Gemeinde Piberbach, Gemeinde Neuhofen (Public)
© Gregor Graf

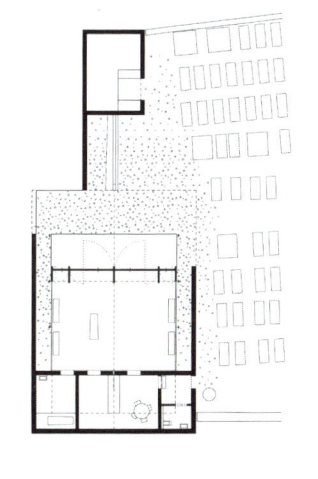

259

The Steirereck at Pogusch by PPAG architects establishes a close relationship with nature, both in the way the architecture utilizes local materials and in how it forms an enclosed human habitat that functions as a regional node in the network of food production. In addition to the farmhouse, stables, solar and biomass power plant, there is a small glass house for the production kitchen, a large glass house for overwintering plants and cabins for overnight accommodation of guests.

Steirereck at Pogusch
› **POGUSCH, AUSTRIA**
2018/2020-2022
Food & Accommodation · 3,700m²
› **PPAG architects**
Anna Popelka, Georg Poduschka
Steirereck Stadtpark GmbH (Private)
© Hertha Hurnaus

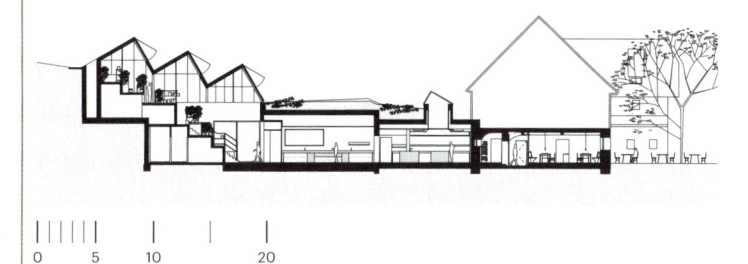

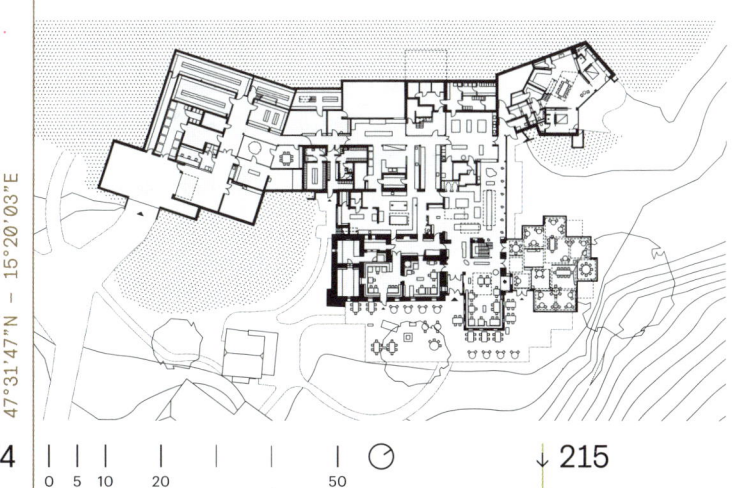

↓ 215

The KIUBO concept consists of a hybrid system that consistently separates the shell from the fitout, combines rent and ownership and offers adaptability to the individual life cycle. The main building structure is implemented using a stationary or mobile support unit in the form of a terminal. The building system is then completed with prefabricated units in the form of individual modules. These modules are connected to the building services of the terminal.

KIUBO

› **GRAZ, AUSTRIA**
2019/2020-2021
Collective housing · 2,696m²
› **Hofrichter-Ritter Architekten**
Gernot Ritter, Veronika Hofrichter-Ritter, Franz Stiegler-Hameter, Fabian Steinberger
ÖWG-Wohnbau (Public)
© Paul Ott

The challenge was to integrate the city boathouse in a spatially and ecologically sensitive way into the green bank of the Mur River in the middle of the historical old town of Graz. The building is constructed as a long, narrow structure on two levels and is placed on the edge of the street to create a public space in front. The design also permits very flexible usages and functions.

City Boathouse

› **GRAZ, AUSTRIA**
2020/2021-2023
Mixed use - Infrastructure & Urban · 240m² · 1,600,000€
› **KUESS Architektur**
Nina Maria Kuess
**Stadt Graz - Sportamt,
City of Graz - Sportamt (Public)**
© Christian Repnik

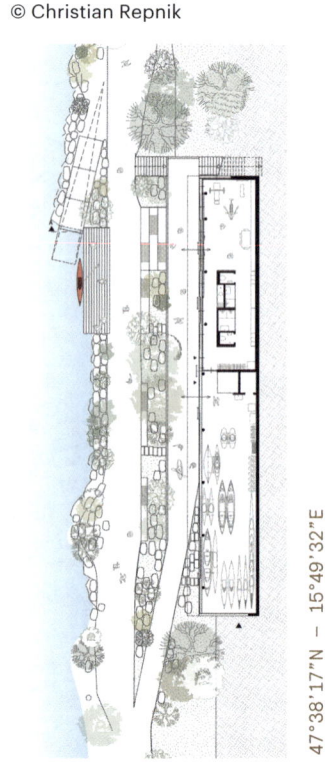

The new location at the Grand-hotel Panhans required the construction of a new concert hall within a tight four-month timeframe due to the hotel's limited space. The viewing plateau at Grand Hotel Panhans served as the new site for a temporary cultural pavilion. Addressing both scheduling constraints and the task of creating a mobile concert hall, the cultural pavilion can be disassembled and relocated in just two weeks.

Cultural Pavilion Semmering

› **SEMMERING, AUSTRIA**
2022/2022
Culture · 420m²
› **Mostlikely Architecture**
Mark Neuner, Christian Höhl
Kultur.Sommer.Semmering GmbH (Private)
© Mostlikely Architecture

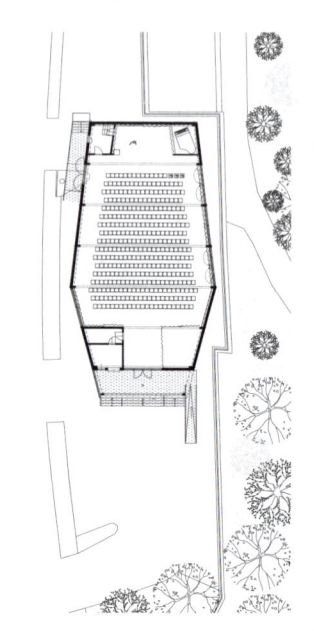

The old Locknbauer farm is situated on a scenic hilltop in southern Austria. The small building ensemble was eventually to be transformed into a winery and production site for a young winemaker. The guiding design principle was to preserve the spatial qualities and character of the existing complex. This allowed for the buildings to blend naturally into the topography and built context, in addition to making reference to the regional architectural traditions.

Locknbauer Winery
› **TIESCHEN, AUSTRIA**
2020/2020-2021
Industrial · 454m²
› **Mascha.Ritter**
Mascha Ritter
Lukas Jahn (Private)
© Simon Oberhofer

Terra Mater Factual Studios is a film production company that has made an international name for itself with nature films. The goal of the new adaptation was to accommodate the growth of the staff and to incorporate the large technical infrastructure of film production into the building at the same time. In the spirit of closeness to nature, the main goal was to meet the organization's demand for sustainability and innovation.

Terra Mater
› **VIENNA, AUSTRIA**
2019/2020-2021
Office · 350m² · 5,700€/m²
› **Berger + Parkkinen Associated Architects**
Alfred Berger, Tiina Parkkinen
Terra Mater Studios (Private)
© Hertha Hurnaus

IKEA Vienna Western Station / IKEA - The Good Neighbour in the City

Vienna, Austria

2017/2019-2021

querkraft architekten

Jakob Dunkl, Gerd Erhartt, Peter Sapp

IKEA Einrichtungenges.m.b.H.

(Private)
Mixed use - Commercial & Offices · 29,480m²

This building is an urban IKEA store with excellent connections to the public transport system, with no car park at all, just 160 trees.

The volume of the building takes a step back on all 4 sides, giving space, air, and sun to the neighbourhood. It offers an inviting rooftop terrace and a large amount of greenery on all the façades, thus cooling down its surrounding significantly.

This building makes an important contribution to the future of a liveable and ecological city and also to the future of retail. It is an urban IKEA with excellent connections to the public transport system, an inviting rooftop terrace and 160 trees on and around the building, all in all it is a good neighbour.

The external shell recalls a set of shelves. This about 4.5-metre-deep, shelf-like zone runs around the building and provides shade, allows spaces to expand, provides room for terraces and greenery, as well as for accessory elements like lifts, escape stairwells, and building services. The IKEA retail store occupies the lower floors, while the Jo&Joe Hostel with

345 beds is located on the top two floors. This mix creates a building that is alive 24 hours a day, 7 days a week.

At the briefing stage, the client already stated its aim: 'We want to be a good neighbour'.

querkraft's approach to achieving this is reflected by a building that represents an added value, also for its surroundings, in an area that was lacking social and green spaces. Now the rooftop terrace is accessible to the public and offers a place to drink coffee and enjoy the view of the city. The building also boasts a large amount of greenery on all the façades, all aspects that contribute to being 'a good neighbour'.

Openness allows interaction

The entrance level is a lively place, a generous void links it to the retail areas that stretch in front of it along Mariahilfer Straße. A void extending right through the interior of the building allows points of visual contact between the different floors.

160 trees on and around the building

The trees on the façade and on the roof have a perceptible impact on the microclimate. As the trees could be placed at different heights and depths in the building more trees could be planted than would be possible on the building's ground area. Computer simulations indicate a relevant 1.5°C temperature decrease.

External shelving

The building's external shell is an outer zone which is about 4.5 metres deep. The shelf-like zone runs around the building and provides shade, but also allows spaces to expand, provides room for terraces and greenery, as well as for accessory elements like lifts, escape stairwells, and building services. All these facilities easily connect, while the ground floors are free of any shafts.

Mixed functions through open floor plans

The reinforced prefabricated concrete columns stand on an 10 × 10-metre grid that allows flexibility when using and designing the spaces. Adaptations can be made easily in order to meet changing demands.

Centralized + efficient building services and heating/cooling systems

To ensure efficient conditioning in the building, the services are based on a simple principle: short distances and direct access. In the building the infrastructure is left visible, which increases the perceived height of the space. The structure is heated and cooled by component activation via district heating system. There are 490.5 m^2 photovoltaic panels on the rooftop terrace with the ability to generate up to 87 kWp.

QUERKRAFT ARCHITEKTEN

264

SHORTLISTED

IKEA VIENNA WESTERN STATION / IKEA - THE GOOD NEIGHBOUR IN THE CITY

Retail floor plan

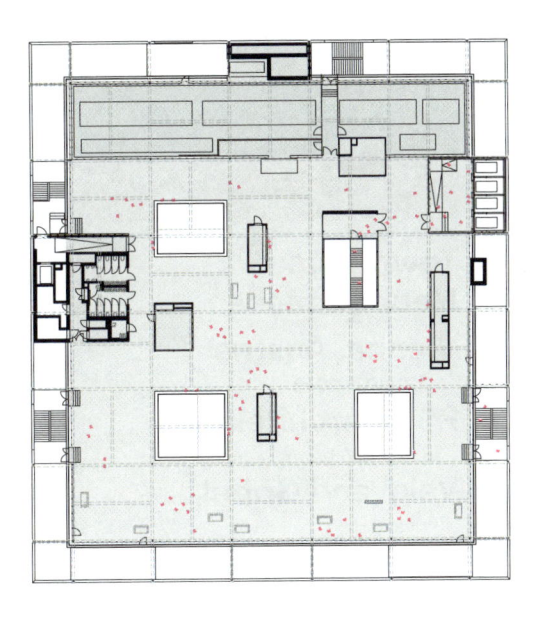

Rooftop plan

QUERKRAFT ARCHITEKTEN

0 5 10   20

Townhouse Neubaugasse
Vienna, Austria
2020/2021-2022
PSLA Architekten
Ali Seghatoleslami, Lilli Pschill
Veigl and Göbel
(Private)
Single house · 172m²

Urban land, as a limited quantitative resource, must be efficiently re-used through qualitative densification. The project offers a fundamental reconfiguration of architectural typologies, incorporating the unbuilt as an integral part of the built structure, resulting in a critical articulation of the entire arsenal of architectural elements.

This townhouse-project was conceived as a hybrid genesis between house and garden and is situated in a narrow courtyard in Vienna's historic 7th district. The building is 4.6m wide and 24m long and is an extension to a 150-year-old house. It is divided into a grid with 20 square fields whose spatial manipulation into sections results in a myriad of windows, spatial intersections, and terraces, offering daylight and panoramic views. The 165-m² building boasts 11 levels, and 16 varying heights for its rooms. The entire built area of the house consists of cascading roofs and terraces that are interconnected by a series of single-flight steel stairs ascending from the garden, resembling airplane steps. The landscaped roofs feature trees, water-retaining plants, lawns, and vertical green spaces, contributing to a cooling effect on the microclimate of the house and courtyard.

The project Is situated along a south-facing fire wall 11 m in height and over 60m in length within a courtyard which is 70m away from the Neubaugasse. The courtyard, as a small-scale oasis, had a major influence on the project's conceptual genesis. Hence more than one-third of the permissible building volume is not built in order to ensure a harmonious built structure and an effective incorporation of the green spaces within the courtyard. Due to the building's narrow width the section takes on the organizational function of the floor plan.

Functions are no longer defined by clear boundaries such as doors and interior walls but are intertwined as an open spatial continuum. None of the 9 cross-sections representing the 18 building's axes are alike, providing the house with multi-sided orientation and internal spatial interaction across floors.

The old asphalt surface in the courtyard was removed and replaced with permeable paving and infiltration trenches. More than a third of the building's primary energy demand is renewably produced on site.

Every structural element is reduced to its smallest dimensions in order to minimize resources. To maximize the usable space a hybrid construction method was employed. The building consists of hollow-core bricks and reinforced concrete slabs for the walls which are 15cm thick, the minimum amount permissible based on the structure, and while the ceiling thickness varies from 18cm to 20cm. The windows and openings in the concrete slabs are arranged in a staggered chessboard pattern creating a structurally three-dimensional monolithic construction.

The building's structural framework reflects the project's final state eliminating the need for additional cladding or interior support structures. Half of the wall surfaces are exposed concrete, while the brick walls are finished with moisture-regulating plaster.

Glass elements on the south-facing façade have been flush-mounted as fixed elements in the outermost layer of the façade thereby gaining interior space.

Thanks to the retention roof structure and the intensively landscaped terraces there is no cooling installed. Rainwater is now directed into and used by the garden rather than directly into the city´s sewer system.

PSLA ARCHITEKTEN

+9.30 m

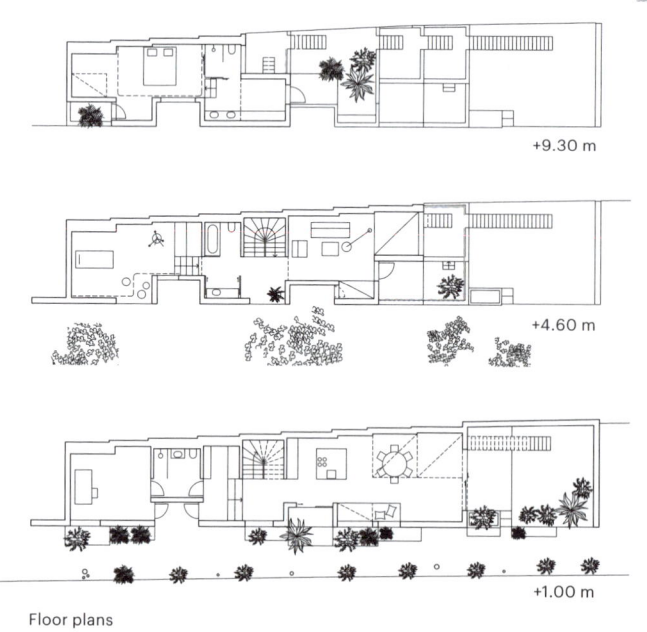

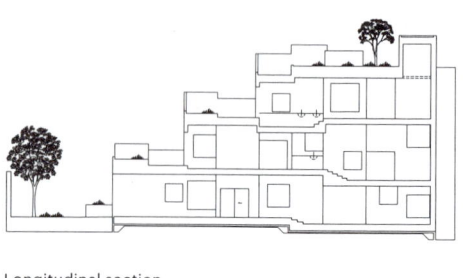

+4.60 m

+1.00 m

Floor plans

Longitudinal section

TOWNHOUSE NEUBAUGASSE

269

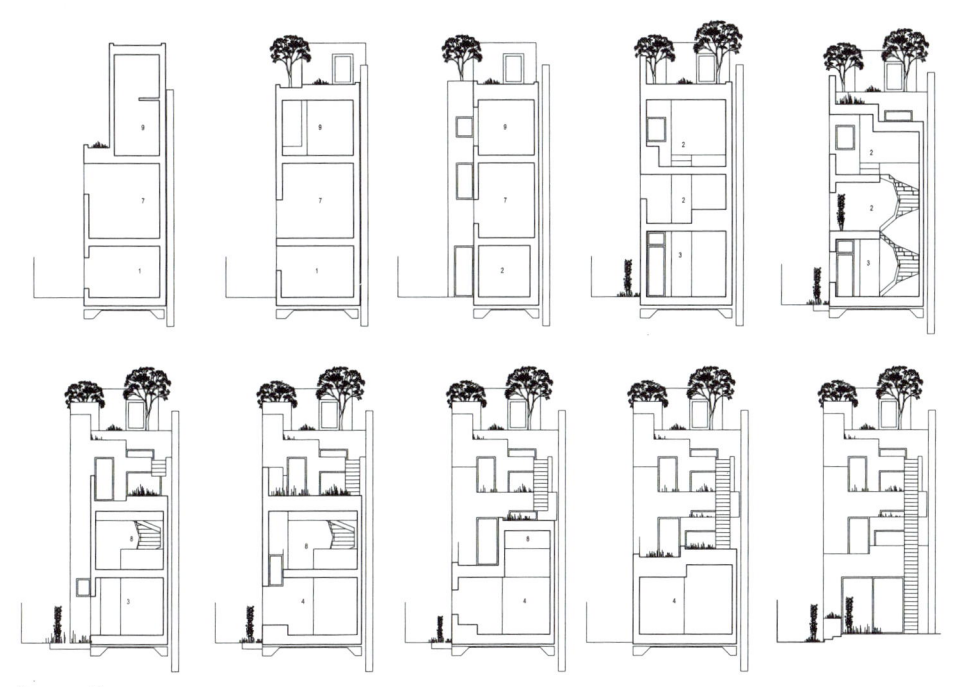

Cross sections

PSLA ARCHITEKTEN

0 1 2   5   10

The project was to include a larger area for public information, exhibition and discussion, as well as an extension of non-public workspaces and meeting rooms. Updates in accessibility, circulation, evacuation, security, fire protection and earthquake resistance were obligatory. The main design idea is based on the logic of the architectural concept by Theophil Hansen and its contemporary continuation. Dialogue orientated solutions with regard to the historical building fabric and heritage status were one of the main challenges that influenced the decisions on materiality, light, dimensions and spacing.

General Renovation of the Austrian Parliament
› VIENNA, AUSTRIA
2016/2017-2022
Government & Civic · 62,000m²
› **Jabornegg & Pálffy**
Christian Jabornegg, András Pálffy
Parlamentsdirektion, Republik Österreich (Public)
© Hertha Hurnaus

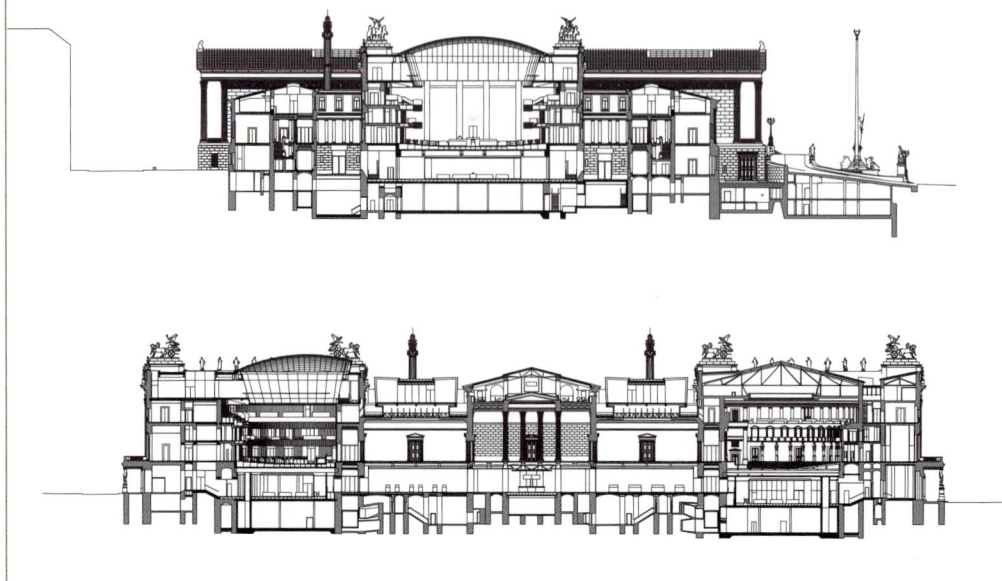

The challenge was to transform a chancellery created in 1914 into a bespoke museum for the 21st century that is full of esprit and accessible to a wide audience, while keeping the building's external appearance and outline.
Centrally located amidst an ensemble of historical buildings between the Albertina and the State Opera, the museum is hidden in the Hanuschhof. It opens itself up to visitors as a delicately balanced ensemble of old and new, with a landscaped museum forecourt and sculpture garden. The facade and side wings were retained, while the central element was completely gutted so its spatial potential could be exploited to create a platform for art derived from the interplay between dimensions, perspectives and spatial circulation.

Museum Heidi Horten Collection

› **VIENNA, AUSTRIA**
2019/2020-2022
Culture · 2,632m²
› **the next ENTERprise Architects**
Ernst J. Fuchs, Marie-Therese Harnoncourt-Fuchs
Palais Goëss-Horten GmbH (Private)
© Lukas Schaller

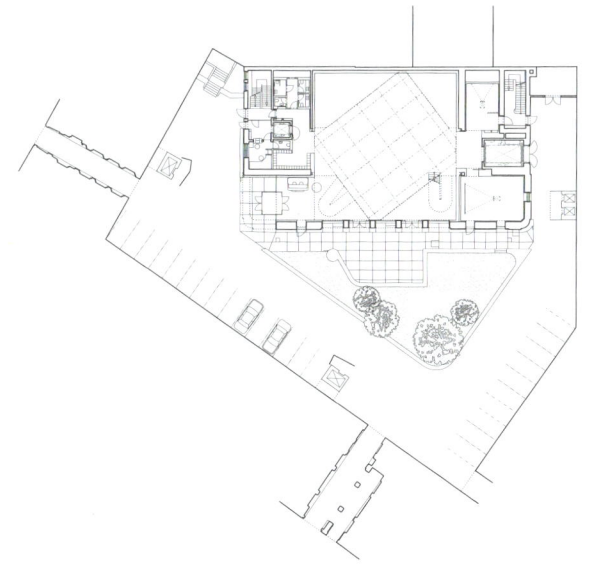

The high-rise ensemble consists of three residential towers in dialogue with each other. In terms of zoning, the towers are connected by a two-story podium that links the Downtown Business Park with the Danube Canal. The podium contains a wide range of communal areas, restaurants, stores and a kindergarten, benefiting both residents and neighbors.

Triiiple Towers

› **VIENNA, AUSTRIA**
2012/2018-2021
Collective housing · 85,350 m²
› **Henke Schreieck Architekten**
Dieter Henke, Marta Schreieck
ARE Austrian Real Estate Development GmbH and Soravia Investment Holding GmbH, ARE Austrian Real Estate Development GmbH (Private)
© Christian Pichlkastner

Within the economically tight cost framework of state-subsidized housing, reinforced concrete continues to play a central role as building material. When used with consideration, the material can contribute to social and economic sustainability. This is achieved by radically reducing the amount of the material to the bare technical necessities in the form of an intelligent set-up. It incorporates sliding walls that easily adapt to different life situations.

Social Housing Aspern H4
› **VIENNA, AUSTRIA**
  2017/2021-2023
  Collective housing · 6,142m²
› **WUP architektur**
  Bernhard Weinberger,
  Andreas Gabriel,
  Helmut Wimmer,
  Raphaela Leu
  WIGEBA (Public)
  © Luiza Puiu

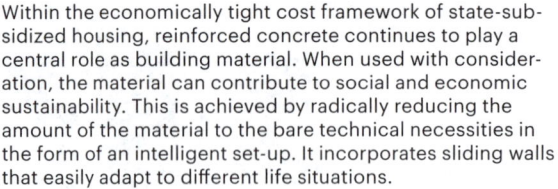

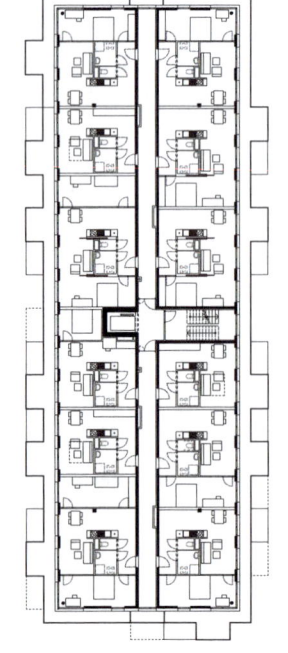

Nestled in the picturesque landscape of Zalacsány, Hungary, the Wellness Pavilion stands as a testament to architectural elegance and its inseparable bond with the surrounding natural environment. This pavilion seamlessly assimilates into the enchanting landscape, creating a sanctuary for well-being. At the heart of the Wellness Pavilion lies a deep appreciation for the intrinsic relationship between architecture and the landscape. The design creates a connection between the built interior and the exterior through the use of natural materials and geometries inspired by the site.

Zalacsány Wellness Pavilion
› **KEHIDAKUSTÁNY, HUNGARY**
  2019/2020-2021
  Sport & Leisure · 735m²
› **Archikon**
  Csaba Nagy, Károly Pólus, Ágnes Tőrös, Krisztina Timár-Major, Miklós Batta
  Zala Springs Hotel and Spa Kft. (Private)
  © Balázs Danyi

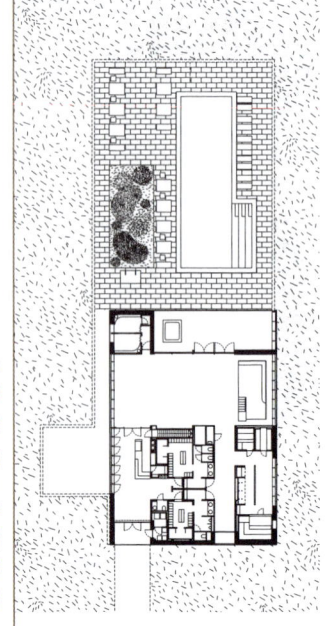

Reconstruction and Extension of the Slovak National Gallery

Bratislava, Slovakia
2014/2016-2022

Architekti B.K.P.Š.
Martin Kusý II., Pavol Paňák, Martin Kusý III., Mária Michalič Kusá, Jana Paňáková

Slovak National Gallery
(Public)
Culture · 27,911m² · 2,357€/m²

The aim of this project was to refurbish the existing architecture of the structure and supplement it with new spaces suitable for the needs of the 21st century. Apart from meeting the programme's requirements, the essential intention was to significantly open the gallery to the city and thus to the public. This area is to be a place for activities that transcend its function as a gallery.

The structure is situated in a prestigious location between the Danube embankment and the city centre. Due to its density, the building is part of its historical urban structure. It consists of contrasting architectural layers of baroque and neoclassicism, though it mainly consists of layers of late modern East European monumental structures added to the existing volumes of the gallery in the 1970s. This dominant part was designed by the distinguished architect Vladimír Dedeček. Through this project, new various use spaces have been added to the area. The project added direct accessibility which had previously been lacking. The materiality of the volumes is dominated mainly by metallic surfaces from the 1970s contrasting with the materials of the baroque section.

The refurbishment and extension of the Slovak National Gallery (ALU) was an unusually complex and multi-layered task. Apart from meeting the programme's new requirements on the limited area of the plot of land, the reconstruction of the late modern period was particularly difficult because the methodology was not already in place. Several shortcomings originating from previous reconstructions and extensions in the 1950s and 1970s also needed to be addressed. A new entrance vestibule was created in the baroque central wing and the exhibition spaces were complemented with a new exhibition hall for large installations and events. The body of the new depository was added to the existing volumes. Originally a relatively closed structure, the building is conceived as an area open to the public through courtyards, passageways, and the permeability of the ground floor spaces. The gallery should serve as a place for a wide range of different activities. The atmosphere of this complex is intended to inspire through the medium of contrasting architectural neighbourhoods and unique exhibition spaces. Within just a few months after its completion in December 2022, the structure had already became a lively, sought-after place in the centre of Bratislava.

In terms of the material concept, different procedures were applied for the different parts of the ensemble. The valuable baroque arcades of the courtyard have been carefully restored. The averted façade of the baroque section was seriously damaged during previous reconstructions. In this reconstruction, the façade was restored not as a replica, but rather in its tectonic essence. The buildings of the late modern period were steel supporting structures. Their façades had to be completely replaced due to their insufficient thermo-physical characteristics. The original red and white colour code of this period was applied. The new aluminium façade elements are partially a replica of the original ones. The former ALU slats with their authentic weathered surface have been installed on the new volume of the depository. Several original surfaces, materials and elements were reused in different positions. Demolished former stone pavement was used as filler in the terrazzo floors of the baroque arcades. Almost all the outdoor public areas are water permeable. The mature trees of the courtyard have been preserved.

↑ 154

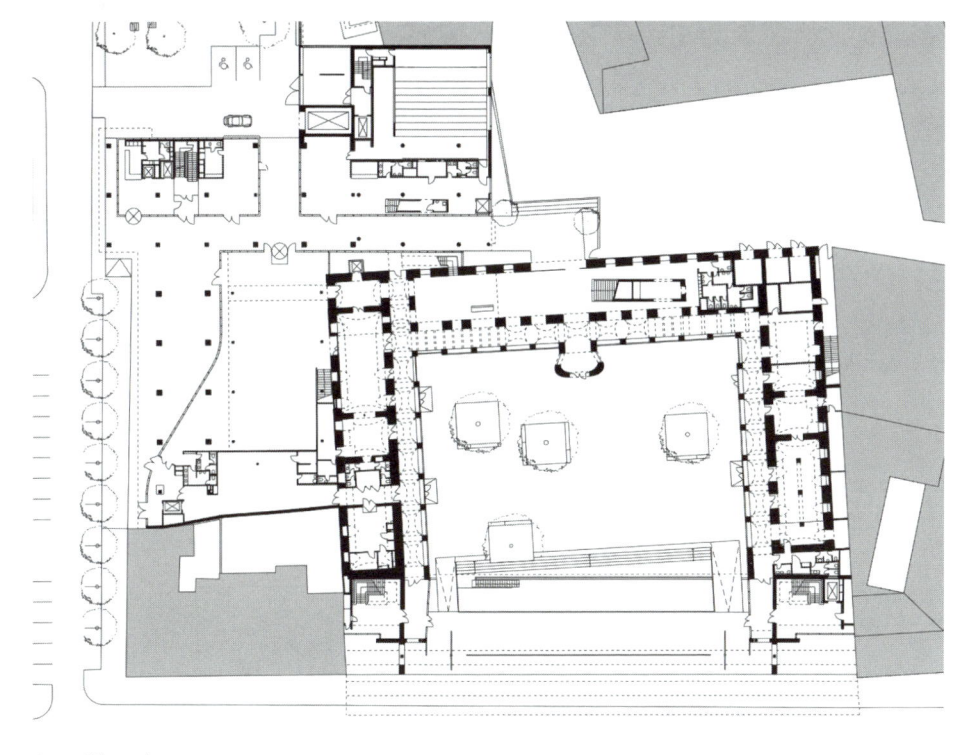

Ground floor plan

ARCHITEKTI B.K.P.Š.

SHORTLISTED

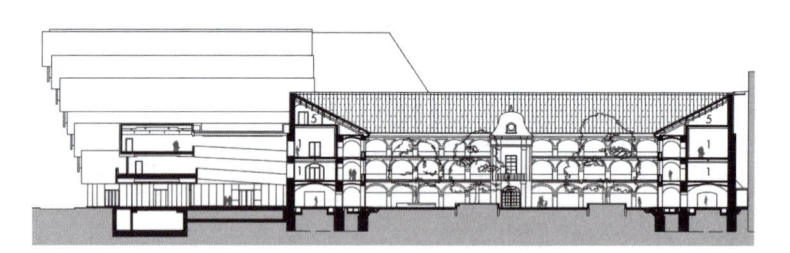

Longitudinal section

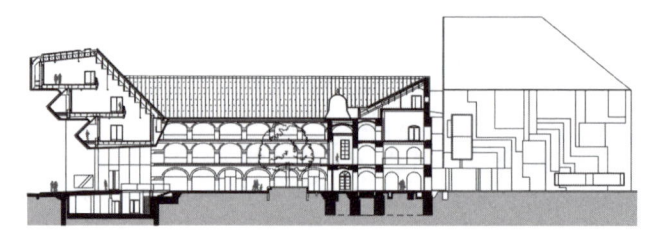

Cross section

RECONSTRUCTION AND EXTENSION OF THE SLOVAK NATIONAL GALLERY

0 5 10 20

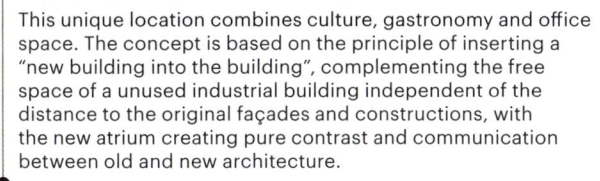

This unique location combines culture, gastronomy and office space. The concept is based on the principle of inserting a "new building into the building", complementing the free space of a unused industrial building independent of the distance to the original façades and constructions, with the new atrium creating pure contrast and communication between old and new architecture.

Conversion of Jurkovič Heating Plant National Cultural Monument

› Bratislava, Slovakia. 2017/2018-2021
  Mixed use - Commercial & Offices · 6,300m² · 2,060€/m²
› **DF CREATIVE GROUP, PAMARCH, Perspektiv**
  Martin Paško, Zuzana Zacharová, Matúš Podskalický, Martina Michalková, Alexandra Havranová, Eva Belláková, Pavol Paulíny, Ján Antal, Barbora Babocká
  Penta Real Estate (Private)
  © Boys Play Nice

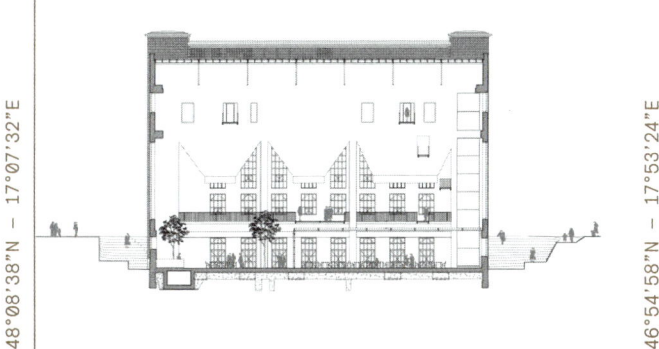

In this project, the deconstruction of roof, façade and plinth showcases the creative and poetic exploration of the relationship between old, ancient and modern. It symbolizes a process of learning from time, with intersecting lines and overlapping layers, culminating in sculptural purity. The design concept is based on a three-layered approach, connecting three archetypal styles of vacation homes found around Lake Balaton. We chose the distinctive elements of the region, thatch and stone.

Summer House

› Tihany, Hungary. 2020/2021-2022
  Single house · 202m² · 4,500€/m²
› **Rapa Architects**
  Levente Arato, Adam Reisz, Krisztian Varga-Koritar
  Helga Katona (Private)
  © Balint Jaksa

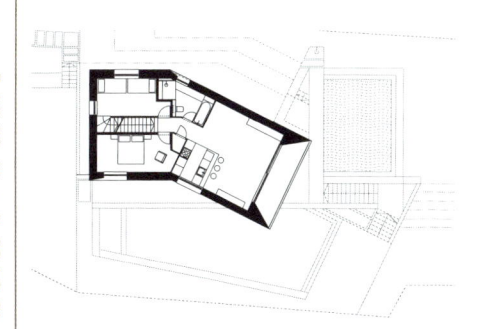

The new residential house is located on the edge of different urban zones, shaped like a sculpture to interact with the different heights of the neighbors. It is a reinvention of a typical Budapest courtyard house. The stepped roof is left "unfinished" to keep it free for the owners' future uses. The contour of the volume is framed by a steel system to integrate the expected diversity. The ground floor is partly occupied by commercial functions and the façade is finished with perforated metal sheets to provide a feeling of accessibility.

Trendo11 Apartment Building
› **BUDAPEST, HUNGARY**
2017/2019-2022
Collective housing · 9,381m²
› **LAB5 architects**
Linda Erdelyi, Andras Dobos, Balazs Korenyi, Virag Anna Gaspar
Trendo Home Ingatlanfejleszto Kft (Private)
© Zsolt Batar

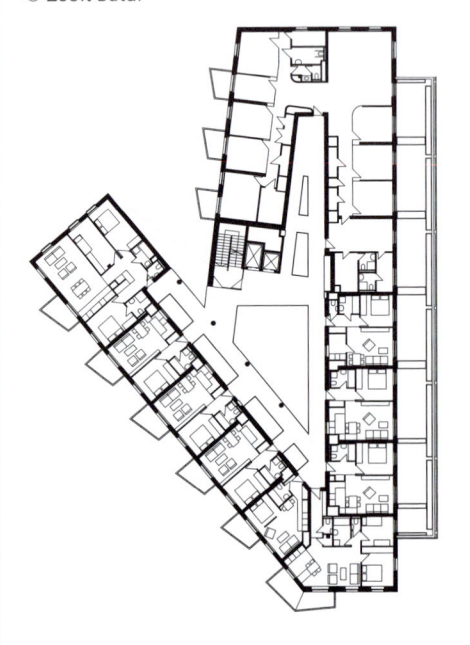

The Budapest-based firm Bánáti + Hartvig Architects expanded steadily in recent years and needed a new office building. To ensure that an ideal workplace would be created, they chose to design it themselves. Two things were borne in mind: to make a building with as small an environmental impact as possible, and to give all who work there a sense of belonging and an inspiring milieu. The building was transformed into an airy, transparent space and its original character was revealed.

The New Office Building of Bánáti + Hartvig Architects
› **BUDAPEST, HUNGARY**
2019/2020-2021
Office · 1,046m²
› **Bánáti + Hartvig Architects**
Béla Bánáti, Lajos Hartvig DLA, Vera Lőcsei
Bánáti + Hartvig Architects (Private)
© Tamás Bujnovszky

The reconstruction of the M3 metro line is one of the most important urban renewal projects in Budapest in the last decade. Simple stairs lead down to an underpass from the surface and further stairs descend to the platform. The gallery level became available through the removal of intermediate stairs leading up to it and its spaces became part of the new main ventilation system. The renewal of the underpass was out of scope, though a new elevator was built to extend the accessible path to the surface.

Reconstruction of the Lehel Tér Metro Station

› BUDAPEST, HUNGARY
2015/2021-2023
Infrastructure · 9,400m² · 2700€/m²
› sporaarchitects, Paragram
Tibor Dékány, Ádám Hatvani, Attila Czigléczki, Balázs Csapó
BKV Zrt (Public)
© Attila Gulyás

The park is located on a unique post-industrial site wedged between prefabricated housing blocks. In the existing dense urban environment, the community had a great need for a new green urban space. Therefore, the park is a combination of unique features that cater to various recreational activities. The central organizing attribute of the park is an asymmetrically shaped lake, which has an ecologically self-cleaning ability thanks to the biodiverse plant-life scattered along its shore and improves the local microclimate. The features are completed by a small pavilion which includes a café and public bathrooms.

Vizafogó Ecopark and Pavilion

› BUDAPEST, HUNGARY
2020/2021-2022
Landscape · 50m²
› Archikon, Objekt
Csaba Nagy, Károly Pólus, Miklós Batta, Bianka Varga, Máté Pécsi, János Hómann, Eszter Ripszám
Budapest Capital 13th District Mayor's Office (Public)
© Balázs Danyi

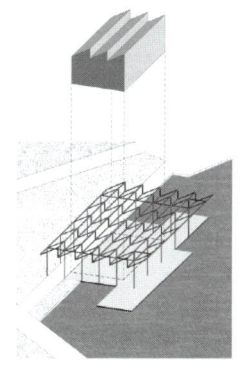

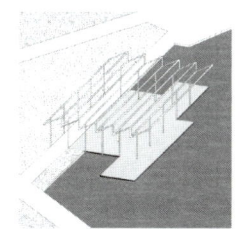

Once built as a fruit storage house with the rocks extracted from its garden, the building was later enlarged with an open archway and used as a weekend house. When Orsi and Viktor first stepped into the garden, it had been deserted for years. Everybody thought the building should be demolished. And yet they knew immediately that their quest for a new home was over.

When we first entered the house, we immediately realized that the long-evolved spatial structure had great potential that must not be lost.

The existing capabilities of the space met all the needs of Orsi, Viktor and their dog, Zara. Due to its size and central position, the original stone fruit storage building became the main living zone, including the living room and the dining area. At the same time, the narrow "archway" provides space for the other additional functions of the house, but not in a subordinate relationship.

Transformation of a 100-year-old Fruit Storage Building

› **SZENTENDRE, HUNGARY**
  2019/2020-2023
  Single house · 125m^2
› **arkt studio, projectroom**
  Gábor Fábián, Dénes Fajcsák, Veronika Juhász
  Orsolya Boros-Orosz, Viktor Boros (Private)
  © Veronika Juhász

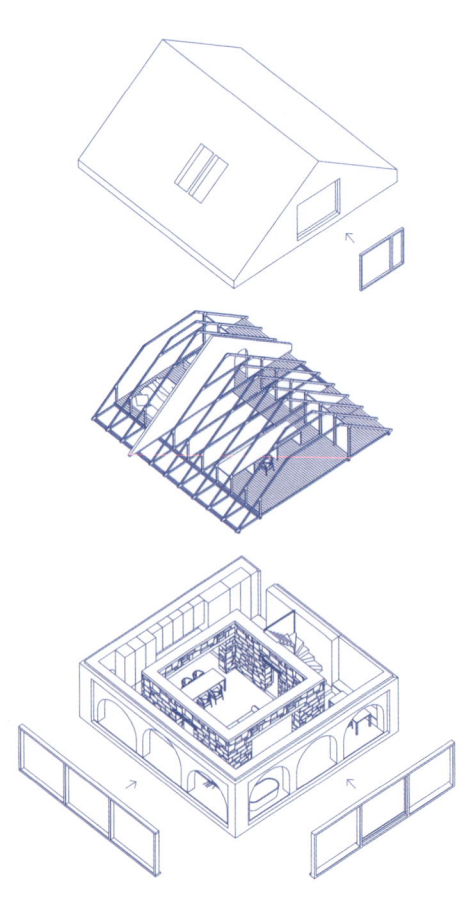

Semmelweis University is a leading higher education institution in Hungary and the Central European region devoted to medicine and health. The aim was to create seminar rooms, demonstration rooms and two large lecture halls. The basic design principles are based on the dialogue with the existing building and have been developed from it. The addition creates a completed inner courtyard. The two buildings are connected on every level and the interior spaces are organized by a central atrium, which is the main spatial element of the new wing.

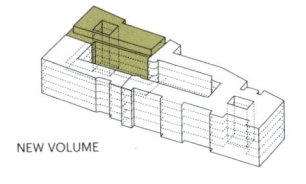

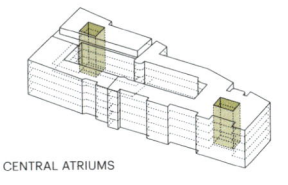

NEW VOLUME

CENTRAL ATRIUMS

CIRCULARITY ON EVERY LEVEL

COMPLETED INNER COURTYARD

Zsuzsanna Kossuth Building of the Faculty of Health Sciences, Semmelweis University

› BUDAPEST, HUNGARY
2016/2020-2022
Education · 4,207m²
› **Studio Fragment**
Zsolt Frikker, Imre Bődi
Semmelweis University (Public)
© Balázs Danyi

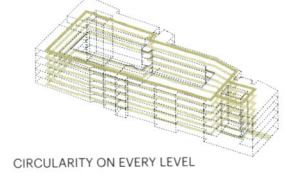

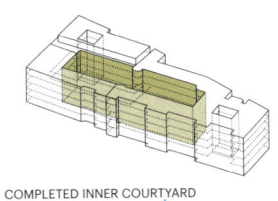

The aim was to create a building that was at once unique, yet simple, rational, yet not boring, striking, yet not ostentatious and economical, yet generous. We decided to create it ourselves, so we would not be left without. When designing the functional relationships, we started from the standards and chose the most rational layout for the low budget, then played with the spaces as building blocks, moving them out to create communal spaces and internal gardens. This dissolved the strict structure of the building, filling the interiors with light and making the building welcoming and bright.

Nest Reformed Kindergarten in Debrecen

› DEBRECEN, HUNGARY
2020/2020-2021
Education · 1,048m² · 1,000€/m²
› **Bíró és Társa Építésziroda**
Béla Bíró, Dániel Fodor, Ferenc Kállay, Béla Nagy
Debrecen-Nagysándor-telepi Református Missziói Egyházközség (Public)
© Attila Varga

Among other goals, the Greek Catholic Eparchy was aimed at creating an emblematic building that expressed their own identity. Consequently, its classic style and modernity were constantly interacting with each other during the design. The museum now completes the framed siting while also providing a closing gesture for the front garden.

The Greek Catholic Museum of Nyíregyháza

› **NYÍREGYHÁZA, HUNGARY**
2020/2021-2022
Culture · 1,857m² · 1,980€/m²
› **Balázs Mihály Építész Muterme**
Mihály Balázs, Márton Nagy, Balázs Falvai, Dávid Török
Görögkatolikus Metropólia (Public)
© Palko Gyorgy

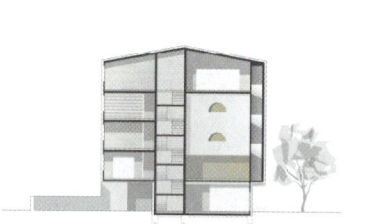

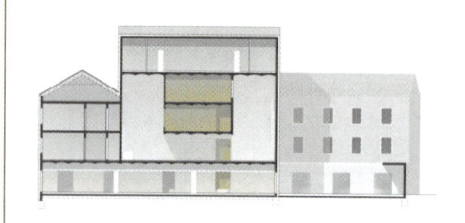

Built in the 15th century, the Firefighters Tower was part of the second medieval precinct of the city. In the early 1870s, the old medieval tower was raised with a new segment, becoming a firehouse to watch for fires in the surrounding area. Built in successive layers, the tower remains an urban observatory through the new age, a place of contemplation and for interpreting urban development. The third age takes place through a discrete, integrated and unitary intervention.

Firefighters' Tower

› **CLUJ-NAPOCA, ROMANIA**
2017/2018-2023
Culture · 365m²
› **Vlad Sebastian Rusu Architecture Office, Octav Silviu Olanescu Architecture Office**
Vlad Sebastian Rusu, Octav Silviu Olanescu, Anamaria Olanescu
Cluj-Napoca Municipality (Public)
© Cosmin Dragomir

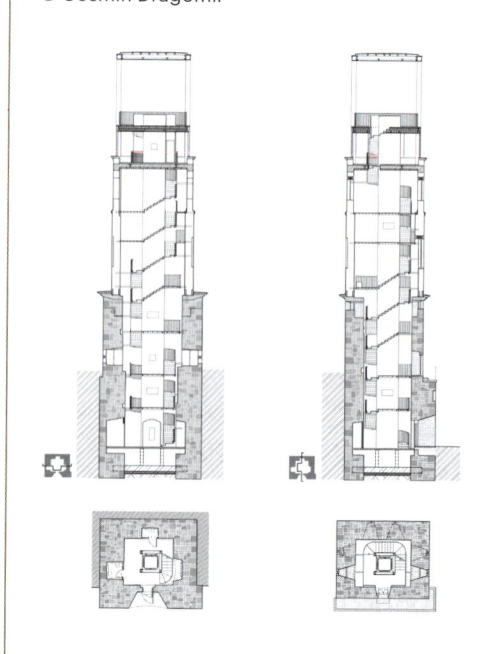

Since the area where the object is designed is surrounded by many buildings of various formats in a rather chaotic environment, we decided to make the architecture as simple and concise as possible, which will unite the ensemble of the square. The vision of the building is intended to emphasize an open and accessible process of solving important issues of the relationship between people and the state. The idea of this project is to make administrative services available, transparent, fast and respectful of each person who applies for them.

Construction of the Centre of Government Services

› **NOVA KAKHOVKA, UKRAINE**
2017/2018-2021
Government & Civic · 766m^2 · 1,130€/m^2
› **Anna Kyrii Architectural Projecting Group**
Anna Kyrii, Iryna Korzh, Maksym Fakas, Vitalii Nechai
Executive Committee of Novokakhovsky City Council (Public)
© Arsen Fedosenko

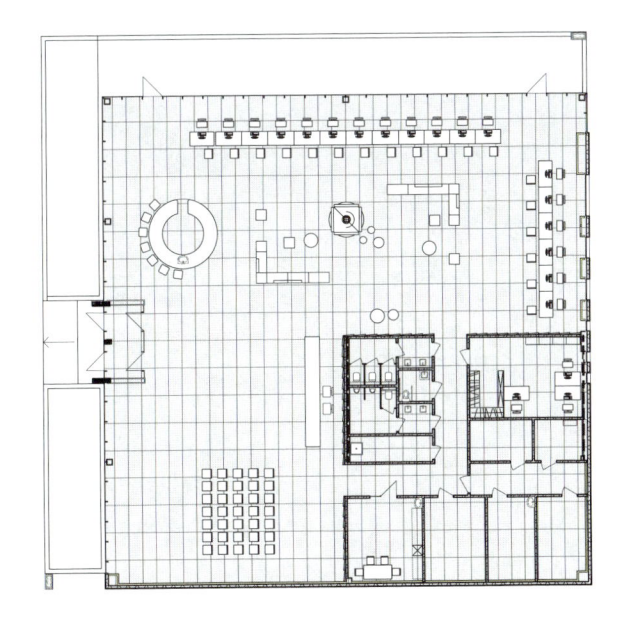

284

From
CHÉNAC-SAINT-
SEURIN-D'UZET
France
45°31'08"N – 0°48'52"W

to
TIMIȘOARA
Romania
45°45'28"N – 21°14'59"E

An existing barn is transformed into a single family house through its complete reconversion and addition of an extension. The project is conceived as a sequence of differentiated volumes, each with its own orientation and distinct characteristics. The pre-existing buildings were originally organized around a shared courtyard with the neighbors to meet the needs of agriculture and animal rearing, thus ignoring the view. The extension hosts the main collective spaces for the family and gives access to a large, covered terrace. The project intends to showcase how old buildings can be brought to life and create unexpected architectural qualities made possible by the coexistence of old and new.

Extension and Reconversion of an Old Farm House Near the Gironde Estuary
› CHENAC-SAINT-SEURIN-D'UZET, FRANCE
2018/2020-2022
Single house · 150m^2 · 1,200€/m^2
› **Martin Migeon Architecture, Anouk Migeon Architecte**
Martin Migeon, Anouk Migeon
SCI l'ESTUAC - Marie Pavy & François Migeon (Private)
© Gion von Albertini

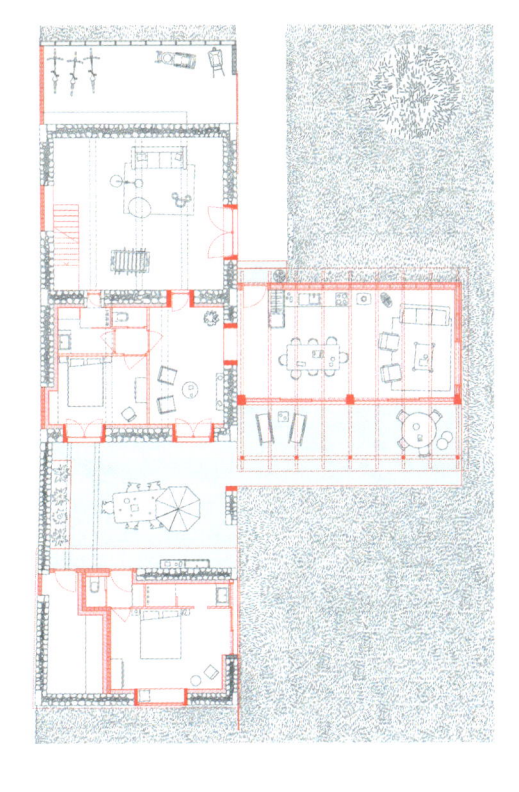

On a hilly terrain cut by the traces of a Roman road and the bed of a stream, two plots of land have been divided. This administrative reality comes in counterpoint to the geology of the land. The house takes its place in this path on the quest to suspend a glass volume in space, hovering above the ground to leave nature undisturbed. At the same time, it takes up equally another duality inherent in the history of the house as transparent belvedere: namely, the holding in dramatic tension of the age-old search for the domus as facing inward to foster family life and the dream of contemplating with invisible barriers the macrocosm beyond the house's transparent walls.

The Grand Bois House
› **TASSIN-LA-DEMI-LUNE, FRANCE**
2020/2021-2022
Single house · 128m²
› **MBL architectes**
Martinez-Barat Sébastien, Lafore Benjamin
Private
© Maxime Delvaux

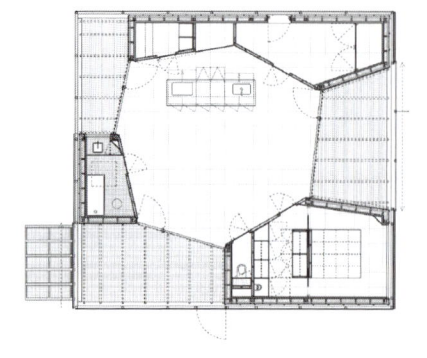

The Orangery explores the possibility of reusing traditional construction methods as an integral part of a contemporary block, at the heart of one of Lyon's major urban renewal projects. The B2 block is divided into five buildings mixing dwellings and offices. The project adopts a strong structural strategy as a common principle: by reducing load-bearing structures to façades and cores in the footsteps of Perret's "ruin structures", living and working become adaptive functions, allowing for functional and meaningful conversion.

The Orangery – B2 Block in Lyon Confluence
› **LYON, FRANCE**
2015/2019-2021
Office · 1,060m² · 2,170€/m²
› **Clément Vergély Architectes, Diener & Diener Architekten**
Clément Vergély, Stefan Jeske
OGIC (Private)
© Erick Saillet

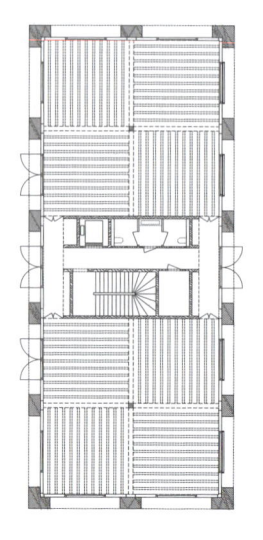

A small house built of wood, straw, lime and salvaged materials stands in the historical context of the small town. The house is cut in two parts: in the shaded part, squeezed against the neighboring house, are the stairs, bathrooms and a small attic. In the other half are the two main rooms, the balcony and the solar panels, facing the sun, and the lake.
In accordance with regulations, the house reproduces the outline of a previously demolished building with very few variations.

Wood and Straw House
› LAVENO MOMBELLO, ITALY
2017/2020-2022
Single house · 85m²
› **Studio Albori**
Giacomo Borella, Emanuele Almagioni, Francesca Riva
Private
© Luca Bosco

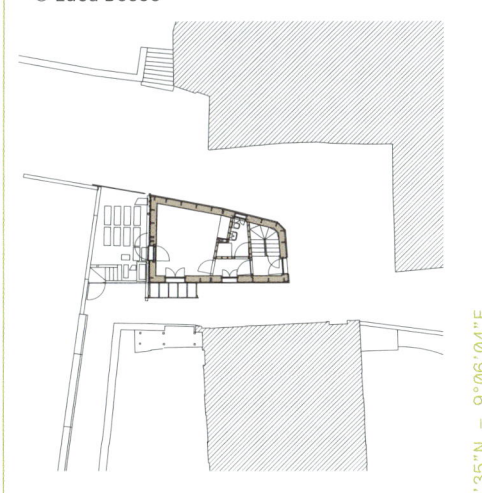

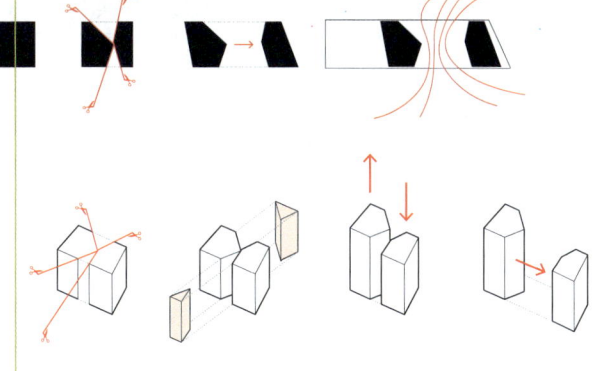

The project is critical of the concept of the gated community. By pulling down the fence, we are giving back a square to the community, which is designed in material and chromatic continuity with the towers that underlines the importance of sharing collective spaces as a key point to strengthen the community's identity. On the sides are two towers for 103 flats, split in two by the public space. The concept for this social housing project puts the community at the forefront, not only giving back a free public space to all but also creating buildings that are adaptable in the future and clad with durable materials, referring to the tradition of Milan.

Affordable Residential Towers
› MILAN, ITALY
2011/2020-2022
Collective housing · 10,850m² · 1,659€/m²
› **C+S Architects**
Carlo Cappai, Maria Alessandra Segantini
Investire sgr (Private)
© Alessandra Bello

This retrofitting project is characterized by its use of innovative technological materials and the search for cutting-edge architectural solutions. The project reinterprets the existing industrial building, formerly occupied by General Electric, by maintaining its main volumes and its character, with the addition of contemporary top-quality elements both on the façade and inside. The intervention emphasizes the building's original shapes and lines by removing any later internal additions and by adapting it to contemporary safety and sustainability criteria, while preserving the reinforced concrete truss design and enhancing the façade's vertical shape. The casing is the result of technological and structural research aimed at lending the building the greatest transparency and indoor brightness.

Luxottica Digital Factory

› Milan, Italy. 2017/2019-2022
 Mixed use - Commercial & Offices · 9,000m²
› **Park Associati**
 Filippo Pagliani, Michele Rossi, Lorenzo Merloni, Michele Versaci, Alessandro Bentivegna, Luna Pavanello, Valeria Donini, Simone Caimi, Marinella Ferrari, Ismail Seleit
 Luxottica Italia Srl (Private)
 ↑ © Lorenzo Zandri
 ↓ © Nicola Colella

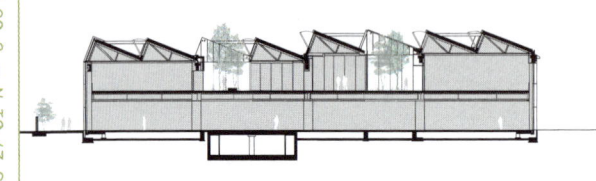

The project sprang from a desire to create a museum with a collection of Etruscan artifacts. Non-conventional architecture was developed underground in reference to the Etruscan tombs of Cerveteri and that civilization's lively relationship with the world beyond death. The experience is given a chiaroscuro effect by large slabs of Pietra Serena stone, while constellations of vases seem to float in mid-air. Upon leaving this space, visitors emerge into the renovated palace, a "newfound home" designed for the rest of the art collection, temporary exhibitions and a restaurant on the top floor.

Art Museum of Fondazione Luigi Rovati

› Milan, Italy. 2016/2018-2022
 Culture · 4,000m² · 6,250€/m²
› **Mario Cucinella Architects**
 Mario Cucinella
 Fondazione Luigi Rovati (Private)
 © Duccio Malagamba

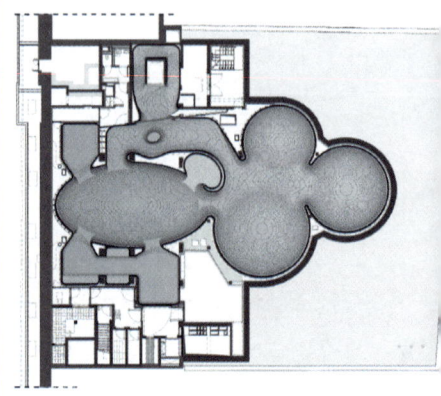

Fieldhouse is a piece of infrastructure wedged between the town's football field and the rocky slopes of Mt. Corno to form a long, low-lying multi-functional structure with a tower for the field floodlights. The design of the Fieldhouse reflects the architecture of local sports facilities and their public character. The long, low-lying structure includes not only the football club's lockers, offices and storage depot, but also a café and an 18-meter lighting tower to replace the requisite field lighting poles, not to mention spaces used by the local Schützen corps. A large terrace extends the café to become a social space for the spectators and the local community.

Fieldhouse: Sports Amenity Facility at the Base of Mount Corno

› Bolzano, Italy. 2017/2021-2022
  Sport & Leisure · 1,080m²
› MoDusArchitects
  Matteo Scagnol
  Municipality of Egna (Public)
  © Gustav Willeit

The project seeks the transformation of a former 19th-century printing factory into a contemporary art gallery, with the broader intent of bringing art into the daily social dynamics of the town. The intervention involves the site and organizes existing stratifications, making evident each era's modifications to the original building. Threshold & Treasure is about the opportunity to act on the limit between people and art, often perceived as hardly accessible.

Threshold and Treasure / Atipografia

› Arzignano, Italy. 2019/2020-2022
  Culture · 1,465m²
› AMAA - Collaborative Architecture Office For Research And Development
  Marcello Galiotto, Alessandra Rampazzo
  Atipografia S.r.l. (Private)
  © Mikael Olsson

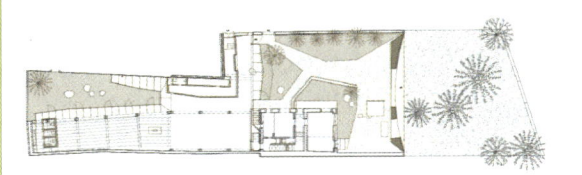

Bivouac Fanton
Auronzo di Cadore, Italy
2015/2018-2021
DEMOGO
Simone Gobbo, Alberto Mottola, Davide De Marchi
CAI – Sezione Cadorina di Auronzo
(Public)
Food & Accommodation · 30m² · 5,675€/m²

The Bivouac Fanton has opened up new and unexplored imagery within architectural debates regarding high altitudes. It does not merely seek a functional resolution, rather it strives to trigger a relationship between man and nature, a deeper relationship that goes beyond the mere satisfaction of a practical need.

The architecture of the Bivouac Fanton is based on the act of inhabiting an oblique space, tracing the line of tension seeking to create a new balance to withstand the unfavourable structure of the mountain. Here man and architecture live in symbiosis with the overhang, they inhabit it by resting on it and breathing in the hypnotic power of deep space. The complexity and fragility of the Alpine environment are addressed through individual actions. The design and development process of the work can be traced back to three key issues: anchoring, suspension, and habitat. These themes intertwine and recompose in the oblique dimension of the Bivouac: here technical and theoretical aspects have fuelled a desire for experimentation at multiple levels. We can find the oblique dimension in the decomposition of the forces on the ground, in the refutation of an artificially flat space.

Designing an outdoor architecture in an extreme territory deprived of human references allows one to focus the attention on the individual dimension of mankind and its relationship with the landscape. Here the minute spatiality of the architecture is confronted with the enormous scale of the surrounding context: the aesthetic of the new bivouac arises from the landscape, from the lines of tension in the existing orography, emerging as a volume hewn from nature, suspended above the slope. The contradiction between anchoring and suspension lives in the ambivalent relationship that keeps them tied together. The structure finds its balance by leaning on the ground, an equilibrium that is both firm and seemingly precarious at the same time. The project develops solutions aimed to produce continuity of experience and test the mixture of protection and risk, nature and artifice, fear and desire that make alpinism so engaging. The dimensions of the bivouac are formed by its sloping habitat, parallel to the ground below it, pointing downhill. The structure forms an inhabitable telescope that frames the surroundings of the Municipality of Auronzo di Cadore and enhances the landscape.

The project aims to define a design solution that guarantees the lowest possible impact on the mountainous context of the Dolomites while providing a self-sufficient habitat to provide impervious shelter to visitors from the conditions of the outside. The anchoring takes place in 3 points, minimising the building's footprint on the ground and making it possible to undo the intervention with the possible removal of the elevated structure thereby restoring the ground to its original orographic conditions. The structure does not touch the soil rather it chooses to lean slightly; this architecture does not touch the ground rather it creates suspension and moves parallel to it, supporting itself and blending into its context. To fulfil the main task of the bivouac, namely, to create a thermally comfortable shelter habitat in extreme climatic conditions, the designers decided to use a high-performance fibreglass shell derived from the nautical construction. This material makes it possible to merge the insulation and load-bearing functions into a single element, minimising the weight of the structure and making it easier to transport and assemble at high altitudes, reducing the total number of trips required.

DEMOGO

292

↑ 169

SHORTLISTED

Site

BIVOUAC FANTON

↓ 233

Floor plan

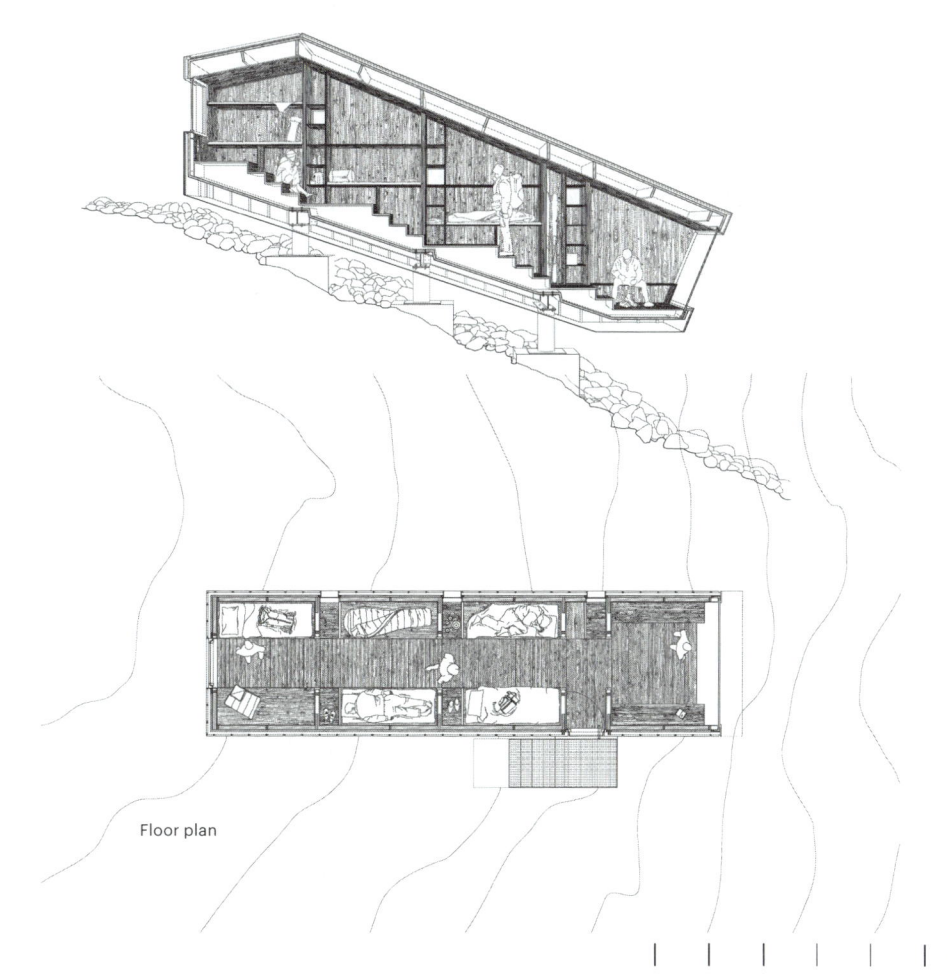

DEMOGO

Bohinj Kindergarten
Bohinjska Bistrica, Slovenia
2020/2021-2023
KAL A, ARREA architecture
Ana Jerman, Janja Šušnjar, Sofia Romeo Gurrea-Nozaleda, Miguel Sotos Fernández-Zúñiga
Občina Bohinj
(Public)
Education · 2,105m²

The Bohinjska Bistrica Kindergarten is a community-driven project fostering education in environmental harmony. Strategically positioned, the kindergarten promotes engagement and strengthens connections with nature. Tradition-based, sustainable construction establishes a caring environment for children and the local community.

The kindergarten in Bohinjska Bistrica is located on the outskirts of the largest settlement in Slovenia's Bohinj Valley. The building is situated on the periphery of the town, next to the Dr. Janez Mencinger Primary School and the Church of St. Nicholas.

The local community had been stressing the need for a new kindergarten to establish a renewed centralized educational infrastructure for years.

The new building and its surroundings have been designed in response to the programmatic and spatial challenge of how to provide spaces for social interaction and free choice for children, while allowing them to actively admire, explore, and experience their local environment. The project is organized around a succession of interconnected technical cores, while being conceived as a continuous playground that integrates indoor and outdoor spaces.

The new building extends the existing town limits of Bohinjska Bistrica, considering the geometric characteristics and orientation of the plot, its surroundings, and the scale of the territory. It emphasizes horizontality through the implementation of three large, south-facing pitched-roof buildings, the result of fragmenting the programme into three distinct volumes. Accordingly, the exterior spaces are simultaneously defined: an open plaza as the main entrance shared with the primary school and three playground areas connected to each other.

The building gradually reduces its scale. The largest two-storey volume (equipment, kitchens, classrooms for 3–6-year-old children) is located to the West, close to the village and it is similar in scale and proportion to the primary school nearby. Meanwhile, the complex gets smaller as it moves East through the gym (a multipurpose space) and the entrance hall, reaching its closest proximity to nature and the rural environment at the eastern end (classrooms for 0–3-year-old children, summer classroom). The three buildings establish a harmonious dialogue between the local culture, the land, and the children's need for a safe and nurturing environment.

The construction takes the local Slovenian tradition of timber construction as an example with the kozolec (drying rack) and the traditional farmhouse as its most representative structures. The same strategy is followed in all the buildings: three main longitudinal glue-laminated timber (GLT) beams that work together with secondary structural half-lapped wooden framing sections to support the high-quality aluminium roof sheets. The entire structure rests on reinforced concrete cores that rise up from a common slab. The façade has been treated with an exterior insulation and finish system (EFICS), vastly improving its energy efficiency. The untreated larch wood cladding will naturally highly resistant to decay and provide a patina that will help the building blend in with the surrounding structures in the future.

The core organizational element of the interior space is based on the traditional Slovenian gank (wooden balcony). This space acts as the backbone of the entire project, both functionally and structurally. This versatile circulation system links the kindergarten spaces together and allows for different configurations, while maintaining simultaneous and flexible use.

KAL A, ARREA ARCHITECTURE

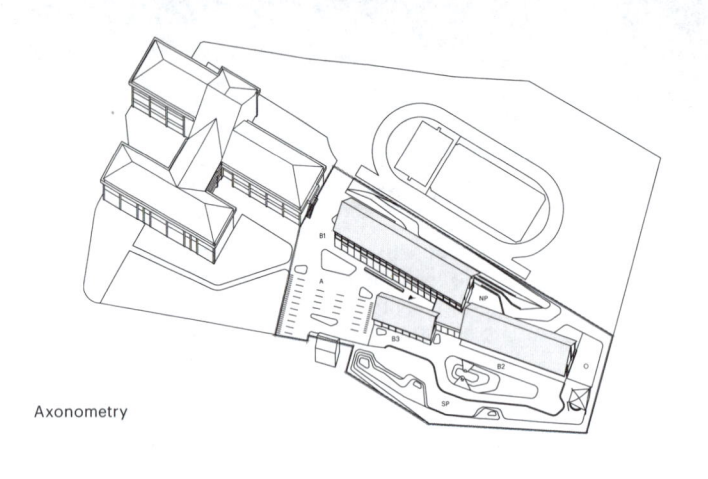

SHORTLISTED

Axonometry

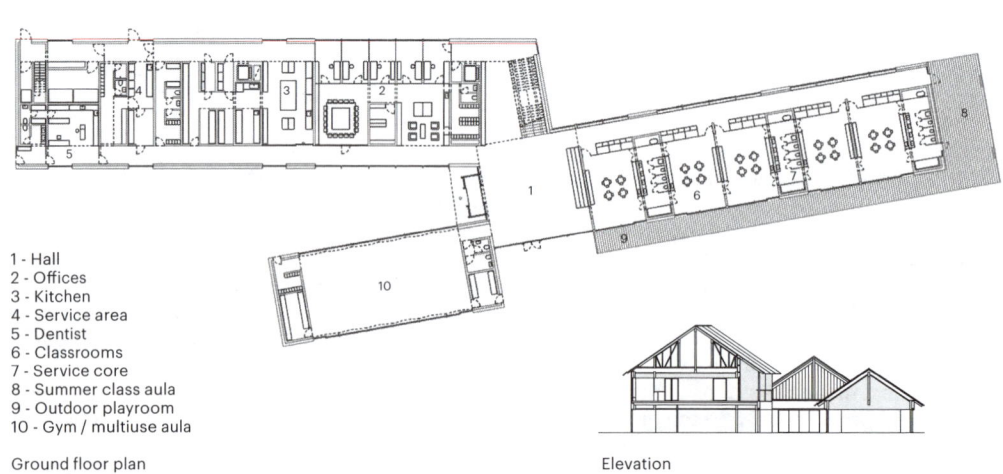

1 - Hall
2 - Offices
3 - Kitchen
4 - Service area
5 - Dentist
6 - Classrooms
7 - Service core
8 - Summer class aula
9 - Outdoor playroom
10 - Gym / multiuse aula

Ground floor plan

Elevation

BOHINJ KINDERGARTEN

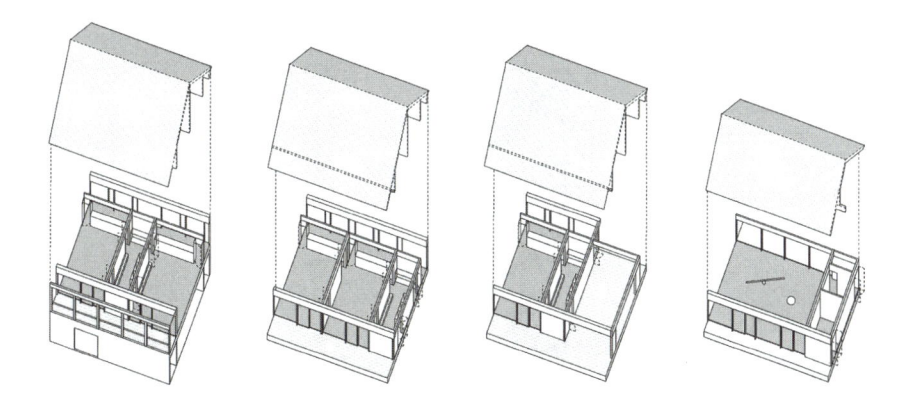

Learning spaces and playground strategies

KAL A, ARREA ARCHITECTURE

Novo Brdo is an affordable housing neighborhood and one of the largest contemporary neighborhoods in Slovenia, with almost 500 non-profit rental apartments. It is key to creating a quality living environment for almost 1,500 new inhabitants, while setting benchmarks for future rental housing projects with a defined financial framework at the same time.

Affordable Housing Neighbourhood Novo Brdo
› LJUBLJANA, SLOVENIA
2016/2019-2022
Collective housing · 42,819m²
› **Dekleva Gregorič Architects**
Lea Kovič, Tina Gregorič, Aljoša Dekleva
Housing Fund of the Republic of Slovenia / SSRS – Stanovanjski Sklad republike Slovenije (Public)
© Miran Kambič

This project is dedicated to fighting poverty and social exclusion among children and promoting values of civic solidarity and social dialogue. This place is neither their home nor school, but something in between, given to them as added value in the formative phase of their lives. The project involves the reconstruction of an area of 380m², dividing it into several parts of different proportions. All spaces are defined by the rawness of the interior and a serving fragment of the purple diagonal wall, making them easily adaptable to hybrid use.

Home for 'My Place Under the Sun'
› RIJEKA, CROATIA
2020/2021-2022
Social welfare · 380m² · 750€/m²
› **'My Place Under the Sun' team**
Ana Boljar, Ida Križaj Leko, Enia Kukoč, Kristijan Mamić, Marin Nižić, Ariana Sušanj, Damian Sobol Turina
CeKaDe - Center for the Culture of Dialog (Private)
© Petar Borovec

The library is created with a new structure that runs around the perimeter of the two-story hall and completely surrounds it. The added structure lets children see the books and the library at all times. The library is designed as light and translucent. The primary school library is a place focused primarily on books. It is accessible both in quiet times and at school breaks, when it suddenly invites pupils in. At the same time, the library space is multifunctional, as it can be transformed into a temporary classroom or a space for storytelling, book presentations, socializing or doing homework.

Open Library
› LJUBLJANA, SLOVENIA
2021/2021-2022
Education · 85m²
› **ARP studio**
Matjaž Bolčina, Ernest Milčinović, Jan Žonta
Municipality of Ljubljana (Public)
© Ana Skobe

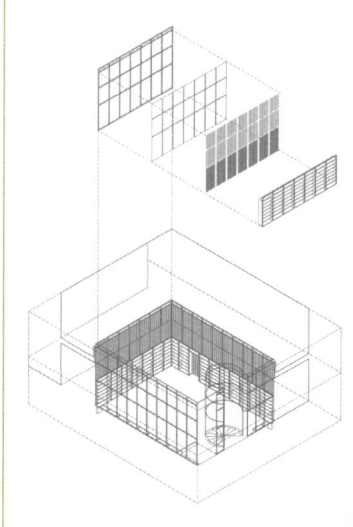

Built in 1828, Cukrarna was one of the first and largest factories in Slovenia. In 1845, it burned down to the outer walls. Scapelab won an international competition in 2009. The key idea was to carve out all internal structures of the building and insert a new, modern entity as a transformative gesture of conversion into a multi-functional space for contemporary art. The ground floor serves as an extension of urban public space, accessible free of charge. Upon entering, visitors are made aware of the gargantuan dimensions of the former factory. The gallery volumes, designed as "white cube" galleries, levitate above the ground floor, hanging from the steel roof structure.

Cukrarna
› **LJUBLJANA, SLOVENIA**
2009/2018-2021
Culture · 5,500m²
› **Scapelab**
Marko Studen, Boris Matić, Jernej Šipoš
Municipality of Ljubljana (Public)
© Miran Kambič

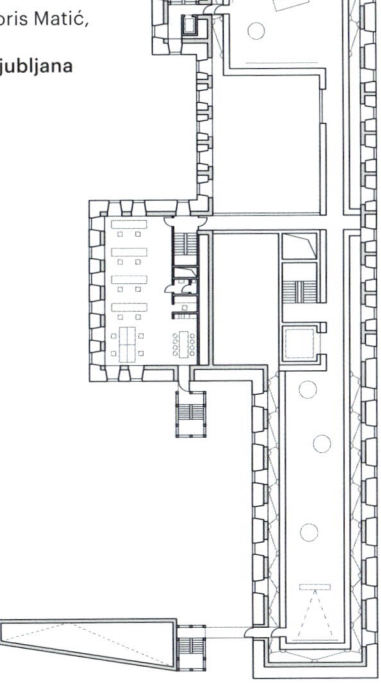

The house consists of two volumes, each with its own gable roof, indicating that the bedrooms and living spaces inside are separate. There is also a third service building. All three volumes together with the existing trees form a mini urban structure, a compositional ensemble of built elements and nature. The house is situated in the row of gardens of the surrounding houses, so we wanted the house to give the impression of a pavilion.

A House for Modest Residence
› **LITIJA, SLOVENIA**
2019/2020-2023
Single house · 140+24m² · 950€/m²
› **Skupaj arhitekti, MKutin arhitektura**
Tomaž Ebenšpanger, Meta Kutin
Helena & Ladislav Muzga (Private)
© Miran Kambič

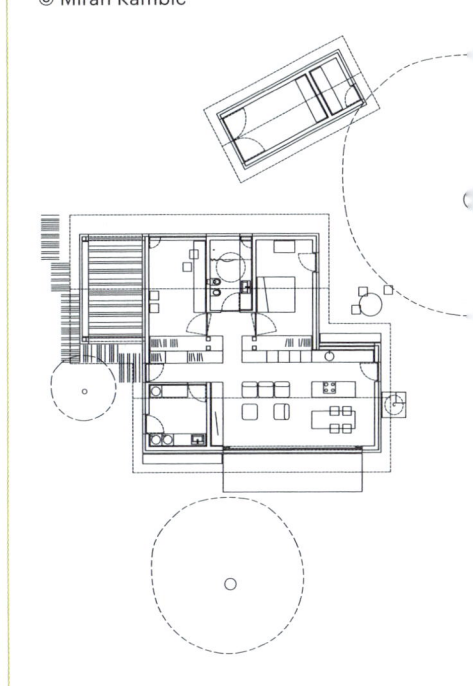

Covering the Remains of the Church of St. John the Baptist in the Žiče Charterhouse

Stare Slemene, Slovenia

2020/2020-2022

MEDPROSTOR, arhitekturni atelje

Rok Žnidaršič, Jerneja Fischer Knap, Samo Mlakar, Katja Ivić, Dino Mujić

Municipality of Slovenske Konjice

(Public)
Culture · 350 m² · 7€/m²

The former upper monastery of the Žiče Charterhouse has stood at the end of the valley since the 12th century. It is a conceptually thought-out solution, which resolves several key points of the half-century-old dilemma concerning the acceptability of interventions in historic building materials and the question of how to protect them.

With this architectural solution, the church has once again become a dominant coherent spatial site with its original dimension recreated, while the floating monolith forms both a physical and symbolic turning point between past interventions and the doctrine of modern cultural heritage protection: the space between a ruin and a reconstruction. The open, movable roof also aptly expresses the intangible value of the collective memory of the last two hundred years when the church was a ruin through the view that rises above the stone walls towards the sky. The architectural intervention re-establishes the historical communication of two spiral staircases, which once led to the upper floors. The two staircases are connected with a new lookout point situated within the gap between the original and secondary north wall.

The renovation had to comply with contemporary technical, programming, and conservation requirements. The construction and restoration interventions in the existing walls were carried out in such a way that they enable the nine-hundred-year-old sacred space to be read chronologically. As part of the renovation, the reconstruction of the demolished part of the northern wall of the church was completed. The largest intervention was the covering of the existing church with a semi-movable folding roof. A hybrid solution, the movable folding roof allows two extremes at the same time: when lowered, it enables the events in the church to run smoothly, regardless of the season and weather, while when raised, it preserves one of the most important intangible features of the ruins, contact with the open sky. For access to the top of the ruins or to the 'loft' of the new roof, new suspended spiral staircases were designed in the existing vertical shafts of the former spiral staircases.

The biggest attraction of the renovation is the movable folding roof, which occupies a special place of significance within the project. It is a rough, high-tech facility, a literal technological 'machine', which acts as a specific architectural tool, intended to preserve a distinctly non-technological, practically immaterial effect, the open sky above the main nave of the church. The extremely pragmatic and modern solution is also intended to preserve the subtle ambience with an open sky, which is the part that is particularly interesting about this extremely material, technical-mechanical solution of the architectural project. The high-tech modern solution in the renovation project does not appear as an apotheosis of the achievements of modern construction, rather it enables an intense phenomenological experience of the immaterial qualities of the remains of the former monastery, while at the same time protecting them from further deterioration. Perhaps precisely because of this, the project's guiding principle could be described as a search for an intersection between the 'matter of the immaterial' on the one hand and the 'immaterial matter' on the other.

MEDPROSTOR, ARHITEKTURNI ATELJE

302

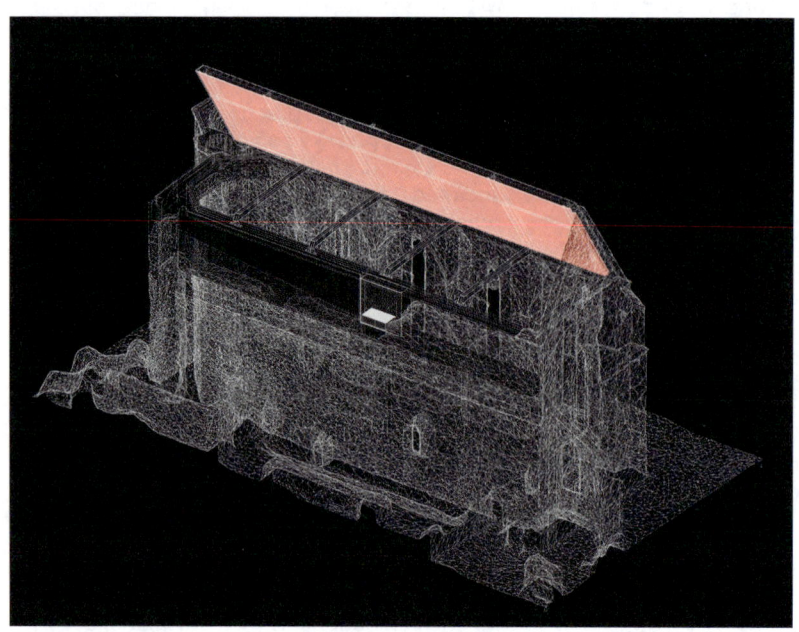

SHORTLISTED

Axonometry

COVERING THE REMAINS OF THE CHURCH OF ST. JOHN THE BAPTIST IN THE ŽIČE CHARTERHOUSE

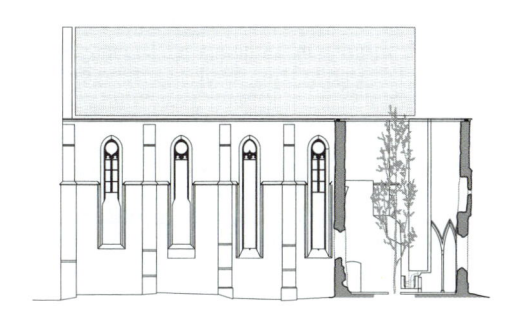

Longitudinal section

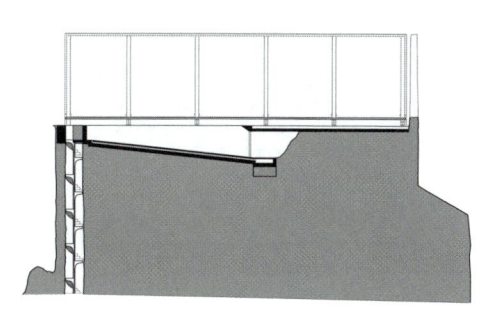

Elevation

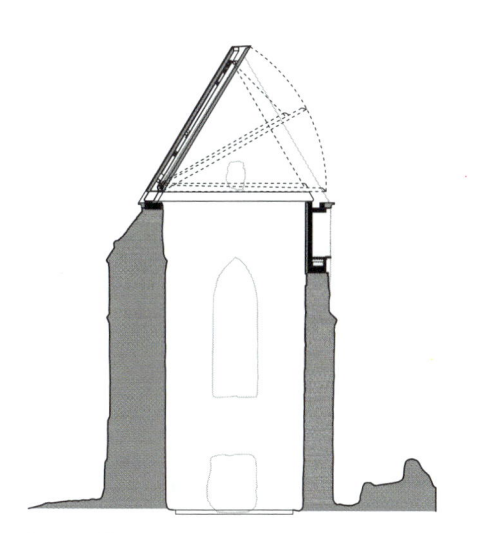

Cross section

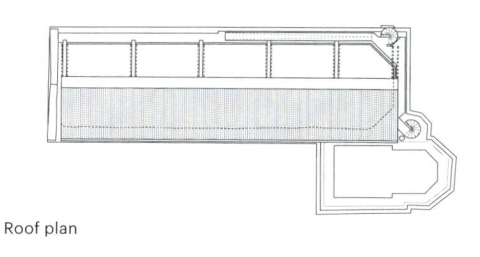

Roof plan

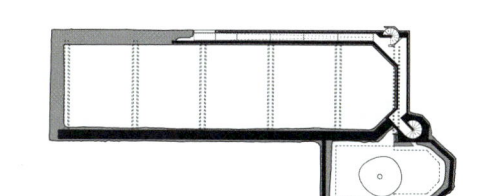

Floor plan

MEDPROSTOR, ARHITEKTURNI ATELJE

Due to the expansion of the vineyard's capacity, it was necessary to expand the winery by building an extension to the existing wine cellar. The extension is interpolated in a way that forms a new ensemble with a green plaza in the center. The winery, with its conception and choice of materials, is integrated into that natural scenery and so becomes an integral part of the ecosystem that surrounds it, preserving the biodiversity. To make wine without interventions, a biodynamic winemaker must use grapes in the way that nature produces them. Just like that, we used each building material in its raw natural state.

Tomac Winery
› **JASTERBARSKO, CROATIA**
2020/2020-2021
Industrial · 603m^2 · 2,305€/m^2
› **DVA ARHITEKTA**
Tomislav Curkovic, Zoran Zidaric
Tomac Winery (Private)
© Sandro Lendler

The essence of the project lies in the transformation of the Old Glassworks and its neighboring public spaces, guided by the vision of creating a vibrant hub for local culture. It transcends mere physical alterations, as its goal is to revitalize the very spirit of Ptuj's historic old town, ensuring its enduring relevance as a cultural focal point. The project's central theme revolves around bridging the old and the new, providing solutions to the challenges posed by the site and the program. The selection of materials, inspired by the diverse character of the old city center, ingeniously incorporates existing elements, thoughtfully reimagined for a contemporary context.

Revitalization of Old Glassworks and Surrounding Urban Areas in Old Town of Ptuj
› **PTUJ, SLOVENIA**
2020/2021-2023
Mixed use - Cultural & Social · 1,361m^2
› **Elementarna, Kolektiv Tektonika**
Ambrož Bartol, Dominik Košak, Miha Munda, Rok Staudacher, Matevž Zalar, Samo Kralj, Darja Matjašec, Katja Mali, Pia Kante
City Municipality of Ptuj (Public)
© Miran Kambič

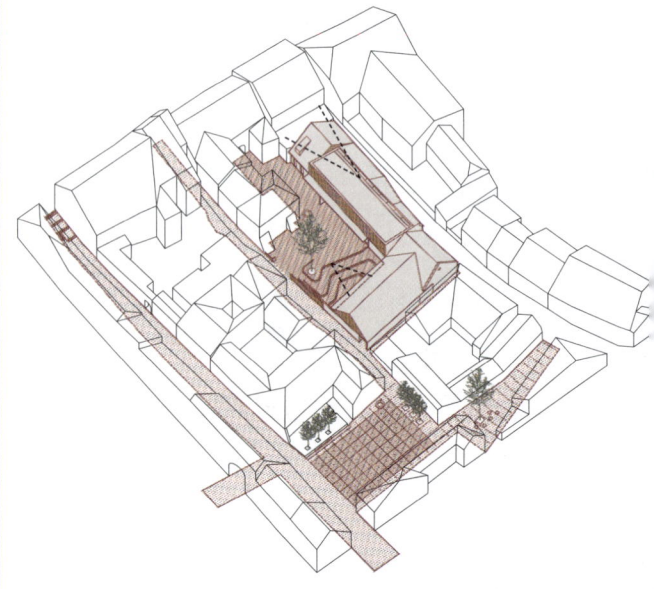

SHORTLISTED

**Riding Hall.
Land Registry
Department of the
Municipal Civil
Court**
Zagreb, Croatia
2019/2020-2022
MORE arhitekture
Davor Busnja
Ministry of Justice
(Public)
Government & Civic · 5,700m²

This Riding Stable was originally part of the Austro-Hungarian military complex and has been transformed into the contemporary space for the Land Registry Department of the Municipal Civil Court in Zagreb. The building is located in the southern part of the forthcoming Justice Square; it is the winning design from an urban and architectural competition for the location.

The reconstruction of the Riding Stable into the Land Registry represents a significant and first transformation of the future Justice Square. The original floor plan dimensions and proportions of the protected building were not sufficient to accommodate the new use. The emphasis was placed on preserving the original composition of the existing Riding Stable whilst adding a new annex. The new transparent steel-glass extension creates a contrast to the existing red building and preserves and showcases its characteristic composition and typological uniqueness.

The former Riding Stable consists of two parts: a large riding hall and a small entrance volume. The sturdy, reconstructed brick building finds its counterpart in the light, transparent steel-glass structure. The former entrance volume becomes a house within the new house. The entrance hall at the junction of the existing building and the new annex functions as a covered outdoor space, with entrances from the south and north, forming a passage between the busy street and the upcoming Justice Square. This conceptual approach interprets the entrance space not just as an entry into the building but as an urban passage.

The structure and spatial proportions of the Riding Stable conditioned the concept of the programme's distribution in the form of strips combined with voids that provide natural lighting. The inserted strips follow the structural grid of the old building and create a spatial and structural rhythm for the new extension.

The project strikes a delicate balance between robust old structure and the careful insertion of the new one, both in terms of programmatic and construction aspects, as well as in the selection and design of used materials. Light plays a crucial role in the organisation of the space. The layout of Riding Stable influenced the concept of the primary spatial layout, establishing a rhythm of programmatic strips combined with voids to provide natural lighting to all workspaces. The existing brick walls of the old building are reflected in the glazed brick of the service cubes and in the translucent membranes of the courtrooms, which are bordered by glass bricks. Wrought iron beams that have been restored, providing support for the roof of the existing building. These beams find their counterpart in the form of steel frames on top of the new annex. They not only support the building's roof and façade but also bear the second floor of the structure.

307

EXISTING
RIVETED IRON BEAMS

2. floor

OFFICE OPEN SPACE

COMPOSITE REINFORCED
SLAB

COURT ROOMS
ADMINISTRATION

LIGHTWEIGHT STEEL
STRUCTURE

STEEL FRAMEWORK

1. floor

OFFICES
OPEN SPACE

REINFORCED CONCRETE
"TABLES"

REINFORCED CONCRETE
"TABLES"

EXISTING MASONRY

COURT ROOMS

REGISTRATION OFFICE

TYPIST OFFICE
TECHICAL SERVICE

ground floor

COUNTER HALL
REGISTRATION OFFICE

RIDING STABLE | entrance - passage | NEW ANNEX

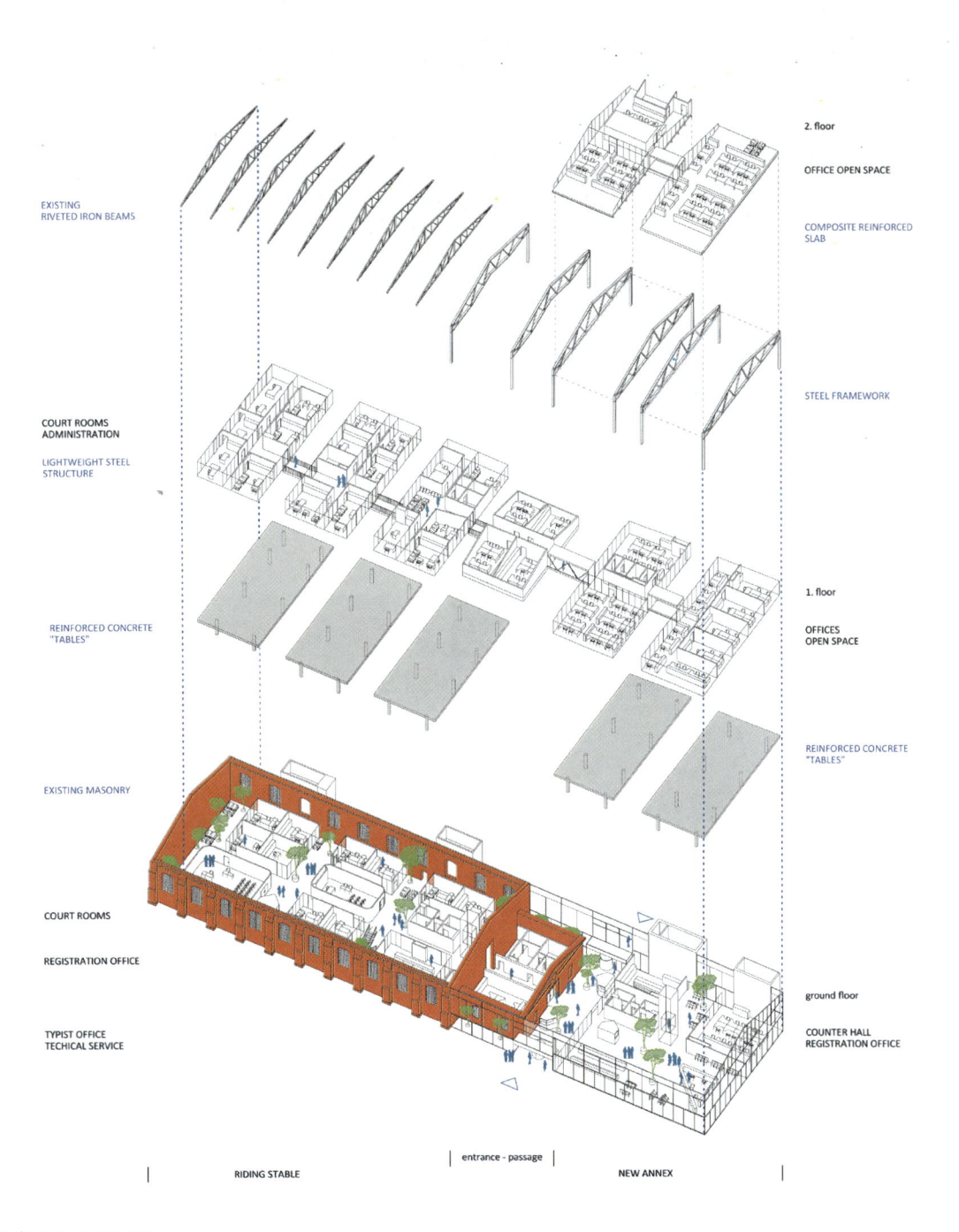

Program diagram axonometry

MORE ARHITEKTURE

308

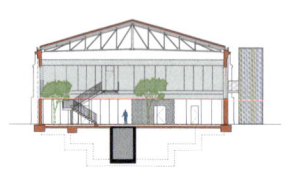

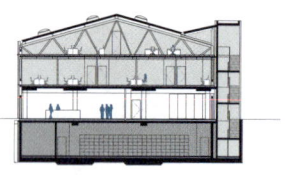

SHORTLISTED

Cross sections

Longitudinal section

RIDING HALL. LAND REGISTRY DEPARTMENT OF THE MUNICIPAL CIVIL COURT   0 5 10   20

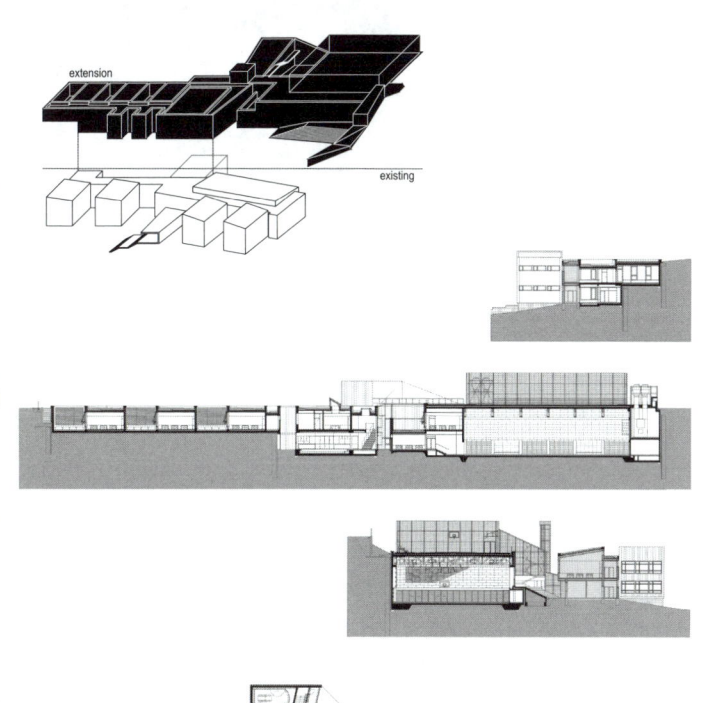

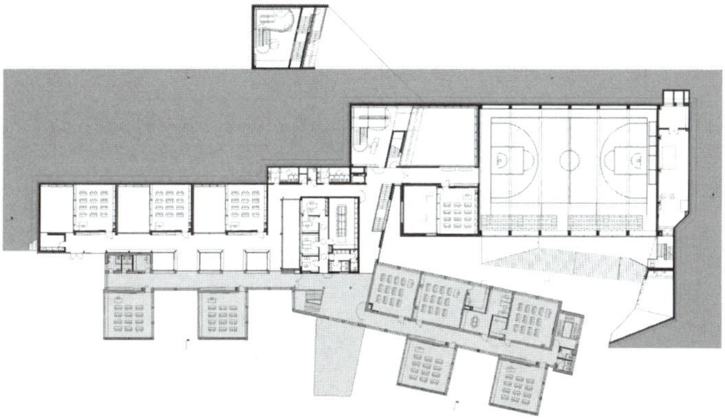

The reconstruction had the goal of adapting the existing school to modern educational content and expanding it with new classrooms, a library, necessary accompanying spaces and a large sports hall. Old pavilion-type classrooms skillfully fit the context, following the rhythm of the neighboring single-family houses, while a block connecting them is placed along the hill. The entire intervention was carried out after extensive earthworks, because there is a height difference of over 20 meters between the old park and the street. The promenade through the old city park wasn't connected to the system of city stairs on the lower side of the street because it was interrupted by the school lot. The project also sought to improve the system of public spaces between the street and the old park. It is crucial that a densely built complex strikes a balance between sometimes conflicting requirements: a sense of spaciousness with plenty of natural light and views, but also the intimacy and privacy of educational spaces. It was the search for that balance that determined the design of the ambience by playing with transparent and translucent surfaces.

Reconstruction and Extension of Primary School Ksaver Sandor Gjalski

› **ZAGREB, CROATIA**
2007/2020-2022
Education · 5,000m² · 2,656€/m²
› **Studio BF**
Željko Golubić, Zoran Boševski, Boris Fiolić
City of Zagreb (Public)
© Robert Leš

The new kindergarten is located at the foot of a north-facing slope, surrounded by corn fields and single-family houses. The context offered an opportunity to explore the relations between institutional and domestic spaces. The kindergarten is a compact single-story volume conceived as a "neighborhood inside a house". The spaces are organized along a central communication axis: children's units are oriented to the south while all other spaces face the north. The central communication axis acts as a kind of "inner street", expanding and overlapping with the multi-purpose hall, the children's wardrobes, an entrance area with space for strollers and a niche for working in small groups.

Kindergarten in Gornja Stubica

› **GORNJA STUBICA, CROATIA**
  2018/2019-2021
  Education · 1,146m²
› **MVA / Mikelić Vreš Arhitekti**
  Marin Mikelić, Tomislav Vreš
  Municipality of Gornja Stubica (Public)
  © Jure Živković

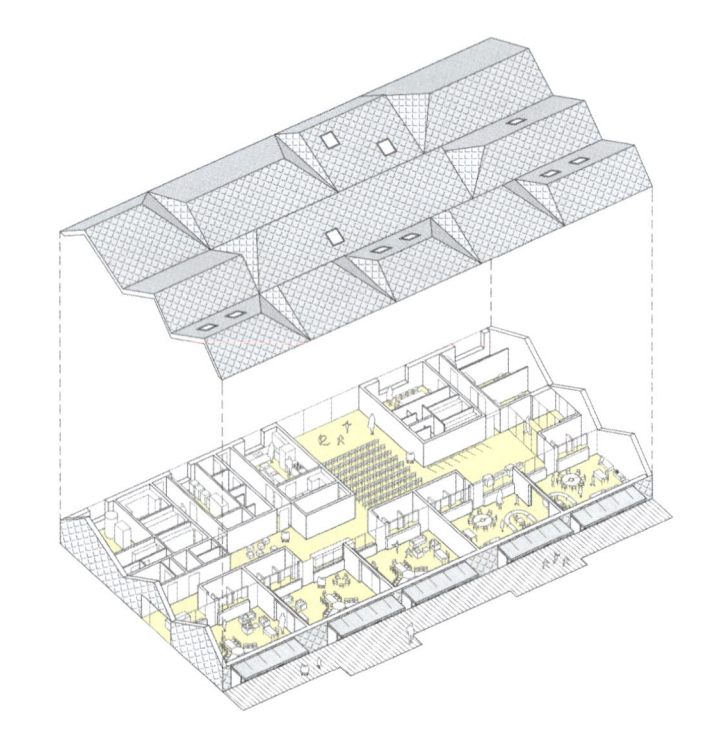

SHORTLISTED

Lonja Wetlands Wildlife Observatories and Visitor Centre

Osekovo, Croatia

2013/2019-2021

roth&čerina

Mia Roth, Tonči Čerina

Park prirode Lonjsko polje

(Public)
Landscape · 430m² · 1500 €/m²

This project aims to allow visitors to explore the unique protected landscape of the Lonja wetlands through a network of entry-points, visitor centres, and observatories placed along the edges of the nature park. The visitor infrastructure embodies centuries of culture adapting to a landscape in constant flux, of anthropogenic and natural symbioses, one that has a border status.

The Osekovo visitor centre samples rural morphologies and tells the stories of its flora and fauna as well as its cultural heritage. It repeats the scales and materials of the surrounding rural morphologies, placing an info-point and administration office in one house, and an exhibition space and auditorium in the other. The two buildings frame a communal square defined by deep trapezoid porticos and denivelations, initiating a focus on rural communal life. To expose the radical changes this environment goes through even closer, a network of observatories has been placed along its edges. They serve as markers and viewpoints for witnessing the slow change of the waters, migrating wildlife, and free-range livestock, but also represent a playful element of the landscape. Their biomorphic language is not explicit, yet it embodies movement, organic form, and traditional tools, echoing familiar local aspects.

Centuries of dynamic symbioses of wild, domesticated, and human species created expressions of a cultural heritage which grew from the relationship of an everchanging landscape and communities synchronizing their way of life with it. The exhibition of the visitor centre presents this unique, centuries old coexistence, condensing a wide ranging sensory introduction before embarking on a visit to the vast wetland. The observatories continue the distinct, upright vertical language of past watchtowers placed along the divides of two empires, hunting box-stands and old observatories, now reframing their role as devices for raising awareness of the importance of this environment. They enable a view of the horizontal wetland and its diverse lifeforms, in which the visitors remain hidden to the wildlife and livestock passing by. Establishing a dialogue of their own, free from direct references, these points act as mediators between the native, the cultural, and the mythic. In a non-hierarchical environment these new points provide a fleeting identity, blurring the borders between the languages of the anthropogenic and the natural.

The Lonja wetlands go through radical changes over the course of a year, with the flooding rhythm attracting birds and fish, feeding oak and ash groves, and providing plains for freely roaming livestock. These species and specific built heritage provide the basis for the materialization of the infrastructure. The structures of both the visitor centre and the observatories utilize contemporary locally sourced materials, repeating vernacular morphologies and techniques. Using available materials, built by local builders, communicated a sense of belonging not only in the project but also in the construction of the network. The main materials in both the centre and the observatories are oak and steel, with additions of ash, chestnut, and larch. The airy space inside each building connecting the ground floor and the gallery is filled with wooden sculptural installations connoting flocks, driftwood, and flux. In the exhibition, a complex ecosystem is interpreted through a combination of analogue interactive exhibits, stories told through digital media, sculptural fragments, and tactile reliefs, communicating the wetlands through traditional materials in new implementations.

LONJA WETLANDS WILDLIFE OBSERVATORIES AND VISITOR CENTRE

ROTH&ČERINA

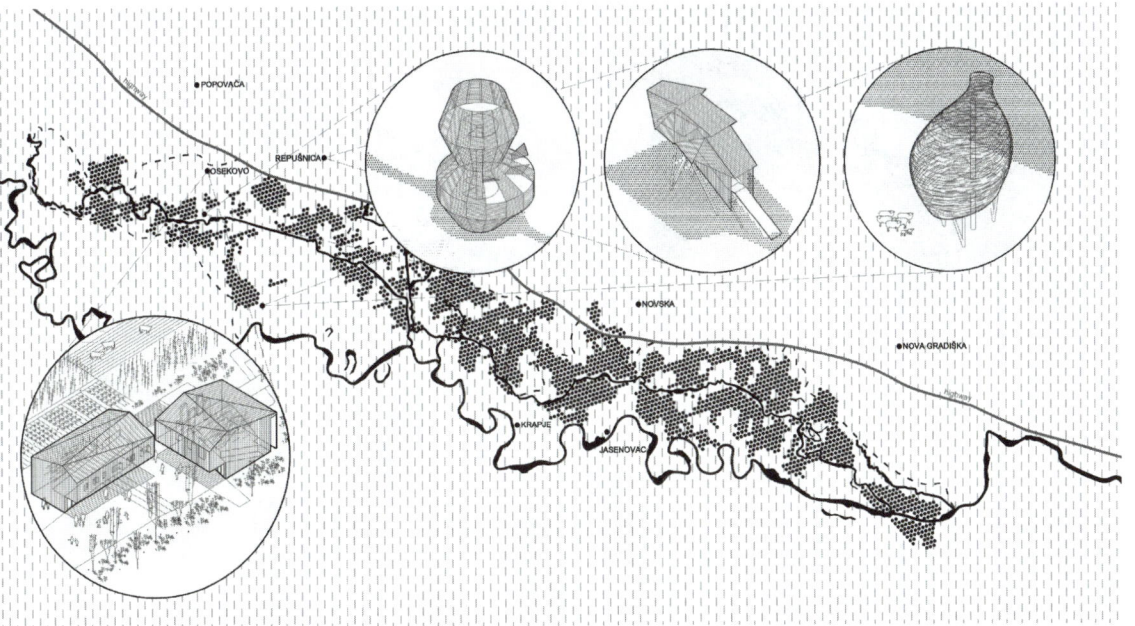

314

SHORTLISTED

Section

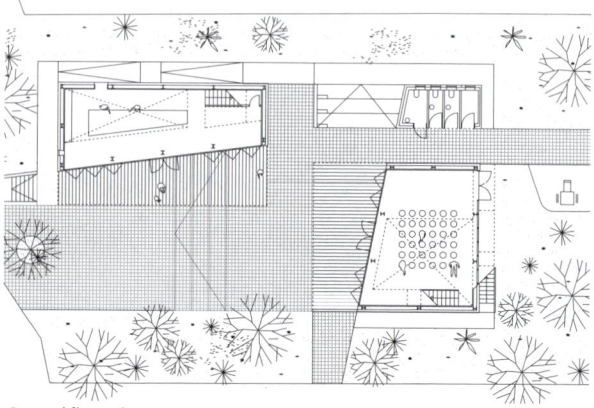

Ground floor plan

LONJA WETLANDS WILDLIFE OBSERVATORIES AND VISITOR CENTRE

The new hall project inherited its former orientation as an important criterion to be integrated with the building's new external and internal layout. The hall has been placed on a lot sloping toward the west and configured to respond to the given urban and topographic determinants. The perimeter around the hall is designed to establish a connection between the school square and the lower plateau with an open court and school parking area for the school bus and vehicles bringing children from neighboring villages. Attention has been paid to incorporating customized prefab elements. Unique types of panels were developed with the outer and inner layer made of pigmented black concrete and thermal isolation between them.

Community Sports Hall
› ZLATAR BISTRICA, CROATIA
 2016/2020-2021
 Sport & Leisure · 2,019m^2 ·
 3,200,000€
› NOP Studio
 Ivan Galic
 Zlatar Bistrica Primary School (Public)
 ↑ © Arxiu NOP Studio
 ↗ © Bosnić+Dorotić

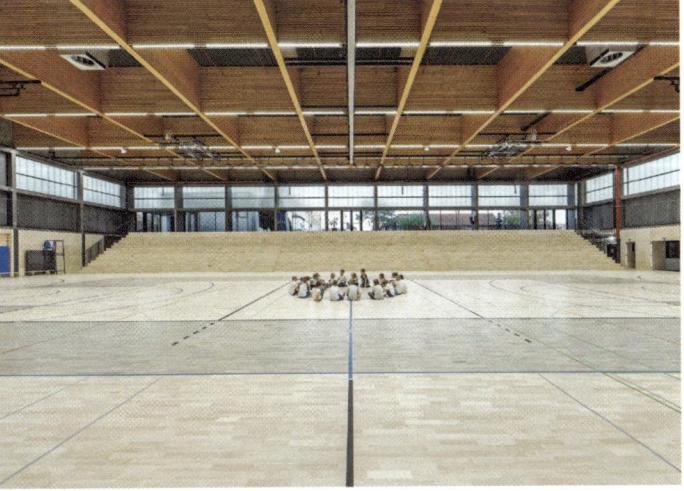

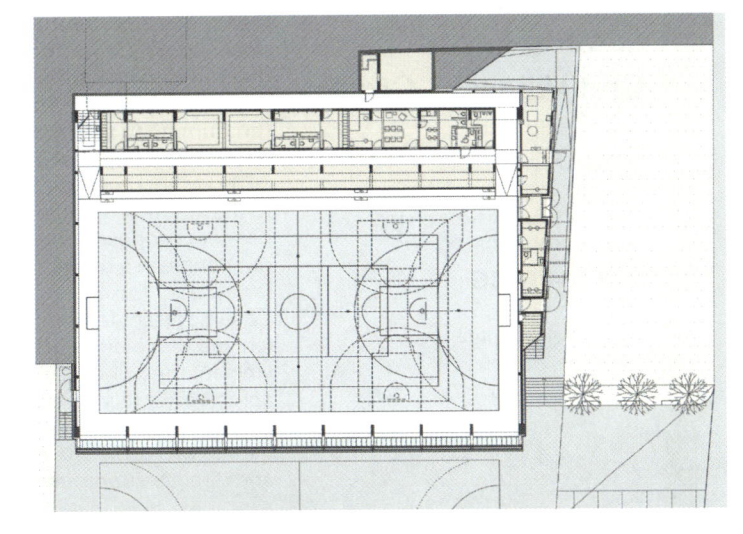

Black Slavonian Eco Pig Farm
Cret Viljevski, Croatia
2019/2020-2021

SKROZ
Margita Grubiša, Marin Jelčić, Daniela Škarica, Ivana Žalac, Zvonimir Marčić

Sin ravnice
(Private)
Industrial · 622,4m²

The Black Slavonian pig is an indigenous Croatian breed. During the 20th century, the number of individuals declined, and it was declared endangered. Fortunately, there is a revived interest in this breed. This farm was designed to accommodate the needs of traditional farming thus aiming to achieve innovative solutions using traditional, local materials.

The architectural project required a farm design according to the strictest organic farming standards. Urban design concept proposes two identical complexes positioned at a right angle in a rotated coordinate system, thus forming the farmyards.

An important factor for the choice of materials was the resilience of the elements that are in direct contact with animals who are fond of digging and biting everything they come across. With this in mind, concrete was selected for the base with a wooden structure above it, and finally, the traditional flat tile was used as a roof cover. Materials are simple, rough, and directly subordinate to the function and context.

Apart from the essential function, the appearance of the buildings is conditioned by the context of the rural Slavonian region, which is visible in the geometry of the roof, the cover of the panes, and in the material and method of treating the façade.

Conceptual design decisions were driven by the need to optimize function. Usually, this type of building is a low-rise with livestock spaces and a passage in the middle. The straw storage space for animal bedding should be right next to the pens. The central passage then serves for feeding the livestock, spreading the bedding, and removing manure after cleaning.

By adding a gallery, the space was rationalized, the breeding process was optimized, and the transportation of manure was eliminated as the plan is to store it in the same building. In addition, movable partitions have been introduced to simplify the building's maintenance, and enabled flexible scenarios adapted to the life within the pens.

The sum of all these parameters and the consideration of the proportions of man, animal and machine, resulted in the section with the highest point in the middle with a double-pitched roof and a central ridge. The roof panes have been broken and dislocated in the ridge, allowing for additional lighting and ventilation in the storage area in the gallery. The extension of the roof pane formed an eave overhanging the outdoor area for sows with their piglets.

The materials chosen for the building had to be resilient and easy to maintain because of the direct contact with porcine animals. With this in mind, raw waterproof concrete was selected for the base with a wooden structure above and galvanized steel partitions. The wooden façade features traditional, commonplace flat tiles used as a roof cover.

Materials are often used in the vernacular architecture of the region of Slavonia.

The wood used is Slavonian oak, a native wood from the region of Slavonia. For this project, the investor bought local wood and it was dried for a year before it could be used as a building material.

The transparency of the façade does not come from the material, but from its geometry. The sequence of wooden laths made of Slavonian oak with interchangeable full and empty fields in two diagonal directions and two planes create a distinctive structure. This structure primarily serves to provide ventilation and protection from the sun, but also functions as a reinterpretation of the geometry of wooden façades found on numerous vernacular outbuildings in Slavonia.

This reinterpretation connects an outbuilding designed by contemporary standards with its environment and built heritage.

SKROZ D.O.O.

318

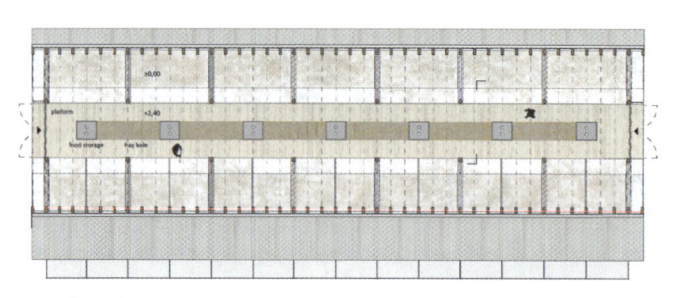

SHORTLISTED

First floor plan

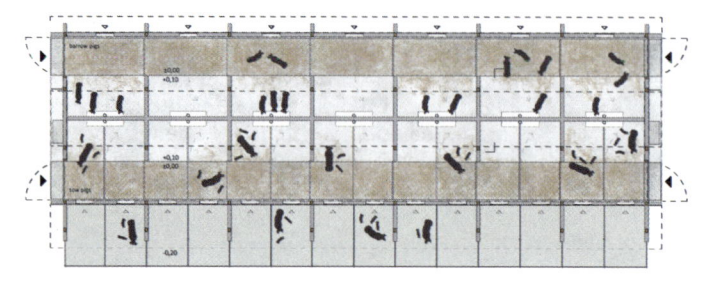

Stable floor plan

BLACK SLAVONIAN ECO PIG FARM

0 5 10   20

↑ 185

THE TYPICAL ORGANISATION OF A STABLE

SEPARATE STORAGE AND BEDDING TRANSPORT — BEDDING ADDING — MANURE REMOVING

MIDDLE CORRIDOR

BEDDING ADDING / BEDDING TRANSPORT
MANURE REMOVING / MANURE TRANSPORT

THE IMPROVED ORGANISATION OF A STABLE

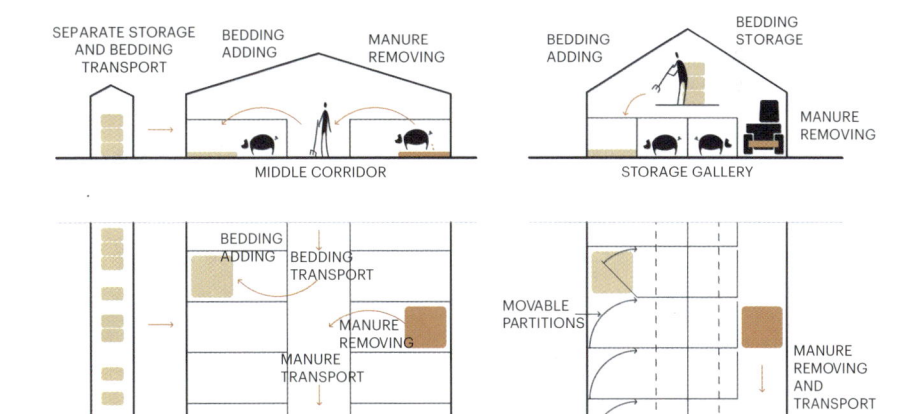

BEDDING ADDING — BEDDING STORAGE — MANURE REMOVING

STORAGE GALLERY

MOVABLE PARTITIONS

MANURE REMOVING AND TRANSPORT

Concept: Organization

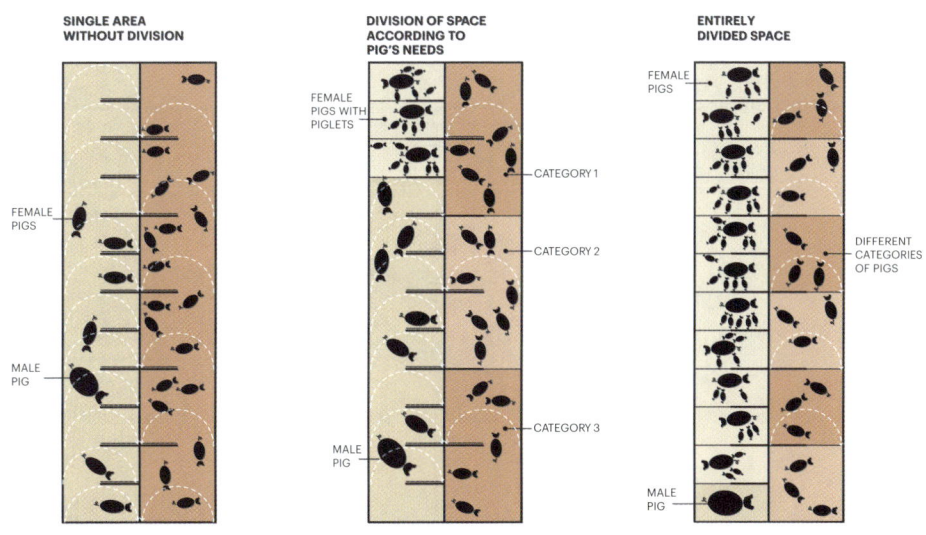

SINGLE AREA WITHOUT DIVISION
FEMALE PIGS
MALE PIG

DIVISION OF SPACE ACCORDING TO PIG'S NEEDS
FEMALE PIGS WITH PIGLETS
CATEGORY 1
CATEGORY 2
CATEGORY 3
MALE PIG

ENTIRELY DIVIDED SPACE
FEMALE PIGS
DIFFERENT CATEGORIES OF PIGS
MALE PIG

Concept: Possible scenearios of stable division enabled by movable partitions

SKROZ D.O.O.   ↓ 239

The urban concept was not to demolish the old market hall nearby. Our suggestion was to find a new function instead. The new building is also organized inside according to a sustainable way of thinking. The pattern of the arches is familiar for people opposed to the radicalism of modernism, whose buildings, which are barely tolerated socially, often become the victim of amortization and demolishment. Early in the designing process, we found two commercial archetypes: the classical Roman basilica and the middle eastern bazaar. Both archetypes appear in the new market hall, though of course in an abstract way. The new market hall is a result of the urban situation, familiar cultural and historical layers and the desire for sustainability.

New Market Hall of Pécs
› PÉCS, HUNGARY
2019/2020-2022
Commerce · 5,625m²
› **GETTO plan, SZTR studio**
Gergely Sztranyák, Tamás Getto
City of Pécs (Public)
↑ © greypixel
↗ © Attila Gulyás

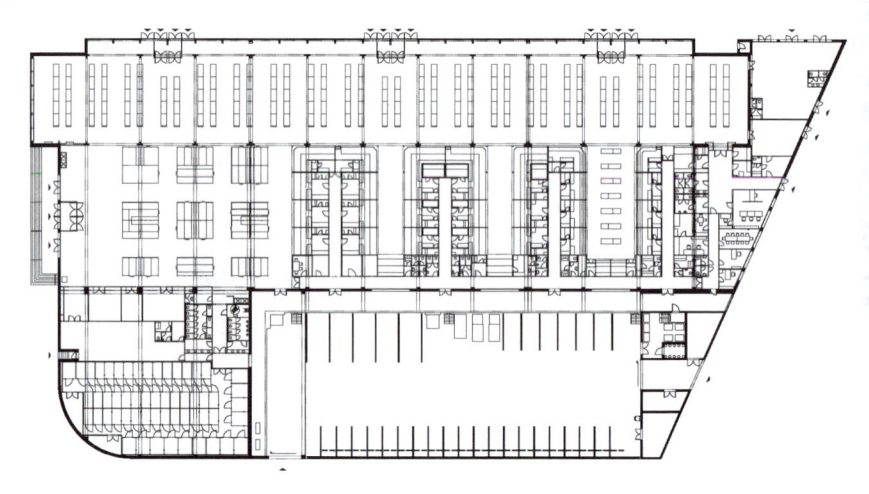

SHORTLISTED

Nursery. 1306 Plants for Timișoara
Timișoara, Romania
2022/2023
MAIO, Studio Nomadic, Studio Peisaj
María Charneco Llanos, Anna Puigjaner Barberá, Alfredo Lérida Horta, Guillermo López Ibáñez, Silvia Tripșa, Victor Popovici, Nicoleta Postolache, Alexandru Ciobotă, Raluca Rusu
Ordinul Arhitectilor din România – Filiala Teritoriala Timis
(Public)
Ephemeral-Society · 486m^2 · 102€/m^2

The proposal is an ephemeral structure that hosts a tree nursery and spaces for public discussions concerning the use of public space and its relationship with greenery. After the structure's limited lifecycle, the trees will be planted around the city according to the citizens' wishes.

Within the frame of Timisoara European Capital of Culture 2023, the proposal takes on a symbolic centrality in the city and therefore aims to be an open test for how public spaces can be used, designed and perceived, where people are invited to understand plants as agents able to regulate the climate in cities but also to boost public engagement.

With an eye fixed on the future urban transformations of the area, the proposal seeks to open new perspectives and debates about the uses and temporalities of the city and its engagement with various communities and institutions.

SHORTLISTED

Built using a logic fully focused on re-use, once dismantled, the intervention will provide new plants for the city. They will be planted according to the agreements made by the citizens and local government.

Timisoara is undergoing a process of urban transformation. The intervention, located in the city centre, had to function for one year as a device to activate urban engagement, opening up new perspectives and debates about the uses and temporalities of the city and its engagement with various communities and institutions.

The installation is located in an extremely sensitive, central, and contested site in the city: precisely where the Revolution sparked in 1989, in Victory Square, a public space that was designed as a promenade but does not really function as a proper square, with its non-accessible, ornamental green area structuring how people circulate and how the space is divided.

Taking the future urban transformations of the area into account, the project is also an invitation to a new understanding of a friendlier and more sustainable public space in which greenery becomes an essential social agent, from its ability to provide drainage to how it allows ecosystems to live together.

The design employs logic based fully on re-use, from its rented scaffolding structure to the plants that will be planted around the city afterwards.

The nursery represents an extended cycle of natural processes. The circuit took shape in the local nursery and, once the installation is dismantled, the nursery will become an open collective garden.

Aware of the role that nature and, more broadly, new forms of urban planning will play in the future of our cities, the landscape architecture firm Studio Peisaj added a deep contextual knowledge of (bio)diverse compositions to the proposal which ranged from local species to the cultural tradition of horticulture in the area.

From another perspective, the project also encompasses the notion of care and includes an educational and social dimension. Gardens were, among other places, educational spaces, places to meet. As contemporary public spaces, they are also spaces for dissent and political struggle.

Map of future installations

NURSERY. 1306 PLANTS FOR TIMIȘOARA

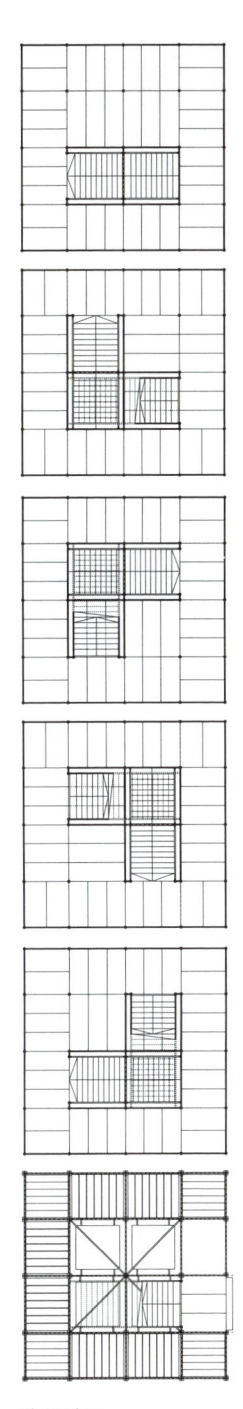

Floor plans

MAIO, STUDIO NOMADIC, STUDIO PEISAJ

324

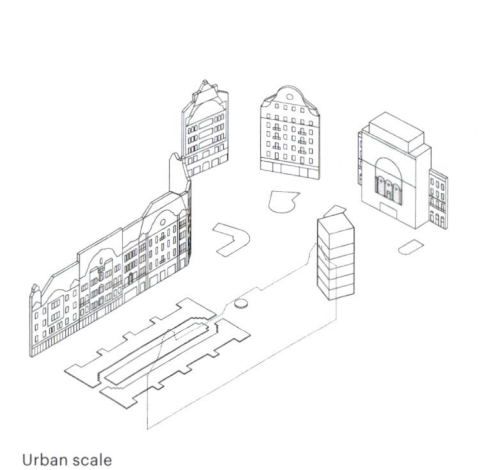

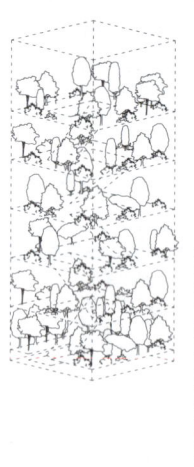

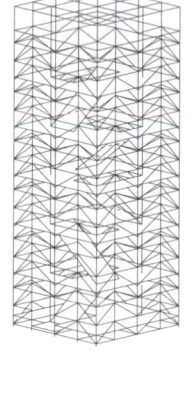

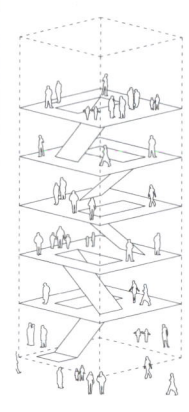

SHORTLISTED

Urban scale

Programmatic diagram

NURSERY. 1306 PLANTS FOR TIMIȘOARA

F.I.D. is a platform for socio-cultural interaction, a meeting space in the Fabric neighborhood. It is contained between the physical boundaries of a participatory architectural installation and the fair play rules of an amateur football tournament. It is a community activation project that aims to stimulate an identity of place and social cohesion. From an architectural perspective, the installation consists of a multi-functional scaffolding and a mini football field made of natural grass. Both constitute a symbolic agora for the neighborhood community, where freedom of expression and community gestures are practiced through sports, events and other spontaneous activities.

F.I.D. Football as Infrastructure of Democracy

› **TIMIȘOARA, ROMANIA**
2022/2022-2023
Society · 4,050m²

› **Casa Jakab Toffler, Atelier VRAC, ISO Birou Arhitectura, Atelier Olimpia Onci**
Gabriel Aurel Boldiș, Laura Adela Borotea, Alexandru Ciobotă, Bogdan Liviu Isopescu, Olimpia Onci-Isopescu, Cristian Andrei Bădescu, Zenaida Elena Florea
Casa Jakab Toffler NGO (Public)
↑ © Marius Vasile
↗ © Caroline Dethier

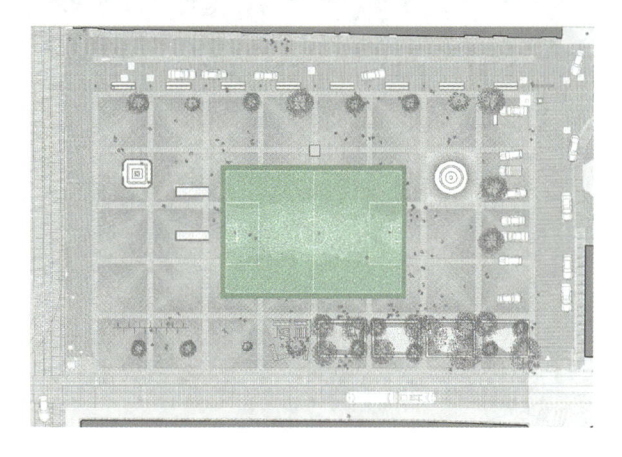

326

From
BORDEAUX
France
44°50'55"N — 0°33'40"W

to
DUMBRAVA VLĂSIEI
Romania
44°38'58"N — 26°06'54"E

This new eco-district is located on the former railway wasteland and the Niel barracks. The Ekko residence includes a building of 49 apartments with a living area covering 3,260 m². It is part of a sustainable and innovative building approach, bringing together a vertical garden with floating trees and apartments under the same roof.
The Niel master plan is governed by bio-climatic town planning rules which favor natural sunshine and lead to a very precise geometric division, imposing on each of the lots to be built in a constrained and complex volume. The Ekko project is designed to respond to the climatic and ecological emergencies of our time, as well as social urgencies, particularly in connection with urban housing.

Ekko

› **BORDEAUX, FRANCE**
 2016/2019-2021
 Collective housing · 3,465m²
› **Duncan Lewis**
 Duncan Lewis, Brigitte Cany Lewis, Isabelle Auriat
 Groupe Launay (Private)
 ↑ © Drone 33
 → © Duncan Lewis

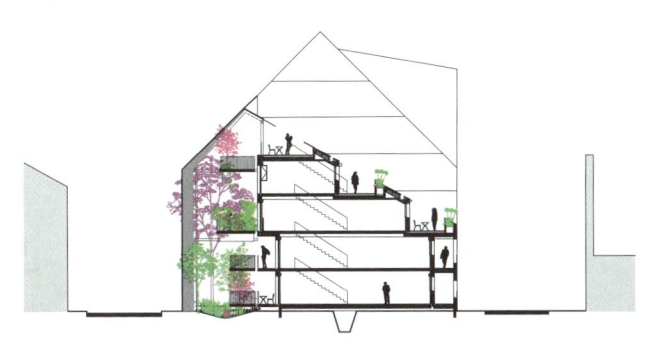

A genuine "Cathédrale des Sports", the building houses spaces for practicing different sports, bringing together in the same volume a climbing complex, a racket zone, a bar area, a fitness area, e-sports and golf. The building is designed to multiply routes and viewing points between the sports, the district and the city. Open to all and offering everyone a spectacular view of the city center and the vineyards, this architectural statement underscores the building's role as part of the geography of the Bordeaux region. Located on the site of the former Soferti factories, in a flooded area, the transparent project opens up 360° to this heterogeneous area undergoing major change. The building is designed as a simple assemblage of low-carbon concrete slabs, beams and columns.

UCPA Sport Station Bordeaux Brazza (The Sports Cathedral)

› BORDEAUX, FRANCE
2016/2021-2023
Sport & Leisure · 15,741m² · 1,236€/m²
› **NP2F**
François Chas, Nicolas Guerin, Fabrice Long, Paul Maitre-Devallon
ADIM Nouvelle Aquitaine (Private)
© Maxime Delvaux

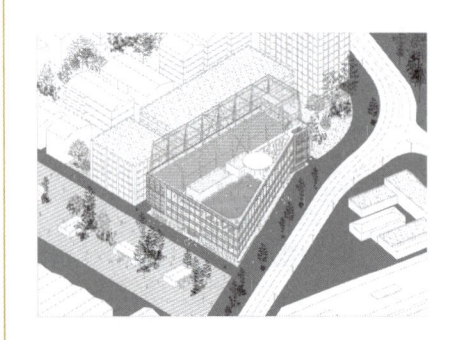

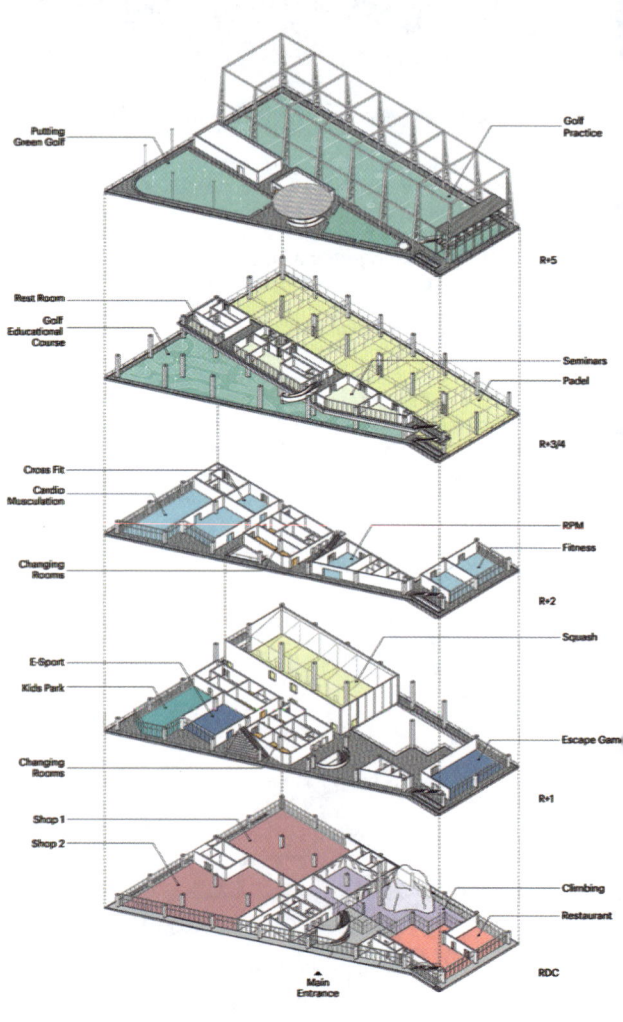

The stone installation will be carried out in a stable, stationary structure, made of metal construction. It will be spread over a space of 96 m², six meters high, and supported by a full plinth on the floor with varying sections connected to the plane of the platform. The cladding of the wall structure and the cover will be made with lightweight materials such as Polystyrene, trying to negate any counterpoint of weight and support. The platform and side walls made of metal construction will be covered with the decorative resin for the floor, applied by spatula and with the fire classification. In the interior, the structure will have a neutral cream color, both on the walls and floor, as well as in the showrooms, while the surface will be painted red.

Chronicle in Stone
› **TURIN, ITALY**
2023/2023
Ephemeral · 96m² · 1,170€/m²
› **MATT ARCHITECT & ASSOCIATES, Ergys Krisiko Studio**
Matilda Pando, Ergys Krisiko
The Albanian Ministry of Culture (Public)
© Matilda Pando

The project is about a two-family building that the property wished to renovate: an isolated, square-plan dwelling composed of a basement, ground floor, first floor and top floor. The architects and the client decided to renovate the existing building without bringing big changes, preferring to build a new independent structure adjacent to it. The demolition of the top floor allowed the new roof to be used as a garden for the new housing unit.

The Hole with the House Around
› **CAMBIANO, ITALY**
2015/2015-2022
Single house · 390m²
› **Elastico Farm**
Stefano Pujatti
Guido Fejles and Paolo Giacomo Fejles (Private)
© Studio Campo

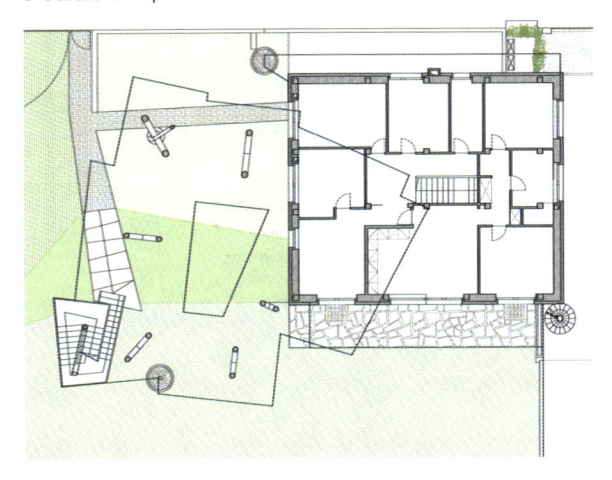

The site is located on the outskirts of Ferrara: an historical jewel of art and architecture, a mix of ancient villages in a landscape that still shows the age-old traditions of the flat Po River Valley. The parish complex acts as a catalyst for the surrounding area, becoming a new center that enhances the identity of the place and promotes socialization, education and interaction. Surrounded by slender trees, the plot creates an intimate and familiar environment where the church's sculptural elements take center stage but engage harmoniously with the surrounding nature. The church is characterized by exceptional volumes and archetypal forms that make it recognizable as a sacred space. Next to the church, the building's profile adopts a more intimate scale to house adjacent spaces for the sacristy, the parish house, a community meeting hall and eight classrooms for various activities. The latter engages with the adjoining school, ensuring a strong connection between the parish complex and its surroundings.

San Giacomo Apostolo Church and Parish Complex

› FERRARA, ITALY
2011/2018-2021
Religion · 1,669m² · 2,200€/m²
› Miralles Tagliabue EMBT
Benedetta Tagliabue, Joan Callis
CEI Conferenza Episcopale Italiana, Parrocchia di San Giacomo Apostolo, Ferrara (Private)
↑ © Marcela Grassi
↗ © Roland Halbe

The project for Palazzo dei Diamanti, a masterpiece of the Italian renaissance, consists of an organic series of interventions aimed at restoring and enhancing the 16th-century complex and at adapting the interior and exterior spaces to the needs of a contemporary museum.
The first intervention concerned the exhibition areas, which have been equipped with new highly technological surfaces behind which all the equipment is hidden. The second intervention consists of the interior design of new spaces in the former Museo del Risorgimento necessary to complete the exhibition activity: a cafeteria, a bookshop and a lecture hall. The third intervention finally concerned the continuity of the paths both inside and outside the building. Between those the most important intervention is the construction of a new loggia that connects the two wings of the palace and mediates between the building and the garden.

Palazzo dei Diamanti Renovation, Restoration and Redevelopment
› **FERRARA, ITALY**
2019/2020-2023
Culture · 4,565m²
› **Labics**
Maria Claudia Clemente, Francesco Isidori
Municipality of Ferrara (Public)
© Marco Cappelletti

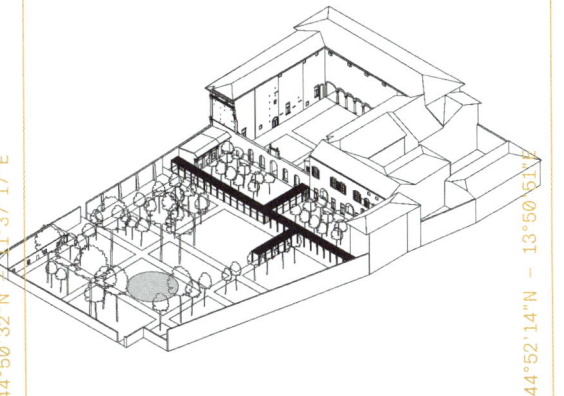

The archaeological remains of the Roman theater are located in the heart of the ancient town of Pula, on the eastern slope of its historical center. The reconstruction project involved a partial restoration of the cavea (seating section), enabling its use for the performing arts.
A new perimeter was built above the traces of a Roman theater. Fragments of lost Platonic order were superimposed on the ancient leftovers. Steel construction was confronted with the stereometric mass of stone. A stage for contemporary performances was introduced in an archeological park. The cultural landscape was immersed in the true nature of culture.

Reconstruction of the Roman Theater
› **PULA, CROATIA**
2013/2020-2022
Culture · 820m² · 4,036€/m²
› **Studio Emil Jurcan**
Emil Jurcan
Archeological museum of Istria (Public)
© Bas Princen

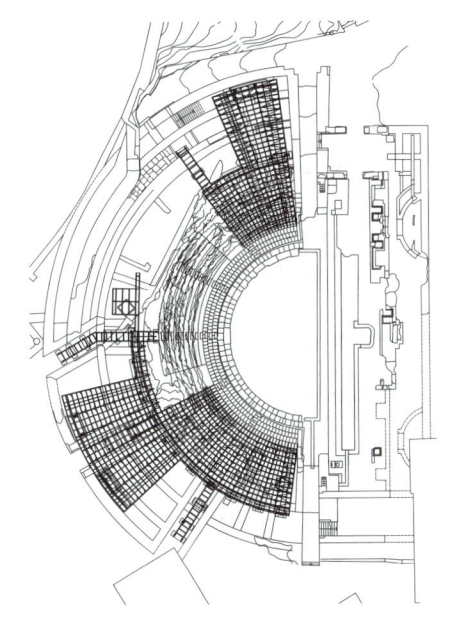

Providur's Palace is the most recently renovated part of an integrated architectural complex in the historical center. A new steel grid, a contemporary intervention within the historical landmarks placed on the roof of the complex, provides the technological, communication and construction backbone of the structure, crucial for the building's viability.
While designing the project to renovate both palaces, the architects decided to keep this precious complex, a frozen image of all the transformations and traumas the buildings experienced through history, in the form in which it was found, and not destroy the existing spatial structure. The overall task for the architects was to create a new and multifaceted interior within the historical compound.

Reconstruction of Providur's Palace
› **ZADAR, CROATIA**
2011/2019-2021
Culture · 5,000m² · 1,760€/m²
› **AB Forum**
Iva Letilovic, Igor Pedisic
City of Zadar (Public)
© Bosnić+Dorotić

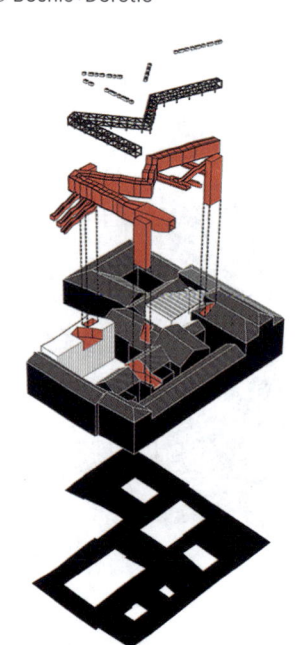

The idea of building a new faculty building has been an aspiration of all its employees since 2011. After the competition, an intervention is planned for the existing building (1889), located on the university campus. The intervention included rehabilitating, reconstructing, extending and upgrading the existing building.
The building's center of gravity is in the intermediate space between the existing building and the new, added part. This spacious inner "street" between the old and the new is a training ground for the interaction between the program and its users.

New Building of the Faculty of Architecture, Civil Engineering and Geodesy
› **BANJA LUKA, BOSNIA - HERZEGOVINA**
2012/2012-2023
Education · 6,900m² · 795€/m²
› **4plus.arhitekti**
Sasha Chvoro, Malina Chvoro
University in Banja Luka (Public)
© Relja Ivanić

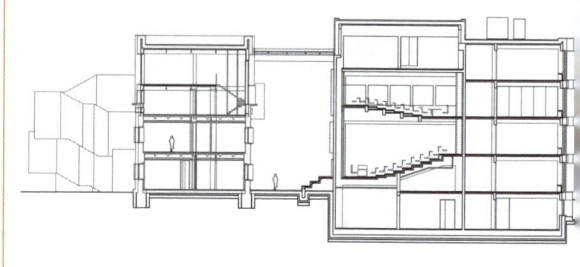

The Pidriš Chapel is an interior design project in a small village near Uskoplje in central Bosnia and Herzegovina. The space has been renovated and its dignity befitting a sacred building has been restored. For a small community like Pidriš, this project was a great success and tangible proof that strength truly resides in unity and collaboration.

The Pidris Chapel Interior
› GORNJI VAKUF- USKOPLJE, BOSNIA - HERZEGOVINA
2021/2022
Religion · 92m² · 330€/m²
› Josipa Skrobo
Josipa Skrobo
Parish of the Assumption of the Blessed Virgin Mary - Uskoplje (Public)
© Fra Josip M Matijanić

The renovation and reconstruction of the house where Ivo Andrić was born is an extremely complex process of planning and thinking about space because it is a very demanding location that is important for the citizens of Travnik and their memory of the place.
The task was to renovate the existing building that represents the birth home of Ivo Andrić and implement a new function in the part that has been upgraded. The existing object was created as a replica of the place where Andrić lived. We rebuilt the entire ground floor and courtyard, while the museum part remained intact both in terms of form and function.

Ivo Andrić's Birth House
› TRAVNIK, BOSNIA - HERZEGOVINA
2020/2020-2021
Culture · 362m² · 750,000€
› Studio Zec, Ledić arhitektura
Amir Vuk Zek, Josip Ledić
Homeland museum Travnik (Public)
© Mala Avlija

This private villa is located deep inside a gorge on a long site bordered by the Lašva River on one side and a very busy motorway on the other side and between two existing buildings, a motel and a petrol station. The idea was to make a house with two faces: the outer one, closed towards the road and a wide protection zone, and the inner one sunlit and facing the river and the forest.

House in Klanac
› ZENICA, BOSNIA - HERZEGOVINA
2018/2019-2021
Single house · 900m² · 1,400€/m²
› Studio Entasis
Vedina Babahmetović
Nermina Čago (Private)
© Anida Kreco

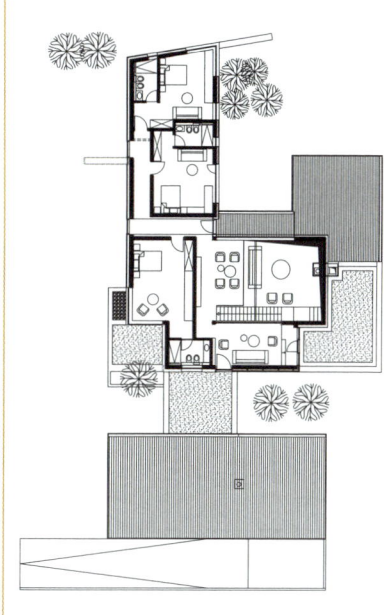

The Hiža Mišljenova house is a reconstruction of an existing house in the village of Puhovac, specific for its tightly connected community of a couple of families, but also for the old Guest Mišljen tombstone that was found there. In the future, the house will be given as a gift to the Puhovac community to serve as the village library.

Hiža Mišljenova House

› **PUHOVAC, BOSNIA - HERZEGOVINA**
2018/2019-2021
Single house · 191m² · 1,800€/m²
› **Studio Entasis**
Vedina Babahmetović
Muamer Spahić (Private)
© Anida Kreco

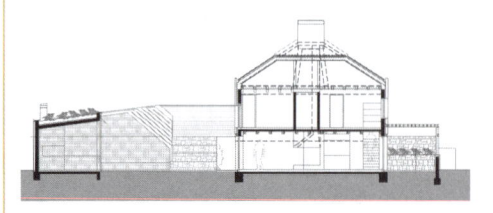

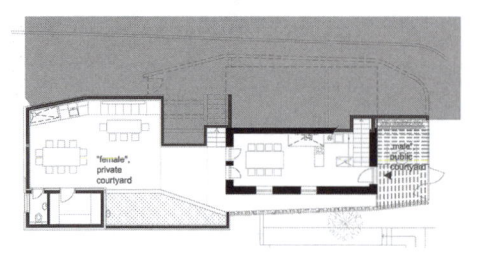

The Regional Housing Program (RHP) defines rules for housing refugees and displaced persons from the territory of the Socialist Federal Republic of Yugoslavia (SFRY) in the territory of its former republics.
The RHP is an essentially encouraging undertaking formally carried out by the construction of housing facilities due to migrations during and after war-related events in the territory of the former SFRY. In the fifth wave of the RHP, conducted in nine municipalities in the Republic of Serbia, the largest facility located in Loznica is the subject of this nomination. The building's volume, content, materialization and form were made consistent with housing standards. Likewise, each of the individual residential buildings is made in standardized architecture, so that they appear on the whole as new, because it is shaped as the same house for all.

Regional Housing Programme for Refugees and Displaced Persons

› **LOZNICA, SERBIA**
2017/2018-2021
Social Welfare · 3,480m²
› **1X2STUDIO**
Zoran Abadic,
Jelena Bogosavljevic
City of Loznica (Public)
© Zoran Abadic

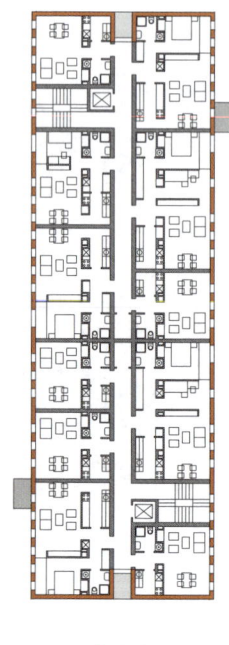

The project is in Belegiš, near the Danube River, which made a great impact on the design concept. It consists of three objects: Object "A" – New School Building (on the site of the old one which has been demolished); Object "B" – Entrance Area (which was rehabilitated); Object "C" – School Gym (which was rehabilitated). The program is an elementary school for children aged 8 to 14.

Vera Miščević Elementary School
› BELEGIŠ, SERBIA
2018/2019-2021
Education · 3,145m²
› **Studio A&D Architects**
Danilo Grahovac, Ivana Mijailović, Jovanka Gojković
Municipality of Stara Pazova (Public)
© Boško Karanović

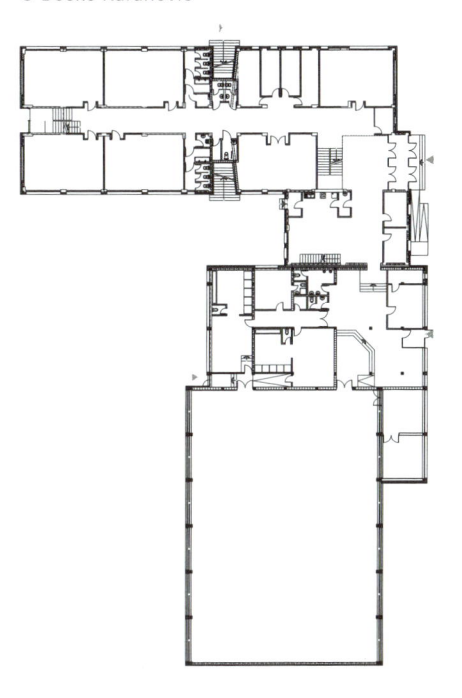

The facility is an innovative hybrid combination of information technology and sustainable construction with the introduction of eco-systems with emphasized green morphologies. The construction is designed as a reinforced skeleton system with concrete cores and panels in central position. The perimeter of the façade is free from the construction to achieve maximum flexibility in façade design and spatial organization.

Office Building, Multinational Company Campus NCR
› BELGRADE, SERBIA
2018/2019-2021
Office · 57,450m²
› **ProAspekt**
Vladimir Lojanica
NCR Campus (Private)
© Relja Ivanić

The Central Building in Pancevo takes a bold approach to multi-family residential architecture. It demonstrates a careful and responsible attitude towards the microenvironment of the city block, contributing significantly to the city's identity while innovatively treating the façade as a new type of living space for each apartment.
In relation to the immediate context of the city center, the Central Building successfully establishes a dialogue between contemporary architecture and its neighbors from past epochs, harmoniously fitting into the eclectic ambiance of Vojvode Radomir Putnik Street. With its vibrant and expressive, pink-colored façade, it evokes memories of traditionally diverse façades of Vojvodina homes, aligning with the recognizable local narrative.

Central
› **PANCEVO, SERBIA**
2019/2020-2021
Collective housing · 3,414m²
› **Danilo Dangubic Architects**
Danilo Dangubić
Probanat izgradnja (Public)
© Miloš Martinović

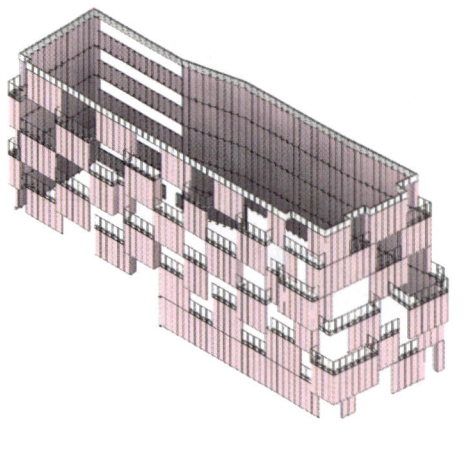

The design approach implies the interpretation of the theme of the townhouse with a tripartite division of the façade and the structure of the building. The selection of the façade treatment and the general concept of materializing the building in a combination of brick, concrete and glass determined the main compositional motif of the frontal façade, where the wide loggias open the apartments to the street.

K26 Manhattan Concept
› **KRAGUJEVAC, SERBIA**
2020/2020-2023
Collective housing · 2,245m² · 1,000€/m²
› **URED STUDIO, re:a.c.t**
Grozdana Sisovic, Dejan Milanovic, Nikola Milanović
RS Gradnja (Private)
© Dejan Milanović

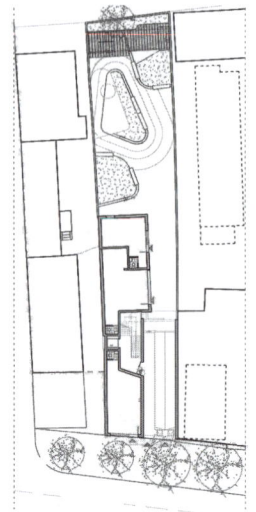

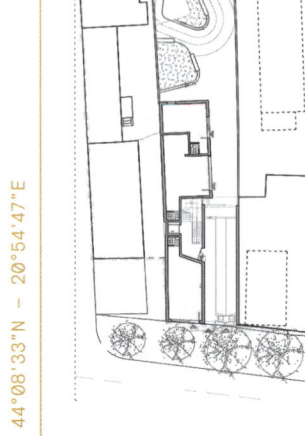

The main design approach was to create comfortable functional and spiritual space for the small Albanian Islamic community at a minimal financial cost. This strategy pushed us to be very modest, starting from the dimensioning of whole volume of the building up to its construction materials.

Mosque in Tupalla
› MEDVEDJA, SERBIA
2020/2020-2021
Religion · 84m² · 650€/m²
› G + A Architects
Arber Sadiki
Muharrem Salihu (Private)
© Aleksandar Stojanovic

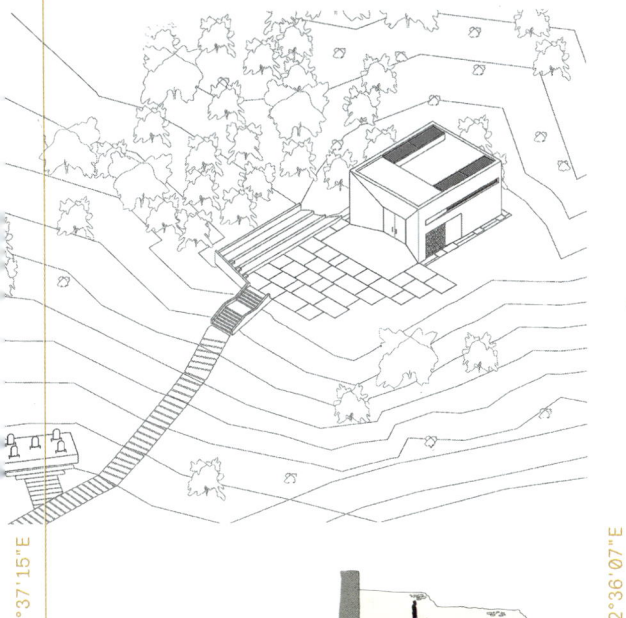

To the west of Kladovo, on the banks of the Danube River, lies Fetislam Fortress, which was declared a Cultural Monument in 1964. The fortress consists of two separate spaces, today known as the Small Town and the Large Town.
Modern interventions were carried out with the aim of revitalizing and increasing the comfort of the space without damaging its authentic structure and monumental properties. The most extensive works to be undertaken involved the construction of a contemporary summer stage in the part of the Small Town closest to the bank of the Danube.

Reconstruction of Fetislam Fortress
› KLADOVO, SERBIA
2020/2020-2021
Culture · 3,000m²
› KOTO, Forma Antika
Slobodan Radovanović, Anica Radosavljević, Uroš Kondić, Katarina Vujanac Ćirković
The Deutsche Gesellschaft für Internationale Zusammenarbeit (GIZ) (Public)
© Nikola Mraković

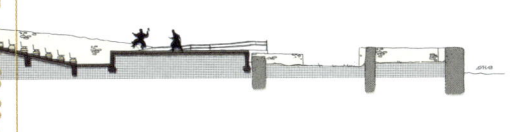

The Constantin Brâncuși Pavilion is composed of a piece of work made entirely of glass, a tribute landmark and an underground space of 1,400m². This underground space includes a gathering area, café, exhibition space and conference area. It is accessible through an amphitheater that opens to the exterior through a harmonic glass wall. The project proposes a cultural program: an international interactive center comprised of two underground floors and one ground floor. It stands 12 meters tall and has a total usable surface area of 1,481m², divided between 81m² above ground and 1,400 m below.

Constantin Brancusi Pavilion
› CRAIOVA, ROMANIA
2010/2014-2022
Culture · 1,481m²
› DSBA
Dorin Stefan
Consiliul judetean Dolj (Public)
© Arthur Zinz, Erwin Szori, Anda Ștefan

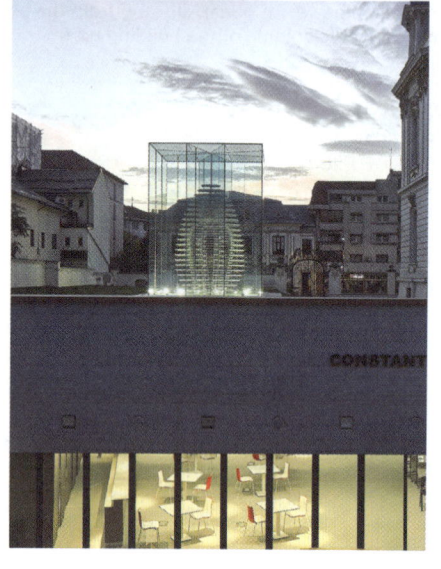

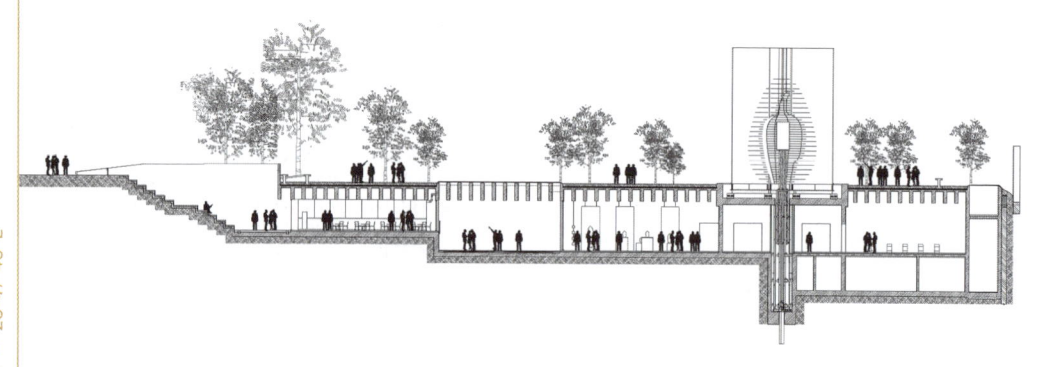

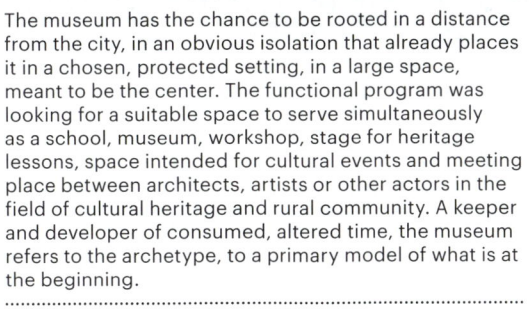

The museum has the chance to be rooted in a distance from the city, in an obvious isolation that already places it in a chosen, protected setting, in a large space, meant to be the center. The functional program was looking for a suitable space to serve simultaneously as a school, museum, workshop, stage for heritage lessons, space intended for cultural events and meeting place between architects, artists or other actors in the field of cultural heritage and rural community. A keeper and developer of consumed, altered time, the museum refers to the archetype, to a primary model of what is at the beginning.

Piscu School Museum and Workshop

› **PISCU, ROMANIA**
2016/2018-2021
Culture · 1,070m²
› **ABRUPTARHITECTURA**
Cosmin Pavel, Cristina Constantin
Gaspar, Baltasar & Melchior Association (Mixed)
↑ © Laurian Ghinitoiu
↗ © Marius Vasile

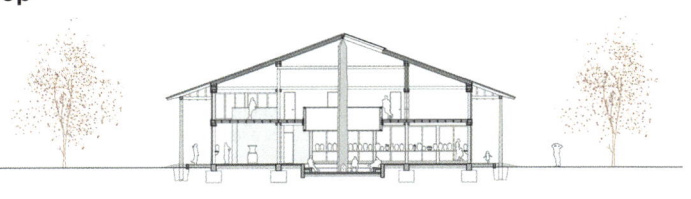

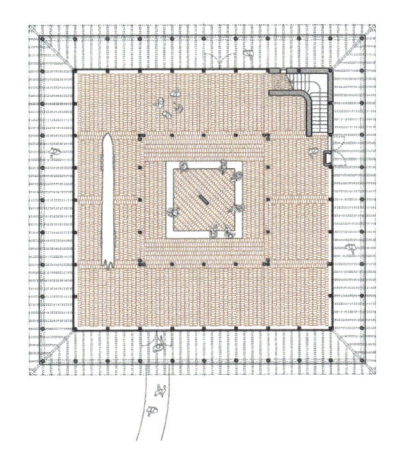

On a narrow street in central Bucharest, in an area affected by the Socialist interventions of the 1970s, this new apartment building takes part in the overlapping of historical and contemporary elements, addressing urban stratification. It attempts to harmonize diverse neighborhood components, offering several types of housing, a co-working space and ground-floor public areas open to the street. Four interconnected architectural modules on an L-shaped lot seamlessly blend with neighboring courtyards, creating a unified urban area. The volume incorporates intermittent interruptions such as a spacious passage and deliberate architectural elements like cutouts, setbacks, terraces and loggias. Materiality emphasizes surfaces, textures and plaster hues, highlighting intricate folds and edges, resulting in layered enclosures and a diversity of used materials.

Urban Spaces 5 / Apartment Building
› **BUCHAREST, ROMANIA**
2016/2019-2022
Collective housing · 9,645m²
› **ADN Birou de Arhitectura**
Bogdan Brădățeanu, Adrian Untaru, Andrei Șerbescu, Valentina Țigâră, Petra Bodea, Mihail Filipenco, Elena Zară
Urban Spaces (Private)
↑↗ © Vlad Pătru
→ © Sabin Prodan

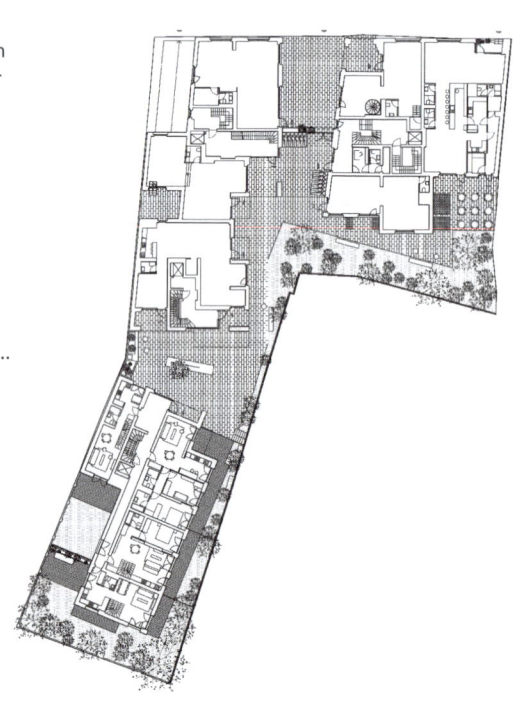

A shadow cast in one place can illuminate insights elsewhere. Set 26 meters below the Plenary Hall of the Romanian Parliament's merged chambers, this light, sound and photography installation becomes a performative rebellion echoing Guy Fawkes's gunpowder plot. It underscores how political decisions impact the built environment.

This is a non-place, an underground dark space, abyssal in its oddity, clearly defined yet seemingly endless, where infinity echoes in the concrete structure's reverberations, extending through a maze of doors and walls, almost inaccessible; a space that is so secure that it almost becomes prohibited. The curatorial concept suggests converting this never used underground technical space, devoid of natural light, from a building classified as a "military objective with armed guard" into a temporary exhibition.

Cities that Transform
› **BUCHAREST, ROMANIA**
2021/2023
Ephemeral - Cultural & Social · 2,500m² · 6€/m²
› **VICEVERSA**
Dorin Ștefan Adam, Laurian Ghinițoiu
N/A Self initiated (Mixed)
© Laurian Ghinițoiu

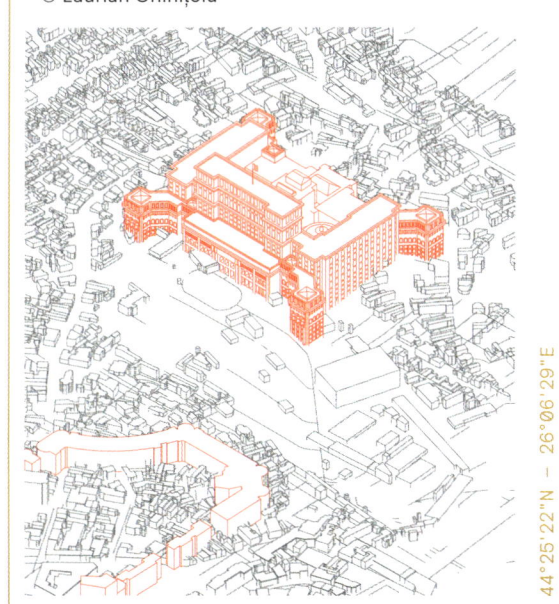

In the back of a modernist block of apartments, typical of inter-war Bucharest, an extension of collective housing is subtly weaved together. The boulevard-facing the surviving inter-war modernist construction has been restored, so the street front kept the scale with no ostentation. Behind it and against the back of this rather modest house is where the new project starts. The apartments in the new wing do not display any functional simplification, nor do they cover any lacks through design. We had to work with one apartment type and the general unit is implacably shaped by offset withdrawals and urban regulations.

Boemia Apartments
› **BUCHAREST, ROMANIA**
2017/2019-2021
Collective housing · 13,250m²
› **STARH - Birou de arhitectura**
Florian Stanciu, Iulia Stanciu
PRIMA CENTRAL APARTMENTS SRL (Private)
© Laurian Ghinițoiu

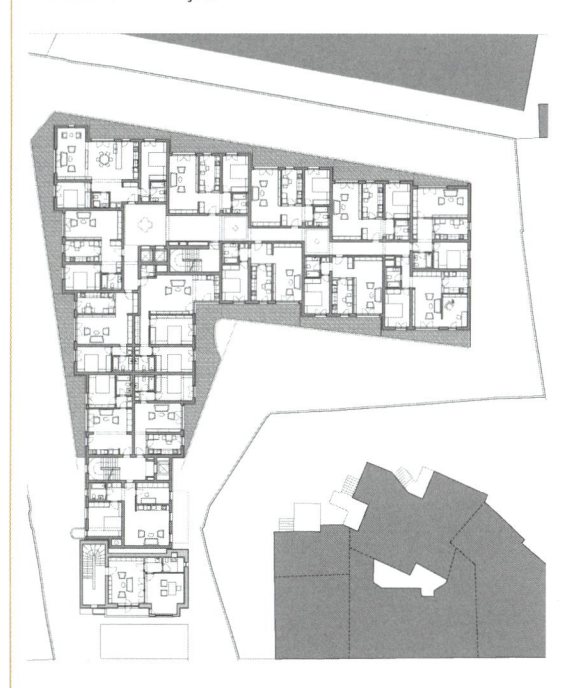

The house in Dumbrava Vlăsiei establishes an approach mainly focused on emphasizing two fundamental elements that make up a suburban home: the rooms and the garden. The project unfolded based on this simple limitation: the house should contract itself, freeing up as much land as possible and making room for Grădina cu camera ("The Garden with Rooms").

House in Dumbrava Vlăsiei

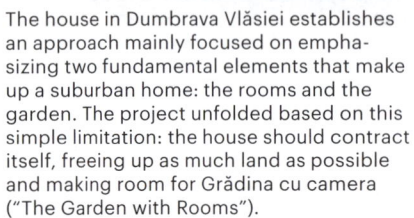

› **DUMBRAVA VLĂSIEI, ROMANIA**
  2018/2021-2023
  Single house · 206m² · 1,350€/m²
› **Alt. Corp.**
  Cosmin Georgescu, Cosmin Gălățianu, Alexandru Cristian Beșliu, Octavian Bîrsan, Andrei Theodor Ioniță
  LORECO INVESTMENTS SRL (Private)
  © Cosmin Georgescu

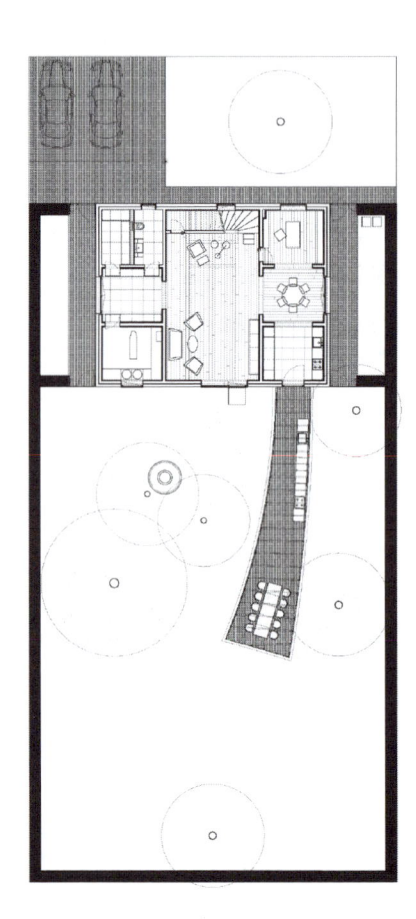

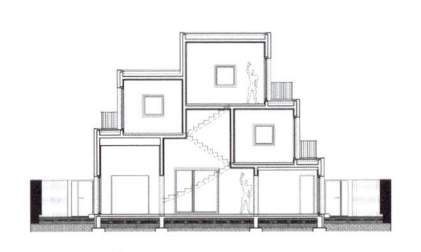

344

From
SANTIAGO
DE COMPOSTELA
Spain
42°52'13"N — 8°31'33"W

to
VARNA
Bulgaria
43°13'01"N — 27°54'46"E

The works for the Cidade da Cultura Opera Theatre were interrupted some time ago. Years later, Fundación Cidade da Cultura decided to reuse, set up and complete the existing structure for the new Fontán Building to host research and university facilities. The clients' and architects' main objective is to improve users' lives and daily working standards.
We set out the Fontán Building as a "meta-project": an architectural design defined by high-accuracy structural and technical elements that create the interior space, conceived in such a schematic way that allows a wide range of functional solutions throughout the building's lifetime since the opening configuration. This requires high layout flexibility and the first step for that purpose is a clear definition of internal circulation, as well as an efficient and adequate MEP and the rest of the facilities' infrastructure, all to provide free use and flexible space arrangement. The Fontán Building can also be explained by the creation of a waterline established by road access from the parking area to the loading dock and pedestrian walkways and adding a cross path running north to south through the building, from the library to the CINC building.

Fontán Building
› **SANTIAGO DE COMPOSTELA, SPAIN**
  2017/2018-2022
  Culture · 13,317m^2 · 1,142.82€/m^2
› **Perea, Suárez y Torrelo, Arquitectos**
  Andrés Perea, Elena Suárez Calvo, Rafael Fernández Torrelo
  Xunta de Galicia (Public)
  © Ana Amado

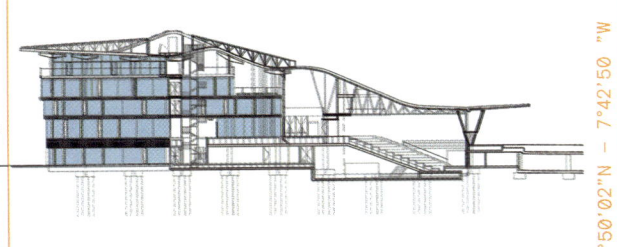

The Camino de Santiago crosses the Castro de Castromaior on its way to Compostela. The center is proposed as an invitation to discover the Castro. A stop on the way for pilgrims to rest, an atrium protected from the sun and the rain, from which to observe how far they have walked and how much walking remains. The center is always visitable and inhabitable without the need for permanent staff, since this should be an unaffordable burden for the budget of a small city council like Portomarín. This is a low-cost public facility with almost no maintenance that, like Galician rural churches, must be taken care of by the residents of the village. It is a structure without a birth certificate or author, rooted in the earth like some wise piece of popular architecture. This is a stop on the Camino de Santiago that becomes landscape.

Interpretation Centre Castromaior
› **CASTROMAIOR, SPAIN**
  2016/2019-2022
  Culture · 322m^2 · 417,3€/m^2
› **Carlos Pita**
  Carlos Pita
  Ministerio de transportes, movilidad y agenda urbana (Public)
  © Juan Rodríguez

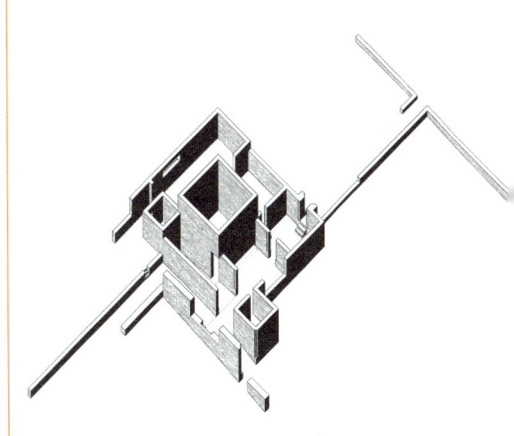

Daycare Centre for Young People with Autism Spectrum Disorder

Derio, Spain
2021/2022

AV62 Arquitectos
Juan Antonio Foraster

APNABI
(Mixed)
Health · 426m²

The project involves a new daycare centre for young people with autism spectrum disorders (ASD) in Derio, Bizkaia. The facility features a large outdoor space where young people will have a close experience with agriculture and gardening techniques and knowledge.

The proposed architecture pays heed to concepts related to ecological awareness, respect for the environment, and total sustainability (energy, environmental, social, cultural, and economic). The building thus seeks to integrate the group of people with ASD in the municipality, while opening up to the citizens of Derio, as well as to provide them with training for future entry into the workforce.

This type of approach is the appropriate scenario so that this sensitive group can receive greater opportunities for growth and development, when combined with all the associated educational programmes. Apnabi thus fulfils its mission of providing support and strategies that guarantee a comprehensive, personalized response to people with

ASD, facilitating their personal and social development as part of their daily life in a collaborative manner.

Located in a peripheral area of the municipality close to the highway, a residential area, and a sector with companies linked to agricultural experimentation, the new centre faces the challenge of creating a quiet space that facilitates the daily activity of people with ASD and at the same time, a space that can be occasionally open to the neighbourhood

The building programme is divided into a large outdoor space that functions as a 'square' and a series of 'interior' workshops with a wooden structure where related educational activities will be carried out, a multipurpose space, a living space and place for rest, a kitchen accessible only to the staff in charge, a dining room, as well as indoor and outdoor common spaces.

The project proposes an array of workshops within a greenhouse. This system offers several advantages for the whole, from a spatial, experiential, and sustainability point of view.

The building has a 'bioclimatic envelope', a system comparable to that of an agricultural greenhouse, which regulates how much solar radiation is captured as well as the building's ventilation by means of automatic openings and closings of the envelope. The outer skin adapts automatically, opening or closing depending on the temperature, humidity, wind, and external solar radiation to achieve the best bioclimatic and hygrothermal conditions at all times.

348

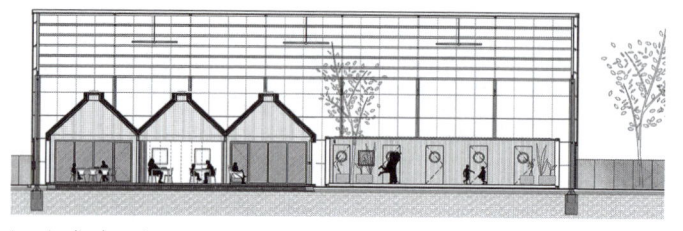

SHORTLISTED

Longitudinal section

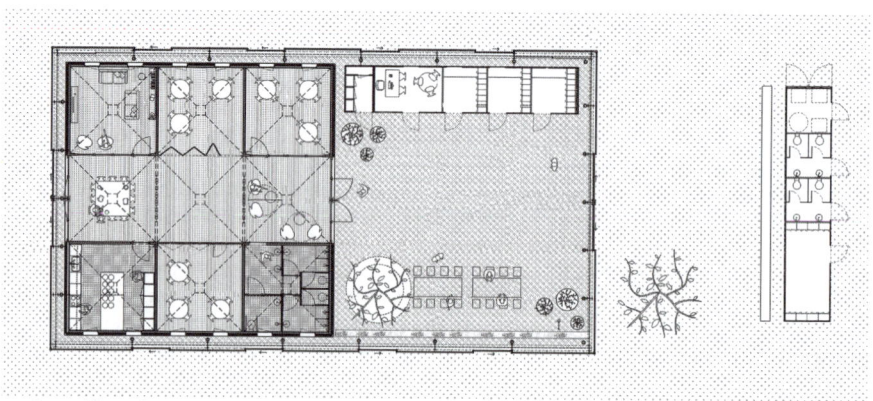

Ground floor plan

DAY CENTRE FOR YOUNG PEOPLE WITH AUTISM SPECTRUM DISORDER

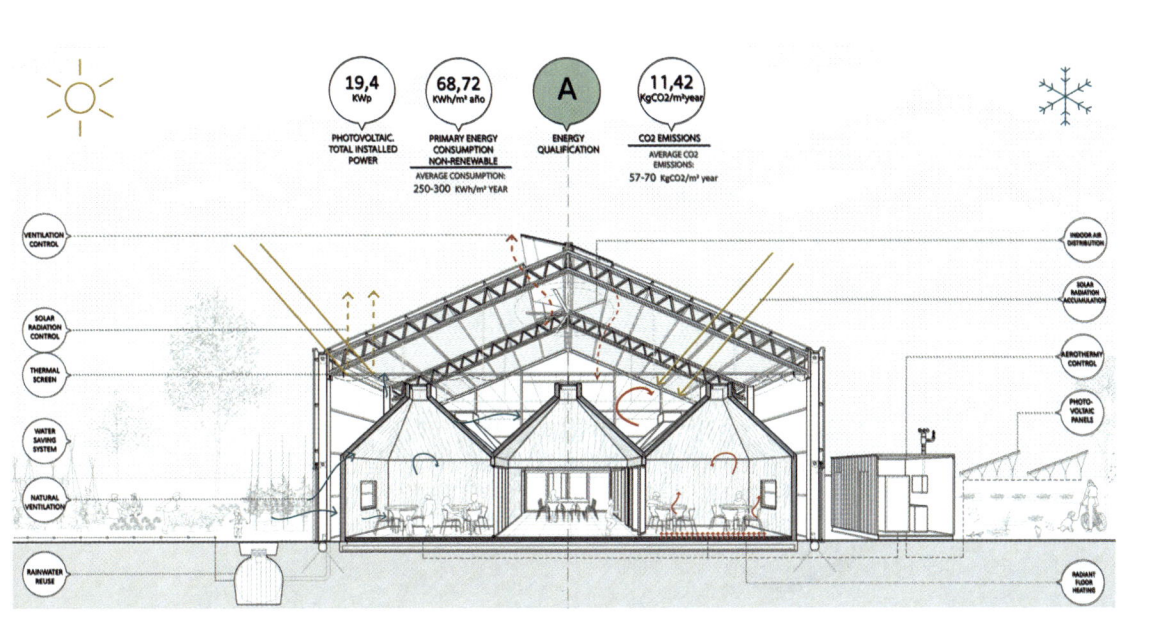

Bioclimatic section

AV62 ARQUITECTOS

The ground floor of a former sock factory is transformed into an artists' workshop.
A courtyard is created by demolishing part of the concrete slab of the first floor. A single gate allows access to the workshop via the courtyard. The rest of the existing post-beam concrete structure is preserved and exposed. A railing made of galvanized corrugated iron connects the courtyard from the terrace of the first floor. A large steel accordion window creates a limit between the interior and the new exterior. The windows overlooking the streets are replaced by double-glazed windows mounted on the façade.

T16
› **TOULOUSE, FRANCE**
 2022/2022-2023
 Office · 140m² · 400€/m²
› **BAST**
 Sebastien Girard (Private)
 © BAST

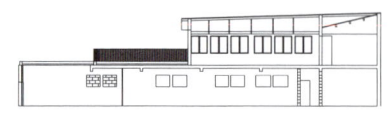

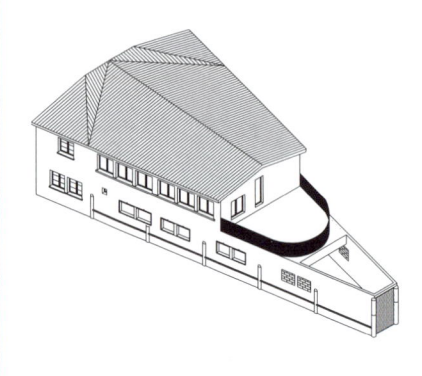

The Forestry House is built to host the offices of Cosylva's forest technicians. It is made of local wood, harvested from the cooperative members forest, mobilizing local crafts and savoir-faire.
Located on the border of a banal business park and a parcel of oak woodland, the building fits into the existing landscape, replacing a tarmac slab, a sad vestige of the previous activity. The L-shaped plan reflects this duality and makes it explicit in the expression of the façades, one more austere (zinc cladding, transom windows) and the other more domestic, with large office windows opening onto the surrounding vegetation and wooden walkway.

The Forestry House
› **CARCASSONNE, FRANCE**
 2019/2020-2022
 Office · 342m² · 2,885€/m²
› **PAUEM atelier**
 Pauline Chauvet, Emanuele Francesco Moro
 Coopérative forestière de l'Aude - Cosylva 11 (Private)
 © Mary Gaudin

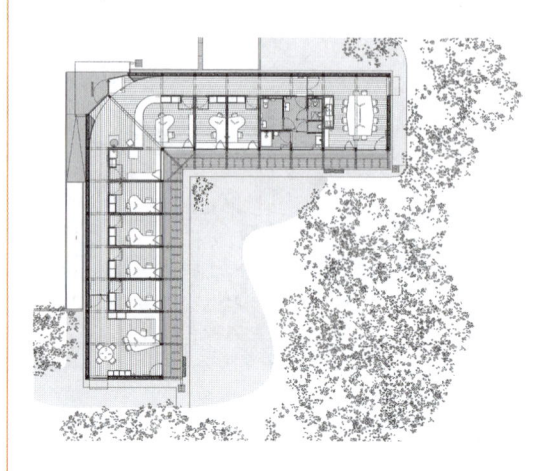

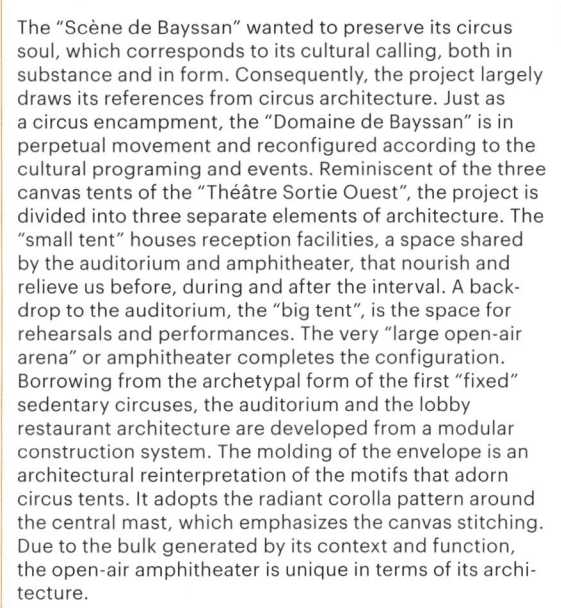

The "Scène de Bayssan" wanted to preserve its circus soul, which corresponds to its cultural calling, both in substance and in form. Consequently, the project largely draws its references from circus architecture. Just as a circus encampment, the "Domaine de Bayssan" is in perpetual movement and reconfigured according to the cultural programing and events. Reminiscent of the three canvas tents of the "Théâtre Sortie Ouest", the project is divided into three separate elements of architecture. The "small tent" houses reception facilities, a space shared by the auditorium and amphitheater, that nourish and relieve us before, during and after the interval. A backdrop to the auditorium, the "big tent", is the space for rehearsals and performances. The very "large open-air arena" or amphitheater completes the configuration. Borrowing from the archetypal form of the first "fixed" sedentary circuses, the auditorium and the lobby restaurant architecture are developed from a modular construction system. The molding of the envelope is an architectural reinterpretation of the motifs that adorn circus tents. It adopts the radiant corolla pattern around the central mast, which emphasizes the canvas stitching. Due to the bulk generated by its context and function, the open-air amphitheater is unique in terms of its architecture.

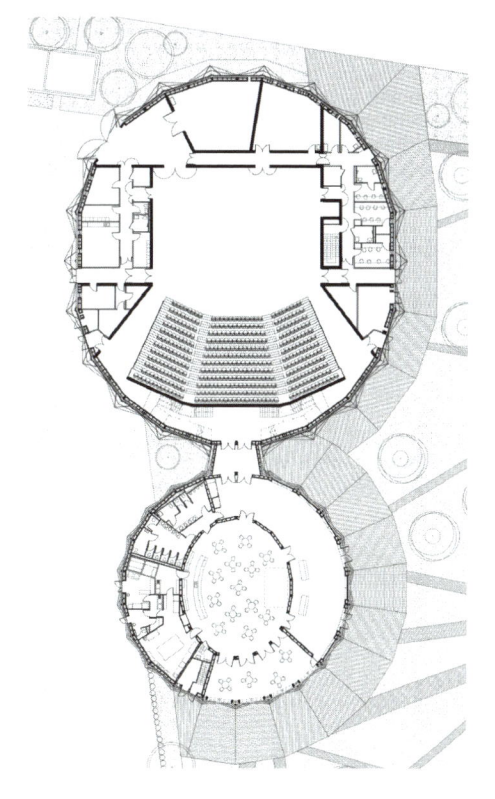

Performance Hall and Open Air Amphitheatre

› Béziers, France. 2018/2019-2021
  Culture · 4,500m²
› **K ARCHITECTURES**
  Karine Herman, Jérôme Sigwalt
  Department Of Herault (Public)
  © Sophie Oddo

Located at the bow of a new subdivision at the city entrance of Gignac-la-Nerthe, the project proposes to integrate social housing by using a special materiality. The architectural design proposes two volumes that seek to harmonize with the surrounding urban context of isolated and grouped houses. The project and its typological distribution make it possible to offer eight housing units on this plot. Built in massive stone, the edifice resonates with the village's vernacular constructions. The outside spaces are designed in a wooden structure and complete the accommodation with places to contemplate the Nerthe massif. Stones from the neighboring quarries compose the façade and mark the place with a particular atmosphere. The raw material expresses its strength.

8 Intermediate Social Housing Units

› Gignac - la Nerthe, France. 2017/2020-2021
  Collective housing · 1,036m² · 2,040€/m²
› **Atelier Régis Roudil Architectes**
  Régis Roudil
  3F SUD (Mixed)
  © Florència Vesval

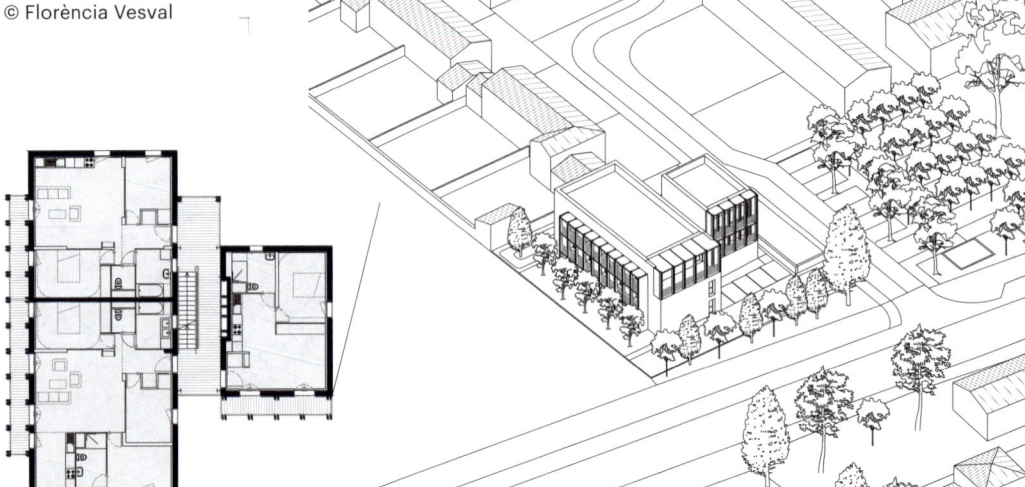

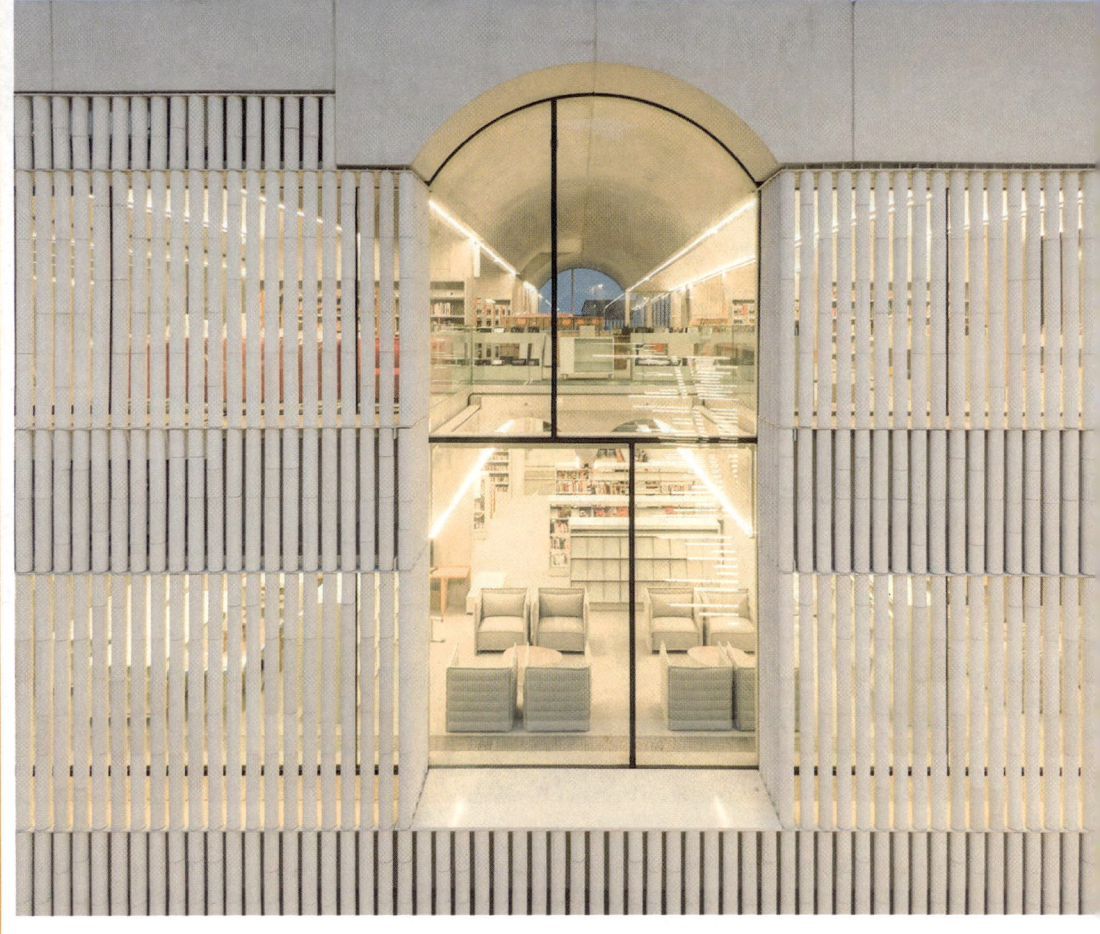

Média Library Charles Nègre

Grasse, France

2011/2014-2022

Beaudouin Architectes, Ivry Serres Architecture

Emmanuelle Beaudouin, Laurent Beaudouin, Aurélie Husson, Ivry Serres

City of Grasse

(Public)
Education · 4,423m² · 2,900€/m²

The media library in Grasse is imbued with the strength of a poetic project within the tortuous density of this mediaeval town, visible by its presence, discreet in its volumes and materials.

The town of Grasse is made up of narrow streets and colourful finishes. The public buildings, in white stone, are notable for elements that emerge from the urban fabric, including the bell tower of Notre-Dame du Puy Cathedral, the Clock Tower, and the Sarrazine Tower. The Charles Nègre Media Library draws strength from the city's substance and the subtle echoes of the vernacular language. The library is inspired by the relationships between these monuments and the urban fabric to assert itself as a place from which one can gaze out over Grasse and its steep landscape. Dominated by the silhouette of a new belvedere tower, the media library offers a vista of the old town from its top floor terrace. By drawing on the sources of the urban structure, it creates tensions, brushes, and closeness. As a counterpoint, the library has renewed the visual openings onto the neighbourhood and the distance. The structure is a key element of a more global urban project that reshapes pedestrian relationships and public spaces in a degraded city centre.

The elements of the programme are independent and distributed over several access levels, reappropriating four buildings while preserving the structures and façades. A common foyer gives access to the exhibition room and the auditorium located below the pedestrian crossing. The opening of an arcade into an existing building allows entry to the square and pedestrians to pass by the water tank that faces the exhibition hall. While this tank was a strong constraint, it was used when drafting the project, thereby creating a public square and a reflecting pool. Today it is partially covered by the overhang of the media library, which highlights the main entrance. A ramp suspended above the passage extends the alley inside the media library, inviting visitors to take an architectural walk through the levels. From the hall, where a luminous fault crosses the upper levels, the media library has clear spaces, permeable to light and fresh air in the summer. The filter of the fluted white concrete columns of the envelope deployed on six levels filters the natural light and this large-scale variation of the Provençal claustra protects the glass façade located in the back.

The site's multiple constraints are linked to archaeological excavations, the stability of the soil and existing structures, seismic conditions, and the reuse of old houses. The vaulted structure of this concrete building, founded entirely on piles, allows for the large cantilever that covers the tank. The precisely designed walls were cast in place while sails connected to the circulation cores balance the overhang. This homogeneous system balances the masses, while the bracing and the architectural concrete vaulted floors give a constructive and aesthetic truth to this project.

MÉDIA LIBRARY CHARLES NÈGRE

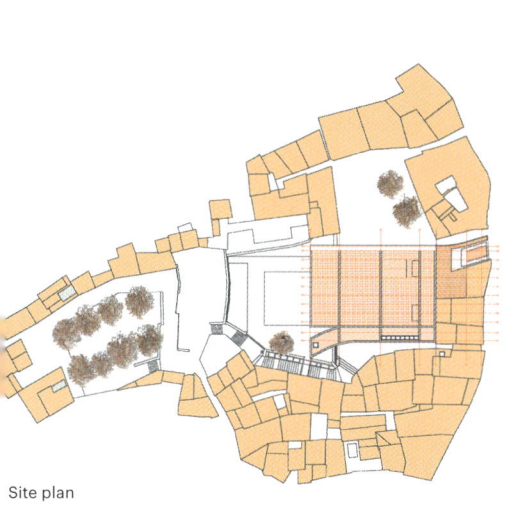

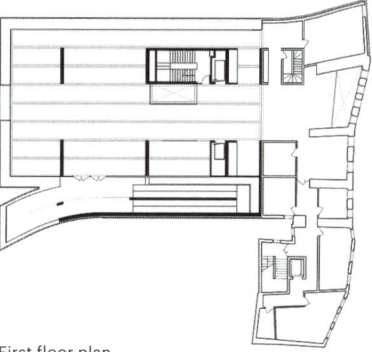

First floor plan

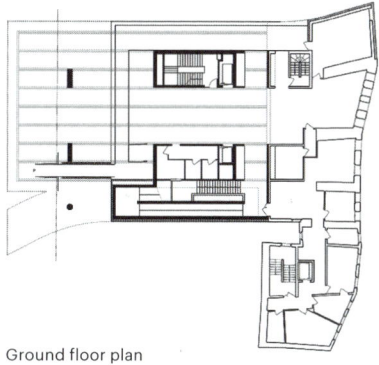

Ground floor plan

B3 floor plan

Site plan

BEAUDOUIN ARCHITECTES, IVRY SERRES ARCHITECTURE

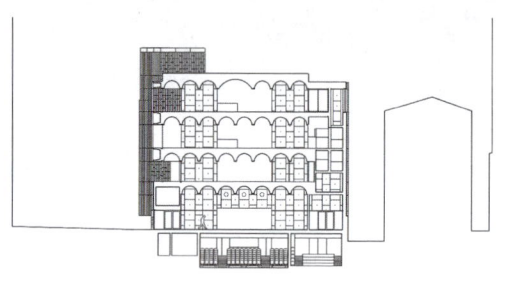

Cross section

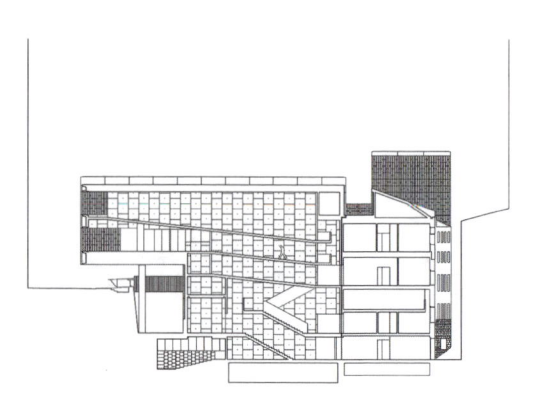

Longitudinal section

MÉDIA LIBRARY CHARLES NÈGRE

The project is located in Orbetello, Maremma, in southern Tuscany, adjacent to an existing Ente Maremma farm built in the modernist Agrarian Reform. Tuscany's stringent building regulations dictate specific design choices that perpetuate an "in-style" revival. These regulations impose a commodified, tourist-oriented image requiring pitched roofs, artificial ornamentation and faux stone facades to maintain a fabricated pastoral ideal. Anonima Agricola challenges this stereotypical perception by embracing generic agricultural materials. It unveils the neglected modernist essence that shaped this territory in the postwar period. By refusing predefined authenticity, the project fosters a new ecological imagination. Material choices blend bioclimatic principles with generic, ordinary elements as an antidote to the Disneyfication process.

Anonima Agricola

› ORBETELLO, ITALY
2020/2021-2022
Single house · 120m² · 1,200€/m²
> **Captcha Architecture**
Margherita Marri, Jacopo Rosa
Francesco Grassi (Private)
© Piercarlo Quecchia

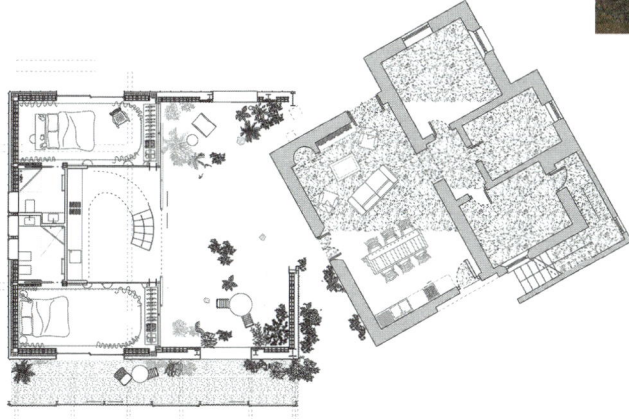

The hospitality structure of Camplus San Pietro is located in the heart of Rome next to the Vatican City. It offers the possibility of long and short term stays in symbiosis with nature and the urban context. Students can stay during the academic year and tourists can stay all year round.
The six-story building, a former health facility, has been restored, refurbished, and redesigned. It hosts 120 guest rooms and encourages guests to lead a sustainable lifestyle and to be in direct contact with nature. The interior design of this refurbishment project is characterized by a sophisticated contrast between the Brutalist style of the building; sculpture-like elements, such as the staircase or the slim metal structure system in each guest room; and nature, which is visually introduced into the building thanks to the large window openings. The main furniture pieces like the bed, closet and kitchenette are embedded in the metal structure, optimizing the three-dimensional space, taking advantage of the vertical direction and clearly dividing the daytime and nighttime areas. This generates a comfortable space without clutter and a loft feeling.

Camplus San Pietro
› ROME, ITALY
2017/2019-2022
Collective housing ·
4,000m² · 2,000€/m²
› **Roselli Architetti Associati**
Riccardo Roselli
Fondazione CEUR (Private)
© Luigi Filetici

This traditional house is located in the settlement of Lepetani, which historically developed on the northwest slope of Vrmac at the entrance to the Bay of Kotor. The building is designed as a house within a house, with a double front façade: the original stone facade as the historical layer and the structural façade as the new layer. The connection between these two facades is established with steel terraces and bridges from the windows of the stone walls to the structural façade, making the window a gateway to the terrace. This spatial arrangement extends all the way to the roof, without disrupting the traditional appearance of the building and the row, while creating a new and different approach to the treatment of old houses.

House Lepetane
› KOTOR, MONTENEGRO
2021/2021
Single house · 401m²
› **Enforma**
Nikola Novakovic, Ana Mičić
Latković family (Private)
© Milos Martinovic

This is a seaside house divided into two apartments connected by a common plateau with an open kitchen. The entire architecture is conceived as a kind of sequence of the Mediterranean city. The author's intention was to form a central open space as a reason for organizing sitting and eating in accordance with the project assignment.

Family House Bigovo 3
› KOTOR, MONTENEGRO
2017/2020-2021
Single house · 161m²
› **BiroVIA**
Verica Krstic, Vasilije Milunovic, Jelena Ivanovic Vojvodic
Private investor (Private)
© Vladan Stevovic

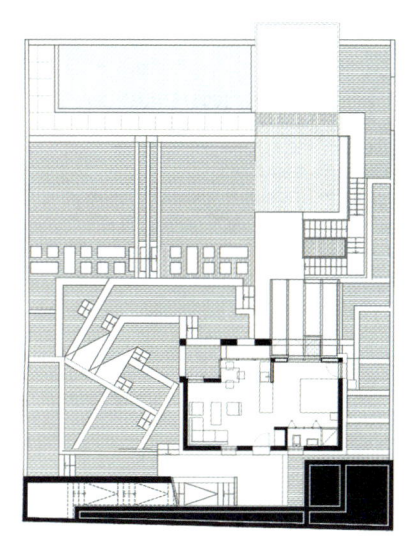

The designed building is located right on Kotor-Budva intercity road. This detached building with southwest-southeast orientation is comprised of a ground floor and two upper floors. The simplified form was endowed with a green semi-atrium on the first floor, viewed from most of the premises. The covered main entrance that leads to the furniture show room is located on the ground floor of the building, on the south-east side. The function of this building is adapted to contemporary operations, with transformable office spaces in the upper floors. There is an open-air terrace on the building roof.

Betula Design Centre
› KOTOR, MONTENEGRO
2019/2020-2022
Office · 870m²
› **Studio Synthesis architecture & design**
Sonja Radović Jelovac
Simes Inzenjering / Katarina Milic (Private)
© Relja Ivanic

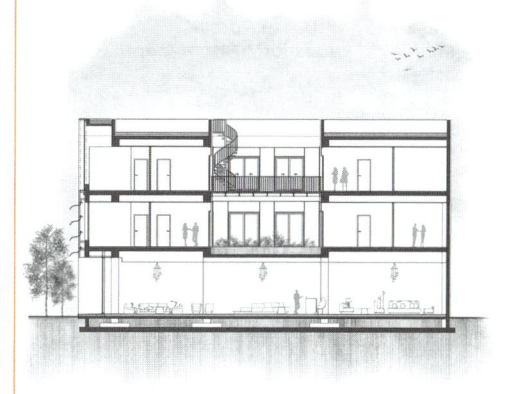

↑ 241 ↑ 243

The project is the result of a competition held in 2020. It is the first primary school built after fifteen years in the capital of Montenegro, where the number of children in schools is twice as large as planned. It is also an exception, as the authors could follow their project from beginning to end. The location is a deregulated construction area where, in addition to family houses, there are neglected agricultural lands, gardens, orchards, greenhouses, etc. The public space of the settlement is reduced to a chaotic network of poorly connected roads.
Considering the complexity and different constructive systems of the program, the authors decided to divide the required gross area of the school complex into two independent volumes: the school and the sports hall. In this way, a seemingly strict concept was formed: two programs, two constructions, two houses.

Primary School "Novka Ubovic"
› PODGORICA, MONTENEGRO
2020/2021-2022
Education · 8,800m² · 1,000€/m²
› **BIRO 81000**
Ivan Jovićević, Dušan Đurović
Ministry of Education of Montenegro (Public)
© Relja Ivanić

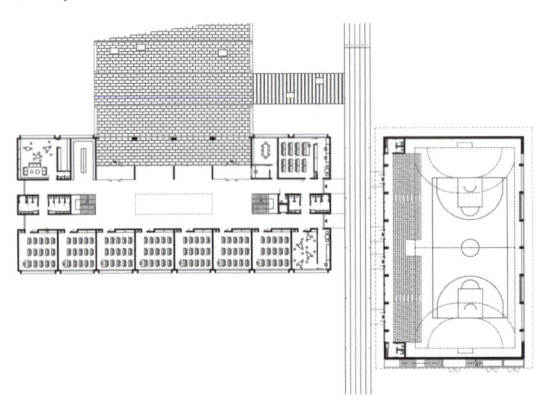

The building is organized through three above-ground and two underground floors. The central communication and service core represents the pivot of the function that develops from the underground garage, through the two-story entrance hall on the ground floor with accompanying exhibition content and up to the floors where various administrative services are organized. The planned contents of the administration together with conference rooms are organized in reduced parallelopipeds, executed on the first floor as a consequence of proper consideration of the horizontal regulation and distance from the neighboring buildings.

Business Centre "Glosarij"
› PODGORICA, MONTENEGRO
2019/2020-2022
Office · 4,400m²
› **Studio GRAD**
Veljko Radulović, Đorđe Gregović
Glosarij d.o.o. (Private)
© Relja Ivanić

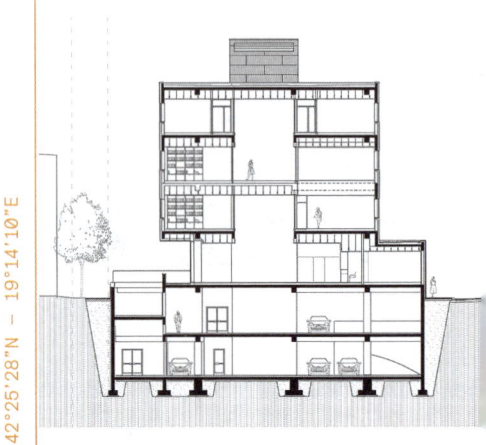

The academy building is located in the park that surrounds the existing small academy building. The building has three floors and penetrates the ground, preserving its existing green and topography. The entrance was organized through the square along the public road. From the two-story reception hall, you enter the underground main gallery and climb to the central two-story hall, which is lit at the top. Public spaces of the academy and office are organized around it. The main conference hall is focused on the park. Archives and technical rooms are located in the basement of the facility.

Montenegrin Academy of Sciences and Arts

› PODGORICA, MONTENEGRO
2019/2020-2022
Education · 4,974m²
› **Studio GRAD**
Veljko Radulović, Đorđe Gregović, Branislav Gregović
The government of Montenegro (Public)
© Relja Ivanić

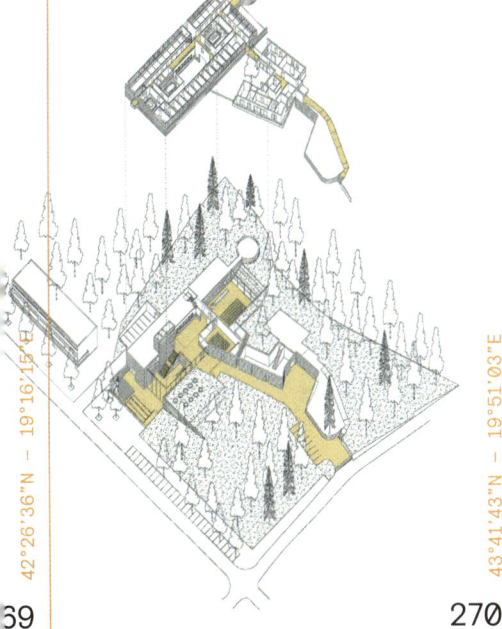

The building only has a ground floor, located so it can be viewed from all sides, opening up views of the river and the road to the Podvrh monastery. The facility is accessed via a driveway connected to the parking lot. It is functionally differentiated into two zones, right and left, which "open" towards the river. The right side includes a restaurant with a sanitary block, while the left side has an info-desk with a souvenir shop, a museum-exhibition area, a presentation hall, an infirmary and a service. The administrative tract is located at the entrance to the facility, which allows direct and unhindered access to employees. The aforementioned units are integrated by a covered opened hall construction made of steel, which becomes a gathering point for visitors.

Visitor Centre "Đalovića Pećina"

› BIJELO POLJE, MONTENEGRO
2019/2021-2022
Food & Accommodation · 500m² · 1,700€/m²
› **ARHINGinzenjering**
Jasmina Kujović Salković, Elvira Alihodžić Muzurović
Administration for Capital Projects (Public)
© Lejla Hadžibegović

SHM house has been designed focusing on the concrete requirements of the client, trying to create a rational articulation of living spaces in direct relation with daily base activities. In a total of 196 square meters of gross floor space, it offers garage spaces for two cars, a living room with a dining area and a kitchen, as well as three bedrooms with a bathroom. Taking advantage of the easy slope of terrain, a garage and a technical room are located in the basement, with direct access from the main floor. The ground floor has two separate units organized into daily living spaces and bedrooms.

SHM House
› **GREMNIK, KOSOVO**
2021/2021-2022
Single house · 196m² · 750€/m²
› **G + A Architects**
Arber Sadiki
Shaban Maxharraj (Private)
© Arben Llapashtica

Due to their functions, storage facilities are not usually treated on a human scale. We wanted to change how they are perceived through our way of thinking and design. This is a project in which architecture combines and reformulates industrial language to generate new spaces for work and other related activities.
These spaces are designed to enable a variety of functions, leading to the need to create a worker-friendly space and one easy to access for every user. This flexible way of design simplifies the process of adapting the user's space to their needs. With the intentions of making the most out of the location, the buildings are in harmony with their surroundings, creating a strategic point inside Prishtina's industrial zone and thereby initiating a somewhat diverse environment regarding its use.

Prishtina Business Centre
› **PRISTINA, KOSOVO**
2021/2021-2022
Mixed use - Commercial & Offices · 10,000m² · 550€/m²
› **LSN Architects**
Lulzim Nuza, Florian Shala, Sado Kolić
"Dumnica Group" (Private)
© Leonit Ibrahimi

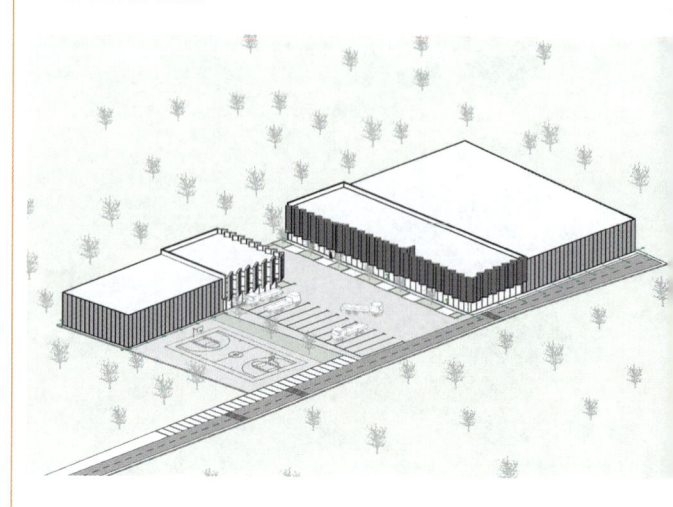

The volume of the building is in regular geometric shapes, where the module stands out against the volume, giving character to the construction both in the architectural aspect and in the functional aspect. The characteristic of the object is that the modules are created in such a way that the interplay of shadow and light takes place both inside and outside the object. The building has an administrative and multimedia function and will be used for various multicultural events, scenography, a shooting space and administrative work.

AMC Multimedia
› **PRISTINA, KOSOVO**
   2020/2021-2022
   Mixed use - Commercial & Offices · 4,266m²
› **Maden Group**
   Ideal Vejsa, Rashit Zeneli, Agon Elezi
   AMC Corporation (Private)
   © Leonit Ibrahimi

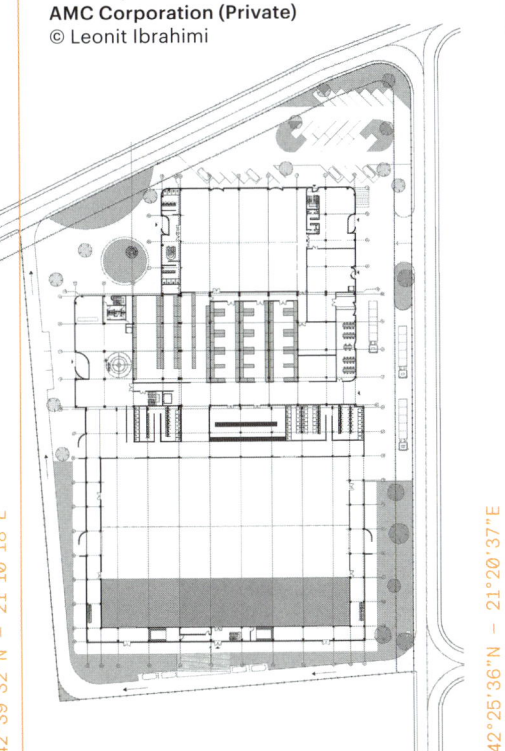

The envisaged kindergarten has been designed to accommodate up to 175 children. The edifice is equipped with two principal entrances, both leading to the central core of the building. The form of a circle was chosen as appropriate and logical, allowing equal distance to the center, visibility, better sunlight and a softened presence in the space. Due to the availability of the plot only on one side, the existence of an internal traffic ring around the building was of exceptional importance for vehicle access and according to fire protection standards. The site is accessed from its highest point. From here, the logical elevation of the ground floor, where the user rooms are located, is the same. That is why the building is distributed according to the development of the plot towards the southeast, where the "green valley" stretches.

Volkovo Kindergarten
› **SKOPJE, NORTH MACEDONIA**
   2018/2019-2021
   Education · 4,920m²
› **Prima Inzenering**
   Filip Koneski, Danica Spasevska
   Gjorche Petrov Municipality (Public)
   © Boris Jurmovski

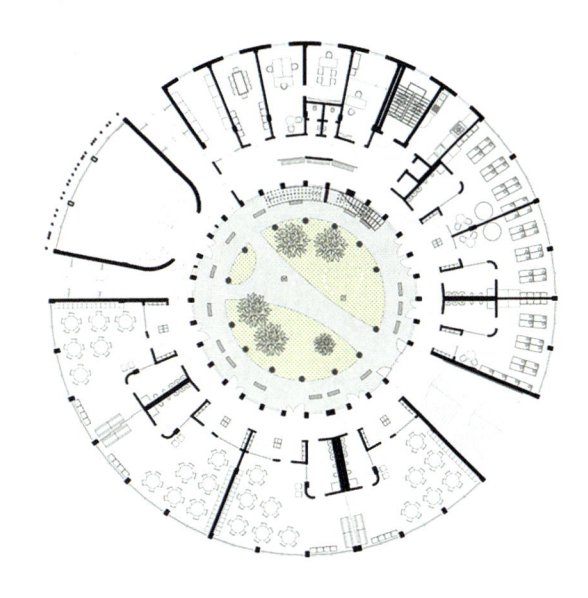

MAH is a single-family house on two levels located in Bardovci, Skopje. Spread over an impressive gross floor area on a spacious plot of approximately 860m², this modern residence embodies elegance and functionality. The house displays a contemporary aesthetic with a flat roof and large windows that allow abundant natural light to flood the interior spaces. The use of wooden façade panels adds a touch of warmth to the design, creating a harmonious blend of modernity and attractive charm.

MAH House
› **SKOPJE, NORTH MACEDONIA**
2019/2019-2021
Single house · 650m²
› **PROXY**
Nikola Kungulovski, Medina Gicikj
Martin Kochkov (Private)
© Nikola Kungulovski

The May Apartments building is located on Banjaluchka Street no. 20 in the Karposh neighborhood in Skopje, the Republic of North Macedonia. The urban block that includes this building is part of planned and already built family houses, i.e. low-rise residential structures up to four floors.

May Apartments
› **SKOPJE, NORTH MACEDONIA**
2019/2020-2022
Collective housing · 2,000m²
› **BMA - Besian Mehmeti Architects**
Besian Mehmeti
Elitte Living LLC (Private)
© Vase Petrovski

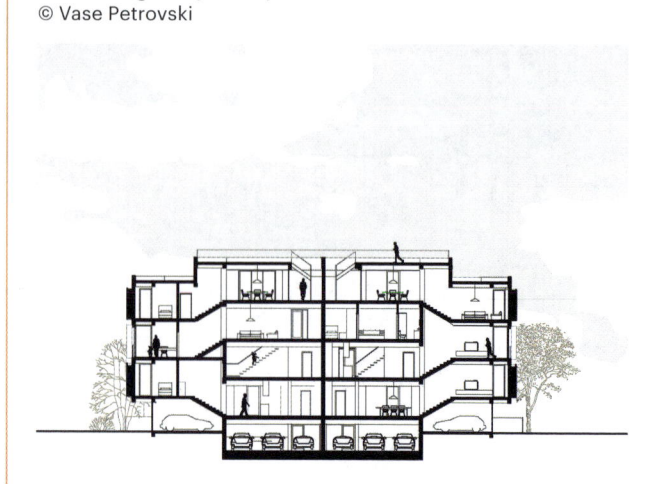

The CHP House represents a free-standing family house located on the south side of the foot of Vodno mountain. It is in the village of Dolno Sonje, a half-hour drive from the city center of Skopje. It is meant to be used as a holiday house and a residential house, considering its short distance to the city. The architectural concept of the house is somewhere between a suburban house and country house. The building style of the house and its aesthetics interact with its surroundings, as well as with 21st-century building ethics.

CHP House

› **SKOPJE, NORTH MACEDONIA**
2017/2018-2023
Single house · 243m²
› **Attika Architects, Volart**
Bojan Tasev, Nikola Tomevski, Simon Papesh
Private (Private)
© Gerro Petrovski Amanito

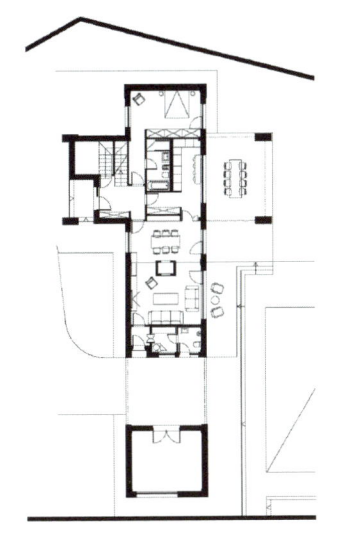

Designed for the largest retailers of tiles and sanitary ware in the country, this showroom with a warehouse is a place where several world brands are exhibited and represented. The building itself provides a total reimagining of traditional stores and our attempted reinterpretation of domestic architectural heritage in a building with a different function. Inspired with a simplified interpretation of old Macedonian architecture, using the traditional elements of Ohrid house, built in a tight location with overhanging volumes used to capture the light, the volume of our building is defined with a composition of multiple prisms with different materialization and spatial disposition.

Showroom and Distribution Centre with Warehouse Balkanija

› **SKOPJE, NORTH MACEDONIA**
2020/2020-2023
Commerce · 4,001m² · 500€/m²
› **Syndicate Studio**
Ilija Bozinovski, Dejan Sekulovski, Mia Shirik, Sashe Neshik, Katina Sutoglu
Balkanija MM dooel Kumanovo (Private)
© Vladimir Sekulovski

The house is situated in a neighborhood known for its narrow streets, HO SHI MIN, in the municipality of Butel, in the city of Skopje. The settlement is characterized by multi-layered materiality, irregular two-gable and four-gable roofs and small window openings. BB House sublimates these motifs into another dimension of architectural plastic representation, favoring a minimalistic glare from the outside and a dynamic composition from the inside.

BB House
› **SKOPJE, NORTH MACEDONIA**
2020/2020-2021
Single house · 130m²
› **BINA [bureau of inventive architecture]**
Bekir Ademi, Amine Ademi
Nimetula Sinani (Private)
© Boris Jurmovski

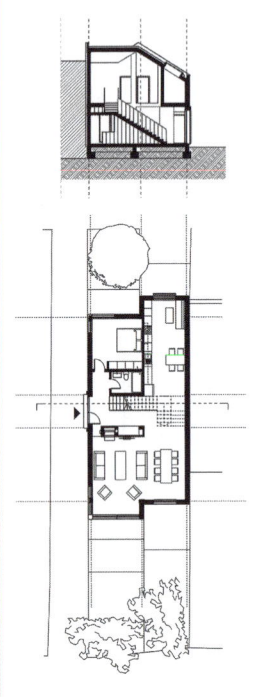

The main design principle is to create connections with the outdoor space, the yard and the greenery. This was achieved by placing the building on the elevated part of the terrain. At this junction, large glass canvases form a transparent visual border between the interior and the exterior. Consequently, the central mass of the building is elevated, creating different perspectives and interrupting the long horizontal structure, while separating different programmatic scenarios at the same time.

Villa for Contemporary Living
› **VELES, NORTH MACEDONIA**
2019/2020-2022
Single house · 425m²
› **Biro 60B, Arhitektura Nova**
Elena Pazardzievska Ristovska, Marija Dimitrievska Cilakova
Sahsko Lazarov (Private)
© Boris Jurmovski

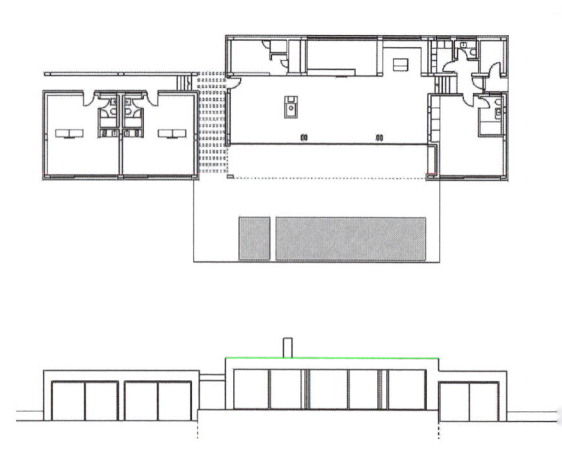

The Bankya central mineral bath is a national cultural monument and one of the most significant bath buildings in Bulgaria, dating from the early 20th century. The main goal of the project is to adapt the historical building as a spa center, meeting modern requirements, while respecting and emphasizing its cultural value.
The challenges were determined by finding a way to reuse the historic building. A specific approach, considering the possibilities of minimal intervention in the original, has been applied to areas with high architectural value in the interior and the exterior.

Conservation, Restoration and Socialization of the Central Mineral Bath "Bankya"
› **BANKYA, BULGARIA**
2018/2018-2022
Food & Accommodation · 5,250m² · 644€/m²
› **Georgiev Design Studio**
Chavdar Georgiev
Bankya municipality (Public)
© Ivan Shishiev

The project aims to provide an office building with flexible spaces for rent for a private investor. The building plot is located in a high-density area in the historical center of the city of Sofia. The main goal of the project is to create a contemporary workspace that integrates the new building into the existing urban fabric in a smooth and sensitive way.

MIR Office Building
› **SOFIA, BULGARIA**
2020/2020-2022
Office · 3,950m²
› **bureau XII**
Milena Filcheva, Peter Torniov
PTM Bojinov & Bojinov (Private)
© Boris Missirkov

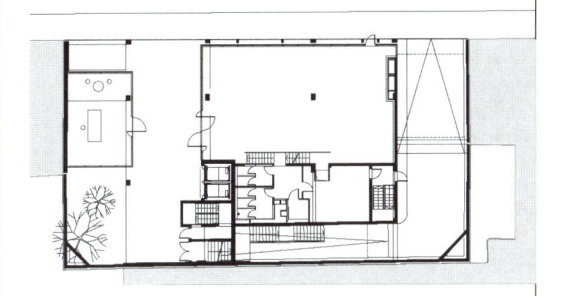

The Mill was initially built in the nearby village around 1933. Later, it was moved to Karpachevo and rebuilt where it stands now. After it closed down, it was abandoned and suffered serious damage due to the lack of maintenance.

The main aim of the project was to adapt and repurpose the abandoned building into a cultural center, adopting the principles of "honest" intervention and sustainable architecture. The project aimed to conserve the raw rural aesthetics of the original premises while integrating its new function in a holistic and sensible manner to meet new needs. The balance between its authentic spirit and atmosphere and the contemporary footprint is an essential part of the design concept. The sustainable aspect was achieved by using local resources and natural materials and by recycling available ones.

Cultural Information Centre "The Mill"

› **KARPACHEVO, BULGARIA**
  2020/2021-2022
  Food & Accommodation · 250m² · 200€/m²
› **Studio Nada**
  Antonina Tritakova, Georgi Sabev
  Devetaki Plateau Association (Public)
  © Todor Todorov

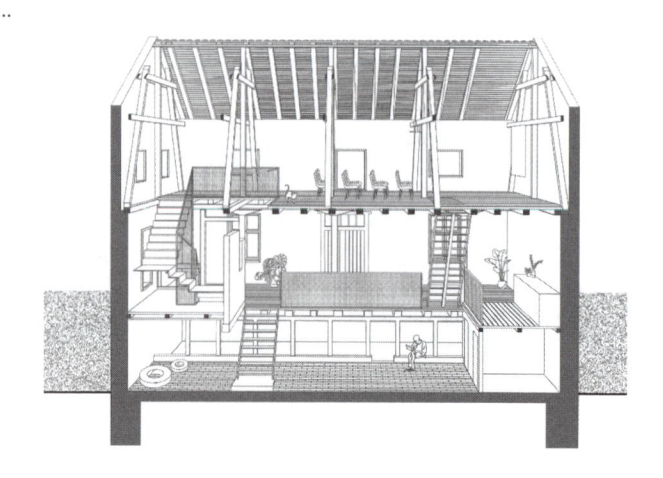

An unsightly space in the city core of Burgas has become a vibrant place for recreation, social contacts and cultural life. Combining nostalgia and modernity, the project restores the value of the street in the historical urban fabric, providing a convenient pedestrian connection between the central city square and the city central pedestrian zone.

The program envisaged transforming the unsightly space into a vibrant place for recreation, social contacts and cultural life by removing the temporary pavilions, introducing greenery and building a pavilion for the Association of the Masters of Folk Art Crafts to serve as a meeting point and a platform for various events.

Renovation of Aleko Konstantinov street

› **BURGAS, BULGARIA**
  2018/2021-2021
  Urban planning · 111m² · 293€/m²
› **Urbana Architects**
  Rositsa Zlatanova, Galina Milkova, Vladimir Milkov
  Burgas Municipality (Public)
  © Galina Milkova

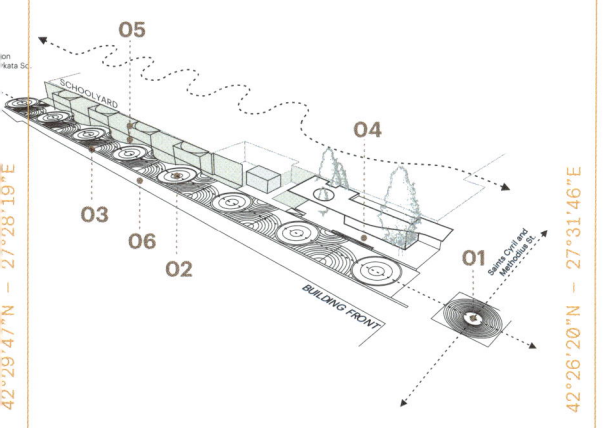

The ethnographic houses are part of a bigger complex aimed at creating a public space with added value for both fishermen and visitors, promoting the traditional fishermen's craft and sustainable fishing practices, fostering cultural exchange and supporting locals by creating new jobs.

The houses are inspired by the original environment in the village. It consists of rows of housing structures facing artificial canals where the boats are.

The houses are DIY architecture with the spontaneous and informal use of materials and structures like containers, sheds, diverse panels, found objects and self-made decorations.

Buildings for Ethnographic Exibitions in the Cultural and Tourist Complex Chengene Skele

› **BURGAS, BULGARIA**
  2019/2020-2021
  Food & Accommodation · 243m² · 1,000€/m²
› **MOTTO architectural studio**
  Mariana Sarbova, Desislava Stoyanova
  Municipality of Burgas (Public)
  © Georgi Georgiev

The house is located near the Black Sea town of Sozopol on a plot with a sweeping sea view. The project consists of the partial reconstruction and complete visual transformation of the existing house. The old house was built around 15 years ago in a style imitating authentic Sozopol architectural elements and materials: a multitude of inclined roofs with tiles, façade planking and tile cladding, bay windows and arches. The contractor wanted to achieve the exact opposite effect and have contrasting, memorable, minimalistic and contemporary architecture.

Private House in Sozopol
› **SOZOPOL, BULGARIA**
2021/2021-2022
Single house · 540m²
› **Simple Architecture**
Alexander Yonchev
Anonymous (Private)
© Assen Emilov

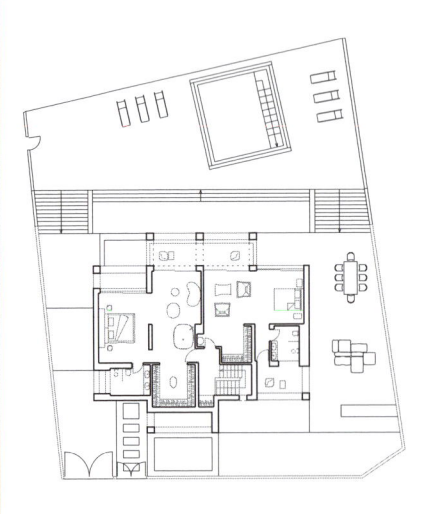

Located near two reputable state universities, this mixed-use building incorporates the functions of a student accommodation, a hotel and a conference center. Campus 90 responds to local and foreign students' increased interest in education in the city of Varna and changes the character of the neighborhood.
A significant challenge of the project was to provide a new functional program to the partially completed structure of the building. The client's initial intention was to build a high-rise office building. Construction began in 2008 and was interrupted by the global financial crisis (2008). Over 10 years later, the scope of the project was changed to a student accommodation building. The project was entirely redesigned, including with structural strengthening.

Campus 90
› **VARNA, BULGARIA**
2020/2020-2022
Mixed use - Cultural & Social · 16,575m²
› **E-Arch Studio**
Martin Hristov, Galina Baleva-Hristova, Ina Dineva
Patishta i mostove LTD (Private)
© Martin Hristov

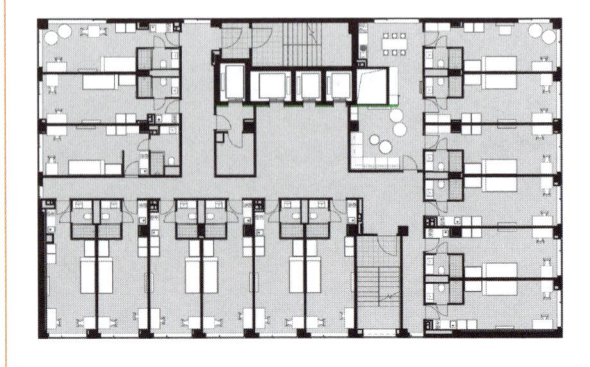

Karin Dom emerged from an open competition in late 2019. Its aim was to provide a dedicated home for the non-profit organization Karin Dom, which delivers expert services to children with special needs and their families.
Karin Dom was once situated in a lush, expansive seaside garden in Varna. However, the central location of the new site posed size constraints and we were further challenged by budget limitations. In response, we embraced three essential design principles: first, we crafted a compact building, preserving ample greenery and creating an inviting garden in the constrained site. Second, we regarded nature as a vital educational element, nurturing a profound connection both indoors and outdoors. Open ground floors and generous upper-level windows establish a constant visual link with the outside, immersing occupants in the natural world. Third, we emphasized spaces for interaction. An expansive atrium connected floors, welcoming abundant natural light, and a central staircase became a communal meeting point.

Karin Dom
› **VARNA, BULGARIA**
  2020/2021-2022
  Health · 2,810m^2 · 585€/m^2
› **unas studio**
  Bilyana Asenova, Saša Ciabatti
  Foundation Karin Dom (Private)
  © Georgi Milev

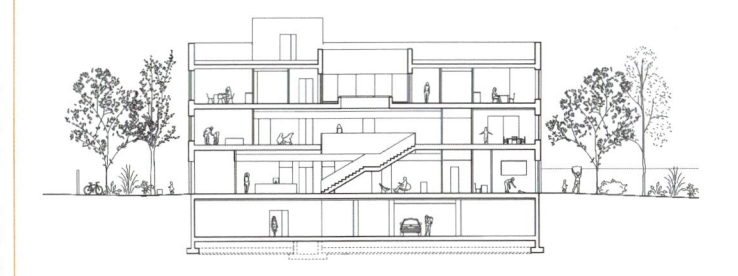

372

From
AVEIRO
Portugal
40°36'55"N — 8°45'01"W

to
TBILISI
Georgia
41°41'17"N — 44°48'16"E

The traditional wooden houses of the region painted in bold colors, the ocean, the lagoon and the sky reflected in the mirroring waters gave us the leitmotif. The limited budget for the renovation of this beach apartment gave rise to a radical answer: a single color for the whole space, for all architectural elements. The program is divided clearly in the core, separating the private zones from the open social area. A low-height corridor with moving panels allows for different uses, simultaneously. A long worktop, where one can cook, unifies the social area leading us to the balcony with its view of the dunes. The monochrome is like a backdrop that highlights life.

Monochrome Apartment
› **AVEIRO, PORTUGAL**
2021/2022-2022
Single house · 68m²
› **JCS ARCH+**
João Carmo Simões, Daniela Sá
Private
↑ © JCS
→ © Matilde Travassos

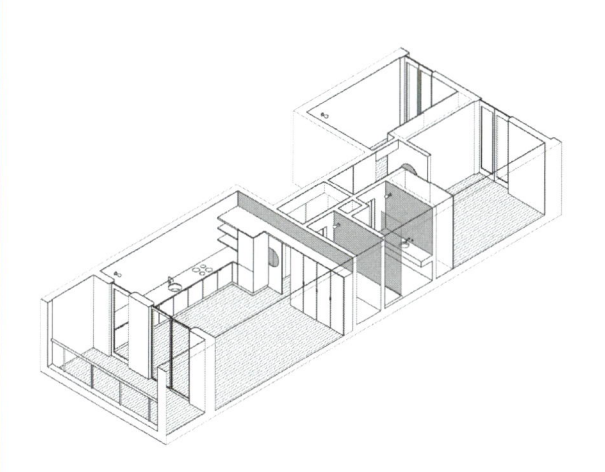

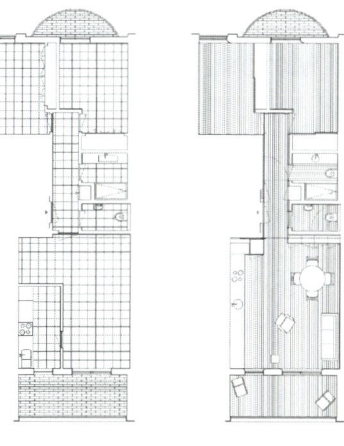

Before

After

Escadinhas Footpaths
Matosinhos, Portugal
2022/2022
Paulo Moreira Architectures, Verkron
Paulo Moreira, Verkron
Bairros Saudáveis
(Public)
Ephemeral -Society · 1,100m² · 83,33€/m²

This project links architecture, art, and the natural world. The structure involves a network of pedestrian footpaths linking the hilly neighbourhood of Monte Xisto to the River Leça in Matosinhos. The initiative demonstrates the added value that low-budget projects can bring to neglected urban spaces in our cities.

The public space and urban renewal project brought together a multidisciplinary team of architects, artists, local builders, and stakeholders. The steps leading to Rua das Escadinhas, an unusual urban device connecting the upper and lower levels of the western hill of Monte Xisto, were rehabilitated. Following the path that links the bottom of the steps to the Leça River, an old ruin was rebuilt and transformed into a seating area enveloped by nature. The project, developed within the framework of Bairros Saudáveis initiative, was designed by Paulo Moreira Architectures, together with the Verkron collective, and carried out by local builders. The final result lends an artistic dimension to the project that enhances its appeal.

The project aims to 'stitch together' the uneven topography of Monte Xisto, which is poorly connected to the surrounding area. Despite its geographical proximity to the Leça River valley and the centre of the parish, the neighbourhood is isolated by the lack of access. Through a comparatively modest investment in a context of social and territorial exclusion, the project aimed to improve the neighbourhood's access to the surrounding natural environment. During the first phase of the building work, the steps leading to Rua das Escadinhas, an unusual urban device connecting the upper and lower levels of the western hill of Monte Xisto, were rehabilitated. Following the path that links the bottom of the steps to the Leça River, an old ruin was rebuilt and transformed into a seating area enveloped by nature. The meticulous rehabilitation of the site, which included adding benches in every 'room', has encouraged people to spend time there and transformed it into a place for socialising.

Lasting a year, the construction was carried out by local builders who are residents of the neighbourhood. The steps and handrail were repaired and a new border between the public steps and the private land adjoining them was created in the form of benches, allowing the stairs to be used as a place for rest. Cleaning the area of the old ruins was a huge challenge. The sheer amount of rubbish, debris, and vegetation that had accumulated for more than forty years made it impassable and unusable by local people. The cleaning operation extended beyond the building: the riverbanks were also cleaned up and the natural landscape was enhanced. Once the rubbish and debris had been removed, small-scale interventions restored the site's original character, undoing the precarious interventions carried out over the years.

PAULO MOREIRA ARCHITECTURES

376

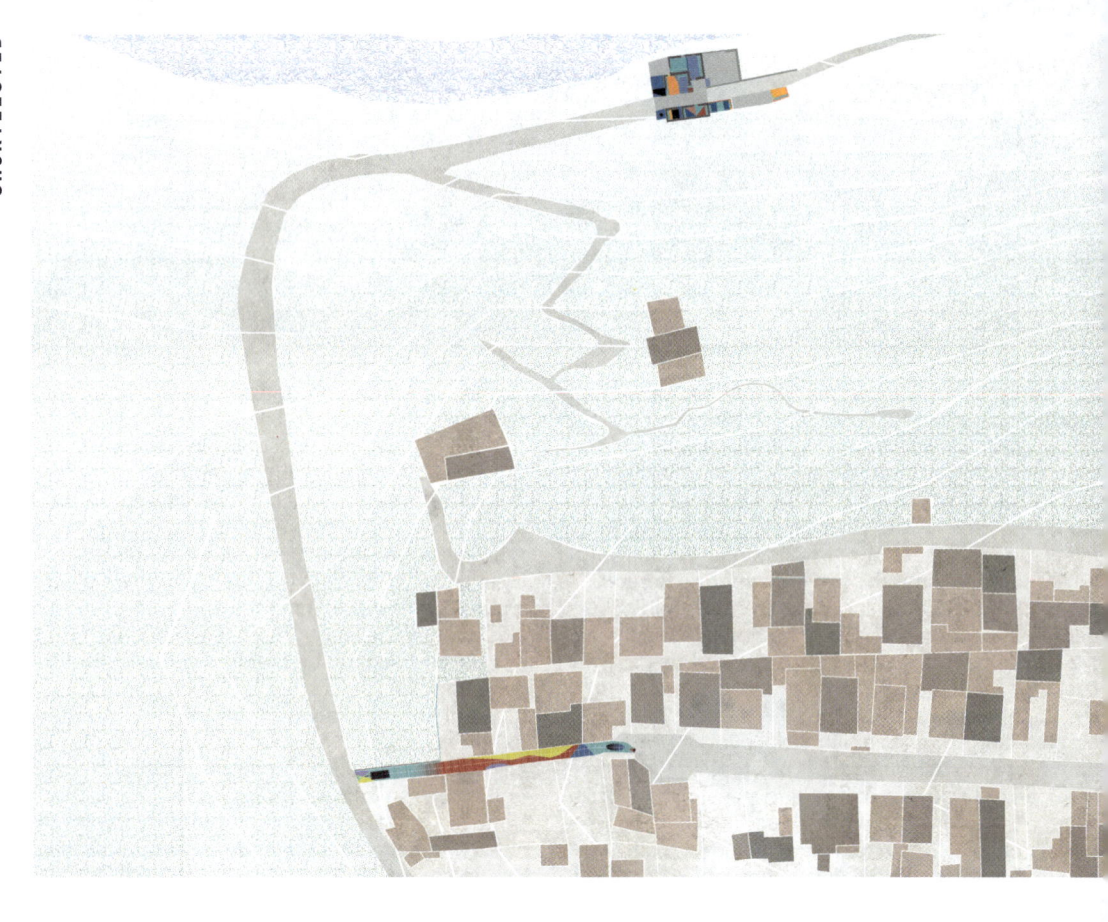

SHORTLISTED

ESCADINHAS FOOTPATHS

PAULO MOREIRA ARCHITECTURES

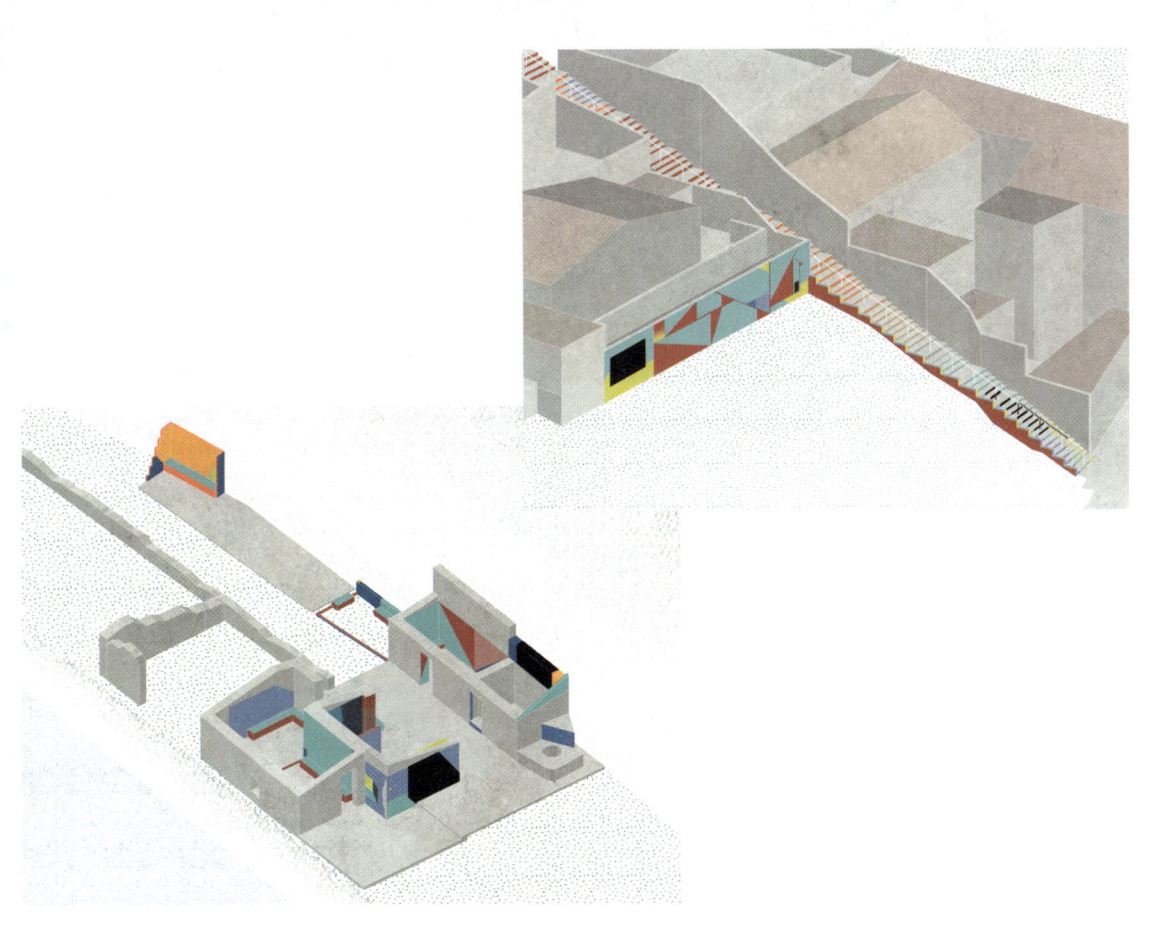

General Silvinhas Building
Porto, Portugal
2016/2019-2022
ATA Atelier, ENTRETEMPOS
Tiago Antero, Vitor Fernandes
Zhiang Zhou
(Private)
Collective housing · 1,378m²

The General Silveira building is a mixed collective housing and commercial project located in a classified block in Porto's city centre that, between the haze of memory and the increasingly contemporary city. The building was founded in the inexorable circumstance that dictates its formal lexicon.

The General Silveira building's design is based on a morphological model that characterizes housing in Porto. Through the design of 4 smaller-scale volumes, which are contiguous 2 by 2 and separated by a courtyard inside the block, the proposal volumetrically functions as 4 buildings, evoking the memory of the 4 pre-existing fractions as well as the predominant scale of the surrounding urban fabric, integrating itself into the city's typological housing matrix. However, the intention is not to mimic the architectural language of the late 19th and early 20th centuries but rather to design a contemporary style of architecture that seeks to reinterpret the relationships of proportion, materiality, and form.

The initial concern was the interconnectivity of the whole design since access to the interior of the city block from the streets was strongly impacted by the conditions. Schematically, the typical distribution of 4 apartments per floor evokes the 4 original plots, in a morphological corollary that results in 4 hipped roofs, creating the 5th floor of the project. The ground floor is physically and visually permeable, acting as a mediating space between the public and the private, the moment where commerce and housing converge and the streets interconnect.

In a strong compromise between adapting to the needs of the present and intervening in existing heritage, the project introduces a profound improvement in terms of accessibility. This feature begins from the outside, through two accesses at the level of each of the streets, allowing entry to a courtyard cut into the interior, where there is a central stairwell and an elevator that is the centrepiece of the project, not only because of its impact on the perception of the space, but above all, because this is the element that defines all the altimetric relationships with the surroundings, namely cornices, eaves, dormers, balconies, and openings.

Environmental sustainability has also been addressed throughout the project, especially with passive systems that reduce the building's ecological footprint. The implementation of a central courtyard, where the vertical accesses are located, not only allows the introduction of natural lighting in the areas furthest from the streets but also makes cross ventilation possible in all the commercial and residential units, which is vitally important for the health of the spaces. The houses are accessed from this outdoor patio via galleries, taking advantage of this ventilation and natural lighting. Finally, the metrics of the elevations, the choice of the tile pattern and colour, and the distance between openings refer to the dynamic and tectonic design of the adjacent buildings. The Genius Loci is the inexorable circumstance that dictates the formal lexicon.

Considering that an intervention in a historic and classified area such as this always requires a sensitive and careful process between improving the quality of the spaces and inserting them appropriately into the urban surroundings the project sought a compromise between the dictates of the past and the new ethical and environmental needs of the present.

ATA ATELIER. ENTRETEMPOS

380

SHORTLISTED

Diagram

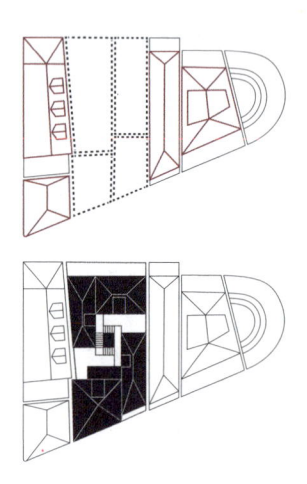

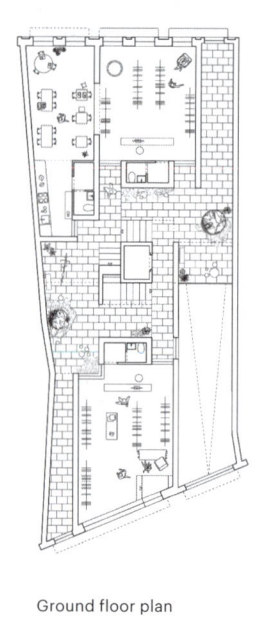

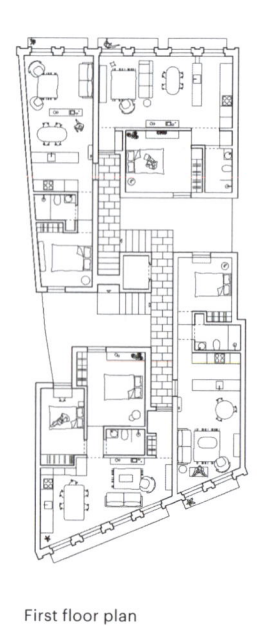

Ground floor plan

First floor plan

GENERAL SILVINHAS BUILDING   0 1 2 5   10   20

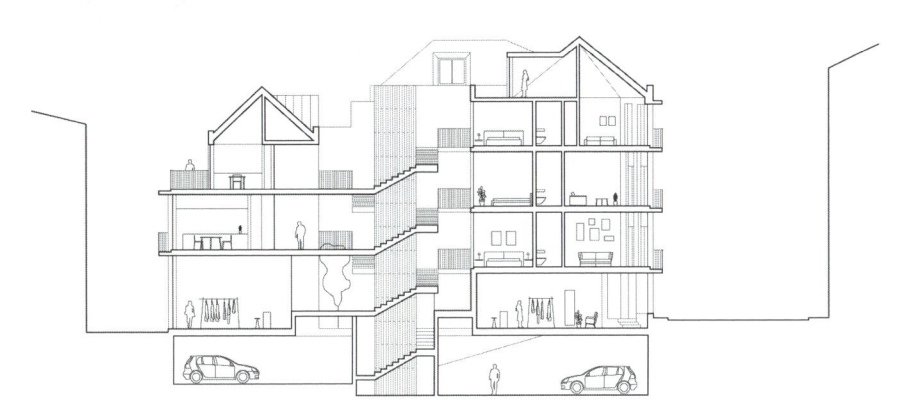

Cross section

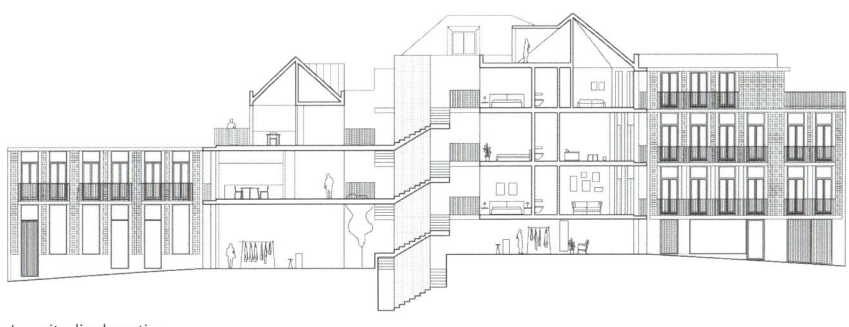

Longitudinal section

ATA ATELIER. ENTRETEMPOS

The architectural idea guiding the project is based on the hotel's aim to be immersed in its surroundings, preserving its belonging to the urban context that gives it meaning. The pre-existing complex consists of three volumes of old wine warehouses scaled along the escarpment that descends to the river, plus a building on the upper floor where the hotel's reception is located. A new floor is added to each of the three warehouses, but designed in continuity with them by form and construction system, making the change almost imperceptible. The complexity of the project lies in how it distributes and articulates the program along the 12 floors resulting from the maintenance of the pre-existing buildings and their extension.

Vincci Ponte de Ferro Hotel
› VILA NOVA DE GAIA, PORTUGAL
2013/2018-2021
Food & Accommodation · 7,989m²
> **José Gigante Arquitecto**
José Manuel Gigante, Manuel Fernando Santos
RSR Singular Assets Europe SOCIMI, S.A. (Private)
© Marta Maria Ferreira / Luís Ferreira Alves

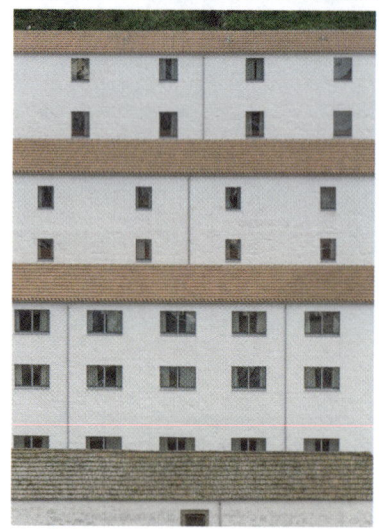

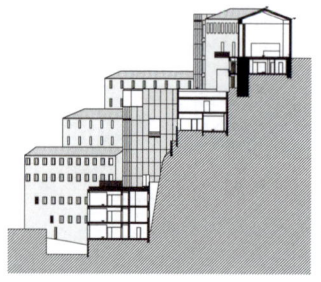

Cross section

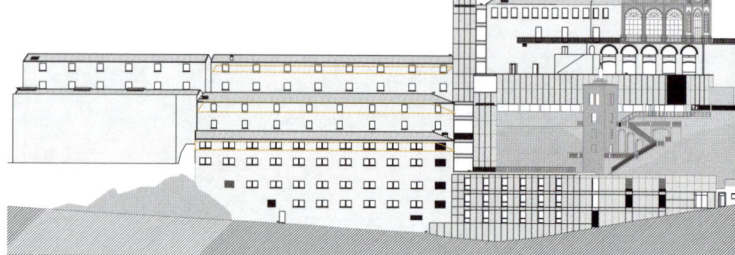

North elevation

The classification of the Mercado do Bolhão in Porto as a "monument of public interest" recognizes the heritage value of two inseparable dimensions – the building and the activity. The proposed intervention in the 1914-1917 market building is based on the restoration and enhancement of the building and the modernization required to meet the demands of the central and daily fresh produce market activity in Porto. This transformative action, which is attentive to existing values, seeks to restore the building's identity and consistency, open the market to the city and update its function, which in a constant balance between tangible and intangible heritage.

Rehabilitation of the Bolhão Market

› **PORTO, PORTUGAL**
 2014/2018-2022
 Commerce · 21,340m^2 · 25,700,000€
› **Nuno Valentim, Arquitectura e Reabilitação**
 Nuno Valentim Lopes, Rita Machado Lima, Frederico Eça, Margarida Carvalho, Juliano Ribas
 Go Porto, Gestão e Obras do Porto, EM (Public)
 © Marta Maria Ferreira

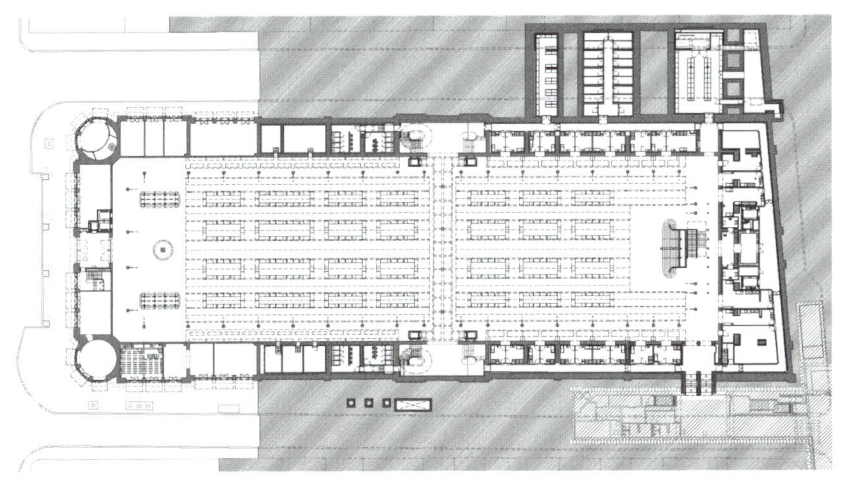

Cinema Batalha, a 1940s project by architect Artur Andrade, had great symbolic significance as a landmark of resistance to the dictatorship's impositions of form and substance. Its prominence transformed it into an affirmation of contemporary times and of cinema, the last of the arts. The project is based on the desire to highlight the importance of the building in its context and to establish it as a landmark of modern architecture, as well as the expectation of it becoming the center of important cultural activity in the city.

Rehabilitation of Cinema Batalha
› **PORTO, PORTUGAL**
2017/2019-2022
Culture · 2,635m² · 1,962.16€/m²
› **Atelier 15**
Alexandre Alves Costa, Sergio Fernandez, Miguel Ribeiro
GO Porto - Gestão e Obras do Porto, EM (Public)
© Guilerme Oliveira

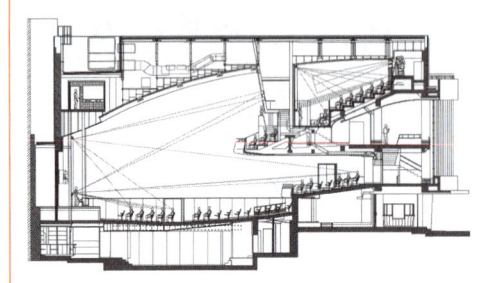

The ESAP/CESAP campus is structured with three buildings to be built in different phases. Phase I involved the renovation and transformation of an abandoned factory destined for the ESAP academic building. The economic limitations and the need to house the new academic facilities in a very short time were important constraints that significantly influenced the construction program. Consequently, the first phase of the works focused on the renovation and transformation of the pre-existing building in order to shorten the construction time while providing comfortable and efficient spaces with as little resources as possible. Nevertheless, these conditions, although difficult, ended up creating a dynamic of participation and collaborative interaction among the entire school community, enriching the project and allowing new ideas to be implemented very quickly.

ESAP – Oporto School of Art
› **PORTO, PORTUGAL**
2021/2021-2022
Education · 4,209m² · 1,000€/m²
› **Cannatá & Fernandes**
Michele Cannatà, Fátima Fernandes, João Carreira
CESAP – Cooperativa de Ensino Superior Artístico do Porto (Private)
© Portugal Fashion

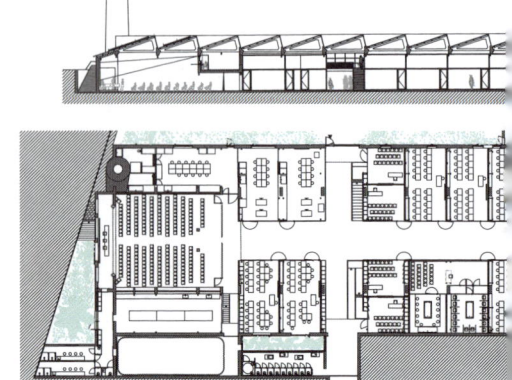

The project is a territorial gesture that looks at the city in a broader context, using the detail of the program and its complexity as a solution to establish the generic relationship of all the artificial and natural elements of the place and their articulated replacement in the urban map. The program's distribution is based on the basic idea of simplicity. Given the functional complexity of the various components on so many levels (distributive, organic, mechanical and infrastructural), the project attempts to simplify the program by breaking it in a regulated and sequential plot, with a portico, extended over the layout area and summarized in a perceptible matrix in the structure and, consequently, in the architectural language.

Campanhã Intermodal Terminal
› **PORTO, PORTUGAL**
2017/2019-2022
Mixed use - Infrastructure & Urban · 19,000m^2
› **Brandão Costa Arquitectos**
Nuno Brandão Costa
Go Porto, Porto Municipality (Public)
© Francisco Ascensão

EMERGING FINALIST

**Piódão Square
and Tourist Office**
Piódão, Portugal.
2018/2020-2022
Branco del Rio
João Branco, Paula del Rio
Câmara Municipal Arganil
(Public)
Mixed use · Infrastructure & Urban · 1,767m²
· 238 €/m²

40°13'45"N – 7°49'30"W

The only flat, open area of the steep sloping village of Piódão has regained its dignity as a welcoming place for people to gather. What was previously a parking lot has been redesigned, paved, and given partial shade using traditional materials and techniques. The space was given back to its people in line with the town's material and building culture.

The project rehabilitates and reconfigures one of Piódão's square as well as its tourist office building.

The village of Piódão is located in the Serra do Açor, in central Portugal. Its houses made of schist traversed by steep, narrow streets form an amphitheatre on a northwest-facing escarpment.

In its lower part, the Cónego Manuel Fernandes Nogueira square is the town's only unobstructed, flat, open space and it serves as the main access point to the village

Over the years, the space has been taken over by cars as a parking lot. The project returns the space to the people as the village's gathering place, encouraging friendly exchanges and social interaction.

The materials and building solutions used in both the tourism office and the square came from the local surroundings. There is, thus, a certain feeling that nothing was done, that it has always been as it is.

The primary goal was to remove cars and give the space back to people. By doing so, the space was freed from obstacles and its limits were requalified and redefined.

First, a grid of cherry trees at the entrance changes the sequence upon arriving to the village. After the first contact with the village, at a distance by car during which one can recognize the settlement within its landscape, the trees delay the second order of understanding of the town as a whole: the village appears to be elevated from its foundation. This plant "filter" also protects and withdraws the square from the road, preventing cars from circulating.

Secondly, the newly paved surface of the square, built using schist, with no uneven patches or curbs, reinforces the square's new pedestrian character, and ensures universal accessibility. The formal complexity of the space, which lacks directionality, is approached with the introduction of a large central circle, with the church at its axis, which circumscribes the bust and the existing trees.

The different elements that make up the square, the church façade and the stone foundation on which it stands, the tourist office and the small houses with restaurants and cafes, are arranged around this new soft centrality.

The architectural intervention, both inside and outside the Tourist Office, aimed to clean and clear up the existing building, removing elements and additions. A new shed protects the entrances to the building and contributes to a unitary image of the whole.

The project strove to act silently.

The existing trees, the statue, and the public lighting were all preserved.

The new pavement was built using the same material and technique as the whole village, schist, following a tradition mastered by local builders.

The trees at the entrance of the square are cherry trees, which are native to the region.

The two porches, on the entrances to the Tourist Office and Public Toilets, were built with a delicate structure of metallic columns and wooden beams, and covered with a roof of slate slabs, like all the roofs in the village.

The overall approach to the design aims to contribute to an arrangement where it is difficult to grasp what is new and what is old, thereby ensuring that the locals' connection to the place remains unchanged.

The project sought to forge a connection between cultural and material sustainability, hopefully contributing to encouraging new inhabitants to settle in this very withdrawn interior part of the country.

PIÓDÃO SQUARE AND TOURIST OFFICE

BRANCO DEL RIO

EMERGING FINALIST

PIÓDÃO SQUARE AND TOURIST OFFICE

Before intervention

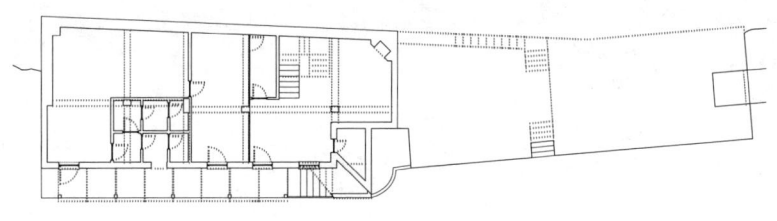

Ground floor plan

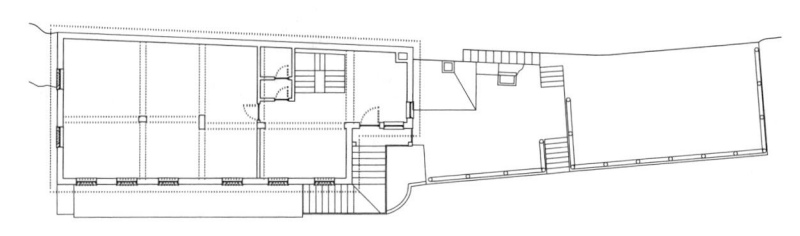

First floor plan

After intervention

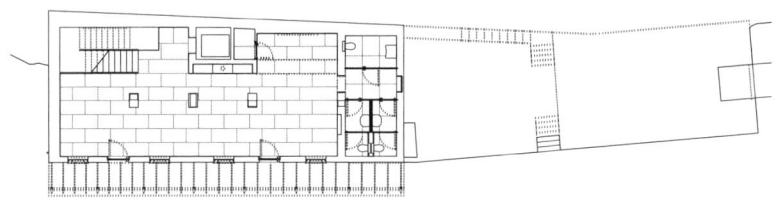

Ground floor plan

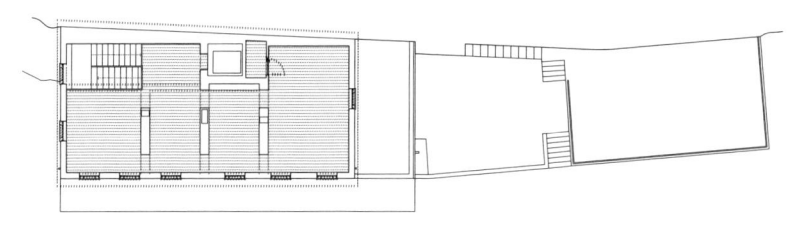

First floor plan

BRANCO DEL RIO   0 1 2   5   10   20

PIÓDÃO SQUARE AND TOURIST OFFICE

BRANCO DEL RIO

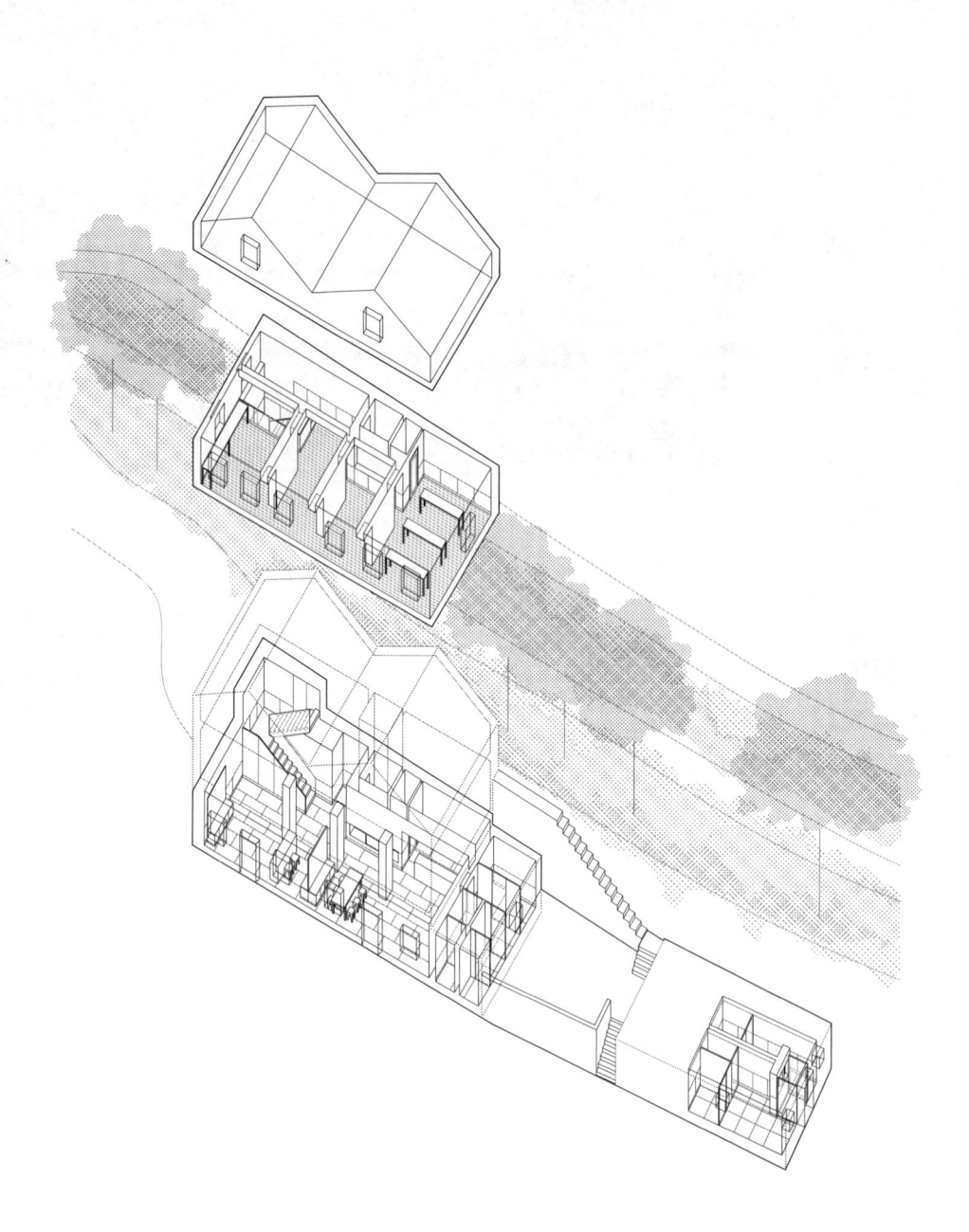

PIÓDÃO SQUARE AND TOURIST OFFICE

BRANCO DEL RIO

PIÓDÃO SQUARE AND TOURIST OFFICE

BRANCO DEL RIO

PIÓDÃO SQUARE AND TOURIST OFFICE

A Difficult Equation for Piódão Square and Tourist Office

"What is this village? Is it for the people who live here, or for the foreigners who come to see it? Is it more of a nativity scene or a Euro Disney?" [1]

Pedro Baía

PhD architect, editor, professor and researcher. Founder and director of Circo de Ideias publisher. Researcher at CEAU and professor at FAUP and DA/UAL.

These questions reveal the complexities faced by architects João Branco and Paula del Rio in designing the village square and tourist office in Piódão. This project was the subject of various issues related to authenticity, identity, craftsmanship, heritage, popular culture, representation, tourism, and mobility.

Piódão represents a difficult equation to solve: on the one hand, there is the mythical notion of the historic, idealized village that needs to be preserved; on the other, the practical reality of the daily lives of the people who live and work there.

Through reflections on the cultural and symbolic factors that define this village and community, the architects developed a thoughtful, challenging, and mindful strategy. Initial visits to the site and preliminary meetings with political representatives, residents, and retailers were crucial in understanding the complex context in which they would be operating.

In terms of its status as a mythical historic village, Piódão has a magical aura that evokes a nostalgic connection to the deep roots and origins of Portugal, far away from the city, progress, and technology. From this point of view, the village represents an ancestral heritage that has managed to escape the aggressive pace of modern life. Considered one of the most beautiful villages in Portugal, Piódão can be compared to a nativity scene, with its small schist houses set on terraces in the mountains, marked by the voids of the houses, black slate roofs, narrow streets and steps, and the brilliant white of the church at the centre.

The argument for maintaining the authenticity of the historic village is part of the process of constructing an identity created for touristic and economic purposes. In the past, the schist houses of this region were the poorest dwellings, while whitewashed houses were the richest due to the higher cost of the materials and difficulty of access through the mountains. Schist constructions, as the only locally available material, were a sign of poverty, and lime finishes were a luxury only the church and some families could afford.

In recent decades, the situation has turned on its head. It is now more accessible and practical to build with concrete, brick, plaster, and ceramic tiles than with traditional schist and slate techniques, which require specialized labor and knowledge. To reinforce the image of a historic, authentic mountain village with an identity underscored by characteristic regional stone, there has been a new appreciation for local stone houses and an incentive to remove plaster and tiles.

[1] João Branco, in Sérgio Costa Andrade, "A arquitectura invisível que dá vida nova à aldeia histórica do Piódão", *Público*, 9 de Março de 2024. — https://www.publico.pt/2024/03/09/culturaipsilon/noticia/arquitectura-invisivel-vida-nova-aldeia-historica-piodao-2082520

[2] Paula del Rio, in Sérgio Costa Andrade, "A arquitectura invisível que dá vida nova à aldeia histórica do Piódão", *Público*, 9 de Março de 2024. — https://www.publico.pt/2024/03/09/culturaipsilon/noticia/arquitectura-invisivel-vida-nova-aldeia-historica-piodao-2082520

"Our project was designed more for the local people, not for Instagram photos." [2]

In practical day-to-day reality, the village functions like a machine. It needs to accommodate and distribute the waves of tourists arriving daily by car and bus to restaurants, cafes, terraces, and local accommodation, as well as handle the loading and unloading of deliveries for retailers and residents. Before the architects stepped in, the space at the entrance to Piódão, at the foot of the village, was overrun by traffic and served as a parking lot. The main access to the village and its attractive space in front of the main church was thus de-characterized, with the village lacking a designated public area.

The architects' project sought to restore dignity to the entrance to the village, by proposing a pedestrianized square flush to the ground without any steps or curbs. Their intervention saw the introduction of schist paving and a large paved circle aligned with the church steps that also encompassed a monument and existing trees, which formed a meeting space and created newfound centrality between the church, the tourism office, and the restaurants.

Along the main road to the village, cherry trees— typical of the region— were planted to demarcate the square and protect it from traffic noise. Near the church, sober and discreet metal railings were installed to act as new handrails for the steps up to the church level, and protective barriers near the bridge and stream running below the square.

The architects' project for the square was completed with the design of the new tourist office, one of the most delicate aspects of the whole equation. The new office was designed from an existing building, following a picturesque model of evocative mountain simulations.

The most illustrative example of this simulation can be found on the building's top floor, with two windows facing the square, each aligned with an overhead ridge. In reality, there is no access to the top floor, and the wooden-framed windows are unusable. They are fake, serving only to create a facade that suggests two individual houses, each with its own gable roof. This is a scene-setting tactic: the seeking out of a picturesque mountain identity to convey the comforting authenticity of a historic village and meet tourists' expectations.

When tackling this design equation, the architects decided to follow the narrative of the historic village, maintaining the local stone and the building's original silhouette, while still presenting a contemporary project. They maintained the gable roofs and the inaccessible top floor with the two false windows. Their intervention in the building retained the concrete structure of the former hotel, but opened up the existing layout by eliminating walls, stairs, and annexes, as well as closing off and introducing new doors and windows. The tourist office's exhibition space was enhanced with new paving, and a more articulated compartmentalization with improved circulation spaces and light sources.

"A new canopy, built using the traditional system of a wooden structure with slate slabs, protects the building's entrances and helps maintain the image of a unified ensemble."[3]

On the outside, the new tourist office features a key element for understanding the project's commitment to resolving this difficult equation. The canopy's design, in its simplicity and elegance, illustrates the overall tone of the approach adopted by the architects in the balanced design developed for Piódão: respecting local materials, caring for the historic village's character, seeking unity in the ensemble, spatial redefinition, and contemporary expectations.

    Finally, the design of the square – marked by its paved circle – represents an open space available to be used by everyone. It is free and welcoming, unifying, and conciliatory, embodying both ancient and modern features. This delicate, thoughtful gesture invites and welcomes all who pass by, from tourists to residents, and from politicians to retailers.

[3] Branco Del-Rio Arquitects website. — https://www.branco-delrio.com/projects/praca-e-posto-de-turismo-piodao

Municipal Pools
Castromonte, Spain
2020/2021

Óscar Miguel Ares. Contextos de Arquitectura y Urbanismo
Oscar Miguel Ares Álvarez

Ayuntamiento de Castromonte
(Public)
Sport & Leisure · 500m² · 900€/m²

Depopulation is one of the great endemic problems in the central area of our country, the area has come to be known as 'Empty Spain'.

The project not only aims to create architecture, but above all it seeks to create a space. This multifunctional structure (in which the swimming pools are just one among other elements) is a place to meet and discuss for a small municipality of 309 inhabitants that seemed fated to disappear. The strategy of creating a public structure serves not only to stake a claim for a certain level of social justice for smaller population centres against larger cities, but also to avoid the population from draining even further by making these villages more attractive. This will encourage people who once abandoned the village to return together with their children.

The municipal swimming pools are a synthesis of the municipal's two most characteristic realities. Thus, its composition is based on the dialogue of the two natures that coexist surrounding the hamlet in the current context of field and municipality. On the one hand, uncut stone is used in its long walls emulating the tradition of walls and fences that identify the municipality. On the other hand, the technological reality of wind farms that emerge between wheat fields has been reinterpreted. This is achieved by the seemingly aerial arrangement of a prefabricated beam roof.

The building floor plan is configured by a succession of parallel masonry walls, which are crafted according to traditional techniques. The roof, composed of Art Wind beams, seeks to symbolize the other world of wind turbines and industrialization, that have been part of the Montes Torozos ecosystem for some time now.

The beams playfully rise over the masonry, embracing it and the ground with their shadows. The structure evokes the memory of shady summers. The shadows mend, mingle, and sustain the structure.

Except for the roof beams, homegrown materials and traditional techniques were used to implement the structure. All the materials are locally sourced, since none have been produced more than 80km away (the prefabricated beams). We can thus speak of a true local economy and recycling project.

There are two worlds of construction. The first refers to the traditional load-bearing walls that were built by dismantling local existing walls and using demolition material. Creating these walls involved recovering and reinforcing the stone placement with traditional techniques and local trades. Furthermore, an in-situ concrete girder was projected between the roof and the prefabricated beams. Seeking to blend in with the stone, extracted gravel was used, which was mixed with white cement. Its surface was washed afterwards, which made it possible to connect the concrete texture with the masonry.

The second world, the world of the beams, is a simile of the vertical blades of the local wind turbines. This time they are lying down, intentionally arranged in an open way between their interstices. This system is used to generate the pronounced shadows that run throughout the indoor space.

MUNICIPAL POOLS

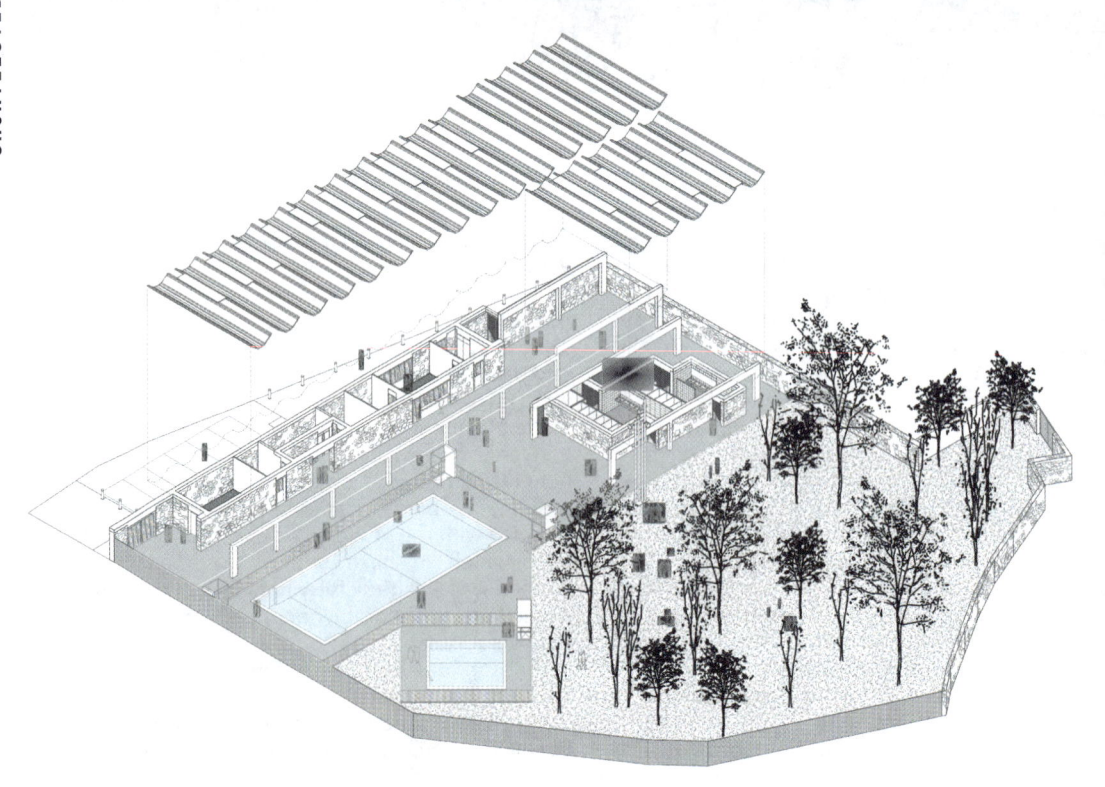

Ground floor plan

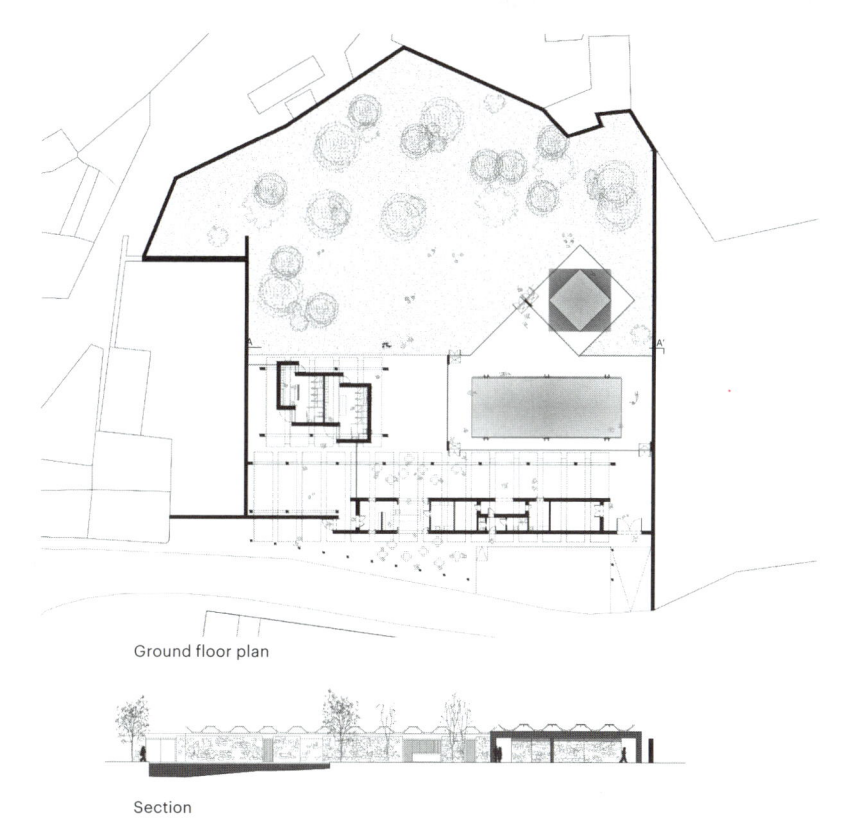

Section

ÓSCAR MIGUEL ARES. CONTEXTOS DE ARQUITECTURA Y URBANISMO

For the new School of Arts, located in a plot that used to be part of a convent's orchards, a courtyard system was replicated to generate an "other space" for creation. Towards the city, the building shows itself as an architecture of walls, which continues the traditional architecture of the adjacent convent; towards the inside, it merges as an architecture of patios full of light and life. The project strives to be respectful of its historical context. However, it houses a space for creativity, youth and dreams. The essence of the project is the materialization of this duality.

Art School of Valladolid

› **VALLADOLID, SPAIN**
2017/2020-2022
Education · 6,173m²
› **estudio Primitivo González**
Primitivo González, Noa González Cabrera, Ara González Cabrera
**Consejería de Educación,
Junta de Castilla y León (Public)**
© Luis Díaz Díaz

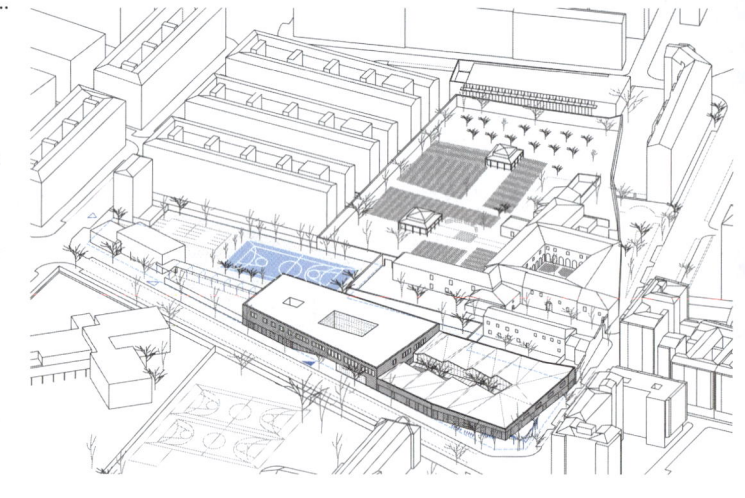

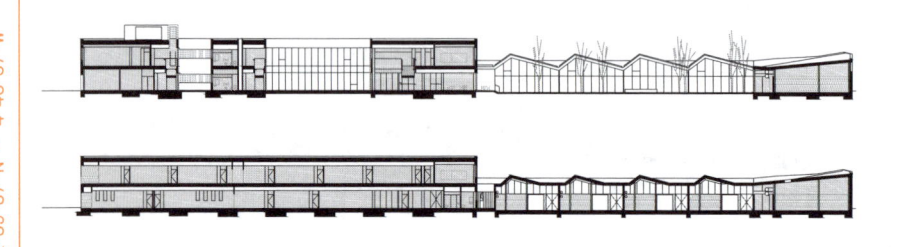

A building sensitive to the urban situation, its height and volumetric configuration seeks to adapt to the surroundings, notably by reducing its scale. This is achieved by staggering the building, a meandering floor plan articulated by three open courtyards and large checkerboard-patterned openings in the façade. LaScala is a building comprising of 100 social housing units. The exterior galleries leading to the units are considered an extension of the plot's open space, serving as a social gathering place with natural ventilation and lighting, just like its inviting ground-floor gardens connected to the street.

"Lascala" NSA6 100 Social Housing

› MADRID, SPAIN
 2010/2017-2021
 Collective housing · 10,547m^2
› MARMOLBRAVO, MADhel
 Mauro Bravo, Marina del Marmol, Daniel Bergman, Miguel Herraiz
 EMVS Empresa Municipal de la Vivienda y Suelo de Madrid (Public)
 © Pedro Pegenaute

Reggio School
Madrid, Spain
2018/2020-2022
Andrés Jaque / Office for Political Innovation
Andrés Jaque
Reggio School
(Private)
Education · 5,942m² · 1,497€/m²

The design, construction, and use of the Reggio School is intended to extend beyond the sustainability paradigm to engage with ecology as an approach where environmental impact, interspecies alliances that transcend humanity, material mobilization, collective governance, and education intersect through architecture.
The design of the school was developed in conversation with teachers, students, and parents, as a participatory process that incorporated their ideas, concerns, and sensitivities.

Shunning homogenization and unified standards, the architecture of the school aims to become a multiverse where the layered complexity of the environment becomes readable and experiential.

The school operates as an assemblage of different climates, ecosystems, architectural traditions, and regulations. As a result, the school stacks an array of diverse architectural designs, fostering a teaching environment that spurs curiosity and collective-self-education.

Located adjacent to the linear Valdebebas Public Park, the school minimizes its overall construction and land use by expanding its physical exercise, science, and courses into the public park. In this way, education takes shape as a process of social interaction (instead of seclusion, exclusivity, and segregation) contributing social heterogeneity and tolerance-building, while also activating the public space as a place of lively intergenerational interaction.

1. STACKING LAYERS OF DIVERSITY AS SELF-EDUCATION. The ground floor classrooms engage with the land. The higher levels are where students coexist with an exuberant greenhouse fuelled by reclaimed water. Exploring the school's richness is how kids become more mature.

2. AN ASSEMBLY AT THE HEART OF THE SCHOOL. The second floor, formalized as a large void opened through landscape-scale arches to the surrounding ecosystems, is conceived as the school's main social and governance assembly space.

Small gardens included across the building nurture insects, butterflies, birds and bats, striving to repair the ecosystems of the neighbouring park which lost its biodiversity due to the massive use of pesticides in the surrounding private suburban gardens. The school is an instrument that provides care for and helps to regenerate the public ecosystems of which it forms part.

3. MAKING MECHANICAL SYSTEMS VISIBLE AS A SOURCE OF EDUCATION. All services are unapologetically visible. They are an opportunity for students to question how their bodies and social interactions depend on water, energy, and the exchanges and circulation of air.

ANDRES JAQUE / OFFICE FOR POLITICAL INNOVATION

The design employs a low budget strategy to reduce its environmental impact based on these principles:

1. VERTICAL DESIGN TO REDUCE LAND USAGE. Instead of a building that spreads out horizontally (as is typical in schools), the vertical design reduces its foundations and sanitary systems to 27% of what would normally be required.
2. RADICALLY REDUCED CONSTRUCTION. No cladding, no drop ceilings, no raised technical floors, no wall lining, and no ventilated façades are used in this naked building. The amount of material used in the facades, roofs, and interior partitions has been reduced by 48% by inventing a projected-cork facade that provides both insulation, weatherproofing, and finishing.
3. A THICK CORK LAYER ACTS AS INSULATION AND A BASE FOR LIFE THAT EXTENDS BEYOND HUMANS. The irregular surface of the cork is designed to allow organic material to accumulate. This envelope will provide a habitat to microbiological, fungi, plant, and animal life.
4. MORE THINKING, LESS MATERIAL. The building's structure has been shaped, analysed and dimensioned so that the thickness of the loading walls can be reduced by an average of more than 150 mm compared to conventional reinforced concrete structures.

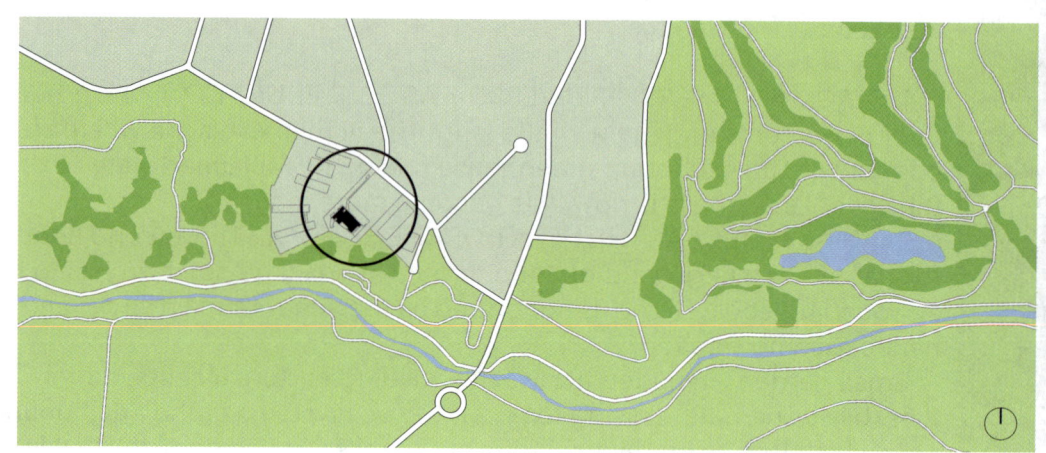

Siteplan

ANDRES JAQUE / OFFICE FOR POLITICAL INNOVATION

REGGIO SCHOOL

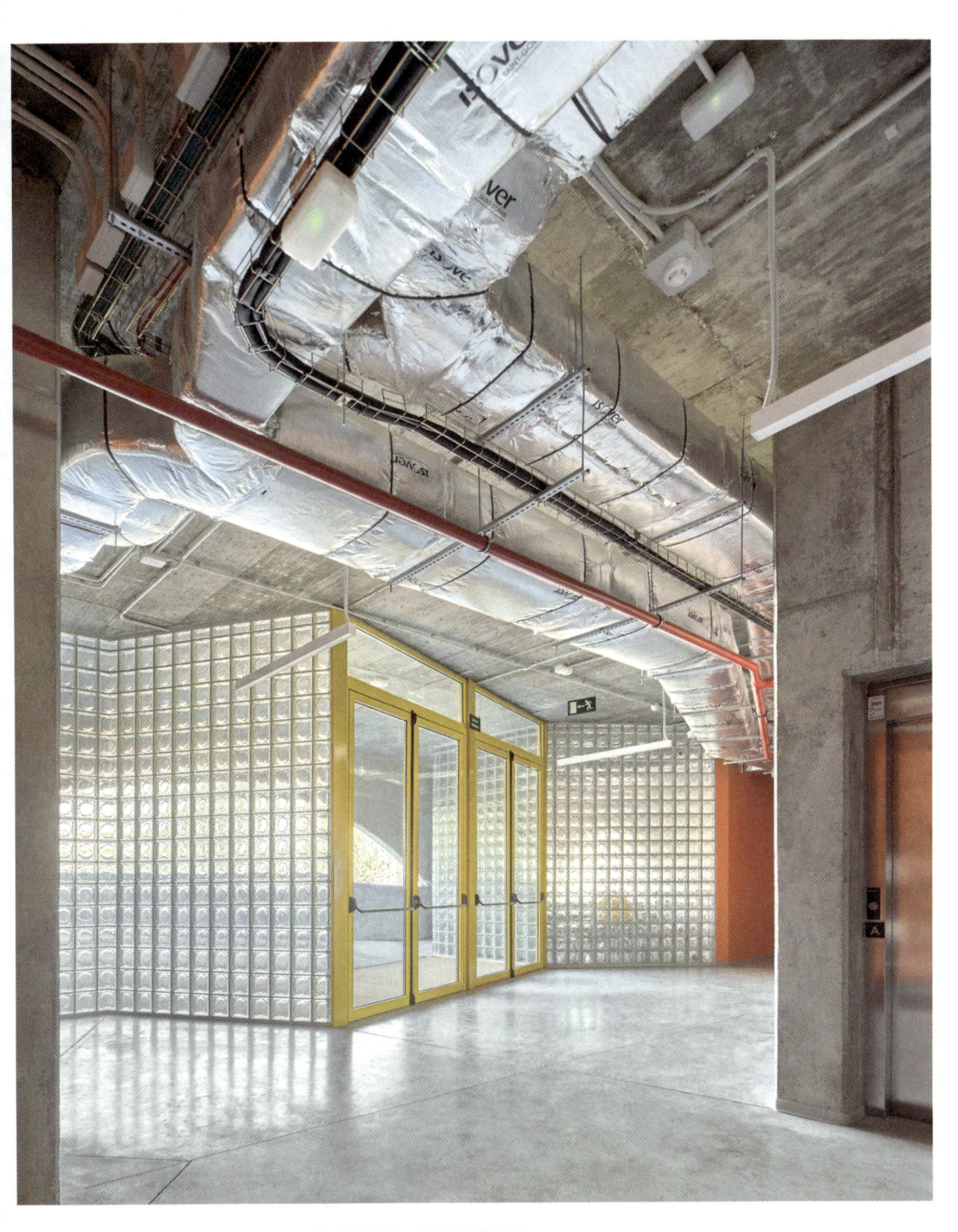

ANDRES JAQUE / OFFICE FOR POLITICAL INNOVATION

414

FINALIST

Floor plan level 5

Floor plan level 2

REGGIO SCHOOL

Floor plan level 6

Floor plan level 3

ANDRES JAQUE / OFFICE FOR POLITICAL INNOVATION

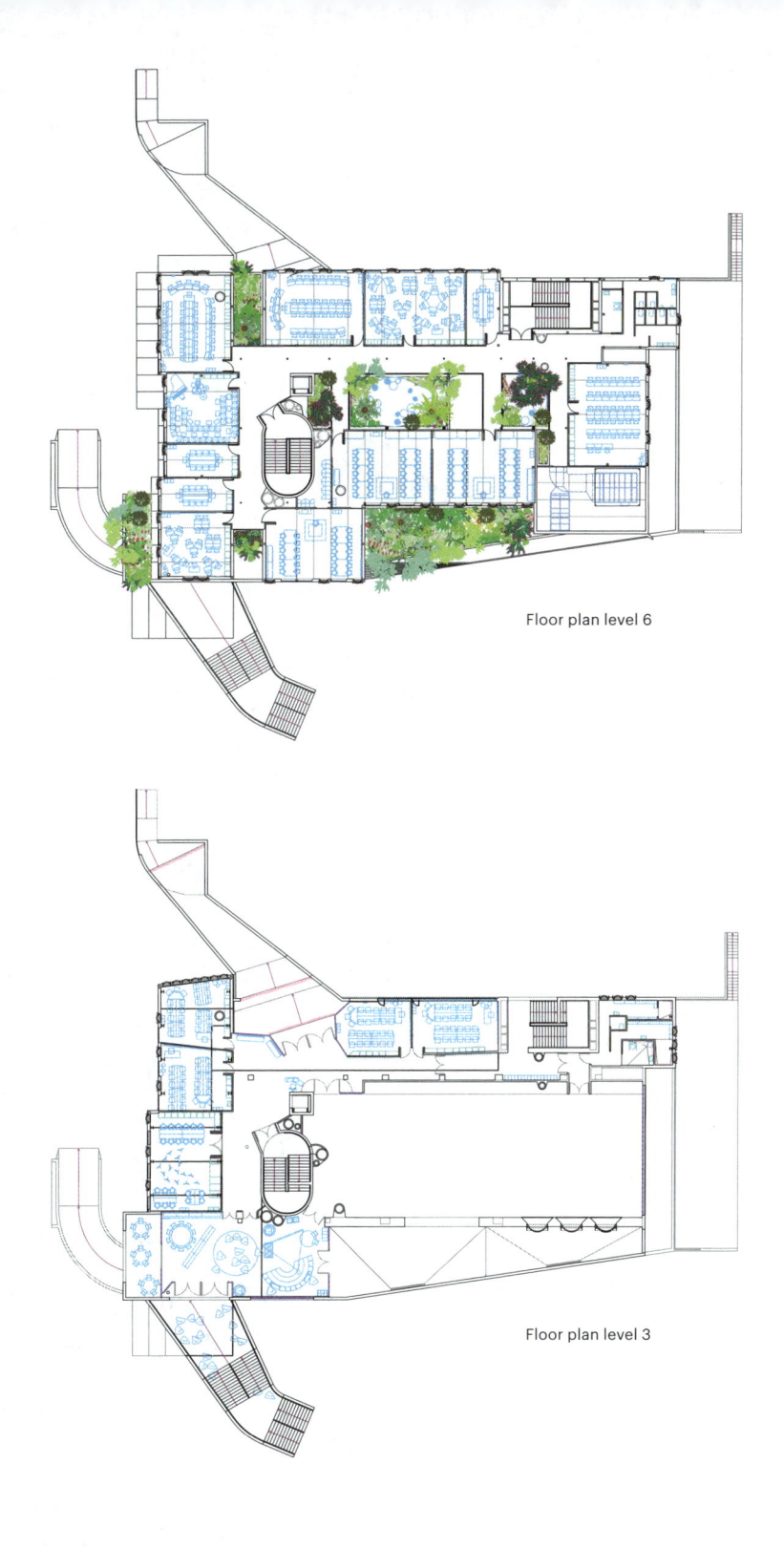

REGGIO SCHOOL

ANDRES JAQUE / OFFICE FOR POLITICAL INNOVATION

REGGIO SCHOOL

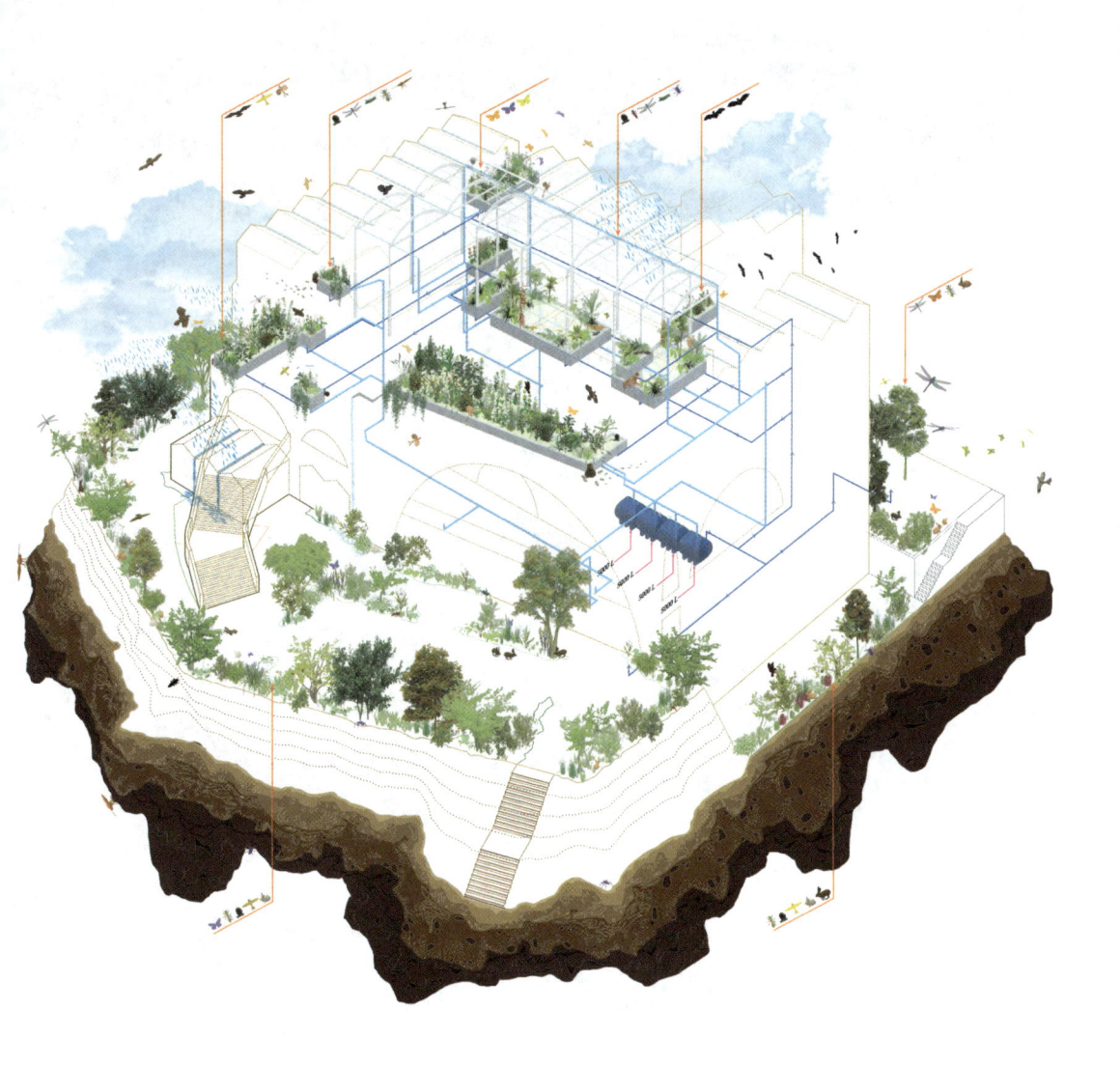

Bioclimatic diagram

ANDRES JAQUE / OFFICE FOR POLITICAL INNOVATION

REGGIO SCHOOL

ANDRES JAQUE / OFFICE FOR POLITICAL INNOVATION

REGGIO SCHOOL

Rainforest? Turn left after the drawbridge! Inside Madrid's eye-popping living school

"Pupils asked for a building without walls that was like a garden and a spaceship. The dazzling result, housed within a living skin for insects and fungi, is one of the most inventive schools ever built."

Oliver Wainwright

Writer and photographer based in London. Architecture and design critic of The Guardian since 2012.

Article previously published in The Guardian 17th January 2023 https://www.theguardian.com/artanddesign/2023/jan/17/reggio-school-andres-jaque-madrid-rainforest-zig-zag

'It looks like a robot made of butter," was one pupil's reaction when they saw their new school for the first time. They were not wrong. Standing on the northern outskirts of Madrid, in the suburb of Encinar de los Reyes, the Reggio school is a surreal sight, rising from its sloping plot like a big, buttery machine for learning.

Lumpy, yellowish, room-sized blocks appear to be stacked up on a frame of concrete shelves, with rows of beady bubble windows bursting through their gungey surfaces, like eyes emerging from the gloop. The blocks leave gaps where lush gardens sprout, while polished metal ducts poke up from the zigzag rooftop, like the chimneys of a cartoon factory. Down below, the concrete base is sliced open with gaping arches, stretched wide and squeezed tight, as if the building is flexing its muscles.

There can be few schools that make children look forward to Monday mornings as much as this dreamy multi-storey temple of curiosity. It is the work of Spanish architect Andrés Jaque, whose practice, the Office for Political Innovation, has carved out a niche over the last two decades for provocative, mischievous research projects, often taking the form of videos and installations, alongside a series of quirky private projects, ranging from a hedonistic villa in Ibiza to a climate-tuned courtyard house in Murcia, and a beguilingjoggers' cafe in Madrid. Jaque (pronounced "HA-kay") a smiley 51, juggles life as the recently appointed dean of Columbia University's graduate school of architecture in New York, where he has lived for the last 10 years, with running a small office in Madrid – a combination he balances, "by only ever working on one project at a time," he says, "and putting everything into it." This is the practice's first building of this scale, and it doesn't disappoint.

It began with an intense period of research, listening to the desires of the pupils (500 of them, aged from two to 18) and their vocal team of hands-on teachers, in a collaborative two-year process (including 20-hour meetings about the colour of handrails).

"A school with no walls," was one child's dream. "I want many different routes to get around," said another. "I want it to feel like a garden," added a third. "Or a spaceship. And not be too big, so I can get to know it easily." The teachers, meanwhile, wanted a building that could be used as a teaching tool, and a game, and never feel quite finished. "The architecture should prompt the imagination," as Jaque puts it, "and inspire the students to ask questions about the world."

The collaborative process sprung from the school's radical outlook, as a bastion of the Reggio-Emilia method, an educational approach first developed in postwar northern Italy. It follows the principle that children should not be seen as empty vessels to be filled with learning, but active participants in defining their own curriculum. Emphasis is placed on encouraging curiosity, with pupils, teachers and parents engaged in a back-and-forth adventure of discovery. Crucially, the physical environment is imagined as "the third teacher", with spaces configured to encourage interaction, open-ended exploration, and connection with the outdoors.

Built for a modest €8m (about €1,100 per square metre), Jaque's design embodies all of this and more. It is one of the most inventive school buildings of the century, breaking ground in everything from its layout, to the use of materials and its relationship to the natural world.

The theatrics begin at the entrance, where children arrive across a drawbridge-like deck through one of the arched openings, and soon find themselves standing in a colossal hall, or "agora". Conceived as a gym, theatre and assembly hall in one, the room has a heroic scale, divided by a curtain and open to the outdoors through a 20-metre wide archway, with a second arch on the shorter end, glazed with glass bricks. The wide opening leads to a covered loggia, with views out over the playground and green valley beyond, and connects to the library, imagined as a kind of extension of the playground. Portable seat-desks can be arranged on an outdoor staircase, "so you can sit and read at break time," says Jaque, "and not be forced to play football".

From here, you get a good view of the building's blobby, buttery surface, which turns out to be a natural cork mixture, pulverised and sprayed on to the walls to form a thick insulating jacket – with twice the thermal properties that Madrid's regulations require. Specifically developed for this project, it is unlike any other cladding around, with a texture somewhere between gritty, earthen plaster and sponge. It has an alluring, tactile quality, covering the building in globular lumps, forming creases and folds as it splurges around the corners, with the look of supersized Play-Doh.

Beyond providing insulation, this 15cm-thick coat is intended to take on a life of its own, becoming a habitat for fungi, insects and other organisms to flourish in its nooks and crannies. Rainwater is designed to run down the facade, following the clefts in the cork, nourishing whatever microbial lifeforms take hold. Other schools might reach for the pressure-washer, but this one will embrace the grime. "I hope it will become like the surface of a tree," says Jaque, "full of life."

The idea of the building as an armature for "more than human" life (an ongoing theme in Jaque's work) recurs throughout the school. On the landings, windows look out between the classrooms into recessed gardens, each designed to attract a different form of wildlife, from butterflies to birds and bees, in spaces that are specifically inaccessible to humans, so the creatures can be observed undisturbed.

The third floor, meanwhile, is home to a miniature temperate rainforest, which rises two storeys in a covered courtyard, with laboratories and workshops accessed off a deck around the edge. There is something poetic about coming out of a biology class to be confronted with a lush botanical garden and its attendant insects, and it serves an environmental purpose, too. As an enclosed greenhouse space, it helps to heat the classrooms in winter and cool them in summer, with ventilation hatches in the translucent barrel-vaulted roof.

Younger pupils have already begun to colonise the forest floor, building a model cardboard city between the ferns. "This is a collaborative project initiated by a second-grade student," notes a sign, in classic Reggio style. "Together, the pupils discussed the buildings their city must have, elected a mayor and organised a collective management strategy." Will the next step be unleashing their skills on the building itself?

It could certainly take it. Throughout, the architecture operates as a didactic tool, with the structure and services left exposed, so you can see how it all works. Pleasure has been taken in the artful composition of foil-wrapped ducts and pipes, their housings painted in cheerful colours and assembled in a playful industrial bricolage. The lower concrete levels are left raw, like an ancient Roman foundation, while the lightweight steel framework of the upper stories is exposed, the diagonal white struts creating an inverted mock-Tudor effect against the green-painted walls. "It is a literal stack of architectural traditions," says Jacque.

The much agonised-over colour palette ranges from an olive-cream dining room, offset with bright yellow window frames, to terracotta walls with fleshy salmon handrails (a nod to Jim Stirling's postmodern Clore gallery at Tate Britain), and pistachio-hued science labs. It all feels unusually grown up, intentionally avoiding the usual infantilising school colour palette: Jaque says the teachers "wanted colours that would be difficult to name".

Elsewhere, there are walls of glass bricks and hollow terracotta blocks – an everyday building material in Spain – but laid on their sides, covered with plaster, then ground back to reveal the blocks' extruded internal pattern. The effect is striking, creating a fine-lined graphic herringbone pattern, and a texture that helps with acoustics, as well as revealing how the walls are made. Similarly, the porridgy fireproof coating, required to protect steel columns and beams, is left exposed, but smoothed at child height to avoid grazing, creating a subtle line that echoes around the building.

The concrete might represent a high level of embodied carbon ("it was the only economical choice," says Jaque), but efforts have been made to reduce the amount used, with the arched openings and porthole cutouts allowing more slender walls and lowering the quantity of steel reinforcement needed. By ditching the usual plasterboard linings and suspended ceilings, the architects say they reduced the overall amount of building material by about 40%. "Nakedness became our religion," says Jaque, with a giggle. "We are unapologetically enjoying the hidden parts of architecture." Much of the school is open to the elements too, reducing the need for heating and cooling, with just the labs requiring air conditioning.

A less obvious form of sustainability comes in the fact that these architects enjoy using materials that others do not. The office has a knack for exploiting surplus supplies, sourcing things that might have been lying in a warehouse for years as dead stock, long out of fashion. The bubble windows, for example, were originally manufactured as roof lights for trailers, for which there is now little demand. "We always adapt the design to what we can find," says Jaque. "It's like mining new materials – and celebrating the potential of quotidian things."

The result is that these ordinary parts, lovingly assembled with meticulous care and childlike imagination, have created one of the most extraordinary schools around.

El Roser Social Centre is a pioneering facility in Spain designed to bring the social services of the city together in one place. The chosen location is the city's old prison, built in 1929. Having closed in the mid-20th century, it was recovered for a social use totally opposite to its original purpose. The project recovers the constructive essence of the building. In this way, the original structure and typology, which had been concealed, were uncovered to highlight them and to evoke an image of architectural austerity in keeping with the center's nature. The conceptualization of the project has also facilitated the building's integration into the urban context to which it belongs.

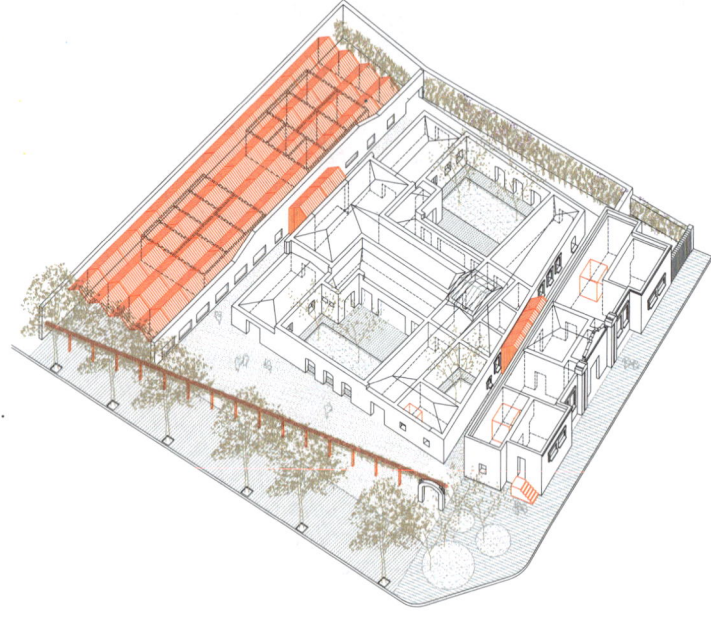

El Roser Social Centre

› Reus, Spain. 2018/2020-2021
  Social welfare · 1,323m²
› **Josep Ferrando Architecture, Gallego Arquitectura**
  Josep Ferrando, David Recio, Xavier Gallego
  Reus City Council (Public)
  © Adrià Goula

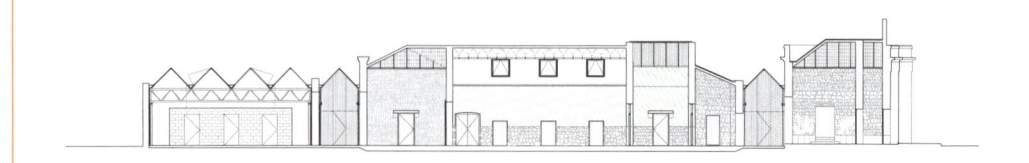

Social Housing 1737
Gavà, Spain
2019/2020-2022
HARQUITECTES
David Lorente, Josep Ricart, Roger Tudó, Xavier Ros
IMPSOL (Metropolitan Institute of Land Development and Property Management)
(Public)
Collective housing · 16,509m^2

The volumetric organization of this project encourages the biological and recreational continuity between the Serra de les Ferreres area and the Llobregat Agricultural Park in Gavà, Catalonia, complementing longitudinal circulation with new transversal connections that facilitate access to the block.

Opening the interior corners of the complex prevents potentially unsafe dead zones, while the staggered buildings adapt to the natural slope of the plot of land. Only the paths leading to the stairs receive minimal paving; the rest of the land is used as a drainage area to manage the water cycle and help to ensure the growth of native shrubs and almond, carob, and olive trees.

As the plot provides beautiful views and pleasant surroundings, an additive system generates the building and intensifies the relationships between the inhabited spaces and their environs. All the rooms face outward, toward the landscape. At the same time, however, these rooms enclose a cloister-like central atrium that concentrates the services and circulations, giving generous natural light and cross ventilation to all the spaces.

The project shapes 3 continuous rings – terrace, programme, and circulation – with the compact vertical communication cores placed inside the atrium to serve 4 dwellings per level. This layout yields 136 apartments. The central atrium, a sheltered and slightly tempered space, ventilates the stairwell, endows the dwellings with nuance, and makes the residences more comfortable.

Each apartment is shaped by a series of identical non-hierarchical modules, each 10.6 m², which can be used as a living room, kitchen, or bedroom, with outward-facing transition spaces surrounding each room. Along the outer wall, a continuous 1.5-metre-wide balcony runs toward the atrium while an almost symmetrical corridor space acts as a glazed porch and converts bathrooms, storage space, or lounge room annexes. Designed as a dense plinth, the ground floor does not use the atrium directly. More conventional, compact typologies are employed to resolve the vestibules, following the same spatial matrix.

Wood and plant life complement the materiality of the concrete outer walls. A hybrid structure with screens and concrete slabs separates the dwellings, combined with slim structural concrete pillars that permit short, efficient spans, and characterize the space in each room.

The building uses reinforced concrete in the structural elements, and although it is a material with a high level of CO_2 emissions, the structure has been designed by optimizing the sections, with small spans and pillars also defining the façade. The fact that the concrete structure has a longer lifespan should be taken into consideration, which means that the impact of CO_2 emissions due to building in concrete is spread out over more years.

429

HARQUITECTES

430

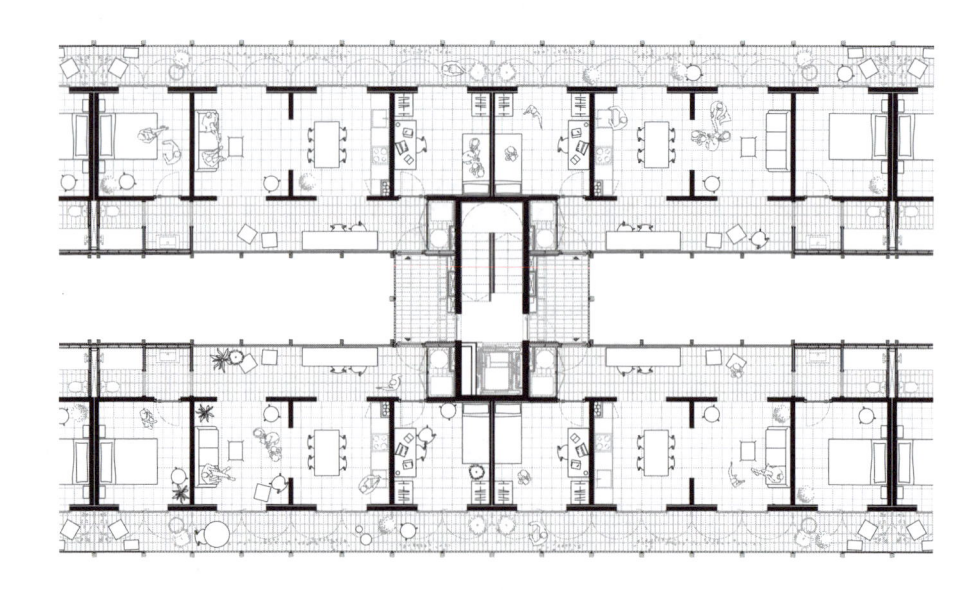

SHORTLISTED

SOCIAL HOUSING 1737

This five-story housing project develops several social strategies that aim to improve urban connectivity, social equity and sustainability. The building consists of a compact volume with four facades and an interior courtyard that provides all rooms with a window towards the exterior. This interior courtyard also acts as a climatic buffer, allowing crossed ventilation in summer and warming the interior air during the winter, reducing the use of cooling and heating. The apartments are composed of generic spaces of similar dimensions that adapt to changes in their inhabitants' vital needs. This inclusive typology aims to escape from a housing scheme where spaces are predestined for a specific use and a predetermined family model.

40 Social Apartments for Rent
› **SANT FELIU DE LLOBREGAT, SPAIN**
2018/2021-2023
Collective housing · 5,366m^2
› **MAIO**
María Charneco Llanos, Anna Puigjaner Barberá, Alfredo Lérida Horta, Guillermo López Ibáñez
IMPSOL - Àrea Metropolitana de Barcelona (AMB) (Public)
© José Hevia

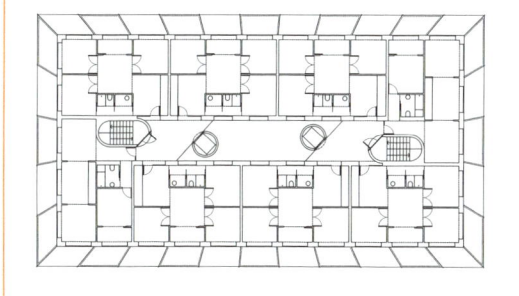

The extension arises from the idea of occupying the original vacant space that remains between a summer house and the golf clubhouse. Occupying this empty space allows maintaining and intensifying the porous and narrow urban rhythm that defines the street, Carrer de Villà. A new small light wooden house addition, which follows the morphology of the neighboring houses, nestles among ancient trees above a permeable concrete structure. The reform is based on the basic principle of sustainability: "never demolish". Maintaining the existing house and renovating have allowed a generous dialogue between two similar forms of architecture with different construction shapes.

Garden House Extension and Reform in Between. In Between Houses, in Between Trees
› **SANT CUGAT DEL VALLÈS, SPAIN**
2017/2020-2022
Single house · 417m^2 · 2,000€/m^2
› **BAILORULL**
Manuel Bailo Esteve, Rosa Rull Bertran
Private
© José Hevia

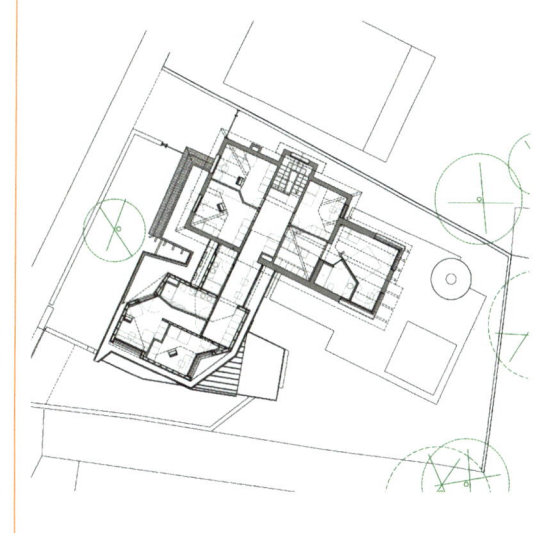

The House-Factory Natura Bisse aims to modernize the opacity of traditional industrial buildings. The corporative building houses offices, a showroom and production areas for a cosmetic company. The geographical and topographical advantage of the selected plot (Barcelona Synchrotron Park) allowed us to create a sequence of terraces in all the stories of the building. The architecture of Natura Bissé meets two aims, representing the values of the brand and the qualities of the activities carried out there. The result is a well-integrated building with a compact and flexible interior design.

House-Factory Natura Bissé
› **CERDANYOLA DEL VALLÈS, SPAIN**
2017/2018-2021
Industrial · 15,373m² · 18,134,454€
› **TDB ARQUITECTURA**
Juan Trias de Bes Mingot, Marta Pascual, Carlos García
Natura Bissé International SA (Private)
© Alejo Bague

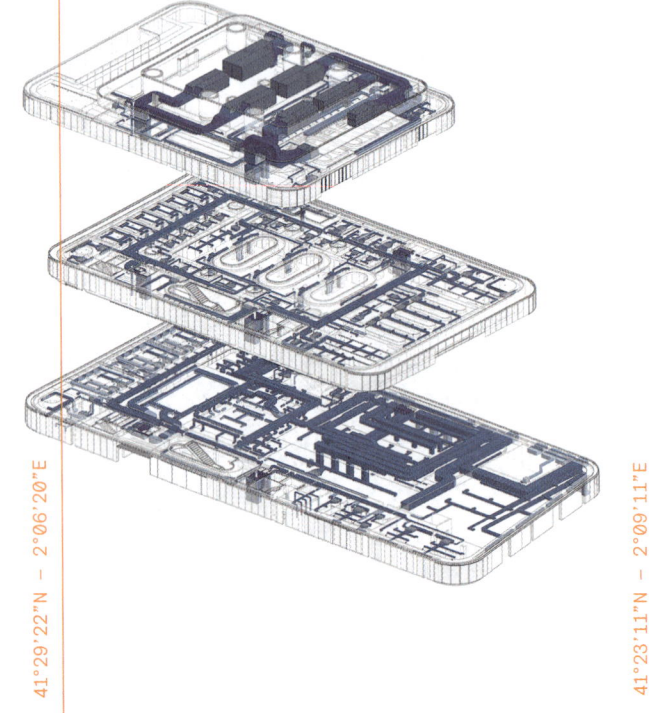

The different stories pervading this symbolic building have been as important to its rehabilitation as its material legacy. Built in 1864, La Carboneria became well known in 2008 due to squatters. Large-scale graffiti was painted on its façade. After the squatters' forced evacuation in 2014, it became a graphic and political icon of Barcelona. In 2015, Barcelona City Council listed it and ordered the restoration of its four façades to their original state. La Carboneria's uncommon geometry is due to an intense conflict between urban planner Ildefons Cerdà and Barcelona City Council in the 19th-century. Our design resurrects that past.

La Carboneria (Casa Tarragó)
› **BARCELONA, SPAIN**
2019/2019-2022
Collective housing · 1,200m² · 1,516€/m²
› **Office for Strategic Spaces (OSS)**
Ángel Borrego Cubero
Lesing Spain LWP S.L. (Private)
© OSS

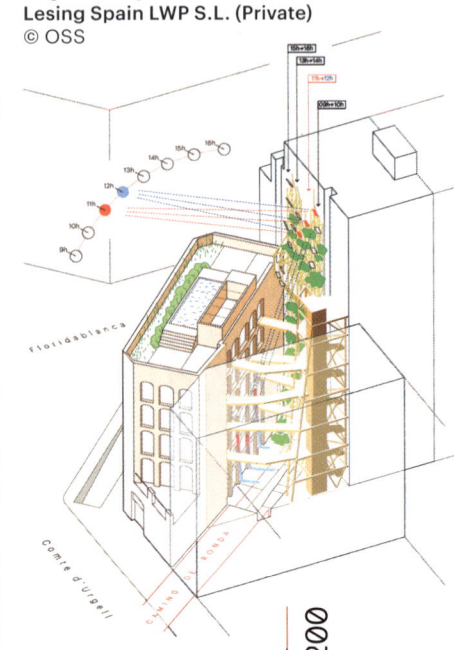

↑ 259

To situate the building in its historical context, the use of ceramic materials goes back to the old industrial buildings in Poblenou. The front volume with its bronze structural façade with large plate-glass windows and an institutional character has a split-level ground floor and five floors and intermediates with the neighboring buildings, forming the frontage of Avinguda Diagonal. The second volume acts as an entrance atrium to the new lobby of the residential building. The tower block displays great slimness on the façades located on Passeig de Gràcia and Avinguda Diagonal, becoming ever slenderer at its extremities.

Passeig de Gràcia 109-111. Mandarin Residences & Casa Seat
› BARCELONA, SPAIN
  2018/2019-2022
  Mixed Use - Cultural & Social · 18,000m²
› OAB Office of Architecture in Barcelona
  Carles Ferrater
  KKH PROPERTY INVESTORS (Private)
  © Joan Guillamat

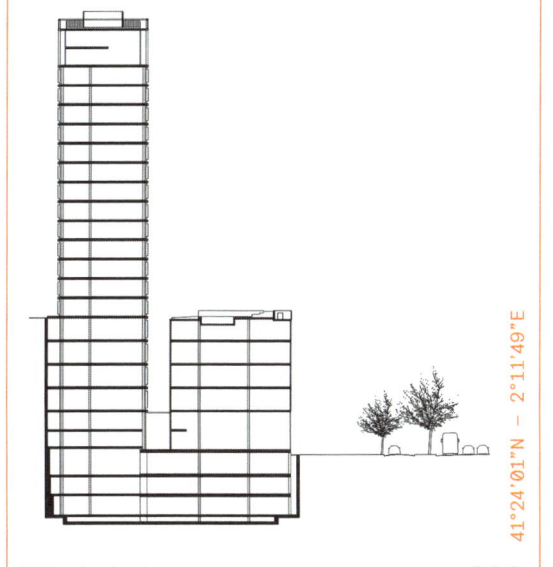

433

This is an office building that recovers the industrial nature of one of the districts of Barcelona. The use of ceramic materials goes back to the old industrial buildings in Poblenou, to situate the building in its historical context. The streets of a traditional European city are known for the regular continuity of their façades, openings and colors. It is in this homogeneity that public space becomes comfortable, when the city opts for a common design instead of an architecturally individualistic approach, thereby creating a shared space. In this context, architectural form decides to borrow the morphology of Barcelona's traditional architecture, and specifically the verticality of its balconies, embellishments and eaves. This gives a more human scale to the building and enables all windows to be opened to let in fresh air and to look out onto the street, improving the exchange between the user and the outside.

Pallars 180
› BARCELONA, SPAIN
  2018/2019-2022
  Office · 15,111m² · 1,067.65€/m²
› BAAS arquitectura
  Jordi Badia
  Conren Tramway Cinco, SL (Private)
  © Gregori Civera

EMERGING WINNER

Gabriel García Márquez Library
Barcelona, Spain
2015/2019-2022
SUMA Arquitectura
Elena Orte, Guillermo Sevillano
BIMSA Barcelona Municipality
(Public)
Education · 4,170m² · 2,239.82€/m²

41°25'02"N – 2°11'60"E

↓ 341

The García Márquez library is a pioneering, landmark building that is the culmination of a three-decade-long plan for building these facilities in Barcelona. The library serves a working class and vindictive neighbourhood, one which had lacked significant investment for years. The neighbourhood had demanded its own "palace for the people" and it now enjoys the "best new library in the world", according to IFLA.

The library's sculpted form evokes blocks of stacked books with folded pages. The building sits on an elevated plaza that allows pedestrians to move freely and features cantilevers over the open area, creating an urban lounge that extends the neighbourhood's pedestrian and cultural axis, enclosed by large trees that predate the structure.

The library offers a reinterpretation of the characteristic chamfer of Barcelona's Eixample to a street crossing that is now Plaça Carmen Balcells. The 45º geometry of the chamfer also follows a north-south axis and underscores the entire library, with a triangular courtyard and cores, and an envelope that seeks indirect light in its facades and skylights, shunning frontal views of the police station while looking out at the trees lining the street.

The 4,294-m2 facility is spread out over 5 floors around three vertical cores and a central triangular atrium with zenithal lighting.

The site is a small rectangular plot at a crossing of two secondary streets, behind a police station. The limited footprint entails a higher number of floors, though these never exceed the tree canopy, while the elevated ground floor allows for light and independent uses on the lower floor through the rear garden.

The building sits on three cores around a triangular courtyard, connected by an array of timber trusses, which house the more independent spaces and free up open-plan areas. The geometry and position of the cores encourage circulation in and around the atrium, multiplying the views and pathways through the library while turning the void into a centripetal and connective space with a spiral staircase.

The project was accompanied by a programmatic research project to redefine the contemporary library model. For its Ecosystems collection, the architects analyzed formal and informal situations, both local and global, and then combined and designed them holistically to foster the experience of accessing, exchanging, and producing knowledge. From the Agora-Showcase to the Forum of Ideas and the Palace of Reading, the library is a landscape, a Spiral of Encounters, where everyone can find their own place.

The library boasts numerous passive and active energy-efficiency and sustainability strategies accredited with the LEED Gold certification, including the atrium that acts as a solar chimney; a lightweight, ventilated fiberglass envelope with resins that optimizes solar protection and natural lighting; industrialized, prefabricated construction systems; low emission materials and greenhouse gas storage from structural wood; photovoltaic panels; recycled rainwater, and more.

The timber structure not only solves the load-bearing requirements, but also helps define the spaces, orients them, and organizes visuals and pathways to circulate through the structure, defines their scale and character, and is designed holistically together with the rest of the architectural and programmatic elements to form a coherent ecosystem.

The structural ensemble is fundamentally resolved with exposed laminated and cross-laminated timber (the largest exposed volume in Europe as of the date of construction), combined with singular and reinforcing steel elements, as well as joinery and assembly evocative of cabinetmakers. The result combines warmth, lightness, and visual permeability.

GABRIEL GARCÍA MÁRQUEZ LIBRARY

SUMA ARQUITECTURA

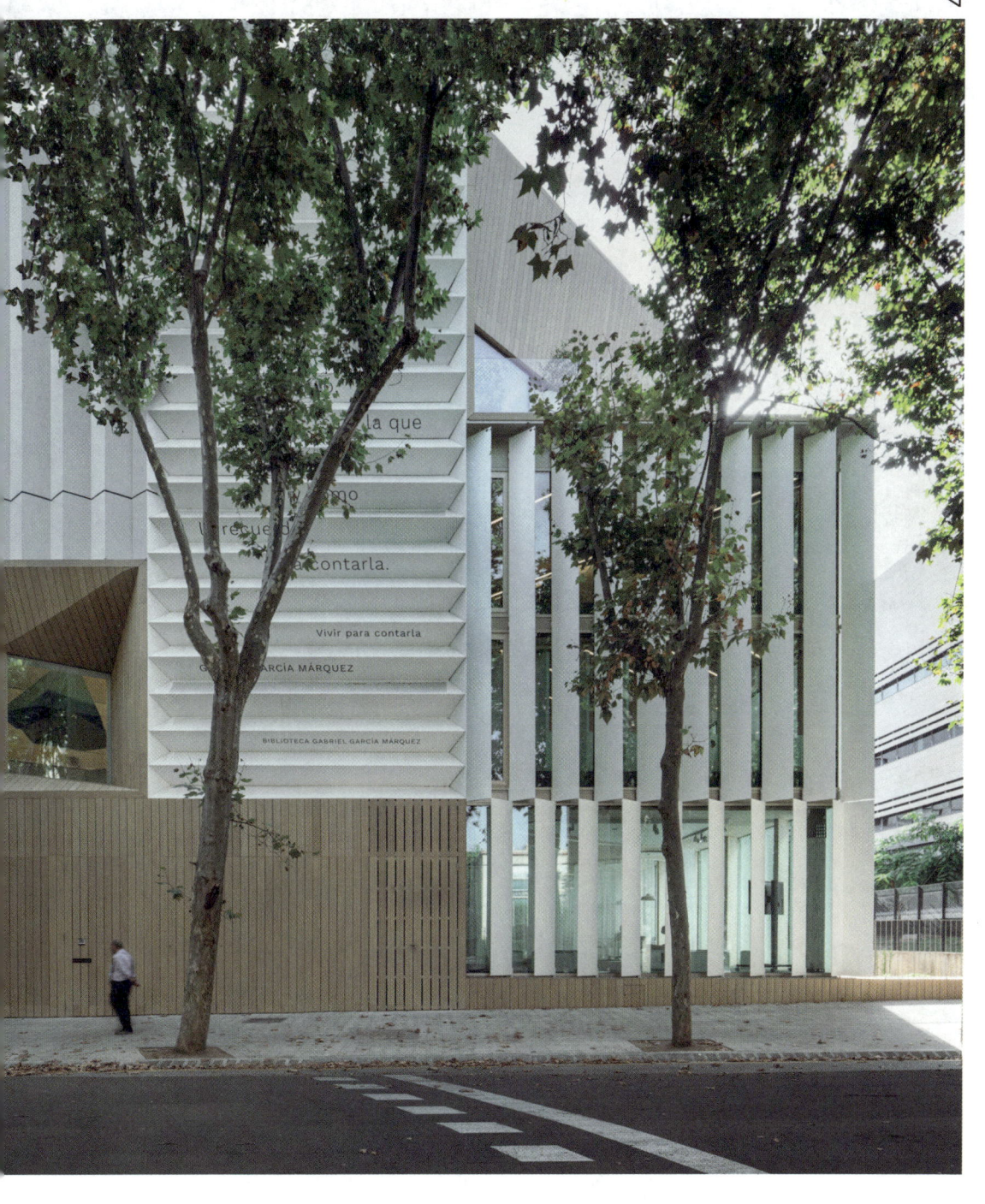

EMERGING WINNER

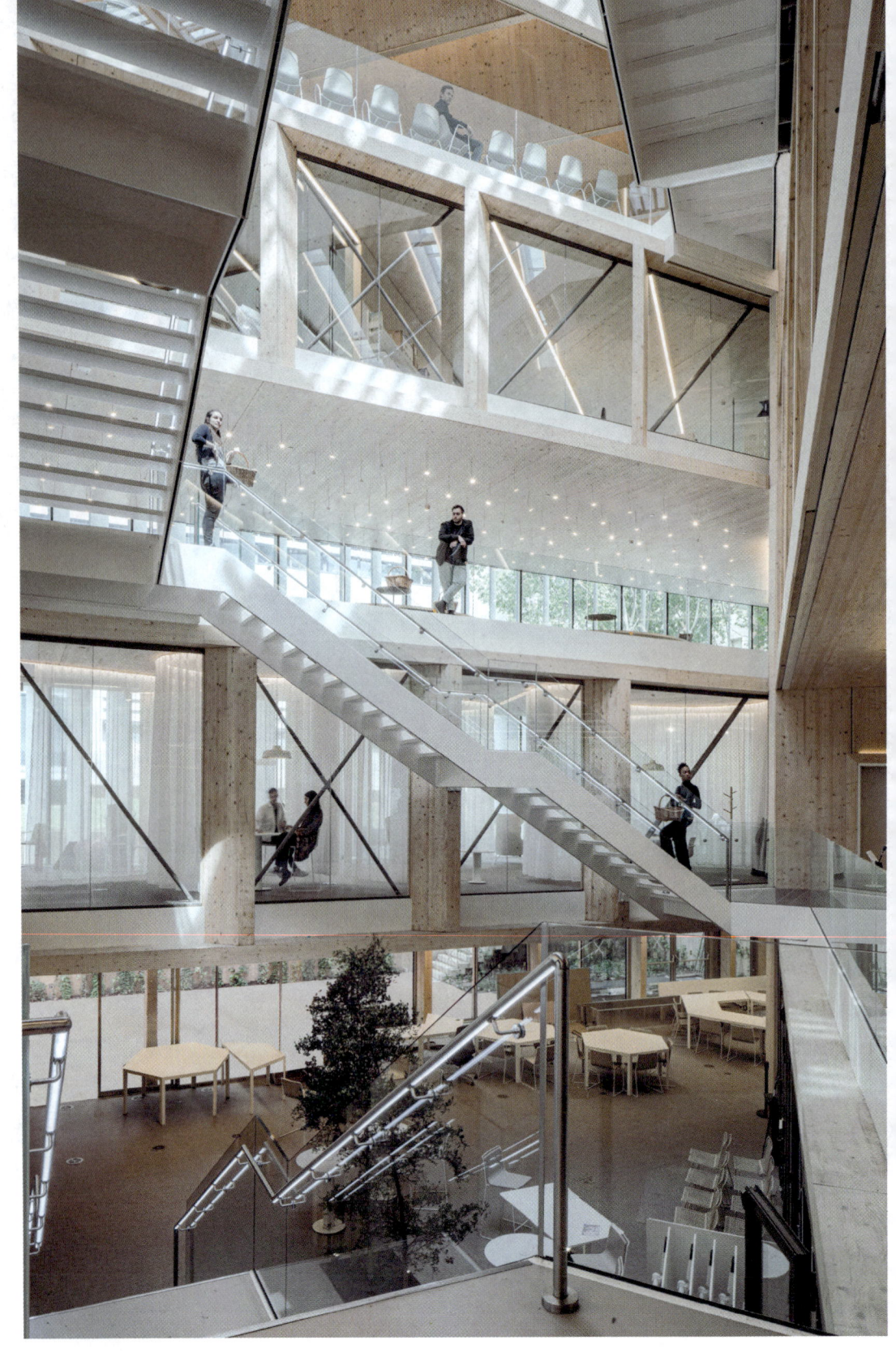

GABRIEL GARCÍA MÁRQUEZ LIBRARY

441

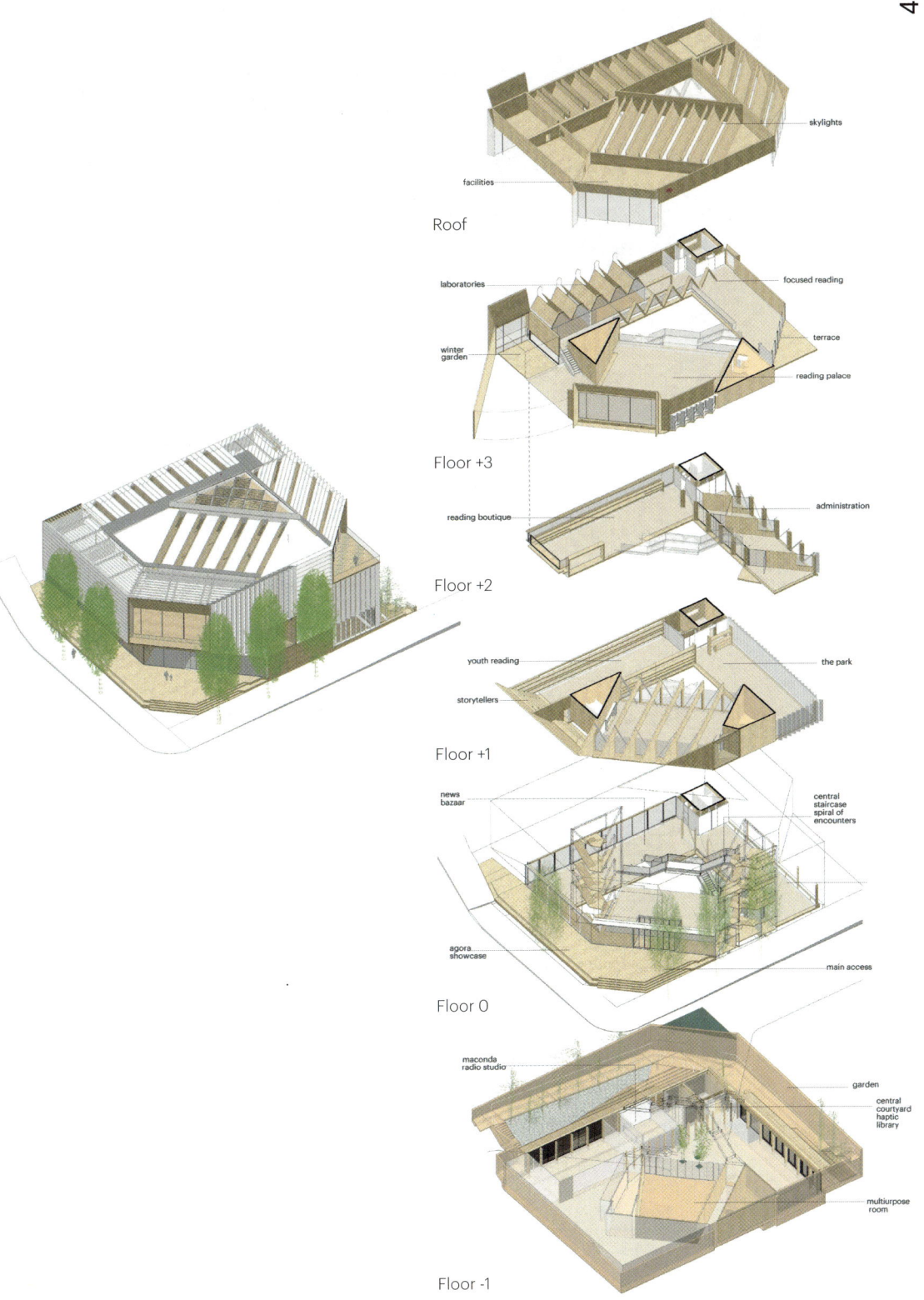

Roof
- skylights
- facilities

Floor +3
- laboratories
- winter garden
- focused reading
- terrace
- reading palace

Floor +2
- reading boutique
- administration

Floor +1
- youth reading
- storytellers
- the park

Floor 0
- news bazaar
- agora showcase
- central staircase spiral of encounters
- main access

Floor -1
- maconda radio studio
- garden
- central courtyard haptic library
- multiurpose room

SUMA ARQUITECTURA

Exploded axonometry

442

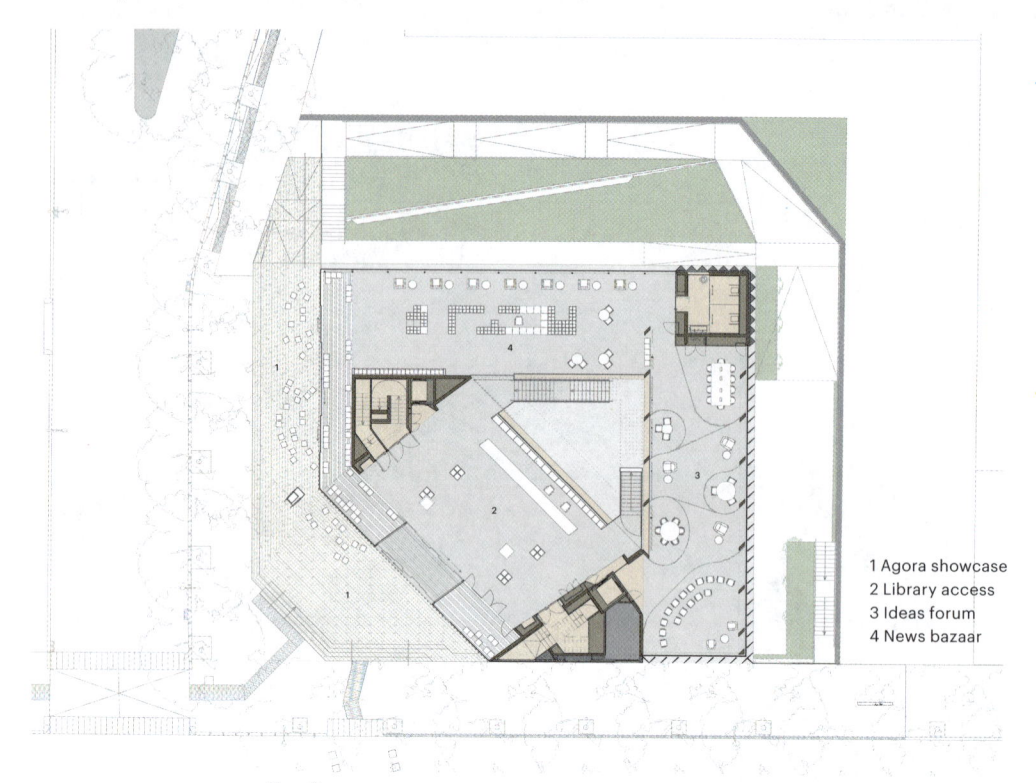

EMERGING WINNER

Floor 0
Library access

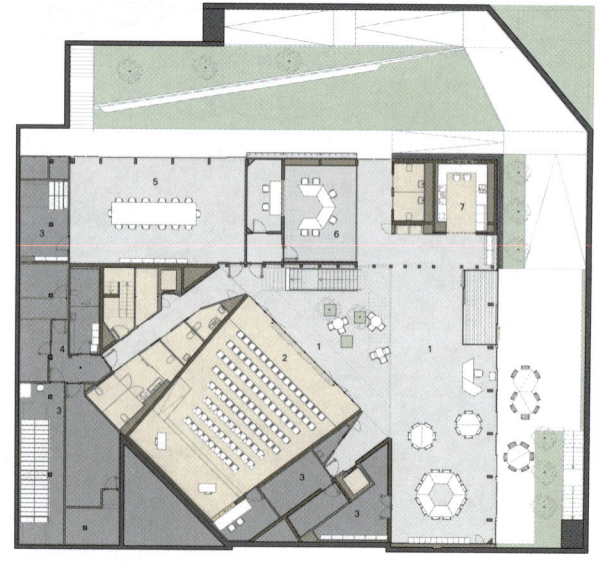

1 Agora showcase
2 Library access
3 Ideas forum
4 News bazaar

Floor -1
Multipurpose room -
archive

1 Atrium
2 Multipurpose space
3 Warehouse
4 Backstage
5 Archive
6 Radio
7 Kitchen

GABRIEL GARCÍA MÁRQUEZ LIBRARY

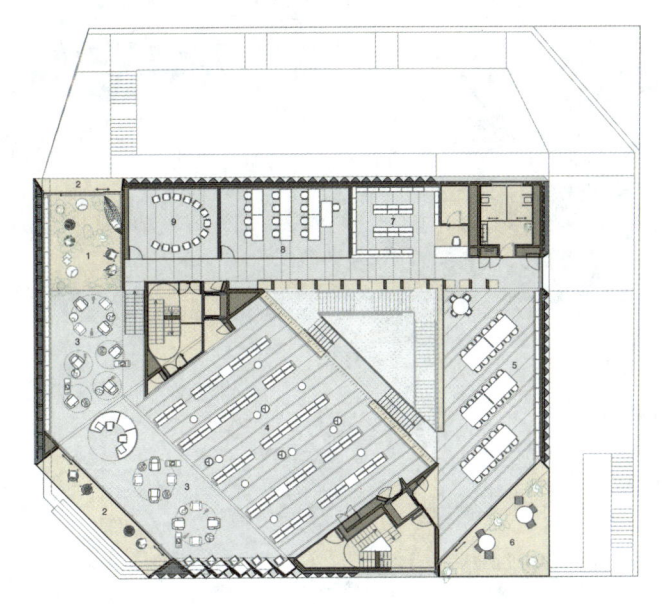

1 Winter garden
2 Balcony
3 Homely reading
4 Reading palace
5 Focused study room
6 Terrace
7 Knowledge space
8 Multimedia space
9 Classroom

Floor +3
General library

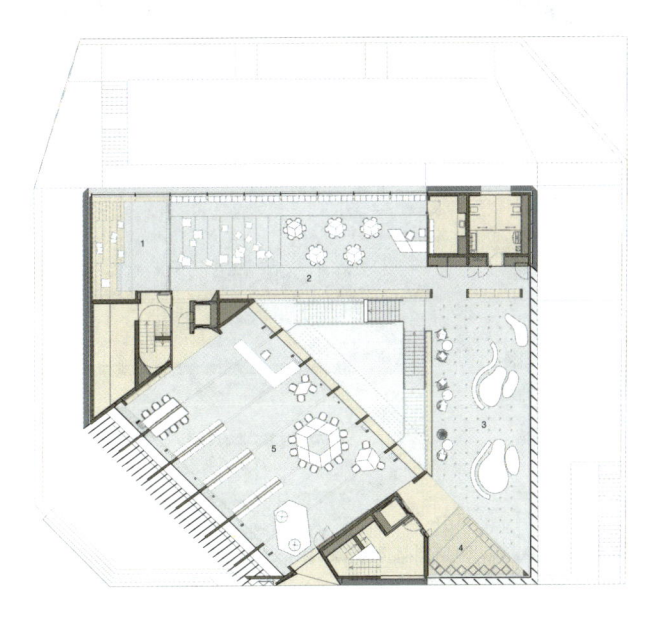

1 Storyteller's corner
2 Young readers
3 The park
4 Kiosk/comic corner
5 Children's/youth library

Floor +1
Children's library

SUMA ARQUITECTURA

444

EMERGING WINNER

Cross section

GABRIEL GARCÍA MÁRQUEZ LIBRARY

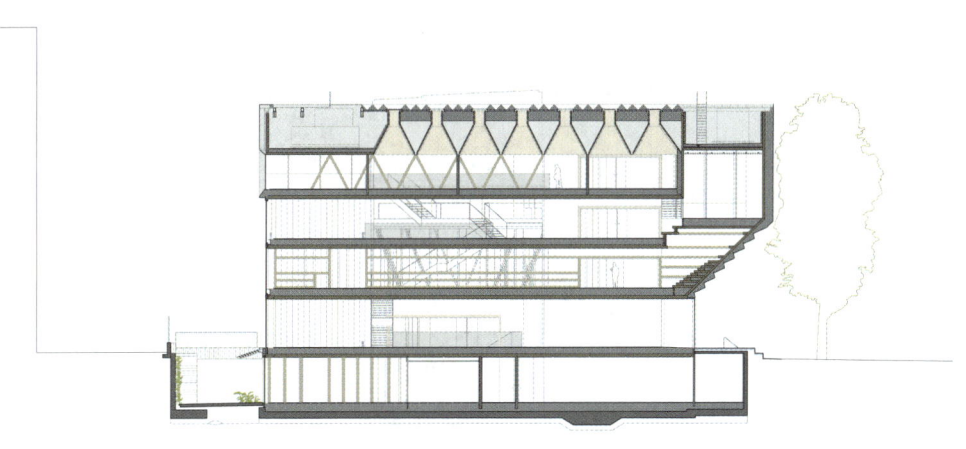

Cross section

SUMA ARQUITECTURA

445

GABRIEL GARCÍA MÁRQUEZ LIBRARY

Shadows and Reflections from the Gabriel García Márquez Library in Sant Martí de Provençals

Josep Lluís Blàzquez
Art Historian. Director of the architecture programme "Perspectiva" on Catalunya Ràdio.

'On a corner plot that used to be home to a colony of street cats there now stands this grand space that appears to view itself as an exotic bird, bang in the middle of two mass-produced residential blocks built with questionable materials during the era of *developmentalism*."

Since winning the Barcelona City Award for architecture in February 2023 and right up to its most recent award, the EUmies Awards 2024 for emerging architects, the praise and accolades heaped on the Gabriel García Márquez Library in the Sant Martí de Provençals neighbourhood haven't stopped pouring in. During this time, I had the pleasure of speaking to the project's creators, Elena Orte and Guillermo Sevillano from SUMA Arquitectura, on two occasions, in February 2023[1] and May 2024[2].

In the interim between these two prizes, the project also received the award for "Public Library of the Year" by the International Federation of Library Associations and Institutions (IFLA)[3], and the prize for architecture at the 2023 FAD Awards[4] – not to forget the NAN[5] award for "best facility" already garnered in 2022. These two years, therefore, have given us plenty of opportunity to be regaled with the outstanding qualities of this project through its laundry list of prizes… But not only this, it's also had the chance to be tested out as a fully-fledged civic facility by those best placed to assess a work of architecture – its users – whose ever-increasing usage and footfall since opening have proved it to be a resounding success, so much so that an extension may even be in order.

The library, however, has not only being on the receiving end of praise and accolades in this time. In fact, just around the same time it was awarded the EUmies Awards, the building was also the subject of controversy due to the cracks emerging in some of the large glass partitions surrounding it, which although don't jeopardise the structure of the building or pose any short-term threat, does mean the glass will eventually have to be replaced at a cost that is no mere drop in the ocean. Indeed, ever since its inception the project has grappled with the risks involved in building a structure with wooden foundations on a vast expanse of clay soil, which was far more extensive than could ever have first been predicted. Intrepid, therefore, is yet another of the qualities that could be used to define it.

Sant Martí de Provençals is a neighbourhood largely forgotten by the successive Barcelona city councils over the last 30 years, and this library was initially little more than a measly investment aimed only at quelling voices, while the district's more glamorous neighbourhoods – the ones occupying the area from Gran Via out to the coast – absorbed the lion's share of Barcelona's entire public and private investments. Meanwhile, the mountain-side

[1] https://www.ccma.cat/3cat/conversem-amb-els-arquitectes-de-suma-guanyadors-del-premi-ciutat-de-barcelona-2022/audio/1162291/

[2] https://www.ccma.cat/3cat/suma-arquitectura-gustav-dusing-i-max-hacke-guanyadors-dels-premis-mies-van-der-rohe-2024/audio/1205964/

[3] https://www.ifla.org

[4] https://arquinfad.org/premisfad/edicions-anteriors/?edicio/2023/obra/11488/

[5] https://nanarquitectura.com/2022/11/18/premios-nan-arquitectura/22442#biblioteca-gabriel-garc%C3%ADa-marqu%C3%A9z-de-suma-arquitectura

SUMA ARQUITECTURA

of the neighbourhood, just four streets up from the library, is also enjoying the large-scale regeneration of the Rec Comtal canal area and the large intermodal hub that is La Sagrera, along with all the residential and community spaces of high architectural quality that come with it. The inhabitants of Sant Martí de Provençals are still grappling to come to terms with the emerging reality of what being squashed in the middle of this marvellous, speculative urban sandwich may imply: the library has already been on the receiving end of certain, acerbic epithets on behalf of the local population, such as the "Centre Pompidou of Sant Martí" or the "Guggenheim of La Verneda".

On a corner plot that used to be home to a colony of street cats – duly registered by the local council and enjoying their accompanying citizen's rights – there now stands this grand space that appears to view itself as an exotic bird, bang in the middle of two mass-produced residential blocks built with questionable materials during the era of *developmentalism*. With feigned nonchalance, the brand-spanking new building also views itself as a herald of new times to come; times of social change and transformation for certain neighbourhoods whose residents – for better or for worse – still nurture the memory of the proud yet tarnished community that emerged in Barcelona as a result of the great migrations of the 1950s, 60s and 70s.

Although I've said that the investment was made to quell voices, it would be unfair not to point out that it was also an ambitious investment which saw the new library become one of Barcelona's largest, enjoying third place in terms of its total surface structure (4,000m² over its six floors), and also one of the most ample in terms of its documental holdings, which stood at some 40,000 items when the library first opened.

While wandering around the building and pondering some of these vagaries of history, I'm suddenly struck by the memory of the great architect and urban planner of late 20th-century Barcelona, Oriol Bohigas – and especially his 1957 text *Elogi de la barraca* ("In Praise of the Shack"), in which he discusses the dignity and effort with which newcomers to the city built their shacks in these neighbourhoods: their first home. Thirty-five years later, while Bohigas held the post of Barcelona's head of culture from the 1992 Olympic Games through to 1994, the Barcelona Library Plan 1998-2010 was formed. In this respect, the Gabriel García Márquez Library not only boasts a significant collection of Latin-American literature, it's also the result of the goals set forth in this plan, and the extensive professional capabilities developed by the city's network of libraries over these past 30 years. One of the plan's main initial aims was for there to be public libraries in all the city's neighbourhoods, as well as for the accessibility of information to the general public – an objective that made perfect sense at a time when Internet was still not openly available to everyone and… some people still even read books! This new plan was both a challenge and commitment on behalf of the city, which eventually paid dividends when it was designated a UNESCO "City of Literature" in 2015.

Indeed, the projects architects, Elena and Guillermo from SUMA Arquitectura, openly acknowledge that the library would never have been possible without the brilliant minds behind the city's network of libraries, along with all the human talent that was involved in this long trajectory. The awards it has amassed in under two years are also testament to SUMA's ability to integrate itself harmoniously and without fanfare into the fabric of this network, bringing along with it new ideas and inspiration.

If we extend our vision further beyond Barcelona to look at some of the other public libraries erected across the globe over the past decades, there are indeed some real gems: we need look no further than IFLA's 2023 Public Library of the Year Awards, when SUMA's project was up against marvels such as the Valvasor Library Krško in Slovenia, the Parramatta Library in Australia, and Shanghai Library East in China. The (public) library is one of the building types most prone and receptive to experimentation and innovation – a point of convergence and interaction for local cultures and lifestyles that demands much more commitment than a museum or cultural centre. Now in the full throes of the 21st century, the era of PDFs and eBooks, building a "house of books" (not to mention filling it with users) constitutes a bold display of resistance against the alienation created by virtual worlds and the monotonous spaces and commercial franchises spawned by the globalisation of our cities. Moreover, it also incurs the challenge of reformulating the model over and over again, in accordance with the characteristics of the location and community where it's to be built. It's due to this final point that the libraries of today's cities are excellent drivers for social cohesion and revitalising urban environments. In this sense, the Gabriel García Márquez Library of Sant Martí de Provençals is an enrichment project that goes further beyond the scope determined by Barcelona's network of public libraries for almost thirty years.

Over recent years, Elena and Guillermo have been busy making the rounds with projects that include a library and multi-purpose centre in Fuerteventura, a proposal for another library in Barcelona (in the Sant Gervasi neighbourhood) and a humanities library for Sapienza University in Rome. Architects, like people, are fruit of a past that, depending on the case, will either spurn or shackle them. Like people, an architect can either build upon or scupper the legacy they've been dealt, but more important is the legacy they leave behind for their successors, as this provides the inspiration for the future buildings to come. The next chapter for Barcelona lies with a monumental library – one of the largest in Europe that will comprise some 18,000m^2 and a collection of 660,000 books – in the precincts of the city's Estació de França. They say it could be completed before 2030.

SUMA ARQUITECTURA

This five-story residential building has six apartments, a penthouse and two commercial premises. The building core contains the staircase, elevator shaft and services and is positioned at the center of an irregular-shaped plot. The staircase thereby offers a range of different perspectives of the city that change as you head upwards and the design brings natural light and ventilation to the shared spaces. This layout frees up the perimeter space, meaning there can be two flats on each floor that each have ventilation from two façades. On the top level, where there is just one penthouse flat, the circular geometry of the spiral staircase is revealed in its entirety and the living space is articulated around it.

Llacuna Residential Building

› **BARCELONA, SPAIN**
2019/2020-2021
Collective housing · 700m² · 2,000€/m²
› **ARQUITECTURA-G**
Aitor Fuentes Mendizabal, Jonathan Arnabat Vila, Igor Urdampilleta Plasencia, Jordi Ayala Bril
Proyecto Llacuna 6 SL (Private)
© José Hevia

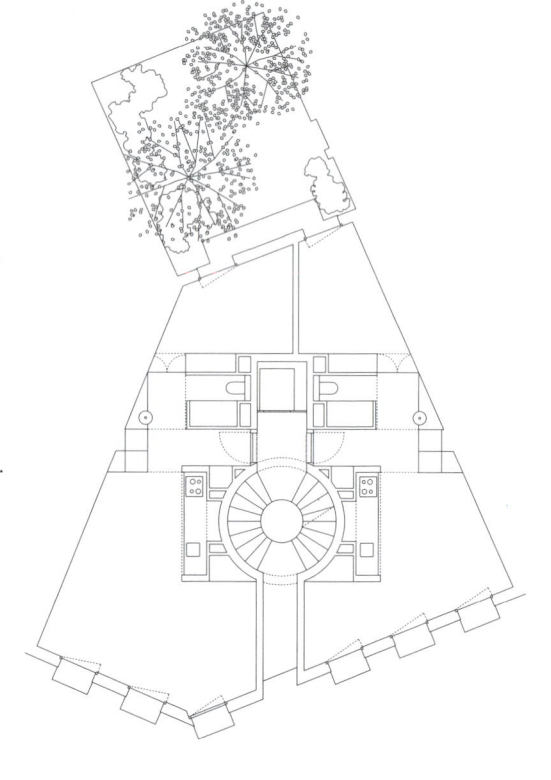

FINALIST

Rebirth of the Convent Saint-François
Sainte-Lucie-de-Tallano, France. 2018/2019-2022
Amelia Tavella Architectes
Amelia Tavella
Collectivité de Corse
(Public)
Culture · 12,00m² · 1,800€/m²

41°41'44"N – 9°03'58"E

The French studio, Amelia Tavella Architectes, renovated and extended a 15th-century convent on the island of Corsica, adding volume to the structure with perforated copper.
Built in 1480, the partially ruined Convent of Saint-Francois is positioned on a hill overlooking a village and mountainous landscape.

"I believe in invisible, higher forces. The Convent of Saint-Francois of Sainte-Lucie de Tallano, built in 1480, is part of this belief. Housed high up, on its promontory, the site was a defensive castle before it became a place of prayer, of retreat, chosen by monks aware of the absolute beauty of the site. Faith strives for the sublime.", says Amelia Tavella.

With its back to the cemetery, the convent overlooks the village it watches over. An olive grove is like a collar at its feet. Here beats the heart of Alta Roca.

The beauty here is religious, supernatural.

Nature has grown within the building. Siamese nature slipped between the stones and then transformed into a suit of plant-based armor that protects against erosion and collapse. Amelia has honored this nature that must have protected the dormant edifice long before its resurrection: "I chose to keep the ruins and replace the part that had been torn, the phantom part, with copper work which will become the Maison du Territoire. I walked in the footsteps of the past, connecting beauty to faith, and faith to art, moving minds from before to a form of modernity that never alters or destroys the past. The ruins are marks, vestiges, and imprints; they also tell about the foundations and a truth, they were beacons, cardinal points that directed our choices.

I have always built this way on my island of Corsica, like an archaeologist who brings together what was with what is and what will happen. I do not remove; I hang, bind, affix, and slide, resting on the initial ground, on the original work: the copper reveals the stone, the monument and it makes the ruiniform, poetic state sacred.

A ruin is an x-ray image of a polished structure undone by time.
The convent finds herself magnified , because held by a reversible copper frame, itself doomed to transform, skate, become second skin and have a story.

I liked the idea of a possible return to ruin, the idea that the copper could be undone. This possibility is a courtesy, one that pays respect to the past, to Corsican heritage.

I built the Maison du Territoire by aligning myself with the original massing. By mimicry, I reproduced the silhouette of the pre-existing building."

Site plan

AMELIA TAVELLA ARCHITECTES

454

FINALIST

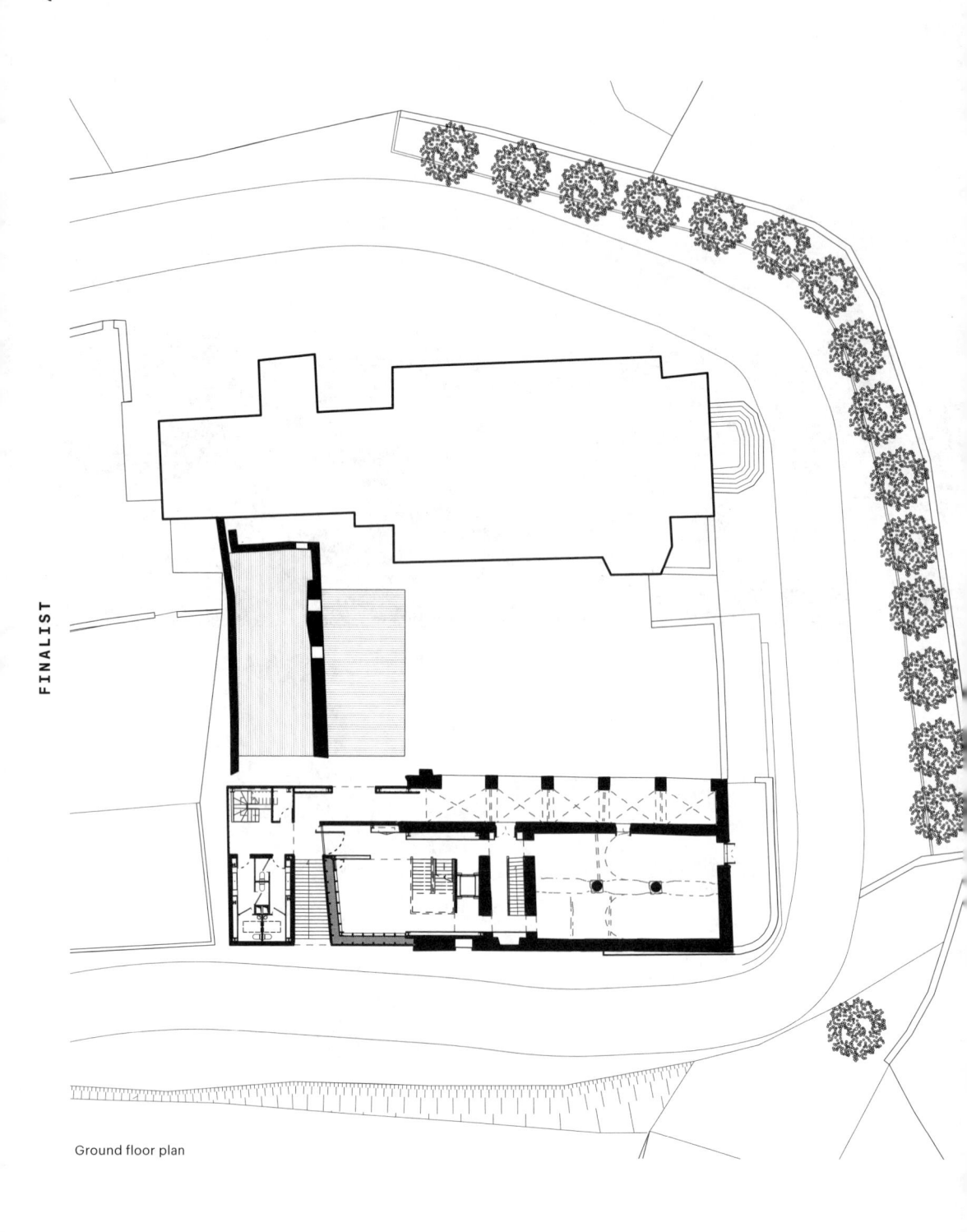

Ground floor plan

REBIRTH OF THE CONVENT SAINT-FRANÇOIS

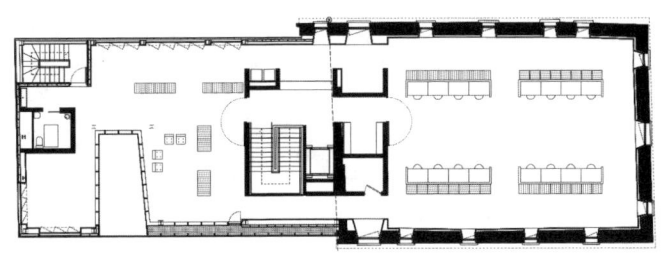

Second floor plan

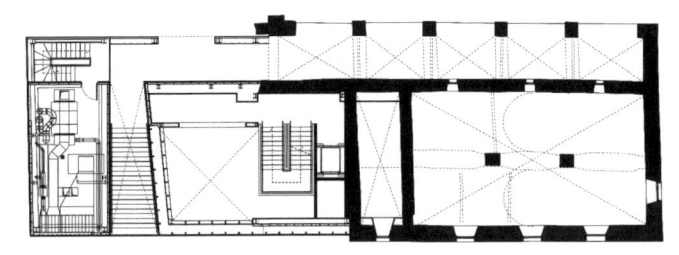

First floor plan

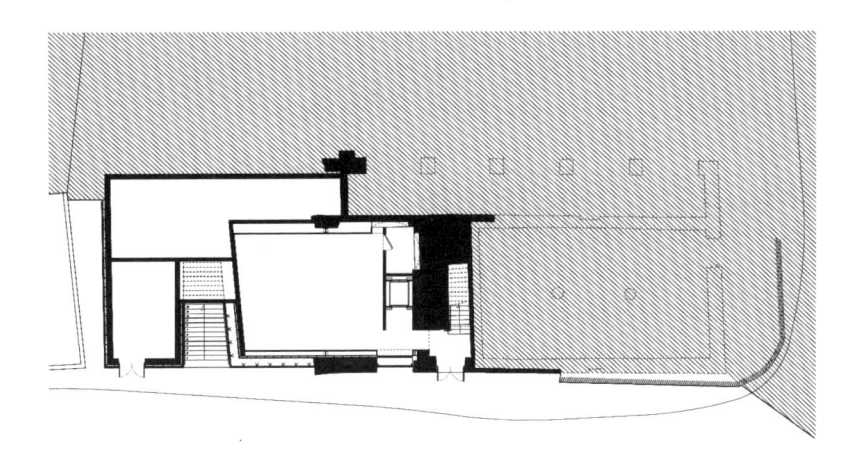

AMELIA TAVELLA ARCHITECTES

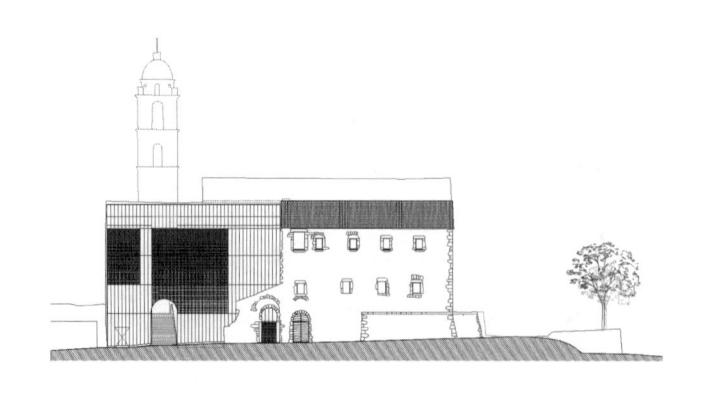

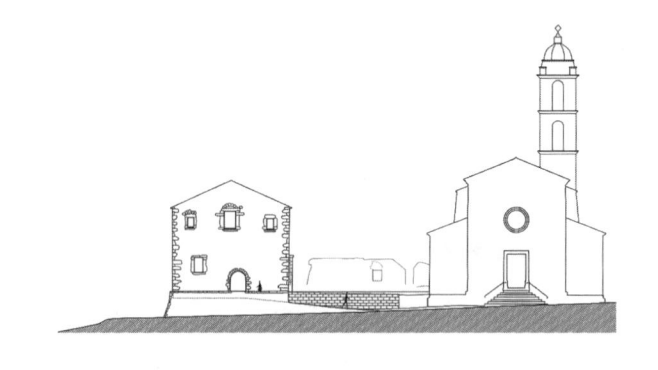

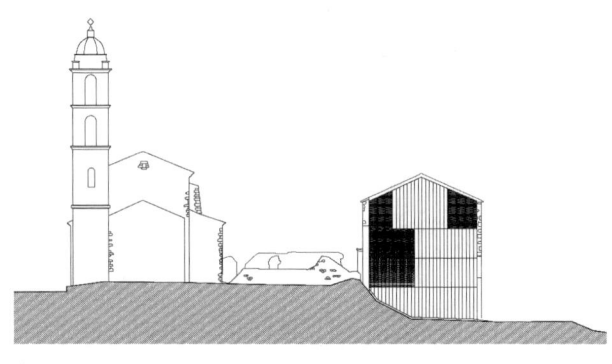

Elevations

REBIRTH OF THE CONVENT SAINT-FRANÇOIS

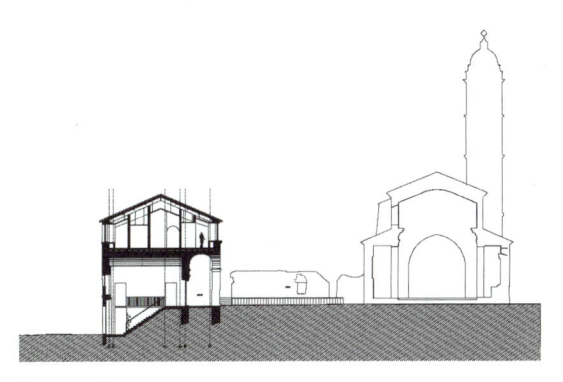

Cross section

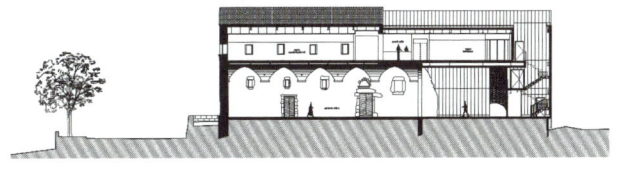

Longitudinal section

AMELIA TAVELLA ARCHITECTES

REBIRTH OF THE CONVENT SAINT-FRANÇOIS

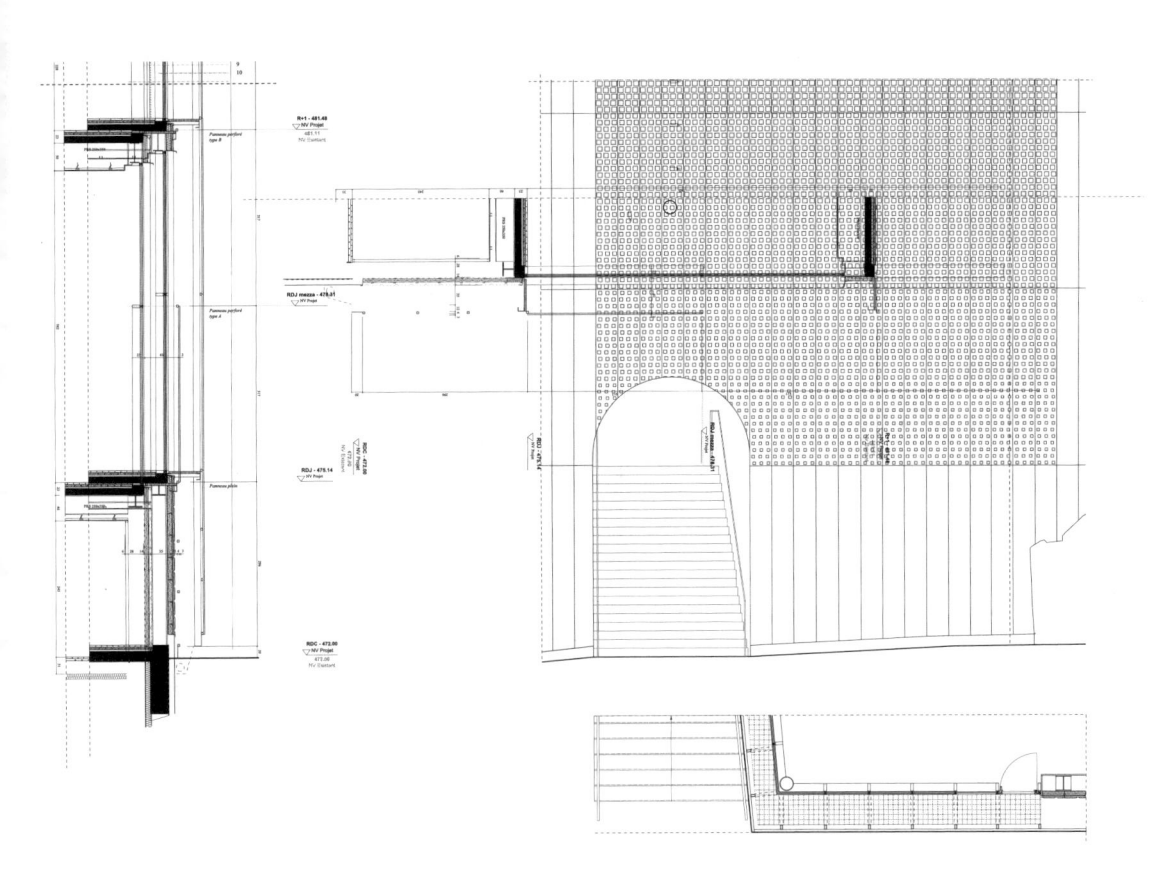

Details

AMELIA TAVELLA ARCHITECTES

FINALIST

Section

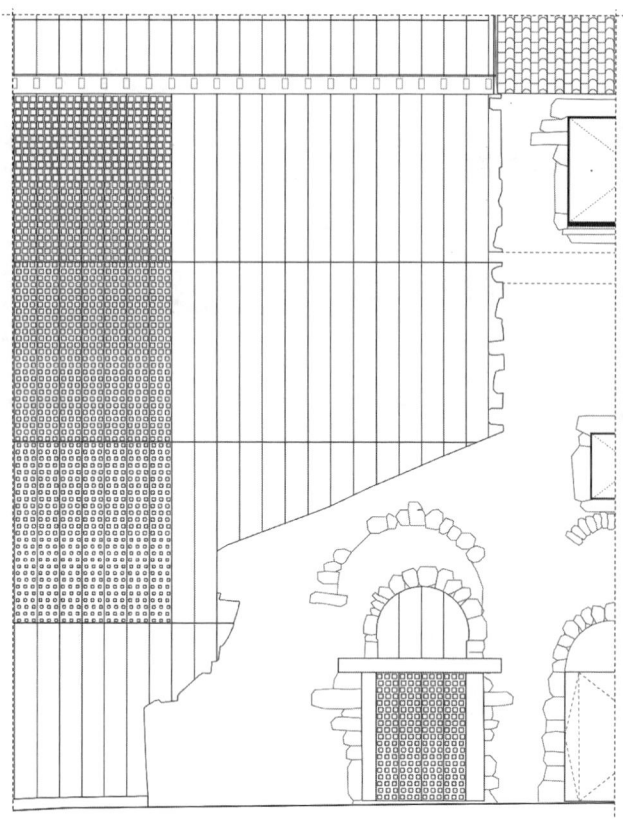

North elevation

REBIRTH OF THE CONVENT SAINT-FRANÇOIS

AMELIA TAVELLA ARCHITECTES

462

FINALIST

REBIRTH OF THE CONVENT SAINT-FRANÇOIS

Vortex

Nina Bouraoui
Franco-Algerian writer

We must believe in the superior forces of the Invisible. These forces guide us and reveal things to us. It is they who bring us to the convent of Saint-François in Sainte-Lucie-de-Tallano via a mysterious vortex that could be the powerful heart of Alta Rocca.

Here, everything pulses, coming and going like the sea that surrounds the earth environment. Here, everything is movement. Everything here seems supernatural. The beauty of the mountains, the sun and the rains that crash down here, the beauty of the movement of the clouds, the beauty of the olive grove that forms a collar, the beauty of the village below the convent, all bear witness to the stories of the past and to the stories yet to come.

Here everything challenges human beings. Everything is vast and limitless. Everything commands respect and communion.

There is a poetic architecture: one that envelops without undoing, embraces without hurting and transforms without destroying. This architecture bends to nature, honouring it and paying tribute to it. This architecture is delicate and maybe even supernatural. Amelia Tavella connected with the wonders of the convent of Saint-François, originally a castle built in 1480 before it became a home for monks. She walked through the remains. She grazed its sacredness. She spoke with the dead. She bowed to what was, inventing what is and what will be.

It is not a trifling thing to move the stones and to build from the ruins. The architect became an archaeologist in her native land of Corsica. She is committed to the memory of the place, her childhood and its legends. Above all, architects are undoubtedly repairers. They heal the past.

The restoration of the convent of Saint-François is an act and declaration of love. The part torn from the convent had to be magnified so it could exist again; taking another form, using another material, Amelia Tavella brought it back to life with precious copper. Between the stones, horn is now being used in the space, thereby serving as the hidden backbone of the new building. Copper skin against stone skin: the two fit together and extend outwards, making us think of a graft rather than something added on.

Like a balm, the copper soothes the stone. Like a mirror, the stone reflects the light from the copper. The second skin is the cathedral, which pierces high above and captures the sparkling of the stars through the play of mashrabiyyas. The building at the top of the hill protects its cemetery and those who live there. Neither exists without the other.

In the centre of the convent, we can still hear the voices of the monks and priors. Amelia Tavella has brought two times together: the time past and the time yet to come. Her obsession is gentle and does not rush anything. Extending and opening what was closed, the ruins become the home of the surrounding territory.

It is a double metamorphosis, affecting both the place and its author.

Just like the stone, the copper will withstand the assault of time and its changes will have the status of an imprint. This is not a new convent. It is a rebirth. The stone is wedded to the copper and the copper supports the stone, not as a guardian but as a revelator. Here the mechanics of the materials and elements unfold. A *museum* stands here.

AMELIA TAVELLA ARCHITECTES

The project's goal is to offer an educational tool based on the context and location itself. Indeed, considering the space's dimensions, the views of the city and the landscape and the opportunity for children to engage with nature and the building's raw materiality, all aspects have been carefully considered to encourage curiosity and early learning in children. The human becomes the main operator interacting with the building.

The Montlaur Nursery in Bonifacio
› BONIFACIO, FRANCE
2016/2018-2023
Education · 1,322m² · 2,482€/m²
› **Buzzo Spinelli**
Isabelle Buzzo, Jean-Philippe Spinelli
Bonifacio Municipality (Public)
© Aldo Amoretti

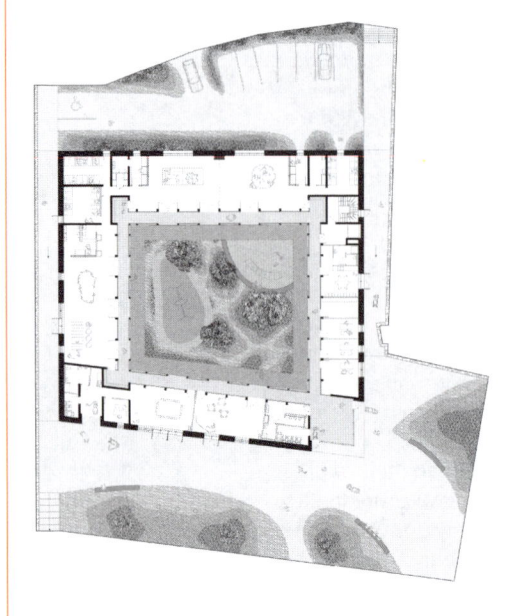

Eco Park Durres is a large public park built on a former landfill that posed a serious environmental problem for the city. The primary function of the project was to solve an environmental emergency problem, but it was not solely understood as a technical one that could have been fixed with a fenced sanitary landfill. It was understood also as a social issue that required a more complex strategy focused on solving environmental problems, creating public recreational spaces for the city and promoting ecological awareness among the citizens.

Eco Park Durres (1st Phase)
› DURRES, ALBANIA
2019/2021-2023
Landscape · 144,000m²
› **Casanova+Hernandez Architecten**
Helena Casanova, Jesus Hernandez
INTEGRATED ENERGY (Private)
© Alvis Mine

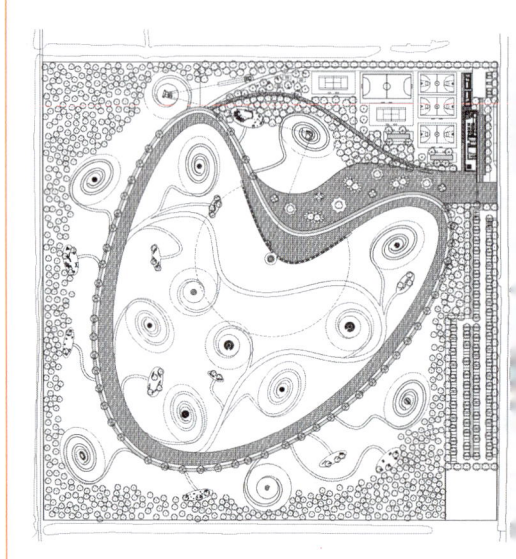

The project aimed to reconstruct the Lasgush Poradeci school, which was severely damaged by the November 2019 earthquake. The main goal was to design a new school with increased capacity, which would not only serve a larger number of students, but also the entire community with new facilities and public spaces. Similar to the old school, both primary and secondary grade students would use the building, so the school was divided into two main buildings with separate entrances and connected on the upper floors to provide independent and safe flows of movement for students of different age groups. The functional and volumetric design solution was based on analysis of the urban and environmental conditions.

'Lasgush Poradeci'' Secondary School
> TIRANA, ALBANIA
2020/2021
Education · 7,593m² · 570 €/m²
> ASArchitects
Ani Tola, Antonela Saliaj, Geri Bisha, Sonila Semini, Sabina Sheshi
Municipality of Tirana(Public)
© Evisa Kasaj

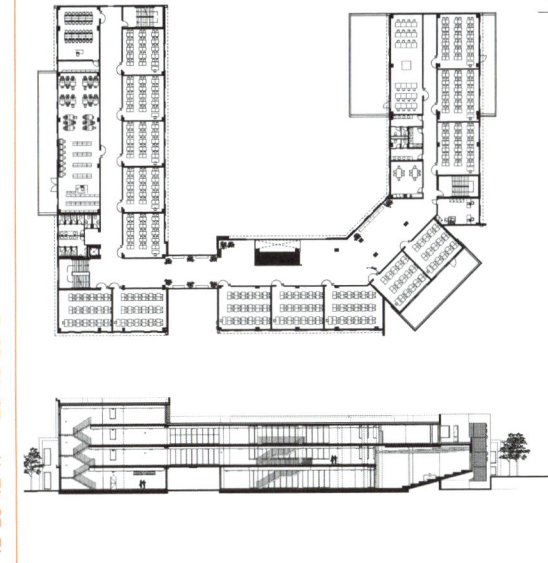

The project site in Golem offers a unique opportunity not only to present a new landmark in relation to the beautiful beach of Golem, but also to harmoniously blend its natural and residential character. As the Meteor lands in the western part of the intervention site, it creates a new magnetic field and allows a new public space to be born. Its position respects the vector of the street, allowing visitors to enjoy the sea view with an open horizon, while creating a new sense of monumentality and asymmetrically redefining the former "roundabout".

Meteor Public Space
> DURRES, ALBANIA
2022/2022-2023
Urban Planning · 4,000m²
> IXI architecture
Saimir Kristo, Iva Guço, Xhoana Kristo, Iris Hyka
Ministry of Culture of Albania (Public)
© Besmir Domi

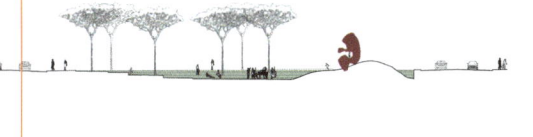

The renovation project of the National Theatre of Opera, Ballet and Folkloric Ensemble (NTOBFE) aspires to strengthen the education of a social life and our consciousness regarding collective cultural memory. Even though the NTOBFE is an important historical building, it was in poor and non-aesthetic conditions when the design began. With this renovation, we aimed to bring into focus a modern vision of theatrical experience in Albania. We tried to find a balance between old and new, through architectural elements that convey their transition in time, their timeline. This design achieves the best of international acoustic standards and technologies.

National Theatre of Opera, Ballet and Popular Ensemble
› TIRANA, ALBANIA
2016/2020-2021
Culture · 13,809m²
› Atelier 4
Olsi Efthimi, Altin Premti, Alban Efthimi
Ministry of Culture, Albania (Public)
© Marelin Topciu

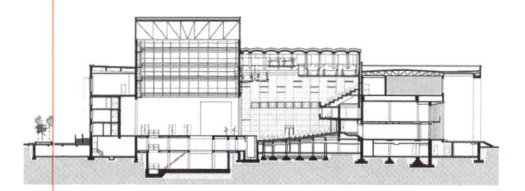

The design renovates the Brutalist monument in the heart of Albania's capital city, once the showpiece of Communist dictator Enver Hoxha. For many Albanians, the Pyramid is a symbol of victory over the regime and MVRDV's design was inspired by how they had reclaimed the building. The concrete structure is reused, the atrium and its surroundings have been made green and a small village of cafes, studios, workshops and classrooms has opened. The Pyramid is therefore expected to become a new hub for Tirana's cultural life and a symbol for the new generation.

Pyramid of Tirana
› TIRANA, ALBANIA
2018/2021-2023
Culture · 11,835m²
› MVRDV, iRI
Winy Maas, Agolli Gent
Albanian-American Development Foundation (AADF); Municipality of Tirana; Albania Ministry of Culture (Mixed)
© Ossip van Duivenbode

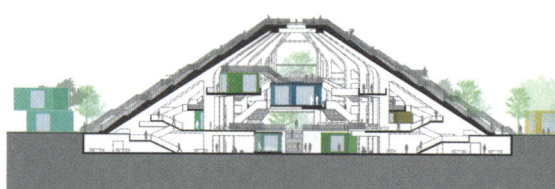

The steep terrain on which the building was built was challenging and the slope and the dense urban conditions influenced the basic elements of its design. Conceptually, the building has been treated as a "House of Peace", where its primary and simple form has undergone a sculptural process of cuts and clefts to give it a contemporary and dynamic appearance. These features include a large panoramic roof terrace, as well as an impressive main entrance. Other distinctive features allow for the entry of natural light into the underground floors, which are used for offices and conference rooms.

Embassy of Peace
› **TIRANA, ALBANIA**
2017/2019-2021
Mixed use - Cultural & Social · 3,735m² · 1,035€/m²
› **AVatelier**
Armand Vokshi
FFPBB (Private)
© Evisa Kasaj

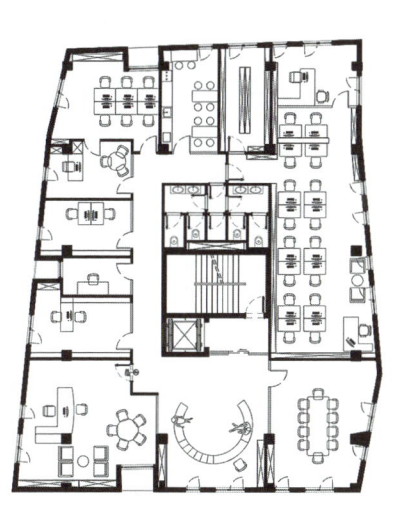

Designed meticulously to obtain a balanced result between functionality, variability and quality, this project embodies a distinctive volumetric configuration that complements its surroundings. Several considerations, such as the way of use, the distribution of the premises and the plot's orientation contributed to its final volumetric configuration. The volume is conceived as a series of interconnected cubes located along the central axis of the building with a longitudinal extension that is separated between them by hollow strips of windows on either side, oriented to the east and west.

Tirana Business Centre
› **TIRANA, ALBANIA**
2020/2020-2021
Commerce · 6,230m² · 550€/m²
› **Smart Studio**
Florian Nepravishta
AV-7 sh.p.k. (Private)
© Florian Nepravishta

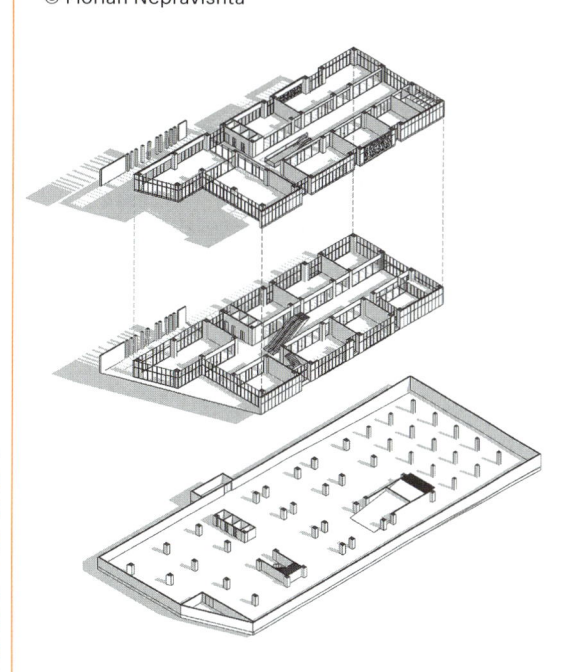

The regeneration of the listed monument Agora Modiano aims to regain its role as the Thessaloniki's central food market and a landmark in the heart of the city.
We approached the project as a process of alternating between the research phase, the evaluation phase and the design phase, focusing on the interpretation of the predominant concepts of the monument. We identified them as: simplicity, rhythm, light, lightness, materiality and people. We wanted to redefine and reinforce qualities, which the monument had in its original form and life, highlighting its atmosphere as the powerful quality that it possessed in its entirety. The new materials are intended to highlight the existing ones.

The Regeneration and Reinterpretation of the Agora Modiano Listed Monument

› **THESSALONIKI, GREECE**
 2017/2020-2022
 Food & Accommodation · 5,505m2
› **Morpho Papanikolaou|SPARCH architects**
 Morpho Papanikolaou
 F.L.S. Private Company | FAIS GROUP (Private)
 © Olga Deikou

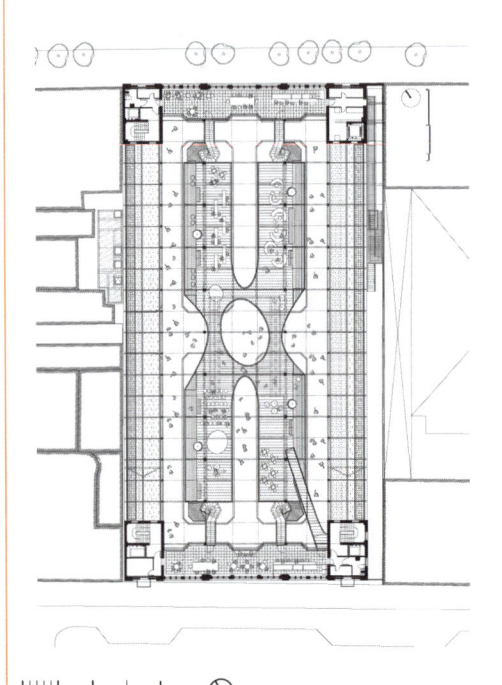

The regeneration of Fanarioton Square echoes beyond its boundaries, as it completely reconfigures the basis of Thessaloniki's most prominent historical axis, revealing the city's historical layering, restoring its continuity and reintroducing its monuments to the public. Starting from an existing but incoherent street junction, the design team adopted an integrated approach to deliver a balanced, accommodating and sustainable public space by carefully levelling surfaces, enhancing greenery and shaping organically flowing routes and paths with the use of natural, low-maintenance materials.

Revelation and Highlighting of Thessaloniki's Monumental Axis

› **THESSALONIKI, GREECE**
 2018/2019-2021
 Urban planning · 7,500m² · 160€/m²
› **Makridis Associates**
 Thodoris Makridis, Petros Makridis, Eleanna Makridou, Alkistis Stergiani Kartsiou, Martha Georgakakou, Vasileios Tsigkas
 Municipality of Thessaloniki (Public)
 © Kimberley Powell

The site is located in a densely vegetated area on the borders between the forest and the city. The design approach was to create a unique child-centered space and to translate the educational targets set by the institution into architecture. With schoolchildren as the main users in mind, the goal of the design was to create a simple and intimate place where children perceive the building as their home and the outdoor space as their yard: a school atmosphere that strikes a balance between the children's expression and their development in an adult environment.

Anatolia Elementary School
› **THESSALONIKI, GREECE**
2019/2021-2022
Education · 4,345m²
› **Morpho Papanikolaou|SPARCH architects**
Morpho Papanikolaou
Anatolia College Trustees (Mixed)
© Konstantinos Pappas

This project is an ongoing effort of adaptive forestry and meadow management practices. The family desired a landscape of light, shadow and seasonal change. They wanted a safe place where their young daughter could learn about the natural environment by interacting with the landscape and its species as she grows. It includes forest planting, stairs and a meadow that bridges the home to the surrounding Kojori forestlands and the greater Vere River Valley. The work aims to spark demand for endemic forest species, the growth of local nurseries and supply chains and minimal maintenance methods that increase herbaceous biodiversity and enhance soil health. The project foregrounds species behavior and facilitates local horticultural knowledge through on-site learning and ongoing documentation.

Betania Forest Garden
› **BETANIA, GEORGIA**
2023/2023
Landscape · 800m²
› **Ruderal**
Sarah Cowles, Benjamin Hackenberger, Giorgi Nishnianidze
Confidential (Private)
© Grigori Sokolinsky

Tbilisi Urban Forest (Narikala Ridge Forest)
Tbilisi, Georgia
2021/2022
Ruderal
Sarah Cowles, Benjamin Hackenberger, Christian Moore, Giorgi Nishnianidze
Tbilisi City Hall
(Public)
Landscape · 550,000m²

In 2020, city leaders in Tbilisi initiated a project to replant the Tbilisi Urban Forest with a biodiverse palette of endemic, climate-adapted species. Ruderal developed and tested a novel approach to urban afforestation that integrates ecology, technology, and aesthetics via two planting projects within the 700-hectare territory.

The Tbilisi Urban Forest aims to improve biodiversity in the habitat, build resilience to climate change, and provide new recreational opportunities for citizens and tourists. In the mid-20th century, Soviet planners planted pine monocultures to reduce erosion and cool the city. The aging pines suffered significant die-off from pests and fungi, posing a fire hazard and public safety risk. The design and research team selected two pilot areas: The Narikala Ridge, a north-facing cliffside bridging the historic city centre to the National Botanical Garden of Georgia, and Okrokana, a south-facing slope in a peri-urban settlement in the hills above Tbilisi, to test new approaches to afforestation.

Ruderal adapted the work of environmental scientists to create detailed spatial plans for coherent 'patches' of plant communities adapted to different soil and slope conditions. The patches integrate existing trees with new saplings, shrubs, and specimen trees that are grafted into the microtopography and the soil pockets carved out for the initial pine plantations of the mid-20th century. The diversity of species and vertical heterogeneity of the trees plated provide cover for wildlife.

The scale and complexity of the project required new tools to manage the large spatial dataset and model typical scenarios. Ruderal developed a parametric planting design tool in Grasshopper that reconciles typical planting conditions with precise site-specific spatial data. The tool allows designers to rapidly visualize the patches at different scales, adapt, and optimize species mixes relative to the nursery inventory, and to simulate the interaction of diverse species over time. Ruderal will adapt the work from the pilot project to the remaining territory and other afforestation projects in Europe and beyond.

The saplings, shrubs, and tree specimens for the project are grown in Georgian nurseries and collected from local seed stocks, unlike other municipal projects that rely on imported trees and shrubs. By using local species and seed stocks, the project links the city to the surrounding ecological context and supports a growing network of native plant nurseries. Drawing from this network of local nurseries, rather than importing species from abroad, significantly reduces the project's carbon footprint.

The afforestation approach includes an additional layer of 'nurse plants' to increase the new seedlings' survival rate. Each new sapling is surrounded and supported by nurse plant seedlings (mainly Cotinus coggygria) which provide shade, shelter from the wind, and protection from herbivores and improve the soil quality by adding organic matter and nutrients. Additionally, the faster-growing nurse plants provide the first visual evidence of the project's scale and effect. After one year, the irrigation and planting project has seen nascent plant communities emerge, including planted and volunteer species suppressed by the former pine canopy.

RUDERAL

SHORTLISTED

TBILISI URBAN FOREST (NARIKALA RIDGE FOREST)

473

RUDERAL

474

From
LISBON
Portugal
38°42'55"N — 9°09'23"W

to
NICOSIA
Cyprus
35°9'08"N — 33°22'57"E

The project is part of a single-family house program aimed at achieving a timeless architectural expression. The design is a departure from the existing building, integrating parts of the former facade in the renovated morphology. The space was designed as a three-dimensional structure, characterized by interior volume and openness to the exterior, following the filtered light of the patio. The house spacing sequence is fluid, avoiding strict compartments.

House in Santa Isabel
› **LISBON, PORTUGAL**
2016/2018-2021
Single house · 394m²
› **Domitianus Arquitetura**
Paulo Tormenta Pinto, Rosa Maria Bastos
Private
© Inês d'Orey

The project undertakes the rehabilitation of a mid-19th century residential building into four dwellings, two of which are duplexes. The project is intended to be another stage in the building's evolution, a contemporary unfolding in the reading that will be made of it, as if it were a palimpsest. The design strategy is developed and driven by the dichotomy between two periods: that of the initial construction and that of the present day.

Andaluz Houses
› **LISBON, PORTUGAL**
2016/2018-2022
Collective housing · 490m² · 900€/m²
› **PLCO arquitectos**
Pedro Lagrifa de Oliveira
jorge do ó + pedro oliveira (Private)
© Eduardo Nascimento

The project is formed by two old warehouses unified into a single space. Outside, the ruined appearance and the traces of the past are maintained; while inside, the walls create a white, bright space: the house. Two gardens shape the relationship between inside and outside. In the double-height interior, a central space is occupied by two staircases. An archetypal volume exists within the space under a ceiling shaped by the negative space of the rooftop pool. The house is defined within this space by the relationship with the pool volume and the existing walls.

House in Barreiro
› BARREIRO, PORTUGAL
2015/2018-2023
Single house · 653m² · 1,531€/m²
› **Aires Mateus e Associados**
Francisco Aires Mateus, Manuel Aires Mateus
João Feijão (Private)
© Joao Guimaraes

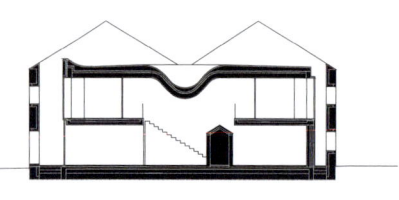

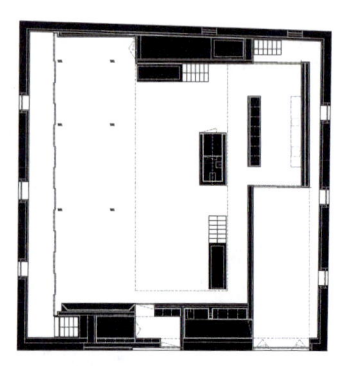

The property includes three areas: a ridge, a plateau and a valley that reaches the sea. The intervention respects the area without altering it, allowing the experience of the natural environment to merge with the hotel. Two approaches emerge: building-territory and architecture-way. The territory is the basis of the hotel and leads to selective transformation. The hotel goes beyond the building, using the terrain and creating a network of paths that allows users to experience the entire territory. A repetitive module, adapted to the topography, defines the space and offers an individual experience that unites the idea of a retreat. It integrates the sea, the plain and the sky, harnessing light from all directions. The color choices are integrated with nature. Each space is part of the whole, a tree in the forest, unique and unpredictable.

Praia do Canal Nature Resort
› ALJEZUR, PORTUGAL
2008/2018-2023
Food & Accommodation · 6,972m²
› **Atelier Bugio**
João Favila Menezes
Herdade da Praia do Canal - Empreendimentos Turísticos e Florestais (Private)
© Leonardo Finotti

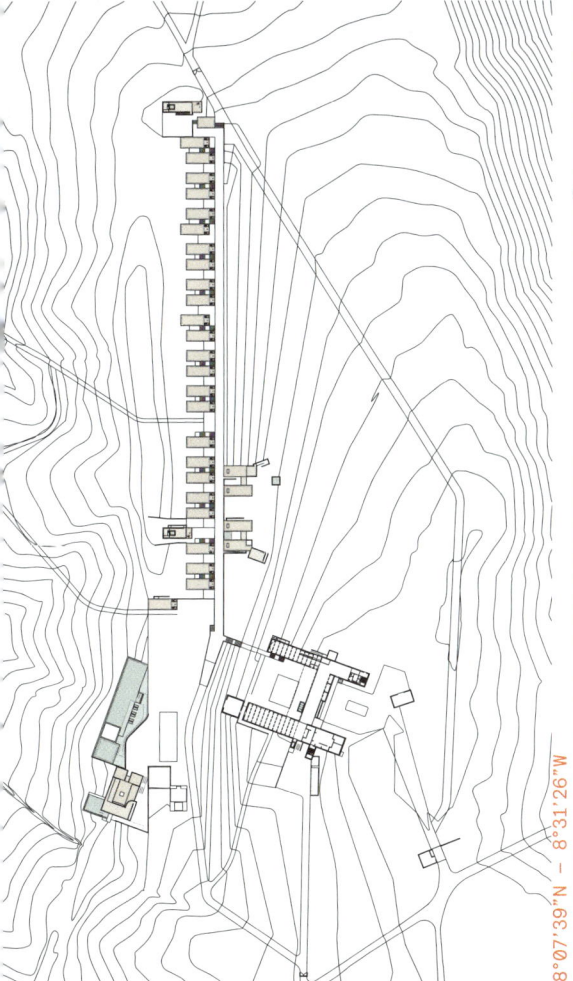

The house emerges from the figure of an extensive water tank attached to a wall, as if it were a resonance box of the entire landscape. On the other side of the wall the social spaces and two fresco rooms are kept, places of transition between interior and exterior, considered foundational for the daily life of the house. Earth tones take over the walls both inside and outside, making it totally adapted to the natural Alentejo scenery.

House in Grândola

› **GRÂNDOLA, PORTUGAL**
2016/2021-2022
Single house · 375m²
› **Bak Gordon Arquitectos**
Ricardo Bak Gordon
Private
© Francisco Nogueira

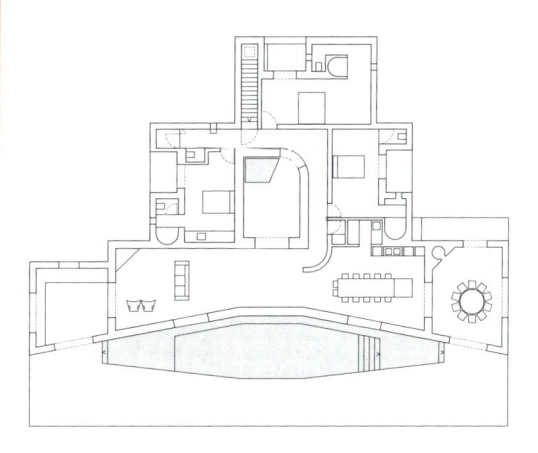

The project for this protected landscape and architectural complex has sought to recover the industrial significance of the Almadraba's fishing activity. The rehabilitation is divided in three areas: firstly the ruined jetty, secondly the chimney and the tar pit and thirdly the path between both banks of La Flecha.

The ruined jetty was a floodplain piece built with local stones as a dam that we rebuilt according to Roman construction methods. The rehabilitation of the boiler, the chimney, the tar pit and the drain started according to philological criteria, thanks to the fact that its state of conservation allowed us to deduce the construction techniques and finishes. Finally, the high landscape value suggests carrying out a wooden pedestrian path that enables an accessible path between the two banks.

Landscape Adaptation and Intervention in the Almadraba of Nueva Umbría

› **LEPE, SPAIN**
2018/2021-2022
Landscape · 1,511m² · 252€/m²
› **Sol89**
Juan Jose López de la Cruz, María González García
Dirección General de Ordenación del Territorio, Urbanismo y Agenda Urbana. Consejería de Fomento, Articulación del Territorio y Vivienda. Junta de Andalucía (Public)
© Fernando Alda

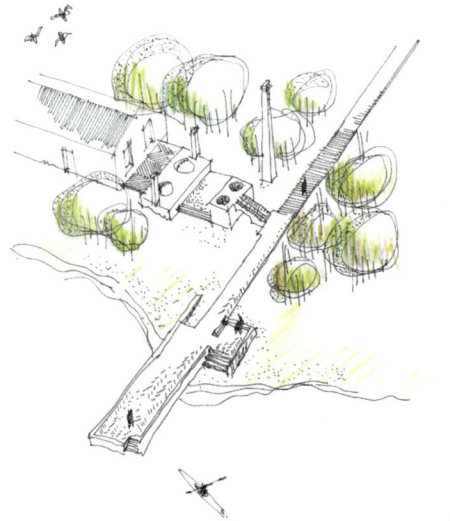

The main goal of the project is to try to achieve an iconic building that contributes representativeness and values to a currently peripheral urban environment, based on the resolution of an extremely simple program. The program, which consists of stands, changing rooms, offices and attached premises, is distributed along the perimeter of the track. This stereotomic basement is built in black concrete, showing the heaviness of being filled with a program and therefore how it belongs to the earth. In contrast, the tectonic part, which is detached from the earth, is a light backlit polycarbonate box levitating above the track. Between them is a void, a space that mediates between both concepts.

Sports Hall "La Unión"

› **SAN JOSÉ DE LA RINCONADA, SPAIN**
2021/2022-2023
Sport & Leisure · 3,410m² · 720€/m²
› **NGNP Arquitectos, MLOPEZ arquitectos**
José Antonio Plaza Cano, Juan Carlos Herrera Pueyo, Enrique Naranjo Escudero, Manuel López Sánchez, José Carlos Oliva Gómez
Ayuntamiento de la Rinconada (Public)
© Jesús Granada

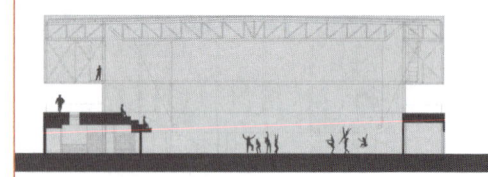

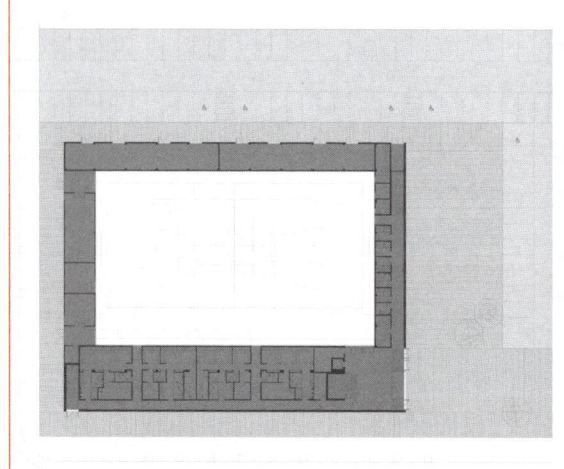

Synapse House is an experimental sustainable housing project that advocates for open domestic interactions. Its star-shaped floor plan organizes domestic uses around two interconnected halls, illuminated from skylights. Like in a neuronal network, several branches spread out from the nucleus towards the exterior. The assignment was to design a sustainable, four-room house with a minimum carbon footprint for a couple with three children. Some of the main ideas for the project included maximizing the filtering surfaces, considering the implications of orientation and softening interior-exterior permeabilities.

Synapse House
› **SEVILLE, SPAIN**
2019/2020-2023
Single house · 210m² · 2,000€/m²
› **Baum Lab**
Miguel Gentil Fernández, Marta Barrera Altemir, Javier Caro Domínguez
Private
© Javier Orive

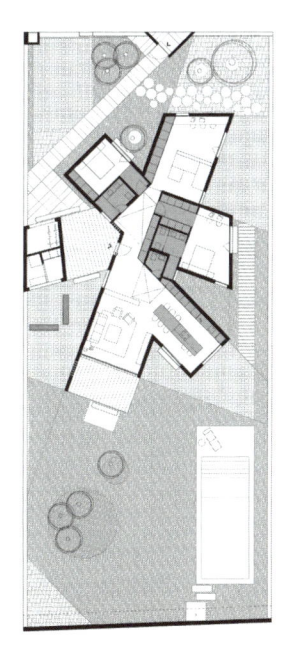

As part of a homogeneous urban fabric, entirely listed as heritage, this project had to address the restoration of the neoclassical town hall, its connection with several more recent structures behind it and the overall functional reorganization of the new resulting complex. The intervention solves the new program by connecting the 18th-century building and the more recent municipal services building with a new volume that allows for a unified reading of the entire ensemble. The new building completes the block and presents itself to the street hermetically. In contrast, it subtly steps up in section as it climbs to its roof, improving interaction with the historic façade.

Rehabilitation and Expansion of the Town Hall of Fuentes de Andalucía
› **FUENTES DE ANDALUCÍA, SPAIN**
2017/2020-2022
Government & Civic ·
1,029m² · 1,105€/m²
› **Laguillo Arquitectos**
Ignacio Laguillo Diaz
Consejeria de Fomento, Articulación del Territorio y Vivienda. Junta de Andalucía (Public)
© Fernando Alda

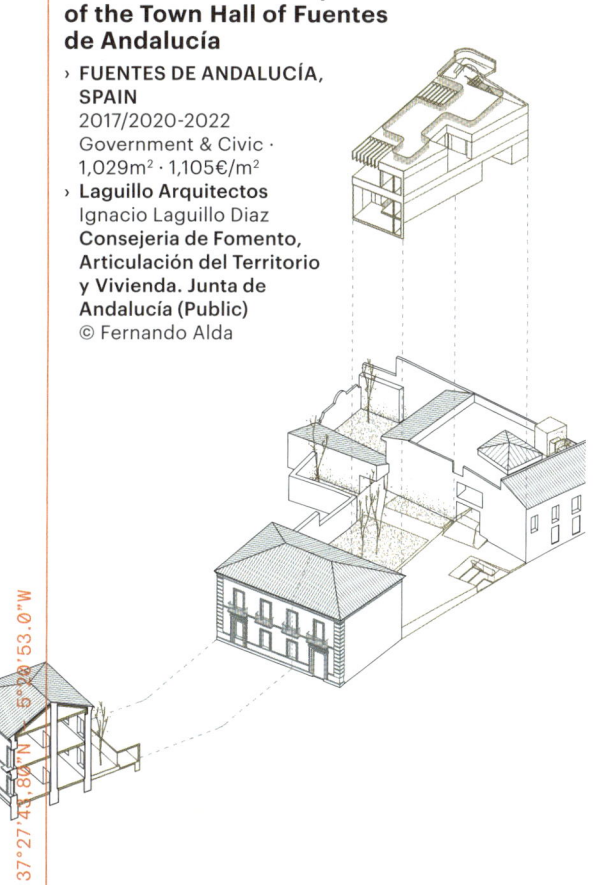

The library is in a park on the border of a wide avenue that covers the railway network. The plan adapts to the 18th-century gardens, respecting the existing trees unfolding its height from the traffic road to the park. The image towards the park is lightened by a deep balcony that extends in the first level the reading spaces to the garden between the treetops, introducing the vision of the park facing south and casting shade on the basement. The interior is a continuous space under a plied metal roof with deep skylights and metal curtains as means of absorbing sound.

Córdoba Public Library
› **CÓRDOBA, SPAIN**
  2007/2014-2021
  Education · 7,194m² · 2,200€/m²
› **Paredes Pedrosa Arquitectos**
  Ángela García de Paredes, Ignacio García Pedrosa
  Ministry of Culture of Spain (Public)
  © Roland Halbe

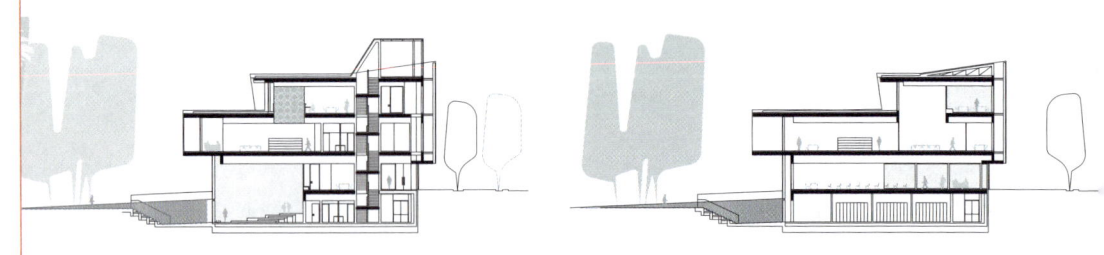

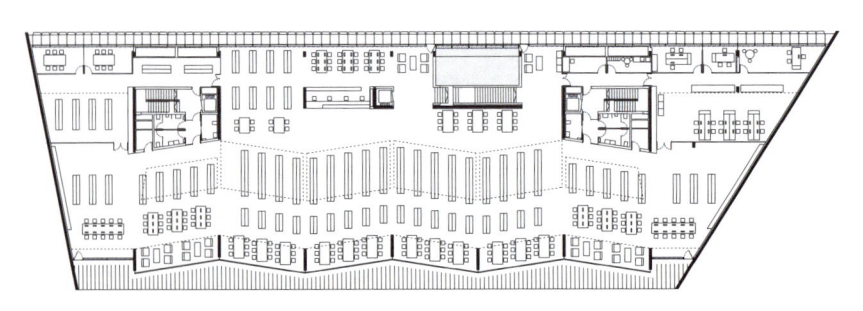

This is a teaching building that lines the street, inviting pedestrians to enter from the public space into the unique realm of educational function. The architecture divided into two structures: one suspended and hermetic, made of white ceramic for teaching, researching and social activities; and a vitreous, permeable body in contact with the ground for public functions. This concept gives rise to the idea of a grand architectural tree or forest where teaching and learning can take place among its branches. The entire building features courtyard-walls of light that connect the covered lower and exterior levels with the upper level open to the sky.

New Faculty of Psychology and Speech Therapy

› **MÁLAGA, SPAIN**
   2016/2017-2021
   Education · 31,639m^2 · 953€/m^2
› **LLPS Arquitectos**
   Eduardo Pérez Gómez, Miguel Ángel Sánchez García
   University of malaga (Public)
   © Javier Callejas Sevilla

The project recovers the construction tradition of the corner dome with which the farmhouses were built in this region located between Extremadura, Castile and Andalusia. These domes of great solidity and thermal inertia, made with the stones that give the name to the valley, with the constructive and functional logic of storing the heavy grain on the upper floor and inhabiting the lower floor, are now made of concrete with metal formwork.

"Wildlife Observatory" in Los Pedroches

› **CÓRDOBA, SPAIN**
   2019/2020-2022
   Culture · 879m^2 · 1,067.15€/m^2
› **Rafael de La-Hoz Arquitectos**
   Rafael de La-Hoz Castanys
   Iñigo Diaz de Berricano Gonzalez (Private)
   © Alfonso Quiroga

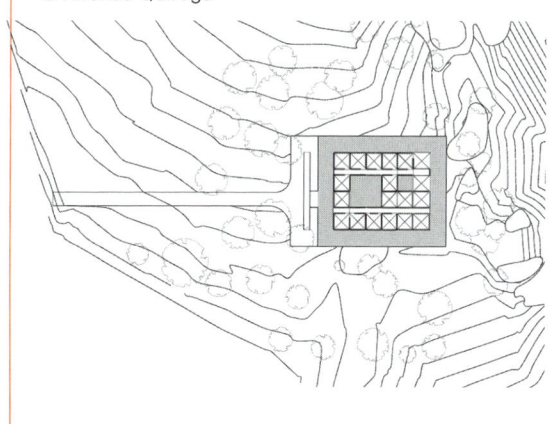

The project relies on Mojacar's difficult topography to solve the domestic spaces at different levels. Each floor opens onto a terrace with views of the sea. The house is built with local construction systems. The exterior in white lime gives the façade a material continuity with the context. Local limestone is used for the wet areas. The reinforced concrete structure allows the pillar system to be adapted to the complex geometry of the plot. The house has been designed with economical solutions and based on an economy of proximity.

House in Mojácar
› MOJÁCAR, SPAIN
2018/2022
Single house · 350m^2
› **Alberto Campo Baeza, Modesto Sánchez Morales**
Alberto Campo Baeza, Modesto Sánchez Morales
José Luís González Martínez (Private)
© Javier Callejas

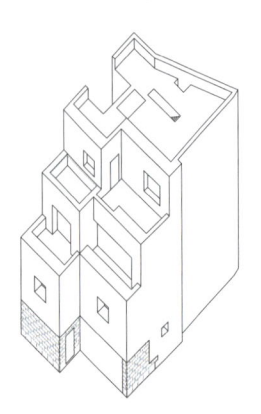

Aimed at creating a center for interpreting the photographer's work and spreading knowledge about this artistic discipline, the project explores the duality between old and new. It stives to preserve the remains of the original house while generating a modernized space at the same time in a constant tension between preservation and rupture. The building also requires complex environmental conditions (humidity, temperature, etc.), as is necessary for a contemporary museum.

Toni Catany International Photography Centre
› LLUCMAJOR, SPAIN
2018/2019-2021
Culture · 1,200m^2 · 1,750€/m^2
› **mateo arquitectura**
Josep Lluís Mateo
Government of the Balearic Islands (Department of Culture) and Spanish Ministry of Culture (Public)
© Aldo Amoretti

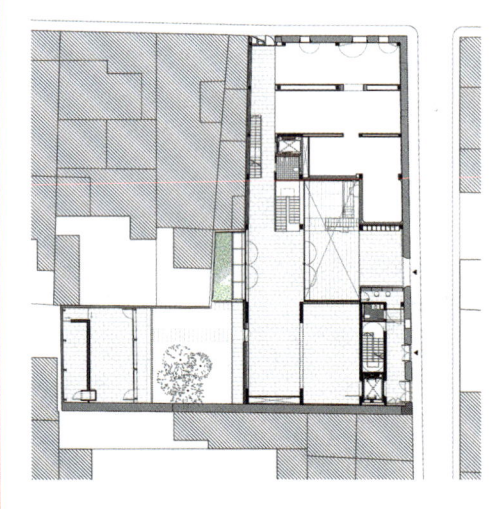

Living in Lime
42 Social Housing
Son Servera, Spain
2009/2020-2023

peris+toral arquitectes
Marta Peris, José Toral

IBAVI - Institut Balear de l'Habitatge
(Public)
Collective housing · 5,766m² · 1,106.08€/m²

Inspired by vernacular architecture and using local ecological materials, this social housing building blends environmental and social strategies that aim for sustainability. The patios, gardens, and liveable streets encourage social interactions and enhance the building's thermodynamic performance.

The elevated streets feature a sequence of small courtyards to provide cross-ventilation and lighting to the homes that flank both sides of the walkway, while the remaining homes are through-units with a dual orientation. The space-forming structure consists of load-bearing walls, unfolding into a diagonal floor plan. The housing typology does not distinguish between day and night areas, separating the rooms, each at one end of the floor plan, while the through-living room connects both façades, linking different spaces without losing the unity of the area through long diagonal sight lines. The living room and kitchen extend the centre of gravity of the floor plan, looking outward through two intermediate spaces: a sun-catching terrace on the façade, serving as a winter garden, and a wooden lattice screen to have privacy on the walkway.

The atmosphere of the village, characterized by marés sandstone walls with hidden gardens behind them, has greatly influenced both the choice of materials and the building's design. The plot's location on the edge of the village, its proximity to the historical centre, and the small scale of the neighbouring plots suggest a dual-scale approach. The building is carried out in two volumes, aligning with the perimeter streets, the façade frontage is reduced to minimize its impact on the old town. This approach creates two diagonal voids at opposite corners of the plot. Two courtyards, one based on inert mineral and the other on plant life, serve as intermediate spaces with distinct character, accompanying both entrances and the communal rooms of the building. The volume is staggered in response to the plot's slope. The inclined Arabic tile roofs, the façade openings, and the walls extending the building's base are key to its integration into the surroundings. The walkway aggregation creates elevated streets that mirror the village streets' proportions, promoting social interactions among residents.

The façade is designed with self-supporting local sandstone (marés), 10 cm thick, which increases to 20 cm to form openings and lintelled arches, and to 40 cm thick in the walls. Two types of stone are used: a harder, heavier, and more resistant white stone for areas in contact with the ground, and a lighter, sandier type for the upper parts.

The load-bearing walls have been built with ceramic pieces baked with biomass from the local industry, using hollow H20 bricks. Given the low apparent density of this material, the bricks were placed with their hollow sections aligned vertically to fill them with sand, thereby increasing their mass and inertia. This solution addresses acoustics between neighbours with a single layer. To properly seal the joints and ensure the hygrothermal properties to the wall, it has been coated on both sides with a lime mortar plaster at least 15 mm thick.

The white concrete slabs are lightened, revealing the in-situ ribs with a unidirectional logic. The formwork has been reused as the base for the structure of the sloping roof.

The walkways are resolved with a 10 cm thick cork ETICS, External Thermal Insulation Composite Systems, coated with lime plaster.

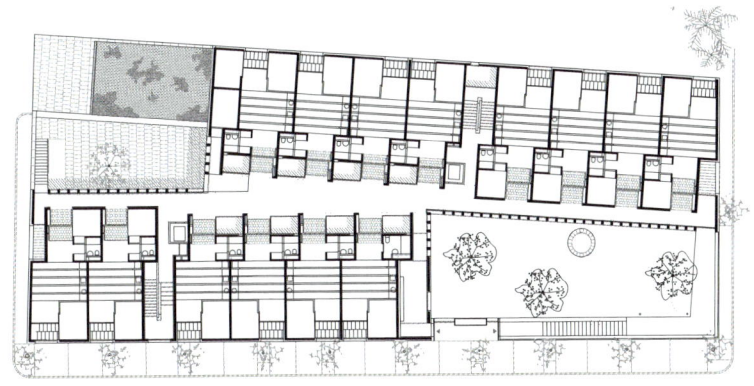

Ground floor

PERIS+TORAL ARQUITECTES

486

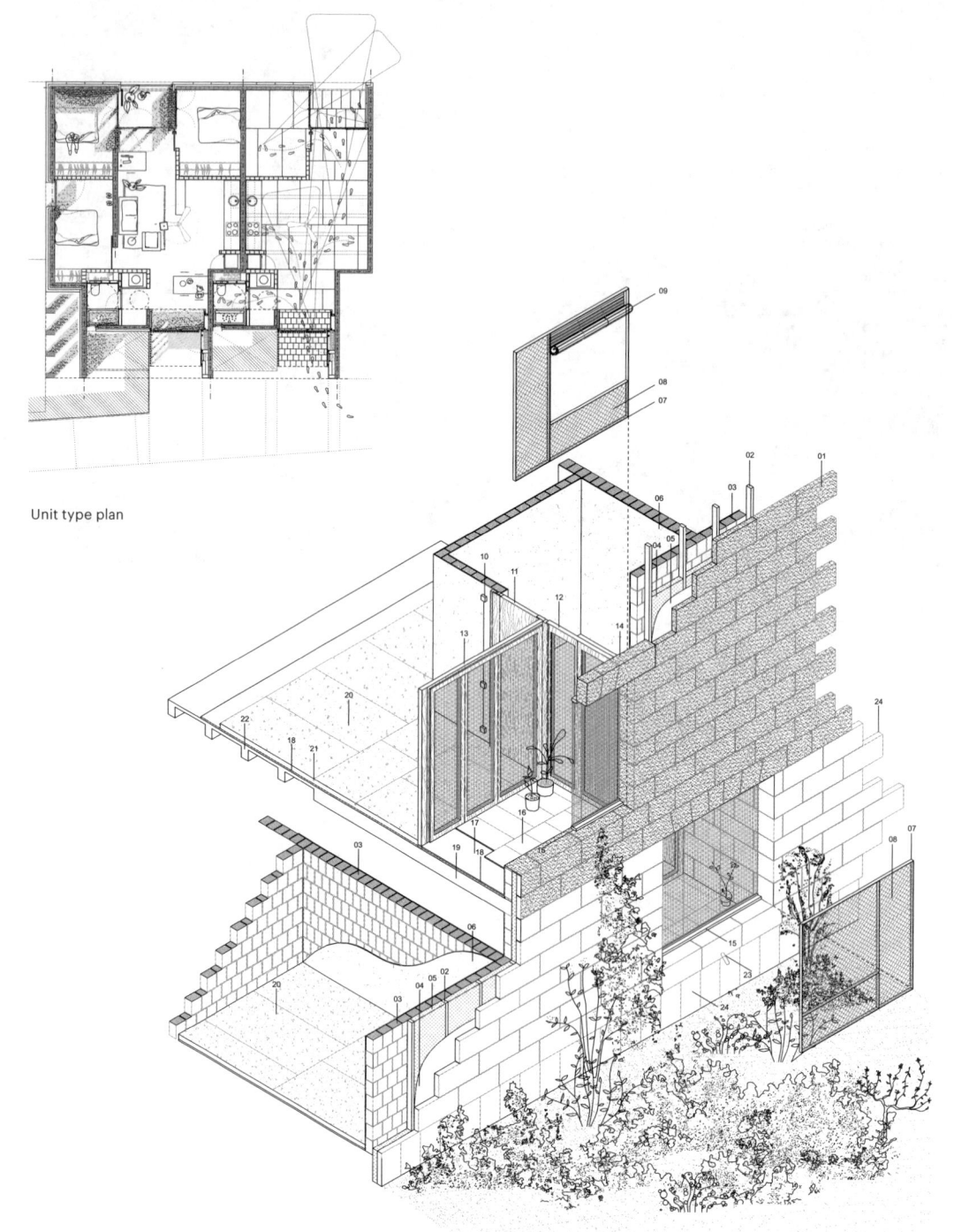

SHORTLISTED

Unit type plan

01. Marés stone Vilafranquer 10x40x80cm
02. Pine frame 50x100mm
03. Load - bearing wall of H20 ceramic block fired with biomass, filles with sand
04. Breathable waterproof sheet
05. Recycled cotton thermal insulation e=10cm
06. Projected lime plaster with seashells e=15mm
07. Galvanized steel frame e=5mm
08. Metal mesh
09. Alicantina type Soria pine roller blind
10. Surface mechanisms with galvanized tube
11. Larch three-layer door e=40mm
14. Vilafranquer type marés lintel archof e=20cm
15. Glass curtain for solar collection without vertical profiles, folding on the side
16. Stone pavement Santanyi e=30mm
17. Waterproofing with waterproof mortar
18. Rock wool acoustic insulations e=30mm with high density <10MN/m3
19. White concrete slab e=25cm
20. White concrete floor, polished e=8cm
21. Pavement expansion joints
22. Unidirectional whote concrete ribbed slab
23. Galvanized steel gargoyle

LIVING IN LIME. 42 SOCIAL HOUSING

↑ 310

Villa B, built on the remains of an abandoned stone building that had fallen into ill repair, transforms an abandoned structure in the historical city into a dwelling of contemporary standards. Repairing parts of the existing structure and adding a new layer of architecture, the renovated house was formed by carefully peeling off layers that had been added over time. Highlighting the original qualities, the building is given a new life. The materials were consciously chosen to be sustainable and enduring. In the new parts, local stone from a quarry nearby and Nordic spruce complement each other forming an interesting pair of materials of a contrasting nature.

Villa B
› **CIUTADELLA DE MENORCA, SPAIN**
2018/2019-2022
Single house · 600m²
› **OOPEAA Office for Peripheral Architecture**
Anssi Lassila
Private
© Marc Goodwin

487

The Screen goes beyond mere structural simplicity, challenging norms while innovating without compromise. It reimagines workspaces by prioritizing openness, natural illumination and the occupants' well-being, along with modular design, abundant brightness and daring aesthetics. This contemporary high-rise, spanning 23,000 square meters, offers flexible office spaces for lease with a deliberate emphasis on modularity and flexibility to facilitate seamless integration for future occupants.

The Screen
› **TUNIS, TUNISIA**
2011/2014-2023
Office · 23,000m²
› **ARK-architecture, AUDA**
Bilel Khemakhem, Mohamed Khemakhem, Mohamed Nejib Saadallah
ZEN Immobiliere (Private)
© Bilel Khemakhem

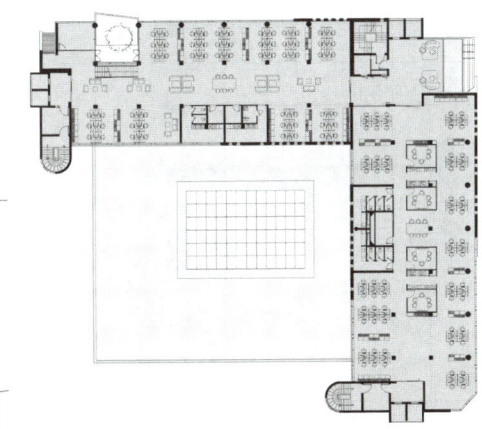

Chris Briffa devised a design for a building that would function as both a place for practicing architecture and a domicile. Over several years, with myriad conceptual permutations, the structure was transformed into his home and studio, retaining distinct identities and addressing diverse needs within the confines of a historical urban neighborhood.

Casa Bottega
› **VALLETTA, MALTA**
2015/2018-2022
Single house · 473m²
› **Chris Briffa Architects**
Chris Briffa
Chris Briffa (Private)
© Aldo Amoretti

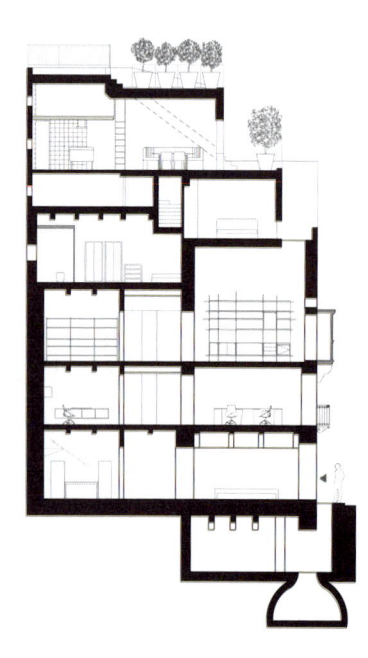

Amidst the island's growing sprawl of vacation homes, the users wanted to revitalize an old olive grove and accommodate family gatherings and holidays, but also theater rehearsals and yoga workshops without removing any tree. This condition shaped the complexity of the spaces and the "village" that was created: intertwining outdoor, semi-outdoor and indoor spaces and events beneath shaded areas like outdoor kitchens, lounges and dining areas. The complex consists of the main residence and five domed guest houses. One dome and a two-story "watchtower" with an accessible roof form the main residence by means of glass curtain walls that ensure an inner heated space (for the living/dining room and kitchen), while allowing the flow of the terraced land to traverse the entirety of the house. The indoor-outdoor continuity creates spaces that value living in the countryside.

Vacation House in an Oliveyard
› **MEGANISI, GREECE**
2018/2019-2021
Single house · 291m²
› **Hiboux architecture**
Dimitris Theodoropoulos, Maria Tsigara, Maria Marianna Xyntaraki
Private
© Yannis Drakoulidis

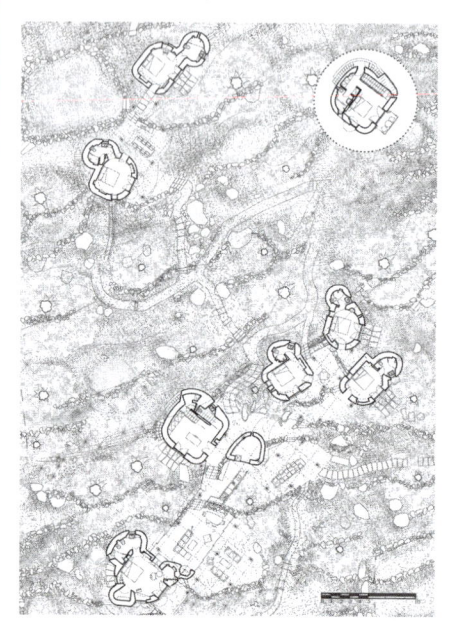

The project favors urban densification and the adoptive reuse of neglected places in the city for a more ecological and affordable way of life. It becomes a contemporary interpretation of the traditional Athenian house where an exterior room would act as the center of daily life, creating a precious feature in the city, adding value and reducing the need for enclosed meters squared. A semi-built room on the roof of a typical building in Athens was transformed into a complete house for three people, urban nomads who spend extended periods of the year here.

Ignatiou Apartment
› **ATHENS, GREECE**
2020/2021-2022
Single house · 25m²
› **Point Supreme**
Marianna Rentzou, Konstantinos Pantazis
Elisa Ly, Jérôme Combe, Marcello Rodio
(Private)
© Filip Dujardin

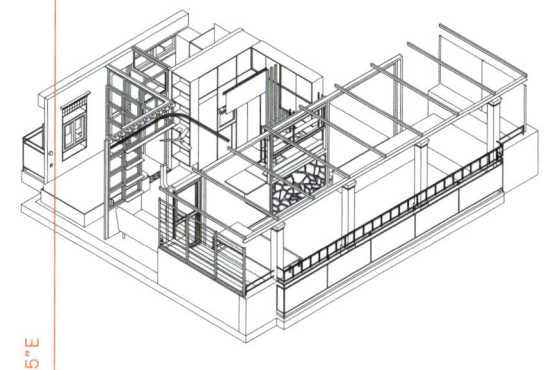

The project is viewed as an experiment, suggesting that it explores new ideas or concepts in both construction and the integration of architectural forms within the city. It is inspired by the movement of the sea and waves and seeks to incorporate these concepts into a residential building, specifically the balconies of an Athenian apartment building. Balconies can be a significant architectural element, offering outdoor spaces for residents and contributing to the overall aesthetics and functionality of the building. The design of the building draws inspiration from the movement and patterns of the sea and waves. This could manifest in various ways, such as the shape of the building, the materials used or the way light and shadows interact with the structure. The project attempts to adapt the concepts of movement and flow to the scale of a residence.

The Seashore Rise
› **GLYFADA, GREECE**
2019/2020-2022
Single house · 491m² · 3,000€/m²
› **314 Architecture Studio**
Pavlos Chatziangelidis
Euphoria Residences (Private)
© Panagiotis Voumvakis

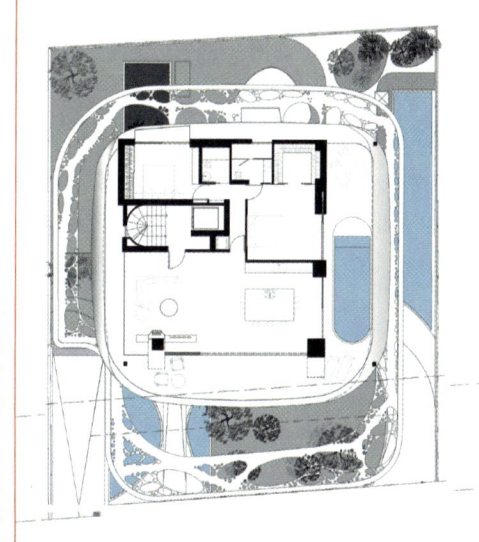

The eLement office building gets its name from its L shape. It is a building that talks about movement and nature. It consists of a ground floor and four floors above ground for offices, as well as a two-story underground parking area. The internal layout is simple and straightforward, with a connecting lobby in the middle to allow for different tenant occupancy. All work spaces have natural light and ventilation. Perforated aluminum louvres protect these spaces from the sun while allowing uninterrupted views to the outside.

eLement – New Office Building

› **MAROUSI, GREECE**
2019/2020-2022
Office · 13,857m^2
› **RS SPARCH**
Rena Sakellaridou
Prodea Investments (Private)
© Yiorgis Yerolymbos

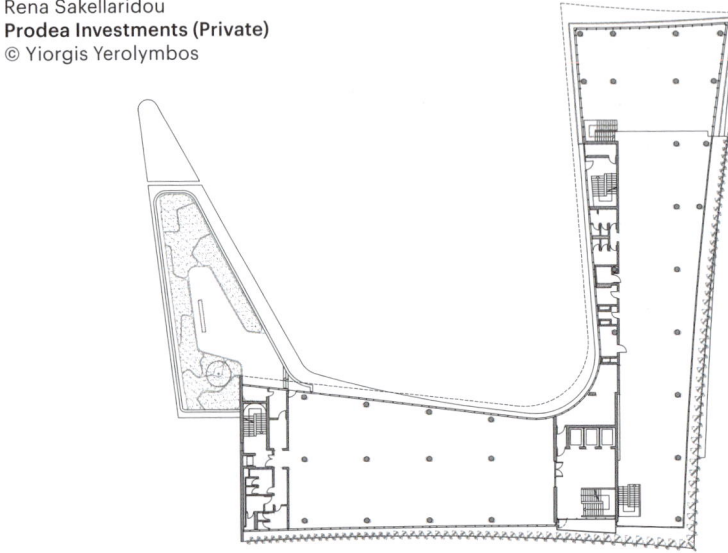

An existing 40-year-old office building is stripped back to its structure and completely reimagined for the present. What used to be a confusing and run-down muddle of geometric clashes is now untangled and rearticulated as if the building were composed of twelve separate buildings, each with its own cladding logic and interior atmosphere. The building is reoriented to take advantage of its location adjacent to a natural park, with large new openings cut into the existing solid walls to open up views, but also to bring in more natural light.

Art 1 Offices
> **ATHENS, GREECE**
> 2020/2021-2022
> Office · 2,300m^2 · 2.6M€
> **Neiheiser Argyros**
> Ryan Neiheiser, Xristina Argyros
> **Hellenic Properties (Private)**
> © Lorenzo Zandri

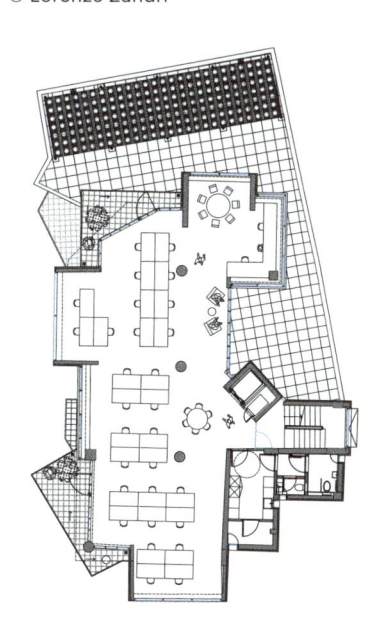

In a peripheral area that still retains its farming character, which is slowly being abandoned, an old orchard is adapted into a vacation garden. This is an act of maintenance with minimal intervention where the garden is defined as an open-air house and a single room shelters the needs for a simple life in the countryside.

Vacation Garden with a Room
> **KEA, GREECE**
> 2016/2016-2022
> Single house · 30m^2
> **Alexandros Fotakis Architecture**
> Alexandros Fotakis, Nicoletta Caputo
> **Private (Private)**
> © Alina Lefa

Homa features three independent lodgings with two bedrooms, outdoor spaces and private pools. Inspired by the island's rich mining history, it is designed around three elements: POINT (natural light-filled entrances), LINE (linear pathways) and PLANE (expansive terraces). The hotel blends seamlessly with the landscape, utilizing the natural plot curvature for privacy and sea views. Its construction materials, including earthy plaster, concrete furniture, wood and natural rocks, celebrate the island's natural essence and mining heritage.

Homa Vagia Boutique Hotel

› VAGIA, GREECE
2020/2021-2022
Food & Accommodation · 180m^2 · 2,700€/m^2
› MOLD architects
Iliana Kerestetzi, Maria Vretou, Konstantinos Vlachoulis
UNDISCLOSED (Private)
© Panagiotis Voumvakis

The main goal was to experiment with alternative forms instead of the archetypical Cycladic architecture model, yet still respecting all the basic elements that comprise its character. When one thinks of the Greek Islands and its vernacular architecture, scattered and stacked white boxes come to mind. The first step was to challenge this morphological preconception by imagining the main two facades of the house being formed as "xerolithies". They start low and gradually develop a sufficient height for a house. They move gently closer and away from the slope and independently from one another, forming spaces between them. To achieve this, all the functions of the house were placed sequentially, making the structure long and narrow.

Xerolithi

› SERIFOS, GREECE
2018/2019-2021
Single house · 250m^2 · 2,200€/m^2
› Sinas Architects
George Sinas
MEK Anaptixiaki (Private)
© Yiorgos Kordakis

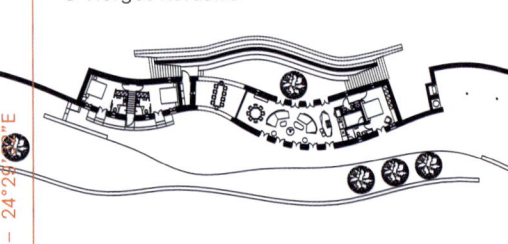

The building rests on the hillside and adapts to the topography and the terrain's morphology. Large transverse walls penetrate the slope. These walls form the backyards and give continuity to the interior of the house towards the landscape. Spaces created between the walls define the entrance, organize the garden and provide space for a water element and a sheltered courtyard. These spaces flow from the interior and are shaped by the walls. The walls are visible only from the east side of the plot, so the living scenario is revealed upon entering the residence. A path crosses them, which connects the thematic sections. The path unfolds parallel to the path inside the house, forming views towards the sea and the living areas.

Louria

› **AGAIRIA, GREECE**
2018/2019-2021
Single house · 215m^2
› **react architects, Kometka Architecture Studio**
Yiorgos Spiridonos, Natasha Deliyianni, Andreas Androulakakis, Tatiana Tzanavari
Leone Gabardella (Private)
© Panagiotis Voumvakis

In a plot with significant slope and southern orientation, we decided to create a partly subterranean residence on two floors. The goal is to alter the natural landscape to the least extent possible in combination with the reassimilation of the local vegetation in the intervention areas. The aim was to weave both the hardscape and softscape of the building into the natural Mykonian landscape. As a result, the entity that was created is not visible from the street. The Latypi project converses with the archetypical architectural legacy as well as the Cycladic terrain, situating itself as a contemporary intervention within the landscape. The concept is inspired by the local sculptural tradition, which has produced timeless artworks throughout the centuries.

Latypi Residence

› **MYKONOS, GREECE**
2018/2020-2022
Single house · 349,65m^2
› **A31 Architecture Construction**
Praxitelis Kondylis
ORIZON Development (Private)
© George Fakaros

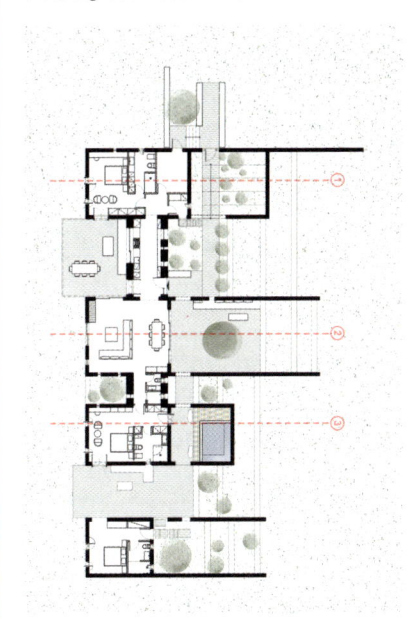

Liknon
Samos, Greece
2020/2020-2022

K-Studio
Dimitris Karampatakis,
Christos Spetseris, Stavros Kotsikas,
Marina Leventaki

Metaxa
(Private)
Food & Accommodation · 380m²

Liknon is a landmark that showcases the origins of the liquor brand Metaxa which are tightly bound to the culture of high-quality goods and winemaking on the island of Samos. The traditional concept of a museum dissolves into a walk-through around the vineyard.

Aiming to connect the Metaxa brand to its roots, Liknon is located in a 100-year-old vineyard in Samos, an island with a rich culture and a long tradition of high-quality goods and winemaking.

In order to craft a positive projection of the company's future, the brand decided to take a nostalgic look back, to celebrate its origins and unique product, and to highlight its most precious ingredient, the fortified sweet muscat wine.

This story could be told nowhere else other than the very same ancient vineyard where Spyros Metaxas developed his precious spirits based on the fragrant notes of sweet muscat grapes, a specialty to the terroir of Samos.

Spreading beneath the traditional village of Vourliotes, 800 m above sea level and subject to the northern *meltemi* wind, the vineyard sprawls down the valley on a sequence of stonewall-held plateaus. This man-made productive landscape was formed by collecting and artfully placing the rocks of the site in a manner that tamed the slope into terraces from which the grapes could then be cultivated.

The architectural brief for the brand's home that guests could visit in order to explore Metaxa's site, values, history, and heritage included the intention to offer an immersive experience into the vine's environment for a thorough understanding of the past, as well as the brand's future direction. The design aimed to celebrate and enhance the sense of being there and enjoying the unique qualities that distinguish Metaxa, making it such a complex spirit in terms of aroma and character.

The brand's story tells itself as visitors are invited to explore different aspects of the vineyard, from the productive processes all the way to users' enjoying the goods at a well-stocked table.

Our proposal aimed to accentuate and preserve the dominant feature of the terraced landscape by carving out a route along the stonewalls and embedded enclosures throughout them. As opposed to creating a building, we peppered the terraced valley with structures that stitch into and take a cue from the pre-existing topography, in order to guide visitors through a curated, yet spontaneous experience to activate their senses.

The architecture of this scenery is an extension of the productive dry stone terraces where the vines grow, and it borrows from the dynamic and roughness of the natural and traditional productive landscape in order to blend into the valley.

The existing language of undulating stone ribbons extends to embrace interior spaces and courtyards that stitch subtly into their surroundings in a simple fashion by gradually modifying their scale and presence. By employing the original craftsmanship of stone-stacking as found in Samos, we managed to recreate the spontaneity of the surroundings in geometry and materiality, thereby blending into the valley with a roughness and dynamic borrowed from the natural and traditional productive landscape.

More than anything, Liknon attempts to achieve continuity, to approach that which is previously existing with minimum intervention while covering any man-made trail to the greatest extent possible. The brief itself aspired to illustrate the knowledge of the primitive practices of winemaking and of handmade landscaping for better natural growth. The concept of the building serves this purist pursuit by camouflaging the architecture and healing any wounds to the natural tissues.

The building techniques follow the traditional principles of stonewalls that support and tame the natural slope. Local stone is arranged into spines that create plateaus where human agricultural activity can flourish. Local craftsmen employed this artful technique that their predecessors had taught them, thus engaging the island's workforce during the building phase.

PERGOLA

TERRACES

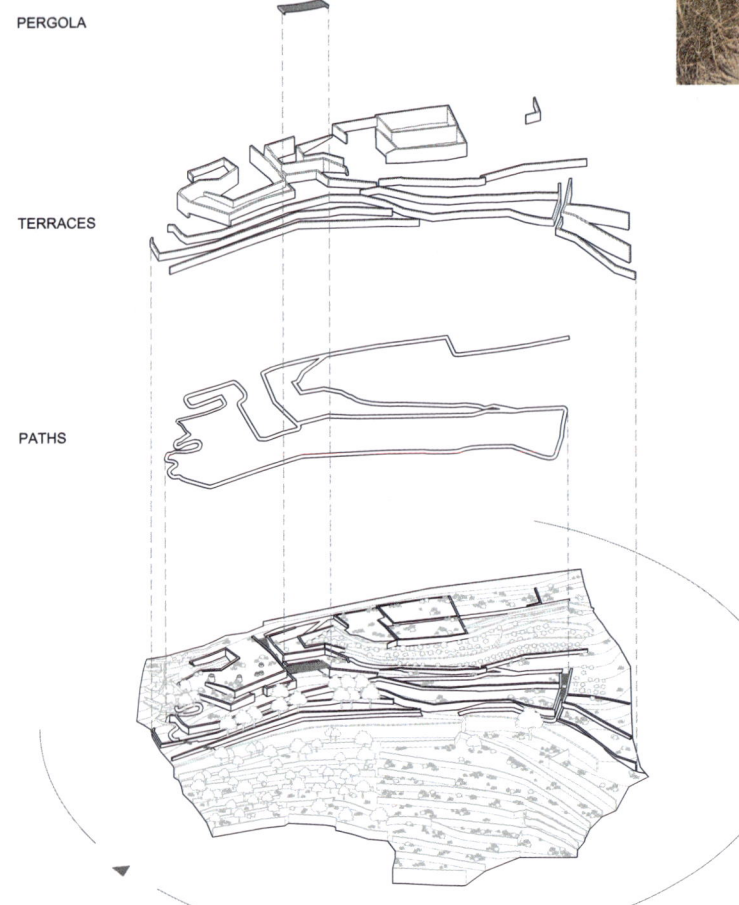

PATHS

SHORTLISTED

LIKNON

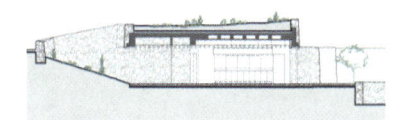

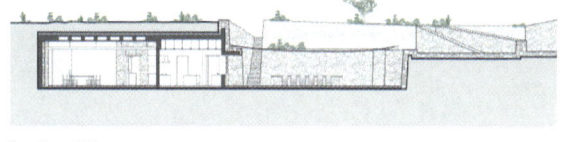

Section AA'

Section BB'

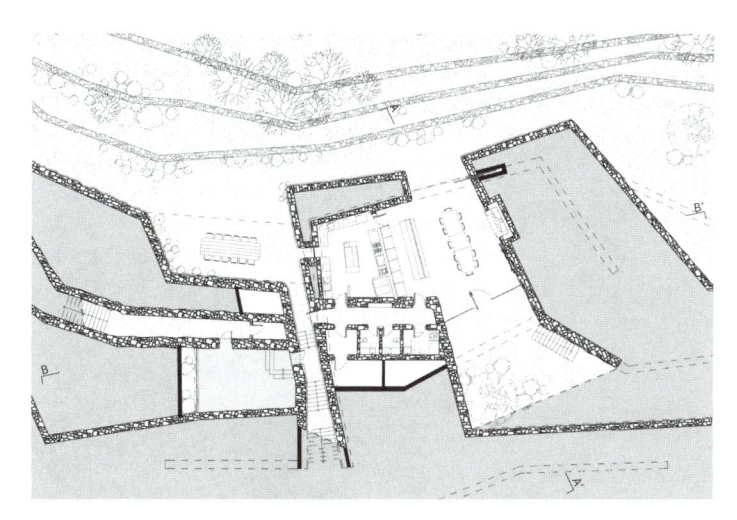

Floor plan

K-STUDIO

Even though the various archeological sites of Kato Paphos appear as distinct areas today, they were once considered part of the historical city of Nea Paphos. This project attempts to resurrect that understanding by proposing a masterplan for the entire area, which includes several immediate and tangible architectural interventions. The intent is to ignite the process of bringing these seemingly distinct areas together.

Archeological Sites
› **PAPHOS, CYPRUS**
2014/2017-2022
Mixed use - Infrastructure & Urban · 7,652m²
› **Simpraxis, Π Square**
Christos Christodoulou, Panayiotis Panayi, Marios Christodoulides
Paphos Municipality (Public)
© George Rahmatoulin

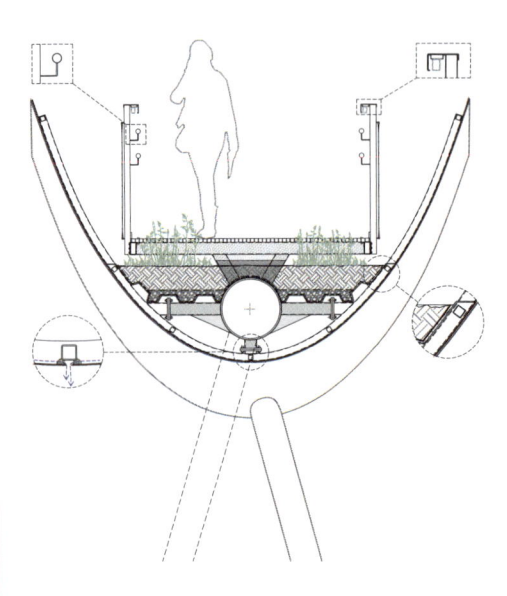

The house is built in a plot full of olive trees. The architect's main goal was to protect as many trees as possible and integrate the residence. Hence the residence is "inserted" among the olives and sits surrounded in a sea of silver green. This design aims to blend seamlessly with nature, especially the olive-filled plot, fostering unity between the environment and living spaces. It emphasizes coexistence and ecological respect, offering functional comfort. The house harmoniously merges with the olive grove, becoming part of the landscape.

House in Olive Grove
› **PAPHOS, CYPRUS**
2018/2019-2021
Single house · 210m²
› **Vardas Studio**
Andreas Vardas
Marios & Christina Karystiou (Private)
© George Christodoulou

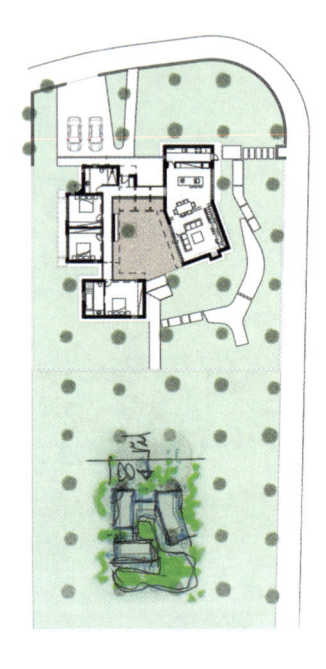

The main volume of the project is inspired by the compact form and small openings of the *koulas*, consisting of two levels of indoor space and a third level without a roof, operating as roof garden and giving the sense of a room open to the sky. A secondary linear volume, which expands the functional spaces of the ground floor, differentiates as form and materiality, emphasizing the height of the main volume and its dynamic presence.

The Koulas Project
› LIMASSOL, CYPRUS
2017/2020-2021
Single house · 170m²
› **Alexis Papadopoulos Architectural Practice**
Alexis Papadopoulos, Maria Protou, Despo Anagiotou
Marcel Seys & Sonia Bosman (Private)
© Mariana Bisti

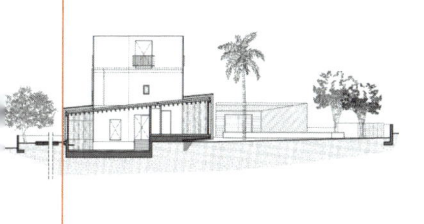

This renovation and contemporary extension of a listed house built in 1904 investigates notions of privacy and interaction among its tenants, as well as perceptions of scale and intimacy within a private dwelling. The spaces of the existing house are used as communal areas, including for food preparation. The two contemporary additions, whose outer shells remain continuously perceptible from within, include sleeping quarters, bathing and exercise areas.

House 0410
› NICOSIA, CYPRUS
2018/2019-2022
Single house · 209m²
› **Marios Christodoulides**
Marios Christodoulides
Marios Christodoulides & Miranda Christou (Private)
© Christos Papantoniou

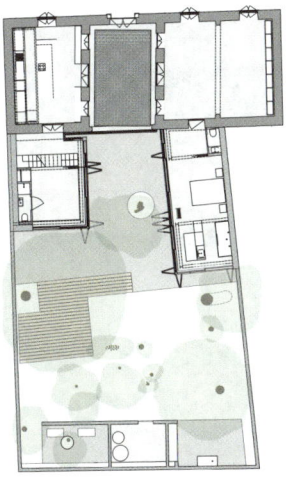

The project focuses on the evolution of the traditional courtyard. It is organized in a way that the interior and the exterior, the natural and artificial environments merge together in fluid sequences of spaces and paths. The peripheral network of courtyards, the bioclimatic behavior of the house, the vivid playfulness of the ins and outs, the multiple spatial layering and depths contribute to the social and environmental behavior of the building.

Living in 'Aphrodite'
› NICOSIA, CYPRUS
2017/2020-2022
Single house · 500m² · 1,750€/m²
› **Yiorgos Hadjichristou**
Yiorgos Hadjichristou
Tonia Bayada, Vasilis Vasiloudes (Private)
© Kyriaki Christofidou.JPG

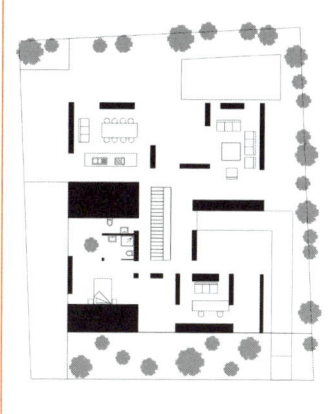

On a symbolic site adjacent to the fenced "green line" that crosses the island, the project gathers the formerly dispersed municipal departments into one building. Archaeological excavations revealed antiquities dating back to the Copper Age, leading to a prolonged design process from which the current project evolved. Offices for the city administration, weddings and planning combine with spaces extending the given brief: a panoramic walkway, a room open to the sky, shaded outdoor spaces and a multi-use hall for events outside office hours. The aim is to engage the civic building within a democratic space open for use, permeable to pedestrians and allowing for an exchange of views, literally and metaphorically.

Nicosia Municipality Town Hall
› **NICOSIA, CYPRUS**
 2015/2020-2023
 Government & Civic · 6,000m² · 2,350€/m²
› **Irwin Kritioti Architecture**
 Richard Dickon Irwin, Margarita Kritioti
 Nicosia Municipality (Public)
 © George Rahmatoulin

The house is built on the traces of a ruined building in a high-density refugee settlement. The restrictive building regulations applied in these sites indicate a complex condition, raising questions about their readjustment to contemporary ways of residential living. An open dialogue is developed between the building and the existing urban landscape that offers a vast range of spatial and visual conditions.

Domus Laetitiae / House in a Refugee Settlement
› **NICOSIA, CYPRUS**
 2019/2021-2022
 Single house · 164m² · 1,000€/m²
› **Studio Kyriakos Miltiadou**
 Kyriakos Miltiadou
 Stylianos Solomou (Private)
 © Maria Efthymiou

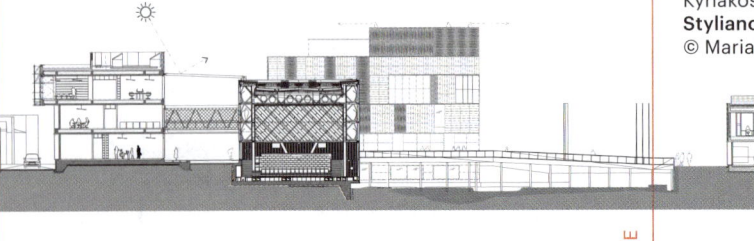

502

From
SANTA CRUZ
DE TENERIFE
Spain
28°27'27"N - 16°15'20"W

El Tanque Garden is the ecological restoration of a post-industrial area that endows the Cabo Llanos neighborhood of Santa Cruz de Tenerife with its first green public space. Created around a former oil refinery tank, reused as a cultural space since 1997 and protected industrial heritage since 2014, this banana tree garden recalls the agricultural landscape prior to industrialization, staging the city as a place of coexistence of different times, cultures and sensibilities that have shaped the identity of Santa Cruz de Tenerife. What used to be contaminated underused land, though part of a protected heritage compound, is now a leafy garden, offering a public space for social cohesion, reconnection with nature and cultural heritage.

Before

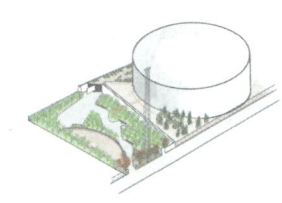

After

El Tanque Garden
› **SANTA CRUZ DE TENERIFE, SPAIN**
2022/2021-2022
Landscape · 2,563m² · 188€/m²
› **Fernando Menis**
Fernando Menis
Consejería de Educación, Universidades, Cultura y Deportes del Gobierno de las Islas Canarias, Dirección General de Patrimonio Cultural (The Government of the Canary Islands) (Public)
© Simona Rota

504

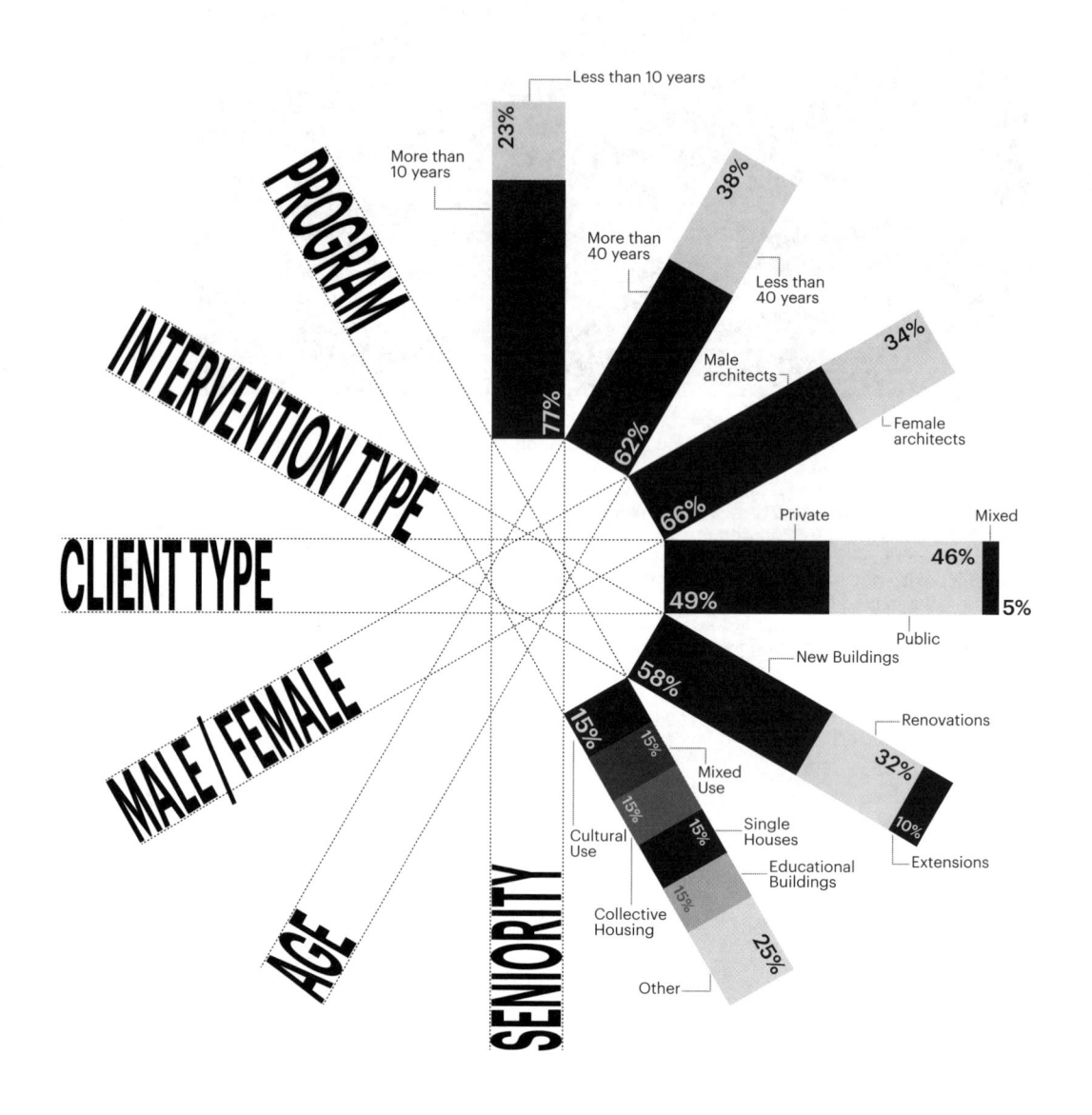

EPILOGUE

Bringing the Conversations Around

The works in this book represent only a portion of what has been built in Europe over the last two years. They have been deemed outstanding for numerous reasons and deserve special attention as they improve different aspects of the world we live in and thus become conversation starters.

The awards ceremony in the Barcelona Pavilion, the talks, the exhibition, the documentary and this publication are the starting point for many activities that aim to improve the conditions of our surroundings. This is possible by exchanging know-how throughout Europe and beyond and by discussing topics that have an impact on each and every one of us living on Earth as well as on the planet itself.

- A total of 456 studios and 1,116 people are the creators of these works, 62% of whom are over 40 years old. The most experienced architect was born in 1937 while the youngest was born in 2000 and 77% of the studios where these people work have been around for more than 10 years.
- 66% of the architects are men and 34% are women.
- 49% of the works have been developed for private clients, 46% are commissioned by public bodies and 5% by a public-private partnership.
- 58% are new buildings, 32% are the result of renovating what is already there and 10% involve extensions.
- 28% of these works can be found in well-established urban areas, 26% in peripheries, 22% in historic centres, 14% in rural areas and 10% in industrial parts of cities and towns.
- Mixed use, cultural use, single houses, collective housing and educational buildings each account for approximately 15% of the works, constituting 75% of the total.
- The longest design required 17 years to be built, while the average is 4 years. Several works, however, have taken less than a year to be conceptualised and built.

These partial figures, the group of works that have been built, the jury proceedings, the texts from this publication, the digital archive, the videos and the exhibitions all show certain trends that can be compared to previous years and help spark conversations. The Out & About programme also helps stimulate dialogue. This programme opens the doors of the shortlisted works so that everybody can get to know more about them with the architects, clients and people involved. The travelling exhibition, which comes in various formats, and the archive that has taken shape since 1988 strengthen the local conversations about the role of architecture and architects, the social and ecological opportunities, policymaking, how urban and rural areas change and relate, and much more. These conversations have become a pillar in order to advance towards a shared culture of architecture. Next year, Architecture & the Media will continue the debate on how the media plays a role in portraying architecture while the collaboration with the LINA architecture platform will open up an array of visions on architecture. This will provide numerous opportunities to a broad diversity of contributors who are merging with the organisation of the Young Talent Award, while the start of the following cycle of the Architecture and Emerging Award will help shape a continuous and common legacy together. The EUmies Awards are built by each and every person in Europe and are attentively observed by those beyond. Therefore, we all have an amazing responsibility. We thank you all and we will continue counting on you.

Ivan Blasi
Director EUmies Awards

CONVERSATIONS AND DEBATES

EXHIBITIONS

CEREMONY

VISITS

510

COLOPHON

Works per countries

ALBANIA

Eco Park Durres (1st Phase)
Durres, Albania
Casanova+Hernandez Architecten
» 314 / p. 464

Meteor Public Space
Durres, Albania
IXI architecture
» 316 / p. 465

Embassy of Peace
Tirana, Albania
AVatelier
» 319 / p. 467

Lasgush Poradeci. Secondary School
Tirana, Albania
ASArchitects
» 315 / p. 465

National Theatre of Opera, Ballet and Popular Ensemble
Tirana, Albania
Atelier 4
» 317 / p. 466

Pyramid of Tirana
Tirana, Albania
iRI, MVRDV
» 318 / p. 466

Tirana Business Centre
Tirana, Albania
Smart Studio
» 320 / p. 467

AUSTRIA

Possibility Space instead of Building Waste
Bergheim, Austria
smartvoll Architekten
» 171 / p. 258

City Boathouse
Graz, Austria
KUESS Architektur
» 176 / p. 260

Kiubo
Graz, Austria
Hofrichter-Ritter Architekten
» 175 / p. 260

Mortuary
Kematen an der Krems, Austria
Moser und Hager Architekten
» 173 / p. 259

Steirereck at Pogusch
Pogusch, Austria
PPAG architects
» 174 / p. 259

New Mozarteum Foyers
Salzburg, Austria
maria flöckner und hermann schnöll
» 172 / p. 258

Cultural Pavilion Semmering
Semmering, Austria
Mostlikely Architecture
» 177 / p. 260

Locknbauer Winery
Tieschen, Austria
Mascha.Ritter
» 178 / p. 261

General Renovation of the Austrian Parliament
Vienna, Austria
Jabornegg & Pálffy
» 182 / p. 270

IKEA Vienna Western Station / IKEA – the Good Neighbour in the City
Vienna, Austria
querkraft architekten
» 180 / p. 262

Museum Heidi Horten Collection
Vienna, Austria
the next ENTERprise Architects
» 183 / p. 271

Social Housing Aspern H4
Vienna, Austria
WUP architektur
» 185 / p. 272

Terra Mater
Vienna, Austria
Berger + Parkkinen Architects
» 179 / p. 261

Townhouse Neubaugasse
Vienna, Austria
PSLA Architekten
» 181 / p. 266

Triiiple Towers
Vienna, Austria
Henke Schreieck Architekten
» 184 / p. 271

BELGIUM

Brussels Beer Project
Anderlecht, Belgium
OFFICE Kersten Geers David Van Severen
» 107 / p. 185

Open Air Swimming Pool Flow
Anderlecht, Belgium
Pool is Cool, Decoratelier Jozef Wouters
» 106 / p. 181

Het Steen
Antwerp, Belgium
noAarchitecten
» 110 / p. 190

Hospital ZNA Cadix
Antwerp, Belgium
Robbrecht en Daem architecten,
VK architects+engineers
» 111 / p. 194

Bruges Meeting & Convention Centre
Bruges, Belgium
META architectuurbureau,
Souto Moura - Arquitectos
» 97 / p. 170

Wetlands - Chevetogne
Chevetogne, Belgium
Atelier Paysage
» 114 / p. 196

WORKS PER COUNTRIES

Fire Station, Multi-Purpose Space, and Emergency Housing
Dilbeek, Belgium
Bureau Bouwtechniek, Studio SNCDA
» 104 / p. 176

Arthouse Timelab
Ghent, Belgium
a2o
» 101 / p. 173

Cohousing Jean
Ghent, Belgium
ectv architecten
» 102 / p. 174

Repurposing Winter Circus Mahy
Ghent, Belgium
aNNo architecten, Atelier Kempe Thill - Architects and Planners, Baro Architectuur, SumProject
» 100 / p. 173

Paddenbroek Educational Rural Centre
Gooik, Belgium
jo taillieu architecten
» 103 / p. 175

Share and Reuse Factory
Kortrijk, Belgium
ATAMA
» 98 / p. 171

Honkhuis - Small-Scale Assisted Living
Leuven, Belgium
360 architecten
» 112 / p. 195

Jtb House
Leuven, Belgium
BLAF architecten
» 113 / p. 195

Residence ARC
Liège, Belgium
Artau architectures
» 116 / p. 197

Amal Amjahid - Community Facility Along the Canal
Sint-Jans-Molenbeek/Molenbeek-Saint-Jean, Belgium
&bogdan
» 109 / p. 186

Duchesse. Reconversion of Industrial Buildings in Residential Units
Sint-Jans-Molenbeek/Molenbeek-Saint-Jean, Belgium
NOTAN OFFICE
» 108 / p. 185

Karreveld
Sint-Jans-Molenbeek/Molenbeek-Saint-Jean, Belgium
AgwA
» 105 / p. 180

BOSNIA-HERZEGOVINA

New Building of the Faculty of Architecture, Civil Engineering and Geodesy
Banja Luka, Bosnia - Herzegovina
4plus.arhitekti
» 236 / p. 332

The Pidris Chapel Interior
Gornji Vakuf-Uskoplje, Bosnia - Herzegovina
Josipa Skrobo
» 237 / p. 333

Hiža Mišljenova House
Puhovac, Bosnia - Herzegovina
Studio Entasis
» 240 / p. 334

Ivo Andrić's Birth House
Travnik, Bosnia - Herzegovina
Ledić arhitektura, Studio Zec
» 238 / p. 333

The House in Klanac
Zenica, Bosnia - Herzegovina
Studio Entasis
» 239 / p. 333

BULGARIA

Conservation, Restoration and Socialization of the Central Mineral Bath "Bankya"
Bankya, Bulgaria
Georgiev Design Studio
» 281 / p. 367

Buildings for Ethnographic Exibitions in the Cultural and Tourist Complex Chengene Skele
Burgas, Bulgaria
MOTTO architectural studio
» 285 / p. 369

Renovation of Aleko Konstantinov street
Burgas, Bulgaria
Urbana Architects
» 284 / p. 369

Cultural Information Centre "The Mill"
Karpachevo, Bulgaria
Studio Nada
» 283 / p. 368

MIR Office Building
Sofia, Bulgaria
bureau XII
» 282 / p. 367

Private House
Sozopol, Bulgaria
Simple Architecture
» 286 / p. 370

Campus 90
Varna, Bulgaria
E-Arch Studio
» 287 / p. 370

Karin Dom
Varna, Bulgaria
unas studio
» 288 / p. 371

CROATIA

Black Slavonian Eco Pig Farm
Cret Viljevski, Croatia
SKROZ
» 224 / p. 316

Kindergarten in Gornja Stubica
Gornja Stubica, Croatia
MVA - Mikelić Vreš Arhitekti
» 221 / p. 310

Tomac Winery
Jasterbarsko, Croatia
DVA ARHITEKTA
» 217 / p. 304

Lonja Wetlands Wildlife Observatories and Visitor Centre
Osekovo, Croatia
roth&čerina
» 222 / p. 311

Reconstruction of the Roman Theater
Pula, Croatia
Studio Emil Jurcan
» 234 / p. 331

Home for 'My Place Under the Sun'
Rijeka, Croatia
My Place Under the Sun Team
» 212 / p. 298

Reconstruction of Providur's Palace
Zadar, Croatia
AB Forum
» 235 / p. 332

Reconstruction and Extension of Primary School Ksaver Sandor Gjalski
Zagreb, Croatia
Studio BF
» 220 / p. 309

Riding Hall. Land Registry Department of the Municipal Civil Court
Zagreb, Croatia
MORE arhitekture
» 219 / p. 305

Community Sports Hall
Zlatar Bistrica, Croatia
NOP Studio
» 223 / p. 315

CYPRUS

The Koulas Project
Limassol, Cyprus
Alexis Papadopoulos Architectural Practice
» 357 / p. 499

Domus Laetitiae / House in a Refugee Settlement
Nicosia, Cyprus
Studio Kyriakos Miltiadou
» 361 / p. 500

COLOPHON

House 0410
Nicosia, Cyprus
Marios Christodoulides
» 358 / p. 499

Living in 'Aphrodite'
Nicosia, Cyprus
Yiorgos Hadjichristou
» 359 / p. 499

Nicosia Municipality Town Hall
Nicosia, Cyprus
Irwin Kritioti Architecture
» 360 / p. 500

Archeological Sites
Paphos, Cyprus
Simpraxis, Square
» 355 / p. 498

House in Olive Grove
Paphos, Cyprus
Vardas Studio
» 356 / p. 498

CZECH REPUBLIC

Kloboucká Lesní Company Headquarters
Brumov-Bylnice, Czech Republic
Mjölk architekti
» 152 / p. 225

Reconstruction of Pavilion Z
České Budějovice, Czech Republic
A8000
» 149 / p. 222

Research Library of South Bohemia Extension
České Budějovice, Czech Republic
Kuba & Pilař architekti
» 150 / p. 223

Lázně Bělohrad Town Hall
Lázně Bělohrad, Czech Republic
re:architekti
» 124 / p. 202

IGI Vratislavice - Library and Community Centre
Liberec, Czech Republic
atakarchitekti
» 122 / p. 201

Low-Threshold Club
Nová Paka, Czech Republic
atakarchitekti
» 123 / p. 201

Plato Contemporary Art Gallery
Ostrava, Czech Republic
KWK Promes
» 153 / p. 226

Gočár's Gallery in Pardubice
Pardubice, Czech Republic
TRANSAT architekti
» 125 / p. 202

Kunsthalle
Prague, Czech Republic
Schindler Seko architekti
» 121 / p. 200

DENMARK

New Aarch
Aarhus, Denmark
A. Enggaard, Aarhus School of Architecture, ADEPT, Danish Building and Property Agency, Rolvung og Brønsted Arkitekter, TriConsult, Vargo Nielsen Palle
» 36 / p. 80

Åben Brewery
Copenhagen, Denmark
pihlmann architects
» 43 / p. 84

House of Martial Arts
Copenhagen, Denmark
entasis
» 42 / p. 84

Egedammen Kindergarten
Gladsaxe, Denmark
BBP Arkitekter
» 41 / p. 83

Herning Folk High School
Herning, Denmark
HH Herning, SLETH
» 34 / p. 79

Codan – Office and Warehouse
Køge, Denmark
Johansen Skovsted Arkitekter
» 39 / p. 82

H.C. Andersen's House
Odense, Denmark
Kuma & Associates Europe
» 37 / p. 81

Flugt – Refugee Museum of Denmark
Oksbøl, Denmark
BIG - Bjarke Ingels Group
» 34 / p. 79

Stevns Klint Experience
Rødvig, Denmark
Kristine Jensens Landscape, Praksis
» 40 / p. 83

Faber's Factories
Ryslinge, Denmark
Arcgency
» 38 / p. 81

Ilulissat Icefjord Centre
Ilullisat, Denmark (Greenland)
Dorte Mandrup
» 1 / p. 41

ESTONIA

Mustjala Retirement Home and Daycare Centre
Mustjala, Estonia
molumba
» 25 / p. 69

Woodwork and Technology Centre in Rakvere
Rakvere, Estonia
KUU architects
» 21 / p. 64

Tondiraba Park
Tallinn, Estonia
AB Artes Terrae
» 15 / p. 59

Son of a Shingle – Vaksali Pedestrian Bridge and Underpasses
Tartu, Estonia
PART architects
» 33 / p. 74

Viimsi Artium
Viimsi, Estonia
KAVAKAVA
» 14 / p. 59

Restaurant O
Viljandi, Estonia
kuidas.works
» 31 / p. 73

FINLAND

Academy of Fine Arts, Mylly
Helsinki, Finland
JKMM Architects
» 18 / p. 61

Dance House Helsinki
Helsinki, Finland
ILO arkkitehdit, JKMM Architects
» 16 / p. 60

Hopealaakso Daycare Centre
Helsinki, Finland
AFKS Architects
» 20 / p. 63

Little Finlandia
Helsinki, Finland
Pikku-Finlandia Studio, Aalto University
» 17 / p. 61

Serlachius Art Sauna
Mänttä-Vilppula, Finland
BAX studio, Mendoza Partida, Planetary Architecture
» 4 / p. 44

Chappe Art House
Raseborg, Finland
JKMM Architects
» 13 / p. 58

Helsinki Airport Departures and Arrivals Building
Vantaa, Finland
ALA Architects
» 19 / p. 62

Ylivieska Church
Ylivieska, Finland
K2S Architects
» 3 / p. 44

FRANCE

Performance Hall and Open Air Amphitheatre
Béziers, France
K ARCHITECTURES
» 259 / p. 351

WORKS PER COUNTRIES

The Montlaur Nursery in Bonifacio
Bonifacio, France
Buzzo Spinelli
» 313 / p. 464

Ekko
Bordeaux, France
Duncan Lewis
» 228 / p. 327

UCPA Sport Station Bordeaux Brazza (The Sports Cathedral)
Bordeaux, France
NP2F
» 229 / p. 328

From Offices to Housing: 112 Paris Street
Boulogne-Billancourt, France
La Soda
» 135 / p. 210

The Forestry House
Carcassonne, France
PAUEM atelier
» 258 / p. 350

Extension and Reconversion of an Old Farm House Near the Gironde Estuary
Chenac-Saint-Seurin-d'Uzet, France
Anouk Migeon Architecte, Martin Migeon Architecture
» 200 / p. 285

8 Intermediate Social Housing Units
Gignac - la Nerthe, France
Atelier Régis Roudil Architectes
» 260 / p. 352

Média Library Charles Nègre
Grasse, France
Beaudouin Architectes, Ivry Serres Architecture
» 261 / p. 353

School in Heudebouville - Normandy
Heudebouville, France
HEMAA ARCHITECTES
» 132 / p. 207

The Orangery - B2 Block in Lyon Confluence
Lyon, France
Clément Vergély Architectes, Diener & Diener Architekten
» 202 / p. 286

Roof Extension for a Single-Family House
Malakoff, France
Forme
» 136 / p. 210

Le Pont des Arts – Cultural Pole
Marcq-en-Baroeul, France
HBAAT - HART BERTELOOT ARCHITECTURE TERRITOIRE,
V+ (Bureau Vers plus de bien-être)
» 96 / p. 169

Glass Blowing and Cultural Centre of Meisenthal
Meisenthal, France
FREAKS, SO-IL
» 146 / p. 217

Early Childhood Facilities and a Garden
Menucourt, France
Nicolas Simon Architectes
» 133 / p. 208

Jean Lamour Gymnasium
Nancy, France
Studiolada Architects
» 144 / p. 215

Learning Centre for polytechnic University
Palaiseau, France
DREAM, Nicolas Laisné Architectes, OXO architectes, Sou Fujimoto Architects
» 134 / p. 209

A Common House
Pantin, France
Plan Común
» 139 / p. 213

Morland Mixité Capitale
Paris, France
David Chipperfield Architects Gesellschaft von Architekten
» 138 / p. 212

Nursery 24-bed
Paris, France
Atelier Régis Roudil Architectes
» 137 / p. 211

The Good, the Bad and the Ugly - Artist's Studio
Saint Langis-lès-Mortagne, France
Didier Fiuza Faustino - Mésarchitecture
» 131 / p. 207

Refurbishment and Extension of a Community Swimming Pool
Saint-Méen-Le-Grand, France
RAUM
» 165 / p. 251

Rebirth of the Convent Saint-François
Sainte-Lucie-de-Tallano, France
Amelia Tavella Architectes
» 312 / p. 451

The Grand Bois House
Tassin-la-Demi-Lune, France
MBL architectes
» 201 / p. 286

T16
Toulouse, France
BAST
» 257 / p. 350

The Vendegies-sur-Écaillon Nursery School
Vendegies-sur-Écaillon, France
Studio RIJSEL
» 99 / p. 172

GEORGIA

Betania Forest Garden
Betania, Georgia
Ruderal
» 324 / p. 469

Tbilisi Urban Forest (Narikala Ridge Forest)
Tbilisi, Georgia
Ruderal
» 325 / p. 470

GERMANY

Ausbauhaus Südkreuz ("House to Be Extended")
Berlin, Germany
Praeger Richter Architekten
» 85 / p. 154

Blue Hour at Spreepark
Berlin, Germany
modulorbeat
» 89 / p. 160

Building Community Kurfürstenstrasse
Berlin, Germany
June14 Meyer-Grohbrügge & Chermayeff
» 84 / p. 150

Edge Suedkreuz Berlin
Berlin, Germany
TCHOBAN VOSS Architekten
» 86 / p. 155

Floating University Berlin
Berlin, Germany
Floating e.V. Association
» 87 / p. 156

Spore Initiative
Berlin, Germany
AFF Architekten
» 88 / p. 160

Study Pavilion on the Campus of the Technical University of Braunschweig
Braunschweig, Germany
Gustav Düsing, Büro Hacke
» 83 / p. 132

Woof & Skelle: Building Ensemble for Social Housing and Kindergarten | Ellener Hof
Bremen, Germany
ZRS Architekten Ingenieure
» 82 / p. 131

Machine Hall
Irschenhausen, Germany
Florian Nagler Architekten
» 167 / p. 255

Light Rail Tunnel
Karlsruhe, Germany
allmannwappner
» 147 / p. 218

Karl's Eye Pavilion
Kassel, Germany
Christoph Hesse Architects
» 120 / p. 200

Kunstraum Kassel
Kassel, Germany
Innauer Matt Architekten
» 119 / p. 199

COLOPHON

Dantebad II - Housing
Munich, Germany
Florian Nagler Architekten
» 168 / p. 256

Munich Volkstheater
Munich, Germany
LRO
» 169 / p. 257

Campusro
Rosenheim, Germany
ACMS Architekten
» 170 / p. 257

Extension Starnberg District Office
Starnberg, Germany
Auer Weber Assoziierte
» 166 / p. 255

Calwer Passage
Stuttgart, Germany
ingenhoven associates
» 148 / p. 222

Rieckshof Photo Studio
Uckermark, Germany
HELGA BLOCKSDORF / ARCHITEKTUR
» 90 / p. 161

New Construction of Kreisarchiv Viersen
Viersen, Germany
DGM Architekten
» 117 / p. 198

Reorganization and Refurbishment of Leeste Cooperative Comprehensive School
Weyhe, Germany
REMKE PARTNER INNENARCHITEKTEN mbB
» 81 / p. 131

Bob Campus
Wuppertal, Germany
raumwerk.architekten
» 118 / p. 198

GREECE

Louria
Agairia, Greece
Kometka Architecture Studio, react architects
» 352 / p. 493

Art 1 Offices
Athens, Greece
Neiheiser Argyros
» 348 / p. 491

Ignatiou Apartment
Athens, Greece
Point Supreme
» 345 / p. 489

The Seashore Rise
Glyfada, Greece
314 Architecture Studio
» 346 / p. 489

Vacation Garden with a Room
Kea, Greece
Alexandros Fotakis Architecture
» 349 / p. 491

Element – New Office Building
Marousi, Greece
RS SPARCH
» 347 / p. 490

Vacation House in an Oliveyard
Meganisi, Greece
Hiboux architecture
» 344 / p. 488

Latypi Residence
Mykonos, Greece
A31 ARCHITECTURE CONSTRUCTION
» 353 / p. 493

Liknon
Samos, Greece
K-Studio
» 354 / p. 494

Xerolithi
Serifos, Greece
Sinas Architects
» 351 / p. 492

Anatolia Elementary School
Thessaloniki, Greece
Morpho Papanikolaou - SPARCH architects
» 323 / p. 469

Revelation and Highlighting of Thessaloniki's Monumental Axis
Thessaloniki, Greece
MAKRIDIS ASSOCIATES
» 322 / p. 468

The Regeneration and Reinterpretation of the Agora Modiano Listed Monument
Thessaloniki, Greece
Morpho Papanikolaou - SPARCH architects
» 321 / p. 468

Homa Vagia Boutique Hotel
Vagia, Greece
MOLD architects
» 350 / p. 492

HUNGARY

Reconstruction of the Lehel Tér Metro Station
Budapest, Hungary
Paragram, sporaarchitects
» 192 / p. 279

The New Office Building of Bánáti + Hartvig Architects
Budapest, Hungary
Bánáti + Hartvig Architects
» 191 / p. 278

Trendo11 Apartment Building
Budapest, Hungary
LAB5 architects
» 190 / p. 278

Vizafogó Ecopark and Pavilion
Budapest, Hungary
Archikon, Objekt
» 193 / p. 279

Zsuzsanna Kossuth Building of the Faculty of Health Sciences, Semmelweis University
Budapest, Hungary
Studio Fragment
» 195 / p. 281

Nest Reformed Kindergarten in Debrecen
Debrecen, Hungary
Bíró és Társa Építésziroda
» 196 / p. 281

Zalacsány Wellness Pavilion
Kehidakustány, Hungary
Archikon
» 186 / p. 272

The Greek Catholic Museum of Nyíregyháza
Nyíregyháza, Hungary
Balázs Mihály Építész Muterme, dmb műterem
» 197 / p. 282

New Market Hall of Pécs
Pécs, Hungary
GETTO plan, SZTR studio
» 225 / p. 320

Transformation of a 100-year-old Fruit Storage Building
Szentendre, Hungary
arkt studio, projectroom
» 194 / p. 280

Summer House
Tihany, Hungary
Rapa Architects
» 189 / p. 277

IRELAND

Ballyblake House
Ballyblake, Ireland
Steve Larkin Architects
» 63 / p. 112

Middleton Park Gate Lodge
Castletown Geoghegan, Ireland
TAKA
» 62 / p. 111

Passage House
Cork, Ireland
O'Donnell + Tuomey
» 61 / p. 111

Annesley Gardens
Dublin, Ireland
Metropolitan Workshop
» 69 / p. 115

Bottleworks
Dublin, Ireland
Henry J Lyons
» 72 / p. 121

WORKS PER COUNTRIES

Dominick Hall
Dublin, Ireland
Cotter & Naessens Architects, Denis Byrne Architects
» 68 / p. 114

Electricity Supply Board Headquarters
Dublin, Ireland
Grafton Architects, O'Mahony Pike Architects
» 71 / p. 120

Ladyswell Square
Dublin, Ireland
ABK Architects
» 65 / p. 113

O'Devaney Gardens Regeneration Phase 1
Dublin, Ireland
Dublin City Council - City Architects Department
» 66 / p. 113

Printing House Square
Dublin, Ireland
McCullough Mulvin Architects, O'Mahony Pike Architects
» 70 / p. 119

Printmaking Studio, Grangegorman
Dublin, Ireland
Plus Architecture, Scullion Architects
» 67 / p. 114

Writer's Room
Dublin, Ireland
Clancy Moore
» 73 / p. 121

The Thatch
Kildare, Ireland
Karen Brownlee Architects
» 64 / p. 112

ITALY

Threshold and Treasure / Atipografia
Arzignano, Italy
AMAA - Collaborative Architecture Office For Research And Development
» 208 / p. 289

Bivouac Fanton
Auronzo di Cadore, Italy
DEMOGO studio di architettura
» 209 / p. 290

Fieldhouse: Sports Amenity Facility at the Base of Mount Corno
Bolzano, Italy
MoDusArchitects
» 207 / p. 289

The Hole with the House Around
Cambiano, Italy
Elastico Farm
» 231 / p. 329

Palazzo dei Diamanti Renovation, Restoration and Redevelopment
Ferrara, Italy
Labics
» 233 / p. 331

San Giacomo Apostolo Church and Parish Complex
Ferrara, Italy
Miralles Tagliabue EMBT
» 232 / p. 330

Wood and Straw House
Laveno Mombello, Italy
Studio Albori
» 203 / p. 287

Affordable Residential Towers
Milan, Italy
C+S Architects
» 204 / p. 287

Art Museum of Fondazione Luigi Rovati
Milan, Italy
Mario Cucinella Architects
» 206 / p. 288

Luxottica Digital Factory
Milan, Italy
Park Associati
» 205 / p. 288

Anonima Agricola
Orbetello, Italy
Captcha Architecture
» 262 / p. 257

Camplus San Pietro
Rome, Italy
Roselli Architetti Associati
» 263 / p. 258

Chronicle in Stone
Turin, Italy
Ergys Krisiko Studio, MATT ARCHITECT & ASSOCIATES
» 230 / p. 329

KOSOVO

SHM House
Gremnik, Kosovo
G + A Architects
» 271 / p. 362

AMC Multimedia
Pristina, Kosovo
Maden Group
» 273 / p. 363

Prishtina Business Centre
Pristina, Kosovo
LSN Architects
» 272 / p. 362

LATVIA

Social Services Centre Perle
Cēsis, Latvia
ĒTER
» 30 / p. 72

Avoti Office Building
Lizums, Latvia
MADE ARHITEKTI
» 32 / p. 73

Learning Centre in Mārupe
Marupe, Latvia
Good Pattern
» 26 / p. 69

Brewery 'Manufaktūra'
Riga, Latvia
SAMPLING
» 28 / p. 70

Ogre Central Library and Marriage Registry
Riga, Latvia
PBR
» 29 / p. 71

Ola Foundation
Riga, Latvia
UPB
» 27 / p. 70

Science Centre Vizium
Ventspils, Latvia
Arhitekta J. Pogas birojs, Audrius Ambrasas Architects
» 24 / p. 68

LITHUANIA

Nemunas Island Bridge-Plaza
Kaunas, Lithuania
About Architecture, Dominykas Daunys, Isora x Lozuraityte Studio
» 49 / p. 103

Žalgiris Arena Multifunctional Water Sports Centre
Kaunas, Lithuania
E. Miliūno studija
» 50 / p. 104

Aqua Urban Fabric Salos-1 in Svencele
Svencele, Lithuania
DO ARCHITECTS
» 48 / p. 102

FF2 Optics House
Vilnius, Lithuania
Isora x Lozuraityte Studio
» 53 / p. 106

House Krivis with Gallery
Vilnius, Lithuania
Studija Lape
» 57 / p. 108

Lojoteka. Educational Media Centre
Vilnius, Lithuania
INBLUM architects, Senamiesčio projektai
» 55 / p. 107

Museum of Urban Wooden Architecture
Vilnius, Lithuania
JSC Vilniaus Planas
» 58 / p. 108

COLOPHON

Pilaite High-School (Gymnasium)
Vilnius, Lithuania
DO ARCHITECTS
» 51 / p. 105

Reconstruction of Vilnius Central Post Office into ISM University
Vilnius, Lithuania
A2SM, Senojo miesto architektai
» 54 / p. 106

School Reconstruction Project
Vilnius, Lithuania
Senojo Miesto Architektai
» 56 / p. 107

Transformation of Soviet Kindergarten "Peledziukas"
Vilnius, Lithuania
DO ARCHITECTS
» 52 / p. 105

Family Retreat House Vasara
Zarasai, Lithuania
HEIMA architects
» 59 / p. 109

Multifunctional Hall on Lake Zarasas Island
Zarasai, Lithuania
Šarūno Kiaunės projektavimo studija
» 60 / p. 109

LUXEMBOURG

E22sspiu!
Esch-sur-Alzette, Luxembourg
2001
» 141 / p. 214

Lodging in Lasauvage
Lasauvage, Luxembourg
Anouck Pesch Architecte
» 140 / p. 213

Repairing Villa Kutter
Luxembourg, Luxembourg
DIANE HEIREND ARCHITECTES
» 143 / p. 215

Domaine Claude Bentz
Remich, Luxembourg
Studio Jil Bentz
» 145 / p. 216

Conversion of the Gonner House into a Shelter
Rumelange, Luxembourg
hsa - heisbourg strotz architectes
» 142 / p. 214

MALTA

Casa Bottega
Valletta, Malta
Chris Briffa Architects
» 343 / p. 488

MONTENEGRO

Visitor Centre "Đalovića Pećina"
Bijelo Polje, Montenegro
ARHINGinzenjering
» 270 / p. 361

Betula Design Centre
Kotor, Montenegro
Studio Synthesis architecture & design
» 266 / p. 359

Family House
Kotor, Montenegro
BiroVIA
» 265 / p. 359

House Lepetane
Kotor, Montenegro
Enforma
» 264 / p. 358

Bussiness Centre "Glosarij"
Podgorica, Montenegro
Studio GRAD
» 268 / p. 360

Montenegrin Academy of Sciences and Arts
Podgorica, Montenegro
Studio GRAD
» 269 / p. 361

Primary School "Novka Ubovic"
Podgorica, Montenegro
BIRO 81000
» 267 / p. 360

NORTH MACEDONIA

BB House
Skopje, North Macedonia
BINA - Bureau of Inventive Architecture
» 279 / p. 366

CHP House
Skopje, North Macedonia
Attika Architects, Volart
» 277 / p. 365

MAH House
Skopje, North Macedonia
PROXY
» 275 / p. 364

May Apartments
Skopje, North Macedonia
BMA - Besian Mehmeti Architects
» 276 / p. 364

Showroom and Distribution Centre with Warehouse Balkanija
Skopje, North Macedonia
Syndicate Studio
» 278 / p. 365

Volkovo Kindergarten
Skopje, North Macedonia
Prima Inzenering
» 274 / p. 363

Villa for Contemporary Living
Veles, North Macedonia
Arhitektura Nova, Biro 60B
» 280 / p. 366

NORWAY

Haukeland Bybanen (Light-rail Train) Station
Bergen, Norway
3RW Arkitekter
» 5 / p. 47

Edholmen Marina and Restaurant
Fredrikstad, Norway
Jensen & Skodvin Architects
» 9 / p. 53

Weekend House Hjeltnes
Lindesnes, Norway
Knut Hjeltnes Sivilarkitekter
» 22 / p. 67

Extension to Raubergstølen Mountain Lodge
Lom, Norway
Jensen & Skodvin Architects
» 6 / p. 47

Munch Museum
Oslo, Norway
estudioHerreros
» 8 / p. 49

The New National Museum in Oslo
Oslo, Norway
Klaus Schuwerk Architect
» 7 / p. 48

POLAND

Targ Blonie / Food Market
Błonie, Poland
Pracownia Architektoniczna Aleksandra Wasilkowska
» 92 / p. 162

Footbridge for Bikes and Pedestrians
Dobczyce, Poland
Biuro Projektów Lewicki Łatak
» 157 / p. 244

LPP Fashion Lab - Fashion Laboratories Building
Gdansk, Poland
JEMS Architekci
» 47 / p. 102

Extension of the Building of the State Music School in Jastrzębie-Zdrój with a Concert Hall
Jastrzębie Zdrój, Poland
SLAS architekci
» 155 / p. 243

Public Multi-Family Housing Assembly
Łowicz, Poland
GDA ŁUKASZ GAJ, PA+U Rafał Mazur
» 91 / p. 161

Miedzianka Shaft
Miedzianka, Poland
KWK Promes
» 126 / p. 203

WORKS PER COUNTRIES

Redevelopment and Modernization of the National Library of Poland in Warsaw
Warsaw, Poland
KONIOR STUDIO, SOKKA
» 95 / p. 167

School for Children from Ukraine - Adaptation of the Floor in the Office Building
Warsaw, Poland
xystudio
» 94 / p. 166

Warsaw Breweries
Warsaw, Poland
JEMS Architekci
» 93 / p. 166

PORTUGAL

Praia do Canal Nature Resort
Aljezur, Portugal
Atelier Bugio
» 329 / p. 476

Monochrome Apartment
Aveiro, Portugal
João Carmo Simões Architecture+
» 289 / p. 373

House in Barreiro
Barreiro, Portugal
Aires Mateus e Associados
» 328 / p. 476

House in Grândola
Grândola, Portugal
Bak Gordon Arquitectos
» 330 / p. 477

Andaluz Houses
Lisboa, Portugal
PLCO arquitectos
» 327 / p. 475

House in Santa Isabel
Lisboa, Portugal
Domitianus Arquitetura
» 326 / p. 475

Escadinhas Footpaths
Matosinhos, Portugal
Paulo Moreira Architectures, Verkron
» 290 / p. 374

Square and Tourist Office
Piódão, Portugal
Branco del Rio
» 297 / p. 386

Campanhã Intermodal Terminal
Porto, Portugal
Brandão Costa Arquitectos
» 296 / p. 385

ESAP - Oporto School of Art
Porto, Portugal
Cannatá & Fernandes
» 295 / p. 384

General Silveira Building
Porto, Portugal
ATA Atelier, ENTRETEMPOS
» 291 / p. 378

Rehabilitation of Cinema Batalha
Porto, Portugal
Atelier 15
» 294 / p. 384

Rehabilitation of the Bolhão Market
Porto, Portugal
Nuno Valentim - Arquitectura e Reabilitação
» 293 / p. 383

Vincci Ponte de Ferro Hotel
Vila Nova de Gaia, Portugal
José Gigante Arquitecto
» 292 / p. 382

ROMANIA

Boemia Apartments
Bucharest, Romania
STARH - Birou de arhitectura (Florian & Iulia Stanciu)
» 252 / p. 341

Cities that Transform
Bucharest, Romania
VICEVERSA
» 251 / p. 341

Urban Spaces 5 / Apartment Building
Bucharest, Romania
ADN Birou de Arhitectura
» 250 / p. 340

Firefighters' Tower
Cluj-Napoca, Romania
Octav Silviu Olanescu Architecture Office, Vlad Sebastian Rusu Architecture Office
» 198 / p. 282

Constantin Brancusi Pavilion
Craiova, Romania
DSBA
» 248 / p. 338

House in Dumbrava Vlăsiei
Dumbrava Vlăsiei, Romania
Alt. Corp.
» 253 / p. 342

Piscu School Museum and Workshop
Piscu, Romania
ABRUPTARHITECTURA
» 249 / p. 339

F.I.D. Football as Infrastructure of Democracy
Timișoara, Romania
Atelier Olimpia Onci, Atelier VRAC, Casa Jakab Toffler, ISO Birou Arhitectura
» 227 / p. 325

Nursery. 1306 Plants for Timișoara
Timișoara, Romania
MAIO, Studio Nomadic, Studio Peisaj
» 226 / p. 321

SERBIA

Elementary School "Vera Miščević"
Belegiš, Serbia
Studio A&D Architects
» 242 / p. 335

Office Building, Multinational Company Campus NCR
Belgrade, Serbia
ProAspekt
» 243 / p. 335

Reconstruction of Fetislam Fortress
Kladovo, Serbia
KOTO
» 247 / p. 337

K26 Manhattan Concept
Kragujevac, Serbia
re:a.c.t, URED STUDIO
» 245 / p. 336

Regional Housing Programme for Refugees and Displaced Persons
Loznica, Serbia
1X2STUDIO
» 241 / p. 334

Mosque in Tupalla
Medvedja, Serbia
G + A Architects
» 246 / p. 337

Central
Pancevo, Serbia
Danilo Dangubic Architects
» 244 / p. 336

SLOVAKIA

Conversion of Jurkovič Heating Plant National Cultural Monument
Bratislava, Slovakia
DF CREATIVE GROUP, PAMARCH, Perspektiv
» 188 / p. 277

Reconstruction and Extension of the Slovak National Gallery
Bratislava, Slovakia
Architekti B.K.P.Š.
» 187 / p. 273

Jelšava Cabins
Jelšava, Slovakia
2021 Architects
» 158 / p. 245

City Hall Leopoldov
Leopoldov, Slovakia
zerozero
» 151 / p. 224

Uhrovec Castle – Operation Building
Uhrovské Podhradie, Slovakia
ô, Slovak Technical University - Faculty of Architecture and Design - Institute of History and Theory of Architecture and Restoration of Monuments
» 154 / p. 242

COLOPHON

Villa Bôrik
Žilina, Slovakia
LABAK, PLURAL
» 156 / p. 244

SLOVENIA

Bohinj Kindergarten
Bohinjska Bistrica, Slovenia
ARREA architecture, KAL A
» 210 / p. 294

A House for Modest Residence
Litija, Slovenia
MKutin arhitektura, Skupaj arhitekti
» 215 / p. 299

Affordable Housing Neighbourhood Novo Brdo
Ljubljana, Slovenia
Dekleva Gregorič Architects
» 211 / p. 298

Cukrarna
Ljubljana, Slovenia
Scapelab
» 214 / p. 299

Open Library
Ljubljana, Slovenia
ARP studio
» 213 / p. 298

Revitalization of Old Glassworks and Surrounding Urban Areas in Old Town of Ptuj
Ptuj, Slovenia
Elementarna, Kolektiv Tektonika
» 218 / p. 304

Covering the Remains of the Church of St. John the Baptist in the Žiče Charterhouse
Stare Slemene, Slovenia
MEDPROSTOR arhitekturni atelje
» 216 / p. 300

SPAIN

Gabriel García Márquez Library
Barcelona, Spain
SUMA Arquitectura
» 310 / p. 434

La Carboneria (Casa Tarragó). The Rehabilitation of a Historic Barcelona Residential Building
Barcelona, Spain
Office for Strategic Spaces (OSS)
» 307 / p. 432

Llacuna Residential Building
Barcelona, Spain
ARQUITECTURA-G
» 311 / p. 450

Pallars 180
Barcelona, Spain
BAAS arquitectura
» 309 / p. 433

Passeig de Gràcia 109-111. Mandarin Residences & Casa Seat
Barcelona, Spain
OAB Office of Architecture in Barcelona
» 308 / p. 433

Interpretation Centre Castromaior
Castromaior, Spain
Carlos Pita
» 255 / p. 345

Municipal Pools
Castromonte, Spain
Óscar Miguel Ares. Contextos de Arquitectura y Urbanismo
» 298 / p. 402

House-Factory Natura Bissé
Cerdanyola del Vallès, Spain
TDB ARQUITECTURA
» 306 / p. 432

Villa B
Ciutadella de Menorca, Spain
OOPEAA Office for Peripheral Architecture
» 341 / p. 487

Córdoba Public Library
Córdoba, Spain
Paredes Pedrosa Arquitectos
» 335 / p. 480

Wildlife Observatory in Los Pedroches
Córdoba, Spain
Rafael de La-Hoz Arquitectos
» 337 / p. 481

Day Centre for Young People with Autism Spectrum Disorder
Derio, Spain
AV62 Arquitectos
» 256 / p. 346

Rehabilitation and Expansion of the Town Hall of Fuentes de Andalucía
Fuentes de Andalucía, Spain
Laguillo Arquitectos
» 334 / p. 479

Social Housing 1737
Gavà, Spain
HARQUITECTES
» 303 / p. 427

Landscape Adaptation and Intervention in the Almadraba of Nueva Umbría
Lepe, Spain
Sol89
» 331 / p. 478

Toni Catany International Photography Centre
Llucmajor, Spain
mateo arquitectura
» 339 / p. 482

Lascala. NSA6 100 Social Housing
Madrid, Spain
MADhel, MARMOLBRAVO
» 300 / p. 407

Reggio School
Madrid, Spain
Andrés Jaque - Office for Political Innovation
» 301 / p. 408

New Faculty of Psychology and Speech Therapy
Málaga, Spain
LLPS Arquitectos
» 336 / p. 481

House in Mojácar
Mojácar, Spain
Alberto Campo Baeza, Modesto Sánchez Morales
» 338 / p. 482

El Roser Social Centre
Reus, Spain
Gallego Arquitectura, Josep Ferrando Architecture
» 302 / p. 426

Sports Hall "La Unión"
San José de la Rinconada, Spain
MLOPEZ arquitectos, NGNP Arquitectos
» 332 / p. 478

Garden House Extension and Reform in Between. In Between Houses, in Between Trees
Sant Cugat del Vallès, Spain
BAILORULL
» 305 / p. 431

40 Social Apartments for Rent
Sant Feliu de Llobregat, Spain
MAIO
» 304 / p. 431

El Tanque Garden
Santa Cruz de Tenerife, Spain
Fernando Menis
» 362 / p. 503

Fontán Building
Santiago de Compostela, Spain
Perea, Suárez y Torrelo, Arquitectos
» 254 / p. 345

Synapse House
Seville, Spain
Baum Lab
» 333 / p. 479

Living in Lime - 42 Social Housing
Son Servera, Spain
peris+toral.arquitectes
» 340 / p. 483

Art School of Valladolid
Valladolid, Spain
estudio Primitivo González - e.G.a
» 299 / p. 406

SWEDEN

Merkurhuset
Gothenburg, Sweden
Bornstein Lyckefors Arkitekter - NOW: Olsson Lyckefors Arkitektur
» 23 / p. 67

WORKS PER COUNTRIES

Hage
Lund, Sweden
Brendeland & Kristoffersen architects, Price & Myers
» 46 / p. 86

Gjuteriet
Malmö, Sweden
Kjellander Sjöberg
» 44 / p. 85

Twelve Houses
Malmö, Sweden
Förstberg Ling
» 45 / p. 85

Sara Cultural Centre
Skellefteå, Sweden
White arkitekter
» 2 / p. 43

Liljevalchs+
Stockholm, Sweden
Wingårdh Arkitektkontor
» 11 / p. 54

Meeting Place Mariatorget - St Pauls Church
Stockholm, Sweden
Spridd
» 10 / p. 53

House on a Hill
Värmdö, Sweden
Tham & Videgård
» 12 / p. 58

THE NETHERLANDS

Art Pavilion M.
Almere, The Netherlands
Studio Ossidiana
» 80 / p. 127

De Warren Cooperative Housing
Amsterdam, The Netherlands
Natrufied architecture
» 78 / p. 125

Haut Amsterdam
Amsterdam, The Netherlands
Team V Architectuur
» 76 / p. 123

Jonas
Amsterdam, The Netherlands
Orange Architects
» 77 / p. 124

Renovation 94 Houses Van der Pekbuurt Amsterdam
Amsterdam, The Netherlands
Ibelings van Tilburg Architecten
» 75 / p. 123

Forest Bath Housing
Eindhoven, The Netherlands
Gaaga
» 115 / p. 197

Museum Singer Laren
Laren, The Netherlands
Bedaux de Brouwer Architecten
» 79 / p. 126

Little C
Rotterdam, The Netherlands
CULD (JVST + Juurlink & Geluk), INBO
» 74 / p. 122

TUNISIA

The Screen
Tunis, Tunisia
ARK-architecture, AUDA
» 342 / p. 487

UKRAINE

Katerynoslavski Residential Complex
Dnipro, Ukraine
Filimonov&Kashirina Architects
» 164 / p. 249

Club Town 12
Ivano-Frankivsk, Ukraine
Atelier Architecture+, GaidART
» 163 / p. 249

Co-haty – Pilot Project of Adaptation of a Vacant Dormitory for IDP Housing
Ivano-Frankivsk, Ukraine
METALAB, Urban Curators
» 162 / p. 248

Fayna Town (Stage 5)
Kyiv, Ukraine
Archimatika
» 127 / p. 203

MOT (Module of Temporality)
Kyiv, Ukraine
balbek bureau
» 129 / p. 204

Reitarska Circle
Kyiv, Ukraine
Emil Dervish
» 128 / p. 204

Dwelling House «Baltiyska Hall»
Lviv, Ukraine
SHEREMETA ARCHITECT GROUP
» 159 / p. 246

Office Centre On 5 sq. Petrushevych
Lviv, Ukraine
Andriy Asanov architecture&design studio
» 160 / p. 246

Temporary housing for refugees "Unbroken Mothers»
Lviv, Ukraine
Sulyk Architects
» 161 / p. 247

Construction of the Centre of Government Services
Nova Kakhovka, Ukraine
Anna Kyrii Architectural Projecting Group
» 199 / p. 283

13 Detached Family Houses for IDP
Staryi Bykiv, Ukraine
District #1, Individual Intrepreneur Oleksandr I. Petrenko
» 130 / p. 205

COLOPHON

Works per studios

&bogdan
—Amal Amjahid – Community Facility Along the Canal
Oana Bogdan
» 109 / p. 186

1X2STUDIO
—Regional Housing Programme for Refugees and Displaced Persons
Zoran Abadic, Jelena Bogosavljevic
» 241 / p. 334

2001
—E22sspiu!
Philippe Nathan, Sergio Carvalho, Julie Lorang
» 141 / p. 214

2021 Architects
—Jelšava Cabins
Peter Lényi, Ondrej Marko, Marián Lucky, Lenka Borecká
» 158 / p. 245

314 Architecture Studio
—The Seashore Rise
Pavlos Chatziangelidis
» 346 / p. 489

360 architecten
—Honkhuis - Small-Scale Assisted Living
Jan Mannaerts, Kris Buyse, Greet Houben, Katrijn De Jonghe
» 112 / p. 195

3RW Arkitekter
—Haukeland Bybanen (Light-rail Train) Station
Sixten Rahlff, Espen Rahlff, Jerome Picard, Catarina De Almeida Brito, Reka Bankuti-Toht, Lars Cohen, Elida Mosquera
» 5 / p. 47

4plus.arhitekti
—New Building of the Faculty of Architecture, Civil Engineering and Geodesy
Sasha Chvoro, Malina Chvoro
» 236 / p. 332

A. Enggaard
—New Aarch
Gert Hedegaard
» 36 / p. 80

a2o
—Arthouse Timelab
Luc Vanmuysen, Jo Berben, Ingrid Mees, Bart Hoylaerts, Stefaan Evers, Wout Sorgeloos, Killian Nekeman, Jonas Knapen, Fréderique Hermans
» 101 / p. 173

A2SM
—Reconstruction of Vilnius Central Post Office into ISM University
Aurimas Sasnauskas, Sla Malenko, Joris Sykovas, Radvile Samackaite
» 54 / p. 106

A31 ARCHITECTURE CONSTRUCTION
—Latypi Residence
Praxitelis Kondylis
» 353 / p. 493

A8000
—Reconstruction of Pavilion Z
Martin Krupauer, Daniel Jeništa, Pavel Kvintus, Petr Hornát
» 149 / p. 222

Aalto University
—Little Finlandia
Pekka Heikkinen
» 17 / p. 61

Aarhus School of Architecture
—New Aarch
Kristine Leth, Torben Nielsen
» 36 / p. 80

AB Artes Terrae
—Tondiraba Park
Merle Karro-Kalberg, Heiki Kalberg, Tanel Breede
» 15 / p. 59

AB Forum
—Reconstruction of Providur's Palace
Iva Letilovic, Igor Pedisic
» 235 / p. 332

ABK Architects
—Ladyswell Square
John Parker, Criona Nangle
» 65 / p. 113

About Architecture
—Nemunas Island Bridge-Plaza
Vano Ksnelashvili
» 49 / p. 103

ABRUPTARHITECTURA
—Piscu School Museum and Workshop
Cosmin Pavel, Cristina Constantin
» 249 / p. 339

ACMS Architekten
—Campusro
Christian Schlüter-Vorwerg, Laura Heidelauf, Jonathan Vogt
» 170 / p. 257

ADEPT
—New Aarch
Martin Krogh, Martin Laursen, Anders Lonka, Simon Poulsen
» 36 / p. 80

ADN Birou de Arhitectura
—Urban Spaces 5 / Apartment Building
Bogdan Brădățeanu, Adrian Untaru, Andrei Șerbescu, Valentina Țigâră, Petra Bodea, Mihail Filipenco, Elena Zară
» 250 / p. 340

AFF Architekten
—Spore Initiative
Sven Froehlich, Martin Froehlich, Ulrike Dix, Monic Frahn
» 88 / p. 160

WORKS PER STUDIOS

AFKS Architects
—Hopealaakso Daycare Centre
Jari Frondelius, Jaakko Keppo, Juha Salmenperä, Mikko Liski, Erika Siikaoja, Soile Heikkinen
» 20 / p. 63

AgwA
—Karreveld
Harold Fallon, Benoît Vandenbulcke, Benoît Burquel, Hélène Joos, Nicky Vancaudenberg, Julien Delmotte, Thomas Montulet, Sofie Devriendt, Ali Ismail, Juliette Lucarain, Dorothée Fontignie, Hannelore Thomas, Marie Pirard
» 105 / p. 180

Aires Mateus e Associados
—House in Barreiro
Francisco Aires Mateus, Manuel Aires Mateus
» 328 / p. 476

ALA Architects
—Helsinki Airport Departures and Arrivals Building
Samuli Woolston, Antti Nousjoki, Juho Grönholm
» 19 / p. 62

Alberto Campo Baeza
—House in Mojacar
Alberto Campo Baeza
» 338 / p. 482

Alexandros Fotakis Architecture
—Vacation Garden with a Room
Alexandros Fotakis, Nicoletta Caputo
» 349 / p. 491

Alexis Papadopoulos Architectural Practice
—The Koulas Project
Alexis Papadopoulos, Maria Protou, Despo Anagiotou
» 357 / p. 499

allmannwappner
—Light Rail Tunnel
Manfred Sauer, Vasko Petkov, Christian von Arenstorff, Julia Behm, Katrin Bell, Christian Boland, Frank Karlheim, Marion Arnemann, Helge Birke, Tobias Bösl, Ivonne Eitel, Dimitra Giannikopoulou, Nicole Hansmeier, Eva Hartl, Xaver Heltai, Leila Hussein, Henrike Jahns, Eisuke Kawai, Sebastian Kordowich, Kerstin Liese-Schaich, Maria Mesa Izquierde, Marc Ottinger, Mirko Petzold, Bernine Pryor, Muslima Rafikova, Adrian Stadler, Olga Fraile Vasallo, Jakob Wolfrum, Rouven Würfel, Bertram Landwerlin
» 147 / p. 218

Alt. Corp.
—House in Dumbrava Vlăsiei
Cosmin Georgescu, Cosmin Gălățianu, Alexandru Cristian Beșliu, Octavian Bîrsan, Andrei Theodor Ioniță
» 253 / p. 342

AMAA - Collaborative Architecture Office for Research and Development
—Threshold and Treasure / Atipografia
Marcello Galiotto, Alessandra Rampazzo
» 208 / p. 289

Amelia Tavella Architectes
—Rebirth of the Convent Saint-François
Amelia Tavella
» 312 / p. 451

Andres Jaque - Office for Political Innovation
—Reggio School
Andrés Jaque
» 301 / p. 408

Andriy Asanov architecture&design studio
—Office Centre On 5 sq. Petrushevych
Andriy Asanov, Yuriy Nazaruk, Taras Salo, Vitalii Nesterenko, Taras Andrushko, Oleksandr Davydyuk
» 160 / p. 246

Anna Kyrii Architectural Projecting Group
—Construction of the Centre of Government Services
Anna Kyrii, Iryna Korzh, Maksym Fakas, Vitalii Nechai
» 199 / p. 283

aNNo architecten
—Repurposing Winter Circus Mahy
Stijn Cools
» 100 / p. 173

Anouck Pesch Architecte
—Lodging in Lasauvage
Anouck Pesch
» 140 / p. 213

Anouk Migeon Architecte
—Extension and Reconversion of an Old Farm House Near the Gironde Estuary
Anouk Migeon
» 200 / p. 285

Arcgency
—Faber's Factories
Mads Møller, Camilla Lemb Nielsen, David Kofod
» 38 / p. 81

Archikon
—Zalacsány Wellness Pavilion
Csaba Nagy, Károly Pólus, Ágnes Törös, Krisztina Timár-Major, Miklós Batta
» 186 / p. 272
—Vizafogó Ecopark and Pavilion
Csaba Nagy, Károly Pólus, Miklós Batta, Bianka Varga
» 193 / p. 279

Archimatika
—Fayna Town (Stage 5)
Aleksandr Popov, Dmytro Vasiljev, Mykola Morozov, Samir Khuder, Varvara Bebeshko, Anna Kornilova
» 127 / p. 203

Architekti B.K.P.Š.
—Reconstruction and Extension of the Slovak National Gallery
Martin Kusý II., Pavol Paňák, Martin Kusý III., Mária Michalič Kusá, Jana Paňáková
» 187 / p. 273

ARHINGinzenjering
—Visitor Centre "Đalovića Pećina"
Jasmina Kujović Salković, Elvira Alihodžić Muzurović
» 270 / p. 361

Arhitekta J. Pogas birojs
—Science Centre Vizium
Juris Poga, Astra Poga
» 24 / p. 68

Arhitektura Nova
—Villa for Contemporary Living
Marija Dimitrievska Cilakova
» 280 / p. 366

ARK-architecture
—The Screen
Bilel Khemakhem
» 342 / p. 487

arkt studio
—Transformation of a 100-year-old Fruit Storage Building
Gábor Fábián, Dénes Fajcsák, Veronika Juhász
» 194 / p. 280

ARP studio
—Open Library
Matjaž Bolčina, Ernest Milčinović, Jan Žonta
» 213 / p. 298

ARQUITECTURA-G
—Llacuna Residential Building
Aitor Fuentes Mendizabal, Jonathan Arnabat Vila, Igor Urdampilleta Plasencia, Jordi Ayala Bril
» 311 / p. 450

ARREA architecture
—Bohinj Kindergarten
Ana Jerman, Janja Šušnjar
» 210 / p. 294

Artau architectures
—Residence ARC
Vincent Thiry, Virginie Vinamont, Roland Coulon, Jocelyne Jacobs, Morgan Delvaux, Christophe Klubert
» 116 / p. 197

ASArchitects
—'Lasgush Poradeci' Secondary School
Ani Tola, Antonela Saliaj, Geri Bisha, Sonila Semini, Sabina Sheshi
» 315 / p. 465

COLOPHON

ATA Atelier
—General Silveira Building
Tiago Antero
» 291 / p. 378

atakarchitekti
—IGI Vratislavice – Library and Community Centre
Jiří Janďourek, Ondřej Novák
» 122 / p. 201
—Low-Threshold Club
Jana Janďourková Medlíková, Jiří Janďourek
» 123 / p. 201

ATAMA
—Share and Reuse Factory
Carolien Pasmans, Bram Aerts
» 98 / p. 171

Atelier 4
—National Theatre of Opera, Ballet and Popular Ensemble
Olsi Efthimi, Altin Premti, Alban Efthimi
» 294 / p. 466

Atelier 15
—Rehabilitation of Cinema Batalha
Alexandre Alves Costa, Sergio Fernandez, Miguel Ribeiro
» 317 / p. 384

Atelier Architecture+
—Club Town 12
Yaroslav Doroshenko
» 163 / p. 249

Atelier Bugio
—Praia do Canal Nature Resort
João Favila Menezes
» 329 / p. 476

Atelier Kempe Thill - architects and planners
—Repurposing Winter Circus Mahy
Oliver Thill, André Kempe
» 100 / p. 173

Atelier Olimpia Onci
—F.I.D. Football as Infrastructure of Democracy
Olimpia Onci-Isopescu
» 227 / p. 325

Atelier Paysage
—Wetlands – Chevetogne
Etienne Cellier
» 114 / p. 196

Atelier Régis Roudil Architectes
—Nursery 24-bed
Régis Roudil
» 137 / p. 211
—8 Intermediate Social Housing Units
Régis Roudil
» 260 / p. 352

Atelier VRAC
—F.I.D. Football as Infrastructure of Democracy
Cristian Andrei Bădescu, Zenaida Elena Florea
» 227 / p. 325

Attika Architects
—CHP House
Bojan Tasev, Nikola Tomevski, Simon Papesh
» 277 / p. 365

AUDA
—The Screen
Mohamed Khemakhem, Mohamed Nejib Saadallah
» 342 / p. 487

Audrius Ambrasas Architects
—Science Centre Vizium
Audrius Ambrasas, Vilma Adomonytė, Justas Jankauskas, Jonas Motiejūnas, Viktorija Rimkutė
» 24 / p. 68

Auer Weber Assoziierte
—Extension Starnberg District Office
» 166 / p. 255

AV62 Arquitectos
—Day Centre for Young People with Autism Spectrum Disorder
Juan Antonio Foraster
» 256 / p. 346

AVatelier
—Embassy of Peace
Armand Vokshi
» 319 / p. 467

BAAS arquitectura
—Pallars 180
Jordi Badia
» 309 / p. 433

BAILORULL
—Garden House Extension and Reform in Between. In Between Houses, in Between Trees
Manuel Bailo Esteve, Rosa Rull Bertran
» 305 / p. 431

Bak Gordon Arquitectos
—House in Grândola
Ricardo Bak Gordon
» 330 / p. 477

Balázs Mihály Építész Muterme
—The Greek Catholic Museum of Nyíregyháza
Mihály Balázs
» 197 / p. 282

balbek bureau
—MOT (Module of Temporality)
Slava Balbek, Alla Vitas-Zahargevska, Anastasiia Partyka, Nata Kurylenko
» 129 / p. 204

Bánáti + Hartvig Architects
—The New Office Building of Bánáti + Hartvig Architects
Béla Bánáti, Lajos Hartvig DLA, Vera Lőcsei
» 191 / p. 278

Baro Architectuur
—Repurposing Winter Circus Mahy
Geert Willemyns
» 100 / p. 173

BAST
—T16
» 257 / p. 350

Baum Lab
—Synapse House
Miguel Gentil Fernández, Marta Barrera Altemir, Javier Caro Domínguez
» 333 / p. 479

BAX studio
—Serlachius Art Sauna
Boris Bežan
» 4 / p. 44

BBP Arkitekter
—Egedammen Kindergarten
Ebbe Wæhrens
» 41 / p. 83

Beaudouin Architectes
—Média Library Charles Nègre
Emmanuelle Beaudouin, Laurent Beaudouin, Aurélie Husson
» 261 / p. 353

Bedaux de Brouwer Architecten
—Museum Singer Laren
Pieter Bedaux, Joyce Verstijnen, Dennis Schuurkes, Thomas Bedaux, Thom Hoevenaar, Cees de Rooij, Nick van Esch, Luuk Laurijsen, Martijn Rasenberg
» 79 / p. 126

Berger + Parkkinen Architects
—Terra Mater
Alfred Berger, Tiina Parkkinen
» 179 / p. 261

BIG - Bjarke Ingels Group
—Flugt – Refugee Museum of Denmark
Finn Nørkjær, Ole Elkjær-Larsen, Frederik Lyng, Bjarke Ingels, Frederik Skou Jensen
» 34 / p. 79

BINA - Bureau of Inventive Architecture
—BB House
Bekir Ademi, Amine Ademi
» 279 / p. 366

Biro 60B
—Villa for Contemporary Living
Elena Pazardzievska Ristovska
» 280 / p. 366

BIRO 81000
—Primary School "Novka Ubovic"
Ivan Jovićević, Dušan Đurović
» 267 / p. 360

Bíró és Társa Építésziroda
—Nest Reformed Kindergarten in Debrecen
Béla Bíró, Dániel Fodor, Ferenc Kállay, Béla Nagy
» 196 / p. 281

BiroVIA
—Family House
Verica Krstic, Vasilije Milunovic, Jelena Ivanovic Vojvodic
» 265 / p. 359

WORKS PER STUDIOS

Biuro Projektów Lewicki Łatak
—Footbridge for Bikes and Pedestrians
Kazimierz Łatak, Piotr Lewicki
» 157 / p. 244

BLAF architecten
—Jtb House
Lieven Nijs, Bart Vanden Driessche
» 113 / p. 195

BMA - Besian Mehmeti Architects
—May Apartments
Besian Mehmeti
» 276 / p. 364

Branco del Rio
—Square and Tourist Office
João Branco, Paula del Río
» 297 / p. 386

Brandão Costa Arquitectos
—Campanhã Intermodal Terminal
Nuno Brandão Costa
» 296 / p. 385

Brendeland & Kristoffersen architects
—Hage
Geir Brendeland, Olav Kristoffersen, Thomas Skinnemoen
» 46 / p. 86

Bureau Bouwtechniek
—Fire Station, Multi-Purpose Space, and Emergency Housing
» 104 / p. 176

bureau XII
—MIR Office Building
Milena Filcheva, Peter Torniov
» 282 / p. 367

Büro Hacke
—Study Pavilion on the Campus of the Technical University of Braunschweig
Max Hacke
» 83 / p. 132

Buzzo Spinelli
—The Montlaur Nursery in Bonifacio
Isabelle Buzzo, Jean-Philippe Spinelli
» 313 / p. 464

C+S Architects
—Affordable Residential Towers
Carlo Cappai, Maria Alessandra Segantini
» 204 / p. 287

Cannatà & Fernandes
—ESAP – Oporto School of Art
Michele Cannatà, Fátima Fernandes, João Carreira
» 295 / p. 384

Captcha Architecture
—Anonima Agricola
Margherita Marri, Jacopo Rosa
» 262 / p. 357

Carlos Pita
—Interpretation Centre Castromaior
Carlos Pita
» 255 / p. 345

Casa Jakab Toffler
—F.I.D. Football as Infrastructure of Democracy
Gabriel Aurel Boldiş, Laura Adela Borotea, Alexandru Ciobotă
» 227 / p. 325

Casanova+Hernandez Architecten
—Eco Park Durres (1st Phase)
Helena Casanova, Jesus Hernandez
» 314 / p. 464

Chris Briffa Architects
—Casa Bottega
Chris Briffa
» 343 / p. 488

Christoph Hesse Architects
—Karl's Eye Pavilion
Christoph Hesse, Michela Quadrelli
» 120 / p. 200

Clancy Moore
—Writer's Room
Andrew Clancy, Colm Moore
» 73 / p. 121

Clément Vergély Architectes
—The Orangery – B2 Block in Lyon Confluence
Clément Vergély, Stefan Jeske
» 202 / p. 286

Cotter & Naessens Architects
—Dominick Hall
David Naessens, Louise Cotter
» 68 / p. 114

CULD (JVST + Juurlink & Geluk)
—Little C
Cor Geluk, Jaakko van 't Spijker
» 74 / p. 122

Danilo Dangubic Architects
—Central
Danilo Dangubić
» 244 / p. 336

Danish Building and Property Agency
—New Aarch
Lisa Sørensen
» 36 / p. 80

David Chipperfield Architects Gesellschaft von Architekten
—Morland Mixité Capitale
David Chipperfield, Felger Christoph
» 138 / p. 212

Decoratelier Jozef Wouters
—Open Air Swimming Pool Flow
Jozef Wouters
» 106 / p. 181

Dekleva Gregorič Architects
—Affordable Housing Neighbourhood Novo Brdo
Lea Kovič, Tina Gregorič, Aljoša Dekleva
» 211 / p. 298

DEMOGO studio di architettura
—Bivouac Fanton
Simone Gobbo, Alberto Mottola, Davide De Marchi
» 209 / p. 290

Denis Byrne Architects
—Dominick Hall
Denis Byrne
» 68 / p. 114

DF CREATIVE GROUP
—Conversion of Jurkovič Heating Plant National Cultural Monument
Martin Paško, Zuzana Zacharová, Matúš Podskalický, Martina Michalková, Alexandra Havranová, Eva Bellákova
» 188 / p. 277

DGM Architekten
—New Construction of Kreisarchiv Viersen
Bernd Volkenannt
» 117 / p. 198

DIANE HEIREND ARCHITECTES
—"Repairing" Villa Kutter
Diane Heirend
» 143 / p. 215

Didier Fiuza Faustino - Mésarchitecture
—The Good, the Bad and the Ugly – Artist's Studio
Didier Fiuza Faustino, Mazoyer Pascal, Fabre Marie-Hélène
» 131 / p. 207

Diener & Diener Architekten
—The Orangery – B2 Block in Lyon Confluence
» 202 / p. 286

District #1
—13 Detached Family Houses for IDP
Andrii Kopylenko, Andrii Titarenko
» 130 / p. 205

dmb műterem
—The Greek Catholic Museum of Nyíregyháza
Dávid Török, Márton Nagy, Balázs Falvai
» 197 / p. 282

DO ARCHITECTS
—Aqua Urban Fabric Salos-1 in Svencele
Andre Baldisiute, Sabina Grincevičiūtė, Algimantas Neniškis, Kasparas Žiliukas, Gilma Teodora Gylytė, Ignas Uogintas, Gediminas Aismontas, Milda Gustainė, Justas Paicius, Emilija Deksnytė, Marija Steponavičiūtė, Grasilda Mintaučkytė, Laura Gaudutytė, Edvinas Skiestenis, Emilija Martinkevič
» 48 / p. 102

—Pilaite High-School (Gymnasium)
Andre Baldisiute, Sabina Grincevičiūtė, Algimantas Neniškis, Kasparas Žiliukas, Gilma Teodora Gylytė, Justas Paicius, Aurimas Lenktys, Solveiga Buozelyte, Karolis Grigaitis, Mikas Kauzonas, Gerda Nevulyte, Roberta Zvirblyte, Vytenis Stasiunas
» 51 / p. 105

—Transformation of Soviet Kindergarten "Peledziukas"
Andre Baldisiute, Sabina Grincevičiūtė,

Algimantas Neniškis, Julija Čiapaitė-Jurevičienė, Ignas Uogintas, Justina Jauniškytė, Domantas Baltrūnas, Karolina Čiplytė, Vadim Babij, Gilma Teodora Gylyte, Justas Paicius
» 52 / p. 105

Dominykas Daunys
—Nemunas Island Bridge-Plaza
Dominykas Daunys
» 49 / p. 103

Domitianus Arquitetura
—House in Santa Isabel
Paulo Tormenta Pinto, Rosa Maria Bastos
» 326 / p. 475

Dorte Mandrup
—Ilulissat Icefjord Centre
Dorte Mandrup-Poulsen
» 1 / p. 41

DREAM
—Learning Centre for polytechnic University
Dimitri Roussel
» 134 / p. 209

DSBA
—Constantin Brancusi Pavilion
Dorin Stefan
» 248 / p. 338

Dublin City Council - City Architects Department
—O'Devaney Gardens Regeneration Phase 1
Ali Grehan, Matt Shelton, Madeline Hallinan
» 66 / p. 113

Duncan Lewis
—Ekko
Duncan Lewis, Brigitte Cany Lewis, Isabelle Auriat
» 228 / p. 327

DVA ARHITEKTA
—Tomac Winery
Tomislav Curkovic, Zoran Zidaric
» 217 / p. 304

E-Arch Studio
—Campus 90
Martin Hristov, Galina Baleva-Hristova, Ina Dineva
» 287 / p. 370

E. Miliūno Studija
—Žalgiris Arena Multifunctional Water Sports Centre
Aurimas Ramanauskas, Vytautas Miliūnas, Vaidas Zabulionis
» 50 / p. 104

ectv Architecten
—Cohousing Jean
Els Claessens, Tania Vandenbussche
» 102 / p. 174

Elastico Farm
—The Hole with the House Around
Stefano Pujatti
» 231 / p. 329

Elementarna
—Revitalization of Old Glassworks and Surrounding Urban Areas in Old Town of Ptuj
Ambrož Bartol, Dominik Košak, Miha Munda, Rok Staudacher, Matevž Zalar, Samo Kralj
» 218 / p. 304

Emil Dervish
—Reitarska Circle
Emil Dervish
» 128 / p. 204

Enforma
—House Lepetane
Nikola Novakovic, Ana Mičić
» 264 / p. 358

entasis
—House of Martial Arts
Christian Cold, Signe Cold
» 42 / p. 84

ENTRETEMPOS
—General Silveira Building
Vitor Fernandes
» 291 / p. 378

Ergys Krisiko Studio
—Chronicle in Stone
Ergys Krisiko
» 230 / p. 329

estudio primitivo gonzález
—Art School of Valladolid
Primitivo Gonzalez, Noa González Cabrera, Ara González Cabrera
» 299 / p. 406

estudioHerreros
—Munch Museum
Juan Herreros, Jens Richter
» 8 / p. 49

ĒTER
—Social Services Centre Perle
Dagnija Smilga, Karlis Berzins, Niklavs Paegle
» 30 / p. 72

Fernando Menis
—El Tanque Garden
Fernando Menis
» 362 / p. 503

Filimonov&Kashirina Architects
—Katerynoslavski Residential Complex
Sergij Filimonov, Natalia Kashirina
» 164 / p. 249

Floating e.V. Association
—Floating University Berlin
Katherine Ball, Felix Wierschbitzki, Florian Stirnemann, Lorenz Kuschnig, Sarah Bovelett, Benjamin-Foerster, Jeanne Asrtup Chavaux
» 87 / p. 156

Florian Nagler Architekten
—Machine Hall
Florian Nagler
» 167 / p. 255

—Dantebad II - Housing
Florian Nagler
» 168 / p. 256

Forme
—Roof Extension for a Single-Family House
Clément Maitre, Robinson Neuville
» 136 / p. 210

Förstberg Ling
—Twelve Houses
Mikael Ling, Björn Förstberg
» 45 / p. 85

FREAKS
—Glass Blowing and Cultural Centre of Meisenthal
Yves Pasquet, Cyril Gauthier, Guillaume Aubry
» 146 / p. 217

G + A Architects
—Mosque in Tupalla
Arber Sadiki
» 246 / p. 337
—SHM House
Arber Sadiki
» 271 / p. 362

Gaaga
—Forest Bath Housing
Stevelink Esther, Arie Bergsma
» 115 / p. 197

GaidART
—Club Town 12
Volodymyr Gaidar
» 163 / p. 249

Gallego Arquitectura
—El Roser Social Centre
Xavier Gallego
» 302 / p. 426

GDA ŁUKASZ GAJ
—Public Multi-Family Housing Assembly
Łukasz Gaj
» 91 / p. 161

Georgiev Design Studio
—Conservation, Restoration and Socialization of the Central Mineral Bath "Bankya"
Chavdar Georgiev
» 281 / p. 367

GETTO plan
—New Market Hall of Pécs
Tamás Getto
» 225 / p. 320

Good Pattern
—Learning Centre in Mārupe
Guntis Zingis, Kristina Reinberga
» 26 / p. 69

Grafton Architects
—Electricity Supply Board Headquarters
Philippe O'Sullivan, Ger Carty, Yvonne Farrell, Shelley McNamara, Matt McCullagh, Donal O'Herlihy, Ivan O'Connell, Shane Twohig, Leah Hogan,

WORKS PER STUDIOS

Briain Moriarty, Eibhlín Ní Chathasaigh, James Rossa O'Hare, Kieran O'Brien, Simona Castelli, David Healy, Petrina Tierney, Alanah Doyle, Anne Henry, Aonghus Mc Donnell, Fiona Hughes, Steven Connolly, Brenda Leonard, Conor McHugh, Terry Murphy, Andrea Doyle, Alex Doran
» 71 / p. 120

Gustav Düsing
—Study Pavilion on the Campus of the Technical University of Braunschweig
Gustav Düsing
» 83 / p. 132

HARQUITECTES
—Social Housing 1737
David Lorente, Josep Ricart, Roger Tudó, Xavier Ros
» 303 / p. 427

HBAAT - Hart Berteloot Architecture Territoire
—Le Pont des Arts – Cultural Pole
Mathieu Berteloot, Heleen Hart
» 96 / p. 169

HEIMA architects
—Family Retreat House Vasara
Povilas Žakauskas, Povilas Daugis, Elena Gaidelytė, Rūta Kazenaitė
» 59 / p. 109

HELGA BLOCKSDORF / ARCHITEKTUR
—Rieckshof Photo Studio
Helga Blocksdorf
» 90 / p. 161

HEMAA ARCHITECTES
—School in Heudebouville – Normandy
Pierre Martin-Saint-Etienne, Charles Hesters
» 132 / p. 207

Henke Schreieck Architekten
—Triiiple Towers
Dieter Henke, Marta Schreieck
» 184 / p. 271

Henry J Lyons
—Bottleworks
Richard Doorly, Miriam Corcoran, Marc Golden
» 72 / p. 121

HH Herning
—Herning Folk High School
Anne Marie Mau, Jens Thomas Arnfred
» 34 / p. 79

Hiboux architecture
—Vacation House in an Oliveyard
Dimitris Theodoropoulos, Maria Tsigara, Maria Marianna Xyntaraki
» 344 / p. 488

Hofrichter-Ritter Architekten
—Kiubo
Gernot Ritter, Veronika Hofrichter-Ritter, Franz Stiegler-Hameter, Fabian Steinberger
» 175 / p. 260

hsa - heisbourg strotz architectes
—Conversion of the Gonner House into a Shelter
Michel Heisbourg, Bob Strotz
» 142 / p. 214

Ibelings van Tilburg Architecten
—Renovation 94 Houses Van der Pekbuurt Amsterdam
Marc Ibelings, Tim Schuijt
» 75 / p. 123

ILO arkkitehdit
—Dance House Helsinki
Kati Murtola, Pia Ilonen
» 16 / p. 60

INBLUM architects
—"Lojoteka". Educational Media Centre
Dmitrij Kudin, Laura Malcaitė, Marija Stonytė-Izdelé
» 55 / p. 107

INBO
—Little C
Bert van Breugel
» 74 / p. 122

Individual Intrepreneur Oleksandr I. Petrenko
—13 Detached Family Houses for IDP
Oleksandr Petrenko
» 130 / p. 205

ingenhoven associates
—Calwer Passage
Christoph Ingenhoven
» 148 / p. 222

Innauer Matt Architekten
—Kunstraum Kassel
Sven Matt, Markus Innauer
» 119 / p. 199

iRI
—Pyramid of Tirana
Agolli Gent
» 318 / p. 466

Irwin Kritioti Architecture
—Nicosia Municipality Town Hall
Richard Dickon Irwin, Margarita Kritioti
» 360 / p. 500

ISO Birou Arhitectura
—F.I.D. Football as Infrastructure of Democracy
Bogdan Liviu Isopescu
» 227 / p. 325

Isora x Lozuraityte Studio
—Nemunas Island Bridge-Plaza
Petras Išora-Lozuraitis
» 49 / p. 103
—FF2 Optics House
Petras Išora – Lozuraitis, Ona Lozuraitytė –Išorė
» 53 / p. 106

Ivry Serres Architecture
—Média Library Charles Nègre
Ivry Serres
» 261 / p. 353

IXI architecture
—Meteor Public Space
Saimir Kristo, Iva Guço, Xhoana Kristo, Iris Hyka
» 316 / p. 465

Jabornegg & Pálffy
—General Renovation of the Austrian Parliament
Christian Jabornegg, András Pálffy
» 182 / p. 270

JCS arch+
—Monochrome Apartment
João Carmo Simões, Daniela Sá
» 289 / p. 373

JEMS Architekci
—LPP Fashion Lab – Fashion Laboratories Building
Maciej Miłobędzki, Jerzy Szczepanik-Dzikowski, Marcin Sadowski, Zygmunt Borawski, Łukasz Kuciński, Katarzyna Kuźmińska, Maria Mermer, Grzegorz Moskała, Anna Świderska, Nina Wójcicka
» 47 / p. 102
—Warsaw Breweries
Paweł Majkusiak, Olgierd Jagiełło, Marek Moskal, Marcin Sadowski, Maciej Rydz, Grzegorz Artymiński, Izabela Bednarska, Zygmunt Borawski, Tytus Brzozowski, Mieszko Burmas, Małgorzata Charazińska, Łukasz Chaberka, Anna Dubois, Aleksandra Dutkowska, Marcin Giemza, Wojciech Gruszczyński, Michał Iwaniuk, Szamil Jachimczyk, Katarzyna Janczura, Rafał Jóźwiak, Radosław Kacprzak, Urszula Kos, Łukasz Krzesiak, Katarzyna Kuźmińska, Magdalena Litaszewska, Beata Momot, Grzegorz Moskała, Marta Najder, Bartłomiej Najman, Maciej Olczak, Mariusz Olszewski, Katarzyna Piotrowska, Maks Potapow, Agnieszka Rokicka, Aleksandra Rusin, Łukasz Stępnik, Bartosz Śniadowski, Marta Świątek-Piziorska, Anna Świderska, Mateusz Świętorzecki, Piotr Waleszkiewicz, Izabela Wencel, Marcin Zaremba, Agata Żak
» 93 / p. 166

Jensen & Skodvin Architects
—Extension to Raubergstølen Mountain Lodge
Jan Olav Jensen, Øystein Skorstad, Knut Borgen, Halvard Amble
» 6 / p. 47
—Edholmen Marina and Restaurant
Torunn Golberg, Jan Olav Jensen, Øystein Skorstad, Sigrid Moldestad, Knut Borgen, Thomas Knigge
» 9 / p. 53

JKMM Architects
—Chappe Art House
Asmo Jaaksi, Juha Mäki-Jyllilä, Samuli Miettinen, Teemu Toivio, Teemu Kurkela, Gerrie Bekhuis
» 13 / p. 58
—Dance House Helsinki
Asmo Jaaksi, Juha Mäki-Jyllilä, Samuli Miettinen, Noora Liesimaa, Teemu Kurkela, Harri Lindberg
» 16 / p. 60
—Academy of Fine Arts, Mylly
Asmo Jaaksi, Juha Mäki-Jyllilä, Samuli Miettinen, Teemu Toivio, Katja Savolainen, Noora Liesimaa, Päivi Meuronen, Teemu Kurkela, Jussi Vepsäläinen
» 18 / p. 61

jo taillieu architecten
—Paddenbroek Educational Rural Centre
Jo Taillieu
» 103 / p. 175

Johansen Skovsted Arkitekter
—Codan – Office and Warehouse
Sebastian Skovsted, Søren Johansen
» 39 / p. 82

José Gigante Arquitecto
—Vincci Ponte de Ferro Hotel
José Manuel Gigante, Manuel Fernando Santos
» 292 / p. 382

Josep Ferrando Architecture
—El Roser Social Centre
Josep Ferrando, David Recio
» 302 / p. 426

Josipa Skrobo
—The Pidris Chapel Interior
Josipa Skrobo
» 237 / p. 333

JSC Vilniaus Planas
—Museum of Urban Wooden Architecture
Vincas Brezgys, Rūta Astasevičiūtė
» 58 / p. 108

June14 Meyer-Grohbrügge & Chermayeff
—Building Community Kurfürstenstrasse
Johanna Meyer-Grohbrügge, Sam Chermayeff
» 84 / p. 150

K ARCHITECTURES
—Performance Hall and Open Air Amphitheatre
Karine Herman, Jérôme Sigwalt
» 259 / p. 351

K-Studio
—Liknon
Dimitris Karampatakis, Christos Spetseris, Stavros Kotsikas, Marina Leventaki
» 354 / p. 494

K2S Architects
—Ylivieska Church
Niko Sirola, Mikko Summanen, Kimmo Lintula
» 3 / p. 44

KAL A
—Bohinj Kindergarten
Sofia Romeo Gurrea-Nozaleda, Miguel Sotos Fernández-Zúñiga
» 210 / p. 294

Karen Brownlee Architects
—The Thatch
Karen Brownlee
» 64 / p. 112

KAVAKAVA
—Viimsi Artium
Indrek Peil, Siiri Vallner
» 14 / p. 59

Kjellander Sjöberg
—Gjuteriet
Ola Kjellander, Stefan Sjöberg, Sylvia Neiglick, Johan Pitura, Hannes Haak, Simon Estié, Pär Hädefält, Sebastian Mardi
» 44 / p. 85

Klaus Schuwerk Architect
—The New National Museum in Oslo
Klaus Schuwerk
» 7 / p. 48

Knut Hjeltnes Sivilarkitekter
—Weekend House Hjeltnes
Knut Hjeltnes
» 22 / p. 67

Kolektiv Tektonika
—Revitalization of Old Glassworks and Surrounding Urban Areas in Old Town of Ptuj
Darja Matjašec, Katja Mali, Pia Kante
» 218 / p. 304

Kometka Architecture Studio
—Louria
Andreas Androulakakis, Tatiana Tzanavara
» 352 / p. 493

KONIOR STUDIO
—Redevelopment and Modernization of the National Library of Poland in Warsaw
Tomasz Konior, Dominik Koroś
» 95 / p. 167

KOTO
—Reconstruction of Fetislam Fortress
Slobodan Radovanović, Anica Radosavljević, Uroš Kondić, Katarina Vujanac Ćirković
» 247 / p. 337

Kristine Jensens Landscape
—Stevns Klint Experience
Kristine Jensen
» 40 / p. 83

Kuba & Pilař architekti
—Research Library of South Bohemia Extension
Ladislav Kuba, Tomáš Pilař, Kateřina Jechová, Patrik Obr
» 150 / p. 223

KUESS Architektur
—City Boathouse
Nina Maria Kuess
» 176 / p. 260

kuidas.works
—Restaurant O
Hannes Praks, Henri Papson, Andrea Tamm, Maria Helena Luiga
» 31 / p. 73

Kuma & Associates Europe
—H.C. Andersen's House
Yuki Ikeguchi, Kengo Kuma
» 37 / p. 81

KUU architects
—Woodwork and Technology Centre in Rakvere
Joel Kopli
» 21 / p. 64

KWK Promes
—Miedzianka Shaft
Robert Konieczny, Michał Lisiński, Dorota Skóra, Krzysztof Kobiela, Magdalena Orzeł-Rurańska, Klaudia Księżarczyk, Magda Bykowska
» 126 / p. 203
—Plato Contemporary Art Gallery
Robert Konieczny, Michał Lisiński, Dorota Skóra, Tadeáš Goryczka, Marek Golab-Sieling, Agnieszka Wolny-Grabowska, Krzysztof Kobiela, Adrianna Wycisło, Mateusz Białek, Jakub Bilan, Wojciech Fudala, Katarzyna Kuzior, Damian Kuna, Jakub Pielecha, Magdalena Orzeł-Rurańska, Elżbieta Siwiec, Anna Szewczyk, Kinga Wojtanowska, Karol Knap
» 153 / p. 226

La Soda
—From Offices to Housing: 112 Paris Street
Bernard Valentin, Latour Helene
» 135 / p. 210

LAB5 architects
—Trendo11 Apartment Building
Linda Erdelyi, Andras Dobos, Balazs Korenyi, Virag Anna Gaspar
» 190 / p. 278

LABAK
—Villa Bôrik
Michal Marcinov
» 156 / p. 244

Labics
—Palazzo dei Diamanti Renovation, Restoration and Redevelopment
Maria Claudia Clemente, Francesco Isidori
» 233 / p. 331

WORKS PER STUDIOS

Laguillo Arquitectos
—Rehabilitation and Expansion of the Town Hall of Fuentes de Andalucía
Ignacio Laguillo Diaz
» 334 / p. 479

Ledić arhitektura
—Ivo Andrić's Birth House
Josip Ledić
» 238 / p. 333

LLPS Arquitectos
—New Faculty of Psychology and Speech Therapy
Eduardo Pérez Gómez, MIguel Angel Sanchez Garcia
» 336 / p. 481

LRO
—Munich Volkstheater
Arno Lederer, Jórunn Ragnarsdóttir, Marc Oei, Katja Pütter
» 169 / p. 257

LSN Architects
—Prishtina Business Centre
Lulzim Nuza, Florian Shala, Sado Kolić
» 272 / p. 262

MADE ARHITEKTI
—Avoti Office Building
Mikelis Putrams, Linda Krumina
» 32 / p. 73

Maden Group
—AMC Multimedia
Ideal Vejsa, Rashit Zeneli, Agon Elezi
» 273 / p. 363

MADhel
—"Lascala" NSA6 100 Social Housing
Daniel Bergman, Miguel Herraiz
» 300 / p. 407

MAIO
—Nursery. 1306 Plants for Timișoara
María Charneco Llanos, Anna Puigjaner Barberá, Alfredo Lérida Horta, Guillermo López Ibáñez
» 226 / p. 321
—40 Social Apartments for Rent
María Charneco Llanos, Anna Puigjaner Barberá, Alfredo Lérida Horta, Guillermo López Ibáñez
» 304 / p. 431

MAKRIDIS ASSOCIATES
—Revelation and Highlighting of Thessaloniki's Monumental Axis
Thodoris Makridis, Petros Makridis, Eleanna Makridou, Alkistis Stergiani Kartsiou, Martha Georgakakou, Vasileios Tsigkas
» 322 / p. 468

maria flöckner und hermann schnöll
—New Mozarteum Foyers
Maria Flöckner, Hermann Schnöll
» 172 / p. 258

Mario Cucinella Architects
—Art Museum of Fondazione Luigi Rovati
Mario Cucinella
» 206 / p. 288

Marios Christodoulides
—House 0410
Marios Christodoulides
» 358 / p. 499

MARMOLBRAVO
—"Lascala" NSA6 100 Social Housing
Mauro Bravo, Marina del Marmol
» 300 / p. 407

Martin Migeon Architecture
—Extension and Reconversion of an Old Farm House Near the Gironde Estuary
Martin Migeon
» 200 / p. 285

Mascha.Ritter
—Locknbauer Winery
Mascha Ritter
» 178 / p. 261

mateo arquitectura
—Toni Catany International Photography Centre
Josep Lluís Mateo
» 339 / p. 482

MATT ARCHITECT & ASSOCIATES
—Chronicle in Stone
Matilda Pando
» 230 / p. 429

MBL architectes
—The Grand Bois House
Sébastien Martinez-Barat, Benjamin Lafore
» 201 / p. 286

McCullough Mulvin Architects
—Printing House Square
Valerie Mulvin
» 70 / p. 119

MEDPROSTOR arhitekturni atelje
—Covering the Remains of the Church of St. John the Baptist in the Žiče Charterhouse
Rok Žnidaršič, Jerneja Fischer Knap, Samo Mlakar, Katja Ivić, Dino Mujić
» 216 / p. 300

Mendoza Partida
—Serlachius Art Sauna
Héctor Mendoza, Mara Partida
» 4 / p. 44

META architectuurbureau
—Bruges Meeting & Convention Centre
Niklaas Deboutte, Eric Soors
» 97 / p. 170

METALAB
—Co-haty – Pilot Project of Adaptation of a Vacant Dormitory for IDP Housing
Anna Pashynska, Tetyana Pashynska, Nasar Dnes, Maryana Baran, Bohdan Volynskyi
» 162 / p. 248

Metropolitan Workshop
—Annesley Gardens
Neil Deely, Jonny McKenna, Denise Murray, Sharon Chatterton, Ozan Balcik
» 69 / p. 115

Miralles Tagliabue EMBT
—San Giacomo Apostolo Church and Parish Complex
Benedetta Tagliabue, Joan Callis
» 232 / p. 330

Mjölk architekti
—Klobouckά Lesní Company Headquarters
Jan Mach, Jan Vondrák, Filip Cerha
» 152 / p. 225

MKutin arhitektura
—A House for Modest Residence
Meta Kutin
» 215 / p. 299

MLOPEZ arquitectos
—Sports Hall "La Unión"
Manuel López Sánchez, José Carlos Oliva Gómez
» 332 / p. 478

Modesto Sánchez Morales
—House in Mojacar
Modesto Sánchez Morales
» 338 / p. 482

modulorbeat
—Blue Hour at Spreepark
Marc Günnewig, Jan Kampshoff
» 89 / p. 160

MoDusArchitects
—Fieldhouse: Sports Amenity Facility at the Base of Mount Corno
Matteo Scagnol
» 207 / p. 289

MOLD architects
—Homa Vagia Boutique Hotel
Iliana Kerestetzi, Maria Vretou, Konstantinos Vlachoulis
» 350 / p. 492

molumba
—Mustjala Retirement Home and Daycare Centre
Johan Tali, Karli Luik, Priit Rannik, Annika Lill
» 25 / p. 69

MORE arhitekture
—Riding Hall. Land Registry Department of the Municipal Civil Court
Davor Busnja
» 219 / p. 305

Morpho Papanikolaou - SPARCH architects
—The Regeneration and Reinterpretation of the Agora Modiano Listed Monument
Morpho Papanikolaou
» 321 / p. 468

—Anatolia Elementary School
Morpho Papanikolaou
» 323 / p. 469

Moser und Hager Architekten
—Mortuary
Michael Hager, Anna Moser
» 173 / p. 459

Mostlikely Architecture
—Cultural Pavilion Semmering
Mark Neuner, Christian Höhl
» 177 / p. 260

MOTTO architectural studio
—Buildings for Ethnographic Exibitions in the Cultural and Tourist Complex Chengene Skele
Mariana Sarbova, Desislava Stoyanova
» 285 / p. 369

MVA - Mikelić Vreš Arhitekti
—Kindergarten in Gornja Stubica
Marin Mikelić, Tomislav Vreš
» 221 / p. 310

MVRDV
—Pyramid of Tirana
Winy Maas
» 318 / p. 466

My Place Under the Sun Team
—Home for 'My Place Under the Sun'
Ana Boljar, Ida Križaj Leko, Enia Kukoč, Kristijan Mamić, Marin Nižić, Ariana Sušanj, Damian Sobol Turina
» 212 / p. 298

Natrufied Architecture
—De Warren Cooperative Housing
Boris Zeisser, Anja Verdonk
» 78 / p. 125

Neiheiser Argyros
—Art 1 Offices
Ryan Neiheiser, Xristina Argyros
» 348 / p. 491

NGNP Arquitectos
—Sports Hall "La Unión"
José Antonio Plaza Cano, Juan Carlos Herrera Pueyo, Enrique Naranjo Escudero
» 332 / p. 478

Nicolas Laisné Architectes
—Learning Centre for polytechnic University
Nicolas Laisné
» 134 / p. 209

Nicolas Simon Architectes
—Early Childhood Facilities and a Garden
Nicolas Simon
» 133 / p. 208

noAarchitecten
—Het Steen
An Fonteyne, Philippe Viérin, Jitse van den Berg
» 110 / p. 190

NOP Studio
—Community Sports Hall
Ivan Galic
» 223 / p. 315

NOTAN OFFICE
—Duchesse. Reconversion of Industrial Buildings in Residential Units
Karam Frédéric
» 108 / p. 185

NP2F
—UCPA Sport Station Bordeaux Brazza (The Sports Cathedral)
François Chas, Nicolas Guerin, Fabrice Long, Paul Maitre-Devallon
» 229 / p. 328

Nuno Valentim - Arquitectura e Reabilitação
—Rehabilitation of the Bolhão Market
Nuno Valentim Lopes, Rita Machado Lima, Frederico Eça, Margarida Carvalho, Juliano Ribas
» 293 / p. 383

ô
—Uhrovec Castle – Operation Building
Martin Varga, Martin Kvitkovsky
» 154 / p. 242

O'Donnell + Tuomey
—Passage House
Sheila O'Donnell, John Tuomey
» 61 / p. 111

O'Mahony Pike Architects
—Printing House Square
Valerie Mulvin
» 70 / p. 119
—Electricity Supply Board Headquarters
James Pike, Derbhile McDonagh, Eoin Synnot, Dean Wallace, Karen King, Michael Hussey
» 71 / p. 120

OAB Office Of Architecture in Barcelona
—Passeig de Gràcia 109-111. Mandarin Residences & Casa Seat
Carles Ferrater
» 308 / p. 433

Objekt
—Vizafogó Ecopark and Pavilion
Máté Pécsi, János Hómann, Eszter Ripszám
» 193 / p. 279

Octav Silviu Olanescu Architecture Office
—Firefighters' Tower
Octav Silviu Olanescu, Anamaria Olanescu
» 198 / p. 282

Office For Strategic Spaces (OSS)
—La Carboneria (Casa Tarragó). The Rehabilitation of a Historic Barcelona Residential Building
Angel Borrego Cubero
» 307 / p. 432

OFFICE Kersten Geers David Van Severen
—Brussels Beer Project
David Van Severen, Kersten Geers
» 107 / p. 185

Olsson Lyckefors Arkitektur
—Merkurhuset
Andreas Lyckefors, Johan Olsson, Per Bornstein, Fabian Sahlqvist, Viktor Stansvik, Johanna Engloo, Johan Häggqvist, Ergin Can, Rebecca Wallin, Viktor Fagrell, Ainhoa Etxeberria, Karin Pallarp, Marina Pettersson, Joel Gödecke, Edvard Nyman, David Svahn, Ola Sjöberg
» 23 / p. 67

OOPEAA Office For Peripheral Architecture
—Villa B
Anssi Lassila
» 341 / p. 487

Orange Architects
—Jonas
Jeroen Schipper, Patrick Meijers, Paul Kierkels, Elena Staskute
» 77 / p. 124

Óscar Miguel Ares. Contextos de Arquitectura y Urbanismo
—Municipal Pools
Oscar Miguel Ares Álvarez
» 298 / p. 402

OXO Architectes
—Learning Centre for Polytechnic University
Manal Rachdi
» 134 / p. 209

PA+U Rafał Mazur
—Public Multi-Family Housing Assembly
Rafał Mazur
» 91 / p. 161

PAMARCH
—Conversion of Jurkovič Heating Plant National Cultural Monument
Pavol Pauliny
» 188 / p. 277

Paragram
—Reconstruction of the Lehel Tér Metro Station
Balázs Csapó
» 192 / p. 279

Paredes Pedrosa Arquitectos
—Córdoba Public Library
Ángela García de Paredes, Ignacio García Pedrosa
» 335 / p. 480

Park Associati
—Luxottica Digital Factory
Filippo Pagliani, Michele Rossi, Lorenzo Merloni, Michele Versaci, Alessandro Bentivegna, Luna Pavanello, Valeria Donini, Simone Caimi, Marinella Ferrari, Ismail Seleit
» 205 / p. 288

WORKS PER STUDIOS

PART architects
—Son of a Shingle – Vaksali Pedestrian Bridge and Underpasses
Sille Pihlak, Siim Tuksam
» 33 / p. 74

PAUEM atelier
—The Forestry House
Pauline Chauvet, Emanuele Francesco Moro
» 258 / p. 350

Paulo Moreira Architectures
—Escadinhas Footpaths
Paulo Moreira
» 290 / p. 374

PBR
—Ogre Central Library and Marriage Registry
Rūdis Rubenis, Valdis Onkelis
» 29 / p. 71

Perea, Suárez y Torrelo, Arquitectos
—Fontán Building
Andrés Perea, Elena Suárez Calvo, Rafael Fernández Torrelo
» 254 / p. 345

peris+toral arquitectes
—Living in Lime - 42 Social Housing
Marta Peris, Jose Toral
» 340 / p. 483

Perspektiv
—Conversion of Jurkovič Heating Plant National Cultural Monument
Ján Antal, Barbora Babocká
» 188 / p. 277

pihlmann architects
—Åben Brewery
Søren Pihlmann, Anna Wisborg
» 43 / p. 84

Pikku-Finlandia Studio
—Little Finlandia
Jaakko Torvinen, Havu Järvelä, Elli Wendelin
» 17 / p. 61

Plan Común
—A Common House
Felipe De Ferrari, Nissim Haguenauer, Kim Courrèges, Sacha Discors
» 139 / p. 213

Planetary Architecture
—Serlachius Art Sauna
Pekka Pakkanen, Anna Kontuniemi
» 4 / p. 44

PLCO arquitectos
—Andaluz Houses
Pedro Lagrifa de Oliveira
» 327 / p. 475

PLURAL
—Villa Bôrik
Martin Jančok, Michal Janák, Zuzana Kovaľová, Ruslan Dimov
» 156 / p. 244

Plus Architecture
—Printmaking Studio, Grangegorman
Gavin Wheatley
» 67 / p. 114

Point Supreme
—Ignatiou Apartment
Marianna Rentzou, Konstantinos Pantazis
» 345 / p. 489

Pool Is Cool
—Open Air Swimming Pool Flow
Paul Steinbrück
» 106 / p. 181

PPAG architects
—Steirereck at Pogusch
Anna Popelka, Georg Poduschka
» 174 / p. 259

Pracownia Architektoniczna Aleksandra Wasilkowska
—Targ Blonie / Food Market
Aleksandra Wasilkowska
» 92 / p. 162

Praeger Richter Architekten
—Ausbauhaus Südkreuz ("House to Be Extended")
Jana Richter, Henri Praeger
» 85 / p. 154

Praksis
—Stevns Klint Experience
Mads Bjørn Hansen
» 40 / p. 83

Price & Myers (Civil And Structural Engineering)
—Hage
Tim Lucas, Ian Shepherd
» 46 / p. 86

Prima Inzenering
—Volkovo Kindergarten
Filip Koneski, Danica Spasevska
» 274 / p. 363

ProAspekt
—Office Building, Multinational Company Campus NCR
Vladimir Lojanica
» 243 / p. 335

projectroom
—Transformation of a 100-year-old Fruit Storage Building
Gábor Fábián, Dénes Fajcsák, Veronika Juhász
» 194 / p. 280

PROXY
—MAH House
Nikola Kungulovski, Medina Gicikj
» 275 / p. 364

PSLA Architekten
—Townhouse Neubaugasse
Ali Seghatoleslami, Lilli Pschill
» 181 / p. 266

querkraft architekten
—IKEA Vienna Western Station / IKEA – the Good Neighbour in the City
Jakob Dunkl, Gerd Erhartt, Peter Sapp
» 180 / p. 262

Rafael De La-Hoz Arquitectos
—"Wildlife Observatory" in Los Pedroches
Rafael de La-Hoz Castanys
» 337 / p. 481

Rapa Architects
—Summer House
Levente Arato, Adam Reisz, Krisztian Varga-Koritar
» 189 / p. 277

RAUM
—Refurbishment and Extension of a Community Swimming Pool
Julien Perraud, Benjamin Boré, Thomas Durand
» 165 / p. 251

raumwerk.architekten
—Bob Campus
Ragnhild Klußmann, Marc Hübert
» 118 / p. 198

re:a.c.t
—K26 Manhattan Concept
Grozdana Sisovic, Dejan Milanovic
» 245 / p. 336

re:architekti
—Lázně Bělohrad Town Hall
Michal Kuzemenský, David Pavlišta, Ondřej Synek, Jan Vlach, Jiří Žid, Vojtěch Ružbatský
» 124 / p. 202

react architects
—Louria
Yiorgos Spiridonos, Natasha Deliyianni
» 325 / p. 493

REMKE PARTNER INNENARCHITEKTEN mbB
—Reorganization and Refurbishment of Leeste Cooperative Comprehensive School
Sascha Remke, Tanja Remke
» 81 / p. 131

Robbrecht en Daem architecten
—Hospital ZNA Cadix
Paul Robbrecht, Hilde Daem, Johannes Robbrecht
» 111 / p. 194

Rolvung og Brønsted Arkitekter
—New Aarch
Jakob Bronsted
» 36 / p. 80

Roselli Architetti Associati
—Camplus San Pietro
Riccardo Roselli
» 263 / p. 358

COLOPHON

roth&čerina
—Lonja Wetlands Wildlife Observatories and Visitor Centre
Mia Roth-Čerina, Tonči Čerina
» 222 / p. 311

RS SPARCH
—Element – New Office Building
Rena Sakellaridou
» 347 / p. 490

Ruderal
—Betania Forest Garden
Sarah Cowles, Benjamin Hackenberger, Giorgi Nishnianidze
» 324 / p. 469

—Tbilisi Urban Forest (Narikala Ridge Forest)
Sarah Cowles, Benjamin Hackenberger, Christian Moore, Giorgi Nishnianidze
» 325 / p. 470

SAMPLING
—Brewery 'Manufaktūra'
Manten Devriendt, Liene Jākobsone
» 28 / p. 70

Šarūno Kiaunės projektavimo studija
—Multifunctional Hall on Lake Zarasas Island
Šarūnas Kiaunė, Asta Kiaunienė, Vytis Obolevičius, Ugnė Valatkevičiūtė
» 60 / p. 109

Scapelab
—Cukrarna
Marko Studen, Boris Matić, Jernej Šipoš
» 214 / p. 299

Schindler Seko architekti
—Kunsthalle
Jan Schindler, Ludvík Seko, Zuzana Drahotová
» 121 / p. 200

Scullion Architects
—Printmaking Studio, Grangegorman
Declan Scullion
» 67 / p. 114

Senamiesčio projektai
—"Lojoteka". Educational Media Centre
Ramūnas Buitkus, Indrė Šukytė
» 55 / p. 107

Senojo Miesto Architektai
—Reconstruction of Vilnius Central Post Office into ISM University
Diana Sabaliauskiene, Sara Lucinskiene
» 54 / p. 106

—School Reconstruction Project
Daina Ferguson, James Ferguson
» 56 / p. 107

SHEREMETA ARCHITECT GROUP
—Dwelling House «Baltiyska Hall»
Mykola Sheremeta, Oles Kuzo, Ostap Halko
» 159 / p. 246

Simple Architecture
—Private House
Alexander Yonchev
» 286 / p. 370

Simpraxis
—Archeological Sites
Christos Christodoulou, Marios Christodoulides
» 355 / p. 498

Sinas Architects
—Xerolithi
George Sinas
» 351 / p. 492

SKROZ
—Black Slavonian Eco Pig Farm
Margita Grubiša, Marin Jelčić, Daniela Škarica, Ivana Žalac, Zvonimir Marčić
» 224 / p. 316

Skupaj Arhitekti
—A House for Modest Residence
Tomaž Ebenšpanger
» 215 / p. 299

SLAS architekci
—Extension of the Building of the State Music School in Jastrzębie-Zdrój with a Concert Hall.
Aleksander Bednarski, Mariusz Komraus
» 155 / p. 243

SLETH
—Herning Folk High School
Søren Leth, Rasmus Therkildsen, Hans Bruun Olesen, Niels Eli Kjær Thomsen, Bente Ulrikke Weinreich, Nanna Østergaard Christensen, Troels Voer Hørup
» 34 / p. 79

Slovak Technical University - Faculty of Architecture and Design - Institute of History and Theory of Architecture and Restoration of Monuments
—Uhrovec Castle – Operation Building
Pavol Paulíny
» 154 / p. 242

Smart Studio
—Tirana Business Centre
Florian Nepravishta
» 320 / p. 467

smartvoll Architekten
—Possibility Space instead of Building Waste
Christian Kircher, Philipp Buxbaum, Dimitar Gamizov, Olha Sendetska, Viola Habicher
» 171 / p. 258

SO-IL
—Glass Blowing and Cultural Centre of Meisenthal
Jing Liu, Florian Idenburg, Ilias Papageorgiou
» 146 / p. 217

SOKKA
—Redevelopment and Modernization of the National Library of Poland in Warsaw
Katarzyna Sokołowska
» 95 / p. 167

Sol89
—Landscape Adaptation and Intervention in the Almadraba of Nueva Umbría
Juan Jose López de la Cruz, María González García
» 331 / p. 478

Sou Fujimoto Architects
—Learning Centre for polytechnic University
Sou Fujimoto
» 134 / p. 209

Souto Moura - Arquitectos
—Bruges Meeting & Convention Centre
Eduardo Souto de Moura
» 97 / p. 170

sporaarchitects
—Reconstruction of the Lehel Tér Metro Station
Tibor Dékány, Ádám Hatvani, Attila Czigléczki
» 192 / p. 279

Spridd
—Meeting Place Mariatorget – St. Pauls Church
Klas Ruin, Jakob Wiklander, Ola Broms Wessel, Winnie Westerlund
» 10 / p. 53

STARH - Birou De Arhitectura (Florian & Iulia Stanciu)
—Boemia Apartments
Florian Stanciu, Iulia Stanciu
» 252 / p. 341

Steve Larkin Architects
—Ballyblake House
Steve Larkin
» 63 / p. 112

Studija Lape
—House Krivis with Gallery
Tomas Lape, Edvinas Kaltanas, Emilija Liudvinavičiūtė, Ieva Viliūtė
» 57 / p. 108

Studio A&D Architects
—Elementary School "Vera Miščević"
Danilo Grahovac, Ivana Mijailović, Jovanka Gojković
» 242 / p. 335

Studio Albori
—Wood and Straw House
Giacomo Borella, Emanuele Almagioni, Francesca Riva
» 203 / p. 287

WORKS PER STUDIOS

Studio BF
—Reconstruction and Extension of Primary School Ksaver Sandor Gjalski
Željko Golubić, Zoran Boševski, Boris Fiolić
» 220 / p. 309

Studio Emil Jurcan
—Reconstruction of the Roman Theater
Emil Jurcan
» 234 / p. 331

Studio Entasis
—The House in Klanac
Vedina Babahmetović
» 239 / p. 333
—Hiža Mišljenova House
Vedina Babahmetović
» 240 / p. 334

Studio Fragment
—Zsuzsanna Kossuth Building of the Faculty of Health Sciences, Semmelweis University
Zsolt Frikker, Imre Bődi
» 195 / p. 281

Studio GRAD
—Bussiness Centre "Glosarij"
Veljko Radulović, Đorđe Gregović
» 268 / p. 360
—Montenegrin Academy of Sciences and Arts
Veljko Radulović, Đorđe Gregović, Branislav Gregović
» 269 / p. 361

Studio Jil Bentz
—Domaine Claude Bentz
Jil Bentz
» 145 / p. 216

Studio Kyriakos Miltiadou
—Domus Laetitiae / House in a Refugee Settlement
Kyriakos Miltiadou
» 361 / p. 500

Studio Nada
—Cultural Information Centre "The Mill"
Antonina Tritakova, Georgi Sabev
» 283 / p. 368

Studio Nomadic
—Nursery. 1306 Plants for Timișoara
Silvia Tripșa, Victor Popovici, Nicoleta Postolache
» 226 / p. 321

Studio Ossidiana
—Art Pavilion M.
Giovanni Bellotti, Alessandra Covini
» 80 / p. 127

Studio Peisaj
—Nursery. 1306 Plants for Timișoara
Alexandru Ciobotă, Raluca Rusu
» 226 / p. 321

Studio RIJSEL
—The Vendegies-sur-Écaillon Nursery School
Edouard Cailliau, Thomas Lecourt
» 99 / p. 172

Studio SNCDA
—Fire Station, Multi-Purpose Space, and Emergency Housing
Sara Noel Costa De Araujo
» 104 / p. 176

Studio Synthesis Architecture & Design
—Betula Design Centre
Sonja Radović Jelovac
» 266 / p. 359

Studio Zec
—Ivo Andrić's Birth House
Amir Vuk Zek
» 238 / p. 333

Studiolada Architects
—Jean Lamour Gymnasium
Christophe Aubertin, Xavier Géant
» 144 / p. 215

Sulyk Architects
—Temporary housing for refugees "Unbroken Mothers"
Taras Sulyk
» 161 / p. 247

SUMA Arquitectura
—Gabriel García Márquez Library
Elena Orte, Guillermo Sevillano
» 310 / p. 434

SumProject
—Repurposing Winter Circus Mahy
Paul Lievevrouw
» 100 / p. 173

Syndicate Studio
—Showroom and Distribution Centre with Warehouse Balkanija
Ilija Bozinovski, Dejan Sekulovski, Mia Shirik, Sashe Neshik, Katina Sutoglu
» 278 / p. 365

SZTR studio
—New Market Hall of Pécs
Gergely Sztranyák
» 225 / p. 320

TAKA
—Middleton Park Gate Lodge
Alice Casey, Cian Deegan
» 62 / p. 111

TCHOBAN VOSS Architekten
—Edge Suedkreuz Berlin
Sergei Tchoban, Stephan Lohre
» 86 / p. 155

TDB ARQUITECTURA
—House-Factory Natura Bissé
Juan Trias de Bes Mingot, Marta Pascual, Carlos García
» 306 / p. 432

Team V Architectuur
—Haut Amsterdam
Jeroen van Schooten, Do Janne Vermeulen, Thomas Harms, Bart-Jan Hopman, Job Stuijt, Onno van Ark, Coen Ooijevaar
» 76 / p. 123

Tham & Videgård
—House on a Hill
Bolle Tham, Martin Videgård
» 12 / p. 58

the next ENTERprise Architects
—Museum Heidi Horten Collection
Ernst J. Fuchs, Marie-Therese Harnoncourt-Fuchs
» 183 / p. 271

TRANSAT architekti
—Gočár's Gallery in Pardubice
Petr Všetečka, Robert Václavík, Karel Menšík, Tereza Novotná
» 125 / p. 202

TriConsult
—New Aarch
Søren Ibsen
» 36 / p. 80

unas studio
—Karin Dom
Bilyana Asenova, Saša Ciabatti
» 288 / p. 371

UPB
—Ola Foundation
Uldis Pilēns
» 27 / p. 70

Urban Curators
—Co-haty – Pilot Project of Adaptation of a Vacant Dormitory for IDP Housing
Anastasiya Ponomaryova, Varvara Yagnysheva, Bohdan Volynskyi
» 162 / p. 248

Urbana Architects
—Renovation of Aleko Konstantinov Street
Rositsa Zlatanova, Galina Milkova, Vladimir Milkov
» 284 / p. 369

URED STUDIO
—K26 Manhattan Concept
Nikola Milanović
» 245 / p. 336

V+ (Bureau Vers Plus de Bien-Être)
—Le Pont des Arts – Cultural Pole
Thierry Decuypere, Jörn Aram Bihain
» 96 / p. 169

Vardas Studio
—House in Olive Grove
Andreas Vardas
» 356 / p. 498

Vargo Nielsen Palle
—New Aarch
Jonas Snedevind Nielsen, Mathias Palle, Brian Vargo
» 36 / p. 80

Verkron
—Escadinhas Footpaths
Colectivo Verkron
» 290 / p. 374

VICEVERSA
—Cities that Transform
Dorin Ștefan Adam, Laurian Ghinițoiu
» 251 / p. 341

VK architects+engineers
—Hospital ZNA Cadix
Steven Wallays, Tom Debacker, Kim Debeyser
» 111 / p. 194

Vlad Sebastian Rusu Architecture Office
—Firefighters' Tower
Vlad Sebastian Rusu
» 198 / p. 282

Volart
—CHP House
Bojan Tasev, Nikola Tomevski, Simon Papesh
» 277 / p. 365

White arkitekter
—Sara Cultural Centre
Robert Schmitz, Oskar Norelius, Maria Orvesten, Patrik Buchinger
» 2 / p. 43

Wingårdh Arkitektkontor
—Liljevalchs+
Gert Wingårdh
» 11 / p. 54

WUP architektur
—Social Housing Aspern H4
Bernhard Weinberger, Andreas Gabriel, Helmut Wimmer, Raphaela Leu
» 185 / p. 272

xystudio
—School for Children from Ukraine - Adaptation of the Floor in the Office Building
Marta Nowosielska, Dorota Sibińska, Filip Domaszczyński
» 94 / p. 166

Yiorgos Hadjichristou
—Living in 'Aphrodite'
Yiorgos Hadjichristou
» 359 / p. 499

zerozero
—City Hall Leopoldov
Irakli Eristavi, Pavol Silla, Juraj Cerveny
» 151 / p. 224

ZRS Architekten Ingenieure
—Woof & Skelle: Building Ensemble for Social Housing and Kindergarten | Ellener Hof
Monique Bührdel, Carolin Senftleben, Marine Miroux, Samuel Reichl, Lisa-Marie Kolbinger, Tobias Bieger, Riccardo Fanton
» 82 / p. 131

Π Square
—Archeological Sites
Panayiotis Panayi
» 355 / p. 498

EUMIES AWARDS

Architecture Winners 1988—2022

1988	**Borges & Irmão Bank.** ÁLVARO SIZA Vila do Conde, Portugal © Eugeni Bofill
1990	**Stansted Airport.** FOSTER + PARTNERS London, United Kingdom © Dennis Gilbert
1992	**Municipal Sports Stadium.** BONELL I GIL Badalona, Spain © Hisao Suzuki
1994	**Waterloo International Station.** NICHOLAS GRIMSHAW & PARTNERS London, United Kingdom © Jo Reid and John Peck
1996	**French National Library.** DOMINIQUE PERRAULT ARCHITECTE Paris, France © Georges Fessy
1998	**Art Museum of Bregenz.** BÜRO PETER ZUMTHOR Bregenz, Austria © Hélène Binet
2001	**Kursaal Centre.** RAFAEL MONEO Donostia, Spain © F.O.A.T.
2003	**Car Park and Terminus Hoenheim North.** ZAHA HADID ARCHITECTS Strasbourg, France © Hélène Binet
2005	**Netherlands Embassy.** OMA Berlin, Germany © Phil Meech
2007	**MUSAC.** MANSILLA + TUÑÓN ARQUITECTOS León, Spain © Luis Asín
2009	**Norwegian Opera & Ballet.** SNØHETTA Oslo, Norway © Chrsitopher Hagelund
2011	**Neues Museum.** DAVID CHIPPERFIELD Berlin, Germany © Jörg von Bruchhausen
2013	**Harpa. Reykjavik Concert Hall and Conference Centre.** HENNING LARSEN ARCHITECTS, STUDIO OLAFUR ELIASSON, BATTERÍIÐ ARCHITECTS Reykjavik, Iceland © Nic Lehoux
2015	**Szczecin Philharmonic Hall.** BAROZZI VEIGA Szczecin, Poland © Barozzi / Veiga
2017	**Deflat Kleiburg.** NL ARCHITECTS, XVW ARCHITECTUUR Amsterdam, The Netherlands © Stijn Brakkee

2019		**Transformation of 3 Housing Blocks, 530 Dwellings - Grand Parc Bordeaux.** LACATON & VASSAL ARCHITECTS; FRÉDÉRIC DRUOT ARCHITECTURE; CHRISTOPHE HUTIN ARCHITECTURE Bourdeaux, France © Philippe Ruault
2022		**Town House - Kingston University.** GRAFTON ARCHITECTS London, United Kingdom © Dennis Gilbert

Emerging Winners 2001-2022

2001		**Kaufmann Holz AG Distribution Centre.** FLORIAN NAGLER ARCHITEKTEN Bobingen, Germany © Stefan Müller-Naumann
2003		**Scharnhauser Park Town Hall.** JÜRGEN MAYER H. Ostfildern, Germany © David Frank
2005		**BasketBar.** NL ARCHITECTS Utrecht, The Netherlands © Luuk Kramer
2007		**Department of Mathematics. Faculty of Physics and Mathematics.** BEVK PEROVIĆ ARHITEKTI Ljubljana, Slovenia © Miran Kambič
2009		**Gymnasium 46° 09 N / 16° 50 E.** STUDIO UP Koprivnica, Croatia © STUDIO UP
2011		**Collage House.** BOSCH.CAPDEFERRO.ARQUITECTURA Girona © José Hevia
2013		**Red Bull Music Academy / Nave de Música Matadero** LANGARITA-NAVARRO ARQUITECTOS Madrid, Spain © Luis Díaz Díaz
2015		**Luz House.** ARQUITECTURA-G Cilleros, Spain © José Hevia
2017		**Navez - 5 Social Units as Northern Entrance of Brussels.** MSA / V+ Schaarbeek, Belgium © Serge Brison
2019		**E26 (school refectory).** BAST Montbrun-Bocage, France © BAST
2022		**La Borda - Cooperative Housing.** LACOL Barcelona, Spain © IMHAB

EUMIES AWARDS

Young Talent Winners 2016-2023

2016

A Symbiotic Relation of Cooperative Social Housing and Dispersed Tourism in Habana Vieja. IWO BORKOWICZ
Faculty of Architecture. KU Leuven

GeoFront. POLICARPO DEL CANTO BAQUERA
Madrid School of Architecture. Polytechnic University of Madrid

S'lowtecture. TOMASZ BROMA
Faculty of Architecture. Wrocław University of Science and Technology

2018

Deplorable Framework. MATTHEW GREGOROWSKI
The Cass Faculty of Art Architecture and Design. London Metropolitan University

Neue Bauakademie Berlin. HENDRIK BRINKMANN
College of Architecture, Media and Design. Berlin University of the Arts

Perdido (Lost) - P.R.U.S. of Madrid. JULIO GOTOR VALCÁRCEL
Madrid School of Architecture. Polytechnic University of Madrid

The Bank of England: a Dialectical Project. LOED STOLTE
Faculty of Architecture and the Built Environment. Delft University of Technology

2020

Oasi. ÁLVARO ALCÁZAR DEL ÁGUILA, ROSER GARCIA, EDUARD LLARGUÉS, SERGIO SANGALLI
Vallès School of Architecture. Polytechnic University of Catalonia

Off the Grid. WILLEM HUBRECHTS
Faculty of Engineering Science. University of Leuven

Stage for the City. MONIKA MARINOVA
School of Art, Architecture and Design. London Metropolitan University

Three Places to Inhabit the Mountain Range in the Maule Region.
MARIA JESÚS MOLINA, PÍA MONTERO, ANTONIA OSSA
School of Architecture. University of Talca

2023

Eden Archipelago. MARÍA DE LA O MOLINA PÉREZ-TOMÉ
Madrid School of Architecture. Polytechnic University of Madrid

Peripheral Cartographies. LAURA HURLEY
School of Engineering and Architecture, SEFS. University College Cork & Munster Technological University

Valter. DINKO JELECEVIC
Faculty of Architecture. Graz University of Technology

Open Winner

Earth Bound. SHAHA RAPHAEL
School of Architecture. Architectural Association

COLOPHON

Jury, Advisory Committee, Independent Experts, National Associations, 2024

Jury Members

Frédéric Druot, President
Architect, researcher and artist.
Founder of Frédéric Druot Architecture (FDA) in Paris

Martin Braathen
Architect and Senior Curator of Architecture at the National Museum, Oslo

Pippo Ciorra
Architect, critic and professor.
Senior Curator for MAXXI Architettura in Rome

Tinatin Gurgenidze
Architect, urban researcher, curator, and author. Co-founder and one of the artistic directors of the Tbilisi Architecture Biennial

Adriana Krnáčová
Writer and politician.
In 2014-2018 she served as Mayor of Prague

Sala Makumbundu
Architect. Managing partner at Christian Bauer & Associés Architectes (CBA) in Luxembourg

Hrvoje Njiric
Architect, professor and lecturer.
Founder of njiric+ arhitekti in Zagreb

Advisory Committee

Architekturzentrum Wien, Vienna
Angelika Fitz, Director

CIVA, Brussels
Nikolaus Hirsch, Artistic Director

Danish Architecture Centre, Copenhagen
Kent Martinussen, CEO

DESSA Gallery, Ljubljana
Maja Ivanic, Director

German Architecture Museum, Frankfurt
Peter Cachola Schmal, Director

Fundació Mies van der Rohe, Barcelona
Anna Ramos, Director

Hungarian Contemporary Architecture Centre, Budapest
Samu Szemerey, Co-founder and Content Director

Cité de l'architecture et du patrimoine, Paris
Francis Rambert, Director

Museum of Architecture, Wroclaw
Michał Duda, Curator

Museum of Estonian Architecture, Tallinn
Karen Jagodin, Director

Museum of Finnish Architecture, Helsinki
Carina Jaatinen, Director

Museum of Architecture and Design, Ljubljana
Maja Vardjan, Director

National Museum of Art, Architecture and Design, Oslo
Martin Braathen, Senior Curator

RIBA, London
Carmen Mateu, Head of Awards

The Berlage, Delft
Salomon Frausto, Director of Studies

Triennale di Milano, Milan
Lorenza Baroncelli, Director

COLOPHON

Independent Experts

Stefanos Antoniadis
Benjamin Aubry
José Juan Barba
Justin Baroncea
David Basulto
João Belo Rodeia
Nina Berre
Ana Boranieva
Chris Briffa
Hendrik Brinkmann
Nathalie Brison
Marco Brizzi
Michael Cosmas
Margaux Darrieus
Alexandra Demetriu
Ana Dobrasinovic
Oleg Drozdov
Marc Duboisa
Beate Engelhorn
Aurora Fernández Per
Jorge Figueira
Fabrizio Gallanti
Georgi Georgiev
Martynas Germanavičius
Stefan Ghenciulescu
Diane Gray
Michael Hayes
Florian Heilmeyer
Manuel Henriques
Angelika Hinterbrandner
Nikoloz Japaridze
Viara Jeliazkova
Boris Brorman Jensen
Karolina Jirkalová
Gabriele Kaiser
Audrys Karalius
Juulia Kauste
Martin Keiding
Ana Kosi
Kateryna Kozlova
Saimir Kristo
Kristian Krog
Ivane Ksnelashvili
Mateja Kurir
Ruta Leitanaite
Janis Lejnieks
Carl-Dag Lige
Laura Linsi
Ivan Mata
Pablo Millán Millán

Štefan Moravčík
Henrieta Moravcíková
Maroje Mrduljas
Nataliia Mysak
Marco Navarra
Anh-LinhNgo
Sandra O'Connell
Shane O'Toole
Osamu Okamura
Vassilos P. Batzokas
Ewa P. Porebska
Lucia Pedrana
Spiros Pengas
Paola Pierotti
Levente Polyák
Danica Prodanovic
Jelena Prokopljevic
Moisés Puente
Carlos Quintáns
Bekim Ramku
Giulia Ricci
Ibai Rigby
Romana Ring
Mika Savela
Emmett Scanlon
Enida Setka
Gigi Shukakidze
Rachele Stefano
Iwan Strauven
Levente Szabo
Marcin Szczelina
Anahit Tarkhanyan
Andre Tavares
Massimiliano Tonelli
Hubert Trammer
Alexandra Trofin
Elša Turkušić
Margit Ulama
Marta Urbańska
Sandro Valentino
Hanne Van Reusel
Xander Vermeulen
  Windsant
Rasmus Waern
Sofie Willems
Finn Williams
Anna Yudina
Frano Petar Zovko
Artis Zvirgzdins

National Associations

Shoqata e Arkitekteve të Shqipërisë, Albania
Հայաստանի ճարտարապետների միություն, Armenia
Bundeskammer der Architekten und Ingenieurkonsulenten, Austria
Koninklijke Federatie van de Architectenverenigingen van België / Conseil National de l'Ordre des Architectes, Belgium
Asocijacija Arhitekata u Bosni u Hercegovini, Bosnia and Herzegovina
Съюз на архитектите в България / Камарата на архитектите в България, Bulgaria
Udruženje Hrvatskih Arhitekata, Croatia
Σύλλογος Αρχιτεκτόνων Κύπρου, Cyprus
Česká komora architektů, Czech Republic
Akademisk Arkitektforening / Danske Arkitektvirksomheder, Denmark
Eesti Arhitektide Liit, Estonia
Suomen Arkkitehtiliitto, Finland
Union Nationale des Syndicats Français d'Architectes / Syndicat de l'Architecture / Conseil pour l'International des Architectes Français, France
Georgian Union of Architects – საქართველოს არქიტექტორთა კავშირი, Georgia
Vereinigung Freischaffender Architekten Deutschlands / Bund Deutscher Baumeister, Architekten und Ingenieure / Bund Deutscher Architekten / Bundesarchitektenkammer, Germany
Τεχνικό Επιμελητήριο Ελλάδας / Συλλογοσ Αρχιτεκτονων Διπλωματουχων Ανωτατων Σχολων Πανελληνια Ενωση Αρχιτεκτονων, Greece
Magyar Építész Kamara, Hungary
Arkitektafélag Íslands, Iceland
Royal Institute of Architects of Ireland, Ireland
Consiglio Nazionale degli Architetti, Planificatori, Paesaggisti e Conservatori, Italy
Asociacioni i Arkitektëve të Kosovës, Kosovo
Latvijas Arhitektu savienības, Latvia
Lietuvos architektų sąjunga / Lietuvos architektų rūmai, Lithuania
Ordre des Architectes et des Ingénieurs-Conseils, Luxembourg
Kamra tal-Periti, Malta
The Union of Architects of Moldova, Moldova
Savez arhitekata Crne Gore, Montenegro
Bond van Nederlandse Architecten / Bureau Architectenregister, The Netherlands
Асоцијација на архитекти на Македонија, North Macedonia
Arkitektbedriftene i Norge / Norske arkitekters landsforbunds, Norway
Stowarzyszenie Architektów Polskich, Poland
Ordem dos Arquitectos, Portugal
Udruženje Arhitekata Srbije, Republic of Serbia
Ordinul Arhitecților din Romania, Romania
Slovenská komora architektov, Slovakia
Zbornica za arhitekturo in prostor Slovenije, Slovenia
Consejo Superior de los Colegios de Arquitectos de España, Spain
Sveriges Arkitekter / Innovationsföretagen, Sweden
Ordre des architectes Tunisie, Tunisia
National Union of Architects of Ukraine, Ukraine

CREDITS

European Union Prize for Contemporary Architecture Mies van der Rohe Awards

Committee of Honour

Iliana Ivanova
European Commissioner for Innovation, Research, Culture, Education and Youth

Laia Bonet
Second Deputy Mayor in charge of the Area of Ecology, Urban Planning, Infrastructure and Mobility and President of the Fundació Mies van der Rohe

Sabine Verheyen
Member of the European Parliament, Chairwoman of the Committee on Culture and Education

Pia Ahrenkilde Hansen
Directorate-General for Education, Youth, Sport and Culture – European Commission

Ruth Schagemann
President of the Architects' Council of Europe (ACE)

Oya Atalay Franck
President of the European Association for Architectural Education (EAAE)

Advisory Committee

Architekturzentrum Wien, Vienna
Angelika Fitz, Director

CIVA, Brussels
Nikolaus Hirsch, Artistic Director

Danish Architecture Centre, Copenhagen
Kent Martinussen, CEO

DESSA Gallery, Ljubljana
Maja Ivanic, Director

German Architecture Museum, Frankfurt
Peter Cachola Schmal, Director

Fundació Mies van der Rohe, Barcelona
Anna Ramos, Director

Hungarian Contemporary Architecture Centre, Budapest
Samu Szemerey, Co-founder and content director

Cité de l'architecture et du patrimoine, Paris
Francis Rambert, Director

Museum of Architecture, Wroclaw
Michał Duda, Director

Museum of Estonian Architecture, Tallinn
Karen Jagodin, Director

Museum of Finnish Architecture, Helsinki
Carina Jaatinen, Director

Museum of Architecture and Design, Ljubljana
Maja Vardjan, Director

National Museum of Art, Architecture and Design, Oslo
Martin Braathen, Senior Curator

RIBA, London
Carmen Mateu, Head of Awards

The Berlage, Delft
Salomon Frausto, Director of Studies

Triennale di Milano, Milan
Lorenza Baroncelli, Director

European Commission

European Commissioner for Innovation, Research, Culture, Education and Youth
Iliana Ivanova

Directorate-General for Education, Youth, Sport and Culture

Director-General
Pia Ahrenkilde Hansen

Deputy Director-General
Normunds Popens

Director for Culture and Creativity
Georg Häusler

Policy Officer. Creative Europe Programme
Jutta Kastner

www.ec.europa.eu/creative-europe
f @CreativeEuropeEU
x @europe_creative

Fundació Mies van der Rohe

Ajuntament de Barcelona
Gobierno de España. Ministerio de Fomento
Generalitat de Catalunya. Departament de Territori i Sostenibilitat
Col·legi d'Arquitectes de Catalunya (COAC)
Escola Tècnica Superior d'Arquitectura de Barcelona (ETSAB)
Fira Barcelona
Museum of Modern Art (MoMA)
Stiftung Preußischer Kulturbesitz

President
Laia Bonet

Vice President
Maria Rosa Alarcón

Director
Anna Ramos

Executive Director
Antoni Garijo

Director of Prizes and Programmes
Ivan Blasi

Curatorship
Anna Sala Giralt

Register and Exhibition Coordination
Jordi Garcia

Archive and Collection
Txell Cuspinera

Communication
Anna Bes

Programme Management
Adriana Mas

Administration
Arnau Cabeza
Clara Moreno
Pilar Moyano
Roser Olóndriz

MvdR Pavilion Management
Víctor Sánchez

MvdR Pavilion Visitor Assistance
Sergi Carreras
Ruth Castilla
Manuel Luque
Marc Quintana
Antoni Santiago

Bookshop and shopmies.com
Raúl Martínez
Alex Raya

Collaborators
Norhan Essebbahi
Cristina Fernández
Oriol Palomeque
Júlia Sabater
Maria Ventura

www.eumiesawards.com
@eumiesawards
(Facebook, X, Instagram, Linkedin, Youtube)

Organised by
Co-funded by the European Union
fundació mies van der rohe barcelona

Institutional partners
ace

Strategic partner
world-architects.com Profiles of Selected Architects

Partners
JUNG JANSEN Steel Systems

With the support of
USM ALMA

Venue partner in Venice:
European Cultural Centre

COLOPHON

IMPRINT

Catalogue

Published by
Fundació Mies van der Rohe

Editors
Ivan Blasi
Anna Sala Giralt

Graphic Design
spread: David Lorente-Tomoko Sakamoto

Assistance
Oriol Palomeque
Júlia Sabater
Maria Ventura

Translation and proofreading
Textos BCN

Printing
Gràfiques Ortells. Barcelona

Distribution
Fundació Mies van der Rohe
www.shopmies.com
Artbook
www.artbook.com

All content (text and images) related to the projects included in this publication has been provided and licensed by the respective authors of the works.

Copyright of this edition
© 2024 Fundació Mies van der Rohe.
All rights reserved. No part of this publication may be reproduced, distributed, or transmitted in any form or by any means, including photocopying, recording or other electronic or mechanical methods, without the prior written permission of Fundacio Mies van der Rohe.

ISBN 978-84-127721-9-7
DL B 14706-2024

Printed and bound in the European Union.

We thank all the architect's offices for their valuable collaboration and permission to publish the documents.
We thank all the photographers who have wonderfully portrayed the works and have allowed us to use them.

Fundació Mies van der Rohe
Provença 318, pral. 2a
08037 Barcelona
www.miesbcn.com
FB/X/IG/IN: @FundacioMies

**European Union Prize for Contemporary Architecture –
Mies van der Rohe Awards 2024**
www.eumiesaward.com
FB/X/IG/IN: @EUmiesAwards

Mies van der Rohe Pavilion
Av. Francesc Ferrer i Guàrdia 7
Parc de Montjuïc
08038 Barcelona

Photographic Credits

Cover
Front © Leonhard Clemens
Back © Jesús Granada

Munch Museum
75-78 © Einar Aslaksen

Liljevalchs+
80-83 © Christoffer Grimshorn

Son of a Shingle – Vaksali Pedestrian Bridge and Underpasses
100-103 © Tõnu Tunnel

Hage
112 © Thomas Skinnemoen
116-117, 122-123, 125 (top), 126
© Geir Brendeland
120, 121, 124, 125 (bottom) © Peter Westrup

Annesley Gardens
143-145 © Ste Murray

Art Pavilion M.
155 © Studio Ossidiana
156-158 © Riccardo De Vecchi

Study Pavilion on the Campus of the TU Braunschweig
161 © Leonhard Clemens
163, 167 (top), 170, 171, 172-173 © Iwan Baan
166, 167 (bottom), 174 © Lemmart

Building Community Kurfürstenstrasse
178-180 © Laurian Ghinitoiu

Floating University Berlin
184 © Lena Giovanazzi
185 © Daniel Seiffert
186, 187 © Mor Arkadir

Targ Blonie / Food Market
190-193 © Nate Cook

Fire Station, Multi-Purpose Space, and Emergency Housing
204-207 © Philippe Braquenier

Open Air Swimming Pool Flow
209, 211, 212 © Annemie Augustijns
210 © POOL IS COOL

Amal Amjahid - Community Facility Along the Canal
214-217 © Corentin Haubruge

Het Steen
218, 219 (top), 220 © Kim Zwarts
219 (bottom) © Felixarchief
221 (top) © Stijn Bollaert
221 (bottom) © noAarchitecten

Light Rail Tunnel
246-248 © Brigida González

PLATO Contemporary Art Gallery
254, 256-257, 258, 266, 267 © Juliusz Sokołowski
260, 261, 262, 263, 265 © Jakub Certowicz

Refurbishment and Extension of a Community Swimming Pool
279-282 © Charles-Bouchaib

IKEA Vienna Western Station / IKEA – the Good Neighbour in the City
290-293 © Hertha Hurnaus

Townhouse Neubaugasse
294, 295, 296 (top right) © Lukas Schaller
296 (top left), 297 © Simone Bossi

Reconstruction and Extension of the Slovak National Gallery
301-304 © Matej Hakar

Bivouac Fanton
318-321 © Iwan Baan

Bohinj Kindergarten
322-325 © Luis Diaz Diaz

Covering the Remains of the Church of St. John the Baptist in the Žiče Charterhouse
328-331 © Miran Kambič

Riding Hall. Land Registry Department of the Municipal Civil Court
333-336 © Bosnic + Dorotic

Lonja Wetlands Wildlife Observatories and Visitor Centre
339-342 © Marko Mihaljević

Black Slavonian Eco Pig Farm
344-347 © Bosnic + Dorotic

Nursery. 1306 Plants for Timișoara
349-352 © Laurian Ghinitoiu

Day Centre for Young People with Autism Spectrum Disorder
374-377 © José Hevia

Média Library Charles Nègre
381, 382, 383, 384 (top) © Fernando Guerra
384 (bottom) © Agathe Rosa

Escadinhas Footpaths
402-405 © Ivo Tavares Studio

General Silveira Building
406-409 © José Campos

Square and Tourist Office in Piódão
414, 420, 421, 424-425 © Frederico Martinho
417, 423, 426 © do mal o menos

Municipal Pools
430 © Eugeni Bach
431 © Héctor Fernández
432-433 © Ana Amado

Reggio School
436-450 © José Hevia

Social Housing 1737
455-458 © Adrià Goula

Gabriel García Márquez Library
462-474 © Jesús Granada

Rebirth of the Convent Saint-François
479-490 © Thibaut Dini

Tbilisi Urban Forest (Narikala Ridge Forest)
498 © Luka Tavzarashvili
499 © George Kolbaia
501 © Sarah Cowles

Living in Lime - 42 Social Housing
513-516 © José Hevia

Liknon
524-527 © Claus Brechenmacher & Reiner Baumann

ACKNOWLEDGEMENTS

The European Union Prize for Contemporary Architecture / Mies van der Rohe Awards is possible because of the confidence and the support of the European Commission – Creative Europe programme – and the Barcelona City Council – Ecology, Urban Planning and Mobility-Architecture, Landscape and Heritage. For 38 years they have been travelling partners in the construction of this cross-cutting project.

We are truly thankful to Mrs. Iliana Ivanova, European Commissioner for Innovation, Research, Culture, Education and Youth, Mrs. Pia Ahrenkilde Hansen, Directorate-General for Education, Youth, Sport and Culture - European Commission, Mrs. Sabine Verheyen, Member of the European Parliament, Chairwoman of the Committee on Culture and Education, Mr. Jaume Collboni, Mayor of Barcelona and Mrs. Laia Bonet, President of Fundació Mies van der Rohe.

We would like to thank the people who saw us through this book; to all those who provided support, talked things over, read, wrote, offered comments, allowed us to quote their remarks and assisted in the editing, proofreading and design.

We would like to express our gratitude to those who stand with us day after day and who have supported and encouraged us despite all the time it took us away from them, especially Diego and Pau.

A special gratitude to the Jury members with whom we have had many intense discussions throughout our many days together.

We want to thank all the people in the architects' offices and the experts for their valuable collaboration. A special mention to Gustav Düsing, Max Hacke, Elena Orte, Guillermo Sevillano, Geir Brendeland, Olav Kristoffersen, Thomas Skinnemoen, Tim Lucas, Ian Shepherd, Andrés Jaque, Roberto González, Robert Konieczny, Michał Lisiński, Dorota Skóra, Tadeáš Goryczka, Marek Golab-Sieling, Agnieszka Wolny-Grabowska, Krzysztof Kobiela, Adrianna Wycisło, Mateusz Białek, Jakub Bilan, Wojciech Fudala, Katarzyna Kuzior, Damian Kuna, Jakub Pielecha, Magdalena Orzeł-Rurańska, Elżbieta Siwiec, Anna Szewczyk, Kinga Wojtanowska, Karol Knap, Amelia Tavella, Alice Kopp, João Branco and Paula del Río, for their invaluable support and energy in providing us with texts, images, stories and all kinds of documents and knowhow.

The clients of the winning and finalist works have also been of crucial assistance for the documentation of their projects: Torsten Markgräfe, Bettina Nöhren, Tatjana Schneider and the students and people from TU Braunschweig; Neus Castellano, Director of the Gabriel García Márquez library and the whole team; the PLATO Gallery team and the City of Ostrava; Lena Sjostrand, Mats Persson and White Arkitekter from Lund; Collectivité de Corse/Cullettività di Corsica and the Village of Sainte-Lucie-de-Tallano/Santa Lucìa d'Attallà; Eva Martín, Director of the Colegio Reggio and its professors, students and staff; and the people from the villages of Arganil and Piódão.

We would like to thank James Payne, Peter Cachola Schmal, Bartosz Haduch, Michał Haduch, Pedro Baía, Oliver Wainwright, Josep Lluís Blàzquez, and Nina Bouraoui for their wonderful insightful texts. The photographers have provided us with special interpretations of architecture and we are very thankful for their work.

David and Tomoko, working with you as graphic designers is a pleasure.

We are grateful to the teams of fantastic people working in those companies who have supported this project for a long time and those that have recently joined it.

Last and not least: we apologize to all those who have been with us over the course of these last months and whose names we have failed to mention.

COLOPHON